Who's Who
in the
Old Testament

together with the Apocrypha

JOAN COMAY

J M DENT
LONDON

© 1971, 1993 by Joan Comay

First published 1971 by Weidenfeld & Nicolson

First published in paperback 1993

Typeset by Datix International Limited, Bungay, Suffolk

Printed in England by Clays Ltd, St Ives plc

J M Dent Ltd
The Orion Publishing Group
Orion House
5 Upper St Martin's Lane
London WC2H 9EA

British Library Cataloguing-in-Publication Data

ISBN: 0 460 86134 4

Who's Who in the Old Testament
together with the Apocrypha

Contents

Author's preface

A scholar approaches the Old Testament in much the same spirit as an archaeologist attacks a site inhabited over several ages. He takes into account that the present text has evolved over a lengthy period, is woven together from different sources and has been constantly re-edited in the light of changing concepts. He will try to retrace this process – to sort out the different historical and literary strata and to interpret each element in relation to the time and place of its origin. In this way it becomes possible to analyse a biblical character in historical depth.

However, such a strictly scholastic treatment is not the intention of the present work. In general, the events relating to specific characters are set out as a straightforward narrative derived from the text, and designed to bring out the human interest of the story. In many cases, notes and comments are added that sketch in the general background or touch on the problems of interpretation that have occupied the scholars, without presuming to resolve them. It is not laid down whether each person in the Bible really existed in historical fact, or only in folk-mythology, or as fictional characters in tales written for moral purposes.

A few more points may help to explain the method of presentation:

As a rule, the biblical narrative and its historical setting are fully dealt with under the heading of the main character, while under each subordinate character the relevant events are briefly retold.

It is doubtful whether either the nations or the pagan deities mentioned in the Old Testament have a place in a Who's Who devoted to individual human beings. For convenience of reference, they have been included, but briefly.

The meanings of personal names have been given in those cases where the derivation is reasonably clear.

The following abbreviations have been used:

Acc.	Accadian	Gk.	Greek
Ass.	Assyrian	Heb.	Hebrew
Bab.	Babylonian	Pers.	Persian
Egypt.	Egyptian		

It is difficult to be precise about biblical dates. Generally, the older the period the more conjectural are the dates. It is essential in a work of this kind to adhere to one single chronological table and that given in the new Jerusalem Bible has been used as a basis. Where no approximate date or even century can be given the term 'date unknown' has been used. Here again no judgment is implied on the question whether the character had an historical existence or is legendary. This refers particularly to the chapters in Genesis before Abraham.

Author's acknowledgments

The author would particularly like to thank the advisory editors, Rabbi Michael Graetz and Revd Dr Leonard Cowie, who while not always in agreement with me on matters of interpretation have provided invaluable comments and suggestions. Dr Meir Gertner, of the Near and Middle Eastern Department, School of Oriental and African Studies, and his two assistants, Mr S. Sharvit and Mr J. Dean, supplied extremely helpful advice on the derivations of the names.

I am also deeply indebted to Jonathan Cowan for his research assistance with the mass of small entries; to Diane Kagan and Nomi Miller for their patient checking of quotations and references; and to Pauline Cooperstone without whose rapid and accurate typing and retyping of drafts this work could not have been completed in the given time.

As usual my long-suffering husband and children provided much-needed encouragement.

Introduction to the Old Testament

The Books of the Old Testament

The Old Testament contains the ancient literature of the Hebrew people. The works in it were composed and re-edited over a period of more than a thousand years, up to about the end of the 3rd century BC.

Other Near Eastern civilizations, such as the Egyptian and the Babylonian, produced religious and historical writings, legal codes, legends and folk-tales, prophecies, proverbs and poetry. But only the Hebrews wove them into a sacred anthology. What resulted was not so much an historical work in the modern sense, as a religious epic. The covenant between a small people and a universal God was the central theme, and all events were related to it. When neighbouring nations oppressed them, when the imperial armies of the ancient world trampled upon them, when they were afflicted by plague or bad harvests, it was because the Lord was angry with the Israelites for their transgressions. Even kings had to obey the Law, for it was God's Law. Perhaps for this reason, the Hebrews portrayed their own forefathers with remarkable honesty, and refused to make saints or demigods of them. Jacob can trick his old, blind father into giving him Esau's blessing; and David, the national hero, can behave shamefully over Bathsheba. It is this quality which makes the Old Testament so intensely human a chronicle.

The most venerable part of the Old Testament is the Pentateuch, or the Five Books of Moses. Its ultimate form was a blend of four early written versions: the 'J' Document, compiled in the southern kingdom of Judah in the 10th century BC; the 'E' Document, compiled in Ephraim in the northern kingdom of Israel in the 9th and 8th centuries BC; the Book of Deuteronomy (the 'D' Document), dating from the 7th century BC; and the material introduced by the priestly writers (the 'P' Document) about the time of the Exile.

Chronicles, produced about the 4th century BC, drew its material partly from Genesis, Exodus, Numbers and Joshua, and mainly from the Books of Samuel and Kings. This material was rewritten in a way that suited the Chronicler's didactic purpose. Ezra and Nehemiah are usually regarded as a continuation of Chronicles.

The final editing of the Books of Joshua, Judges, Samuel and Kings took place only in the post-Exilic period.

These multiple sources of the Old Testament, dating from different periods and reflecting changes in religious and social ideas, explain the problems of interpretation that face biblical scholars.

The Hebrew Bible is divided into three sections: the Law (Pentateuch), the Prophets and the Writings. The Pentateuch was canonized – i.e. accepted in final form as a sacred text – about 400 BC; the Prophets about 200 BC; and the Writings about AD 90. In that year, the scope and arrangement of the Hebrew Bible was settled by the Rabbinical Council of Jamnia. This step was prompted by the destruction of Jerusalem and the Second Temple by the Romans, in AD 70.

The oldest extant edition in the Hebrew language is the Masoretic Text finalized in Tiberias in the 9th century AD ('Masorah' means tradition). This is still the standard Hebrew Bible in general use today. It is a remarkable fact that the Isaiah scrolls discovered in a Dead Sea cave in 1947 are almost identical with the Masoretic Text, although they date from ten centuries earlier.

The accepted Jewish translation into the English language is that of the Jewish Publication Society of America, published in 1914.

The Books are listed below in the order in which they appear with their abbreviations in brackets. They also have the Hebrew equivalents in brackets, except for those bearing the names of persons.

The Law (Torah)	Genesis (Gen.)	(Bereishit)
	Exodus (Exod.)	(Shemot)
	Leviticus (Lev.)	(Vayikrah)
	Numbers (Num.)	(Bamidbar)
	Deuteronomy (Deut.)	(Devarim)

The Prophets (Nevi'im)   The Earlier Prophets:

Joshua (Josh.)	
Judges (Judg.)	(Shoftim)
1 Samuel (1 Sam.)	(Shmuel Alef)
2 Samuel (2 Sam.)	(Shmuel Beth)
1 Kings (1 Kgs.)	(Melachim Alef)
2 Kings (2 Kgs.)	(Melachim Beth)

The Later Prophets:

Isaiah (Isa.)
Jeremiah (Jer.)
Ezekiel (Ezek.)

The Twelve Minor Prophets:

Hosea (Hos.)	Nahum (Nahum)
Josel (Joel)	Habakkuk (Hab.)
Amos (Amos)	Zephaniah (Zeph.)
Obadiah (Obad.)	Haggai (Hag.)
Jonah (Jonah)	Zechariah (Zech.)
Micah (Mic.)	Malachi (Mal.)

The Writings (Ketuvim)		
	Psalms (Ps.)	(Tehillim)
	Proverbs (Prov.)	(Mishlei)
	Job (Job)	
	Song of Songs (S. of S.)	(Shir-ha-Shirim)
	Ruth (Ruth)	
	Lamentations (Lam.)	(Ichah)
	Ecclesiastes (Eccles.)	(Kohelet)
	Esther (Esther)	
	Daniel (Dan.)	
	Ezra (Ezra)	
	Nehemiah (Neh.)	
	1 Chronicles (1 Chr.)	(Divrei ha-Yamim Alef)
	2 Chronicles (2 Chr.)	(Divrei ha-Yamim Beth)

The Bible is known in Hebrew as the 'Tanach', a word made up of the initials of the three above sections.

By early tradition, the Hebrew Bible consisted of 'The Twenty-four Books', since Samuel, Kings, the Twelve Prophets, Ezra-Nehemiah, and Chronicles were each regarded as one Book.

The Greek Bible

In the 3rd century BC the Septuagint, a Greek translation of the Hebrew Bible, was produced in Alexandria, Egypt, for the use of the large Jewish community residing there. Egypt was then under Greek influence, being ruled by the Ptolemaic dynasty descended from one of the generals of Alexander the Great. The work is regarded as having been initiated by the king himself, and colourful legends have clustered round its obscure early history. Septuagint means the Version of the Seventy, from the number of elders who were said to have been brought from Jerusalem for the purpose. From the surviving texts, it is clearly the work of various translators, and is uneven in quality.

The Greek Bible continued to be amplified, and became the Old Testament in general use in the early Christian Church. The earliest comprehensive manuscript of the Septuagint dates from the 4th century AD. It included not only the books of the Hebrew canon, with some omissions and additions, but also additional Jewish works, mostly written in the 2nd and 1st centuries BC in Hebrew, Aramaic and Greek. These writings later became known as the Apocrypha, from a Greek word meaning 'hidden' or 'spurious'.

The Latin Bible

In the 4th century AD St Jerome, working in Bethlehem, produced the Latin translation of the Bible known as the Vulgate. He wished to limit the Old Testament to the Hebrew canon, but was overruled by the Church, and most of the Apocrypha were included, though they were termed 'deutero-canonical'. Their inclusion was confirmed by the Council of Trent (1546) and by the Vatican Council (1870). The books of the Apocrypha not accepted into the Latin Bible were 1 and 2 Esdras and the Prayer of Manasseh.

The Latin Bible continues to be used by the Roman Catholic Church. Recently, authoritative modern translations have been published in French (*La Bible de Jérusalem*, 1956), and in English (The Jerusalem Bible, 1966).

The Protestant Bible

In his German translation of the Bible (1534), Martin Luther reverted to the opinion of St Jerome about the canon of the Old Testament. He relegated the Apocrypha to a separate section at the end of the Old Testament, since they were not holy scripture but 'good and useful for reading'.

The same attitude was taken in the early English translations, such as Wycliffe (c. 1382), Coverdale (1535), the Greek Bible (1539), the Geneva Bible (1560), and the Bishops' Bible (1568). These were forerunners of the Authorized Version or King James Bible, published in 1611. It became the classic English Bible, and had a profound effect on the thought and literature of the English-speaking world.

In the course of time, the Authorized Version (AV) lagged increasingly behind biblical scholarship, archaeology and the increased knowledge of ancient Hebrew and Greek. Moreover, some of its magnificent language became archaic. A Revised Version (RV) was published in 1885. After World War II a Revised Standard Version (RSV) was produced in the United States and the Old Testament section appeared in 1952. It is from the RSV that the quotations and spelling of names have been taken for the present work.

From the beginning of the 20th century, a number of translations were brought out in modern colloquial English by Protestant, Catholic and Jewish scholars. In 1947, a joint commission was set up by the Protestant Churches in the British Isles, to prepare a fresh and authoritative translation into modern English from the original sources. It was published in 1970 as the New English Bible (NEB).

In the Protestant versions, the Books of the Old Testament appear in the following order, which differs in certain respects from the arrangement in the Hebrew Bible, though the individual Books are the same.

Genesis	2 Chronicles	Daniel
Exodus	Ezra	Hosea
Leviticus	Nehemiah	Joel
Numbers	Esther	Amos
Deuteronomy	Job	Obadiah
Joshua	Psalms	Jonah
Judges	Proverbs	Micah
Ruth	Ecclesiastes	Nahum
1 Samuel	Song of Solomon	Habakkuk
2 Samuel	Isaiah	Zephaniah
1 Kings	Jeremiah	Haggai
2 Kings	Lamentations	Zechariah
1 Chronicles	Ezekiel	Malachi

To sum up: The Hebrew Bible contains thirty-nine works, regarded as constituting 'Twenty-four Books'.

In the Septuagint the Old Testament included additional books or parts of books, dating from the 2nd and 1st centuries BC.

The Latin Bible incorporated eleven of these works, known as 'deutero-canonical'.

The Protestant Bible reverted to the Hebrew canon (though not in the same order), with fifteen additional works printed separately as Apocrypha.

The physical setting

The Land of the Bible has a remarkably varied landscape. There are five distinct regions: the coastal plain, the central hill country, the Jordan valley, the plateau east of the Jordan, and the Negev in the south.

The fertile coastal plain is flat and sandy, with a good supply of water from underground springs. It was well settled from the earliest times. The northern part was occupied by the Phoenicians, and the southern part by the Philistines from the 12th century BC.

Inland from the coast are rolling limestone hills two to three thousand feet high. The Valley of Jezreel divides them into two areas – the Galilee highlands in the north, and the mountains of Samaria and Judea in the centre. The Israelites settled mainly in the hill region.

The deep Jordan Valley is part of the longest rift in the earth's surface, running across the Red Sea and into the heart of Africa. The Jordan river flows from Mount Hermon through the Sea of Galilee and ends in the Dead Sea, 1,300 feet below sea level.

East of the Jordan Valley and the Dead Sea, a steep escarpment leads to the open Transjordan plateau. In this area lay the kingdoms of Edom, Moab and Ammon, and the tribes of Reuben, Gad and part of Manasseh were settled.

The northern part of the Negev round Beersheba is a sparse plain dotted with low scrub. It becomes bleaker and more rugged further south. The Hebrew patriarchs were typical of the nomads who have inhabited this region down the ages.

The ancient route from Egypt to Mesopotamia ran via Gaza up the coastal plain, and cut through a strategic pass into the Jezreel Valley, continuing across the Jordan to Damascus. The other main route, the King's Highway, ran east of the Dead Sea and the Jordan River. It was from this side that Joshua invaded Canaan.

Chronology

BC	General	Israelite	Main Biblical Characters
			ADAM AND EVE
			NOAH
		The Creation and the Flood (Gen. 1–11)	
		The Patriarchs and the Sojourn in Egypt 1800–1250 BC (Gen. 12–Exod. 1)	
			ABRAHAM, ISAAC AND JACOB
		The patriarchs in Canaan: c. 1800–1700	
		The Israelites in Egypt: c.1700–1250	JOSEPH
			JOB
		Israelite forced labour	
2000	**Egyptian domination** *Middle Bronze Age: 2100–1550*		
1800			
1700	Hyksos regime in Egypt: 1720–1560 New Kingdom in Egypt: 1560–715 *Late Bronze Age: 1550–1200* Tel el-Amarna Letters		
1300	Rameses II: 1301–1234	**The Exodus and the Conquest** 1250–1200 (Exod., Lev., Num., Deut., Josh.) The Exodus: c. 1250 The Law at Sinai The Conquest: c. 1220–1200	MOSES AARON JOSHUA
1250	Egyptian control weakens		

BC	General	Israelite	Main Biblical Characters
1200	Egypt: 20th Dynasty: *c.* 1200–1085 *Iron Age I:* 1200–900	**The Judges** 1200–1030 (Judg., 1 Sam. 1–7, Ruth) Allocation and settlement of Israelite tribal areas: 1200–1025 Wars of Ehud, Deborah, Gideon and Jephthah Exploits of Samson	EHUD, DEBORAH GIDEON
	Philistines settle on Palestine coast	Migration of tribe of Dan War against Benjamin The story of Ruth	JEPHTHAH, SAMSON RUTH
1100	Assyrian hegemony in Mesopotamia Rise of Aramean kingdoms (Damascus, Zobah, Hamath)	Philistine victory at Apek and capture of Ark	
1050	21st Egyptian Dynasty: 1085–945	Samuel appears: *c.* 1040	SAMUEL
		The Monarchy 1030–931 (1 and 2 Sam., 1 Kgs., 1 and 2 Chr.) Reign of Saul: *c.* 1030–1010 Victories over Ammonites, Philistines, Amalekites Saul and David Defeat and death at Mt Gilboa	SAUL
	Struggle with Philistines	Reign of David: *c.* 1010–970 Capture of Jerusalem Victories and expansion Alliances with Hamath and Tyre Revolt of Absalom Solomon appointed successor	DAVID
950		Reign of Solomon: *c.* 970–931 Building of Temple and palace Red Sea trade route Visit of Queen of Sheba	SOLOMON

BC	General	Israelite		Main Biblical Characters
		Solomon's death and split in kingdom		
	22nd (Libyan) Dynasty in Egypt Shishak I: 945–935	**The Two Kingdoms** 931–587 (1 and 2 Kgs., 2 Chr., Amos, Hos., Isa., Mic., Jer.)		
		Israel: 931–721	**Judah:** 931–587	
	Shishak's campaign in Palestine	Jeroboam I: 931–910	Rehoboam: 931–913	JEROBOAM REHOBOAM
		Nadab: 910–909	Abijah: 913–911	
	Iron Age 2: 900–600	Baasha: 909–886	Asa: 911–870	
	Ben-hadad I, king of Damascus	Elah: 886–885		
		Zimri: 885		
		Omri: 885–874 Founds Samaria		OMRI
	Ben-hadad II, king of Damascus	Ahab: 874–853 Wars against Damascus	Jehoshaphat: 870–848	AHAB ELIJAH JEHOSHAPHAT
	Assyrian domination Shalmaneser III: 858–824 Victory over 12 kings at Kharkar, 853	Ahaziah: 853–852 Jehoram: 852–841	Jehoram: 848–841 Ahazia: 841	
850	Mesha, king of Moab		Athalia: 841–835	ELISHA
	Shalmaneser III, invades Palestine	Jehu: 841–814	Joash: 835–796	JEHU
800	Ben-hadad III, king of Damascus	Jehoahaz: 814–798 Joash: 798–783 Jeroboam II: 783–743	Amaziah: 796–781 Uzziah: 781–740	
750	Tiglath-pileser III: 745–727	Zechariah: 743 Shallum: 743		JEROBOAM II, UZZIAH AMOS HOSEA
	Rezin, king of Damascus	Menahem: 743–738 Pekahiah: 738–737	Jotham: 740–736 Ahaz: 736–716	ISAIAH MICAH

Main Biblical Characters

General

Israelite

Main Biblical Characters

BC	General	Israelite	Main Biblical Characters
	Shalmaneser V: 726–722 Sargon II: 721–705	Pekah: 737–732 Tiglath-pileser occupies Galilee Hoshea: 732–724 Fall of Samaria: 721 Deportation of inhabitants	
		Rezin and Pekah besiege Jerusalem	HEZEKIAH
		Hezekiah: 716–687	
700	Sargon defeats Egyptians at Rafiah: 720 Sargon takes Ashdod, 711 Sennacherib: 704–681	Shiloh tunnel Assyrians invade Judah: 701 Manasseh: 687–642 Tribute paid to Assyria	JONAH TOBIT JOSIAH ZEPHANIA NAHUM
650	Esarhaddon: 680–669 Lower Egypt occupied: 671 Ashurbanipal: 668–621	Amon: 642–640 Josiah: 640–609 Religious reforms	
	Fall of Nineveh: 612		JEREMIAH HABAKKUK
	Campaign of Pharaoh Neco Judean defeat at Megiddo: 609	Jehoahaz: 609 Jehoiakim: 609–598	
600	Babylonian domination Battle of Carchemish – end of Assyrian Empire: 605 Nebuchadnezzar: 604–562	Jehoiachin: 598 Jerusalem surrenders; Jehoiachin deported Zedekiah: 598–587 Siege of Jerusalem: 589 Fall of Jerusalem: 587 Deportations Gedaliah assassinated Judea a Babylonian province	DANIEL
	Siege of Tyre: 588–575		

BC	General	Israelite	Main Biblical Characters
		The Exile and the Return 587–331 BC (Ezek., Isa. 40–55, Zeph., Nahum, Hab., Ezra, Neh., Hag., Zech., Obad., Joel, Mal., Esther) Exile in Babylonia Fresh deportations: 582	EZEKIEL 'SECOND ISAIAH'
550	**Persian domination** Cyrus, king of Medes and Persians: 549–529 Capture of Babylon: 539 Cambyses: 529–522 Conquest of Egypt	Edict of Cyrus: **Return: 538** Foundations of Second Temple: 537 Zerubbabel as governor	ZERUBBABEL HAGGAI ZECHARIAH
	Darius I: 522–486 Organization of Empire Battle of Marathon: 490	Second Temple built: 520–515	
500	Xerxes I (Ahasuerus): 486–465 Defeat at Salamis: 480 Artaxerxes I Longimanus: 465–423		ESTHER JUDITH
450		Ezra's mission: 458 (if under Artaxerxes I) Mission of Nehemiah: 445–425 Walls of Jerusalem rebuilt Religious reforms	EZRA NEHEMIAH OBADIAH JOEL MALACHI
400 350	Artaxerxes II Mnemon: 404–358	Ezra's mission: 398 (if under Artaxerxes II) Code of Laws	
	Alexander the Great Conquests: 336–323 End of Persian Empire: 331 Ptolemaic dynasty in Egypt: 323–30 Seleucid dynasty in Syria and Mesopotamia: 312–64	**The Hellenistic Period** 331–63 (1 and 2 Macc., Dan. 11)	

BC	General	Israelite	Main Biblical Characters
300	Septuagint in Alexandria	Judea under Ptolemies: 301–197	
250			
200	Antiochus III: 223–187	Judea under Seleucids: 197–142	
		Antiochus III sanctions Jewish religious autonomy	
	Defeats Egyptians at Panias: 198	Temple pillaged: 170	
	Defeated by Romans at Magnesia: 188	Persecution of Jews: from 167	
	Antiochus IV Epiphanes: 175–163	Mattathias starts revolt in Modi'in: 167	
	Egyptian campaigns: 170, 168	Judas Maccabeus becomes leader: 166	JUDAS MACCABEUS
		Victories of Judas: 166–164	
		Rededication of Temple: Dec. 164	
	Antiochus V Eupator: 163–162	Lysias besieges Jerusalem: 162	
	Demetrius I Soter: 162–150	Judas defeated and killed: 160	
		Jonathan, high priest and ethnarch: 163–142	JONATHAN THE MACCABEE
150	Alexander Balas: 150–145	Captured and killed: 143–142	
	Demetrius II: 145–138		
	Antiochus VI: 145–142		
	Tryphon: 142–138	Simon, high priest and ethnarch: 143–134	SIMON THE MACCABEE
	Antiochus VII: 138–129	Judea becomes autonomous: 142	
	Demetrius II: 129–125 (second reign)	John Hyrcanus I, high priest and ethnarch: 134–104	
100	Pompey's eastern campaigns: 66–62	Pompey takes Jerusalem: 63	
		End of Hellenistic Period and Beginning of Roman Period	

NB The main biblical characters have been placed in the chronology as far as possible in the periods that correspond to the biblical account. This does not imply that each of them exists in history.

A

Aaron *c.* 13 century BC. Brother of Moses and first high priest.

Aaron was the son of Amram and Jochebed, of the priestly tribe of Levi. He was older than his brother Moses by three years, though younger than their sister Miriam. He married Elisheba, the daughter of Amminadab of the tribe of Judah, and had four sons: Nadab, Abihu, Eleazar and Ithamar.

When the Lord ordered Moses to go to Pharaoh and ask him to let the Israelites leave Egypt, Moses pleaded that 'I am slow of speech and of tongue.' (Exod. 4:10) The Lord told him that Aaron his brother would serve as his spokesman, for 'I know that he can speak well.' (Exod. 4:14)

Aaron went into the wilderness and met Moses. The two brothers embraced, and Moses repeated the Lord's commandments. They then sent for the Israelite elders. Aaron informed them that the Lord was about to release them from their slavery, and convinced them by performing magic signs.

Moses and Aaron appeared before Pharaoh, and at first asked for permission for the Israelites to journey into the wilderness to hold a feast to their God. Pharaoh refused, and increased the burdens of the Hebrew slaves, who then blamed the brothers for these new hardships. Once again they appeared before Pharaoh to urge their plea. To impress Pharaoh with a miracle, Aaron threw down his rod and it turned into a serpent. Pharaoh sent for his sorcerers who performed the same feat 'but Aaron's rod swallowed up their rods'. (Exod. 7:12)

Aaron's role in the infliction of some of the ten plagues that followed is recorded in Exodus (Chapters 7, 8 and 9). By stretching out his rod at the behest of Moses, he brought on the first three plagues (blood, frogs and lice). Together they were involved in producing the sixth plague (boils) and the eighth one (locusts). Only Moses is mentioned in connection with the other five. Pharaoh finally yielded to the demand to 'let my people go'. Aaron was then eighty-three years old and Moses eighty.

After their dramatic crossing of the Red (or Reed) Sea, the Israelites were attacked in the desert by fierce Amalekite nomads. All day Moses sat on a hill-top while Aaron and Hur (Miriam's son) stood on either side of him and held up his hands grasping the sacred rod, until the attackers were repulsed.

Moses went up Mount Sinai to receive the Ten Commandments leaving Aaron and Hur in charge of the encampment. When Moses did not appear at the appointed time, the people became rebellious and demanded of Aaron: 'Up, make us gods, who shall go before us; as for this Moses ... we do not know what has become of him.' (Exod. 32:1) Aaron told them to bring him whatever gold items they had, and he fashioned a golden calf as a tangible object of worship for them. He proclaimed a feast for the following day and the people sacrificed, ate, drank and 'rose up to play' (Exod. 32:6).

On his return, the outraged Moses smashed the stone tablets he was carrying. He destroyed the calf and upbraided Aaron, who replied defensively: 'Let not the anger of my lord burn hot; you know the people, that they are set on evil.' (Exod. 32:22)

It was after this that the Ark of the Law and the tabernacle were constructed, and Aaron and his sons ordained as priests.

Two hundred and fifty of the Israelites, led by Korah, a Levite, revolted against the leadership of Moses and Aaron, claiming that all members of the congregation were holy. The earth split open and swallowed up the mutinous group. Moses placed a stave from each of the tribes overnight in the Tabernacle, with the Levites represented by that of Aaron. Next morning, it was seen that Aaron's rod alone had sprouted blossom, 'put forth buds ... and it bore ripe almonds' (Num. 17:8). This demonstrated the special status of the priesthood and the Levites.

Before the Children of Israel entered the Promised Land, they reached Mount Hor, near the southern end of the Dead Sea. The Lord told Moses to take Aaron up the mountain, together with his son Eleazar. Aaron's vestments were placed upon Eleazar, who succeeded him as high priest. Aaron then died, at the age of one hundred and twenty-three. The Israelites mourned him for thirty days.

Aaron figures in the biblical account as sharing with Moses the receipt of God's commands, the performance of miracles, and leadership over the people. Despite this close association in authority, Aaron lacked the spiritual grandeur that made Moses the central figure of the Old Testament.

AARON AND THE PRIESTHOOD

Scholars are generally of the opinion that the earlier traditions about the Exodus, as reflected in the J and E Documents, give Aaron a minor role, and do not refer to his priestly function at all. A professional priesthood was developed in Jerusalem under the monarchy, and was centred on the Temple. Two priestly orders came into being, both claiming descent from Aaron – the Zadokites, through Aaron's son Eleazar; the Aaronites, through Aaron's son Ithamar. After the Return, and under the influence of Ezra's reforms, the Zadokites became the dominant priesthood, and the Aaronites or Levites were relegated to the status of Temple servants and lesser country priests.

The special role of the priesthood, and the details of Temple worship, were elaborated in the P (priestly) Document in the post-exilic period, in about the 4th century BC. It is mainly from this late source that these themes were injected into the Books of Exodus, Leviticus and Numbers. Aaron's importance as the founder of the priesthood and the first high priest was thereby magnified in retrospect. [The main part of the story of Aaron is told in the Books of Exodus, Leviticus and Numbers.]

Abagtha c. 5 century BC. One of the seven chamberlains of Ahasuerus, king of Persia, sent to bring Queen Vashti to the king's banquet to show off her beauty. [Esther 1:10, 11]

Abda (Heb. 'servant') *1. c.* 10 century BC. Father of Adoniram who was the member of King Solomon's household in charge of the levy of labour for public works. [1 Kgs. 4:6]
2. see OBADIAH 9.

Abdeel (Heb. 'servant of God') c. 7 century BC. Father of Shelemiah, who was ordered by King Joiakim to arrest the prophet Jeremiah and his scribe Baruch. [Jer. 36:26]

Abdi (Heb. 'servant') *1. c.* 10 century BC. Grandfather of Ethan, one of the chief musicians of King David. [1 Chr. 6:44]
2. c. 8 century BC. The father of Kish, a Levite who sanctified himself and helped cleanse the Temple in the reign of Hezekiah. [2 Chr. 29:12]

3. 5 century BC. Descendant of Elam, who divorced his non-Jewish wife in the time of Ezra. [Ezra 10:26]

Abdiel (Heb. 'servant') *c.* 8 century BC. Father of Ahi and son of Guni, he was head of a family of Gadites living in Gilead during the period of Jeroboam II, king of Israel. [1 Chr. 5:15]

Abdon (Heb. 'servile') *1. c.* 12 century BC. Son of Hillel, a Pirathonite from the land of Ephraim, he judged Israel for eight years and had forty sons and thirty nephews who rode on seventy asses. [Judg. 12:13–15]
2. date unknown. Son of Shashak, a Benjaminite leader who lived in Jerusalem. [1 Chr. 8:23–25]
3. c: 11 century BC. Son of Jeiel, a Benjaminite leader and uncle of King Saul. [1 Chr. 8:30; 9:36]
4. c. 7 century BC. The son of Micah, he was sent by King Josiah to consult the prophetess Huldah. Also called Achbor. [2 Kgs. 22:12, 14; 2 Chr. 34:20]

Abednego (Bab. 'servant of Nego' [a Babylonian god]) *c.* 6 century BC. The Babylonian name given to Azariah, one of the four young men of Judah taken off to Babylon by the orders of King Nebuchadnezzar. When the four refused to worship or serve the Babylonian gods, Nebuchadnezzar, in great rage, ordered them cast into the fiery furnace. They were delivered by an angel and walked out unhurt. [Dan. 1–3]

Abel (Heb. 'son') date unknown. The younger son of Adam and Eve. Abel was a shepherd, while his elder brother Cain became a tiller of the soil. When the two brothers came to present their offerings to the Lord, the lambs of Abel were preferred to the produce of Cain. Cain was so angry that he killed his brother Abel, thus committing the first murder recorded in the Bible.

The story of Cain and Abel is re-garded as expressing the age-old strife in the Near East between the desert nomads with their flocks and herds, and the settled cultivators. The story has its roots in the primitive custom of ritual human sacrifice to propitiate the gods and ensure the fertility of the soil, on which the life of the community depended.

Clearly, the story of Cain and Abel represents a stage in human society that had evolved far beyond the primitive beginnings, and it is only in a legendary sense that the two of them were re-garded as the 'children' of the first human beings. *See* CAIN [Gen. 4]

Abi (Heb. 'progenitor') *c.* 8 century BC. Daughter of Zachariah, she became the wife of Ahaz, king of Judah, and the mother of his successor, King Hezekiah. Also called Abijah. [2 Kgs. 18:2; 2 Chr. 29:1]

Abialbon *see* ABIEL 2.

Abiasaph (Heb. 'father added [a son]') *c.* 13 century BC. A son of Korah and a descendant of Kohath of the tribe of Levi, he was head of a family of Kora-hites who went out of Egypt with Moses. When his father Korah led a rebellion against Moses and Aaron in the wilderness and died unnaturally, Abi-asaph and his brothers were not punished. His descendants were keepers at the gates of the Tabernacle in the reign of King David. Also called Ebiasaph. [Exod. 6:24; 1 Chr. 6:37; 9:19]

Abiathar (Heb. 'father of excellence') *c.* 11 century BC. High priest during the reign of David.

Abiathar was a young priest at the sanctuary town of Nob, just outside Jerusalem, and the son of the head priest Ahimelech. When Saul heard David had been helped by them, he had all the priests of Nob rounded up and slain and the town destroyed. Only Abiathar escaped and managed to join the outlawed David in the mountains. David pledged himself to look after Abiathar: 'Stay with me, fear not; for he that seeks my life seeks your life; with me you shall be in safekeeping.' [1 Sam. 22:23]

Abiathar stayed with David throughout his guerrilla days and then came to Jerusalem with him. Here David made him one of the two high priests, the other being Zadok. At the time of Absalom's revolt, they tried to follow David from Jerusalem with the Ark, but he asked them to turn back and keep him posted of developments, using their sons as runners. After the defeat and death of Absalom, the two high priests encouraged the leaders of Judah to call for the return of David.

When David was aged and losing his hold on affairs, Abiathar supported the abortive bid of the eldest surviving prince, Adonijah, to usurp the throne. Solomon, a younger son, was crowned instead.

David died shortly after and Solomon succeeded him. Because of his loyalty and long service to David, Abiathar's life was spared. But Solomon banished him from Jerusalem: 'Go to Anathoth, to your estate.' (1 Kgs. 2:26) [1 Sam. 22:20–23; 2 Sam. 15:24; 1 Kgs. 1, 2, 4; 1 Chr. 15:11, 18:16; 24:6; 27:34]

Abida (Heb. 'father of knowledge') c. 17 century BC. Son of Midian, he was a grandson of Abraham and his wife Keturah. [Gen. 25:4; 1 Chr. 1:33]

Abidan (Heb. 'father of judgment') c. 13 century BC. Son of Gideoni and a leader of the tribe of Benjamin, he was appointed by Moses to number the tribe of Benjamin for military service and led the contingent as they marched through the wilderness. [Num. 1:11; 2:22; 7:60–65; 10:24]

Abiel (Heb. 'God is my father') 1. c. 11 century BC. Son of Zeror of the tribe of Benjamin, he was the grandfather of King Saul and of Abner his commander. [1 Sam. 9:1; 14:51]
2. c. 10 century BC. The Arbathite warrior in the army of King David who was distinguished for his bravery. Also called Abialbon. [2 Sam. 23:31; 1 Chr. 11:32]

Abiezer (Heb. 'father of help') 1. c. 13 century BC. A leader of the tribe of Manasseh recorded in the census by Moses who would be given a share in the land of Israel, after the conquest of Joshua. Also called Iezer. [Num. 26:30; Josh. 17:2; 1 Chr. 7:18]
2. c. 10 century BC. A warrior from Anathoth in King David's army distinguished for his bravery. He commanded a division during the ninth month of each year. [2 Sam. 23:27; 1 Chr. 11:28; 27:12]

Abigail (Heb. 'father of joy') 1. c. 11 century BC. Wife of Nabal and later of King David.

When Samuel died, David went into the wilderness to escape King Saul. While there he learned of a man named Nabal and sent ten men to ask him for a contribution to their support, and they were rudely turned away. After this was told to Nabal's wife Abigail, who was both beautiful and wise, she realized at once that this insult would mean an attack on her husband's life. Loading up asses with food, she slipped out without telling her husband, intercepted David and his men, and pleaded with them to accept the gift. David agreed and turned back. Abigail hastened home and that night attended a party given by Nabal. Because he got drunk she was unable to tell him what she had done until next morning. He then had a heart attack and died about ten days later.

When David heard of this death he asked Abigail to become his wife, and she agreed. David fled to Gath to escape Saul's wrath, and she went with him.

When the Amalekites invaded from the south she was taken prisoner, but was rescued by David. After Saul's death on the battlefield they moved to Hebron, where Abigail bore David a son called Chileab (Daniel). [1 Sam. 25; 30; 2 Sam 2:2; 3:3; 1 Chr. 3:1]

2. c. 11 century BC. Sister of King David and the mother of Amasa, the commander of the army of Absalom. [2 Sam. 17:25; 1 Chr. 2:16, 17]

Abihail (Heb. 'father of strength') *1. c.* 13 century BC. Father of Zuriel, chief of the Levite family of Merarites, who were appointed to pitch their camp on the northern side of the Tabernacle and were also given the task of carrying certain parts of the Tabernacle during the wanderings in the wilderness of the children of Israel. [Num. 3:35]

2. date unknown. The wife of Abishur, a Jerahmeelite from the tribe of Judah. [1 Chr. 2:29]

3. date unknown. The son of Huri, a leader of the tribe of Gad living in the land of Bashan, east of the river Jordan. [1 Chr. 5:14]

4. c. 10 century BC. Mother of Mahalath, a wife of King Rehoboam of Judah, she was the daughter of David's brother Eliab. [2 Chr. 11:18]

5. c. 5 century BC. Father of Esther who became queen of Persia. [Esther 2:15; 9:29]

Abihu (Heb. 'God is father') c. 13 century BC. Second son of Aaron and Elisheba and nephew of Moses, Abihu was chosen to become a priest in the Tabernacle in the wilderness. Later Abihu and his elder brother Nadab burnt forbidden incense to the Lord and died immediately. [Exod. 6:23; 24:1, 9; 28:1; Levit. 10:1, 2; Num. 3:2, 4; 26:60, 61; 1 Chr. 6:3; 24:1–2]

Abihud (Heb. 'father of praise') c. 16 century BC. Son of Bela and a grandson of Benjamin. [1 Chr. 8:3]

Abijah (Heb. 'God is my father') *1. c.* 16 century BC. A son of Becher and a grandson of Benjamin, he and his family were heads of the tribe and mighty warriors. [1 Chr. 7:8]

2. c. 11 century BC. Son of the prophet Samuel, he and his brother Joel were judges in Beersheba and known to take bribes and act corruptly. The elders of Israel asked Samuel to give them a king to succeed Samuel rather than let his sons rule over Israel. [1 Sam. 8:2; 1 Chr. 6:28]

3. Second king of Judah after the monarchy split, he reigned 913–11 BC. Abijah was the son and successor of Rehoboam, king of Judah. His mother was Maacah, the daughter of Abishalom.

Abijah claimed the whole of the divided kingdom, on behalf of the house of David. He defeated the forces of Jeroboam, king of Israel, which enabled the Judeans to expand their territory and occupy the southern hills of Ephraim, including the important religious centre of Bethel.

After a brief three-year reign Abijah died, leaving a family of fourteen wives, twenty-two sons and sixteen daughters. He was succeeded by his son Asa. Also called Abijam. [1 Kgs. 14:31; 15:1–8; 1 Chr. 3:10; 2 Chr. 11:20, 22; 12:16; 13]

4. c. 10 century BC. The young son of Jeroboam 1, king of the northern kingdom of Israel, who fell mortally sick. Jeroboam sent his wife in disguise to the prophet Ahijah to ask whether the child would live and was told that he would die as soon as she returned to the capital city of Tirzah. Ahijah's prophesy came true and all the people of Israel mourned the child's death. [1 Kgs. 14:1–17]

5. c. 10 century BC. A priest in the reign of King David who was responsible for the eighth turn of service in the Tabernacle in Jerusalem. [1 Chr. 24:10]

6. see ABI

7. 6 century BC. A priest of Judah who returned with Zerubbabel from exile in Babylon. [Neh. 12:4, 17]

8. *c.* 5 century BC. One of the priests of Judah who signed the solemn covenant in the time of Nehemiah. [Neh. 10:7]

Abijam *see* ABIJAH *3*.

Abimael (Heb. 'God is my father') date unknown. Son of Joktan and a descendant of Shem, Noah's second son. [Gen. 10:26, 28; 1 Chr. 1:20, 22]

Abimelech (Heb. 'the King [God] is my father') *1. c.* 17 century BC. King of Gerar. Abraham, en route to Egypt, passed off Sarah as his sister. But when she was taken into the king's harem, the Lord warned Abimelech in a dream to return Sarah to Abraham and Abimelech sent Sarah and Abraham on their way with precious gifts. Abimelech made a pact with Abraham concerning the well at Beer-sheba, and later made arrangements with Isaac about water and grazing rights.

Abimelech, probably a successor with the same name, had a similar experience with Isaac and his wife Rebekah, who was also passed off as his sister. [Gen. 20:2–18; 21:22–32; 26:1–30]
2. *c.* 12 century BC. The son of Gideon, victor over the Midianites, and of a Canaanite woman from Shechem referred to as his concubine. On his father's death, he made a bid to become king of that region. Shechem, the main city, had a mixed population – partly Israelites and the rest native Canaanites who had remained there after Joshua's conquest. Abimelech saw the path to power through his tie with his mother's people. The elders of Shechem agreed to support him and provided him with funds – seventy pieces of silver from the treasury of the local deity, Baal-berith (Lord of the Covenant). Abimelech used this money to hire a band of cut-throats from among the town vagrants. With these mercenaries he descended on his 70 brothers, seized them and had them killed 'upon one stone' (Judg. 9:5). The

only one to escape this mass fratricide was Gideon's youngest son Jotham, who managed to hide himself.

All the leading citizens of Shechem gathered at the town's meeting-place, an oak tree next to a pillar, and proclaimed Abimelech their king. Suddenly Jotham appeared on nearby Mount Gerizim and shouted down at the throng. He told them the parable of the trees that wanted a king. The honour was accepted only by the thorny bramble, fire from which consumed the whole forest. Jotham prophesied that this would happen with Abimelech and his supporters. Before he could be seized, Jotham again made his escape.

Abimelech ruled for three years, basing himself not in Shechem itself but in the fortified place of Arumah, a few miles away in the hills. Discontent grew up among the Shechemites, and revolt was sparked by a certain Gaal, the son of Ebed, who had come into town and had gained the confidence of the local leaders. (Gaal evidently belonged to the native Canaanite stock.)

At the instance of Zebul, the governor of the town, Abimelech sent four companies of armed men to take up positions outside the town gate. In the clash that followed, some of Gaal's followers were killed and the rest were chased back as far as the city gate.

After that encounter Zebul felt strong enough to expel Gaal and his brethren from the town. Abimelech came back next day with reinforcements to take his revenge upon the rebellious city. Two companies of soldiers fell upon the people working in the fields, while Abimelech with the third company seized the city gate to cut off their retreat. He then fought his way into the city, laid it waste and killed all the inhabitants found in it. Salt was thrown on the smouldering ruins – the symbol of complete destruction.

About a thousand people were in the 'migdal' or tower of Shechem, and took refuge in the stronghold of the temple standing in it. Unable to take this strongly fortified structure by assault, Abimelech tore a branch from a tree, told his men to follow suit, and set fire to the citadel, killing everyone in it.

He then marched against the neighbouring town of Thebez, that was presumably also involved in the revolt. The townspeople shut themselves in the fortified tower. As Abimelech approached it to set it alight, a woman hurled down part of a millstone. It fell on Abimelech's head, fatally injuring him. He ordered his young armour-bearer to kill him with his sword, lest it be said that Abimelech was slain by a woman. With their leader dead, his followers scattered and returned to their homes. 'Thus God requited the crime of Abimelech, which he committed against his father in killing his seventy brothers.' (Judg. 9:56)

The ruins of the ancient citadel of Shechem have recently been excavated at the southern entrance to the valley in which Nablus (Shechem) stands. The town of Thebez probably stood on the site of the present Arab hill-town of Tubaz. [Judg. 8, 9; 2 Sam. 11:21]

3. c. 11 century BC. A name used perhaps erroneously in the title of Psalm 34 for Achish, the Philistine king of Gath to whom David fled from the wrath of Saul. [1 Sam. 21:10; Ps. 34:1]

4. see ACHISH *1.*

Abinadab (Heb. 'father of nobility') *1. c.* 11 century BC. Villager of Kiriath-jearim and a member of the tribe of Judah in whose house the Ark was placed after the Philistines had in desperation returned it to the Israelites hoping to avoid further horrors. Abinadab kept it for three months and his son Eleazer looked after it. Two other sons, Uzzah and Ahio, drove the cart that brought the Ark to Jerusalem. [1 Sam. 7:1; 2 Sam. 6:3, 4; 1 Chr. 13]

2. c. 11 century BC. The second son of Jesse and a brother of David, he fought in Saul's army and witnessed the slaying of Goliath by David. [1 Sam. 16:8; 17:13; 1 Chr. 2:13]

3. c. 11 century BC. Son of King Saul and brother of Jonathan, he was killed with his father and brother when the Philistines defeated the Israelites on Mount Gilboa in the Galilee. [1 Sam. 31:2; 1 Chr. 10:2]

Abinoam (Heb. 'father is good') *c.* 12 century BC. Father of Barak of the tribe of Naphtali. [Judg. 4:6, 12; 5:1, 12]

Abiram (Heb. 'exalted father') *1. c.* 13 century BC. Son of Eliab, of the tribe of Reuben, he and his brother Dathan were the leading conspirators behind the rebellion of Korah against Moses while in the wilderness. The earth opened and the plotters were swallowed up. [Num. 16:1, 12, 24, 25, 27; 26:9; Deut. 11:6]

2. c. 9 century BC. Eldest son of Hiel of Bethel, he died because his father rebuilt Jericho, thus invoking the curse of Joshua. [1 Kgs. 16:34]

Abishag *c.* 10 century BC. A beautiful young Shunammite chosen to minister to King David when he was old. After David's death, his son Adonijah asked permission to marry her, and as a result of his request King Solomon had him killed, fearing this was a threat to his throne. [1 Kgs. 1:3, 15; 2:17, 21, 22]

Abishai (Heb. 'father of gift') *c.* 11 century BC. Eldest son of Zeruiah, King David's sister, and the brother of David's tough commander Joab, and of Asahel. He was a daring warrior utterly loyal to David and to Joab. During David's outlaw days he went with him stealthily into the camp of King Saul at Hachilah. When they reached the sleeping king, Abishai urged David to kill him but David refused to raise his hand against the Lord's anointed. When David became king, Abishai was one of the thirty mighty men who formed

David's bodyguard and was second-in-command to Joab. He aided Joab in the ruthless slaying of Abner in revenge for the death of their brother Asahel, and commanded a part of Joab's army in the victorious battle against the Ammonites who had insulted King David's messengers of goodwill. He saved the king's life when David joined his men in battle against the Philistines and Ishbibenob, the giant, tried to kill him with his great spear. In one battle Abishai is credited with having killed single-handed 300 of the enemy. Loyal to David in the civil war caused by Absalom, Abishai joined in the pursuit of Sheba son of Bichri and later helped to crush the last vestige of rebellion against David who then became king again of a united Israel. He seems to have died before Joab as his name does not appear at the death of David nor at the inauguration of his son King Solomon. (1 Sam. 26; 2 Sam. 3:30; 10:10; 16:9; 18:12; 19:11; 20:6; 21:17; 23:18; 1 Chr. 2:16; 11:20; 18:12; 19:11, 15]

Abishalom (Heb. 'father of peace') *c.* 10 century BC. Father-in-law of King Rehoboam of Judah, and the father of Maacah, the king's favourite wife. Also called Absalom and Uriel. [1 Kgs. 15:2, 10; 2 Chr. 11:20; 13:2]

Abishua (Heb. 'father of deliverance') *1. c.* 16 century BC. Son of Bela and a grandson of Benjamin. [1 Chr. 8:4]
2. date unknown. Son of Phinehas and great-grandson of Aaron, the high priest, he was an ancestor of Ezra. [1 Chr. 6:4, 5, 50; Ezra 7:5]

Abishur (Heb. 'father of protection') date unknown. Son of Shammai and a leader of Judah, he married Abihail and had two sons. [1 Chr. 2:28]

Abital (Heb. 'father of dew') *c.* 10 century BC. A wife of King David and the mother of Shephatiah, one of the six sons of David born to him in Hebron. [2 Sam. 3:4; 1 Chr. 3:3]

Abitub (Heb. 'father of goodness') date unknown. Son of Shaharaim and a leader of the tribe of Benjamin. [1 Chr. 8:11]

Abner (Heb. 'father of light') *c.* 11 century BC. Abner, the son of Ner, was King Saul's cousin and the able commander of his army. After Saul's death in battle, Abner retired eastward across the river Jordan with the remnant of his forces, set up his camp at Mahanaim, and there proclaimed Saul's weak son Ishbosheth as king.

Abner advanced again into the territory of Benjamin and at the Pool of Gibeon, north-west of Jerusalem, he met the army of David under his commander Joab. Abner and Joab agreed on a trial of strength between twelve picked men from either side. When all these men were killed leaving the issue still undecided, general fighting broke out in which Abner's army was routed.

In their flight, Abner himself was pursued by Asahel, Joab's youngest brother. Abner shouted to him to leave him alone: 'Why should I smite you to the ground? How then could I lift up my face to your brother Joab?' (2 Sam. 2:22) Asahel persisted and Abner was forced to kill him.

Abner became angry with Ishbosheth who accused him of misconduct with one of Saul's concubines. Disillusioned with the weakling he had himself made king, Abner sent messengers to make his peace with David: 'Make your covenant with me, and behold, my hand shall be with you to bring over all Israel to you.' (2 Sam. 3:12) David made one condition, that his wife Michal, Saul's daughter, should be returned to him, and Abner forced her brother Ishbosheth to agree.

Before seeing David, Abner conferred with the leaders of the northern tribes, and agreed with them to unite the country under David. The union was sealed when Abner and twenty men went to Hebron to tell David. David gave him and his retinue a feast and then Abner went off to rally all of Israel to the banner of David.

When Joab returned from an expedition, he tried without success to turn David against Abner. Joab then sent a messenger after Abner asking him to return and killed him in revenge for Joab's brother Asahel.

David was angry and shocked when he heard the news. Abner was buried at Hebron and David ordered a public funeral for him. The king himself walked behind the coffin, wept over the grave, and fasted. All the country understood that David had had no hand in Abner's murder. [1 Sam. 14:50; 17:55–8; 20:25; 26:13–16; 2 Sam. 2–4; 1 Chr. 26:28, 27:20]

Abraham (Heb. 'father is exalted') *c.* 18–16 centuries BC. First patriarch, Abraham was the founder of the Hebrew nation. In Jewish, Christian and Moslem tradition, he emerges as a father-figure – dignified, firm in his faith, humane, respected by the local rulers wherever he went. He moves slowly and majestically across the Near Eastern world of nearly four thousand years ago, from Mesopotamia to Egypt. The main setting for his story is the central hill country in the Land of Canaan promised to him and his seed by God.

Abram (as he was first called) came originally from 'Ur of the Chaldeans' (Gen. 11:28), a Sumerian city in the Euphrates valley, near the head of the Persian Gulf. With his father Terah, his wife Sarai (later Sarah) and his nephew Lot, he moved up the river till they came to rest in Haran, a trading centre in northern Aram (as Syria was then called). The family settled in this area, and here Terah died.

At Haran the Lord appeared to Abram and told him to leave for 'the land that I will show you' (Gen. 12:1) where he would make of Abram 'a great nation' (Gen. 12:2).

With Sarai and Lot he travelled to Canaan, and reached Shechem (the modern Nablus). Abram built an altar there, and another near Bethel (a little north of Jerusalem). The Lord again appeared to him and said: 'To your descendants I will give this land.' (Gen. 12:7) This promise was repeated during Abram's lifetime.

There was a famine in the land, and Abram's party continued to the southwest until they arrived in Egypt, then the granary of the region.

Sarai was a beautiful woman and Abram passed her off as his sister for fear that he might otherwise be killed because of her. Reports of her looks reached Pharaoh, who had her brought into his household, generously compensating her 'brother' with servants and livestock. The Lord intervened with plagues, and when Pharaoh learnt the truth he reproachfully returned Sarai to her husband and urged them to leave. (Later, Abram had a similar experience with Abimelech, king of Gerar, a Philistine city, near Gaza.)

They returned from Egypt to the hills north of Jerusalem. Both Abram and Lot had by this time acquired large herds of cattle, and there was strife between their herdsmen over the limited grazing. Uncle and nephew agreed to part amicably and Lot, given the choice by Abram, headed eastward to the 'Jordan valley' (Gen. 13:10), where stood the two cities of Sodom and Gomorrah. Abram himself settled in the plain of Mamre outside Hebron.

The Lord revealed to Abram that he intended to destroy the wicked cities of Sodom and Gomorrah. Abram pleaded with Him to spare the cities for the sake of the good men who might be among the inhabitants, and after some bargaining, the required minimum number of righteous men was fixed at ten. But in the end even this number was not found. Abram knew that his compassionate pleas had not helped when he saw the smoke rising from the stricken cities.

Sodom and Gomorrah were attacked by four kings from the north, and Lot was among those taken captive. Setting out in pursuit, Abram carried out a night assault near Dan, chased the enemy to a point near Damascus, and returned with the liberated captives. He restored the plunder to the king of Sodom, refusing to accept any of it for himself. Abram was a man of peace and this rescue of Lot was his only recorded martial exploit.

ISAAC AND ISHMAEL

As Abram and Sarai had remained without issue, she proposed that he should have a child with her Egyptian maid Hagar, who bore him a son called Ishmael. When Abram was ninety-nine and Sarai ninety, the Lord appeared to him again and said that henceforth his name would be Abraham, 'for I have made you the father of a multitude of nations' (Gen. 17:5). Sarai's name was changed to Sarah ('princess'). As a physical token of Abraham's covenant with him, the Lord instructed him to circumcise himself and all members of his household, and thereafter every male infant when he was eight days old. (The 'brith millah' – covenant of the circumcision – has been religiously observed by Jews to this day.)

When the Lord told the aged Abraham that Sarah would give birth to a son, he 'fell on his face and laughed' (Gen. 17:17). One hot day Abraham sat in the doorway of his tent at Mamre and saw three strangers approaching. He went forward to offer them hospitality. They were angels who told him once more that Sarah would bear him a son. Sarah overheard this from within the tent, and she too laughed as she was well past child-bearing age. But in due course Isaac (meaning 'he laughed') was born, as had been foretold.

Abraham gave a great feast when the infant was weaned. Sarah was stung by the mockery of Hagar and her son Ishmael, and demanded that Abraham cast them out. Being a kindly man he was greatly troubled, but the Lord told him to do as Sarah had asked, at the same time reassuring him that his descendants through Ishmael would also be a great nation. Abraham provided Hagar with a supply of bread and water and she left with the boy.

Abraham journeyed southward again, into the territory of Abimelech, the Philistine king of Gerar. Trouble over a well (a vital matter in this arid area) brought the two men together in a pact of friendship, consecrated by a solemn swearing ceremony. The place where this happened was named Beersheba (the 'Well of the Swearing').

Abraham's obedience to God was now put to an agonizing test. He was commanded to slay his beloved son Isaac at a distant mountain top as a burnt-offering to the Lord. Abraham set out on his ass, taking with him Isaac, two young servants and some firewood. On the third day they neared the place. Abraham left the two servants with the ass, and continued on foot with Isaac. On the way the puzzled lad said to his father 'Behold, the fire and the wood; but where is the lamb for a burnt offering?' (Gen. 22:7) The old man evaded the question by saying the Lord would provide the lamb.

When they reached the indicated spot Abraham built an altar, placed the bound boy upon the firewood, and took up the knife. At this dread moment the voice of an angel was heard saying: 'Do not lay your hand on the lad ... for now I know that you fear God.' (Gen. 22:12) In a nearby thicket Abraham saw a ram caught by the horns, and the animal was sacrificed instead of the boy. This episode also served to symbolize the rejection in the Hebrew faith of child-sacrifice practised by pagan cults.

When Sarah died at Hebron at the age of one hundred and twenty-seven, Abraham sought a family burying place and purchased from Ephron the Hittite the Cave of Machpelah and the field in which it stood, for four hundred shekels of silver. Here Sarah was laid to rest.

Abraham, now an aged man, concerned himself with finding a wife for Isaac. He sent for the trusted old retainer who managed his household, and confided in him that he did not want Isaac to marry a local Canaanite girl. The servant was instructed to travel to the Haran area from which Abraham had come to Canaan, and to seek a bride for Isaac among his kindred there. He returned with Rebekah, the young granddaughter of one of Abraham's brothers.

Abraham took another wife, Keturah, and had a number of children by her. He appointed Isaac the heir of his possessions, while making provision for his other children, including the sons of his concubines whom he sent to dwell further to the east in order to protect Isaac. Abraham died at the age of one hundred and seventy-five and was buried with Sarah in the Cave of Machpelah in Hebron.

For Jews, the story of Abraham is of national importance, for it marks their transitional beginning as a people and their divine charter to the Land of Israel. In the religious sense, it also symbolizes the break with pagan idolatry and the commitment to monotheism.

In the New Testament, Abraham is held up as the example of the godfearing and righteous man.

Abraham is more revered by Moslems than any other biblical personage, and is known in the Koran as El Khalil, the Friend of God. The Arabs still call Hebron 'El Khalil', and the Cave of Machpelah is sacred to the Moslems as well. The Jaffa Gate in the Old City of Jerusalem, from which the road to Hebron started, is inscribed with a verse from the Koran: 'There is no God but Allah, and Abraham is beloved of Him.' [Gen. 11:26–25:10]

THE CAVE OF MACHPELAH AND THE OAK OF MAMRE

The traditional Cave of Machpelah in Hebron is marked by a huge fort-like structure which was built by King Herod in the 1st century BC. Its outer walls are of great stone blocks rising to a height of more than forty feet. Several additions were made during the Byzantine, Mameluke and Ottoman periods, for this Jewish burial shrine later became holy also to Christians and Moslems. The crenellated battlements and two square corner minarets are Mameluke. The southern part of the enclosure is now a mosque. It was formerly a 12th-century Crusader church, and before that a Byzantine basilica. Six cenotaphs with embroidered silk coverings are said to stand exactly above the burial places in the cave beneath that of the patriarchs and their wives: Abraham and Sarah, Isaac and Rebekah, and Jacob and Leah. A seventh is held by some to mark the resting place of Joseph. Through a grating in the floor may be glimpsed the original cave.

There are fine examples of stained-glass windows from the 12th century AD made of the famous Hebron glass.

A mile away from Machpelah, along a road running off the Bethlehem-Hebron highway, is an old oak tree, barely alive, its branches supported by iron stakes. It has been known since the 12th century AD as Abraham's Oak or the Oak of Mamre. After leaving Lot near Bethel, Abraham 'came and dwelt by the oaks of Mamre, which are at Hebron; and there he built an altar unto the Lord' (Gen. 13:18). The oak stands in the grounds of the Russian Holy Trinity Church, monastery and hospice, built at the end of the last century. [Gen. 11–25; Isa. 41:8]

Absalom (Heb. '[my] father is peace') *l.c.* 10 century BC. Third son of King David.

The poignant story of Absalom concerns a remarkable king caught between his duty to crush rebellion and his love for a brilliant and wayward son.

Absalom was the third son of King David, born in Hebron while David was king of Judah. His mother was Maacah. Tall and handsome, with a flowing mane of hair, 'from the sole of his foot to the crown of his head there was no blemish in him' (2 Sam. 14:25).

He first appears as the avenger of his sister Tamar, who had been violated and then cast aside by Amnon, their half-brother and David's first-born. Absalom consoled his sister and took her into his house. He carefully waited for an opportunity, and two years later arranged a sheep-shearing feast at his country estate to which he invited all David's sons. Absalom's servants, at his instructions, killed the tipsy Amnon. All the rest of the princes hurriedly mounted their mules and returned to the palace. Absalom took refuge with his grandfather, King Talmai.

When Absalom had been in exile for three years, Joab the commander-in-chief, who was his first cousin, persuaded the king to allow the youth to return to Jerusalem. But David, so skilful in the handling of men, was inept in dealing with the son he loved. Having let him come back, he refused to see him. Absalom nursed his resentment for two years, then forced Joab to come and see him by setting his barley field alight. He demanded that Joab arrange for him to be received by the king. David agreed to this. He raised up the son who came and bowed down before him, and kissed him fondly.

On Absalom's part, this reconciliation was more apparent than real. He strove to deflect popular favour away from the king and towards himself. He would stand at the city gates, intercept inhabitants bringing their disputes for judgment and pay them flattering attention; 'so Absalom stole the hearts of the men of Israel' (2 Sam. 15:6).

After a long period of intrigue, of which David seemed unaware, Absalom decided that the time had come to make a bid for power. On a pretext, he proceeded to Hebron with two hundred armed men, while sending secret messengers to his fellow-conspirators among the different tribes to stand ready for the signal of rebellion. In Hebron he was joined by a formidable ally – Ahithophel, David's leading counsellor and a man whose political judgment was regarded as infallible.

The choice of Hebron for the start of the revolt was a shrewd move. It was Absalom's birthplace; it had been David's original capital and the inhabitants felt neglected since he had moved to Jerusalem; it was the centre of David's own tribe of Judah; and it was within easy striking distance of Jerusalem twenty miles away.

David was taken completely by surprise. He made the painful decision to gain time by abandoning Jerusalem and fleeing eastward with his household and palace guard. Absalom entered the capital unopposed. One of his first acts, on Ahithophel's advice, was to symbolize the takeover by having intercourse with the ten concubines David had left behind to take care of the household.

There were others whom the cool-headed David had persuaded to remain behind in Jerusalem, and serve his interests in the heart of Absalom's camp. There were the two high priests Abiathar and Zadok who undertook to keep David informed by using their sons as runners. Also, there was Hushai, another of David's trusted counsellors, whose task it was to gain Absalom's confidence and counteract the guidance of Ahithophel.

Even with Jerusalem in his hands, and the country rallying behind him, Absalom's seizure of power could not be secure as long as King David was at large. Ahithophel urged immediate pursuit that same night, so that David could be caught and liquidated before he had a chance to organize a counter-thrust. Ahithophel had worked too long with David to underrate his capacities. Hushai argued in favour of greater caution. David and the veteran fighters with him, Hushai pointed out, were desperate men, and dangerous 'like a bear robbed of her cubs in the field' (2 Sam. 17:8). To engage them in a hurry would entail too great a risk for Absalom's cause. He would be well advised to recruit and organize a large army from all the tribes, and then face David with overwhelming strength.

Absalom was convinced by Hushai. David thus gained the time he needed to cross the river Jordan into Gilead, and there rebuilt his forces. Ahithophel clearly perceived that the prince to whom he had defected had made a fatal blunder and that his own career was wrecked. He went home and hanged himself.

Absalom appointed as his army commander Amasa, the son of David's sister Abigail, and therefore another first cousin. In due course their troops crossed the Jordan river into Gilead, and took up positions near Ephraim. Here they were attacked and heavily defeated by David's well-trained men, familiar with the difficult terrain of woods and ridges and skilfully commanded by Joab.

In trying to escape Absalom dashed along a forest path on a mule. His thick hair caught in the overhanging branches of a great oak, and he remained dangling in the air while his mule ran away. One of Joab's men spotted him but did not dare touch him, having heard David instructing his commanders that no harm should come to Absalom. The soldier reported what he had seen to Joab, who ruthlessly plunged three darts into the body of Absalom. He was finished off by Joab's men. In this fashion Absalom's revolt, and his dream of power, came to an abrupt and bloody end.

During the battle, David had remained behind in the town of Mahanaim. Runners reached him with the tidings of victory, and his first question was for the safety of Absalom. When told that the young man was dead, he was overcome with grief, crying out repeatedly, 'O my son Absalom, my son, my son Absalom! Would I had died instead of you, O Absalom, my son, my son!' (2 Sam. 18:33) David's throne had been saved, but at a terrible personal price. [2 Sam. 3:3; 13–19; 1 Chr. 3:2]
2. *see* ABISHALOM

Achan (Heb. 'trouble-maker') *c.* 13 century BC. Son of Carmi and a member of the tribe of Judah. After Joshua had conquered the city of Jericho with trumpets and the shouts of the Israelites, he forbade the people to touch any of the booty but Achan disobeyed and secretly stole some of the loot. During the next battle, this time against the city of Ai, Joshua's men were routed and thirty-six of them killed. When Joshua appealed to God to tell him what he had done wrong, the wrathful Lord answered him, 'Israel has sinned; ... they have taken some of the devoted things ...' (Josh. 7:11). Joshua then assembled the twelve tribes, and lots were cast to find out the guilty family. The tribe of Judah was singled out and Joshua went through them family by family until he came to Achan, who confessed that he had stolen a costly Babylonian garment and large amounts of silver and gold which he had hidden in his tent. Joshua sent his men to retrieve the stolen goods and they were spread before the Lord. Then Achan, his entire family and all his possessions, including his animals and the stolen booty were taken into the valley of Achor. 'And all Israel stoned him with stones; they burned them with fire, and stoned them with stones ... then the Lord turned from his burning anger.' (Josh. 7:25, 26) Also called Achar. [Josh. 7; 1 Chr. 2:7]

Achar *see* ACHAN

Achbor (Heb. 'mouse') *1.* date unknown. Father of Baal-hanan, one of the first kings of Edom. [Gen. 36:38, 39; 1 Chr. 1:49]
2. c. 7 century BC. Father of Elnathan, an officer of King Jehoiakim sent to Egypt to seize the prophet Uriah. [Jer. 26:22; 36:12]
3. see ABDON *4.*

Achish (Philistine 'the king gave') *1. c.* 11 century BC. The Philistine king of Gath with whom David twice took refuge. The first time he arrived alone and feigned madness for fear of being recognized. Later, David and his outlaw band were welcomed by Achish as supposed enemies of the Israelite king.

Achish made David governor of Ziklag on the border of the desert. Using this town as a base, David attacked tribes that were hostile to Israel, pretending to Achish that he was raiding towns in Judah.

The Philistines gathered their armies and marched against Israel. When the other Philistine princes saw David and his men among the soldiers of Achish, they protested that the Hebrews might defect in the battle. Achish tried to convince them that David could be trusted, but had to yield to the pressure of his allies. He apologetically asked David to return. Also called Abimelech. [1 Sam. 21:10; 27–29; Ps. 34:1]
2. c. 10 century BC. Son of Maoch, king of Gath in the reign of King Solomon, with whom two of Shimei's slaves sought refuge. [1 Kgs. 2:39, 40]

Achsah (Heb. 'anklet') *c.* 13 century BC. Achsah was the daughter of Caleb, who settled in Hebron and gave her in marriage to Othniel for capturing the neighbouring city of Debir. The shrewd Achsah got her father to add to her dowry of land 'the upper springs and the lower springs' (Josh. 15:19). [Josh. 15:16–19; Judg. 1:12–14; 1 Chr. 2:49]

Adah (Heb. 'ornament') *1.* date unknown. Wife of Lamech and mother of Jabal and Jubal. [Gen. 4:19, 23]
2. c. 16 century BC. A wife of Esau, she was the daughter of Elon the Hittite. Also called Basemath. [Gen. 26:34; 36:2, 4, 10, 16]

Adaiah (Heb. 'adorned by God') *1.* date unknown. Son of Shimei and a leader of the tribe of Benjamin living in Jerusalem. [1 Chr. 8:21]
2. date unknown. An ancestor of Maaseiah, one of the men of Judah living in Jerusalem after the return from exile in Babylon. [Neh. 11:5]
3. see IDDO *3.*
4. c. 9 century BC. Father of Maaseiah, one of the army commanders of Judah sent to overthrow Queen Athaliah and crown Joash as king. [2 Chr. 23:1]
5. c. 7 century BC. Father of Jedidah, the wife of King Amon of Judah and the mother of King Josiah. [2 Kgs. 22:1]
6. c. 5 century BC. Son of Jeroham, he was one of the first priests to serve in the Temple in Jerusalem after the return from exile in Babylon. [1 Chr. 9:12; Neh. 11:12]
7. 5 century BC. A descendant of Bani who divorced his non-Jewish wife in the time of Ezra. [Ezra 10:29]
8. 5 century BC. A son of Binnui who divorced his non-Jewish wife in the time of Ezra. [Ezra 10:39]

Adalia (Pers. 'respectable') *c.* 5 century BC. One of the ten sons of Haman who plotted to kill all the Jews of Persia in the reign of King Ahasuerus. The plot was discovered and Haman and his sons were executed. [Esther 9:8]

Adam (Heb. 'man') date unknown. The first human being.

In five days God created day and night; heaven, earth and the seas; sun, moon and stars; plants, fish and birds. On the sixth day He created the beasts, and then Man in His own image, male and female. The Lord told them to be fruitful and multiply, and gave them dominion over all living things. In this fashion, Chapter 1 of the Book of Genesis tells the story of creation. Man here is the human species, and not a particular individual.

In the second chapter of Genesis there is a different account of the Creation, more vivid and detailed. Though it appears after Chapter 1, this version is of earlier origin. It probably derives from the J (Jehovistic) Document, whereas Chapter 1 may be attributed to the P (priestly) Document written several centuries later by priestly writers for whom the Almighty had become a more abstract concept. In the earlier version the creation of Man is overlaid with the story of a particular man, who in Genesis 3:17 is called Adam for the first time. He has a wife called Eve 'because she was the mother of all living' (Gen. 3:20). (Eve in Hebrew is Chava, which means 'life'.)

According to this earlier and more primitive account, 'the Lord God formed man of dust from the ground, and breathed into his nostrils the breath of life' (Gen. 2:7). God put Adam in the Garden of Eden and created Eve out of one of Adam's ribs to be a helpmeet for him. Adam had been warned not to eat of the fruit of the tree of knowledge of good and evil, but the serpent tempted Eve to try the fruit and she gave some to Adam too. As a result they became ashamed of their nakedness, covered it with fig-leaves and hid from the Lord.

Then God cursed the serpent saying '... upon your belly you shall go, and dust you shall eat all the days of your life' (Gen. 3:14). Human beings and serpents would henceforth be enemies. To Eve God said that she would bring forth children in sorrow, and her husband would rule over her. To Adam He said, '... cursed is the ground because of you ... In the sweat of your face you shall eat bread till you return to the ground;

... you are dust, and to dust you shall return.' (Gen. 3:17–19) Lest they eat also of the tree of life and become immortal, Adam and Eve were driven forth from Eden and their return was barred by cherubim and a flaming sword.

The Bible states that the Garden was 'in Eden in the east' (Gen. 2:8) and the river that flowed from it parted into four: Pishon, Gihon, Tigris and Euphrates. This would place Eden somewhere in Mesopotamia – the ancient Babylonia and the modern Iraq.

After the expulsion, Adam and Eve had three sons – Cain and Abel, and much later, after Abel's murder, Seth. Adam's age when he died is given as nine hundred and thirty years. [Gen. 1–4]

REFLECTIONS ON ADAM AND EVE

The origin of Adam's name has intrigued scholars. The account in Genesis stresses that man was formed out of the earth and would return to it. This bears out the suggestion that the Hebrew word for man, *adam*, was derived from the Hebrew word for earth, 'adama'. The root of both words may be connected with the Hebrew word for 'red' – 'adom'. That would imply a reddish soil or clay in the area where Adam was created.

The belief that the first man was created out of clay was by no means confined to Hebrew mythology. There were similar stories among the ancient Babylonians, Egyptians and Greeks, and parallel folk legends among primitive tribes in many other parts of the world, including Australian aborigines, Maoris, Africans, American Indians and Eskimos.

Adam and Eve are the prototype of the close bond between husband and wife: 'Then the man said, "This at last is bone of my bones and flesh of my flesh ..." Therefore a man leaves his father and his mother and cleaves unto his wife, and they become one flesh.' (Gen. 2:23, 24) This emphasis on the marriage tie was remarkable in ancient times, for men were permitted to take more than one wife, and to have children by concubines.

Granting that primal man evolved from lower species millions of years ago, the legend of Adam and Eve continues to serve as a striking parable of the human condition. Paradise is lost, men must wrest a living by their toil, women bear children in pain, and the grave awaits each mortal being; all men are brothers, for Adam is their common forefather; and all men are equal, for they are all created in the image of God. [Gen. 2–5]

Adbeel (Heb. 'God established') *c.* 17 century BC. Son of Ishmael and a grandson of Abraham, he was leader of a desert tribe. [Gen. 25:13; 1 Chr. 1:29]

Addan 6 century BC. A leader of Judah who returned with Zerubbabel from exile in Babylon but could not trace his ancestry and therefore could not prove that he was a Jew. Also called Addon. [Ezra 2:59; Neh. 7:61]

Addar *see* ARD 2.

Addon *see* ADDAN

Adiel (Heb. 'ornament of God') *1.* date unknown. Ancestor of Adaiah, one of the chief priests in the Temple after the return from Babylon. [1 Chr. 9:12]
2. c. 11 century BC. Father of Azmaveth, the officer in charge of King David's treasuries. [1 Chr. 27:25]
3. c. 8 century BC. One of the leaders of Simeon who drove out the inhabitants from the rich Gedor valley and settled there in the reign of King Hezekiah. [1 Chr. 4:36]

Adin (Heb. 'delicate') *1.* date unknown. Ancestor of a family of Judah who returned with Zerubbabel from exile in Babylon. [Ezra 2:15; 8:6; Neh. 7:20]
2. 5 century BC. A leader of Judah who

signed the solemn covenant in the time of Nehemiah. [Neh. 10:16]

Adina (Heb. 'delicate') *c.* 10 century BC. A warrior from the tribe of Reuben in King David's army who was distinguished for his bravery. [1 Chr. 11:42]

Adlai (Heb. 'God's justice') *c.* 10 century BC. Father of Shaphat, King David's official who was in charge of the royal herds that fed in the valley. [1 Chr. 27:29]

Admatha (Pers. 'military commander') 5 century BC. One of the seven chief princes of Persia whom King Ahasuerus consulted when he wished to punish Queen Vashti for disobeying his orders. [Esther 1:14]

Adna (Heb. 'pleasure') *1.* 5 century BC. A descendant of Pahath-moab who divorced his non-Jewish wife in the time of Ezra. [Ezra 10:30]
2. 5 century BC. Head of a priestly family descended from Harim in the time of Nehemiah. [Neh. 12:15]

Adnah (Heb. 'pleasure') *1. c.* 11 century BC. A warrior of the tribe of Manasseh who deserted from King Saul's army and rallied to David at Ziklag. [1 Chr. 12:20]
2. c. 10 century BC. Commander of a large contingent in the army of King Jehoshaphat of Judah. [2 Chr. 17:14]

Adonijah (Heb. 'my Lord is God') *1. c.* 10 century BC. Fourth son of David, he was born in Hebron to David and Haggith. When David grew old, Adonijah, then the eldest remaining son, decided to take matters into his own hands and have himself proclaimed king. He conferred with Joab, David's commander-in-chief, and with one of the high priests, Abiathar. They gave him their support, and 'he prepared for himself chariots and horsemen, and fifty men to run before him' (1 Kgs. 1:5).

Adonijah invited his brothers (except Solomon) and the city notables to a feast at the spring of En-rogel, down in the valley of Kidron outside the city walls. Here he performed ceremonial sacrifices by the sacred stone called the Serpent's Stone.

The oppostion, led by Nathan the prophet, reacted swiftly. Bathsheba the queen was sent by Nathan to go into David's bedchamber and tell him what Adonijah was doing. She also reminded the king he had promised the throne to her son Solomon. Nathan then appeared and supported Bathsheba.

David decided to abdicate immediately in favour of Solomon and instructed Zadok the other high priest, Nathan and Benaiah the commander of the palace guard, to take Solomon on the king's own mule to the spring of Gihon, also in the valley of Kidron, and in front of the Jerusalem citizens to anoint him king: 'then blow the trumpet, and say, Long live King Solomon!' (1 Kgs. 1:34) When the noise of the crowd rejoicing at Solomon's coronation reached Adonijah's feast, and the company learned that Solomon had already replaced David as king, the guests hurriedly returned to their homes. Adonijah sought sanctuary at the altar and was spared at that time by Solomon.

After David had died and Solomon was firmly established on the throne, Adonijah asked to see Bathsheba. 'And she said, "Do you come peaceably?" He said, "Peaceably".' (1 Kgs. 2:13) He then asked her if she would intervene with her son King Solomon and ask him if he would allow Adonijah to marry Abishag the young Shunammite girl who had looked after David in his old age. Bathsheba agreed to do this. When she entered the royal chamber, Solomon treated her with great deference and seated her to the right of his throne. But when she put forward Adonijah's request, Solomon reacted sharply. Adonijah might as well have asked for the throne, he said. (To take the wife or concubine of a dead or deposed king symbolized a claim to the succession.) King Solomon immediately sent for Benaiah and had his eldest half-brother put to death. [2 Sam. 3:4; 1 Kgs. 1–2]

2. c. 9 century BC. A Levite sent by King Jehoshaphat to teach the Law of God in the cities of Judah. [2 Chr. 17:8]

3. 5 century BC. One of the leaders of Judah in the days of Nehemiah who signed the solemn covenant to observe the Laws of God. [Neh. 10:16]

Adonikam (Heb. 'the Lord raised [for help]') date unknown. The ancestor of a large family that returned with Zerubbabel to Judah from exile in Babylon. [Ezra 2:13; 8:13; Neh. 7:18]

Adoniram (Heb. 'the Lord is exalted') c. 10 century BC. The son of Abda, he was given the unpopular task of levying the forced labour necessary for the royal building programmes. He had been appointed to this task by David and retained by Solomon. By the time Solomon died and his son Rehoboam succeeded him, the population was weary with the constant exactions. The northern tribes revolted against the new king and in the disturbances Adoniram was stoned to death. Sometimes called Adoram and Hadoram. [2 Sam. 20:24; 1 Kgs. 4:6; 5:14; 12:18, 19; 2 Chr. 10:18]

Adonizedek (Heb. 'Lord of righteousness') c. 13 century BC. The king of Jerusalem who formed a military alliance with the rulers of Hebron and the foothill towns of Lachish, Eglon and Jarmuth, to attack the town of Gibeon 'for it has made peace with Joshua and with the people of Israel' (Josh. 10:4). After their defeat by Joshua, Adonizedek and the other four kings hid themselves in a cave but were discovered and put to death. Their bodies were hung on trees until sunset, when they were cut down and buried in the same cave. [Josh. 10]

Adoram *see* ADONIRAM

Adrammelech 1. date unknown. One of the gods of the Sepharvaim, a tribe settled by the Assyrians in Samaria after the exile of the people of Israel. Children were sacrificed to this god. [2 Kgs. 17:31]
2. *c.* 7 century BC. He and his brother Sharezer murdered their father Sennacherib, king of Assyria, while he was at prayer in the house of Nisroch, his god. The two sons escaped to Armenia and their brother Esarhaddon became king in 680 BC. [2 Kgs. 19:37; Isa. 37:38]

Adriel (Heb. 'flock of God') *c.* 10 century BC. Son of Barzillai and the husband of King Saul's daughter Merab. Their five sons were executed by the Gibeonites in revenge for Saul's murder of their people. [1 Sam. 18:19; 2 Sam. 21:8]

Agag *c.* 11 century BC. King of Amalek who was defeated in battle by King Saul. Saul wanted to spare Agag alive but the prophet Samuel 'hewed Agag in pieces' (1 Sam. 15:33) as retribution for Agag's brutality. [1 Sam. 15:8, 9, 32, 33]

Agee (Heb. 'fugitive') *c.* 10 century BC. The father of Shammah the Hararite warrior of King David who stood his ground and killed the Philistines when everyone else had fled. [2 Sam. 23:11]

Agur (Heb. 'gatherer') date unknown. The son of Jakeh who spoke a series of prophecies, collected in the Book of Proverbs, to Ithiel and Ucal. [Prov. 30]

Ahab (Heb. 'father's brother') 1. Seventh king of Israel after the monarchy split, he reigned 874–53 BC. In his twenty-two years on the throne of Israel, Ahab consolidated the dynasty founded in the northern kingdom by his father Omri. He further developed the lines of policy Omri had laid down: co-existence with the southern Hebrew kingdom of Judah; partnership with the Phoenicians on the seaboard; containment of Aram-Damascus to the north-east; and the fostering of commerce and construction at home. Ahab would thus have stood high in the roster of Israelite kings, but for the one aspect of his rule which the biblical chroniclers refused to condone – religious laxity. For them, the central theme in Ahab's record was the fierce onslaught of the prophet Elijah against the alien cult fostered by his queen, Jezebel. For that reason, he is sternly dismissed as having done '... more to provoke the Lord, the God of Israel, to anger than all the kings of Israel who were before him' (1 Kgs. 16:33).

The Phoenicians inhabited the coastal plain which is today Lebanon, with their two major port cities of Sidon and Tyre. They were the most enterprising traders and seafarers in the Mediterranean, with a relatively high level of affluence and skills. Hiram, king of Tyre, had been the friend and business partner of David and Solomon, and Omri had renewed these ties with the contemporary Phoenician ruler Ethbaal. The alliance was cemented by Ahab's marriage to Ethbaal's daughter Jezebel.

She seems to have been a strong-willed woman who dominated her husband and used her position at the Samarian court to promote the Phoenician culture and religion. In the midst of this Hebrew hill-nation, dedicated to the exclusive worship of a single invisible God, there sprang up the cults of the Phoenician Baal, Melkart and the fertility goddess Ashtoreth (Astarte). At the palace Jezebel maintained as her pensioners a huge corps of some four hundred 'prophets of Ball' in the service of these alien creeds. The Bible suggests that Ahab did not merely tolerate Jezebel's activities, but took an active part in them: 'He erected an altar for Baal in the house of Baal, which he built in Samaria.' (1 Kgs. 16:32)

AHAB AND ELIJAH

The revulsion of the faithful was focused by the austere and outspoken prophetic figure of Elijah the Tishbite, from the land of Gilead across the Jordan river. He confronted the king and sternly announced that the wrathful Lord would smite Israel with a prolonged drought: '... there shall be neither dew nor rain these years' (1 Kigs. 17:1). The prophet then escaped across the river.

Two years later, Elijah set out again to see the king. Ahab went out to meet him and greeted him with the words 'Is it you, you troubler of Israel?' (1 Kigs. 18:17) Elijah retorted that it was the royal house that troubled Israel, because they had forsaken the Lord and followed false gods. Elijah demanded an encounter with the prophets of Baal on Mount Carmel in the presence of the people. The king complied. In the famous confrontation that then took place, the foreign priests were confounded and put to death by Elijah. After this crushing victory for the forces of monotheism, the drought broke in a great storm that came sweeping in from the sea. Ahab drove back in his chariot through the pouring rain, with the exulting prophet running ahead of him part of the way with his cloak tucked up above his knees. When Jezebel heard from Ahab what had happened she furiously swore to have Elijah killed. But the prophet once more made his escape.

Jezebel's evil influence over the king was vividly shown in the story of Naboth's vineyard. Ahab had established his winter quarters at Jezreel, a town in the valley of that name, where the climate was milder than at Samaria up in the hills some twenty-five miles to the south. Adjoining the palace grounds at Jezreel was a fine vineyard which the king was anxious to buy or exchange for another elsewhere. The owner, Naboth, was unwilling to part with it as it had been a family inheritance for a long time. Ahab sulked with frustration:

'And he lay down on his bed, and turned away his face, and would eat no food.' (1 Kgs. 21:4) Jezebel arranged for Naboth to be convicted of blasphemy and stoned to death. The ruler then became the legal owner of the property.

No sooner had Ahab taken possession of the vineyard than Elijah descended upon him and cried out: 'Have you killed, and also taken possession? ... In the place where dogs licked up the blood of Naboth shall dogs lick your own blood.' (1 Kgs. 21:19) The prophet then pronounced a curse on Ahab and all his house, predicting that they would be destroyed. The frightened king tore his clothes, dressed himself in sackcloth and fasted. The Lord noted that he had humbled himself in repentance and postponed the doom of the dynasty to Ahab's son and successor.

A black basalt stele (inscribed monument) was discovered a century ago in southern Jordan. It claims that Mesha king of Moab threw off the yoke of Israel after having paid an annual tribute to Omri and Ahab of a 'hundred thousand lambs, and the wool of a hundred thousand rams' (2 Kgs. 3:4). It was presumably to help control Moab that Jericho was refortified in Ahab's reign, after having remained an empty ruin since its destruction by Joshua.

Like his father, Ahab was an energetic builder. He developed the new hill capital of Samaria, founded by Omri. The bible mentions that he built an 'ivory house'. The excavations at Samaria have in fact produced hundreds of ivory carvings that were inlaid in furniture, probably according to the Phoenician fashion of the time. Ahab extended the fortifications of strategic strongholds such as those at Hazor in the eastern Galilee and Megiddo in the Jezreel valley. The extensive stables for chariot and cavalry horses excavated at Megiddo date from his time.

THE SYRIAN WAR

Ahab buttressed the alliance with Judah

by marrying his daughter Athalia to Jehoram, the son and heir of King Jehoshaphat of Judah. Nevertheless, Ahab's forces were unable to block a fresh advance by King Ben-hadad II of Aram-Damascus (Syria), Israel's most oppressive enemy in that period. The Syrian army marched right to the gates of Samaria and laid siege to it. Ahab at first tried to appease Ben-hadad, then rejected his arrogant demands, saying: 'Let not him that girds on his armour boast himself as he that puts it off.' (1 Kgs. 20:11) Ahab launched a surprise attack from the city in the noonday heat. The Syrians were routed, and their king escaped on the back of a chariot horse.

Ben-hadad mustered a fresh army, and took up positions near the town of Aphek on the level ground of the Golan plateau east of the Sea of Galilee. His advisers had pointed out to him that 'their gods are gods of the hills, and so they were stronger than we; but let us fight against them in the plain, and surely we shall be stronger than they.' (1 Kgs. 20:23) This seemed sound military tactics, for the Arameans could deploy their mounted troops against the Israelite highlanders, once they were lured out of their native hills into open country. But in the pitched battle that followed the forces of Aram were again defeated. King Ben-hadad begged for his life and Ahab agreed to spare him on condition that he gave back the occupied Israelite towns and granted Israel trading rights in the bazaars of Damascus. Ahab was plunged into gloom when an unknown prophet told him he would forfeit his life as a consequence of this act of clemency.

After the king of Aram was spared, the Bible states laconically that 'For three years Syria and Israel continued without war.' (1 Kgs. 22:1) The probable explanation for this truce was that both nations were threatened by the new and formidable imperial power of Assyria,

pressing down from the north. In the 'monolith inscription' which survives from the sixth year of the reign of Shalmaneser III, king of Assyria, (853 BC) he boasts of a victory against a league of twelve kings. Among them were both the king of Damascus and 'Ahab the Israelite', who was said to have brought two thousand chariots and ten thousand foot soldiers into the combined army. In fact, the common front did succeed in halting the Assyrian advance for the time being.

When the Assyrian danger receded, King Jehoshaphat of Judah joined forces with Ahab in an expedition to retake the Israelite town of Ramoth-gilead in the land of Gilead, east of the Jordan river. Ben-hadad of Damascus had either not returned this area as he had promised when his life was spared, or he had regained it later.

With the two Hebrew monarchs sitting on thrones at the threshing floor of Samaria, the whole company of prophets appeared before them and assured them of success in the coming battle. Only one prophet was missing, Micaiah, whose unsparing utterances Ahab found hard to tolerate. Prodded by Jehoshaphat, Ahab sent for Micaiah as well. At first the prophet joined in the chorus of encouragement, but when pressed he courageously pronounced his true prediction, which was one of disaster for Ahab. The king ordered the dour pessimist to be flung into jail and kept on bread and water until his own return from the war.

All the same, Ahab's confidence was shaken. Jehoshaphat entered the battle in his royal armour, but Ahab himself was disguised in order to avoid attention. The ruse was effective for a while. The Syrian leader had commanded his troops to concentrate on the king of Israel and at first they mistook Jehoshaphat for their quarry until the Judean king gave his own battle cry. Unfortunately for Ahab, a stray arrow pierced the joint in his armour at the armpit. He ordered his charioteer to withdraw, but the battle was too fierce, and he was propped upright in the chariot facing the enemy until he died at sunset in a pool of blood. When the word spread among his followers they broke off the engagement and retreated back across the river and up to Samaria. Here Ahab was buried, 'And they washed the chariot by the pool of Samaria, and the dogs licked up his blood.' (1 Kgs. 22:38) He was succeeded by his son Ahaziah. [1 Kgs. 16–22; 2 Chr. 18]

Archaeological excavations in 1932 at Samaria brought to light remains of buildings constructed by Kings Omri and Ahab and their successors. On the summit bounded by steep slopes on three sides, Omri built a rectangular citadel, protected by a wall of square stones laid with great skill on levelled beds in the rock. The base courses of sections of this wall are well preserved. There are also remains of the lower city which was built at the same time on the more gradual southern slope of the site. In Ahab's time, or possibly some years later, a city wall of great thickness was thrown up, and sections of this may also be seen today.

Among the finds in the citadel were the carved ivories from Ahab's 'ivory house', some bearing inscriptions in ancient Hebrew script; and scores of ostraca with Hebrew writing discovered in the ruins of what was probably the royal records office. The large well-plastered reservoir found by the archaeologists may have been the 'pool of Samaria' in which was 'washed the chariot' of Ahab after his death on the battlefield at Ramoth–gilead. (1 Kgs. 22:38)
2.c. 6 century BC. Son of Kolaiah, he was a false prophet of Judah in the time of Jeremiah. [Jer. 29:21, 22]

Aharah see EHI

Aharhel date unknown. Son of Harum and a leader of the tribe of Judah. [1 Chr. 4:8]

Ahasbai see UR

Ahasuerus (Pers. 'mighty', 'eye of man') *1. c.* 6 century BC. Father of King Darius of Persia. [Dan. 9:1] *2.* 5 century BC. King of Persia (Xerxes 1) (486–65 BC), who in the third year of his reign gathered together all the leading men of his empire at Shushan (Susa), the capital. Under the influence of wine, Ahasuerus sent his court chamberlains to fetch Queen Vashti, so that her beauty could be displayed to the guests. She refused to come and the angry king, after consultation with his chief counsellors, issued a decree banning Vashti from his presence. He then searched his kingdom for a suitable queen to replace her and chose Esther, the adopted daughter of Mordecai, a Jewish court official.

Esther thwarted the evil designs of Haman the chief minister to kill all the Jews in the kingdom. Ahasuerus had Haman and his sons hanged and promoted Mordecai to chief minister. [Ezra 4:6; Esther 1–3; 6–10]

Ahaz (Heb. 'he grasped') *1.* date unknown. One of the four sons of Micah of the tribe of Benjamin and a descendant of King Saul. [1 Chr. 8:35, 36; 9:41, 42]
2. Twelfth king of Judah after the monarchy split, he reigned 736–16 BC. At the age of twenty, Ahaz succeeded his father Jotham to the throne of Judah.

In the reign of his illustrious grandfather Uzziah, the kingdom had reached the peak of its expansion and strength. Under Ahaz, Judah again declined rapidly and its borders shrank.

Edom, the vassal desert kingdom to the south, successfully revolted. The Philistines regained their lost territory in the coastal plain, and occupied part of the foothills. The Bible attributes these reverses to Ahaz's impiety. He indulged in pagan cults and revived the primitive custom of child sacrifice that was especially associated with the valley (gei) of Hinnom (Gehenna) skirting Jerusalem. He 'even burned his son as an offering, according to the abominable practices of the nations whom the Lord drove out ... And he sacrificed and burned incense on the high places, and on the hills, and under every green tree.' (2 Kgs. 16:3, 4)

The forces of Pekah, king of Israel, and Rezin, king of Aram-Damascus (Syria), invaded Judah, that had refused to join their alliance against the Assyrian threat. They failed to take Jerusalem or to depose Ahaz, but delivered a crippling military blow to Judah and withdrew, carrying with them a great deal of plunder and a number of captives.

Against a strong warning from his adviser, the great prophet Isaiah, Ahaz then decided to appeal for help to the king of Assyria. He sent messengers with gifts to Tiglath-pileser III saying: 'I am your servant and your son. Come up, and rescue me from the hand of the king of Syria and from the hand of the king of Israel, who are attacking me.' (2 Kgs. 16:7) The Assyrians were in no need of this invitation in pursuing their strategy of conquest. In the period 734–2 BC, they smashed the coalition opposing them, occupied Damascus and a large part of the territory of Israel, and thrust down the coastal plain as far as Gaza. Judah was left isolated and maintained itself intact only by submission to the Assyrians and the payment of tribute. In an inscription the Assyrian monarch lists Ahaz among the local kings in the area who delivered to him tribute in the form of 'gold, silver, tin, iron, lead ... gorgeous raiment, the purple apparel of their land.' The latter may be a reference to the famous Tyrian purple extracted from a species of periwinkle on the seacoast, chiefly at the Israelite centre of Dor.

The Book of Kings records that Ahaz went to Damascus to pay his respects to his Assyrian overlord. He was so impressed with an altar he saw there that he sent back detailed instructions to Uriah, the priest of the Temple in Jerusalem, to have an exact replica made. When he returned Ahaz moved to another position the bronze altar erected by Solomon and installed the new one in its place. He may possibly have meant this as a gesture to the Assyrians.

After a reign of twenty years, Ahaz died and was buried in Jerusalem, but not in the royal tombs. He was succeeded by his son Hezekiah, one of the greatest of the Judean kings. [2 Kgs. 15:38; 16:1–20; 17:1; 18:1; 20:11; 23:12; 1 Chr. 3:13; 2 Chr. 27:9; 28:1–27; 29:19; Isa. 1:1; 7:1–12; 14:28; 38:8; Hos. 1:1; Mic. 1:1]

Ahaziah (Heb. 'God sustains') *1.* Eighth king of Israel after the monarchy split, he reigned 853–2 BC. After the death of King Ahab, his eldest son Ahaziah, son of Jezebel, succeeded him briefly on the throne of Israel in Samaria. He distinguished himself only by falling through the latticework of an upper room, seriously injuring himself. He sent messengers to the shrine of the Philistine god Baal-zebub (lord of the flies) at Ekron on the coastal plain to find out whether he would recover. The prophet Elijah intercepted the messengers and angrily asked them if there was no God in Israel that they go seeking the god of Ekron? He predicted that their master would not get up again from his bed.

In a rage the king despatched a company of fifty soldiers to seize the prophet but they were killed by fire from heaven. The same thing happened to a second unit. Elijah returned to the palace with the third unit and personally repeated his dire prophesy to the king, who died soon after.

Ahaziah is also mentioned as having been rebuffed by King Jehoshaphat of Judah when he proposed that his men join the Judean sailors on the vessels plying between Ezion-geber and Ophir. This was a transparent attempt to gain a footing in the southern trade route.

Ahaziah was succeeded by his brother Jehoram. [1 Kgs. 22:51; 2 Kgs. 1; 2 Chr. 20:35, 37]

2. Sixth king of Judah after the monarchy split, he reigned in 841 BC. Ahaziah was the youngest son of King Jehoram of Judah and his queen Athaliah, daughter of King Ahab of Israel. His elder brothers were killed by Philistine and nomad raiders.

At the time that Ahaziah succeeded his father, Judah and Israel were allies in a war against the kingdom of Aram (Syria) with its capital at Damascus. Ahaziah joined King Jehoram of Israel at the battlefront, which was Ramoth-gilead east of the Jordan river. Jehoram was wounded and returned to his winter palace at Jezreel accompanied by Ahaziah. The Israelite commander Jehu staged a coup, and raced back to Jezreel, where the two kings came out to meet him unaware of the danger. Jehu killed Jehoram and then pursued Ahaziah along the Jezreel valley. The Book of Kings says that Ahaziah was wounded in this chase and took refuge in the fortress at Megiddo where he died. Chronicles says that he was caught in Samaria, brought before Jehu and slain. His body was taken to Jerusalem for burial. He had been king for only one year; the throne was now seized by his mother Queen Athaliah. Also called Jehoahaz. [2 Kgs. 8:24–29; 9:16–29; 10:13; 11:1, 2; 12:18; 13:1; 14:13; 1 Chr. 3:11; 2 Chr. 22]

Ahban (Heb. 'brother of the intelligent') date unknown. The elder son of Abishur, a leader of the tribe of Judah, and his wife Abihail. [1 Chr. 2:29]

Aher (Heb. 'another') date unknown. A leader of the tribe of Benjamin. [1 Chr. 7:12]

Ahi (Heb. 'my brother') c. 8 century

BC. Son of Abdiel and a leader of the tribe of Gad, living east of the river Jordan. [1 Chr. 5:15]

Ahiah (Heb. 'God is my brother') 5 century BC. A leader of Judah who signed the solemn covenant in the time of Nehemiah. [Neh. 10:26]

Ahiam (Heb. 'uncle') c. 10 century BC. Son of Sachar the Hararite and a warrior in the army of King David distinguished for his bravery. [2 Sam. 23:33; 1 Chr. 11:35]

Ahian (Heb. 'a [young] brother') date unknown. Son of Shemida and a leader of the tribe of Manasseh. [1 Chr. 7:19]

Ahiezer (Heb. 'brother of help') **1.** c. 13 century BC. Son of Ammishaddai, he was the leader of the tribe of Dan chosen by Moses to take a census and led his contingent in the army of the children of Israel. [Num. 1:12; 2:25; 7:66–71; 10:25]

2. c. 11 century BC. An ambidextrous archer of the tribe of Benjamin who deserted from King Saul's army and joined David at Ziklag. [1 Chr. 12:1–3]

Ahihud (Heb. 'God is praised') **1.** date unknown. Son of Gera, a leader of the tribe of Benjamin. [1 Chr. 8:7]

2. c 13 century BC. Son of Shelomi, he was a leader of the tribe of Asher chosen by Moses to help divide the land of Israel among the tribes. [Num. 34:27]

Ahijah (Heb. 'the Lord's brother') **1.** date unknown. Son of Jerahmeel, a leader of the tribe of Judah. [1 Chr. 2:25]

2. date unknown. Descendant of Ehud, a leader of the tribe of Benjamin. Also called Ahoah. [1 Chr. 8:4, 7]

3. c. 11 century BC. Son of Ahitub and high priest in the reign of King Saul, he was a great-grandson of Eli. [1 Sam. 14:3, 18; 21:1; 22:9]

4. 10 century BC. A prophet from the sanctuary of Shiloh in Ephraim, Ahijah encouraged Jeroboam in his plot against the ageing King Solomon. Jeroboam was the overseer of the labour force from his tribal area that was used in the building operations in Jerusalem. There was growing dissatisfaction in the country at this time over the tax and compulsory labour burdens, and jealousy was building up among the northern tribes against the dominant position of Judah.

One day, Ahijah, wrapped in a new cloak, met Jeroboam on a deserted stretch of road outside Jerusalem, and tore his cloak into twelve pieces denoting the tribes of Israel, and handed ten of them to Jeroboam, saying: 'Take for yourself ten pieces; for thus says the Lord, the God of Israel, "Behold, I am about to tear the kingdom from the hand of Solomon, and will give you ten tribes ..."' (1 Kgs. 11:31).

Jeroboam was condemned to death by Solomon, but fled to Egypt. After Solomon died and was succeeded by his son Rehoboam, he returned, and the ten northern tribes seceded, set up a separate kingdom of Israel and made Jeroboam king. Ahijah's prophecy was thus fulfilled.

The new king restored idol worship, expelled the priestly Levites, who were loyal to the House of David, and in their stead recruited priests from the common people. His infant son became critically ill and he sent the queen in disguise to consult with the prophet Ahijah and find out the fate of his child. Ahijah, now old and nearly blind, was forewarned by the Lord and immediately recognized her. He told her that her son would die, and uttered a curse against the king and all his dynasty because he had departed from the ways of the Lord. The Lord, Ahijah said, would 'utterly consume the house of Jeroboam, as a man burns up dung until it is all gone' (1 Kgs. 14:10). [1 Kgs. 11:29, 30; 12:15; 14:2, 4, 5, 6, 18; 15:29; 2 Chr. 9:29; 10:15]

5. c. 10 century BC. Son of Shisha, he and his brother Elihoreph were secretaries to King Solomon. [1 Kgs. 4:3]

6. c. 10 century BC. Father of Baasha, the army commander of Israel who usurped the throne of Israel from King Nadab. [1 Kgs. 15:27, 33; 21:22; 2 Kgs. 9:9]

7. c. 10 century BC. A Pelonite warrior in the army of King David distinguished for his bravery. [1 Chr. 11:36]

8. c. 10 century BC. The Levite appointed by King David to supervise the treasuries of precious objects dedicated to the Tabernacle. [1 Chr. 26:20]

Ahikam (Heb. 'my brother rose up') *c.* 7 century BC. The son of Shaphan, he was a court official sent by King Josiah with Hilkiah the high priest to consult the prophetess Huldah after a 'book of the law' was discovered in the Temple. She predicted the doom of Judah.

Ahikam's son Gedaliah was appointed by Nebuchadnezzar as the governor of Judah after the fall of Jerusalem in 587 BC. [2 Kgs. 22:14; 2 Chr. 34:20; Jer. 26:24; 39:14; 40:5–16]

Ahilud (Heb. 'born of my brother') *c.* 10 century BC. Father of Jehosphaphat who was court recorder for King David and then for King Solomon. [2 Sam. 8:16; 20 1 Kgs. 4:3, 12; 1 Chr. 18:15]

Ahimaaz (Heb. 'brother of wrath') *1.* date unknown. Son of Zadok, from the line of Aaron, his descendant Azariah served as the high priest in the Temple of Solomon. [1 Chr. 6:9]

2. c. 11 century BC. Father of Ahinoam, one of King Saul's wives. [1 Sam. 14:50]

3. c. 10 century BC. Son of Zadok, King David's high priest, he guarded the Ark of God during Absalom's revolt and acted as a secret messenger for King David. [2 Sam. 15:27; 17:17–22; 18:19]

4. c. 10 century BC. Husband of King Solomon's daughter Basemath, he was one of King Solomon's twelve officers responsible for supplying the provisions for the royal household one month in each year. [1 Kgs. 4:15]

Ahiman (Heb. 'my brother is a gift') *1. c.* 13 century BC. One of the three giants descended from Anak who were driven out of Hebron by Caleb son of Jephunneh. [Num. 13:22; Josh. 15:14; Judg. 1:10]
2. c. 10 century BC. Levite gatekeeper of the Tabernacle in the reign of King David. [1 Chr. 9:17]

Ahimelech (Heb. 'the King [God] is my brother') *1. c.* 11 century BC. The son of Ahitub, he was the head priest at Nob, a priestly sanctuary just outside Jerusalem. When David became a fugitive from King Saul, destitute and unarmed, he took refuge at the sanctuary. Pretending that he was on a secret mission for King Saul, David persuaded the head priest to give him some of the hallowed bread as provisions together with the sword of Goliath which had been preserved at the sanctuary.

The kindly priest was to pay a cruel price for his help to the fugitive. Beside himself with fury at David's escape, the king had all the priests of Nob rounded up and brought before him. Ahimelech protested that he had done nothing wrong. Was not David Saul's son-in-law and 'captain over your bodyguard, and is honoured in your house?' (1 Sam. 22:14)

Saul would not hear any excuses and ordered his servants to kill Ahimelech and the eighty-five other priests. The men refused to 'put forth their hand to fall upon the priests of the Lord' (1 Sam. 22:17), and the grim execution was carried out by the king's Edomite herdsman Doeg. Nob was destroyed with all its inhabitants; only Abiathar, the son of Ahimelech, escaped to join David in the mountains. [1 Sam. 21, 22]
2. c. 11 century BC. A Hittite soldier who joined David's army and went with

him secretly by night into King Saul's camp. [1 Sam. 26:6]

Ahimoth (Heb. 'Moth [Canaanite god] is my brother') date unknown. A leader descended from Kohath. [1 Chr. 6:25]

Ahinadab (Heb. 'noble brother') *c.* 10 century BC. Son of Iddo, he was one of the twelve officers appointed by King Solomon to supply the provisions of the royal household for one month in each year. [1 Kgs. 4:14]

Ahinoam (Heb. 'brother is good') *1. c.* 11 century BC. A daughter of Ahimaaz and a wife of King Saul. [1 Sam. 14:50]
2. c. 11 century BC. David married Ahinoam from Jezreel while he was an outlaw in the wilderness of Paran, and she was the mother of his eldest son Amnon. She, together with David's other wife Abigail and their children, were carried away from Ziklag by the Amalekites. David and his men rescued them. [1 Sam. 25:43; 27:3; 30:5; 2 Sam. 2:2; 3:2; 1 Chr. 3:1]

Ahio (Heb. 'God is my brother') *1.* date unknown. Son of Elpaal and a leader of the tribe of Benjamin. [1 Chr. 8:14]
2. c. 11 century BC. Son of Jeiel of the tribe of Benjamin and an uncle of King Saul. [1 Chr. 8:31; 9:37]
3. c. 10 century BC. Son of Abinadab, he and his brother Uzzah brought the Ark of God from Kiriath–jearim to Jerusalem in the reign of King David. [2 Sam. 6:3, 4; 1 Chr. 13:7]

Ahira (Heb. 'Ra [Egyptian god] is my brother') *c.* 13 century BC. Son of Enan, he was a leader of the tribe of Naphtali chosen by Moses to take a census of the men of Naphtali and led the contingent of his tribe in the army of the children of Israel. [Num. 1:15; 2:29; 7:78–83; 10:27]

Ahiram see EHI

Ahisamach (Heb. 'brother helps') *c*. 13 century BC. Father of Oholiab of the tribe of Dan who helped Bezalel construct the Tabernacle in the wilderness. [Exod. 31:6; 35:34; 38:23]

Ahishahar (Heb. 'Shahar [Canaanite god] is my brother') date unknown. Son of Bilhan and a leader of the tribe of Benjamin. [1 Chr. 7:10]

Ahishar (Heb. 'the King [God] is my brother') *c*. 10 century BC. Superintendent of the royal palace in the reign of King Solomon. [1 Kgs. 4:6]

Ahithophel (Heb. 'Thophel [God] is my brother') *c*. 10 century BC. A Gilonite who was David's leading counsellor and a man of great political judgment. When Absalom decided to unfurl the banner of revolt Ahithophel joined him in the conspiracy. David fled from Jerusalem but his trusted friend Hushai remained behind and pretended to be on Absalom's side, in order to counter Ahithophel's influence. The great adviser was regarded as so sage that 'in those days the counsel which Ahithophel gave was as if one consulted the oracle of God' (2 Sam. 16:23).

The first step Absalom took on Ahithophel's advice, after entering Jerusalem, was to have intercourse with the ten concubines David had left behind – a symbolic act of succession. Ahithophel urged immediate pursuit before David could organize a counter-thrust. He had worked too long with David to underrate his capacities. But Hushai argued in favour of greater caution. 'This time the counsel which Ahithophel has given is not good.' (2 Sam. 17:7) Absalom and the men around him were convinced by Hushai, and David thus gained the time he needed to cross the river Jordan into Gilead and there rebuilt his forces. Ahithophel perceived clearly that the prince to whom he had defected had made a fatal blunder and that his own

career was wrecked '... and he set his house in order, and hanged himself' (2 Sam. 17:23) – the only suicide outside the battlefield mentioned in the Old Testament. [2 Sam. 15:31–37; 16:20–23; 17; 1 Chr. 27:33, 34; Ps. 41:9; 55:12; 109]

Ahitub (Heb. 'brother of goodness') *1. c*. 11 century BC. Grandson of the high priest Eli and father of Ahimelech, chief priest of King Saul. [1 Sam. 14:3; 22:9, 20]
2. c. 10 century BC. Father of Zadok, King David's high priest, he was an ancestor of Ezra. [2 Sam. 8:17; 1 Chr. 6:7, 8; 18:16; Ezra 7:2]
3. date unknown. Son of Amariah, he was a member of a family of high priests of Judah who served in the Temple. [1 Chr. 6:11, 12]
4. date unknown. Ancestor of Azariah, a chief priest who served in the Temple after the return from Babylon. [1 Chr. 9:11; Neh. 11:11]

Ahlai *1.* date unknown. Son of Sheshan, a leader of the tribe of Judah. [1 Chr. 2:31]
2. c. 10 century BC. Father of Zabad, a warrior in the army of King David distinguished for his bravery. [1 Chr. 11:41]

Ahoah *see* AHIJAH 2.

Ahumai (Heb. 'mother's brother') date unknown. The elder son of Jahath and a leader of the tribe of Judah of the families of the Zorathites. [1 Chr. 4:2]

Ahuzzam (Heb. 'possession') date unknown. A son of Ashhur, a leader of the tribe of Judah. [1 Chr. 4:6]

Ahuzzath (Heb. 'possessions') *c*. 17 century BC. A friend of King Abimelech of Gerar who accompanied him when he made his peace covenant with Isaac. [Gen. 26:26]

Ahzai *see* JAHZERAH

Aiah (Heb. 'vulture') *1.* date unknown. Son of Zibeon and a descendant of Seir. [Gen. 36:24; 1 Chr. 1:40]
2. c. 11 century BC. Father of Rizpah who was King Saul's concubine. [2 Sam. 3:7; 21:8]

Akan *see* JAAKAN

Akkub (Heb. 'insidious') *1. c.* 10 century BC. A gatekeeper of the Ark in the reign of King David and an ancestor of a family of Levites who returned to Jerusalem with Zerubbabel from exile in Babylon in 538 BC. [1 Chr. 9:17; Ezra 2:42, 45; Neh. 7:45; 11:19; 12:25]
2. date unknown. Son of Elioenai of the tribe of Judah and a descendant of King David. [1 Chr. 3:24]
3. c. 5 century BC. A Levite who explained the Law to the people of Judah after Ezra had read out the Law of Moses in the market-place. [Neh. 8:7]

Alemeth (Heb. 'covering') *1. c.* 16 century BC. Son of Becher and a grandson of Benjamin, he was a leader of the tribe and a mighty warrior. [1 Chr. 7:8]
2. date unknown. Son of Jehoaddah of the tribe of Benjamin, and a descendant of King Saul. [1 Chr. 8:36; 9:42]

Aliah date unknown. An Edomite leader descended from Esau. Also called Alvah. [Gen. 36:40; 1 Chr. 1:51]

Alian (Heb. 'tall') date unknown. Son of Shobal and a leader of a Horite clan. Also called Alvan. [Gen. 36:23; 1 Chr. 1:40]

Allon (Heb. 'oak') date unknown. Son of Jedaiah and a leader of the tribe of Simeon. [1 Chr. 4:37]

Almodad (Heb. 'God is friend') date unknown. Son of Joktan and a descendant of Shem. [Gen. 10:26; 1 Chr. 1:20]

Alvah *see* ALIAH

Alvan *see* ALIAN

Amal (Heb. 'labour') *c.* 16 century BC. Son of Helem and a grandson of Asher, he and his family were leaders of the tribe and mighty warriors. [1 Chr. 7:35]

Amalek date unknown. Son of Eliphaz and a descendant of Esau, he was the traditional ancestor of the Amalekites, the fierce tribe who became bitter enemies of the children of Israel. [Gen. 36:12, 16; 1 Chr. 1:36]

Amariah (Heb. 'God says') *1.* date unknown. Ancestor of Athaiah, one of the first men to settle in Jerusalem after the return from exile in Babylon. [Neh. 11:4]
2. c. 11 century BC. Son of Meraioth the priest and father of Ahitub, his grandson was Zadok, King David's high priest. [1 Chr. 6:7, 52; Ezra 7:3]
3. c. 10 century BC. Son of Azariah, King Solomon's high priest, and father of Ahitub. [1 Chr. 6:11]
4. c. 10 century BC. A Levite descended from Hebron who served in the Tabernacle in the reign of King David. [1 Chr. 23:19; 24:23]
5. c. 9 century BC. High priest of King Jehoshaphat of Judah, he was chief judge in all religious matters. [2 Chr. 19:11]
6. c. 8 century BC. One of the Levites who helped distribute the tithes and freewill offerings among the Levites in the cities of Judah during the reign of King Hezekiah. [2 Chr. 31:15]
7. 6 century BC. A priest who returned to Judah with Zerubbabel from exile in Babylon. [Neh. 12:2, 13]
8. c. 6 century BC. Great-grandfather of the prophet Zephaniah. [Zeph. 1:1]
9. 5 century BC. A son of Binnui who divorced his non-Jewish wife in the time of Ezra. [Ezra 10:42]
10. 5 century BC. A leading priest of Judah who signed the solemn covenant in the time of Nehemiah. [Neh. 10:3]

Amasa *1. c.* 10 century BC. The son of David's sister Abigail and commander of the forces of his cousin Absalom in the revolt against David. His army was defeated in Gilead and Absalom killed by Joab. David kept him as commander in place of Joab, who later treacherously stabbed him to death. His body lay in the road until one of Joab's young men dragged it into a field and spread a cloak over it. [2 Sam. 17–20; 1 Chr. 2:17]
2. c. 8 century BC. Son of Hadlai, he was a leader of Ephraim who urged the release of the men of Judah captured in battle by King Pekah of Israel. [2 Chr. 28:12]

Amasai (Heb. 'burdensome') *1.* date unknown. A Levite descended from Kohath, he was the father of Mahath and an ancestor of the prophet Samuel. [1 Chr. 6:25, 35]
2. c. 11 century BC. Leader of a group of thirty men who deserted from King Saul's army and joined David at Ziklag, and swore allegiance to David on behalf of his men. [1 Chr. 12:18]
3. c. 10 century BC. A priest who blew a trumpet during the celebrations in the reign of King David when the Ark of God was taken up to Jerusalem. [1 Chr. 15:24]

Amashsai (Heb. 'burdensome') *c.* 5 century BC. Son of Azarel, he was one of the first priests to settle in Jerusalem after the return from exile in Babylon in the time of Nehemiah. [Neh. 11:13]

Amasiah (Heb. 'whom God bears') *c.* 9 century BC. Son of Zichri, he commanded a large force of men in the army of King Jehoshaphat of Judah. [2 Chr. 17:16]

Amaziah (Heb. 'strength of the Lord') *1.* date unknown. Son of Hilkiah, the Levite, and an ancestor of Ethan, King David's musician. [1 Chr. 6:45]

2. Ninth king of Judah after the monarchy split, he reigned 796–81 BC.

Amaziah, the son of King Joash of Judah and his wife Jehoaddan of Jerusalem, succeeded to the throne at the age of twenty-five after the murder of his father by two court officials, with the connivance of the priesthood. When he was firmly established, he had the murderers executed, though was careful to spare their children in accordance with the Mosaic injunction: 'The fathers shall not be put to death for the children, nor the children be put to death for the fathers; but every man shall die for his own sin.' (2 Kgs. 14:6)

Amaziah carried out a census of all men over twenty in his kingdom as a basis for conscripting an army. He led his forces southward and defeated the Edomites in the Valley of Salt – the canyon running down from the Dead Sea. This victory gave him control of the ancient routes to Moab, east of the Dead Sea, to the mining area of Punon in the Arabah rift and to the Gulf of Akaba. Amaziah then advanced to the north-east and captured the fortified Edomite centre of Sela (the Rock). He brought back with him to Jerusalem the stone gods of the conquered Edomites.

Amaziah now felt strong enough to send a message to King Joash of Israel, challenging him to a military trial of strength. Joash scornfully advised Amaziah not to invite trouble for his kingdom and himself. A war started, and quickly ended with the defeat of the forces of Judah at Beth-shemesh, on the western outskirts of Judah, and the capture of Amaziah himself. Joash marched up to Jerusalem, battered down a large part of the city wall and returned to Samaria, taking with him hostages and plundered treasure from the Temple and the palace. Amaziah was left in his ravaged capital.

In due course a revolt broke out against Amaziah. He fled to Lachish in the lowlands near the coastal plain, where the conspirators followed and killed him. They brought his body on a horse to Jerusalem for burial.

He was succeeded by his sixteen-year-old son Uzziah. [2 Kgs. 12:21; 13:12; 14:1–21, 23: 15:3; 1 Chr. 3:12; 2 Chr. 24:27; 25; 26:1, 4]

3. *c.* 8 century BC. Father of Joshah, a leader of Simeon who settled in the rich Gedor valley in the reign of King Hezekiah. [1 Chr. 4:34]

4. *c.* 8 century BC. Priest of Bethel who complained to King Jeroboam II of the seditious comments made by the prophet Amos and asked Amos to leave the royal city of Bethel and prophesy elsewhere. [Amos 7:10–14]

Ami (Heb. 'my uncle') *c.* 10 century BC. A servant of King Solomon whose descendants returned with Zerubbabel from exile in Babylon. Also called Amon. [Ezra 2:57; Neh. 7:59]

Amittai (Heb. 'God of truth') *c.* 8 century BC. Father of the prophet Jonah. [2 Kgs. 14:25; Jonah 1:1]

Ammiel (Heb. 'God is my uncle') *1. c.* 13 century BC. Son of Gemalli, the leader of the tribe of Dan, he was one of the twelve men sent by Moses to spy out the Promised Land. [Num. 13:12]

2. *c.* 11 century BC. Father of Machir who befriended both King David and Jonathan's lame son Mephibosheth. [2 Sam. 9:4, 5; 17:27]

3. *c.* 10 century BC. A gatekeeper of the Tabernacle in the reign of King David. [1 Chr. 26:5]

Ammiel *see* ELIAM *1.*

Ammihud (Heb. 'uncle [God] of praise') *1. c.* 13 century BC. A leader of the tribe of Ephraim and the great-grandfather of Joshua. His son was Elishama, who marched at the head of his tribe in the army of the children of Israel in the wilderness. [Num. 1:10; 2:18; 7:48–53; 10:22; 1 Chr. 7:26]

2. *c.* 13 century BC. Father of Shemuel, the leader of the tribe of Simeon appointed by Moses to share out the land of Israel among the tribes. [Num. 34:20]

3. *c.* 13 century BC. Father of Pedahel, the leader of the tribe of Naphtali appointed by Moses to share out the land of Israel among the tribes. [Num. 34:28]

4. *c.* 10 century BC. Father of Talmai, king of Geshur, to whom Absalom fled after he murdered his half-brother Amnon. [2 Sam. 13:37]

5. *c.* 6 century BC. Father of Uthai, one of the first men of Judah to settle in Jerusalem after the return from exile in Babylon. Also called Uzziah. [1 Chr. 9:4; Neh. 11:4]

Amminadab (Heb. 'uncle [God] of nobility') *1. c.* 13 century BC. Father of Nahson, a leader of the tribe of Judah, and of Elisheba, Aaron's wife. [Exod. 6:23; Num. 1:7; 2:3; 7:12–17; Ruth 4:20; 1 Chr. 2:10]

2. date unknown. Son of Kohath, the Levite, and an ancestor of the prophet Samuel. [1 Chr. 6:22]

3. *c.* 10 century BC. Son of Uzziel, he was head of a group of Levites who helped bring the Ark of God to Jerusalem in the time of King David. [1 Chr. 15:10, 11]

Ammishaddai (Heb. 'uncle [God] is Almighty') *c.* 13 century BC. Father of Ahiezer a Danite who was chosen by Moses to take a census of the men in his tribe fit to be soldiers in the army of the children of Israel. [Num. 1:12; 2:25; 7:66, 71; 10:25]

Ammizabad (Heb. 'uncle [God] has given') *c.* 10 century BC. Son of David's warrior Benaiah who later commanded his father's division. [1 Chr. 27:6]

Ammonites A fierce people living north-east of the Dead Sea who were bitter enemies of Israel. They were the traditional descendants of Ben-Ammi,

the second son of Lot through his incestuous relationship with his younger
daughter. [Gen. 19:38; Num. 21:24;
Deut. 2:19, 20, 37; Josh. 13:10; Judg. 3;
13; 1 Sam. 11; 14; 2 Sam. 8; 10; 11; 12;
23; 1 Kgs. 11; 14; 2 Kgs. 23; 24; 1 Chr.
11; 18; 19; 20; 2 Chr. 12; 20; 24; 27;
Ezra 9:1; Neh. 2; 4; 13; Ps. 83:7; Isa.
11:14; Jer. 9; 27; 40; 41; 49; Ezek. 21;
25; Dan. 11:41; Amos 1:13; Zeph. 2:8,
9]

Amnon (Heb. 'trustworthy') *1. c.* 10 century BC. King David's eldest son who
seduced his half-sister Tamar and was
killed in revenge by her brother Absalom. [2 Sam. 3:2; 13:1–39; 1 Chr. 3:1]
2. date unknown. Son of Shimon and a
leader of the tribe of Judah. [1 Chr.
4:20]

Amok (Heb. 'deep') 6 century BC. Head
of a family of priests who returned to
Judah with Zerubbabel from exile in
Babylon. [Neh. 12:7, 20]

Amon (Heb. 'trustworthy') *1.* date unknown. Amon was the local god for the
city of Thebes. When Thebes conquered
the city states of Lower Egypt in about
1700 BC, Amon became the national
god of the Egyptians. He was regarded
as the god of fertility and later the sun-
god. [Jer. 46:25]
2. see AMI
3. *c.* 9 century BC. Governor of Samaria,
he arrested and imprisoned the prophet
Micaiah after he had foretold the disaster that would befall King Ahab of Israel
at Ramoth-gilead. [1 Kgs. 22:26; 2 Chr.
18:25]
4. Fifteenth king of Judah after the monarchy split, he reigned 642–40 BC. Amon
was the son of King Manasseh of Judah
and of Meshullemeth daughter of Haruz
of Jotbah. He succeeded his father at
the age of twenty-two, and continued
the idolatrous practices that had marked
Manasseh's reign. After two years on
the throne he was assassinated by some

of his officials. The conspirators were in
turn put to death by the people, and
Amon's eight-year-old son Josiah succeeded to the throne. [2 Kgs. 21:18–26;
1 Chr. 3:14; 2 Chr. 33:20–25; Jer. 1:2;
25:3; Zeph. 1:1]

Amorites (Bab. 'westerners') A powerful people in pre-biblical times, they
originated from and ruled in north-west
Mesopotamia. Some began infiltrating
into Canaan in the early centuries of the
2nd millennium BC, and by the time
Joshua appeared they were well en-
trenched in the land. There was thus
considerable fighting between them and
the Israelites. Many of them remained
after Joshua's conquest. In the time of
King Solomon, they were made 'a forced
levy of slaves' (1 Kgs. 9:21). [Gen. 10;
14; 15; 48; Exod. 3; 23; 33; 34; Num.
13; 21; 22; 32; Deut. 1; 2; 3; 4; 7; 20;
31; Josh. 2; 3; 5; 7; 9; 10; 11; 12; 13;
24; Judg. 1; 3; 6; 10; 11; 1 Sam. 7:14; 2
Sam. 21:2; 1 Kgs. 4;9; 21; 1 Chr. 1:14;
2 Chr. 8:7; Ezra 9:1; Neh. 9:8; Ps.
135:11; 136:19; Amos 2:9, 10]

Amos (Heb. 'burden') *c.* 775–50 BC.
First of the literary prophets.
    Amos lived in Tekoa, a village in the
Judean hills about six miles south of
Bethlehem. Uzziah ruled at the time in
the southern kingdom of Judah and Jeroboam II in the northern kingdom of
Israel. Amos was a sheep-farmer, and
also gathered the fruit of the sycamore
tree (a kind of fig). His first appearance
as a prophet was at a festival in the
town of Bethel, in the kingdom of Israel.
His opening words thundered a grim
warning to the merrymakers: 'The Lord
roars from Zion, and utters his voice
from Jerusalem; the pastures of the shepherds mourn, and the top of Carmel
withers.' (Amos 1:2)
    For the Hebrew kingdoms, this was a
period of relative peace and prosperity.
What Amos saw were the negative results of this relaxation: luxurious living

for the rich, exploitation of the poor, loose moral standards, corruption in public life, and religious observance based on ritual rather than real piety. It was against these abuses that he was called upon to preach.

He also sensed that the Hebrews were blind to the Assyrian danger looming up far to the north: 'Woe to those who are at ease in Zion, and to those who feel secure on the mountain of Samaria.' (Amos 6:1)

It is hardly surprising that Amos's fierce attack on the establishment was resented. After his first appearance at Bethel, the local priest sent a complaint to King Jeroboam accusing the preacher of sedition. 'Amos has conspired against you in the midst of the house of Israel; the land is not able to bear all his words. For thus Amos has said, "Jeroboam shall die by the sword, and Israel must go into exile away from his land."' (Amos 7:10, 11)

Apparently the authorities failed to take action, and the priest himself tried to persuade Amos to leave. 'O seer, go, flee away to the land of Judah, and eat bread there, and prophesy there.' (Amos 7:12) (These words implied that Amos was one of the wandering soothsayers who supported themselves from the credulous.) Amos replied indignantly that he was not a prophet nor a prophet's son, but had been called by the Lord from his own regular occupations. He repeated his warning in even fiercer terms: 'Therefore thus says the Lord: "Your wife shall be a harlot in the city, and your sons and your daughters shall fall by the sword, and your land shall be parcelled out by line; and you yourself shall die in an unclean land, and Israel shall surely go into exile away from its land."' (Amos 7:17)

The Book of Amos may be divided into three main parts.

The first two chapters deal with the Lord's punishment of the nations. He starts with the neighbouring states of Damascus, Gaza, Tyre, Edom, Ammon and Moab. Their crimes are those of war and violence. The prophet then moves closer to home. The people of the south, Judah, will be punished 'because they have rejected the law of the Lord, and have not kept his statutes' (Amos 2:4). Finally comes the turn of the citizens of Israel to whom he is speaking. Here Amos's wrath rises to a climax and the catalogue of their sins becomes specific and vivid. They are profane, immoral and above all callous and inhuman towards their fellow-men – '... they sell the righteous for silver, and the needy for a pair of shoes' (Amos 2:6).

The next three chapters are warning sermons, each starting with the phrase 'Hear this word ...'. In the remaining chapters, the threats of judgment are built around concrete symbols: the devouring grasshoppers, the consuming fire, the builder's plumbline, the basket of summer fruit and the smitten sanctuary.

In the last few verses of the Book, Amos holds out the hope of a new beginning after the destruction he has prophesied. '"Behold, the eyes of the Lord God are upon the sinful kingdom, and I will destroy it from the surface of the ground; except that I will not utterly destroy the house of Jacob," says the Lord.' (Amos 9:8) 'In that day I will raise up the booth of David that is fallen and repair its breaches, and raise up its ruins, and rebuild it as in the days of old.' (Amos 9:11)

Amos the sheep farmer is usually pictured as a blunt rustic, compared with intellectual urbanites like Isaiah and Jeremiah. It is true that he is familiar with the sights and sounds of country life. Yet at the same time he reveals a wide knowledge of contemporary events, a grasp of political and social issues, and literary skill of a high order.

In the evolving theology of the Old Testament, Amos makes a great leap forward. He is the first to propound the concept of a God who is universal and is not just the tribal deity of the Hebrews. What God demands of man is moral purity and social justice, rather than the rituals and sacrifices of organized religion: 'I hate, I despise your feasts, and I take no delight in your solemn assemblies. Even though you offer me your burnt offerings and cereal offerings, I will not accept them.' (Amos 5:21, 22)

According to Amos, God judges all nations, but has a special covenant with the Hebrews. This makes special demands on them. More than other peoples, they must observe a stern ethical and social code.

Amos was a pioneer in the unique prophetic strain woven into the history of the Hebrew kingdoms over several centuries. Men of God like Amos, Isaiah and Jeremiah served as the moral conscience of the community, and the fearless critics of its rulers. The prophetical books of the Old Testament are among the most sublime ethics and poetry the world has known. [Book of Amos]

Amoz (Heb. 'strong') c. 8 century BC. Father of the prophet Isaiah. [2 Kgs. 19:2; Isa. 1:1]

Amram (Heb. 'uncle [God] is exalted') *1*. c. 13 century BC. Amram was a descendant of Levi, the third son of Jacob and Leah. He married Jochebed and had three children – Miriam, Aaron and Moses. Amram died in Egypt at the age of one hundred and thirty-seven. [Exod. 6:18–20; Num. 3:19; 26:58–59; 1 Chr. 6:2, 3; 24:20]
2. 5 century BC. A descendant of Bani who divorced his non-Jewish wife in the time of Ezra. [Ezra 10:34]

Amraphel c. 18 century BC. Amraphel was king of Shinar and one of the four Mesopotamian kings who defeated an alliance of five local kings from the Dead Sea area in the time of Abraham. They carried off a number of captives, including Abraham's nephew Lot and much booty. Abraham pursued them and rescued the captives and booty.

None of these nine kings has been identified, nor their countries or cities except Elam. [Gen. 14]

Amzi (Heb. 'strong') *1*. date unknown. Son of Bani and descended from Merari. [1 Chr. 6:46]
2. date unknown. Ancestor of Adaiah, one of the chief priests in Jerusalem after the return from exile in Babylon. [Neh. 11:12]

Anah (Heb. '[God] answered') *1*. date unknown. A son of Seir the Horite and a leader of an Edomite clan. [Gen. 36:20, 29; 1 Chr. 1:38]
2. 18 century BC. Father of Oholibamah who married Esau, he was an Edomite leader who discovered hot springs in the desert. [Gen. 36:2, 14, 18, 24, 25; 1 Chr. 1:40, 41]

Anaiah (Heb. '[God] answered') *1*. 5 century BC. A leader of Judah who stood at Ezra's side when he read the Law of Moses to the people in the market-place. [Neh. 8:4]
2. 5 century BC. A leader of Judah who signed the solemn covenant in the time of Nehemiah. [Neh. 10:22]

Anak (Heb. 'long-necked') date unknown. Anak was a very tall man, like his father Arba the legendary founder of Hebron. He founded a race of giants known as Anakim who frightened the spies of Moses by their size: '... and we seemed to ourselves like grasshoppers, and so we seemed to them' (Num. 13:33). They were driven out by Caleb when he was given Hebron and the area round it. Later Joshua swept them out of the hill-country of Canaan and practically exterminated them, though some remnants were found in Gaza, Gath and

Ashdod, after Joshua's time. [Num. 13:22–33; Deut. 9:2; Josh. 15:13–15; 21:11; Judg. 1:20]

Anamim date unknown. One of the sons of Egypt and a grandson of Ham. [Gen. 10:13; 1 Chr. 1:11]

Anammelech (Heb. 'King [God] answers') date unknown. One of the gods of the Sepharvaim, a tribe settled by the Assyrians in Samaria after the exile of the people of Israel. [2 Kgs. 17:31]

Anan (Heb. 'cloud') 5 century BC. A leader of Judah who signed the solemn covenant. [Neh. 10:26]

Anani (Heb. 'my cloud') date unknown. Son of Elioenai of the tribe of Judah and a descendant of King David. [1 Chr. 3:24]

Anath (Canaanite goddess) 12 century BC. Father of Shamgar, a judge over Israel. [Judg. 3:31; 5:6]

Anathoth (Heb. 'answers') *1. c.* 16 century BC. Son of Becher and a grandson of Benjamin, he was a leader of the tribe and a mighty warrior. [1 Chr. 7:8]
2. 5 century BC. A leader of Judah who signed the solemn covenant in the time of Nehemiah. [Neh. 10:19]

Aner *c.* 18 century BC. One of Abraham's three Amorite friends who helped him defeat the five kings who had seized Abraham's nephew Lot. [Gen. 14:13–24]

Aniam (Heb. 'I am the God') date unknown. Son of Shemida and a leader of the tribe of Manasseh. [1 Chr. 7:19]

Anthothijah (Canaanite goddess) date unknown. Son of Shashak, a leader of the tribe of Benjamin living in Jerusalem. [1 Chr. 8:24]

Anub date unknown. Son of Koz, a leader of the tribe of Judah. [1 Chr. 4:8]

Aphiah date unknown. An ancestor of King Saul. [1 Sam. 9:1]

Aphses *see* HAPPIZZEZ

Appaim date unknown. Son of Nadab, a leader of the tribe of Judah. [1 Chr. 2:30, 31]

Ara date unknown. Son of Jether, a leader of the tribe of Asher and a mighty warrior. [1 Chr. 7:38]

Arad (Heb. 'wild ox') date unknown. Son of Beriah, a leader of the tribe of Benjamin living in Jerusalem. [1 Chr. 8:15]

Arah (Heb. 'wandering') *1.* date unknown. Son of Ulla and a leader of the tribe of Asher, his descendants returned to Judah with Zerubbabel from exile in Babylon. [1 Chr. 7:39; Ezra 2:5; Neh. 7:10]
2. 5 century BC. Father of Shecaniah, a leader of Judah, whose daughter married Tobiah, Nehemiah's enemy. [Neh. 6:18]

Aram (Heb. 'high') *1.* date unknown. Son of Shem and a grandson of Noah, he was the traditional ancestor of the Arameans who settled in Syria. [Gen. 10:22, 23; 1 Chr. 1:17]
2. c. 18 century BC. Son of Kemuel and a grandson of Abraham's brother Nahor. [Gen. 22:21]
3. date unknown. Son of Shomer, a leader of the tribe of Asher and a mighty warrior. [1 Chr. 7:34]

Aran date unknown. Son of Dishan and leader of an Edomite clan. [Gen. 36:28; 1 Chr. 1:42]

Araunah *c.* 10 century BC. Owner of a threshing floor. Late in his reign King David took a census of the fighting men throughout his kingdom. But a census was considered unholy (a superstition shared by most primitive communities). The Lord's punishment was a pestilence that killed seventy thousand people. David asked for advice from the prophet Gad who said: 'Go up, rear an altar to the Lord on the threshing floor of Araunah the Jebusite.' (2 Sam. 24:18) When Araunah saw the king coming, he bowed to the ground and asked what he wanted of his servant. David explained that he had come to buy his threshing floor on which he would erect an altar to the Lord so that the plague would be arrested. Araunah, delighted at the honour, provided David with the oxen and the wood for the sacrifice and wanted to give David the floor for nothing. But David refused the gift, bought the floor and the oxen for fifty shekels of silver, built an altar on it and offered up sacrifices. The Lord repented and the pestilence stopped before it reached Jerusalem. Araunah's threshing floor later became the site of Solomon's Temple. Also called Ornan. [2 Sam. 24; 1 Chr. 21; 2 Chr. 3:1]

Arba (Heb. 'four') date unknown. A giant of a man, he was the legendary founder of Kiriath-arba which later became known as Hebron. His descendants were tall men known as Anakim, after his son Anak, and they frightened the scouts of Moses by their size. [Gen. 35:27; Josh. 14:15; 15:13; 21:11]

Ard *1. c.* 16 century BC. Son of Benjamin, he went down to Egypt with his grandfather Jacob. [Gen. 46:21]
2. c. 16 century BC. Son of Bela and a grandson of Benjamin. Also called Addar. [Num. 26:40; 1 Chr. 8:3]

Ardon (Heb. 'fugitive') date unknown. Son of Caleb by his wife Azubah and a leader of the tribe of Judah. [1 Chr. 2:18]

Areli (Heb. 'Ar is my God') 16 century BC. Son of Gad, he went down to Egypt

with his grandfather Jacob. [Gen. 46:16; Num. 26:17]

Aridai (Pers. 'gift of Ari [a tribe]') *c.* 5 century BC. One of the ten sons of Haman who plotted to kill all the Jews in the Persian empire in the reign of King Ahasuerus. The plot was discovered and Haman and his sons were hanged. [Esther 9:9]

Aridatha (Pers. 'gift of Ari [a tribe]') *c.* 5 century BC. One of the ten sons of Haman who plotted to kill all the Jews in the Persian empire in the reign of King Ahasuerus. The plot was discovered and Haman and his sons were hanged. [Esther 9:8]

Ariel (Heb. 'lion of God') 5 century BC. A leader of Judah sent by Ezra to Iddo, to request that Levites be sent to Jerusalem to serve in the Temple. [Ezra 8:16]

Arioch *1. c.* 18 century BC. King of Ellasar and one of the four Mesopotamian kings who defeated an alliance of five local kings from the Dead Sea area in the time of Abraham. They carried off a number of captives, including Abraham's nephew Lot, and much booty. Abraham pursued them and rescued the captives and booty.

None of these nine kings have been identified, and none of their countries or cities except Elam. [Gen. 14]
2. c. 6 century BC. Captain of King Nebuchadnezzar who was ordered to execute all the wise men of Babylon because none could tell Nebuchadnezzar what the dream was that troubled him. Daniel volunteered to recite and explain the dream and Arioch took him to the king. [Dan. 2:14, 24]

Arisai (Pers. 'lives among the Ari [a tribe]') 5 century BC. One of the ten sons of Haman who plotted to kill all the Jews in the Persian empire in the reign of King Ahasuerus. The plot was discovered and Haman and his sons were hanged. [Esther 9:9]

Armoni (Heb. 'belonging to the palace') *c.* 10 century BC. A son of King Saul by his concubine Rizpah, he was put to death by the Gibeonites in the reign of King David to avenge Saul's massacre of the tribe of Gibeon. [2 Sam. 21:8]

Arod *see* ARODI

Arodi (Heb. 'wild ass') *c.* 16 century BC. Son of Gad who went down to Egypt with his grandfather Jacob. Also called Arod. [Gen. 46:16; Num. 26:17]

Arpachshad date unknown. Son of Shem and a grandson of Noah. [Gen. 10:22, 24; 11:11–13; 1 Chr. 1:17, 18, 24]

Artaxerxes I Longimanus (Gk. form of the Pers. 'brave warrior') King of Persia, 465–23 BC. King Artaxerxes of Persia received a letter from the governor of Samaria, protesting against the rebuilding of Jerusalem by the Jews, on the ground that it had always been a rebellious city. He ordered the work to be suspended.

Later, Artaxerxes's Jewish cupbearer Nehemiah obtained permission from his master to go to Jerusalem on a visit and remained for twelve years, becoming governor and rebuilding the walls of the city.

On his mission to Jerusalem, Ezra obtained a decree from Artaxerxes ordering Persian officials to assist him and authorizing a treasury grant. Ezra states that his journey was in the seventh year of King Artaxerxes's reign. The sequence in the Bible suggests that the reference was to Artaxerxes I, but this gives rise to serious problems of interpretation, and some scholars maintain that the king in question was Artaxerxes II Mnemon (404–358 BC). [Ezra 4:6–24; 6:14]

Arza *c.* 9 century BC. Superintendent of the household of King Elah of Israel in whose home the drunken king was murdered by his army commander Zimri. [1 Kgs. 16:9]

Asa (Heb. 'created') *1.* Third king of Judah after the monarchy split, he reigned 911–870 BC. Succeeding his father Abijah as king of Judah, in his long reign of forty-one years he distinguished himself both as a military commander and as a religious reformer.

Early in Asa's reign, Baasha, the king of Israel, advanced to Ramah (just north of Jerusalem) which he started to fortify. To relieve the pressure, Asa sent messengers with gifts of gold and silver to Ben-hadad I, the king of Aram-Damascus, calling for his help. Ben-hadad promptly invaded Israel, and Baasha was forced to withdraw. Asa fortified the towns shielding Jerusalem from the north, Geba and Mizpah. This settled the border between Israel and Judah for some time to come.

A new threat developed from the south. A large expeditionary force from Egyptian Sinai led by Zerah the Cushite (Ethiopian) advanced as far as Mareshah in the Shephelah, but was routed by Asa's Judean spearmen and Benjaminite archers and pursued towards Gaza.

Asa is one of the few Hebrew kings who is commended in the Bible for his pious zeal. 'And Asa did what was good and right in the eyes of the Lord his God.' (2 Chr. 14:2) He stamped out idolatrous practices and restored the Temple in Jerusalem as the centre of worship. It was decreed that unbelievers would be put to death. Asa even stripped of her dignities his grandmother Maacah. (The Bible refers to her as his mother, no doubt because she had acted as queen-mother and regent in his youth.) She had fashioned an obscene idol connected with the cult of the Phoenician fertility goddess Ashtoreth (Astarte), and Asa had this object solemnly burnt in the vale of Kidron in Jerusalem.

Asa developed a disease in the legs, probably dropsy, and there is a hint of reproof about his reliance on doctors and not on prayer alone.

He died in the forty-first year of his reign and was buried in Jerusalem, laid out on a couch 'which had been filled with various kinds of spices prepared by the perfumer's art' (2 Chr. 16:14). He was succeeded by his son Jehoshaphat. [1 Kgs. 15; 16; 22:41, 43, 46; 1 Chr. 3:10; 2 Chr. 14; 15; 16; 17:2; 20:32; 21:12; Jer. 41:9]
2. c. 6 century BC. Father of Berechiah, a Levite who lived in Judah after the return from exile in Babylon. [1 Chr. 9:16]

Asahel (Heb. 'God hath made') *1. c.* 11 century BC. One of the sons of Zeruiah, David's sister. Zeruiah had three sons – Joab, Abishai and Asahel. 'Now Asahel was as swift of foot as a wild gazelle.' (2 Sam. 2:18) He served in David's picked guard of thirty men, and was a commander of an army formation.

After the death of Saul, when Abner's men were routed by those of Joab, Asahel pursued the fleeing Abner, who tried to reason with him: 'Why should I smite you to the ground? How then could I lift up my face to your brother Joab?' (2 Sam. 2:22) But Asahel was determined and Abner was forced to kill him in self-defence. He was buried in Hebron in his father's tomb. Joab never forgave Abner, and later murdered him. [2 Sam. 2:18–3:30; 23:24; 1 Chr. 2:16; 11:26]
2. c. 9 century BC. A Levite sent by King Jehoshaphat to teach the Law of God in the cities of Judah. [2 Chr. 17:8]
3. c. 8 century BC. One of the Levites who supervised the bringing of tithes and offerings into the Temple in the reign of King Hezekiah. [2 Chr. 31:13]
4. 5 century BC. Father of Jonathan, one of the two leaders of Judah who were present when Ezra called on all those who had married non-Jewish women to divorce them. [Ezra 10:15]

Asaiah (Heb. 'created by God') *1. c.* 10 century BC. Son of Haggaiah, a Levite descended from Merari, he helped bring the Ark of God up to Jerusalem and later served in the Tabernacle in the reign of King David. [1 Chr. 6:30; 15:6, 11]
2. c. 8 century BC. One of the leaders of Simeon who drove out the inhabitants of the rich valley of Gedor in the time of King Hezekiah and settled there. [1 Chr. 4:36]
3. c. 7 century BC. Servant of King Josiah of Judah, sent with Hilkiah the priest and Shaphan the scribe to consult the prophetess Huldah. [2 Kgs. 22:12–14; 2 Chr. 34:20]
4. c. 6 century BC. Head of a family of Shilonites who settled in Jerusalem after the return from exile in Babylon. [1 Chr. 9:5]

Asaph (Heb. '[God] sustained') *1. c.* 10 century BC. Son of Berechiah, a Levite, he was appointed by King David as one of the principal officials in charge of the liturgical music used in the public worship in Jerusalem. In later centuries the guild of Temple singers was named after him and claimed to be his descendants. He is mentioned in the titles of twelve Psalms and some may have been composed by him. [1 Chr. 6:39; 9:15; 15:17, 19; 16:5, 7, 37; 25:1–9; 26:1; 2 Chr. 5:12; 20:14; 29:13; 35:15; Ezra 2:41; 3:10; Neh. 7:44; 11:17, 22; 12:35, 46; Ps. 50; 73–83]
2. c. 8 century BC. Father of Joah, the court recorder of King Hezekiah of Judah. [2 Kgs. 18:18, 37; Isa. 36:3, 22]
3. 5 century BC. Keeper of the king's forest in Persia, he was ordered by King Artaxerxes to supply Nehemiah with wood to repair the Temple, the gates and the walls of Jerusalem. [Neh. 2:8]

Asarel (Heb. 'Asher is the God') date

unknown. Son of Jehallelel and a leader of the tribe of Judah. [1 Chr. 4:16]

Asenath (Egypt. 'belonging to the goddess Nath') c. 16 century BC. Daughter of the high priest of the Egyptian temple of On, she became Joseph's wife at Pharaoh's court. They had two sons, Manasseh and Ephraim. [Gen. 41:45, 50; 46:20]

Asharelah (Heb. 'Asher is the God') c. 10 century BC. One of the sons of Asaph, King David's musician, who played musical instruments in the Tabernacle under their father's direction, and took the seventh turn of service. Also called Jesharelah. [1 Chr. 25:2, 14]

Ashbel (Heb. 'man of Baal') c. 16 century BC. Son of Benjamin, he went down to Egypt with his grand-father Jacob. [Gen. 46:21; Num. 26:38; 1 Chr. 8:1]

Asher (Canaanite deity) c. 16 century BC. Eighth son of Jacob. Asher was the second son of Zilpah, the maid of Jacob's wife Leah. Believing herself past child-bearing age, she had given Zilpah to her husband as a concubine; Asher was born in Padan-aram where Jacob was still working as a herdsman for his father-in-law Laban.

Together with his brothers, Asher was involved in the events that led to the selling of his brother Joseph into slavery in Egypt. Later he was one of the ten sons sent by Jacob to buy corn in Egypt, where Joseph had become a leading figure at Pharaoh's court. When Jacob went to settle in Egypt with all his family, it included Asher's four sons and a daughter.

On his deathbed Jacob blessed his sons in turn. Of Asher he said: 'Asher's food shall be rich, and he shall yield royal dainties.' (Gen. 49:20)

Centuries later, in the conquest of Canaan under Joshua, the tribe of Asher was allocated the coastal area of western Galilee, from Mount Carmel to beyond the Ladder of Tyre. In fact the tribe gained control of only a small part of this territory, bordering on the plain of Acre. This fertile area of the Galilee highlands, famous for its olive groves, is reflected in the blessing of Asher by Moses: '... let him dip his foot in oil' (Deut. 33:24). [Gen. 30:13, 35:26; Deut. 33:24; Josh. 17:10, 11; Judg. 5:17; 1 Chr. 2:2; 7:30, 40; Ezek. 48:34]

Asherah This is the Hebrew rendering of Ashirat, the leading goddess of the Phoenician Canaanites and consort of the head of their pantheon. It represented the female principle in the fertility cult. During the reign of King Ahab, his queen, Jezebel of Tyre, who had brought her worship of the Tyrian gods to her adopted land, secured official status for 'the four hundred and fifty prophets of Baal and the four hundred prophets of Asherah' (1 Kgs. 18:19). This led to the dramatic confrontation with Elijah on Mount Carmel. King Josiah destroyed the Asherah idol in Jerusalem. It is occasionally mentioned in the Bible to denote a wooden cult object. It also appears in the plural form, in both genders, as Asherim and Asheroth. [Exod. 34:13; Deut. 7:5; 12:3; 16:21; Judg. 3:7; 6:25–30; 1 Kgs. 14:15, 23; 15:13; 16:33; 18:19; 2 Kgs. 13:6; 17:10, 16; 18:4; 21:3, 7; 23:4, 6, 7, 14, 15; 2 Chr. 14:3; 15:16; 17:6; 19:3; 24:18; 31:1; 33:19; 34:3, 4, 7; Isa. 27:9; Jer. 17:2; Micah 5:14]

Ashhur (Hittite god) date unknown. Son of Caleb the son of Hezron. [1 Chr. 2:24; 4:5]

Ashkenaz date unknown. Son of Gomer and a grandson of Japheth. [Gen. 10:3; 1 Chr. 1:6]

Ashpenaz c. 6 century BC. Chief eunuch of King Nebuchadnezzar of Babylon, whom the king commanded to pick out handsome and clever young men from among the captives of Israel and teach them the Chaldean language so that they might serve in the king's palace. [Dan. 1:3]

Ashtaroth This is the plural Hebrew form for the Canaanite goddess Astarte, one of the dominant female deities of fertility. From the numerous 'Astarte' plaques discovered in archaeological excavations, this goddess was usually represented as naked. The name is often used as a general term for female deities of Canaan. Also called Ashtoreth. [Deut. 1:4; Josh. 9:10; 12:4; 13:12, 31; Judg. 2:13; 10:6; 1 Sam. 7:3, 4; 12:10; 31:10; 1 Kgs. 11:5, 33; 2 Kgs. 23:13; 1 Chr. 11:44]

Ashtoreth *see* ASHTAROTH

Ashvath date unknown. Son of Japhlet, a leader of the tribe of Asher. [1 Chr. 7:33]

Asiel (Heb. 'made by God') date unknown. Ancestor of Jehu, a warrior of the tribe of Simeon who settled in the Gedor valley in the reign of King Hezekiah. [1 Chr. 4:35]

Asnah (Heb. 'thorn-bush') *c.* 10 century BC. Head of a family of Temple servants who returned with Zerubbabel from exile in Babylon. [Ezra 2:50]

Aspatha (Pers. 'given by the [holy] horse') *c.* 5 century BC. One of the ten sons of Haman who plotted to kill all the Jews in the Persian empire in the reign of King Ahasuerus. The plot was discovered and he and his sons were put to death. [Esther 9:7]

Asriel (Heb. 'Asher is the God') *1. c.* 16 century BC. Son of Manasseh and a grandson of Joseph, he was a leader of the tribe. [1 Chr. 7:14]
2. c. 13 century BC. Head of a family of

the tribe of Manasseh to whom an inheritance was given in the land of Israel. [Num. 26:31; Josh. 17:2]

Asshur (Heb. 'land') date unknown. Son of Shem and by tradition the ancestor of the Assyrians. [Gen. 10:22; 1 Chr. 1:17]

Asshurim (Heb. 'lands') *c.* 17 century BC. Son of Dedan and a near descendant of Abraham, he was a leader of a desert tribe. [Gen. 25:3]

Assir (Heb. 'servant of God') *1. c.* 13 century BC. Son of Korah, the Levite who led the revolt against Moses and Aaron in the wilderness. [Exod. 6:24; 1 Chr. 6:22]
2. date unknown. Son of Ebiasaph, a Levite descended from Kohath. [1 Chr. 6:23, 37]

Atarah (Heb. 'crown') date unknown. Wife of Jerahmeel, a leader of the tribe of Judah, and the mother of Onam. [1 Chr. 2:26]

Ater *1.* date unknown. Ancestor of a family of Judah who returned with Zerubbabel from exile in Babylon. [Ezra 2:16; Neh. 7:21]
2. date unknown. Ancestor of a family of Levites, gatekeepers of the Temple, who returned with Zerubbabel from exile in Babylon. [Ezra 2:42; Neh. 7:45]
3. 5 century BC. A leader of Judah who signed the solemn covenant in the time of Nehemiah. [Neh. 10:17]

Athaiah *see* UTHA I.

Athaliah (Heb. 'God is exalted') *1.* date unknown. Son of Jeroham and a leader of the tribe of Benjamin living in Jerusalem. [1 Chr. 8:26]
2. Wife of the eighth king of Judah after the monarchy split, she reigned 841–35 BC. Athaliah was the daughter of King

Ahab of Israel and his domineering Phoenician queen, Jezebel. She was married to Jehoram when he was heir to the throne of Judah, in order to strengthen the alliance between the two kingdoms.

During Jehoram's eight-year reign Athaliah promoted the cult of the Phoenician god Baal as her mother had done in Israel. She was hated by the priesthood and the people.

On Jehoram's death, he was succeeded by his youngest and only surviving son Ahaziah, who was killed a year later in the military coup of Jehu in the kingdom of Israel. On learning of her son's death, Athaliah ruthlessly had all the other royal offspring murdered and seized the throne herself. However, unknown to her, Ahaziah's infant son Joash escaped death, having been rescued and hidden by his aunt Jehosheba, Ahaziah's sister. Later she handed the child to the priest Jehoiada who secretly kept him in the Temple.

When Joash was seven years old Jehoiada carried out a plot whereby the boy was crowned king in the Temple, under the protection of the royal guard. Hearing the trumpet blasts and the shouts of the crowd, Athaliah rushed to the Temple. When she saw the scene there she shouted 'Treason, treason!' The guards seized her, took her outside the Temple precincts and killed her at the Horse Gate of the palace. The crowd then smashed the temple and altar of Baal in the palace and slew Mattan, the priest of Baal.

Athaliah was the only woman to occupy the throne in either of the Hebrew kingdoms. [2 Kgs. 8:26; 11:1–20; 2 Chr. 22; 23; 24:7]
3. *c.* 5 century BC. Father of Jeshaiah who returned with Ezra from exile in Babylon. [Ezra 8:7]

Athlai (Heb. 'God is exalted') *c.* 5 century BC. A son of Bebai, he divorced his non-Jewish wife in the time of Ezra. [Ezra 10:28]

Attai (Heb. 'ready') *1.* date unknown. Son of Jarha, an Egyptian slave, and the daughter of Sheshan, a leader of Judah. [1 Chr. 2:35, 36]
2. *c.* 11 century BC. One of the warriors of the tribe of Gad who deserted from King Saul's army and joined David at Ziklag. [1 Chr. 12:11]
3. *c.* 10 century BC. Son of King Rehoboam of Judah and his favourite wife Maacah. [2 Chr. 11:20]

Azaliah (Heb. 'God has set apart') *c.* 7 century BC. Son of Meshullam and father of Shaphan, King Josiah's secretary. [2 Kgs. 22:3; 2 Chr. 34:8]

Azaniah (Heb. 'whom God hears') 5 century BC. Father of Jeshua a Levite who signed the solemn covenant in the time of Nehemiah. [Neh. 10:9]

Azarel (Heb. 'God helps') *1. c.* 11 century BC. A Korahite warrior who deserted from King Saul's army and joined David at Ziklag. [1 Chr. 12:6]
2. *c.* 10 century BC. A Levite, son of Heman, who took the eleventh turn of service to play musical instruments in the Tabernacle in the reign of King David. Also called Uzziel. [1 Chr. 25:4, 18]
3. *c.* 10 century BC. Son of Jeroham, he was made leader of the tribe of Dan in the reign of King David. [1 Chr. 27:22]
4. *c.* 5 century BC. Father of Amashsai, one of the chief priests in the Temple after the return from exile in Babylon. [Neh. 11:13]
5. 5 century BC. A descendant of Bani who divorced his non-Jewish wife in the time of Ezra. [Ezra 10:41]
6. 5 century BC. A Levite who played a musical instrument at the dedication of the rebuilt walls of Jerusalem in the time of Nehemiah. [Neh. 12:36]

Azariah (Heb. 'whom God aids') *1.* date unknown. A son of Ethan of the tribe of Judah and a grandson of Zerah, he and his family were leaders of the tribe. [1 Chr. 2:8]

2. date unknown. The son of Jehu of the tribe of Judah and the father of Helez, he was descended from the Egyptian slave Jarha whom Sheshan, a leader of Judah, gave in marriage to his daughter. [1 Chr. 2:38, 39]

3. date unknown. The son of Zephaniah the Levite and the father of Joel, he was an ancestor both of the prophet Samuel and of King David's musician Heman. [1 Chr. 6:36]

4. see UZZIAH 1.

5. c. 10 century BC. The high priest in Israel during the reign of King Solomon, he was the son of Zadok. [1 Kgs. 4:2]

6. c. 10 century BC. The son of Nathan and a court official in the reign of King Solomon, he was responsible for supervising the work of the twelve officers of the king who each provided the food for the royal household for one month a year. [1 Kgs. 4:5]

7. c. 10 century BC. The son of Ahimaaz the priest and the father of Johanan, he was the grandfather of Azariah, high priest in King Solomon's Temple. [1 Chr. 6:9]

8. c. 10 century BC. Son of Johanan, the high priest in the Temple in Jerusalem in the reign of King Solomon, he was the father of Amariah and an ancestor of Ezra. [1 Chr. 6:10, 11; Ezra 7:3]

9. c. 10 century BC. The son of Oded and a prophet in the days of Asa, king of Judah, he told the king after his victory over Zerah the Ethiopian that God would be with him as long as he kept the commandments. [2 Chr. 15:1]

10. c. 9 century BC. Two sons of Jehoshaphat, king of Judah, who were put to death by their eldest brother Jehoram when he succeeded to the throne. [2 Chr. 21:2]

11. c. 9 century BC. Son of Jehoram, he was an army commander of Judah who joined the conspiracy led by the high priest Jehoiada to overthrow Queen

Athaliah and crown Joash as king of Judah. [2 Chr. 23:1]

12. c. 9 century BC. Son of Obed, he was an army commander of Judah who joined the conspiracy led by the high priest Jehoiada to overthrow Queen Athaliah. [2 Chr. 23:1]

13. c. 8 century BC. High priest of Judah during the reign of King Uzziah, he led eighty priests into the Temple to order the king not to burn incense on the altar, a privilege reserved exclusively for the priests. Uzziah refused to listen to them but while in the act of burning the incense, he was struck by leprosy and compelled to leave the Temple. [2 Chr. 26:17–20]

14. c. 8 century BC. The son of Johanan and a chief of the tribe of Ephraim in the reign of Pekah, king of Israel, he ordered the men of Israel to return the Jewish captives taken in battle against the kingdom of Judah and personally fed, clothed and transported the captives back to Judah. [2 Chr. 28:12]

15. c. 8 century BC. The son of Jehallelel, he was a Levite who obeyed the command of Hezekiah, king of Judah, to sanctify himself and cleanse the Temple. [2 Chr. 29:12]

16. c. 8 century BC. The father of Joel, a Levite who obeyed the command of Hezekiah, king of Judah, to sanctify himself and cleanse the Temple. [2 Chr. 29:12]

17. c. 8 century BC. The chief priest of the family of Zadok in the reign of Hezekiah, king of Judah, who told the king that so much food had been donated to the Temple as tithes and offerings that the priests and Levites would have more than enough to eat. [2 Chr. 31:10]

18. see UZZIAH 3.

19. c. 7 century BC. Son of Hilkiah, high priest of Judah in the reign of Josiah, king of Judah, he was the father of Seraiah the high priest executed by Nebuchadnezzar when the Babylonians conquered Judah. [1 Chr. 6:13, 14; Ezra 7:1]

20. *c.* 6 century BC. Son of Hoshaiah and a leader of Judah after the Babylonian conquest, he rejected the prophet Jeremiah's advice to stay in Judah and insisted that the people should flee into Egypt. [Jer. 42:3; 43:2]

21. *see* ABEDNEGO

22. *see* SERAIAH **8.**

23. *c.* 5 century BC. The son of Maaseiah the Levite, he repaired part of the walls of Jerusalem opposite his house in the time of Nehemiah. [Neh. 3:23, 24]

24. 5 century BC. A Levite who explained the Law of Moses to the people of Judah after Ezra had read it to the assembled multitude in the marketplace. [Neh. 8:7]

25. 5 century BC. A priest of Judah in the time of Nehemiah who signed the covenant to observe the commands of God. [Neh. 10:2]

26. *c.* 5 century BC. A priest of Judah in the time of Nehemiah who participated in the ceremony of dedicating the rebuilt walls of Jerusalem. [Neh. 12:33]

27. *see* SERAIAH *11.*

Azaz (Heb. 'strong') date unknown. Father of Bela and a leader of the tribe of Reuben. [1 Chr. 5:8]

Azaziah (Heb. 'God makes strong') *1. c.* 10 century BC. A Levite who played a lyre at the celebration when the Ark of God was taken up to Jerusalem in the time of King David. [1 Chr. 15:21]

2. *c.* 10 century BC. Father of Hoshea, he was leader of the tribe of Ephraim in the reign of King David. [1 Chr. 27:20]

3. *c.* 8 century BC. One of the Levites who supervised the bringing of tithes and offerings into the Tabernacle in the reign of King Hezekiah. [2 Chr. 31:13]

Azbuk (Heb. 'devastation') 5 century BC. Father of Nehemiah, the ruler of part of Beth-zur, who helped repair the walls of Jerusalem at the time of the leader Nehemiah. [Neh. 3:16]

Azel (Heb. 'noble') date unknown. Son of Eleasah and a leader of the tribe of Benjamin, he was a descendant of King Saul. [1 Chr. 8:37, 38; 9:43, 44]

Azgad (Heb. 'God is mighty') *1.* date unknown. Ancestor of a large family of Judah who returned with Zerubbabel from exile in Babylon. [Ezra 2:12; 8:12; Neh. 7:17]

2. 5 century BC. A leader of Judah who signed the solemn covenant in the time of Nehemiah. [Neh. 10:15]

Aziel *see* JAAZIEL

Aziza (Heb. 'strong') 5 century BC. A descendant of Zattu who divorced his non-Jewish wife in the time of Ezra. [Ezra 10:27]

Azmaveth (Heb. 'strong unto death') *1. c.* 11 century BC. Members of the tribe of Benjamin famous for their ability to use the bow and the sling with either hand, Azmaveth and his two sons joined the exiled David when he was governor of the Philistine city of Ziklag.

After David became king of the united monarchy, he appointed Azmaveth as the royal treasurer. [2 Sam. 23:31; 1 Chr. 11:33; 12:3; 27:25]

2. date unknown. Son of Jehoaddah of the tribe of Benjamin and a descendant of King Saul. [1 Chr. 8:36; 9:42]

Azriel (Heb. 'help of God') *1.* date unknown. A leader of the tribe of Manasseh and a mighty warrior living east of the river Jordan. [1 Chr. 5:24]

2. *c.* 10 century BC. Father of Jeremoth, who was leader of the tribe of Naphtali in the reign of King David. [1 Chr. 27:19]

3. *c.* 6 century BC. Father of Seraiah who was sent by King Jehoiakim of Judah to arrest the prophet Jeremiah and his scribe Baruch. [Jer. 36:26]

Azrikam (Heb. 'my help has arisen')

1. date unknown. Son of Azel, a leader of the tribe of Benjamin and a descendant of King Saul. [1 Chr. 8:38; 9:44]

2. c. 8 century BC. Commander of the palace of King Ahaz of Judah who was killed in battle by Zichri, a warrior in the army of King Pekah of Israel. [2 Chr. 28:7]

3. c. 6 century BC. A Levite whose descendant Shemaiah settled in Jerusalem after the return from exile in Babylon. [1 Chr. 9:14; Neh. 11:15]

4. date unknown. Son of Neariah of the tribe of Judah and a descendant of King David. [1 Chr. 3:23]

Azubah (Heb. 'helped') *1.* date unknown. First wife of Caleb son of Hezron, she bore him three sons. [1 Chr. 2:18, 19]

2. c. 9 century BC. Wife of King Asa of Judah and mother of King Jehoshaphat his successor. [1 Kgs. 22:42; 2 Chr. 20:31]

Azzan (Heb. 'very strong') *c.* 13 century BC. Father of Paltiel, who was leader of the tribe of Issachar chosen by Moses to help divide up the land of Israel among the tribes. [Num. 34:26]

Azzur (Heb. 'helper') *1. c.* 7 century BC. Father of Hananiah of Gibeon who falsely prophesied that the exile of the leaders of Judah to Babylon would end shortly. He was condemned by Jeremiah who prophesied Hananiah's death within a year. [Jer. 28:1–17]

2. c. 6 century BC. Father of Jaazaniah, a leader of Judah who told the people of Jerusalem that the city would not be destroyed. [Ezek 11:1]

3. 5 century BC. A leader of Judah who signed the solemn covenant in the time of Nehemiah. [Neh. 10:17]

B

Baal (Heb. 'lord') *1.* The chief god of the Canaanites. Baal was worshipped as the god of the elements who brought rain and made the ground fruitful, and sometimes as the god of war. Temples to Baal were established on high places throughout Israel and many of the Children of Israel worshipped there from the days of the Judges. In the reign of King Ahab, Baal-worship became the court religion and led to Elijah's confrontation with the prophets of Baal on Mount Carmel. The worshippers of Baal were later massacred by King Jehu but the influence of Baal remained throughout the period of the first Temple and brought about frequent strictures by the prophets of Israel and Judah. Bel, Belus, Baalim and Merodach were alternative names for Baal and many places were named in honour of Baal. [Num. 22:41; Judg. 2:11; 6:25; 10:10; 1 Kgs. 16:31–33; 18:18–28; 2 Kgs. 10:22; 17:16; Isa. 46:1; Jer. 50:2; 51:44]

2. c. 11 century BC. Son of Jeiel of the tribe of Benjamin and a kinsman of King Saul. [1 Chr. 8:30; 9:36]

3. c. 8 century BC. Son of Reaiah and a leader of the tribe of Reuben, his son Beerah was carried into exile by the Assyrian emperor Tiglath-pileser III. [1 Chr. 5:5]

Baal-berith (Heb. 'lord of the covenant') 12 century BC. The Canaanite god of Shechem in the time of Abimelech, the rebellious son of Gideon the judge. He was also called El-berith. [Judg. 8:33; 9:4, 46]

Baal-hanan (Heb. 'the lord is gracious')

1. c. 13 century BC. Son of Achbor, he was a king of Edom. [Gen. 36:38, 39; 1 Chr. 1:49, 50

2. c. 10 century BC. The Gederite, one of King David's servants in charge of the olive and sycamore trees in the Shephelah. [1 Chr. 27; 28]

Baalim *see* BAAL

Baalis 6 century BC. A chief of the Ammonites in the days of Jeremiah, he sent Ishmael, son of Nethaniah, to kill Gedaliah, the Jewish governor of Judah. [Jer. 40:14]

Baal-zebub (Heb. 'lord of the flies') The name of the local god of the Philistine city of Ekron. When King Ahaziah lay sick and sent messengers to find out from this deity whether he would recover, they were waylaid by the angry prophet Elijah who upbraided them with the words: 'is it because there is no God in Israel to inquire of his word?' (2 Kgs. 1:16). Elijah then foretold the king's death. [2 Kgs. 1:2, 3, 6, 16]

Baana (Heb. 'son of God') *1.* 10 century BC. Son of Ahilud, he was one of King Solomon's twelve officers who provided food for the king for one month in the year. His area of authority included 'Taanach, Megiddo and all Beth-shean'. [1 Kgs. 4:12]

2. 10 century BC. Son of Hushai, he was one of King Solomon's twelve officers who provided food for the king for one month in the year. His area of authority included Asher and Bealoth. [1 Kgs. 4:16]

3. 5 century BC. Father of Zadok who helped repair the walls of Jerusalem in the days of Nehemiah. [Neh. 3:4]

Baanah (Heb. 'son of God') *c.* 11 century BC. *1.* The two fierce sons of Rimmon from Beeroth, Baanah and Rechab, entered the house of Ishbosheth, Saul's son, murdered him and brought his severed head to David at Hebron, hoping to be well rewarded. The shocked David ordered his men to kill them both for having 'slain a righteous man in his own house upon his bed' (2 Sam. 4:11). Their hands and feet were cut off and they were hung up over a nearby pool. David ordered the head of Ishbosheth to be buried in the sepulchre of Abner in Hebron. [2 Sam. 4:2, 5–12]
2. 10 century BC. Father of Heled, one of King David's chosen guard of thirty. [2 Sam. 23:29; 1 Chr. 11:30]
3. 6 century BC. One of the leaders of Judah who returned with Zerubbabel from exile in Babylon. [Ezra 2:2; Neh. 7:7]
4. 5 century BC. One of the leaders of Judah who signed the covenant to observe the Laws of God in the time of Nehemiah. [Neh. 10:27]

Baara (Heb. 'God has seen') date unknown. One of the three wives of Shaharaim of the tribe of Benjamin. [1 Chr. 8:8]

Baaseiah (Heb. 'work of God') *c.* 10 century BC. An ancestor of Asaph, a Levite musician in the Tabernacle in the reign of King David. [1 Chr. 6:40]

Baasha Third king of Israel after the monarchy split, he reigned 909–886 BC. While King Nadab of Israel was involved in a campaign against the Philistines, Baasha the son of Ahijah, from the tribe of Issachar, seized power in a coup and proclaimed himself king. He then put Nadab and all his offspring to death, thereby wiping out the dynasty of Jeroboam. His accession also broke the domination of the tribe of Ephraim in the northern kingdom of Israel.

Baasha invaded Judah, took Ramah on the high ground overlooking Jerusalem from the north, and started to fortify it. Asa, the king of Judah, bribed Benhadad the Aramean ruler to switch sides, and the Syrians invaded Israel from the north, occupying parts of Upper Galilee. Baasha was compelled to abandon the thrust on Jerusalem and rush back. During this period of weakness, the kingdom of Israel also lost its hold on the territories east of the Jordan river, including Moab, that had been part of the empire of David and Solomon.

In spite of his military reverses Baasha retained his throne for twenty-four years. For permitting sinful conduct in religious matters, he was cursed by the prophet Jehu, the son of Hanani, and doom pronounced on his posterity.

Baasha was buried in his capital of Tirzah, north of Shechem. He was succeeded by his son Elah. [1 Kgs. 15–16; 21:22; 2 Kgs. 9:9; 2 Chr. 16; Jer. 41:9]

Bakbakkar 6 century BC. One of the heads of the Levite families that returned from exile in the time of Zerubbabel. [1 Chr. 9:15]

Bakbuk (Heb. 'bottle') date unknown. Ancestor of a family that returned with Zerubbabel to Judah from exile in Babylon. [Ezra 2:51; Neh. 7:53]

Bakbukiah *1.* 6 century BC. One of the Levites who returned to Judah with Zerubbabel from captivity in Babylon. [Neh. 11:17; 12:9]
2. 5 century BC. One of the porters guarding the gates of Jerusalem in the days of Nehemiah. [Neh. 12:25]

Balaam (Gk. from the Heb. *bilam* 'a thing swallowed', or 'ruin') *c.* 13 century BC. A Mesopotamian soothsayer.

Balaam, the son of Beor, was a noted magician who lived in Pethor. Balak the king of Moab sent dignitaries to him with a large reward, invoking his aid against the children of Israel who had pitched their tents in the plains of Moab on their way to the Promised Land. 'Come now, curse this people for me, since they are too mighty for me.' (Num. 22:6)

At first the Lord said to Balaam, 'You shall not go with them; you shall not curse the people, for they are blessed.' (Num. 22:12) He therefore refused the invitation. But when another delegation arrived, God permitted him to go, provided he spoke only the words the Lord would put in his mouth.

As he was riding on his donkey through a vineyard, the animal baulked and refused to go on, and the angry Balaam beat him. When this had happened twice more the Lord 'opened the mouth of the ass, and she said to Balaam, "What have I done to you, that you have struck me these three times?"' (Num. 22:28) Only then did Balaam see that an angel stood in their path with a raised sword in his hand. Balaam threw himself on the ground and gave a solemn undertaking to say only what the Lord wanted.

The king of Moab and his courtiers came out to meet Balaam. Next morning the whole party went up to the heights of Baal, from where the Israelite encampment could be seen in the Jordan valley far below. On Balaam's instructions seven altars were erected and sacrifices made on them. They stood at the first place where, to the king's anger and distress, Balaam blessed the Israelites instead of cursing them. This happened again when they moved on to a second and a third place. To the king's protests Balaam replied that the spirit of God had come upon him. He prophesied that 'a star shall come forth out of Jacob, and a sceptre shall rise out of Israel; it shall crush the forehead of Moab' (Num. 24:17).

Not daring to harm so powerful a soothsayer, the disappointed king returned to his palace and Balaam went home without the promised reward.

In a later story in the Book of Numbers, Balaam reappears in a completely different and more sinister context. While in their camp on the Jordan plain, the Israelites attacked and wiped out some encampments of Midianite nomads, who were held accountable for the immorality and idolatrous practices that had infected the children of Israel. Balaam was among those killed.

In blaming the Midianite women for seducing the Israelites from their faith, Moses said: 'Behold, these caused the people of Israel, by the counsel of Balaam, to act treacherously against the Lord in the matter of Peor, and so the plague came among the congregation of the Lord.' (Num. 31:16)

The apparent contrast in Balaam's behaviour in the two episodes has given rise to many ingenious explanations. It has been suggested that the stories may have derived from different biblical sources at different periods. [Num. 22–4, 31; Deut. 23:4, 5; Josh. 13:22; 24:9, 10; Neh. 13:2; Micah 6:5]

Baladan see MERODACH-BALADAN

Bani (Heb. 'built') *1.* 10 century BC. A Gadite warrior in the army of King David. [2 Sam. 23:36]
2. date unknown. Son of Shemer, he was a Levite descended from Merari and an ancestor of Ethan who ministered in the Tabernacle in the reign of King David. [1 Chr. 6:46]
3. date unknown. A leader of the tribe of Judah whose descendants settled in Jerusalem after the return from exile in Babylon. [1 Chr. 9:4]
4. date unknown. The ancestor of a family who returned with Zerubbabel from exile in Babylon. [Ezra 2:10; 10:29, 34]
5. 5 century BC. The father of Rehum, a

Levite who helped repair the walls of Jerusalem in the time of Nehemiah. [Neh. 3:17]

6. 5 century BC. A Levite in the days of Ezra who explained the Law of Moses to the people of Judah and later signed the covenant to observe the Laws of the Lord. [Neh. 8:7; 9:4, 5; 10:13]

7. 5 century BC. A leader of Judah who signed the covenant to observe the Laws of the Lord in the time of Nehemiah. [Neh. 10:14]

8. 5 century BC. The father of Uzzi who supervised the Temple service of his fellow Levites after the return from Babylon. [Neh. 11:22]

Barachel (Heb. 'God blessed') period of the patriarchs. The Buzite, member of the Ram family and father of Elihu the friend of Job. [Job 32:2, 6]

Barak (Heb. 'lightning') *c.* 12 century BC. Israelite commander who fought against Sisera.

Barak, the son of Abinoam of the tribe of Naphtali, was chosen by the prophetess Deborah to lead the Israelites against the Canaanite general Sisera. Barak gathered his forces and took up his position on Mount Tabor. Sisera's army consisted of nine hundred chariots drawn up in battle array and he assumed that the rebellious Israelite tribesmen would melt back into their hills at this display of martial force. But Deborah said to Barak 'Up! For this is the day in which the Lord has given Sisera into your hand.' (Judg. 4:14)

As Barak and his ten thousand men rushed down the slopes of Mount Tabor, a violent rainstorm flooded the Kishon river and turned the valley into a sea of mud. Their chariots bogged down, and caught completely off-balance, the Canaanite forces were routed and wiped out. Barak pursued the fleeing Sisera and found he had been killed in her tent by Jael the Kenite woman. [Judg. 4, 5]

Bariah (Heb. 'son of God') date unknown. One of the five sons of Shemaiah, a descendant of David. [1 Chr. 3:22]

Barkos (Heb. 'son of Kos [a god]') date unknown. Ancestor of a family which returned with Zerubbabel to Judah from exile in Babylon. [Ezra 2:53; Neh. 7:55]

Baruch (Heb. 'blessed') *1. c.* 6 century BC. Scribe of Jeremiah.

Baruch, the son of Neriah, was the devoted disciple to Jeremiah. He witnessed the deed of transfer of a piece of land bought by Jeremiah from his cousin Hanamel. Some time later, Jeremiah sent for Baruch and dictated a scroll containing his discourses and oracles from the beginning of his ministry. Since Jeremiah had been banned from the Temple area, he sent Baruch to read out the scroll to the crowd of worshippers at the Temple on a special fast day, in the hope that the grim prophecies in it would cause the hearers to repent. Baruch was then summoned to the palace to read the book again before a meeting of officials. Disturbed at its contents, they said to Baruch, 'Go and hide, you and Jeremiah, and let no one know where you are.' (Jer. 36:19) When the enraged king, who had the scroll burnt as it was read to him, ordered their arrest, they were not to be found. At the Lord's command, Jeremiah dictated the scroll over again to Baruch, with additions.

Jerusalem fell in 587 BC and two months later Gedaliah, the governor appointed by the Babylonians, was assassinated. The group of officers loyal to Gedaliah failed to capture the murderer and fearing the Babylonian anger, fled to Egypt, taking Jeremiah and Baruch with them.

Nothing more is known of Baruch's life in Egypt, though it is probable that he remained with his beloved master Jeremiah. [Jer. 32, 36, 43, 45]

2. *c.* 5 century BC. Son of Zabbai the priest, he helped repair the walls of Jerusalem in the days of Nehemiah. He later signed the covenant to observe the Laws of God. [Neh. 3:20; 10:6]

3. *c.* 5 century BC. A leader of the tribe of Judah whose son Maaseiah was one of the first to settle in Jerusalem in the time of Nehemiah. [Neh. 11:5]

Barzillai (Heb. 'iron-maker') *1. c.* 11 century BC. The father of Adriel who married King Saul's daughter Merab. [2 Sam. 21:8]

2. *c.* 10 century BC. When David, fleeing from Absalom, crossed the Jordan river and took refuge in Gilead, Barzillai and several other notables supplied him and his followers with all their needs. They 'brought beds, basins, and earthen vessels, wheat, barley ... honey and curds and sheep and cheese from the herd, ... for they said, "The people are hungry and weary and thirsty in the wilderness."' (2 Sam. 17:28, 29)

When David returned to power, he invited Barzillai to remain with him, but the eighty-year-old Gileadite declined, saying he wanted to die among his own people. He pleaded his age and asked 'Can your servant taste what he eats or what he drinks? Can I still listen to the voice of singing men and singing women?' (2 Sam. 19:35) '... I may die in my own city, near the grave of my father and my mother.' (2 Sam. 19:37) Instead, his son Chimham stayed with David, who asked his successor Solomon to show the family kindness.

In the 6th century BC a family of priests traced their ancestry through his daughter Agia and took his name. [2 Sam. 17:27; 19:31–39; 1 Kgs. 2:7; Ezra 2:61; Neh. 7:63]

Basemath (Heb. 'sweet-smelling') *1. see* ADAH 2.

2. *see* MAHALATH *1*.

3. *c.* 10 century BC. A daughter of King Solomon, she married Ahimaaz, one of the king's twelve officers responsible for supplying the provisions of the royal household. [1 Kgs. 4:15]

Bathsheba (Heb. 'daughter of the oath') *c.* 10 century BC. Wife of David and mother of Solomon. One warm moonlight night early in David's reign, he was unable to sleep and paced restlessly along the roof-top of his palace in Jerusalem. Glancing down over the parapet, he was startled to see a beautiful young woman bathing herself on a nearby roof. On making enquiries he learnt that she was the daughter of Eliam and the granddaughter of his chief counsellor, Ahithophel; and that she was married to Uriah, a Hittite officer serving under Joab in the siege of Rabbah, the capital of Ammon. Yielding to sudden temptation, David sent discreet servants to bring Bathsheba to him and made love to her. She returned inconspicuously to her own home.

A little while later she sent David a message that she had become pregnant. There was only one way to avoid scandal – to let Bathsheba's husband visit her immediately. Uriah was brought back ostensibly to report on the campaign. But he spent his time with his army comrades without going near his wife, and returned to the front after two days. On David's instructions, Joab sent Uriah on a dangerous assault in which he was killed.

When Bathsheba had completed the normal period of mourning, David married the comely young widow who in due course bore a son. 'But the thing that David had done displeased the Lord.' (2 Sam. 11:27) Bathsheba's infant son by David fell sick and died. She bore David a second son, who was named Solomon.

When the boy grew up and David had become old and feeble, Bathsheba gained a promise that Solomon would succeed him on the throne, although he was one of David's younger sons. She and Nathan the prophet told the king that the eldest prince Adonijah was moving to usurp the throne, and David promptly had Solomon crowned as king.

After David's death, Bathsheba brought Solomon a request from Adonijah to wed Abishag the Shunammite, the comely girl who had taken care of the aged David. The young monarch treated his mother with great deference. 'And the king rose to meet her, and bowed down to her; then he sat on his throne, and had a seat brought for the king's mother; and she sat on his right.' (1 Kgs. 2:19) But the request was refused and Adonijah put to death for his presumption.

The love story of David and Bathsheba has had a strong romantic appeal down the ages. Renaissance artists delighted in painting the fair bather on the moonlit rooftop, unwittingly revealing her charms to a sleepless king. Also called Bath-shua. [2 Sam. 11:3; 12:24; 1 Kgs. 1–2; 1 Chr. 3:5; Ps. 51 (title)]

Bath-Shua (Heb. 'daughter of wealth') *1. c.* 16 century BC. A daughter of a Canaanite, Shua, she married Judah and bore him three sons. [Gen. 38:2, 12; 1 Chr. 2:3]
2. see BATHSHEBA

Bavvai 5 century BC. A Levite and son of Henadad, ruler of half the district of Keilah, he helped repair the walls of Jerusalem in the time of Nehemiah. [Neh. 3:18]

Bazlith *see* BAZLUTH

Bazluth 6 century BC. Head of a family who returned to Judah with Zerubbabel from captivity in Babylon. Also called Bazlith. [Ezra 2:52; Neh. 7:54]

Bealiah (Heb. 'Jehovah is the Lord') 11 century BC. One of the Benjaminite warriors who rallied to David at Ziklag when he was pursued by King Saul. [1 Chr. 12:5]

Bebai *1.* date unknown. Ancestor of a large family that returned to Judah with Zerubbabel from exile in Babylon. [Ezra 2:11; 10:28; Neh. 7:16]
2. 5 century BC. One of the signatories of the solemn covenant in the time of Nehemiah. [Ezra 8:11; Neh. 10:15]

Becher (Heb. 'young camel') *1. c.* 16 century BC. Son of Benjamin and a grandson of Jacob and Rachel. [Gen. 46:21; 1 Chr. 7:6, 8]
2. c. 16 century BC. Son of Ephraim and grandson of Joseph. Also called Bered. [Num. 26:35; 1 Chr. 7:20]

Becorath (Heb. 'first fruits') *c.* 11 century BC. An ancestor of King Saul. [1 Sam. 9:1]

Bedad (Heb. 'solitary') date unknown. Father of Hadad, king of Edom. [Gen. 36:35; 1 Chr. 1:46]

Bedan date unknown. Son of Ulam and a descendant of Gilead of the tribe of Manasseh. [1 Chr. 7:17]

Bedeiah (Heb. 'branch of God') 5 century BC. One of the returned exiles who divorced his non-Jewish wife in the time of Ezra. [Ezra 10:35]

Beeliada *see* ELIADA 1.

Beera (Heb. 'a well') date unknown. A son of Zophah, he was a clan leader in the tribe of Asher. [1 Chr. 7:37]

Beerah (Heb. 'a well') 8 century BC. A leader of the tribe of Reuben who was carried into captivity by Tiglath-pileser III, king of Assyria. [1 Chr. 5:6]

Beeri (Heb. 'my well') *1. c.* 16 century BC. Father of Judith, one of Esau's wives. [Gen. 26:34]

2. *c.* 8 century BC. Father of the prophet Hosea. [Hos. 1:1]

Bel *see* BAAL

Bela (Heb. 'destroying') *1.* date unknown. The first king of Edom, he was the son of Beor and his capital city was Dinhabah. [Gen. 36:32, 33; 1 Chr. 1:43, 44]
2. *c.* 16 century BC. Eldest son of Benjamin and a grandson of Jacob and Rachel. [Gen. 46:21; Num. 26:38, 40; 1 Chr. 7:6, 7; 8:1, 3]
3. date unknown. Son of Azaz and a leader of the tribe of Reuben. [1 Chr. 5:8]

Belshazzar (Bab. 'Bel protect the king') *c.* 6 century BC. King of Babylon in the Book of Daniel.

He is described in the Book of Daniel as the son of Nebuchadnezzar and his successor on the throne of Babylon, though historically he was neither. He gave a great feast in the palace attended by all his household and a thousand of his nobles. He sent for the gold and silver vessels from the Temple in Jerusalem that Nebuchadnezzar had brought to Babylon 'and the king and his lords, his wives, and his concubines drank from them' (Dan. 5:3). Suddenly a hand appeared and wrote on the wall of the banqueting chamber the words 'MENE, MENE, TEKEL, and PARSIN' (Dan. 5:25). Nobody could understand this mysterious message and all of them were stricken with terror. The queen remembered Daniel and his ability to interpret dreams and the king sent for him. Daniel interpreted the ominous message as meaning that the king had been weighed and found wanting. He told Belshazzar that he had sinned against the Lord when he drank from the Temple vessels and 'praised the gods of silver and gold, of bronze, iron, wood, and stone, which do not see or hear or know' (Dan. 5:23). Belshazzar was assassinated that night. [Dan. 5; 7:1; 8:1]

Belteshazzar *see* DANIEL

Belus *see* BAAL

Ben-Abinadab *c.* 10 century BC. Son-in-law of King Solomon, he was one of Solomon's twelve officers responsible for supplying the provisions of the king's household. [1 Kgs. 4:11]

Benaiah (Heb. 'the Lord has built') *1. c.* 10 century BC. Captain of David's guard, Benaiah was the son of Jehoiada and came from Kabzeel in Judah. He was a brave soldier and David appointed him captain of his bodyguard. He carried out several feats of bravery such as slaying 'two ariels of Moab ... a lion in a pit on a day when snow had fallen. And he slew an Egyptian ...' (2 Sam. 23:20, 21). Benaiah remained loyal to David through the rebellions of Absalom and of Adonijah. When David was old he sent for him to go with Zadok the priest and Nathan the prophet to anoint Solomon as king of Israel.

On David's death Benaiah transferred his loyalties to Solomon. On the young king's orders he killed Adonijah, Joab and Shimei. Solomon through Benaiah thus succeeded in getting rid of all the men whose loyalty he doubted. Benaiah was appointed commander of the army in place of Joab. [2 Sam. 8:18; 20:23; 23:20-22; 1 Kgs. 1, 2; 4:4; 1 Chr. 11:22-24; 18:17; 27:5, 6]
2. 10 century BC. A warrior from Pirathon of the tribe of Ephraim serving in the army of King David. He was commander of the forces in the eleventh month of each year. [2 Sam. 23:30; 1 Chr. 11:31; 27:14]
3. *c.* 10 century BC. One of the Levites who played musical instruments in the Tabernacle in the reign of King David. [1 Chr. 15:18, 20]
4. *c.* 10 century BC. One of the priests who blew a trumpet before the Ark in the Tabernacle during the reign of King David. [1 Chr. 15:24; 16:6]

5. c. 10 century BC. Father of Jehoiada who succeeded Ahithophel as King David's counsellor. [1 Chr. 27:34]

6. 9 century BC. A Levite descended from Asaph whose grandson, Jahaziel, prophesied victory for King Jehoshaphat of Judah against the armies of the Ammonites and Moabites. [2 Chr. 20:14]

7. 8 century BC. A leader of the tribe of Simeon who drove out the inhabitants of the valley of Gedor and settled there during the reign of King Hezekiah of Judah. [1 Chr. 4:36]

8. c. 8 century BC. One of the Levites who supervised the bringing of tithes and offerings into the Temple in the reign of King Hezekiah. [2 Chr. 31:13]

9. c. 6 century BC. Father of Pelatiah who gave false counsel to the people of Judah and whose death Ezekiel prophesied. [Ezek. 11:1, 13]

10. 5 century BC. Descendant of Parosh, he married a non-Jewish wife and later divorced her in the time of Nehemiah. [Ezra 10:25]

11. 5 century BC. Descendant of Pahathmoab, he married a non-Jewish wife and later divorced her in the time of Nehemiah. [Ezra 10:30]

12. 5 century BC. Descendant of Bani, he married a non-Jewish wife and later divorced her in the time of Nehemiah. [Ezra 10:35]

13. 5 century BC. Descendant of Nebo, he married a non-Jewish wife and later divorced her in the time of Nehemiah. [Ezra 10:43]

Ben-Ammi (Heb. 'son of my people') *c.* 17 century BC. Son of the incestuous relationship between Lot and his younger daughter, Ben-ammi was the father of the Ammonites. [Gen. 19:38]

Ben-Deker *c.* 10 century BC. One of King Solomon's twelve officers responsible for supplying the provisions of the royal household. [1 Kgs. 4:9]

Ben-Geber (Heb. 'son of strength') *c.* 10 century BC. One of King Solomon's twelve officers responsible for supplying the provisions of the royal household. [1 Kgs. 4:13]

Ben-Hadad (Heb. 'son of Hadad [a god]')

1. Ben-Hadad I c. 9 century BC. When Judah was invaded and Jerusalem attacked by King Baasha of Israel, King Asa of Judah sent messengers with gifts of silver and gold to Damascus, to seek the help of Ben-hadad I, son of Tabrimmon and king of Aram, Israel's northern neighbour. Not averse to taking advantage of the quarrel between the two Hebrew kingdoms Ben-hadad invaded Israel and occupied the northern and eastern Galilee. Baasha was forced to abandon his campaign against Judah and hurry back to his capital at Tirzah. [1 Kgs. 15:18, 20; 2 Chr. 16:2–6]

2. Ben-Hadad II c. 9 century BC. Son of Ben-hadad I. A Syrian army led by King Ben-hadad II besieged Samaria, the capital of Israel, but was routed by a surprise attack from the city. Ben-hadad escaped on a chariot horse, but was captured by King Ahab, who spared him on condition that the Galilee towns that had been occupied by his father were returned, and that Israel was given trading rights in the bazaars of Damascus.

Ahab later joined a coalition of local kings led by Ben-hadad against the Assyrians who were advancing from the north under Shalmaneser III. This advance was stopped at the battle of Karkar in 853 BC and the Assyrian danger receded.

Some years later Ben-hadad II was murdered by his army commander Hazael who seized the throne. [1 Kgs. 20; 2 Kgs. 6:24; 8:7–9]

3. Ben-Hadad III c. 9 century BC. King of Aram-Damascus, he was the son of Hazael and succeeded his father on the throne. During his reign, the kingdom of Israel recovered the territory which Hazael had conquered from them. [2 Kgs. 13:24, 25; Jer. 49:27; Amos 1:4]

Ben-Hail (Heb. 'son of valour') *c*. 10 century BC. One of the princes of Judah sent by King Jehoshaphat to teach the Law of God in the cities of Judah. [2 Chr. 17:7]

Ben-Hanan (Heb. 'son of grace') date unknown. A son of Shimon of the tribe of Judah. [1 Chr. 4:20]

Ben-Hesed (Heb. 'son of loving kindness') *c*. 10 century BC. One of King Solomon's twelve officers responsible for supplying the provisions of the royal household. [1 Kgs. 4:10]

Ben-Hinnom *see* HINNOM

Ben-Hur (Heb. 'son of Hur [a god]') *c*. 10 century BC. One of King Solomon's twelve officers responsible for the provisions of the royal household. [1 Kgs. 4:8]

Beninu (Heb. 'our son') 5 century BC. One of the Levites in the days of Nehemiah who signed the solemn covenant. [Neh. 10:13]

Benjamin (Heb. 'son of the south') *1*. *c*. 16 century BC. Youngest son of Jacob.

Benjamin was born to Rachel when Jacob and his family were near Bethlehem on their way to Hebron. The dying Rachel called the baby Benoni ('son of my sorrow') but Jacob renamed him Benjamin.

He was probably too young to have taken part with his brothers in the episode which caused Rachel's elder son Joseph to be sold into slavery in Egypt. Later when there was famine in Canaan, Jacob sent ten of his sons to Egypt to buy food, but refused to let Benjamin go 'for he feared that harm might befall him' (Gen. 42:4).

Joseph, by now the most powerful man in Egypt next to Pharaoh, recognized his brothers though they did not know him. He sent them back with their grain bags full but kept Simeon as hostage for their promise to return with Benjamin, whom he was longing to see. Jacob reluctantly agreed and the brothers returned to Egypt. Joseph gave them dinner, and startled the brothers by seating them correctly according to their age. He sent food from his table to theirs and gave Benjamin five times more than the others.

When the time came to return to Hebron, Joseph commanded his steward to fill their bags with food but put his silver cup in Benjamin's sack. Joseph then sent his men after them and they were brought back under arrest for theft. Joseph upbraided them for the supposed theft and declared as a penalty that Benjamin would have to remain as his bondsman. Judah spoke up insisting that the loss of Benjamin would kill their father, and offered to remain behind instead. Ordering everyone out of the room, Joseph told his brothers who he was, and there was a tearful reunion. Joseph proposed they should fetch their father Jacob and the rest of the family and settle in Egypt. This was done, and when Jacob left Hebron with his entire family, it included the ten sons of Benjamin.

On his deathbed Jacob blessed his sons in turn. Concerning Benjamin, he forecast the martial qualities for which the tribe of that name would be renowned: 'Benjamin is a ravenous wolf, in the morning devouring the prey, and at even dividing the spoil.' (Gen. 49:27) Centuries later, in the conquest of Canaan under Joshua, the tribe of Benjamin was allocated a narrow strip across the Judean hills from the Shephelah to the Jordan valley at Jericho, with Jerusalem (still belonging to the Jebusites) just within its border. Perhaps because of Jerusalem, in the blessing attributed to Moses it is said of Benjamin: 'The beloved of the Lord, he dwells in safety by him.' (Deut. 33:13) Also called Benoni. [Gen. 35; 42–46;

49:27; Exod. 1:3; Deut. 33:12; 1 Chr. 2:2; 7:6]

2. c. 16 century BC. Son of Bilhan and a leader and warrior of the tribe of Benjamin. [1 Chr. 7:10]

3. 5 century BC. One of the descendants of Harim who divorced their non-Jewish wives in the time of Ezra. [Ezra 10:32]

4. 5 century BC. One of the leaders of Judah in the time of Nehemiah who helped repair the walls of Jerusalem and later took part in the ceremony of dedication when the walls had been completely rebuilt. [Neh. 3:23; 12:34]

Beno (Heb. 'his son') c. 10 century BC. Son of Jaaziah, a Levite descended from Merari, he ministered in the Tabernacle in the reign of King David. [1 Chr. 24:26, 27]

Benoni see BENJAMIN 1.

Beor (Heb. 'burning') 1. date unknown. Father of Bela, first king of Edom. [Gen. 36:32; 1 Chr. 1:43]
2. c. 13 century BC. Father of the prophet Balaam. [Num. 22:5; 24:3, 15; 31:8; Deut. 23:4; Josh. 13:22; 24:9; Mic. 6:5]

Bera (Heb. 'son of evil') c. 18 century BC. A king of Sodom who joined four other kings against Chedorlaomer, king of Elam in the time of Abraham (when he was still called Abram). The kings of Sodom and Gomorrah fled and fell in the vale of Siddim which was full of bitumin pits and their flocks and possessions were seized by the victorious enemy. After Abram succeeded in recovering the captives and the possessions, the king of Sodom offered Abram the goods as a reward but he refused to take them. [Gen. 14:1–24]

Beracah (Heb. 'blessing') 11 century BC. One of the Benjaminite warriors who joined David at Ziklag. [1 Chr. 12:3]

Beraiah (Heb. 'the Lord created') date unknown. A son of Shimei and a leader of the tribe of Benjamin who settled in Jerusalem. [1 Chr. 8:21]

Berechiah (Heb. 'God has blessed') 1. 10 century BC. Father of Asaph, a leading singer in the religious services of King David. [1 Chr. 6:39; 15:17]
2. 10 century BC. A gatekeeper of the Ark in the time of King David. [1 Chr. 15:23]
3. 8 century BC. Son of Meshillemoth and one of the leaders of the tribe of Ephraim in the time of King Pekah of Israel and King Ahaz of Judah. When Pekah's forces attacked Judah and brought thousands of captives to Samaria, Berechiah was one of those who supported the prophet Oded against the army and insisted on freeing the captives and returning them to Judah. [2 Chr. 28:8–15]
4. date unknown. Son of Zerubbabel, a descendant of King David. [1 Chr. 3:20]
5. 6 century BC. Son of Asa the Levite, he ministered in the Temple after the return from exile in Babylon. [1 Chr. 9:16]
6. 6 century BC. Father of Zechariah the prophet. [Zech. 1:1, 7]
7. 5 century BC. Son of Meshezabel and father of Meshullam who helped repair the walls of Jerusalem in the time of Nehemiah. [Neh. 3:4, 30; 6:18]

Bered see BECHER 2.

Beri date unknown. Son of Zophah, one of the leaders and 'mighty warriors' (1 Chr. 7:40) of the tribe of Asher. [1 Chr. 7:36]

Beriah (Heb. 'excellent') 1. c. 16 century BC. One of the four sons of Asher and a grandson of Jacob, he accompanied his grandfather into Egypt. [Gen. 46:17; Num. 26:44, 45; 1 Chr. 7:30, 31]
2. c. 16 century BC. Son of Ephraim and a grandson of Jacob, he was born after some of his brothers had been killed by the men of Gath. [1 Chr. 7:23]

3. 10 century BC. Son of Shimei, one of the Levites who served in the Tabernacle in the reign of King David. [1 Chr. 23:10, 11]

4. date unknown. One of the leaders of the tribe of Benjamin living in Aijalon 'who put to flight the inhabitants of Gath'. [1 Chr. 8:13, 16]

Besai date unknown. Ancestor of a family that returned with Zerubbabel to Judah from exile in Babylon. [Ezra 2:49; Neh. 7:52]

Besodeiah (Heb. 'the secret of God') 5 century BC. Father of Meshullam who helped repair the Old Gate of Jerusalem in the time of Nehemiah. [Neh. 3:6]

Bethuel (Heb. 'house of God') *c.* 18 century BC. Father of Rebekah and Laban, and a newphew of Abraham, he gave his daughter in marriage to Abraham's son Isaac. [Gen. 22:22, 23; 24:15, 24, 47; 25:20; 28:2–5]

Bethzur date unknown. Son of Maon and a descendant of Caleb the brother of Jerahmeel. [1 Chr. 2:45]

Bezai *1.* date unknown. Ancestor of a family who returned to Judah with Zerubbabel from captivity in Babylon. [Ezra 2:17; Neh. 7:23]

2. 5 century BC. One of the leaders of Judah who signed the solemn covenant in the time of Nehemiah. [Neh. 10:18]

Bezalel (Heb. 'in the Lord's shadow') *1. c.* 13 century BC. Chief designer of the Tabernacle. Bezalel was the son of Uri, of the tribe of Judah. The Lord told Moses that Bezalel had been chosen to carry out the work on the Tabernacle: 'And I have filled him with the Spirit of God, with ability and intelligence, with knowledge and all craftmanship.' (Exod. 31:3) His gifts included work in gold, silver, stone, wood, embroidery, weaving and engraving. He designed the Tab-

ernacle, the Ark and the furniture. Among the other gifts the Lord gave to Bezalel was the ability to teach his divinely inspired crafts and skills to others. [Exod. 31:2–11; 35:30–35; 36–39; 1 Chr. 2:20; 2 Chr. 1:5]

2. 5 century BC. A descendant of Pahath-moab who divorced his non-Jewish wife in the time of Ezra. [Ezra 10:30]

Bezer (Heb. 'fortification') date unknown. Son of Zophah, he was a leader of the tribe of Asher and a brave warrior. [1 Chr. 7:37]

Bichri (Heb. 'youthful') 10 century BC. Father of Sheba, a Benjaminite who led a revolt against King David. [2 Sam. 20:1]

Bidkar (Heb. 'stabber') *c.* 9 century BC. The aide of Jedu son of Nimshi who assassinated King Joram of Israel and seized the throne. Bidkar threw Joram's body into the vineyard of Naboth. [2 Kgs. 9:25]

Bigtha (Pers. 'gift of God') *c.* 5 century BC. One of the seven chamberlains of King Ahasuerus who was commanded by the drunken king on the seventh day of a feast to bring Queen Vashti before his guests to show off her beauty. [Esther 1:10]

Bigthan (Pers. 'gift of God') *c.* 5 century BC. One of the two doorkeepers of King Ahasuerus who conspired to kill the king. The plot was discovered and the conspirators were executed. Also called Bigthana in the Book of Esther and Gabatha in the Greek Additions to the Book of Esther, in the Apocrypha. [Esther 2:21; 6:2]

Bigthana *see* BIGTHAN

Bigvai *1.* 6 century BC. A leader of Judah who returned with Zerubbabel from exile in Babylon. [Ezra 2:2, 14; 8:14; Neh. 7:7, 19]

2. 5 century BC. A leader of Judah who signed the solemn covenant in the time of Nehemiah. [Neh. 10:16]

Bildad period of the patriarchs. One of Job's friends who remonstrated with him.

Bildad the Shuhite was one of three friends who hurried to comfort Job when they heard of his afflictions. They were shocked to see his changed appearance. They 'rent their robes and sprinkled dust upon their heads toward heaven' (Job. 2:12). They sat down with him without speaking for seven days and seven nights. Then Job began to curse the day he had been born and to protest that his suffering was undeserved. Bildad and the other two tried to console him. They expressed the traditional and pious views about his suffering. Bildad asked him, 'Does God pervert justice? Or does the Almighty pervert the right? . . . God will not reject a blameless man, nor take the hand of evildoers.' (Job 8:3, 20) As Job maintained his innocence, Bildad insisted that if he would only admit his faults God would forgive him: '. . . how can he who is born of woman be clean? Behold, even the moon is not bright and the stars are not clean in his sight.' (Job 25:4, 5)

But Job made no effort to conceal his impatience with Bildad and his other two friends, and utterly rejected their advice to bear his trials with silent fortitude. 'So these three men ceased to answer Job, because he was righteous in his own eyes.' (Job 32:1)

Finally the Lord spoke to Job out of a whirlwind and he was completely overwhelmed and humbled. Then the Lord turned on the three friends and told them that he was angry with them for 'you have not spoken of me wha tis right, as my servant Job has' (Job 42:7). The Lord then instructed them to offer up a burnt sacrifice 'and my servant Job shall pray for you, for I will accept his prayer' (Job 42:8). [Job 2, 8, 18, 25, 42]

Bilgah (Heb. 'cheerfulness') **1.** 10 century BC. A priest in the reign of King David who took the fifteenth turn of service in the Tabernacle. [1 Chr. 24:14]
2. 6 century BC. A priest who returned with Zerubbabel from exile in Babylon. [Neh. 12:5, 18]

Bilgai (Heb. 'cheerfulness') 5 century BC. A priest who signed the solemn covenant in the time of Nehemiah. [Neh. 10:8]

Bilhah (Heb. 'modesty') c. 16 century BC. Rachel's maidservant. When Jacob married Rachel, her father Laban gave her Bilhah to be her servant. Though Jacob loved Rachel very much, she remained childless for a long time. In desperation she asked Jacob to take her handmaid 'that she may bear upon my knees, and even I may have children by her' (Gen. 30:3). Bilhah and Jacob had two sons, Dan and Naphtali, the legendary ancestors of the tribes bearing those names. She later had an illicit affair with Reuben, Jacob's eldest son by his first wife Leah. [Gen. 29:29; 30:3–8; 35:22; 37:2; 46:25; 1 Chr. 7:13]

Bilhan (Heb. 'modest') **1.** date unknown. Son of Ezer and a descendant of Esau, he was a leader of the Horites in the land of Seir. [Gen. 36:27; 1 Chr. 1:42]
2. date unknown. Son of Jediael and a leader of the tribe of Benjamin. [1 Chr. 7:10]

Bilshan (Heb. 'eloquent') 6 century BC. A leader of Judah who returned with Zerubbabel from exile in Babylon. [Ezra 2:2; Neh. 7:7]

Bimhal date unknown. Son of Japhlet, he was a leader of the tribe of Asher and a mighty warrior. [1 Chr. 7:33]

Binea (Heb. 'fountain') date unknown. Son of Moza of the tribe of Benjamin and a descendant of King Saul. [1 Chr. 8:37; 9:43]

Binnui (Heb. 'building') *1.* 6 century BC. Head of a family who returned with Zerubbabel to Judah from Babylon. [Neh. 7:15; 12:8]
2. 5 century BC. Son of Henadad, he helped rebuild the walls of Jerusalem in the time of Nehemiah. He also signed the covenant. [Neh. 3:24; 10:9]
3. 5 century BC. Father of Noadiah, the Levite, who helped weigh the holy vessels brought back to Jerusalem from Babylon in the time of Ezra. [Ezra 8:33]
4. 5 century BC. A descendant of Pahath-moab who divorced his non-Jewish wife in the time of Ezra. His sons did likewise. [Ezra 10:30, 38]

Birsha *c.* 18 century BC. King of Gomorrah in the days of Abraham, who with four other kings was defeated in battle by Chedorlaomer, king of Elam, and his three confederate kings. [Gen. 14:2–24]

Birzaith (Heb. 'son of olive tree') date unknown. Son of Malchiel and a leader of the tribe of Asher. [1 Chr. 7:31]

Bishlam (Heb. 'son of peace') *c.* 5 century BC. A Persian official in Samaria who with others wrote to Artaxerxes I, king of Persia, protesting against the rebuilding of Jerusalem by the Jews after their return from Babylon. [Ezra 4:7]

Bithiah (Heb. 'daughter of the Lord') date unknown. Daughter of a pharaoh who married Mered of the tribe of Judah. [1 Chr. 4:17]

Biztha (Pers. 'eunuch') *c.* 5 century BC. One of the seven chamberlains of King Ahasuerus who was commanded by the drunken king on the seventh day of a feast to bring Queen Vashti before his guests to show off her beauty. [Esther 1:10]

Boaz (Heb. 'strength') *c.* 11 century BC. Husband of Ruth.

Boaz was a well-to-do landowner in the town of Bethlehem. One spring day he went to his barley field, where his servants were reaping the harvest. He noticed that behind them a comely young woman was gleaning the scattered ears left behind by the reapers. He learned on enquiry that she was Ruth, the widow of his relative Mahlon son of Elimelech, and that she had just arrived in Bethlehem from her native land of Moab with her widowed mother-in-law Naomi. Boaz spoke kindly to Ruth and praised her for her devotion to Naomi. He told her to go on gleaning his fields with his servants, where she would not be molested, and invited her to share their food and water.

At the end of the harvest Boaz spent the night on the winnowing floor after the usual feasting. Under Naomi's guidance, Ruth dressed herself in her best clothes and went to lie at the feet of the sleeping Boaz. He woke in the middle of the night and was surprised to find Ruth there. She asked him humbly to spread the edge of his cloak over her as he was a close relative. Boaz was touched and flattered by the way Ruth entrusted herself to him, when she might have gained the attention of younger men; '... for all my fellow townsmen know that you are a woman of worth' (Ruth 3:11). Concerned lest she should be seen with him, Boaz sent Ruth back to Naomi before dawn, with a cloakful of grain.

The same morning Boaz opened discussion with a kinsman who was more closely related to Elimelech. In the presence of ten elders of the town, acting as witnesses, he asked whether the other wanted to buy from Naomi the piece of land that had belonged to Elimelech, and at the same time acquire Ruth as his wife. The relative declined, and Boaz formally declared his intention to do so himself. The agreement was sealed in the customary manner of the times, by taking off and handing over one sandal.

Boaz then married Ruth. A son was born to them whom they called Obed. In due course Obed's son Jesse became the father of King David, who was therefore the great-grandson of Boaz and Ruth. [Book of Ruth; 1 Chr. 2:11, 12]

Bocheru (Heb. 'young') date unknown. A son of Azel, he was a member of the tribe of Benjamin and a descendant of King Saul. [1 Chr. 8:38; 9:44]

Bohan date unknown. A member of the tribe of Reuben after whom a stone was named that marked the boundary between the tribal lands of Benjamin and Judah. [Josh. 15:6; 18:17]

Bukki (Heb. 'void') *1. c.* 13 century BC. Son of Jogli, he was a leader of the tribe of Dan appointed by Moses to take part in dividing the land of Israel among the tribes. [Num. 34:22]
2. date unknown. Son of Abishua, descendant of Aaron the high priest and ancestor of Ezra. [1 Chr. 6:5, 51; Ezra 7:4]

Bukkiah (Heb. 'wasting') *c.* 10 century

BC. One of the fourteen sons of Heman, Levite and musician at religious services in the time of King David, he and his sons took the sixth turn of service. [1 Chr. 25:4, 13]

Bunah (Heb. 'discretion') date unknown. A son of Hezron of the tribe of Judah. [1 Chr. 2:25]

Bunni (Heb. 'built') *1.* date unknown. The ancestor of the Levite Shemaiah who settled in Jerusalem in the time of Nehemiah. [Neh. 11:15]
2. 5 century BC. A Levite in the days of Ezra and Nehemiah, he participated in the service of confession on the public fast day proclaimed by Ezra and later signed the solemn covenant. [Neh. 9:4; 10:15]

Buzi *1. c.* 18 century BC. Second son of Nahor, brother of Abraham, his descendants formed an Arabian desert tribe. [Gen. 22:21]
2. date unknown. One of the ancestors of the Gadites living on the eastern side of the Jordan river. [1 Chr. 5:14]

Buzi 6 century BC. Father of the prophet Ezekiel. [Ezek. 1:3]

C

Cain (Heb. 'spear') date unknown. The first-born of Adam and Eve.

Cain was a tiller of the soil, while his younger brother Abel was a shepherd. When the two brothers came to make their offerings to the Lord, Abel brought young lambs while Cain brought the first-fruits of the field. God rejected Cain's offering but accepted that of Abel. Seeing Cain's wrath, the Lord gave him advice on how to control himself: 'Why are you angry, and why has your countenance fallen? If you do well, will you not be accepted? And if you do not do well, sin is couching at the door; its desire is for you, but you must master it.' (Gen. 4:6, 7) Cain remained angry. He asked Abel to come into the fields and there killed him.

The Lord asked Cain what had happened to Abel, and he replied 'I do not know; am I my brother's keeper?' (Gen. 4:9) The Lord cursed Cain and doomed him to failure as a farmer: 'When you till the ground, it shall no longer yield to you its strength.' (Gen. 4:12) Cain would henceforth become a fugitive and a wanderer across the face of the earth. Cain protested that his punishment was heavier than he could bear, and anyone who found him would slay him. God then put a mark on him so that no one would kill him.

Cain travelled to Nod, east of the Garden of Eden, where he settled down, married and had a son, called Enoch. Cain built a city and named it after his son. Enoch's son was Lamech, and among Cain's great-grandsons were Jabal, ancestor of the tent-dwelling nomads; Jubal, father of music by harp and pipe; and Tubal-cain, master of the metalsmiths.

The story of Cain and Abel derives from ancient and fragmentary traditions that may have been taken over by the Hebrews from the Kenites, the desert nomads from whom Moses acquired his wife. This may explain some of the problems scholars find in the biblical account.

One such problem is that the world of Cain is described as inhabited by other people and not just Adam and Eve and their sons. Thus, when the Lord condemned Cain to be a wanderer and a fugitive, he pleaded that 'whoever finds me will slay me' (Gen. 4:14) and the Lord put a mark on him: 'If any one slays Cain, vengeance shall be taken on him sevenfold.' (Gen. 4:15) Cain then acquired a wife and founded a city in the land of Nod. In the condition of human societies, the story of Cain and Abel marks a stage far advanced from the primitive beginnings. It is only in a legendary sense that Cain and Abel are pictured as the 'children' of the founders of the human race.

The motive for the murder of Abel is perplexing. One theory is that it related to the primitive practice of ritual human sacrifice to propitiate the gods and secure the fertility of the soil, without which the community would starve to death. Part of the punishment for the misguided slaying was, aptly enough, that the ground desecrated by Abel's blood would no longer respond to Cain's cultivation – in other words, the effect was the opposite of that which would have been intended by the sacrifice.

It is not explained why the Lord should have put a mark on Cain to protect him after he had killed his brother; nor is there any indication of the nature of the mark. In a number of primitive societies, it is customary to this day to mark a slayer in a special way, and to banish or isolate him. Such markings include colours painted on the body or face, tattoo marks and incisions, or smearing with mud or dung. Anthropologists surmise that the reason for this practice is to ward off trouble from the spirit of the slain man. In certain tribes even warriors who had killed an enemy in battle must be quarantined or purified afterwards. In some localities it was believed that contact with a murderer would bring misfortune and might even pollute the ground, and this would account for the distinctive marking by which a murderer could be identified on sight. Whatever the explanation for it, the mark of Cain has become a proverbial expression for blood-guilt that cannot be expiated.

However the details may be interpreted, it is clear that the story of Cain and Abel symbolizes the age-old strife in the Near East between 'the Desert and the Sown' – the nomads roaming with their tents and flocks, and the settled tillers of the soil. [Gen. 4]

Calcol (Heb. 'nourishment') *1.* date unknown. A son of Zerah and a grandson of Judah. [1 Chr. 2:6]
2. date unknown. A son of Mahol who was considered exceptionally wise but whose wisdom was surpassed by that of King Solomon. [1 Kgs. 4:31]

Caleb (Heb. 'dog') *1.* date unknown. Brother of Jerahmeel, he was the son of Hezron and the greatgrandson of Judah. His first wife Azubah bore him three sons. After her death he took a second wife, Ephrath, who bore him one son, Hur. Also called Chelubai. [1 Chr. 2:9, 18, 19, 24, 42, 46, 48–50]

2. c. 13 century BC. One of the twelve spies sent by Moses to reconnoitre the land of Canaan. Caleb, the son of Jephunneh, was chosen to represent the tribe of Judah when the Lord commanded Moses to send twelve men 'to spy out the land of Canaan, which I give to the people of Israel' (Num. 13:2). He and Joshua of the tribe of Ephraim came back confident and said to Moses and the people, 'Let us go up at once, and occupy it; for we are well able to overcome it.' (Num. 13:30) But the reports of the other ten were much more discouraging. The gathering was cast into gloom and grumbled at the Exodus, till the wrathful Lord decreed that they should stay wandering in the desert for forty years until that generation had died out. However, as a reward for his faith in the Lord, Caleb would survive: 'But my servant Caleb, because he has a different spirit and has followed me fully, I will bring into the land into which he went, and his descendants shall possess it.' (Num. 14:24)

When the children of Israel finally reached Canaan, Caleb, now eighty-five years of age, reminded Joshua that Moses had promised him the area he had visited as a spy. 'Then Joshua blessed him; and he gave Hebron to Caleb the son of Jephunneh for an inheritance.' (Josh. 14:13) Caleb drove out the three gigantic sons of Anak who were living there. He married his daughter Achsah to his nephew Othniel who took the neighbouring city of Debir (Kiriath-sepher). Achsah persuaded Caleb to include water sources in the land he gave her for her dowry. [Num. 13:6, 30; 14; 32:12; 34:19; Josh. 14:13, 14; 15:13–19; 21:12; Judg. 1:12–15; 1 Chr. 4:15; 6:56]

Canaan (Heb. 'red', 'purple') date unknown. A son of Ham, he was condemned by his grandfather Noah to serve the descendants of his father's brothers Shem and Japheth. [Gen. 9:22–27; 10:6; 1 Chr. 1:8]

Caphtorim date unknown. A son of Egypt and a grandson of Ham, his descendants settled in Caphtor. [Gen. 10:14; 1 Chr. 1:12]

Carkas (Pers. 'vulture') *c.* 5 century BC. One of the seven chamberlains whom Ahasuerus, king of Persia, commanded to bring Queen Vashti to the feast he made in the third year of his reign. [Esther 1:10]

Carmi (Heb. 'vine-dresser') *1. c.* 16 century BC. A son of Reuben and a grandson of Jacob and Leah. [Gen. 46:9; Exod. 6:14; Num. 26:6; 1 Chr. 5:3]
2. c. 13 century BC. Son of Zabdi, of the tribe of Judah. His son Achan took booty following the capture and destruction of Jericho contrary to the express orders of Joshua, and was stoned to death. [Josh. 7:1, 18;1 Chr. 2:7; 4:1]

Carshena (Pers. 'ploughman') 5 century BC. One of the seven princes of Persia and Media who was present at the feast of King Ahasuerus. [Esther 1:14]

Casluhim (Heb. 'fortified') date unknown. A son of Egypt and a grandson of Ham, from whom according to Hebrew tradition the Philistines were descended. [Gen. 10:14; 1 Chr. 1:12]

Chedorlaomer (Elamite 'servant of Lagamar [a god]') *c.* 18 century BC. Chedorlaomer was king of Elam, the important land east of Babylonia. He led the four Mesopotamian kings who defeated an alliance of five local kings from the Dead Sea area in the time of Abraham. They carried off a number of captives, including Abraham's nephew Lot, and much booty. Abraham pursued them and rescued the captives and booty.
    None of these nine kings has been identified, and none of their countries or cities except Elam. [Gen. 14]

Chelal (Heb. 'perfect') 5 century BC. Descendant of Pahath-moab. He divorced his non-Jewish wife in the time of Ezra. [Ezra 10:30]

Chelub (Heb. 'basket') *1.* date unknown. Brother of Shuhah of the tribe of Judah, he was the father of Mehir. [1 Chr. 4:11]
2. 10 century BC. Father of Ezri who was the supervisor of the people who tilled the fields in the reign of King David. [1 Chr. 27:26]

Chelubai *see* CALEB *1.*

Cheluhi 5 century BC. Descendant of Bani, he married a non-Jewish wife and later divorced her in the time of Ezra. [Ezra 10:35]

Chemosh date unknown. The national god of Moab and Ammon. The sacred rites to this god included human sacrifice. Mesha, king of Moab, in the hope of changing the course of the war, offered up his eldest son as a burnt offering after his defeat by the armies of Jehoram, king of Israel, and Jehoshaphat, king of Judah. [Num. 21:29; Judg. 11:24; 1 Kgs. 11:7, 33; 2 Kgs. 3:27; Jer. 48:13]

Chenaanah (Heb. 'merchant') *1.* date unknown. Son of Bilhan of the tribe of Benjamin, he and his family were warrior leaders of the tribe. [1 Chr. 7:10]
2. 9 century BC. Father of Zedekiah, the false prophet who told Ahab, king of Israel, that he would defeat the Syrians in battle at Ramoth-gilead. [1 Kgs. 22:11, 24; 2 Chr. 18:10, 23]

Chenani 5 century BC. A Levite who was a leading worshipper at the solemn fast day proclaimed by Ezra and Nehemiah. [Neh. 9:4]

Chenaniah (Heb. 'made by God') *1.* 10 century BC. A Levite musician in the reign of King David, he supervised the singing of the Levites while the Ark of God was being brought to Jerusalem. [1 Chr. 15:22]

2. 10 century BC. A Levite descended from Izhar, he and his sons supervised the government administration by the judges and public officials in the reign of King David. [1 Chr. 26:29]

Cheran date unknown. Son of Dishon and a descendant of Seir, the Horite. [Gen. 36:26; 1 Chr. 1:41]

Cherethites (Heb. 'executioners') 10 century BC. Part of the bodyguard of King David's army commanded by Benaiah son of Jehoiada. [2 Sam. 8:18; 15:18; 20:23; 1 Kgs. 1:38, 44; 1 Chr. 18:17]

Chesed (Heb. 'gain') c. 18 century BC. Fourth son of Abraham's brother Nahor and his wife Milcah. [Gen. 22:22]

Chidon see NACON

Chileab (Heb. 'like the father') 10 century BC. Second son of King David, born in Hebron, his mother was Abigail, the Carmelitess. Also called Daniel. [2 Sam. 3:3; 1 Chr. 3:1]

Chilion (Heb. 'sickly') c. 11 century BC. Younger son of Elimelech of the tribe of Judah, he and his family left their native town of Bethlehem during a famine in the time of Judges and settled in Moab. Chilion and his elder brother Mahlon married Moabite women, Ruth and Orpah. After the death of Chilion and Mahlon, Ruth went back to Bethlehem with their mother Naomi, and later married their relative Boaz. [Ruth 1:1–5]

Chimham (Heb. 'longing') c. 10 century BC. Chimham was the son of Barzillai, the Gilead notable who befriended and helped David when he fled from Absalom's revolt. The grateful David kept Chimham at his court, and charged Solomon to be kind to Barzillai's offspring. Geruth Chimham, a place near Bethlehem, was named after him. [2 Sam. 19:37–41; Jer. 41:17]

Chislon (Heb. 'hope') c. 13 century BC. A leader in the days of Moses, his son Elidad was appointed to divide the portion of the land of Israel allocated to Benjamin among the members of the tribe. [Num. 34:21]

Col-Hozeh (Heb. 'all seeing') 5 century BC. Son of Hazaiah of the tribe of Judah, his son Shallum was governor of part of Mizpah in the days of Nehemiah and repaired the gate of the fountain and the Pool of Shiloh in Jerusalem. [Neh. 3:15; 11:5]

Conaniah (Heb. 'made by God') **1.** 8 century BC. A Levite appointed by Hezekiah, king of Judah, to supervise the bringing of offerings and tithes into the Temple. [2 Chr. 31:12, 13]

2. 7 century BC. One of the chief Levites of Judah in the reign of King Josiah who donated large quantities of cattle for the Passover offering. [2 Chr. 35:9]

Coniah see JEHOIACHIN

Cozbi (Heb. 'fruitful') c. 13 century BC. Daughter of Zur, a Midianite chief, she was brought by Zimri into the Israelite encampment in the Jordan Valley. The priest Phinehas slew them with a javelin while they were lying together in a tent. The Lord was mollified by this act and lifted the plague he had inflicted on the children of Israel for their immorality. [Num. 25:15, 18]

Cush (Heb. 'black') **1.** date unknown. Eldest son of Ham and a grandson of Noah, he was the father of Nimrod, and by Hebrew tradition regarded as the ancestor of the Cushites, a Negro tribe which settled south of Egypt. [Gen. 10:6, 8; 1 Chr. 1:8–10]

2. *c.* 11 century BC. A Benjaminite soldier in King Saul's army who was sent in pursuit of David. [Ps. 7]

Cushan-Rishathaim *c.* 12 century BC. King of Mesopotamia, he oppressed the children of Israel and forced them to pay heavy tribute for eight years until his hold was broken by Othniel the son of Kenaz, younger brother of Caleb. [Judg. 3:8–10]

Cushi *1. c.* 10 century BC. A soldier in the army of King David, he was sent by Joab, David's army commander, to report to David about the death of Absalom his son and the victory of the king's army against the rebels. [2 Sam. 18:21–32]
2. *c.* 7 century BC. Great-grandfather of Jehudi, who told Baruch to read out the prophecies of Jeremiah to the leaders of Judah. [Jer. 36:14]
3. *c.* 7 century BC. Son of Gedaliah, he was the father of the prophet Zephaniah. [Zeph. 1:1]

Cyrus II (The Great) (Pers. 'son') King of the Medes and the Persians, 559–29 BC. Cyrus II was the son of Cambyses I, king of Anshan, and of Mandane, daughter of King Astyages of the Medes. He succeeded to the throne in 559 BC and rapidly gained control of the surrounding peoples. By 549 BC he had conquered Media. In 539 BC he defeated the Babylonian army and became the ruler of the largest empire the world had seen till then.

Cyrus was a generous conqueror, especially remembered in the Bible for his friendship towards the Jews. 'The Lord stirred up the spirit of Cyrus king of Persia' (2 Chr. 36:22), and he gave the captive Jews he found in Babylon permission to return and rebuild the Temple in Jerusalem. He suggested that those who could not return should help by giving gold, silver, goods and animals to pay for the work. Cyrus also gave orders that the thousands of vessels of the house of the Lord, which Nebuchadnezzar had brought from Jerusalem, should be handed over to the Jews and returned to the Temple. As a result of the active interest Cyrus took in the Jews he is referred to in Isaiah as the 'shepherd' of the Lord (Isa. 44:28) or his 'anointed' (Isa. 45:1).

An excavated cylinder written in cuneiform script refers to an edict of Cyrus authorizing the return of captives 'to the other side of the Tigris'. This cylinder does not refer to the Jews as such, but is consistent with the account in the Book of Ezra. [2 Chr. 36:22, 23; Ezra 1; 4:3; 5:13–17; 6:3; Isa. 44:28; 45:1; Dan. 1:21; 6:28; 10:1]

D

Dagon (Heb. 'corn') Dagon was a Philistine god. Temples were built to him at Gaza, Ashdod and Beth-shean, and his name was incorporated in the city of Beth-dagon, in the Judean foothills. Professor W.F. Albright believes that Dagon was an Accadian god worshipped in the Euphrates valley as early as the 25th century BC.

Three events in the Old Testament took place in shrines to this god: Samson died by pulling down the temple to Dagon in Gaza; many Philistine worshippers were killed when the captured Israelite Ark was placed in the temple of Dagon at Ashdod and the statue of the god fell down; and the head of the slain King Saul was placed in the temple of Dagon at Beth-shean after the Israelite defeat on Mount Gilboa. [Josh. 15:41; Judg. 16:23–30; 1 Sam. 5; 1 Chr. 10:10]

Dalaiah *see* DELAIAH

Dalphon *c.* 5 century BC. One of the ten sons of Haman the Agagite, he joined his father's plot to eliminate all the Jews in Persia. [Esther 9:7]

Dan (Heb. 'judge') *c.* 16 century BC. Fifth son of Jacob. Dan was the elder son of Bilhah, the maid Rachel gave Jacob her husband as a concubine. Together with his brothers, he was involved in the events that led to the selling of their brother Joseph into slavery in Egypt. Later he was one of the ten sons sent by Jacob to buy corn in Egypt, where Joseph had become a leading figure at Pharaoh's court. When Jacob went to settle in Egypt with all his family, it included Dan's son.

On his deathbed Jacob blessed all his sons in turn, and said: 'Dan shall judge his people.' (Gen. 49:16)

In the blessing attributed to Moses, it is said: 'Dan is a lion's whelp, that leaps forth from Bashan.' (Deut. 33:22)

In the conquest of Canaan under Joshua, the small tribe of Dan was allocated an area in the foothills south-west of Ephraim. It was pushed out by Philistine pressure and resettled in the north-east corner of the country. [Gen. 30:6; 35:25; 46:23; 49:16, 17; Exod. 1:4; Num. 26:42; Deut. 33:22; Josh. 19:47; 1 Chr. 2:2]

Daniel (Heb. 'God is my judge') *1. see* CHILEAB
2. c. 6 century BC. Hebrew official at Babylonian court. The Book of Daniel opens with King Nebuchadnezzar of Babylonia instructing his chief eunuch to select a number of boys from noble families and put them through a three-year course of instruction for service as scribes at the court. They were to be physically fit and mentally bright. Daniel was one of the four Jewish boys selected, the other three being Hananiah, Mishael and Azariah. They were given the Babylonian names of Belteshazzar, Shadrach, Meshach and Abednego.

The king ordered that the youths in training should be given food and drink from the royal table. This would have violated the religious dietary laws of the Jewish boys, so Daniel persuaded those in charge to allow them to eat only vegetables and drink only water. At first they were afraid the health of the boys would suffer and the chief eunuch would get into trouble with the king. But a ten-day trial proved they could thrive on the vegetarian diet.

Some years later, the king had a most disturbing dream. When his magicians and wise men could not interpret it he flew into a rage and ordered their death.

In a vision the king's dream was revealed to Daniel. Next morning he was brought before the king, and told him that he had dreamt of a great statue. 'The head of this image was of fine gold, its breast and arms of silver, its belly and thighs of bronze, its legs of iron, its feet partly of iron and partly of clay.' (Dan. 2:32, 33) A stone came hurling out of nowhere and smashed the clay feet, at which the whole statue disintegrated into fine particles that were blown away by the wind. The stone then grew into a great mountain that filled the earth.

Daniel explained that the golden head of the statue was Nebuchadnezzar himself, and the silver, bronze, iron and clay parts represented lesser kingdoms that would succeed the Babylonian one – until all of them were swept away by the kingdom of God that would last forever.

The astounded king exclaimed: 'Truly, your God is God of gods and Lord of kings, and a revealer of mysteries, for you have been able to reveal this mystery.' (Dan. 2:47) He heaped honours and riches on Daniel, who became the chief of all the wise men and governor of the province of Babylon.

Nebuchadnezzar erected a huge golden statue and assembled all the high officials and the notables to prostrate themselves before it to 'the sound of the horn, pipe, lyre, trigon, harp, bagpipe, and every kind of music ...' (Dan. 3:5). Certain courtiers reported to the monarch that the Jews refused to join in this act of idolworship; they referred specifically to Daniel's companions Shadrach, Meshach and Abednego who had been given official positions. The angry king

ordered them to be tied up and flung into a fiery furnace. It radiated such fierce heat that the servants who thrust them in were burnt to death. The Lord sent an angel into the furnace who protected the three young Hebrews. Overwhelmed by this miracle, the king called to them to come out; '... the hair of their heads was not singed, their mantles were not harmed, and no smell of fire had come upon them' (Dan. 3:27). Nebuchadnezzar issued a decree that the mighty God of the Hebrews was to be treated with respect throughout his realm.

Nebuchadnezzar was filled with dread by another ominous dream. In it he saw a tall tree reaching up to the sky. It provided abundant fruit; the birds nested in the branches; and the animals sheltered beneath it. A 'holy one' (Dan. 4:13) came down from heaven and had the tree cut down, leaving only the stump in the ground. The king sent for Daniel, who told him that the tree stood for Nebuchadnezzar himself in all his power and glory. In order to humble him and teach him that the Lord ruled over all, he would be reduced to the level of an animal. He would be driven out of human society, eat grass like an ox and be drenched by the rain and dew. Daniel begged the king to repent and change his ways while there was yet time.

A year later, while the king was boasting of his might, he was attacked by a fit of madness and behaved in the way that Daniel had foretold. When he recovered his sanity he extolled God and was restored to his former greatness.

The next episode in Daniel's story concerns Belshazzar, who is described as Nebuchadnezzar's son and his successor on the throne. He gave a great feast in the palace, attended by all his household and a thousand of his nobles. His princes, wives and concubines drank wine from the vessels from the Temple in Jerusalem that Nebuchadnezzar had brought to Babylon.

Suddenly a hand appeared and wrote on the wall of the banquet chamber the words: 'MENE, MENE, TEKEL, and PARSIN' (Dan. 5:25). Nobody could understand this mysterious message and they were stricken with terror. The queen remembered Daniel and he was brought before Belshazzar. Daniel interpreted the writing on the wall as follows: 'MENE, God has numbered the days of your kingdom and brought it to an end; TEKEL, you have been weighed in the balances and found wanting; PARSIN, your kingdom is divided and given to the Medes and Persians.' (Dan. 5:26, 27, 28) (The three words are Aramaic terms denoting numbers, weight and divisions.)

That night Belshazzar was assassinated 'And Darius the Mede received the kingdom' (Dan. 5:31).

Darius made Daniel once more one of the most powerful men in the kingdom. Those who were jealous of his position tried to discredit him, but were unable to find any fault in his public service. Hoping to hit at him through his faith, they persuaded Darius to issue an edict whereby for thirty days everyone was to worship the king alone, on penalty of being thrown to the lions.

Daniel ignored the order and went on praying to the Lord three times a day in front of his window, which faced in the direction of Jerusalem. His enemies reported this to the king, who was reluctant to impose the punishment but had no option, since '... a law of the Medes and Persians' (Dan. 6:15) was rigid and unalterable. The distressed king had Daniel cast into the den of lions, with a prayer that the Hebrew God would save him. The entrance was blocked with a stone, and the king's seal placed upon it, together with those of his lords.

The king remained awake, fasted all night, and early next morning hurried back to the lions' pit. To his delight Daniel emerged unscathed, saying 'My God sent his angel and shut the lions' mouths, and they have not hurt me' (Dan. 6:22). The king promptly had Daniel's accusers thrown into the den, and this time there was no angel to save them. Darius too issued a proclamation calling for all his subjects to honour the God of Daniel. These simply told tales, set in the Babylon of the 6th century BC, were obviously written down centuries later, since the references to Babylonian rulers are incorrect. But the stories did bear out that God was stronger than alien rulers and would take care of the faithful. That reassurance was needed in the Judea of the 2nd century BC when the Book of Daniel was written, appropriately during the Maccabean revolt against the religious oppression of Antiochus IV Epiphanes (see APOCRYPHA section). Moving from the Babylonian past to the dangerous Judean present, the author's style becomes both more sombre and more obscure. Daniel is now relating his personal visions, in which imaginary creatures symbolize the history of foreign domination of the Jews, culminating in the evils of Antiochus's rule.

In the first vision four beasts come out of the sea. They resemble a lion with eagle's wings, a bear, a leopard and a nameless and terrible monster with ten horns: '... and it had great iron teeth; it devoured and broke in pieces, and stamped the residue with its feet' (Dan. 7:7). There is a great judgment and the fourth beast is slain. The kingdom then passes permanently to the 'people of the saints of the Most High' (Dan. 7:27) and is ruled by a 'son of man' (Dan. 7:13). (The four beasts are interpreted by some as the Babylonian, Median, Persian and Seleucid Greek empires. The ten horns are the successive Seleucid kings, with Antiochus Epiphanes identified as a horn with human eyes and a boastful mouth.)

In a second vision a ram with two horns (Media and Persia) is charged from the west and overcome by a he-goat with a single horn (Greece). The horn (Alexander the Great) is replaced by four others (the successor kingdoms of his generals) and the thrusts of one horn indicate the campaigns of Antiochus. The archangel Gabriel reaffirms that the Messiah will come soon.

In the last and longest of his visions, an angel gives in enigmatic language an outline of the historical events from Alexander the Great to Antiochus Epiphanes. The account is continued into the future, when the existing regime will end in turmoil and upheaval. This collapse will receive 'a little help' – a devious reference to the revolt then in progress. In the troubles to come, the God-fearing whose names were written in the 'book of truth' will be saved, 'And many of those who sleep in the dust of the earth shall awake, some to everlasting life, and some to shame and everlasting contempt' (Dan. 12:2).

In substance, the Book of Daniel is a continuation of the Hebrew prophetic strain that developed over many centuries, and had reached its loftiest expression with Isaiah, Jeremiah and Ezekiel. [Book of Daniel]

3. 5 century BC. A priest of Judah who returned with Ezra from exile in Babylon and signed the solemn covenant. [Ezra 8:2; Neh. 10:6]

Dara date unknown. One of the five sons of Zerah and grandson of Judah. [1 Chr. 2:6]

Darda (Heb. 'thistle') date unknown. A son of Mahol who was considered exceptionally wise but whose wisdom was surpassed by that of King Solomon. [1 Kgs. 4:31]

Darius (Pers. 'he who upholds the good')

1. Darius I, king of Persia, 522–486 BC. Darius the Great, son of Hystaspes, consolidated and organized the huge Persian empire. He authorized the regional governor Tattenai to permit the Jews in Jerusalem to rebuild the Temple, with a contribution from the official tax revenues. Darius also decreed that the animals, wheat, salt, wine or oil required for the priests should be supplied daily so that prayers would be offered 'for the life of the king and his sons' (Ezra 6:10). [Ezra 4, 5, 6; Hag. 1:1, 15; 2:10; Zech. 1:1, 7; 7:1]

2. The Persian king mentioned by Nehemiah may have been Darius II (423–04 BC). [Neh. 12:22]

3. 6 century BC. According to the Book of Daniel, 'Darius the Mede' (Dan. 5:30) became king of Babylon and appointed Daniel one of the three 'presidents' (Dan. 6:2) over the whole kingdom. When the king 'planned to set him over the whole kingdom' (Dan. 6:3), the other two presidents and the princes, jealous of Daniel persuaded Darius to sign a degree that no one in the kingdom was to pray to any other god except the king for thirty days, on pain of being thrown into the lions' den. But Daniel continued to pray to the Lord three times a day. The reluctant king had Daniel thrown into the pit with the lions. The next morning, having fasted all night, the king hurried to the lions' den and to his delight Daniel emerged unscathed. Impressed with the power of the Lord, Darius had Daniel's accusers thrown into the pit and then issued a decree saying that everyone in his kingdom should fear and respect the God of Daniel: 'for he is the living God, enduring for ever' (Dan. 6:26). [Dan. 5:30; 6; 9:1; 11:1]

Darkon (Heb. 'hard') *c.* 10 century BC. A servant of King Solomon whose descendants returned with Zerubbabel from exile in Babylon. [Ezra 2:56; Neh. 7:58]

Dathan (Heb. 'strong') *c.* 13 century BC. Son of Eliab of the tribe of Reuben, he and his brother Abiram joined a conspiracy led by Korah the Levite against the leadership of Moses and Aaron, and together with Korah and all his followers perished in an earthquake. [Num. 16:1–30; 26:9; Deut. 11:6; Ps. 106:17]

David (possibly Heb. 'commander', 'hero') Second king of Israel, *c.* 1010–970 BC.

The small Judean town of Bethlehem was in a flurry. The prophet Samuel was coming, and the citizens did not know why. Samuel was an austere and formidable man of God, of whom the people had stood in awe for a generation. What could this sudden visit portend? When the great man arrived, the fearful elders of the town enquired, 'Do you come peaceably?' (1 Sam. 16:4) and he reassured them that he did. He had 'come to sacrifice to the Lord' (1 Sam. 16:5) and they were required to sanctify themselves and attend.

Jesse, a prosperous and respected sheep-farmer, was specially summoned to the ceremony by Samuel where he and seven of his eight sons were presented to the prophet in turn. When Jesse was asked whether these were all the sons he had, he replied that the youngest one, David, was out tending the sheep. On Samuel's insistence, David was hurriedly brought in – a ruddy, bright-eyed and attractive lad. Samuel anointed his head with oil 'and the Spirit of the Lord came mightily upon David from that day forward' (1 Sam. 16:13). The prophet returned to his home in Ramah, and Bethlehem went back to its quiet, pastoral life.

The background to Samuel's curious act was his estrangement from Saul. He had made Saul king, but turned against him when Saul refused to be an obedient puppet. Guided by the Lord, Samuel chose as the future successor to Saul a gifted but unknown boy in Bethlehem. David's experience of life till then had been confined to tending sheep in the Bethlehem hills and making up songs to accompany his harp. He was soon to be thrust into high places and stirring events, in a way which would exceed even his most poetic imaginings.

THE YOUNG DAVID

After his final break with Samuel, Saul became increasingly subject to fits of melancholy. His worried retainers felt that music might calm the king at such times, and they sought 'a man who is skilful in playing the lyre' (1 Sam. 16:16). One of them then mentioned a lad in Bethlehem who was a skilled musician and the king asked that David be brought to him. Jesse sent him to the palace at Gibeah, bearing a farmer's modest gift of bread, a bottle of wine and a kid. Saul was charmed by young David's good looks and intelligence, and appointed him his armour-bearer. When one of Saul's black moods came upon him, David played to him on his harp 'so Saul was refreshed, and was well, and the evil spirit departed from him' (1 Sam. 16:23). Saul led out his forces against the Philistines, and Jesse's three eldest sons were mobilized. 'David went back and forth from Saul to feed his father's sheep at Bethlehem.' (1 Sam. 17:15)

One day, David was sent by his father to bring victuals from home to his brothers. Jesse prudently included a gift of ten cheeses for their commanding officer. David set out at dawn with these supplies loaded on to a small cart, probably drawn by an ass. Some twelve miles down a ravine from Bethlehem brought him to the Shephelah, the low foothills separating the Hebrews on the mountain plateau from the Philistines on the coastal plain.

In this borderland the two armies now faced each other across a narrow valley through which ran a brook. Neither side would risk an attack across the open ground and up the opposing slope. The Philistines produced a giant soldier from Gath called Goliath, clad in heavy brass armour, carrying a great sword and spear and preceded by a shield-bearer. This human tank paraded daily between the lines, taunting the Israelites and challenging them to send out a champion against him. That was the sight that met David's eyes when he entered the Israelite lines and sought out his brothers. He got talking to a group of soldiers about killing the 'uncircumcised Philistine' (1 Sam. 17:26). His eldest brother Eliab chided David, 'I know your presumption, and the evil of your heart' (1 Sam. 17:28). However, Saul heard these reports and sent for him.

David said stoutly to the king, 'your servant will go and fight with this Philistine' (1 Sam. 17:32). Saul gazed at him in astonishment and brushed aside the idea, 'for you are but a youth, and he has been a man of war from his youth' (1 Sam. 17:33). David maintained that the Lord, who had helped him to slay single-handed a lion and a bear raiding his flock, would protect him against Goliath too. Moved by David's faith, Saul decided to let him try. He made David put on armour and sword, but the boy discarded them, saying he had never worn them before. Instead, he went out equipped only with a stave, a sling and his shepherd's pouch, into which he put five smooth stones carefully selected from the brook.

Goliath could hardly believe his eyes. Lumbering forward, he cried out derisively that he would carve up the youth, and feed his flesh to the birds and beasts. David's sharp tongue mocked the giant, while his nimble feet kept him well out of Goliath's reach. Waiting for the right moment, David hurled a stone from the sling and hit Goliath square in the forehead, so that he fell down stunned. Quick as a cat, David leapt towards Goliath and cut off his head with his own sword. Seeing their champion so abruptly slain, the Philistines started to flee, with the Israelite forces in hot pursuit.

Abner, Saul's general, brought David before the king, who asked him to remain in his service. Saul's son Jonathan was present, and an abiding friendship sprang up between the two men. With a typically warm-hearted gesture, Jonathan took off his own garments and put them on David, together with his sword and bow.

THE GUERRILLA YEARS

David made full use of the dazzling turn in his fortune. He was a success as a military officer, and his fame and popularity grew. When the army returned from the campaign, the women who came to greet the king with dancing and music sang that 'Saul has slain his thousands, and David his ten thousands' (1 Sam. 18:7). The king was angered and 'Saul eyed David from that day on' (1 Sam. 18:9).

In one of his evil moods, while David was playing to him, Saul twice tried to kill him with his javelin. After that he sent David on dangerous missions, hoping he might be slain in battle. Saul let David know that he would gain the hand in marriage of one of the king's daughters if he brought back the foreskins of a hundred Philistine soldiers. Instead of losing his life in the attempt, David accounted for double that number of the enemy, and returned to wed the princess Michal.

As David's prestige grew in the kingdom, Saul's resentment grew with it. He sent men to David's house to kill him, but Michal lowered him out of a window and put a dummy in his bed, pretending her husband was ill. David fled to the aged prophet Samuel in Ramah. Saul sent men to catch him, then arrived in person. Fortunately Saul, who had a strong religious streak, was caught up in the ecstasy of the company of prophets around Samuel, and David was able to escape again.

He secretly contacted Jonathan and told him 'there is but a step between me and death' (1 Sam. 20:3). Jonathan would not believe his father really meant to kill his friend. But Saul's rage when David stayed away from a court banquet left no room for doubt. Jonathan sadly agreed that David had to run for his life. The royal favourite and popular commander had become a harried fugitive.

Alone, destitute and unarmed, David reached the priestly sanctuary at Nob near Jerusalem. He pretended to be on a private mission for the king, and the head priest Ahimelech gave him loaves of the sacrificial bread as provisions, and the sword David had once taken from Goliath. (It had been preserved in the sanctuary.) The kindly priests were to pay a cruel price for this aid: the king had all the priests of Nob rounded up and slain. Only Abiathar, the son of the head priest, escaped and managed to join David in the mountains.

In his desperate flight David slipped into the Philistine city of Gath. Its king Achish was later to be his friend and protector, but now David was in the midst of the enemy. He feigned madness – 'made marks on the doors of the gate, and let his spittle run down his beard' (1 Sam. 21:13) – and got away unharmed.

Some fifteen miles north-east from Gath, David reached the hill country of Adullam, overlooking the spot where as a youth he had triumphed over Goliath. The terrain – rocky gorges, bush and hillside caves – was a natural refuge for the band of about four hundred fugitives and malcontents that now gathered around him. His parents could not share the hardships and dangers of his present life, so he put them beyond Saul's reach under the protection of the king of Moab across the Jordan river.

In the Adullam area stood the small Israelite town of Keilah. When this exposed place was raided by the Philistines, David saw a chance to secure a firm base. His lean guerrillas fell upon the Philistines and routed them; and David quartered his men in the town.

On hearing this, Saul said to himself: 'God has given him into my hand; for he has shut himself in by entering a town that has gates and bars.' (1 Sam. 23:7) But David was not to be trapped. He led his men out of the comfort of city billets and back into the rugged hills.

David headed south-east past Hebron and in among the wooded ridges of Ziph. From here the Wilderness of Judah dropped steeply eastward to the Dead Sea, gleaming far below. The men of Ziph were afraid of Saul's vengeance, and hastened to reveal the presence in their area of these unwelcome bandits. David was forced to move further south to Maon, where Saul's forces caught up with him and cut him off. Saul had to turn back to meet a new Philistine threat, and David used the welcome respite to establish himself in the bleak crags and caves overlooking the Dead Sea shore at En-gedi ('the Spring of the Wild Goat').

Saul came back with three thousand picked men to resume his obsessive search. He entered a dark cave to rest, without knowing that David and some of his men were hiding in its depths. The royal hunter was at the mercy of his quarry! Yet David, against the whispered prodding of his companions, refrained from killing 'the Lord's anointed' (1 Sam. 24:6). Instead, he stealthily cut a piece from the hem of Saul's robe.

As Saul emerged from the cave, David came out behind him and called to him. When Saul turned, David bowed himself to the ground and cried out that he had never done any harm to the king and had in fact just spared his life, as the piece of cloth bore witness. The honest and emotional Saul was much moved. 'You are more righteous than I', he exclaimed, 'for you have repaid me good, whereas I have repaid you evil.' (1 Sam. 24:17) Saul admitted that he expected David to become king of Israel one day and begged him to spare Saul's family when that happened. Saul then withdrew his troops, while David and his men remained in their mountain fastness.

Later, however, Saul resumed his pursuit of David. One night David and his nephew Abishai stole into Saul's slumbering camp and reached the spot where the king was sleeping on the ground. Abishai urged that Saul be killed, but David refused. Instead, they took away with them Saul's spear and water jar. From a nearby hilltop, David shouted taunts at Saul's commander Abner for failing to protect his royal master. When Saul woke and heard what had happened, he was filled with remorse, and cried out, 'behold, I have played the fool, and have erred exceedingly' (1 Sam. 26:21). He addressed David as his son and gave him his blessing. (This story may be a different version of the episode in the cave.)

Like every guerrilla leader, David was careful not to despoil the local farmers, on whose goodwill his band depended for their supplies. At shearing time David sent ten young men to a certain Nabal, a well-to-do sheep-farmer, to seek provisions. They pointed out that Nabal's flocks had been allowed to graze all winter in the hills, unmolested by David's men. Nabal rudely rebuffed them. David led his men towards Nabal's farmstead, vowing he would wipe out everyone he found there. Abigail, Nabal's attractive and clever wife, acted quickly to head them off. Without her husband's knowledge she intercepted David's party, bringing with her several asses loaded with bread, corn, mutton, wine, raisins and figs. David accepted her food and apologies, and turned back. Abigail returned to find Nabal drunk at the feast after the shearing. Next morning she told him how narrowly he had escaped David's wrath. The frightened Nabal suffered a heart attack, from which he died ten days later.

David, always susceptible to feminine beauty and intelligence, had been much attracted by Abigail. He must also have been lonely, for his wife Michal, the daughter of King Saul, had not followed him into exile but had been remarried by her father to someone else. On learning that Abigail had become a widow, David sent messengers asking her to marry him. Abigail promptly set off to join David, accompanied by five handmaidens. He also took another wife, Ahinoam, from the valley of Jezreel, about whose background nothing is known.

The years of precarious survival in the hills of southern Judea were drawing to a close. David knew he could not hold out much longer against Saul's forces. Moreover, he and his now six hundred irregulars had acquired families, which tied them down and made them yearn for a more secure life. David made a difficult decision. With his whole band, he moved westward into the coastal plain and offered his services to the leading Philistine ruler, Achish the king of Gath. What made this easier was that active warfare had died down at that time between the Israelites and their Philistine adversaries.

David was to remain the henchman of Achish for sixteen months. The king appointed him governor of the small border town of Ziklag, on the edge of the Negev desert, half-way between Gath and Beersheba. From this base David and his men carried out raids against the troublesome desert tribes as far as northern Sinai, bringing back captured sheep, cattle, donkeys and camels. To allay doubts about his loyalty, David's reports suggested that these forays were directed at the Israelites and tribes allied with them.

In due course the alliance of Philistine cities resumed the war against Israel. Their army marched north along the coastal plain and into the valley of Jezreel. Achish wanted David and his men to take an active part in the campaign. Fortunately for David, the other Philistine princes did not share Achish's trust in his able Hebrew vassal, and feared he would defect to his own people. They said 'he shall not go down with us to battle, lest in the battle he become an adversary to us' (1 Sam. 29:4). Achish rather apologetically asked David to return to Ziklag with his men.

It took them three days of forced marches to get back, only to find that in their absence the desert nomad Amalekites had raided the town and carried off the women and the children, including David's. The remaining townsmen were bitter against him and threatened to stone him. David mustered his tired men and set off into the desert in hot pursuit. Twenty miles to the south-west they reached the dry watercourse of Besor. A third of the men were too exhausted to carry on and were left behind with the baggage. Then David had a stroke of luck. His men found a young Egyptian who had been adrift in the desert for three days, after having fallen sick and been abandoned by his Amalekite master. Revived with food and water, and given a promise of protection, he led them to the Amalekite raiding party, who were spread out at their ease and making merry over their spoils. David's men fell upon them in the dusk. A number of the younger men escaped on their camels, but the rest of the encampment were wiped out. All the abducted women and children were recovered unharmed, and large flocks and herds captured. The four hundred of David's men who had taken part in this engagement objected to dividing the booty with the two hundred who had remained behind with the baggage. But David decided firmly that each serving soldier should have an equal share and made this a standing rule. On getting back to Ziklag, he sent a good number of the captured animals as gifts to towns in southern Judah that had helped him

during his outlaw years. David was no doubt thinking of future prospects as well as past debts.

DAVID IN HEBRON

The return to his homeland came sooner than David could have expected. There arrived at Ziklag a young Amalekite who had been serving with Saul's army in the north. He was brought before David and blurted out the dreadful news of the Israelite defeat on Mount Gilboa. He claimed that he had himself killed King Saul at the latter's request, and produced Saul's crown and bracelet as proof. He may have expected a reward, but David ordered him to be killed, saying, 'Your blood be upon your head; for your own mouth has testified against you, saying, "I have slain the Lord's anointed"' (2 Sam. 1:16).

David was plunged in grief. Though the king had persecuted him, Saul had united and led his people for two decades and had raised the young David from obscurity to fame. Jonathan had been his closest and most faithful friend. Out of his pain David the poet composed one of the most moving laments in literature:

'Thy glory, O Israel, is slain upon thy
  high places!
  How are the mighty fallen!
Tell it not in Gath,
  publish it not in the streets of
    Ashkelon;
lest the daughters of the Philistines
  rejoice,
  lest the daughters of the
    uncircumcised exult.
Ye mountains of Gilboa,
  let there be no dew or rain upon
    you,
  nor upsurging of the deep!
For there the shield of the mighty
    was defiled,
  the shield of Saul, not anointed
    with oil ...
Saul and Jonathan, beloved and lovely!
  In life and in death they were not
    divided;

they were swifter than eagles,
 they were stronger than lions ...
 I am distressed for you, my brother
  Jonathan;
very pleasant have you been to me;
 your love to me was wonderful,
  passing the love of women.'
    (2 Sam. 1:19–21, 23, 26)

The victory of the Philistines had given them control of northern Israel. With the remnants of his army Abner, Saul's kinsman and general, retreated east of the Jordan river, where he proclaimed as king Saul's eldest surviving son Ishbosheth, a forty-year-old weakling. David seized his chance in this confused situation. He quickly moved back across the frontier to Hebron and was accepted as king of Judah, the largest and most powerful of the Israelite tribes. At the same time, he made a gesture to Saul's memory. Having heard that the men of the town of Jabesh-gilead had retrieved the bodies of Saul and his sons and interred their bones, David sent them a message commending their act.

The united kingdom fashioned by Saul had split in two – Judah in the south and Israel in the north. It would take David many years of patient statecraft to reunite them.

The civil war between the north and the south dragged on, till Abner quarrelled with Ishbosheth and lost patience with the puppet king he had set up. Abner sent messages to David offering to help him become ruler over the whole nation. David made one demand: that Michal, to whom he had been married in his youth, should be restored to him. Whether David still loved her or not, it was clearly of political advantage to renew his family tie with Saul's house. Afraid of Abner, her brother Ishbosheth agreed. Michal's second husband accompanied her sadly to the border.

Having obtained support for David from the elders of the tribes of Israel, Abner came on a visit to Hebron. David received him warmly, and the union was settled.

Joab had been away on a military foray during these developments. On his return, he was taken aback by the pact David had made and murdered Abner. Aghast at this bloody act, David cursed Joab and gave Abner a public funeral in Hebron.

Ishbosheth, too, was murdered by two of his officers, who brought his severed head to David, expecting to be rewarded. David had them put to death, and ordered the head of Ishbosheth to be buried in Abner's tomb.

The elders of all the tribes of Israel now came to Hebron to pledge allegiance to David saying, 'Behold, we are your bone and flesh' (2 Sam. 5:1). He had travelled a long and tortuous path since the day when the prophet Samuel had come to Bethlehem and anointed a shepherd boy's head with oil. David was now thirty years old. He was to rule over the kingdom for nearly forty years more.

JERUSALEM THE CAPITAL

From the time of Joshua, who had failed to capture it, Jerusalem had remained for two and a half centuries a Jebusite enclave in Israelite territory. It was a formidable stronghold, built on a narrow spur surrounded by steep valleys on three sides – the vale of Kidron, the vale of Hinnom and the central valley (subsequently known as the Tyropoeon valley) that would later divide Solomon's Temple Mount from the Upper City. The northern approach was protected by fortifications.

David decided to take the city and make it his capital. It was centrally located between the northern and southern parts of his kingdom, and since it had never been in Israelite hands, was not identified with any one tribe.

The Jebusite defenders adopted a curious strategem. They 'said to David, "you will not come in here, but the blind and the lame will ward you off."'

(2 Sam. 5:6) It has been suggested that the Jebusites were trying to shelter behind the curse that would fall upon those who dared to attack the afflicted. David's men shrank from doing so and he had to promise a reward to the first soldier who would attack in spite of the evil spell. The one who did so was the tough commander Joab himself, and the city fell.

The watchful Philistines reacted to the capture of Jerusalem by marching an army up from the coastal plain – probably through the vale of Sorek, along which the railway now runs. They reached the open ground to the south-west of Jerusalem known as the valley of Rephaim. Here David's troops repulsed them, burning the images they left behind. When they advanced a second time, the Israelites circled round to their rear and fell upon them when the breeze rustling in the treetops signalled the approach of night. The fleeing enemy was chased back to the lowlands.

With his military and political hold on Jerusalem consolidated, David decided to turn it also into the religious centre of the nation, by bringing to it the sacred Ark of the Covenant. Twenty years earlier, the Ark had been returned by the Philistines, and come to rest at Kiriathjearim, about eight miles west of Jerusalem. It was now placed on a cart drawn by two oxen, and set out to the sound of music played on harps, psalteries, timbrels, cornets and cymbals. Along the way a mishap occurred: the oxen jolted the cart, and one of the men walking beside it clutched at the Ark to steady it. He was struck dead by the Lord. The journey was suspended and the Ark was kept in a nearby house for three months. When David felt that the divine displeasure had passed, he brought the Ark to the great tent he had prepared for it in Jerusalem. He himself danced before it clad in a linen ephod, the short apron worn by priests. Michal, Saul's daughter, saw David through a window and berated him afterwards for what she regarded as unseemly conduct in public by her royal husband. David sarcastically flung these reproaches back at her. The quarrel seems to have ended their relationship, for Michal remained childless in David's prolific household.

In those days the number of women in the household was a mark of status for important men. In his outlaw years David had acquired two wives. As king in Hebron he added four more, and had six sons born to him. 'And David took more concubines and wives from Jerusalem, after he came from Hebron; and more sons and daughters were born to David.' (2 Sam. 5:13)

David proceeded to develop the new capital. The ridge on which it stood was enlarged by embankments of earth, and a palace was built with the help of David's ally, Hiram king of Tyre (present-day Lebanon), who sent him cedarwood from the Lebanese mountains, and skilled carpenters and masons.

With the kingdom united and the capital established, David started expanding the territory under Israelite control.

Saul had pushed the Philistines out of the Judean hills after the battle of Michmash. David reduced them even further, occupying Gath and Lachish and penning them into a narrow coastal strip from Gaza through Ashkelon and Ashdod to Joppa (Jaffa).

The kingdoms of Edom and Moab to the south and east of the Dead Sea were subdued, and became tribute-paying vassals. The conquest of Edom gave David access to the Gulf of Akaba that leads into the Red Sea – a maritime route later developed by his son Solomon.

The only campaigns of David treated with some detail in the Bible are those against the Ammonites and their allies, the kings of Aram (Syria). Israel had a bridgehead across the Jordan river in the land of Gilead, which had been held since Joshua by the tribe of Gad and half the tribe of Manasseh. It was a well-watered region lying between the great plateau of Moab to the south and Hauran to the north. East of it was the level country occupied by the Ammonites, with their capital at Rabbah (or Rabbath-ammon, later to become the Greek city of Philadelphia, and today Amman, the capital of the Kingdom of Jordan).

The war on this eastern front was started by an act of provocation by a new Ammonite king, Hanun. David sent him a goodwill mission, but Hanun humiliated the Israelite ambassadors by returning them with half their beards shaved and the lower half of their garments cut off. David reacted by sending his seasoned troops under Joab to attack the Ammonites, who retreated behind the walls of their city.

The Aramean king Hadadezer then sent an army south, under his general Shobach, to the help of his Ammonite allies. David enlarged his regular forces by mobilizing the reserve militia and crossed the Jordan. The crucial battle took place at Helam (probably in the Vale of Succoth) where the Arameans were heavily defeated and Shobach was slain. Their rulers hastened to make peace with Israel, and to bring themselves under David's suzerainty. One consequence was that the Arameans 'feared to help the Ammonites any more' (2 Sam. 10:19). The following year, Joab invaded Ammon and besieged the capital Rabbah, which had a natural defensive position and was strongly fortified.

DAVID AND BATHSHEBA

During this siege, David had stayed behind in Jerusalem. One warm moonlit evening the sleepless king strolled on the roof of the palace and looked down to see a young woman bathing herself on a lower roof. Smitten by her beauty, David made enquiries and learnt that her name was Bathsheba, that she was the granddaughter of one of David's leading counsellors Ahithophel, and that

she was married to Uriah, a Hittite officer on active service with Joab. David discreetly sent for her and made love to her. When Bathsheba let him know that she had become pregnant, David ordered that Uriah report back to him. After talking to him, David told him to go home, and sent round food from the royal kitchen. But Uriah did not rejoin his wife at all, spending that night and the next with the palace guards. Fearful of the scandal if the adultery became known, David sent him back to the front with a sealed letter to Joab, saying, 'Set Uriah in the forefront of the hardest fighting, and then draw back from him, that he may be struck down, and die' (2 Sam. 11:15). Joab accordingly arranged for him to lead a dangerous sortie against a well-defended section of the city wall. In this engagement Uriah was killed. After the regular period of mourning Bathsheba became David's wife and bore him a son.

The prophet Nathan appeared before David and recounted a parable concerning a wealthy man and a poor one who had only one ewe lamb kept as a household pet. When a guest arrived, the rich man killed this lamb, instead of an animal from his own large flock. David cried out that the man who could do such a thing merited death. Nathan pointed at him and declared sternly 'You are the man' (2 Sam. 12:7). He added that David's child by Bathsheba would forfeit its life to redress the wrong. The child fell ill and David fasted and prayed for days, lying prostrate on the ground. But when the baby died, David rose up, broke his fast and refrained from the usual mourning, saying to his surprised retainers, 'why should I fast? Can I bring him back again? I shall go to him, but he will not return to me' (2 Sam. 12:23). Another son was born to David and Bathsheba, and was called Solomon.

David moved up to Rabbah with fresh forces and took personal command of the final successful assault. Ammon became a vassal state, and its men were put to forced labour in stone-cutting and brick-making for David's building operations.

By now, David had carved out an empire stretching in the north beyond Damascus; in the east to the edge of the Arabian desert beyond Ammon and Moab; in the south to the Gulf of Akaba; and in the west to the Mediterranean. Some of the neighbouring rulers made treaties of friendship with him, like the king of Hamath on the Upper Euphrates; Hiram, king of Tyre, on the Phoenician coast (now Lebanon); and the king of Geshur, east of the Sea of Galilee (the Golan Heights).

Israel had become the dominant state in the area between the Nile and the Euphrates valleys. David's strategy had exploited the fact that Egypt's might had declined in the south and that of Assyria had not yet risen in the north.

David's campaigns called for an extensive army organization. The professional backbone was provided by the six hundred seasoned veterans who had been his guerrilla fighters in the early years. They were led by the two sons of David's sister Zeruiah: Joab the commander-in-chief and Abishai his deputy. Thirty of the senior officers formed a kind of army council. There were also foreign mercenaries, some of them Philistine, who had probably attached themselves to David when he was serving Achish the king of Gath.

Around this core of regulars David built up a civilian militia, its members normally being called up for a month each year. According to an unclear passage in Chronicles, 24,000 were called up each month in units supplied by the different tribes. In an emergency there might be a general mobilization of the reserves, as when David crossed the river into Gilead to halt the invading Syrian army under Shobach.

DAVID AND ABSALOM

As David reached the latter part of his forty-year reign, he could look with satisfaction on his achievements. The expanded kingdom was united and prosperous, and had gained peace through victory. But trouble was to descend upon him from within his own household.

The eldest of the princes, and the heir to the throne, was Amnon the son of Ahinoam. Then came Absalom the son of Maacah; and Adonijah, the son of Haggith. (The second son to be born was Chileab the son of Abigail, but he is not mentioned again and may have died as a child.)

Amnon fell in love with his half-sister Tamar, who was Absalom's sister. Pretending to be ill, he asked the king to send her to his quarters to bake some of his favourite cakes. When she refused to go to bed with him, he raped her and then had her thrown out. The dishonoured girl was taken into his home by Absalom, who swore revenge.

Two years later Absalom invited all the king's sons to a sheep-shearing feast at his farm in the hills of Ephraim. When Amnon was drunk, he was killed by the servants on Absalom's orders. The other princes rushed back to Jerusalem to tell David, while Absalom fled to his maternal grandfather, the king of Geshur. David left him banished there, but pined for the attractive son he loved so much.

After three years, the redoubtable Joab – who was David's nephew and Absalom's cousin – found a way to broach the delicate subject. He arranged for a woman from the village of Tekoa to gain an audience with the king. She pretended that she was a widow with two sons, one of whom had killed the other in a quarrel. Her kinsmen demanded that the surviving son should also be put to death. David ruled that the young man should be spared. But when the woman hinted at the parallel with his own son, David suspected that Joab had contrived the story. This Joab admitted, and was told he could fetch Absalom back to Jerusalem.

Yet David could not simply accept Absalom as if nothing had happened. The king refused to see his son, and for the next two years the prince remained in his own home, brooding over his rejection. Then, under pressure from Absalom, Joab gained him access to David, who kissed him in forgiveness.

Outwardly, father and son were now reconciled. But Absalom's resentment was already seeking the path of rebellion. His beauty and charm made him a popular figure, and he used every means to undermine David's authority and gain a following for himself. When he felt the time was ripe, Absalom raised the standard of revolt in Hebron, David's former capital, now neglected. Here he was joined by Ahithophel, David's ablest and most respected counsellor. Absalom had sent his agents to other parts of the country to prepare the ground. Now that he had come into the open, support for his cause was widespread. Absalom prepared to march on Jerusalem.

David's secure world had suddenly collapsed around him. It seems astonishing that he should have been caught so badly off his guard. But a long-established regime is always loath to believe that erosion has set in. Moreover, as a father, David could not imagine that his favourite son could plot his downfall. Now that he faced the truth, David took a prompt but painful decision – to abandon the capital to the rebels, and flee eastwards towards the Jordan river with his family and a band of his most trusted followers.

The wheel had come full circle. The illustrious monarch was once more a fugitive in the wilderness, as he had been so many years before in the time of Saul. David covered his face to hide his tears, as he led his group out of the city, across the Kidron valley and up the Mount of Olives, where he paused to pray for God's help in the dark days ahead.

His cool and resourceful mind was already at work. It was essential for him to plant a fifth column in the rebel camp. The two high priests Abiathar and Zadok had left Jerusalem with him, taking along the sacred Ark of the Covenant. He persuaded them to turn back, and to keep him informed of events, using their sons as messengers. He requested his counsellor Hushai to join Absalom and gain his confidence, in order to counteract the influence of Ahithophel. He also told his Gittite troops to return, but their captain Ittai of Gath refused, and David did not insist.

During this flight, two small incidents depressed David's spirits even more. He was met by Ziba the steward of Mephibosheth, Jonathan's crippled son whom David had protected and reared. Ziba brought two asses laden with provisions, and hinted that his master had gone over to Absalom.

Further along there appeared on the ridge above the road an old Benjaminite called Shimei, a member of the house of Saul. He pelted the party with stones and furiously cursed David as 'a man of blood' (2 Sam. 16:8) whose downfall was deserved. David said resignedly to the angry Abishai, 'Let him alone, and let him curse; for the Lord has bidden him' (2 Sam. 16:11).

East of the Jordan, David made his way to Mahanaim in the land of Gilead. Here he was heartened to find the local population had stood by him. His party had arrived 'hungry and weary and thirsty in the wilderness' (2 Sam. 17:29). They were provided with ample supplies by local leaders, and also by the son of the king of Ammon, further to the east. Having secured a base of operations, David quickly organized an army, and divided it into three formations under the command of Joab, Abishai and Ittai the Gittite.

Absalom recruited large forces, crossed the river and took up battle positions among the wooded ridges of Ephraim. Here David's trained men fell upon them and routed the hastily assembled army with heavy slaughter. Absalom himself was killed by Joab. In this inglorious fashion ended Absalom's brief and tragic rebellion.

David had yielded to the entreaties of his followers that he should stay behind in the town and not risk his person in battle. To his captains he gave one final command, 'Deal gently for my sake with the young man Absalom.' (2 Sam. 18:5)

Runners reached David at the city gate with the tidings of the victory, and his first question was 'Is it well with the young man Absalom?' (2 Sam. 18:29) When told that his beloved and wayward son was slain, he cried out in grief, 'O my son Absalom, my son, my son Absalom! Would I had died instead of you, O Absalom, my son, my son!' (2 Sam. 18:33)

Instead of a victory celebration, David declared a day of mourning. This was more than the unrepentant Joab would tolerate. Bursting into the king's room, he roughly scolded him for caring more about his enemies than his friends, and demanded that he appear before his people if he wanted to keep their allegiance. David stifled his agony and let his political instincts take charge again.

His throne had barely survived insurrection and civil war. He was still beyond the Jordan, an aging king on the eastern perimeter of a confused and divided country. He had to move warily. His return was prepared by the two high priests in Jerusalem who had remained loyal to him. David moved down the river, was ferried across and reached Gilgal on the Jericho plain, where the leaders of Judah came to meet him.

There were others who came to Gilgal. Shimei, the old Benjaminite who had shouted imprecations at the fugitive king, now came to crave pardon. David spared his life, but did not forget. Jonathan's lame son, Mephibosheth, arrived to explain that he had intended to flee with David, but had been deceived by his steward Ziba. The eighty-year-old Gileadite notable Barzillai, who had helped David, accompanied him across the river but declined the king's invitation to settle in Jerusalem, saying he preferred to die in his home town.

The other tribes were indignant that Judah had restored the king without consulting them. Their resentment was whipped up by Sheba, a Benjaminite, who cried, 'We have no portion in David' (2 Sam. 20:1) and led a protest march out of the capital. The kingdom was again on the verge of a split. David sent troops after Sheba. Angry with Joab, he had appointed as his army commander another nephew, Amasa, who had led Absalom's forces. On the road northward in pursuit of the rebels, Amasa was intercepted and murdered by Joab, who took charge of the operation and brought back Sheba's severed head to David. After this abortive revolt, the rule of King David was firmly restored over the whole land.

THE AGING KING

Little is recorded of the remaining years of David's reign.

There was a famine that lasted for three years. It was regarded as a belated punishment for Saul's slaying of a number of the inhabitants of Gibeon, an Amorite hilltown five miles north-west of Jerusalem (today the Arab village of el-Jib). The Gibeonites demanded as an act of atonement that David hand over to them seven of Saul's children and grandchildren. David felt obliged to yield up to them two sons Saul had had by Rizpah, one of his concubines, and five grandsons, the children of Saul's eldest daughter Merab. The Gibeonites hanged all seven, and after this cruel balancing of accounts the famine ended. David made peace with his troubled conscience by bringing back the bones of Saul and Jonathan from Jabesh-gilead, and having them reinterred, together with the bodies of the hanged seven, in the family tomb of Saul's father Kish.

It was during this period too that David decided to take a complete census of all the 'valiant men who drew the sword' (2 Sam. 24:9) throughout the kingdom. The tally was five hundred thousand men for Judah and eight hundred thousand for the rest of the tribes. But head-counting was considered unholy (a superstition shared by most primitive communities). The Lord's punishment was a pestilence that killed seventy thousand people. On the advice of the prophet Gad, David bought the threshing floor of Araunah the Jebusite for fifty silver shekels, built an altar on it and offered up sacrifices. The Lord repented, and the pestilence stopped before it reached Jerusalem. The threshing floor later became the site of Solomon's Temple.

The chronic border warfare with the Philistines flared up again. David was not loath to escape from the burdens of office in the capital, and once more share with his men the hardship and danger of campaigning in the field. But during the engagement 'David grew weary' (2 Sam. 21:15) and when a huge Philistine tried to kill him, he was saved by that tough professional soldier, his nephew Abishai. This narrow escape ended the career of David the warrior, for his men said to him tactfully, 'You shall no more go out with us to battle, lest you quench the lamp of Israel.' (2 Sam. 21:17)

David's vigour became dimmed by age. However many clothes were wrapped around him, he shivered with cold. His servants produced a beautiful maiden, Abishag the Shunammite, and said to David 'Let her lie in your bosom, that my Lord the king may be warm.' (1 Kgs. 1:2) A touching friendship grew up between the aging ruler and the young woman who 'became the king's nurse and ministered to him' (1 Kgs. 1:4).

David withdrew more and more from the active conduct of affairs of state. As old men are wont to do, he spent much time reflecting on his long and eventful life. The pastoral scenes of his childhood blended with the faith in God that had sustained him, and he declared that, 'When one rules justly over men, ruling in the fear of God, he dawns on them like the morning light, like the sun shining forth upon a cloudless morning, like rain that makes grass to sprout from the earth.'

THE SUCCESSION OF SOLOMON

When the king grew old, weary and secluded, the question of the succession to the throne became a pressing one. With Amnon and Absalom both dead, the handsome Adonijah was the next in line, and was regarded as the likely heir to the throne – 'all Israel fully expected me to reign' (1 Kgs. 2:15). Adonijah decided to assert his claim without waiting for the king's death. He was encouraged by Joab the commander-in-chief, and Abiathar the high priest, two of the leading men in the kingdom. They had been with David through thick and thin, from his early outlaw days. Now they wanted to ensure a smooth transition of power, and forestall the claims of Bathsheba for her son Solomon, a much younger prince.

Assured of such powerful support, Adonijah went ahead. He invited his princely brothers and the city notables to a feast at the spring of En-rogel, down in the valley of Kidron outside the city walls. Here he performed ceremonial sacrifices on the sacred Serpent's Stone. Solomon was not invited to take part – nor were Nathan the prophet, Zadok the other high priest, and Benaiah, the captain of the royal guard – all of whom were thought to be associated with Bathsheba's designs. This opposition party reacted swiftly. Bathsheba still retained a strong hold on David, and free access to him. Prompted by Nathan, she entered the king's chamber and told him Adonijah was at that moment usurping the throne he had promised her would go to her son Solomon; David should announce his own successor. Nathan appeared and supported Bathsheba.

David decided the time had come for him to abdicate in favour of the sagacious young Solomon. He instructed Zadok, Nathan and Benaiah to take the youth on the king's own mule down to the spring of Gihon, also in the valley of Kidron, have him anointed, 'then blow the trumpet, and say, "Long live King Solomon!"' (1 Kgs. 1:34) They did so, accompanied by a host of people. When the noise of the crowd rejoicing at the coronation reached Adonijah's company further along the valley, and they learnt that Solomon had already replaced David as king, the guests hurriedly returned to their homes. Adonijah sought sanctuary at the altar, and was spared by Solomon for the time being. The struggle for the succession was over the same day it had begun.

On his deathbed, David imparted his last wishes to Solomon: 'I am about to go the way of all the earth. Be strong, and show yourself a man' (1 Kgs. 2:2); Solomon should follow the Lord's commandments and walk before him in truth, as David had done. He asked Solomon to show special kindness to the children of Barzillai the Gileadite, and to settle accounts with Joab and Shimei.

'Then David slept with his fathers, and was buried in the city of David.' (1 Kgs. 2:10) After a reign of forty years there had passed away 'the oracle of the man who was raised on high, the anointed of the God of Jacob, the sweet psalmist of Israel' (2 Sam. 23:1).

David is the human character most fully and vividly presented in the Old Testament. His Hebrew biographers portrayed their hero complete with all his contradictions. The tough fighter, the shrewd statesman, and the fond husband and father; the unworthy actions prompted by passion or expediency; the sensitive love of beauty, poetry and music; courage and calculation; faith and humbleness of spirit before God – all fuse together in a brilliant and complex man. His faults and errors only serve to throw David's genius into relief.

In David's reign the Hebrew nation reached the peak of its political and military strength. The united kingdom Saul put together from the Israelite tribes was expanded by David into an empire extending from the sea to the desert. After Solomon's death it was to split again into the two small rival kingdoms of Israel and Judah.

[The Story of David is told in 1 Sam. 16–31; the Second Book of Sam.; 1 Kgs. 1, 2]

THE PSALMS OF DAVID

The Book of Psalms, traditionally attributed to David, is an anthology of Hebrew sacred songs and poems. It is placed in the third section of the Old Testament, the Writings ('Ketuvim'). The word 'psalms' is of Greek origin, and denotes the sound of a string instrument. The Hebrew name is 'tehillim' – praises. The themes of the psalms concern not only praise to the Lord, but also personal joy and sorrow, national redemption, festivals and historical events. Their religious fervour and literary power have given the psalms a profound influence down the ages, also in the Christian world.

There has been much dispute among scholars about the age and authorship of these poems, and about their connection with King David. They were probably composed during a thousand years or more of the biblical period. Of the 150 psalms, 73 were marked in the title 'of David' and many are in the first person. Some of these, or parts of them, appear to be of later date than David's reign. However, comparison with other Near Eastern religious poetry of about the same era suggests that some of the poems attributed to David date from his time. Whatever the experts might say, it is natural that popular belief should attribute the whole work to Israel's greatest king, a poet and musician who felt himself to be in close communion with God.

Reliance on the Lord's help for deliverance from enemies, sadness that life is so fleeting, the longing for peace, the concern with the future of the people of Israel, the mystic bond with Jerusalem – all these could be an authentic expression of David's own experiences and feelings. [Book of Psalms]

Debir (Heb. 'oracle') 13 century BC. King of Eglon, he was one of the five Amorite kings who attacked the Gibeonites after they made a pact with Israel. They were defeated by Joshua and hanged on five trees. [Josh. 10:3–26]

Deborah (Heb. 'bee') *1. c.* 17 century BC. Rebekah's nurse, she went with her mistress from Mesopotamia to Canaan where Rebekah married Isaac. Deborah stayed with Rebekah in Canaan and died in Bethel near Jerusalem where she was buried under an oak tree. [Gen. 24:59; 35:8]
2. c. 12 century BC. A judge and prophetess. In the Old Testament there is only one woman whose force of character and sagacity made her a leader in her own right. That was Deborah, who in the 12th century BC led a successful Israelite revolt against Canaanite domination in the northern part of the country.

The story of Deborah's triumph is told in two parallel accounts, one in prose and the other in the form of a stirring ballad or song attributed to Deborah herself. The two are not the same in all details.

Deborah was the wife of one Lappidoth, about whom nothing else is recorded. She was a 'judge', a person whose moral authority was regarded as inspired by the Lord, and was therefore accepted in the settlement of disputes. When the story opens, she is described as habitually seated under a tree between Bethel and Ramah north of Jerusalem where 'the people of Israel came up to her for judgment' (Judg. 4:5).

At that time the Israelites had for twenty years been oppressed in the north by Jabin the Canaanite, king of Hazor, because they 'did what was evil in the sight of the Lord' (Judg. 4:1). The Israelites had been unable to break the Canaanite hold on the fertile Jezreel valley, also known as the Plain of Esdraelon (today it is commonly called the 'Emek' – the 'Valley'). It stretches from west to east across the country, from behind the Carmel range down to the Sea of Galilee and the Jordan river fords.

Commanded by God, Deborah sent for Barak the son of Abinoam, from the tribe of Naphtali in the Galilee highlands. She instructed him to muster the men of Naphtali and Zebulun on the wooded slopes of Mount Tabor, a prominent hump at the north-east corner of the Jezreel valley. The prose account refers only to these two tribes as involved in the battle. However, Deborah's song indicates that she sent out a general call for help, and that contingents were also sent from her own tribe of Issachar, from Ephraim and Benjamin in the central hill country, and from the sub-tribe of Manasseh east of the Jordan. She poured anger on other tribes that failed to respond to her call: Gad, that stayed in Gilead beyond the Jordan; Dan, that remained working in the ships of strangers; Asher, that hung back on the sea coast; and Reuben, on the Moabite plateau of Transjordan, to whom Deborah cried, 'Why did you tarry among the sheepfolds, to hear the piping for the flocks?' (Judg. 5:16)

When summoned by Deborah to take command, Barak answered flatly: 'If you will go with me, I will go; but if you will not go with me, I will not go.' (Judg. 4:8) Deborah agreed to accompany the army.

Barak gathered his force of ten thousand men at Kedesh, his home town, probably on the plateau at the eastern end of the Jezreel valley, overlooking the Sea of Galilee. From here they moved south-west and took up positions on Mount Tabor.

Sisera assembled an army that included nine hundred chariots, and established a base at Harosheth-ha-goiim ('of the Gentiles') (Judg. 4:13), near the defile at the western end of the valley through which the Kishon river flows into Haifa Bay. From here they advanced in battle array along the open plain past the Canaanite strongholds of Megiddo and Taanach.

Sisera no doubt assumed that at this display of martial force, the rebellious Israelite tribesmen would melt back into their hills. But he failed to take into account that the Lord and the weather were on the side of his foes. A violent rainstorm came down suddenly, flooding the Kishon and turning the floor of the valley into mud, which was churned up still further by the prancing horses. With the chariots bogged down and helpless, the Israelite highlanders rushed down on them in a wild charge. Caught completely off-balance, the Canaanite forces were routed and wiped out. Sisera fled and was killed in the tent by Jael a Kenite woman.

Deborah cried in her song of
        triumph:
'From heaven fought the stars,
    from their courses they fought
        against Sisera.
The torrent Kishon swept them away,
    the onrushing torrent, the torrent
        Kishon.
March on, my soul, with might!'
        (Judg. 5:20, 21)

As a result of this victory, the power of King Jabin over the Israelites in the north was broken: 'And the land had rest for forty years.' (Judg. 5:31) [Judg. 4, 5]

Dedan (Heb. 'low') *1.* date unknown. Son of Raamah and a descendant of Ham. [Gen. 10:7; 1 Chr. 1:9]
2. c. 17 century BC. Son of Jokshan and a grandson of Abraham. [Gen. 25:3; 1 Chr. 1:32]

Delaiah (Heb. 'freed by God') *1.* date unknown. One of the seven sons of Elioenai, and a descendant of King David. Also called Dalaiah. [1 Chr. 3:24]
2. 10 century BC. Head of the twenty-third priestly course in the reign of King David. [1 Chr. 24:18]
3. date unknown. Ancestor of a family that returned to Judah from captivity in Babylon with Zerubbabel. Their genealogy was lost and this was regarded as a tragedy. [Ezra 2:60; Neh. 7:62]
4. c. 6 century BC. Son of Shemaiah, he was one of the five leaders to whom Michaiah read the prophecy of Jeremiah against the kingdom of Judah, and who counselled Jeremiah and Baruch to hide themselves from King Jehoiakim. [Jer. 36:12–20, 25]
5. 5 century BC. Son of Mehetabel, he was the father of Shemaiah who was a false prophet in the days of Nehemiah. [Neh. 6:10]

Delilah *c.* 12 century BC. The Philistine woman who betrayed Samson. Delilah was the daughter of a Philistine family in the valley of Sorek, near the village of Mahaneh-dan where Samson lived. When the five Philistine leaders heard that Samson was courting Delilah, they secretly visited her, and promised her eleven hundred pieces of silver from each of them, if she would pry from Samson the secret of his strength.

Three attempts to capture Samson were unsuccessful, as he had teased her by pretending he could be bound by fresh bowstrings, by new ropes or by weaving his hair into a spinning-wheel.

Delilah continued to nag him until 'his soul was vexed to death' (Judg. 16:16) and he told her the truth: because he had been a Nazarene dedicated to holiness from birth, his hair had never been cut, and therein lay his strength.

As soon as Samson fell asleep with his head in her lap, his seven locks were shaved off by a man Delilah had waiting. She woke Samson by crying out that the Philistines were upon him. He sprang up, and not knowing that his strength had gone, turned upon the men she had hidden in the room. This time they overpowered him easily, put out his eyes and brought him in triumph to Gaza.

Samson's betrayal by Delilah has become one of the most familiar tales in the Bible. [Judg. 16]

Deuel (Heb. 'knowledge of God') c. 13 century BC. A leader of the tribe of Gad, his son Eliasaph was appointed by Moses as one of the Gadite commanders of the army of the children of Israel. Also called Renel. [Num. 1:14; 2:14; 7:42, 47; 10:20]

Diblaim (Heb. 'two cakes') 8 century BC. The father of Gomer, the woman who married the prophet Hosea and who symbolized the faithless wife Israel had been to God. [Hos. 1:3]

Dibri (Heb. 'orator') date unknown. A man of the tribe of Dan whose daughter Shelomith married an Egyptian. The son of this marriage cursed God during a quarrel while the children of Israel were in the wilderness, and was put to death. [Lev. 24:11]

Diklah (Heb. 'palm') date unknown. Son of Joktan and a descendant of Noah. [Gen. 10:27; 1 Chr. 1:21]

Dinah (Heb. 'judged') c. 16 century BC.

The daughter of the patriarch Jacob and his wife Leah. While Jacob and his family were living near the town of Shechem (present-day Nablus) on a piece of land bought from Hamor, Shechem, the son of Hamor, fell in love with her and seduced her. Hamor sought permission from Jacob for his son to marry Dinah and further proposed that his clan and Jacob's should intermarry and merge with each other. Concealing their rage at Dinah's seduction, her brothers pretended to agree to Hamor's proposal, if 'you will become as we are and every male of you be circumcised' (Gen. 34:15). This was done, but before the men recovered from the painful operation, Jacob's sons Simeon and Levi killed all the males. 'They slew Hamor and his son Shechem with the sword, and took Dinah out of Shechem's house.' (Gen. 34:26) When Jacob reproached them for this vindictive act they answered him, 'Should he treat our sister as a harlot?' (Gen. 34:31) [Gen. 30:21; 34; 46:15]

Diphath see RIPHATH

Dishan (Heb. 'antelope') *1.* date unknown. Son of Seir the Horite, and an Edomite chieftain. [Gen. 36:21, 28, 30; 1 Chr. 1:42]

Dishon (Heb. 'antelope') *1.* date unknown. Son of Seir the Horite, and an Edomite chieftain. [Gen. 36:21; 1 Chr. 1:38]
2. date unknown. Son of Anah, a descendant of Seir the Horite. [Gen. 36:25; 1 Chr. 1:41]

Dodai (Heb. 'loving') 10 century BC. An Ahohite, who commanded one of King David's twelve armies, used for active service in the second month of each year. [1 Chr. 27:4]

Dodanim (Heb. 'leaders') date unknown. Son of Javan and a great-grand-son of Noah, he settled along the coast of Canaan. [Gen. 10:4; 1 Chr. 1:7]

Dodavah *see* DODAVAHU

Dodavahu *c.* 9 century BC. Father of the prophet Eliezer of Mareshah who criticized King Jehoshaphat of Judah. Also called Dodavah. [2 Chr. 20:37]

Dodo (Heb. 'loving') *1. c.* 12 century BC. Father of Puah of the tribe of Issachar, his grandson Tola judged Israel for twenty-three years. [Judg. 10:1]
2. 10 century BC. Father of Eleazar who was one of King David's three chief officers. [2 Sam. 23:9; 1 Chr. 11:12]
3. 10 century BC. Father of Elhanan of Bethlehem who was one of King David's

chosen guard of thirty soldiers. [2 Sam. 23:24; 1 Chr. 11:26]

Doeg (Heb. 'fearful') *c.* 10 century BC. The Edomite who was chief herdsman to King Saul. Doeg reported to the king seeing David, who had fled from the court, being helped at the priestly sanctuary of Nob. The furious Saul ordered the priests to be killed. Since his own servants shrank from doing so, he turned to Doeg, who slew eighty-five of them. [1 Sam. 21:7; 22]

Dumah (Heb. 'silence') *c.* 17 century BC. Son of Ishmael, grandson of Abraham, and founder of a desert tribe. [Gen. 25:13, 14; 1 Chr. 1:30]

E

Ebal (Heb. 'stone') *1.* date unknown. Son of Shobal and a grandson of Seir the Horite, he was an Edomite leader. [Gen. 36:23; 1 Chr. 1:40]
2. date unknown. Son of Joktan and descendant of Shem. Also called Obal. [Gen. 10:28; 1 Chr. 1:22]

Ebed (Heb. 'servant') *1.* c. 12 century BC. Father of Gaal of the tribe of Ephraim who led an unsuccessful revolt among the people of Shechem against Abimelech, king of Shechem. [Judg. 9:26, 28, 30, 31, 35]
2. c. 5 century BC. Son of Jonathan, he was a leader of Judah who returned from exile in Babylon. [Ezra 8:6]

Ebed-Melech (Heb. 'king's servant') 6 century BC. The Ethiopian servant of King Zedekiah of Judah who obtained the king's permission to release the prophet Jeremiah from the pit into which he had been thrown for preaching surrender to the invading Babylonians. In return Jeremiah promised Ebed-melech that he would not be killed when the Babylonians conquered Jerusalem. [Jer. 38:7–12; 39:16]

Eber (Heb. 'beyond') *1.* date unknown. Descendant of Shem and of Noah. [Gen. 10:21, 24, 25; 1 Chr. 1:18, 19, 25]
2. c. 8 century BC. A leader of the tribe of Gad in Bashan, east of the river Jordan, in the time of King Jeroboam of Israel. [1 Chr. 5:13]
3. date unknown. A son of Elpaal and a leader of the tribe of Benjamin. [1 Chr. 8:12]
4. date unknown. Son of Shashak and a leader of the tribe of Benjamin living in Jerusalem. [1 Chr. 8:22]
5. 5 century BC. One of the chief priests of Judah when Joiakim was high priest in the time of Nehemiah. [Neh. 12:20]

Ebiasaph (Heb. 'God has added') *1.* see ABIASAPH *2.* date unknown. The son of Elkanah, a Levite descended from Kohath, and the father of Assir. [1 Chr. 6:23]

Ecclesiastes (Gk. 'the preacher') c. 3 century BC. The Greek form of the Hebrew word *Kohelet* – the unknown author of the biblical book known as 'Ecclesiastes'.
(See the note on 'Solomon and the Wisdom Books' at the end of the entry on SOLOMON.)

Eden (Heb. 'pleasure') 8 century BC. Son of Joah, he was one of the Levites who obeyed King Hezekiah's command to sanctify himself and cleanse the Temple, and later he helped distribute the free-will offerings among the priests of Judah. [2 Chr. 29:12; 31:15]

Eder (Heb. 'flock') *1.* date unknown. Son of Beriah and a leader of the tribe of Benjamin. [1 Chr. 8:15]
2. c. 10 century BC. A Levite descended from Mushi who ministered in the Tabernacle in the reign of King David. [1 Chr. 23:23; 24:30]

Edom see ESAU

Eglah (Heb. 'heifer') c. 10 century BC. One of King David's wives, she bore him Ithream, David's sixth son. [2 Sam. 3:5; 1 Chr. 3:3]

Eglon (Heb. 'calf-like') *c.* 12 century BC. King of Moab, the territory east of the Dead Sea, in the time of Ehud. With the backing of the Ammonites and the Amalekites (a nomad desert tribe) Eglon pushed westward, occupied the Jericho area, and for eighteen years exacted tribute from the Israelites on the Judean highland.

He was killed at his house in Jericho by Ehud, of the tribe of Benjamin, who plunged a dagger into the belly of the fat king and escaped through the window. Finding the doors shut the servants were afraid to disturb the king and it was some time before 'they took the key and opened them; and there lay their lord dead on the floor' (Judg. 3:25). [Judg. 3]

Egypt date unknown. One of the four sons of Ham and a grandson of Noah, he was regarded as the legendary ancestor of the Egyptians. [Gen. 10:6, 13; 1 Chr. 1:8, 11]

Ehi *c.* 16 century BC. A son of Benjamin, he went down to Egypt at the same time as his grandfather Jacob. He is mentioned only in Genesis but he may be identical with Benjamin's son Ahiram recorded in Numbers, and Aharah in the First Book of Chronicles. [Gen. 46:21; Num. 26:38; 1 Chr. 8:1]

Ehud (Heb. 'God of praise') *1.* date unknown. One of the seven sons of Bilhan and a chief of the tribe of Benjamin. [1 Chr. 7:10; 8:6]
2. c. 12 century BC. A Benjaminite leader and judge. Ehud the son of Gera, of the small tribe of Benjamin, was one of the judges of Israel in the period after Joshua.

The territory of Benjamin extended from the central hill region down into the Jordan valley, round Jericho. Eglon

king of Moab pushed westward across the Jordan, occupied the Jericho area, and exacted tribute from the Israelites on the Judean highlands. This domination was maintained for eighteen years, and was said to be a punishment by the Lord for the lapse of the Israelites into pagan ways.

Ehud was chosen by God to deliver his people. He fashioned a short two-edged dagger and strapped it to his right thigh, where it would be concealed by his robe. (As was common among the Benjaminites, he was left-handed.) He then set out to deliver gifts to Eglon at Jericho, where the obese king was taking his ease. The tribute was presented and Ehud withdrew with his bearers. When they got to the stone quarries at Gilgal, he turned round and went back alone. Finding the king in his upper chamber where it was cool, he said he had an important secret message to deliver. Eglon dismissed the attendants who were present. When they were alone, Ehud said that his message was from God. The king rose to his feet, at which Ehud whipped out the dagger and stabbed Eglon in the belly. Even the hilt sank into the layers of fat. Ehud locked the door from the inside and escaped through the window. Seeing the door shut, the servants thought the king was attending to his needs and were afraid to disturb him. After a while they became worried, opened the door with the key and found their royal master dead upon the floor.

Safely back in the hills, Ehud blew a horn to muster the Israelite fighting men and led them down into the Jordan valley. They seized the fords across the river to cut off the retreat of the Moabites, who were attacked and slain to the last man. 'So Moab was subdued that day under the hand of Israel. And the land had rest for eighty years.' (Judg. 3:30) [Judg. 3]

Eker (Heb. 'offspring') date unknown.

Son of Ram, leader of the tribe of Judah and the grandson of Jerahmeel. [1 Chr. 2:27]

Ela (Heb. 'oak') *c.* 10 century BC. Father of Shimei, one of King Solomon's twelve officers responsible for the king's supplies for one month in the year. [1 Kgs. 4:18]

Elah (Hen. 'oak') *1.* date unknown. One of the Edomite leaders descended from Esau. [Gen. 36:41; 1 Chr. 1:52]
2. c. 13 century BC. Son of Caleb the son of Jephunneh. [1 Chr. 4:15]
3. Fourth king of Israel after the monarchy split, he reigned 886-5 BC. Elah succeeded his father Baasha as king of Israel. His reign was brief and inglorious, for within two years he was murdered while getting drunk in his steward's house. The culprit was one of his army officers, Zimri, who seized the throne. The usurper wiped out all Elah's kin, as had been foretold to Elah's father Baasha by Jehu the prophet. [1 Kgs. 16:1-14]
4. 8 century BC. Father of Hoshea, the last monarch of the northern kingdom of Israel. [2 Kgs. 15:30; 17:1; 18:1, 9]
5. 6 century BC. Son of Uzzi, he was one of the first Benjaminites to settle in Jerusalem following the return from exile in Babylon. [1 Chr. 9:8]

Elam (Ass. 'highland') *1.* date unknown. Eldest of Shem's five sons and a grandson of Noah. [Gen. 10:22; 14:1; 1 Chr. 1:17]
2. date unknown. A head of the tribe of Benjamin. [1 Chr. 8:24]
3. 10 century BC. Fifth son of Meshelemiah, gatekeeper of King David's Tabernacle. [1 Chr. 26:3]
4. date unknown. Ancestor of a large family that returned with Zerubbabel from exile in Babylon. [Ezra 2:7; 8:7; 10:26; Neh. 7:12]
5. date unknown. Ancestor of a large family that returned with Zerubbabel

from exile in Babylon. [Ezra 2:31; Neh. 7:34]
6. 5 century BC. A leader of Judah who signed the solemn covenant in the days of Nehemiah. [Neh. 10:14]
7. 5 century BC. One of the priests who took part in the ceremony of dedication of the rebuilt walls of Jerusalem in the time of Nehemiah. [Neh. 12:42]

Elasah (Heb. 'whom God made') *1. c.* 6 century BC. Son of Shaphan, he was sent by Jeremiah with a letter to the exiles in Babylon prophesying that they would eventually return to Judah but should meanwhile lead a full life in Babylon. [Jer. 29:3]
2. 5 century BC. A priest who divorced his non-Jewish wife in the time of Ezra. [Ezra 10:22]

El-berith see BAAL-BERITH

Eldaah (Heb. 'called of God') *c.* 16 century BC. Son of Midian and a grandson of Abraham and Keturah, he became leader of a tribe in the eastern desert. [Gen. 25:4; 1 Chr. 1:33]

Eldad (Heb. 'loved by God') 13 century BC. One of the two elders of the children of Israel about whose prophecies Joshua complained to Moses. [Num. 11:26-29]

Elead (Heb. 'God has adorned') date unknown. One of the two sons of Ephraim who were killed by the men of Gath while trying to steal their cattle. [1 Chr. 7:21]

Eleadah (Heb. 'God has adorned') *c.* 15 century BC. A leader of the tribe of Ephraim, he was the son of Tahath. [1 Chr. 7:20]

Eleasah (Heb. 'made by God') *1.* date unknown. Son of Helez and a leader of the tribe of Judah. [1 Chr. 2:39. 40]
2. c. 9 century BC. A leader of the tribe of Benjamin and a descendant of King Saul. [1 Chr. 8:37;9:43]

Eleazar (Heb. 'God has helped') *1. c.* 13 century BC. Eleazar was one of the priestly sons of Aaron and Elisheba, and became high priest when Aaron died on Mount Hor and Moses placed his robes on Eleazar.

He took part in Moses's census in Moab and later helped Joshua in dividing the land of Israel among the tribes of Israel. He married one of the daughters of Putiel and they had a son, Phinehas, who became high priest in the time of Joshua. Eleazar was regarded as the ancestor of most high priests and after the return from Babylon, the Zadokite priests traced their descent to him. [Exod. 6:23, 25; 28:1; Lev. 10; Num. 3:1–4, 32; 4:16; 16:37–39; 19:3, 4; 20:25, 26; 25:7–11; 26; 27; 31; 32; 34; Deut. 10:6; Josh. 14:1; 17:4; 19:51; 21:1; 22:13–32; 24:3; Judg. 20:28; 1 Chr. 6:3, 4; 9:20; 24; Ezra 7:5]

2. c. 11 century BC. Son of Abinadab of Kiriath-jearim, he was appointed to look after the Ark of God before it was brought up to Jerusalem. [1 Sam. 7:1]

3. 10 century BC. Son of Dodo the Ahohite, he is singled out as one of three particularly heroic warriors in the army of King David. [2 Sam. 23:9; 1 Chr. 11:12]

4. c. 10 century BC. A Levite descended from Mahli, he had no sons and his daughters married their kinsmein, the sons of Kish. [1 Chr. 23:21, 22; 24:28]

5. 5 century BC. Son of Phinehas the priest, he returned with Ezra to Jerusalem and helped weigh the precious vessels brought back from exile in Babylon. [Ezra 8:33]

6. 5 century BC. Descendant of Parosh who divorced his non-Jewish wife in the time of Ezra. [Ezra 10:25]

7. 5 century BC. A priest who took part in the ceremony of dedication for the rebuilt walls of Jerusalem in the time of Nehemiah. [Neh. 12:42]

Elhanan (Heb. 'grace of God') *1. c.* 10 century BC. A warrior in King David's army who killed Lahmi the brother of the Philistine giant Goliath. [2 Sam. 21:19; 1 Chr. 20:5]

2. c. 10 century BC. Son of Dodo of Bethlehem and a mighty warrior in the armies of King David. [2 Sam. 23:24; 1 Chr. 11:26]

Eli (Heb. 'uplifted') *c.* 11 century BC. High priest at Shiloh. Eli was a descendant of Aaron's son Ithamar and was high priest at the sanctuary of Shiloh in the period of the judges. One day he saw a woman near the altar. Her lips moved but she did not utter a sound. Thinking she was drunk, Eli advised her to 'Put away your wine from you' (1 Sam. 1:14). She explained that she was Hannah, wife of Elkanah, and had come to pray to the Lord because she was barren. Eli said to her, 'Go in peace, and the God of Israel grant your petition which you have made to him.' (1 Sam. 1:17) Soon after she bore a son, Samuel. In gratitude to the Lord she apprenticed him to the priests, 'And the boy ministered to the Lord, in the presence of Eli the priest.' (1 Sam. 2:11)

Late one night Samuel thought he heard Eli calling him. But it was the voice of the Lord who told Samuel that Eli and his household would suffer for the corruption and misdeeds of his two sons, the priests Hophni and Phinehas.

In a battle with the Philistines at Aphek at the edge of the hill country, the Israelites were defeated. The sacred Ark of the Covenant brought by Eli's sons from Shiloh was captured, and they were among the slain. The old priest, now ninety-eight years of age and almost blind, sat in the gateway to hear the story from a runner who had arrived with his clothes torn in mourning. The shock of losing both sons and the Ark was too much for him, and 'Eli fell over backward from his seat by the side of the gate; and his neck was broken and he died' (1 Sam. 4:18). [1 Sam. 1–4; 14:3; 1 Kgs. 2:27]

Eliab (Heb. 'God is father') *1. c.* 13 century BC. Son of Helon and leader of the tribe of Zebulun, he was appointed by Moses to conduct the census of men in his tribe fit for war. [Num. 1:9; 2:7; 7:24-29; 10:16]

2. 13 century BC. Father of Dathan and Abiram of the tribe of Reuben who joined Korah's revolt in the wilderness against the authority of Moses and Aaron. [1 Num. 16:1, 12; 26:8, 9; Deut. 11:6]

3. c. 12 century BC. Son of Nahath the Levite and an ancestor of the prophet Samuel. Also called Eliel and Elihu. [1 Sam. 1:1; 1 Chr. 6:27, 34]

4. c. 11 century BC. Eldest brother of David. Eliab was the eldest son of Jesse and the first to be presented to the prophet Samuel when he visited Bethlehem. Samuel was told by God not to be taken in by the young man's looks or his great height 'for the Lord sees not as man sees; man looks on the outward appearance, but the Lord looks on the heart' (1 Sam. 16:7). Samuel then anointed David, the youngest son, without explaining the reason.

Eliab and two of his brothers served in the army of Saul facing the Philistines in the Vale of Elah. Jesse sent David to take them provisions and to find out how they were faring.

On hearing his young brother talking about killing the Philistine champion Goliath, Eliab turned on him angrily: 'Why have you come down? And with whom have you left those few sheep in the wilderness? I know your presumption, and the evil of your heart.' (1 Sam. 17:28) David turned away from him and talked to other soldiers until Saul heard about the strange youth and sent for him.

Later Eliab's great-granddaughter Nahalath became the wife of Rehoboam, king of Judah. Also called Elihu. [1 Sam. 16:6; 17:28; 1 Chr. 2:13 27:18; 2 Chr. 11:18]

5. c. 11 century BC. A warrior of the tribe of Gad who deserted the army of King Saul and rallied to David's support. [1 Chr. 12:9]

6. c. 10 century BC. One of the Levites in the reign of King David who played musical instruments when the Ark of God was brought to Jerusalem. [1 Chr. 15:18; 16:5]

Eliada (Heb. 'God knows') *1. c.* 10 century BC. One of the sons of King David born to him in Jerusalem. Also called Beeliada. [2 Sam. 5:16; 1 Chr. 3:8; 14:7]

2. c. 10 century BC. Father of Rezon, who led bands of marauders against King Solomon. [1 Kgs. 11:23]

3. c. 9 century BC. A Benjaminite warrior who commanded an army in the forces of King Jehoshaphat of Judah. [2 Chr. 17:17]

Eliahba (Heb. 'hidden by God') *c.* 10 century BC. A soldier from Shaalbon and one of the bravest warriors in the army of King David. [2 Sam. 23:32; 1 Chr. 11:33]

Eliakim (Heb. 'may God raise') *1. c.* 8 century BC. Master of the palace under King Hezekiah of Judah. In 701 BC Sennacherib, king of Assyria invaded Judea and sent his representatives to demand the surrender of Jerusalem. A meeting took place outside the city with a delegation headed by Eliakim. No agreement was reached. The Assyrian envoy shouted out in Hebrew to influence the people on the ramparts. At one point Eliakim said, 'Pray, speak to your servants in the Aramaic language' (2 Kgs. 18:26). Hezekiah sent Eliakim with others to consult Isaiah, the prophet, whose counsel was to stand firm. The Assyrians in fact withdrew without laying siege to the city. In one of his visions, Isaiah calls Eliakim 'a father to the inhabitants of Jerusalem and to the house of Judah' (Isa. 22:21). [2 Kgs. 18:18, 26, 37; 19:2; Isa. 22:20; 36:11, 22; 37:2]

2. 5 century BC. A priest who took part in the service of dedicating the rebuilt walls of Jerusalem in the time of Nehemiah. [Neh. 12:41]

Eliakim *see* JEHOIAKIM

Eliam (Heb. 'God's people') *1. c.* 10 century BC. Father of King David's wife Bathsheba. Also called Ammiel. [2 Sam. 11:3; 1 Chr. 3:5]
2. *c.* 10 century BC. Son of Ahithophel of Gilo, he was a mighty warrior in the army of King David. [2 Sam. 23:34]

Eliasaph (Heb. 'God will increase') *1. c.* 13 century BC. A leader of the tribe of Gad, he was appointed by Moses to conduct the census of the men of Gad fit for war, and then led the contingent. [Num. 1:14; 2:14; 7:42–47; 10:20]
2. *c.* 13 century BC. Son of Lael the Levite, he was head of the family of Gershonites in the wilderness. [Num. 3:24]

Eliashib (Heb. 'restored of God') *1. c.* 10 century BC. A Levite who served in the Tabernacle in the reign of King David and was responsible for the eleventh turn of service. [1 Chr. 24:12]
2. date unknown. Son of Elioenai of the tribe of Judah and a descendant of King David. [1 Chr. 3:24]
3. 5 century BC. Father of Jehohanan in whose home Ezra fasted for the sins of the people of Judah. [Ezra 10:6]
4. 5 century BC. A Levite Temple singer who divorced his non-Jewish wife in the time of Ezra. [Ezra 10:24]
5. 5 century BC. Descendant of Zattu who divorced his non-Jewish wife in the time of Ezra. [Ezra 10:27]
6. 5 century BC. Descendant of Bani who divorced his non-Jewish wife in the time of Ezra. [Ezra 10:36]
7. 5 century BC. High priest of Judah in the days of Nehemiah, he helped rebuild the walls of Jerusalem. He was the father of Joiada. [Neh. 3:1, 20, 21; 12:10; 22; 13:28]

Eliathah (Heb. 'to whom God comes') *c.* 10 century BC. Son of Heman, he and his brothers played musical instruments in the Tabernacle under their father's direction during the reign of King David. [1 Chr. 25:4, 27]

Elidad (Heb. 'beloved of God') *c.* 13 century BC. Son of Chislon, he was made leader of the tribe of Benjamin by Moses and ordered to divide up the inheritance of his tribe after the conquest of the land of Israel. [Num. 34:21]

Eliehoenai (Heb. 'eyes lifted to God') *1. c.* 10 century BC. Son of Meshelemiah and a gatekeeper of the Tabernacle in the reign of King David. [1 Chr. 26:3]
2. 5 century BC. Son of Zerahiah, he returned with Ezra from exile in Babylon. [Ezra 8:4]

Eliel (Heb. 'God is my God') *1. see* ELIAB *3.*
2. date unknown. A leader of the tribe of Manasseh living east of the river Jordan. [1 Chr. 5:24]
3. date unknown. Son of Shimei and a leader of the tribe of Benjamin living in Jerusalem. [1 Chr. 8:20]
4. date unknown. Son of Shashak of the tribe of Benjamin and a leader of the tribe living in Jerusalem. [1 Chr. 8:22]
5. *c.* 11 century BC. One of the warriors of the tribe of Gad who deserted the army of King Saul and rallied to David at Ziklag. [1 Chr. 12:11]
6. 10 century BC. The Mahavite warrior in the army of King David distinguished for his bravery. [1 Chr. 11:46]
7. 10 century BC. Another warrior in the army of King David who was distinguished for his bravery. [1 Chr. 11:47]
8. 10 century BC. Head of a family of Levites descended from Hebron who were appointed by King David to help bring the Ark of God to Jerusalem from Kiriathjearim. [1 Chr. 15:9, 11]
9. *c.* 8 century BC. A Levite who helped supervise the bringing of tithes and

offerings into the Temple in the reign of King Hezekiah. [2 Chr. 31:13]

Elienai (Heb. 'God is my eyes') date unknown. Son of Shimei and a leader of the tribe of Benjamin living in Jerusalem. [1 Chr. 8:20]

Eliezer (Heb. 'help of God') *1. c.* 18 century BC. Steward of Abraham. [Gen. 15:2]
2. c. 16 century BC. Son of Becher and a grandson of Benjamin, he was a leader of his tribe. [1 Chr. 7:8]
3. c. 13 century BC. The younger son of Moses and Zipporah, and ancestor of Shelomoth who was in charge of the sacred gifts dedicated for the maintenance of the Tabernacle in King David's reign. [Exod. 18:4; 1 Chr. 23:15, 17; 26:25]
4. 10 century BC. A priest in the reign of King David who blew a trumpet during the celebrations when the Ark of God was brought up to Jerusalem. [1 Chr. 15:24]
5. 10 century BC. Son of Zichri, he was a leader of the tribe of Reuben in the reign of King David. [1 Chr. 27:16]
6. 9 century BC. Son of Dodavahu of Mareshah, he prophesied the doom of the ships sent by King Jehoshaphat of Judah to Tarshish in a joint venture with King Ahaziah of Israel. [2 Chr. 20:37]
7. 5 century BC. A leader sent by Ezra to Iddo in Casiphia asking him to send Levites to Jerusalem to minister in the Temple. [Ezra 8:16]
8. 5 century BC. Son of a priest, he divorced his non-Jewish wife in the time of Ezra. [Ezra 10:18]
9. 5 century BC. A Levite who divorced his non-Jewish wife in the time of Ezra. [Ezra 10:23]
10. 5 century BC. Descendant of Harim who divorced his non-Jewish wife in the time of Ezra. [Ezra 10:31]

Elihoreph (Heb. 'God his reward') 10 century BC. Son of Shisha, he was a secretary to King Solomon. [1 Kgs. 4:3]

Elihu (Heb. 'he is my God') *1.* period of the patriarchs. One of Job's friends. Elihu, the son of Barachel the Buzite, sat and listened while Job's three friends argued with him. When they fell silent he made three long speeches which covered much the same ground as the others. He too expressed the view that God did not punish good men, only bad ones. If only Job would repent of his sins, God would forgive him. Elihu suggested Job should say to the Lord, 'I have borne chastisement; I will not offend any more; teach me what I do not see; if I have done iniquity, I will do it no more.' (Job 34:31, 32) To the end Job maintained his innocence and demanded a fair trial with the charges against him presented in due form of law.
   Elihu is not mentioned in the epilogue or elsewhere in the text and scholars suggest that the Elihu chapters were not part of the original work, but were inserted at a later date by another author [Job 32–37]
2. see ELIAB *3.*
3. see ELIAB *4.*
4. c. 11 century BC. A captain of the tribe of Manasseh who deserted the army of King Saul and rallied to David's support. [1 Chr. 12:20]
5. 10 century BC. Descendant of Obededom, he was a doorkeeper at the gates of the Tabernacle in Jerusalem in the reign of King David. [1 Chr. 26:7]

Elijah (Heb. 'my Lord is Jehovah') *1. c.* 9 century BC. Hebrew prophet and reformer. Of all the prophets, priests and sages in the Old Testament, none has kept so vivid a hold on the popular mind as Elijah the Prophet – 'Eliyahu ha-Navi' in Hebrew. He is described as appearing mysteriously from an unknown background, fought as a soldier of the Lord against heathen gods, championed the downtrodden, performed his miracles, and vanished up to heaven in a blazing chariot.

The first mention of Elijah is about the year 864 BC, half-way through the reign of Ahab, son of Omri, in the northern kingdom of Israel. King Omri had fostered an alliance with the coastal state of Phoenicia, and these ties of friendship were cemented by Ahab's marriage to Jezebel, daughter of Ethbaal, king of Sidon. Omri had already come under criticism from the devout for his indulgence towards the alien gods and customs of the sophisticated Phoenicians. When Jezebel became queen, she was permitted to promote these trends so actively that the Bible condemns Ahab as the wickedest of the Hebrew kings.

Shrines were openly constructed to Melkart, the Baal (god) of the Phoenicians, and to their fertility goddess Asherah (Ashtaroth, or Astarte), with a pagan temple in the palace at the new hilltop capital of Samaria. Jezebel also maintained four hundred and fifty priests or 'false prophets' of Baal and four hundred prophets of Asherah as part of her household. The Israelite priests and prophets who protested at these pagan ways were suppressed or driven out. Ahab became lax in his own religious observance, and was dominated by his wife.

Suddenly there appeared before the king a wild figure, clad only in a leather loin-cloth and a cloak of hair. He was Elijah the Tishbite, an inhabitant of Gilead, the Israelite province east of the Jordan river. He cried out a dire prediction of drought: 'As the Lord the God of Israel lives, before whom I stand, there shall be neither dew nor rain these years ...' (1 Kgs. 17:1). Before the astonished king could have him arrested and punished, the prophet had gone.

Elijah escaped across the Jordan and hid himself in a desolate spot next to a stream called Cherith. Here he was brought food by the ravens and drank water from the brook until it dried up. By that time the land was gripped by the drought he had foretold as a punishment, and the spectre of famine loomed on the horizon.

At the behest of the Lord, Elijah sought refuge across the Phoenician border and reached the town of Zarephath, seven miles south of the great port-city of Sidon. Near the town gate he saw a poor widow gathering sticks for firewood. He asked her to bring him a drink of water and a piece of bread. She answered that all the food she had for her son and herself was a handful of meal in a jar and a little oil. The prophet told her not to be afraid, for her flour and oil would by a miracle feed all three of them until the drought ended. From then on Elijah lodged in the upstairs room of the widow's humble home.

One day the boy fell ill and died. The distraught mother blamed Elijah and cried out to him: 'You have come to me to bring my sin to remembrance, and to cause the death of my son!' (1 Kgs. 17:18) Without a word, Elijah took the child in his arms, carried him up the stairs and laid him down on his own bed. Three times he stretched out on the small, inert form, praying to God to restore it to life. The child revived.

CONFRONTATION ON MOUNT CARMEL
In the third year Elijah was told by the Lord that the drought was about to break, and he was instructed to present himself again to King Ahab. On his way to Samaria, Elijah met Obadiah the master of the royal household, who had been sent out to search for grazing in the parched countryside. According to Obadiah, the king had hunted everywhere for Elijah, and he was most reluctant to notify Ahab of the prophet's coming; but he eventually agreed.

On receiving the message, the king himself hurried out to meet Elijah and said to him, 'Is it you, you troubler of Israel?' (1 Kgs. 18:17) Elijah flung back that it was not he but Ahab and his household that troubled Israel, for they had forsaken the Lord and worshipped Baal.

The king acceded to Elijah's demand that an assembly of the people be arranged on top of Mount Carmel, in order to witness a trial of strength between the prophet and the priests of Baal who had been brought to Samaria by Jezebel. In the presence of the king, Elijah said to the crowd, 'How long will you go limping with two different opinions? If the Lord is God, follow him; but if Baal, then follow him.' (1 Kgs. 18:21) He then proposed that the prophets of Baal should cut up a bullock and lay the pieces on firewood. He would do likewise, and they would see which divinity would send down fire to consume the sacrifice.

From morning till noon the priests leapt around their altar and cried out to Baal, but there was no answer. Elijah taunted them: 'Cry aloud, for he is a god; either he is musing, or he has gone aside, or he is on a journey, or perhaps he is asleep and must be awakened.' (1 Kgs. 18:27) As the afternoon wore on, the priests became more frenzied, slashing themselves with knives and spears in accordance with their practice until the blood flowed from them. But there was 'no voice; no one answered, no one heeded' (1 Kgs. 18:20).

Towards evening Elijah stepped forward and had the crowd draw closer to him. Using twelve stones, one for each of the tribes of Israel, he rebuilt an old altar to the Lord that had fallen to pieces. He cut up his bullock, laid the pieces on the firewood and dug a trench round the altar. He then had some of the bystanders bring buckets of water which they poured over the altar, drenching the meat and wood and filling the trench. When all was ready, Elijah called, 'Answer me, O Lord, answer me, that this people may know that thou, O Lord, art God, and that thou hast turned their hearts back.' (1 Kgs. 18:37) At that cry, fire came down on to the altar, consumed the sacrifice and the wood, and even licked up the water in the trench. The crowd shouted: 'The Lord, he is God; the Lord, he is God' (1 Kgs. 18:39) and they fell on their faces in awe.

Elijah exploited the dramatic moment to have the priests of Baal seized and dragged down to the small Kishon river in the valley below, where they were all slain.

The prophet told Ahab he could now go home for the rain was approaching. Elijah himself climbed back to the top of the ridge and crouched down with his head between his knees. His servant was sent repeatedly to a point from which he could look out to sea. The seventh time, the servant reported, 'Behold, a little cloud like a man's hand is rising out of the sea.' (1 Kgs. 18:44) Soon the sky darkened and the rain came lashing down in torrents. The king set out in his chariot for his winter palace at Jezreel, at the eastern end of the valley. The exultant prophet bounded ahead of him with his cloak tucked up around his waist.

The confrontation on Mount Carmel ranks as the most dramatic moment in the centuries of struggle between Hebrew monotheism and the seductive pagan cults that constantly eroded it.

But Elijah's victory had put him in grave peril. When the formidable Jezebel heard from Ahab what had happened, she sent a message to the prophet that by the next day he too would be put to the sword, as her priests had been. Once more he fled for his life. This time he headed southwards to Beersheba, the ancient Negeb town in the neighbouring kingdom of Judah. Here he left his servant and headed, solitary and depressed, into the barren wilderness. After walking all day he sank down exhausted under a bush of the desert broom that grows in dry gullies. Giving way to despair, he begged God to let him die.

As had happened before, his bodily needs were miraculously met. While he slept, he dreamt that an angel tapped him on the shoulder, and when he woke he found bread and water to hand. This happened a second time. On the strength of the two scanty meals, Elijah started off on a remarkable forty-day trek across broken desert terrain until he reached Mount Horeb, also known as Mount Sinai, where Moses had first received the Law from the hand of God. Elijah had obviously felt the compulsion to renew his faith at its very source, through a personal revelation from the Lord.

Spending the night in a cave, he heard the voice of God asking what he was doing there. Sadly he replied that the Children of Israel had deserted the Lord, his prophets were being put to death, and only Elijah was left clinging to his faith. For that, they wanted to kill him.

Outside the cave, the landscape was convulsed by gale, earthquake and fire. While Elijah stood in the mouth of the cave with his robe covering his face, the presence of God came to him as a 'still small voice' (1 Kgs. 19:12). The Lord told him to retrace his steps to the wilderness of Damascus. Hazael would become king in Damascus and Jehu in Israel. Their peoples would destroy each other, except for seven thousand faithful Israelites, '... all the knees that have not bowed to Baal, and every mouth that has not kissed him' (1 Kgs. 19:18). Elisha would continue Elijah's life work.

Passing through the Jordan valley on his way back, Elijah came upon the young Elisha ploughing on his father's land. Elijah threw his cloak over the youth, who at once accepted the call to service, and remained his faithful disciple until the end of the great prophet's life on earth.

THE SCOURGE OF KINGS
Elijah was to have one final encounter with his old adversary, Ahab. The king had coveted a vineyard next to his winter palace in Jezreel, but the owner Naboth had refused to part with it. Jezebel had arranged for Naboth to be falsely convicted of blasphemy and stoned to death, whereby his property became vested in the king. When Ahab went to his newly-acquired vineyard, Elijah appeared before him and fiercely denounced him in the name of the Lord: 'Have you killed, and also taken possession?' (1 Kgs. 21:19) The prophet pronounced the doom of Ahab and his whole household, who would be wiped out. As for Jezebel, the dogs would eat her by the walls of Jezreel. Ahab rent his clothes and fasted, and at these signs of repentance, the Lord deferred the fulfilment of Elijah's curse.

After twenty-two years on the throne, Ahab was killed in battle against the Arameans at Ramothgilead, and was succeeded by his son Ahaziah. The following year the new king was badly injured in a fall from the balcony of his palace in Samaria. He sent messengers to consult Baal-zebub, the Philistine God who had his shrine at Ekron on the coastal plain. On the way the messengers were intercepted by Elijah who told them to say to their royal master, 'Is it because there is no God in Israel that you are sending to inquire of Baal-zebub, the god of Ekron? Therefore you shall not come down from the bed to which you have gone, but shall surely die.' (2 Kgs. 1:6)

The angry king sent an officer and fifty soldiers to seize the prophet, but they were wiped out by fire invoked by Elijah from heaven. The same thing happened to the second company of soldiers. The captain of the third detachment flung himself on his knees before Elijah and begged that his life and those of his men should be spared. Elijah accompanied them back to the palace and repeated his words in the presence of the bedridden king. Ahaziah died soon after.

Feeling his end was near, Elijah went

from Gilgal to Bethel and then on to Jericho. At each place he tried to persuade Elisha not to go any further with him, but his disciple refused to be parted from him. Beyond Jericho they came to the banks of the river Jordan. Elijah rolled up his cloak and struck the water with it. It parted immediately so that they were able to cross over dryshod. Elijah then asked Elisha what he desired before his master was taken from him. Elisha answered that he wanted a double portion of Elijah's spirit.

They walked on talking when '... behold, a chariot of fire and horses of fire separated the two of them. And Elijah went up by a whirlwind into heaven.' (2 Kgs. 2:11) As the chariot disappeared from sight, Elisha rent his clothes, then picked up the fallen mantle of Elijah and used it to part the waters again to return across the river.

By Jewish tradition, Elijah has not died, and continues to wander the earth. He will reappear to usher in the Messiah and the final redemption of mankind.

The wonders he worked, and the strange manner of his passing, have surrounded his name with mystic properties. At the Brith Milah (circumcision) of a Jewish child it is the custom to place a chair for Elijah in the hope that he will protect the baby; at the Passover meal, an extra cup of wine is poured for Elijah, and some families draw up an empty chair at the table for him. During the service the door is flung open to let him in. One of the favourite songs of the Passover evening is:

'Elijah the Prophet
Elijah the Tishbite
Elijah the Gileadite
May he come quickly to us
With the Messiah.'

By the alchemy of time, this stern God-driven man became transmuted into a Jewish folk-legend held in popular affection. [1 Kgs. 17–19; 21; 2 Kgs. 1–3:11; 9:36–7; Mal. 4:5]
2. date unknown. Son of Jeroham and a

leader of the tribe of Benjamin living in Jerusalem. [1 Chr. 8:27]
3. 5 century BC. Descendant of Harim the priest, he divorced his non-Jewish wife in the time of Ezra. [Ezra 10:21]
4. 5 century BC. A Levite descended from Elam who divorced his non-Jewish wife in the time of Ezra. [Ezra 10:26]

Elika 10 century BC. A mighty warrior in the armies of King David. [2 Sam. 23:25]

Elimelech (Heb. 'my God is King') c. 11 century BC. A wealthy man of Bethlehem who migrated to Moab during a famine taking with him his wife Naomi and their two sons, one of whom married Ruth. [Ruth 1:1–3]

Elioenai (Heb. 'eyes lifted to God') *1. c.* 16 century BC. Son of Becher and a grandson of Benjamin. [1 Chr. 7:8]
2. date unknown. Son of Neariah of the tribe of Judah and a descendant of King David. [1 Chr. 3:23, 24]
3. c. 8 century BC. One of the leaders of the tribe of Simeon who settled in the rich valley of Gedor during the reign of King Hezekiah after driving out the local inhabitants. [1 Chr. 4:36]
4. 5 century BC. Descendant of Pashhur, the priest, who divorced his non-Jewish wife in the time of Ezra. [Ezra 10:22]
5. 5 century BC. Son of Zattu the Levite, who divorced his non-Jewish wife in the time of Ezra. [Ezra 10:27]
6. 5 century BC. A priest in the time of Nehemiah who took part in the service of dedication for the rebuilt walls of Jerusalem. [Neh. 12:41]

Eliphal (Heb. 'judged of God') 10 century BC. Son of Ur, he was a mighty warrior in the army of King David. Also known as Eliphelet. [2 Sam. 23:34; 1 Chr. 11:35]

Eliphaz (Heb. 'my God is strength') *1. c.* 16 century BC. Eldest son of Esau and his wife Adah. [Gen. 36:4, 11, 12; 1 Chr. 1:35, 36]

2. period of the patriarchs. Eliphaz the Temanite was the eldest of Job's three friends who 'made an appointment together to come to condole with him and comfort him' (Job 2:11). They rent their clothes, sprinkled dust on their heads and sat with him in silence for seven days and nights.

Then Job began to curse the day he was born and to protest that his sufferings were unmerited. Eliphaz and the other two tried to console him, and expressed the traditional and pious views about his affliction: God does not punish good men, only bad ones. As Job continued to rail against God, his three friends got tired of listening to him. Eliphaz answered him angrily, 'Are you the first man that was born? Or were you brought forth before the hills?' (Job 15:7) Finally Eliphaz listed a number of uncharitable acts he falsely attributed to Job.

Job rejected all these arguments. He made no effort to conceal his impatience with Eliphaz and his friends, and utterly refused their advice to bear his trials with silent fortitude. 'So these three men ceased to answer Job, because he was righteous in his own eyes.' (Job 32:1)

Finally the Lord spoke to Job out of a whirlwind and he was completely overwhelmed and humbled. Then the Lord turned on Eliphaz: 'My wrath is kindled against you and against your two friends; for you have not spoken of me what is right, as my servant Job has.' (Job 42:7) The Lord then instructed them to 'offer up for yourselves a burnt offering; and my servant Job shall pray for you, for I will accept his prayer' (Job 42:8). [Job. 2, 4, 15, 22, 42]

Eliphelehu (Heb. 'who exalts God') 10 century BC. A Levite appointed by King David to play the harp during the celebrations when the Ark of God was brought to Jerusalem from Kiriath-jearim. [1 Chr. 15:18, 21]

Eliphelet (Heb. 'God of deliverance') **1.** 10 century BC. One of King David's sons. [2 Sam. 5:16; 1 Chr. 3:8; 14:7]

2. 10 century BC. Another of King David's sons. Also called Elpelet. [1 Chr. 3:6; 14:5]

3. *see* ELIPHAL

4. *c.* 9 century BC. Son of Eshek of the tribe of Benjamin and a descendant of King Saul. [1 Chr. 8:39]

5. 5 century BC. One of the sons of Adonikam who returned with Ezra to Judah from exile in Babylon. [Ezra 8:13]

6. 5 century BC. A descendant of Hashum who divorced his non-Jewish wife in the time of Ezra. [Ezra 10:33]

Elisha (Heb. 'God is salvation') 9 century BC. A prophet in the kingdom of Israel. Elisha was the disciple and successor of Elijah in the crusade against the religious and moral laxity of their time, especially the cult of Phoenician 'baals' (gods). Although they were equally unswerving in the cause of the Lord, there were marked differences of personality between these two holy men. Elijah was stern, forceful and solitary. Elisha could be firm when necessary; but he was a more gentle man, often living with groups of prophets and pursuing his mission by working beneficent wonders.

Elisha was the son of Shaphat, a farmer at Abelmeholah in the Jordan valley south of the Sea of Galilee. One day he was ploughing a field with a wooden plough drawn by oxen, when the noted prophet Elijah came up to him and threw his cloak over the youth. Elisha gladly accepted this symbolic call. He slaughtered two oxen, broke up the plough for firewood, and gave the farm workers a farewell meal. He then took leave of his parents and went off with the prophet.

After Elisha had faithfully served for some years, Elijah felt his end approaching. He went from Gilgal in the Jordan valley up to the sanctuary town of Bethel, and down the mountain once more to Jericho. At each place Elijah tried to persuade Elisha to remain behind, but the devoted younger man refused to do so.

From Jericho the two walked across the barren plain to the Jordan river five miles away. At this spot the stream flows quietly between reeds, bushes and flowering shrubs, before entering the Dead Sea. Some of the Jericho prophets followed them at a distance. Elijah rolled up his cloak and struck the water and it parted, letting them cross dryshod to the other bank. Elijah asked whether his disciple had a final request of him. Elisha replied, 'I pray you, let me inherit a double share of your spirit.' (2 Kgs. 2:9) As they walked on conversing, a fiery chariot appeared drawn by fiery horses. Elijah stepped into the chariot and was carried up to heaven in it by a great whirlwind. Elisha sorrowfully rent his clothes, then picked up Elijah's fallen cloak and retraced his steps. At the river he used the cloak to part the water, as Elijah had done. Seeing this, the waiting prophets hailed him as the successor to Elijah and bowed down before him.

THE WORKER OF MIRACLES

The men of Jericho complained to Elisha that though their town was a pleasant place to live in, the water of their spring had turned foul, making the soil barren and causing miscarriages. Elisha asked for some salt to be brought to him in a new bowl. He threw the salt into the spring and the water became wholesome again. (The spring of Ain es-Sultan, which still accounts for the lushness of the Jericho oasis, is by tradition known as the 'Spring of Elisha'. It is not surprising that this abundance of fresh water gushing out in the desolate Jordan valley was regarded as miraculous by the ancients.)

Elisha set off up the mountain to Bethel. Before he reached the town he met a gang of children who mocked at his bald head. His reaction was astonishingly harsh and curiously out of charac-

ter. He lost his temper and cursed the children, at which two she-bears appeared out of the wood and mauled forty-two of them.

The stories about Elisha show him as living at times in a community of prophets in the Gilgal area, down on the plain of Jericho. Such communities were common — groups of professional holy men or mystics, usually in desert areas, living in conditions of extreme poverty assuaged only by religious ecstasy. The miracles attributed to Elisha while dwelling with the holy brothers are of a minor nature, but throw light on their way of life.

Thus, at a time of famine, they had nothing to eat except the wild plants they could gather; with a handful of meal Elisha made palatable a soup of bitter-tasting and poisonous yellow gourds that one of them had gathered.

While they were chopping down trees on the bank of the Jordan river to make themselves huts, an axe-head fell into the water. The brethren were particularly distressed because the axe had been borrowed. Elisha recovered it by getting it to float up to the surface.

When a farmer in the hills of Ephraim sent Elisha some loaves of barley bread and ears of wheat as 'first fruit' from his field, he miraculously multiplied the food in order to feed a hundred of his hungry fellow-prophets.

A destitute widow was unable to pay her husband's debts, and the creditor claimed her two sons as his bondsmen. She had nothing in the house but a little oil in a jar. Elisha told her to collect a number of empty jars from the neighbours. All of them were miraculously filled from the single jar she had. By selling the oil she was able to redeem the debt and provide for her children and herself.

The kingdom of Moab, on the plateau east of the Dead Sea, had thrown off its allegiance to the kingdom of Israel. King Jehoram of Israel proposed to King

Jehoshaphat of Judah a joint campaign against Moab. The king of Edom, a Judean vassal, was also asked to take part. They took a long detour across the 'Wilderness of Edom' past the southern end of the Dead Sea, in order to attack Moab from the south. But they ran out of water (the key to all desert campaigns) and the troops and baggage animals faced death by thirst. Elisha, who was accompanying them, told them to dig trenches in a certain wadi. By next morning the trenches had filled with water. (Flash floods are not uncommon in the area.)

From afar the Moabite sentries saw the water looking the colour of blood in the early morning light, an illusion increased by the red sandstone rock of the region. They concluded that the allies had been fighting and killing each other and rushed toward the Israelite camp to collect booty. Here they were heavily repulsed and the advance was resumed into the heart of Moab.

Elisha came to live on Mount Carmel with an attendant called Gehazi. Twenty miles away along the Jezreel valley was the small town of Shunem. On his journeys through the town, the prophet would stop for meals in the home of a well-to-do and pious woman. She and her husband built and furnished a small room for him on the roof where the holy man could rest.

Elisha consulted with his servant how he could repay the woman's kindness. The servant pointed out that she had no son and her husband was an elderly man. Elisha sent for her and told her that a son would be born to her within a year. To her great joy the prediction came true.

When the boy was grown, he went out into the fields to his father during the harvest, and was brought home complaining of a blinding headache (possibly due to sunstroke). By nightfall he had died. The bereft mother laid the body on the bed in Elisha's room and closed the door. She then went by donkey to Mount Carmel, flung herself down before the prophet, imploring him to help her. He sent Gehazi ahead with his rod to try and revive the boy and himself followed with the mother. As the laying on of the rod had not helped, the prophet stretched himself seven times over the dead child and put 'his mouth upon his mouth, his eyes upon his eyes, and his hands upon his hands' (2 Kgs. 4:34). The boy revived.

(This story parallels that of Elijah and the widow's son. It illustrates the belief that prophets inspired by God possessed a special life-force that could in suitable cases restore the dead to life.)

Naaman, the army commander of the king of Damascus, contracted the dread disease of leprosy. His wife had an Israelite slave girl who had been taken captive on one of the Aramean incursions into Israel. The girl said there was a prophet in Samaria who would be able to cure him. Carrying lavish presents and a letter from his king to Jehoram, king of Israel, asking him to cure the general, Naaman set out for Samaria with an escort. Jehoram was distressed at this unwelcome visit, fearing that the Syrians were making an impossible demand on him as a pretext to attack him. Elisha sent word that the Aramean commander be brought round to his house. The prophet did not come out to receive the foreign dignitary nor invite him in, but sent a messenger out to tell him that he should bathe seven times in the river Jordan. Naaman was angered at this curt treatment. He snorted, 'Are not Abana and Pharpar, the rivers of Damascus, better than all the waters of Israel? Could I not wash in them, and be clean?' (2 Kgs. 5:12) But his servants persuaded him to follow Elisha's advice, 'and his flesh was restored like the flesh of a little child, and he was clean' (2 Kgs. 5:14).

Naaman came back to Elisha filled with gratitude, and offered him a reward, which the prophet declined. Convinced now that the Hebrew God was the only true one, Naaman asked leave to take two mule-loads of earth back to Damascus with him, so that he could worship the Lord on Israel soil.

Elisha's servant Gehazi was overcome with greed at the thought of the rich gifts his master had spurned. He hurried after Naaman and obtained two bags of silver and two changes of clothes from him, with a concocted story about a couple of needy priests visiting Elisha. The servant hid these gains in the house, but through his occult powers Elisha knew what had happened. He told Gehazi that he may have enriched himself but at the cost of contracting the disease of which Naaman had been cured: 'So he went out from his presence a leper, as white as snow.' (2 Kgs. 5:27)

THE WAR WITH SYRIA

In the fighting with the Arameans (Syrians), Elisha used his supernatural powers for the unexpected purpose of military intelligence. He accurately predicted the time and place of raids planned by the Arameans, so that they were constantly repulsed by the Israelite defenders. The king of Aram declared to his officers that one of them must be a traitor. They replied that the security leaks were due to the Israelite prophet Elisha, then residing in the town of Dothan, ten miles north of Samaria. Under cover of darkness an Aramean task force of chariots and cavalry penetrated as far as Dothan and surrounded the town, with instructions to capture the man of God who had become such a valuable prize.

On rising next morning and finding himself trapped, Elisha invoked the Lord's help. The Aramean troops were temporarily blinded. Elisha then told them they had come to the wrong place and offered to lead them to the man they were seeking. He guided them right into Samaria and handed them over to the king's forces before they recovered

their vision. The king wanted to put them to death, but Elisha dissuaded him, pointing out that they were not really battle captives. Instead, on the prophet's advice, the raiders were fed and returned unharmed across the border. This act of clemency bore fruit in a temporary truce in the fighting.

When the Syrians under the king of Damascus later invaded Israel in force, Elisha was involved in the siege of Samaria. The city was completely cut off and famine-stricken. What little food there was fetched exorbitant prices in the market-place. The desperate King Jehoram blamed Elisha for causing all this suffering through his misplaced faith in the protection of the Lord. The prophet promised that within a day there would be an abundance of barley and flour.

During the night the Syrian army fled in panic, after the Lord had caused them to hear the sound of chariots and a great host, and they thought that Hittite and Egyptian armies had arrived to join forces with the Israelites. The siege was over, and great quantities of abandoned Syrian supplies were left in the hands of the city.

A period of peace seems to have ensued between Israel and Aram, for Elisha is next heard of in Damascus. The King Ben-hadad II was seriously ill. He heard that the renowned Israelite prophet was in his city and sent Hazael, a senior army officer, to consult him, with forty camel-loads of goods as a gift. Elisha gave a cryptic answer: the king would recover from his illness but nevertheless he was about to die.

The prophet reacted strangely to the encounter with Hazael. He seemed to go into a trance, weeping, with his face rigid and his eyes fixed. The bewildered Hazael asked him why he wept. He then predicted that Hazael would become king of Aram, and '... I know the evil that you will do to the people of Israel; you will set on fire their fortresses, and you will slay their young men with the sword, and dash in pieces their little ones, and rip up their women with child.' (2 Kgs. 8:12) The next day Hazael murdered Ben-hadad by smothering him with a wet cloth, and became king in his place. He later occupied all the Israelite territory east of the Jordan, and parts of Israel itself.

Elisha had not forgotten that King Jehoram was the son of Ahab, whose dynasty Elijah had doomed to extinction in the name of the Lord. In the twelfth year of Jehoram's reign, Israel was defending Ramoth–gilead, east of the Jordan, against the king of Aram. The king had gone back to Jezreel to recover from campaign wounds and left the front in charge of a tough and ambitious general, Jehu. Elisha sent a young disciple to inform Jehu that God had selected him to be king, and to anoint his head with oil.

Jehu dashed for Jezreel, killed the king and seized the throne. In the bloody chapter that followed, Jehu extirpated not only Queen Jezebel and all Ahab's family and supporters, but also all the priests and worshippers of the Phoenician baal-cult that Jezebel had spread. Elijah's grim prophecy had been carried out in full measure. Yet Jehu's reign was to prove that this religious purge was at the expense of the national interest. The kingdom was weakened and isolated and lost much territory. Elisha's venture in king-making had been costly.

THE PROPHET'S DEATH

More than fifty years had gone by since the day when Elijah had plucked the young Elisha from his ploughing. Elisha's career since then had spanned for reigns. Jehu's grandson Joash was on the throne when the old prophet lay on his death-bed. The king came to call on him and wept over him. Elisha told him to open the east window and shoot an arrow in the direction of their old enemy Aram. Elisha prophesied that the Arameans would be defeated and turned back at Aphek, east of the Sea of Galilee. He then told the king to strike the ground with his arrows, and Joash did so three times. Elisha complained that he should have done so five or six times, then would he secure total victory; as it was, he would defeat Aram only three times. After these symbolic actions Elisha died.

A brief sequel follows in the Scriptures. Some men carrying a body for burial were surprised by Moabite marauders. They threw the body into Elisha's tomb and fled. On contact with the prophet's bones, the corpse came to life again and stood up. This story was meant to show that Elisha's powers as a worker of miracles persisted even after his death. [1 Kgs. 19;2 Kgs. 2–9; 13]

Elishah (Heb. 'God saves') date unknown. Son of Javan and a descendant of Noah's son Japheth. [Gen. 10:4; 1 Chr. 1:7; Ezek. 27:7]

Elishama (Heb. 'whom God hears') *1. c.* 13 century BC. Son of Ammihud and the grandfather of Joshua, he was appointed by Moses to conduct a census of the men of Ephraim fit for war and led his tribe's contingent. [Num. 1:10; 2:18; 7:48–53; 10:22; 1 Chr. 7:26]
2. 10 century BC. Son of King David. [2 Sam. 5:16; 1 Chr. 3:8; 14:7]
3. see ELISHUA
4. date unknown. Son of Jekamiah and a leader of the tribe of Judah. [1 Chr. 2:41]
5. 9 century BC. A priest in the reign of King Jehoshaphat who taught the Law of God in the cities of Judah. [2 Chr. 17:8]
6. c. 6 century BC. A descendant of the royal family of Judah, his grandson assassinated Gedaliah, the governor of Judah. [2 Kgs. 25:25; Jer. 41:1]
7. c. 6 century BC. Secretary to the leaders of Judah in the reign of King Jehoiakim, in whose room the scroll of Jeremiah's prophecies was kept before it was read to the king. [Jer. 36:12, 20, 21]

Elishaphat (Heb. 'my God judged') *c.* 9 century BC. Son of Zichri, he was one of the Judean officers who on the orders of Jehoiada the high priest executed Queen Athaliah who had usurped the throne. [2 Chr. 23:1]

Elisheba (Heb. 'God her oath') *c.* 13 century BC. Wife of Aaron the high priest, she was the daughter of Amminadab, a leader of the tribe of Judah. [Exod. 6:23]

Elishua *c.* 10 century BC. Son of King David. Also called Elishama. [2 Sam. 5:15; 1 Chr. 3:6; 14:5]

Elizaphan (Heb. 'my God protected') *1. c.* 13 century BC. A Levite head of a family of Kohathites in the wilderness, he and his family were responsible for the Ark of the Tabernacle and some of its appurtenances during the wanderings of the children of Israel. [Num. 3:30; 1 Chr. 15:8; 2 Chr. 29:13]
2. c. 13 century BC. Son of Parnach, he was appointed by Moses to supervise the division of the part of the land of Israel allocated to Zebulun among the members of his tribe. [Num. 34:25]

Elizur (Heb. 'my God is my rock') *c.* 13 century BC. Son of Shedeur, Moses appointed him to conduct the census of the men of Reuben fit for war and he led the contingent of his tribe. [Num. 1:5; 2:10; 7:30–5; 10:18]

Elkanah (Heb. 'provided by God') *1. c.* 13 century BC. One of the sons of Korah of the tribe of Levi who led the revolt in the wilderness against the authority of Moses and Aaron. [Exod. 6:24; 1 Chr. 6:23]
2. c. 13 century BC. Son of Assir and a grandson of Korah the Levite. [1 Chr. 6:23, 25, 36]
3. c. 12 century BC. A judge of Israel for ten years, he was an ancestor of the prophet Samuel. [1 Chr. 6:26, 35]

4. c. 11 century BC. Father of Samuel. Elkanah the son of Jeroham lived in Ramathaim-zophim, the hill country of Ephraim. He had two wives: Hannah who was barren and Peninnah who had several children. Hannah grieved over being childless, and Elkanah said to her: 'Hannah, why do you weep? And why do you not eat? And why is your heart sad? Am I not more to you than ten sons?' (1 Sam. 1:8) The next time the family went to the temple at Shiloh to make their annual sacrifices, she stayed behind and prayed to the Lord. Eli the high priest consoled her.

In due time Hannah bore a child she called Samuel, 'the Lord heard'. When she had weaned him she brought him to Shiloh where he was apprenticed to the priests. Elkanah and Hannah were blessed with five more children. [1 Sam. 1–2; 1 Chr. 6:27, 34]
5. c. 11 century BC. A warrior of the family of the Korahites who deserted the army of King Saul and rallied to David at Ziklag. [1 Chr. 12:6]
6. 10 century BC. One of the two Levites who were gatekeepers for the Ark in the reign of King David. [1 Chr. 15:23]
7. 8 century BC. Chief minister of King Ahaz of Judah, he was killed by Zichri of the tribe of Ephraim in the war between Israel and Judah. [2 Chr. 28:7]
8. date unknown. A Levite whose grandson Berechiah was one of the first to settle in Jerusalem following the return from exile in Babylon. [1 Chr. 9:16]

Elnaam (Heb. 'God his delight') *c.* 10 century BC. Father of Jeribai and Joshaviah, two warriors in the army of King David outstanding for their bravery. [1 Chr. 11:46]

Elnathan (Heb. 'God hath given') *1.* 7 century BC. Father of Nehushta, the mother of King Jehoiachin of Judah. [2 Kgs. 24:8]
2. c. 7 century BC. Elnathan, the son of Achbor, was an official at the court of

King Jehoiakim of Judah. He was sent by the king to bring back from Egypt the prophet Uriah who had predicted doom and fled.

It was Elnathan who pleaded in vain with the king not to destroy the Scroll of Jeremiah's oracles that was being read to him. [Jer. 26:22, 23; 36:25]
3. 5 century BC. Three men, each named Elnathan, leaders of the exile in Babylon, were sent by Ezra to Iddo at Casiphia requesting that he send Levites to serve in the Temple in Jerusalem. [Ezra 8:16]

Elon (Heb. 'oak tree') **1.** *c.* 16 century BC. Father of Adah and father-in-law of Esau. [Gen. 26:34; 36:2]
2. *c.* 16 century BC. Son of Zebulun and grandson of Jacob. [Gen. 46:14; Num. 26:26]
3. *c.* 12 century BC. A judge of Israel for ten years, he was buried in Aijalon. [Judg. 12:11, 12]

Elpaal (Heb. 'God acted') date unknown. Son of Hushim, he was a leader of the tribe of Benjamin. [1 Chr. 8:11, 12, 18]

Elpelet *see* ELIPHELET 2.

Eluzai (Heb. 'God is my castle') *c.* 11 century BC. A Benjaminite warrior who deserted the army of King Saul and rallied to David at Ziklag. [1 Chr. 12:5]

Elzabad (Heb. 'gift of God') **1.** *c.* 11 century BC. A warrior of the tribe of Gad who deserted the army of King Saul and rallied to David's support. [1 Chr. 12:12]
2. 10 century BC. Son of Shemaiah and a gatekeeper of the Tabernacle in the reign of King David. [1 Chr. 26:7]

Elzaphan (Heb. 'protected by God') *c.* 13 century BC. Son of Uzziel, a Levite descended from Kohath and a cousin of Moses, he helped remove the bodies of

Nadab and Abihu from the sanctuary where they had died after burning the forbidden incense. [Exod. 6:22; Lev. 10:4]

Emim (Heb. 'terrors') date unknown. A fierce and powerful tribe living in the land of Canaan in ancient times. [Gen. 14:5; Deut. 2:10]

Enan (Heb. 'eyes') *c.* 13 century BC. A leader of the tribe of Naphtali, he was the father of Ahira who was appointed by Moses as commander of the tribe of Naphtali. [Num. 1:15; 2:29; 7:78, 83; 10:27]

Enoch (Heb. 'dedicated') **1.** date unknown. Eldest son of Cain and a grandson of Adam and Eve. [Gen. 4:17, 18]
2. date unknown. Son of Jared and a descendant of Seth. [Gen. 5:18–24; 1 Chr. 1:3]

Enosh (Heb. 'mortal') date unknown. Son of Seth, the third son of Adam. [Gen. 4:26; 5:6–11; 1 Chr. 1:1]

Ephah (Heb. 'darkness') **1.** *c.* 16 century BC. Son of Midian and a grandson of Abraham and Keturah. [Gen. 25:4; 1 Chr. 1:33; Isa. 60:6]
2. date unknown. Caleb's concubine who bore him three sons. [1 Chr. 2:46]
3. date unknown. Son of Jahdai and a leader of the tribe of Judah. [1 Chr. 2:47]

Ephai (Heb. 'gloomy') 6 century BC. Father of sons who were among the army captains of Judah who rallied to the support of Gedaliah son of Ahikam when the latter was made governor of Judah by the Babylonians. [Jer. 40:8]

Epher (Heb. 'calf') **1.** *c.* 16 century BC. Son of Midian and a grandson of Abraham and Keturah. [Gen. 25:4; 1 Chr. 1:33]
2. date unknown. Son of Ezrah of the tribe of Judah. [1 Chr. 4:17]

3. date unknown. A leader of the tribe of Manasseh living east of the river Jordan. [1 Chr. 5:24]

Ephlal (Heb. 'judgment') date unknown. A leader of the tribe of Judah, he was descended from Perez. [1 Chr. 2:37]

Ephod (Heb. 'clothe') *c.* 13 century BC. Father of Hanniel, a leader of the tribe of Manasseh in the time of Moses who was to supervise the division of their inheritance among the members of the tribe. [Num. 34:23]

Ephraim (Heb. 'fruitfulness') *c.* 16 century BC. Second son of Joseph. Ephraim, like his elder brother Manasseh, was born in Egypt where Joseph had married Asenath, the daughter of the Egyptian high priest of the temple at On.

Years later, after Joseph had brought his father Jacob and the rest of the family to Egypt, he was told his father was ill. He took Manasseh and Ephraim to Jacob's bedside to receive his blessing. The patriarch's sight was failing and when he placed his right hand on the head of Ephraim, the younger son, Joseph sought to correct him. Jacob then explained that Ephraim's descendants would be more important than those of Manasseh. Jacob gave the same importance to these two grandchildren as he did to his sons and they too became founders of tribes.

In the blessing attributed to Moses, Joseph is promised great abundance and power, and it is added that 'such are the ten thousands of Ephraim' (Deut. 33:17).

In the conquest of Canaan under Joshua, the tribe of Ephraim was allocated the central hill area south of Shechem (Nablus) and extending into the coastal plain. [Gen. 41:52; 46:20; 48:1–20; 50:23; Num. 26:28; Deut. 33:17; 1 Chr. 7:20–2]

Ephrath (Heb. 'fruitful') date unknown. A wife of Caleb, who was the son of Hezron, of the tribe of Judah and the mother of Hur. Also called Ephrathah. [1 Chr. 2:19, 50; 4:4]

Ephrathah *see* EPHRATH

Ephron (Heb. 'fawn-like') *c.* 18 century BC. He was the son of Zohar a Hittite, and a landowner in Hebron from whom Abraham bought the Cave of Machpelah as a family burial place. [Gen. 23:8–20; 25:9; 49:29, 30; 50:13]

Er (Heb. 'watchful') *1. c.* 16 century BC. The eldest son of Judah and his wife Bath-shua. Er, who married Tamar, was 'wicked in the sight of the Lord' and died suddenly without children. [Gen. 38:7; 46:12; Num. 26:19; 1 Chr. 2:3, 4]
2. c. 16 century BC. The son of Shelah and a grandson of Judah, he was a chief of the tribe and his descendants were renowned for their production of fine linen. [1 Chr. 4:21]

Eran (Heb. 'watchful') *c.* 16 century BC. Son of Shuthelah and a grandson of Ephraim, he was a chief of the tribe. [Num. 26:36]

Eri (Heb. 'watching') *c.* 16 century BC. Son of Gad and a grandson of Jacob and Zilpah. [Gen. 46:16; Num. 26:16]

Esarhaddon (Ass. 'Asshur has given a brother') King of Assyria, 680–69 BC. Esarhaddon was the son of Sennacherib and the grandson of Sargon II (the Great). He was an able monarch who expanded the Assyrian empire by the occupation of Lower Egypt in 671 BC. Manasseh, king of Judah, was one of the rulers mentioned in Assyrian records as paying tribute to him. [2 Kgs. 19:37; Ezra 4:2; Isa. 37:38]

Esau (Heb. 'hairy, shaggy') *c.* 17

century BC. Elder son of Isaac and Rebekah.

After Isaac's wife Rebekah had been barren for many years, she became pregnant with twins. According to the Biblical account there was conflict between the infants while they were still in the womb and it was foretold that the elder would serve the younger. The first to be born was Esau, who was covered with red hair. He was followed by Jacob, clutching his brother's heel.

Esau grew up as a skilled hunter, while Jacob became a cultivator. One day Esau returned from a hunting trip weak with hunger. He begged his brother for food, and Jacob gave him bread and red lentil soup in return for Esau's surrender of his birthright as the first-born.

At the age of forty Esau took three wives from the local Hittite people, Adah, Oholibamah and Basemath. This was a grief to his parents.

When Isaac was old and nearly blind, he asked Esau, his favourite son, to go hunting and bring him a dish of the venison he liked. He would then, he said, bestow the paternal blessing on him. Rebekah overheard this and determined to get the blessing for Jacob whom she loved best. She prepared a savoury dish of goat's meat and sent it in to her husband with Jacob, having first dressed him in one of Esau's garments and covered his hands and neck with fleece to simulate Esau's hairiness. The old man was deceived and bestowed the blessing on Jacob, declaring that he would be the head of the family after Isaac's death and his brethren would serve him.

When Esau returned and learnt what had happened, he wept bitterly, and begged his father to bless him as well. Isaac replied that Esau would have to serve his brother Jacob, but promised that Esau too would prosper and in due course become independent. Esau, his father added, would live by the sword.

Esau hated Jacob for this betrayal and threatened to kill him. Jacob was sent away to his mother's family in Paddan-aram to escape Esau's revenge, and also to find a wife among his kinsfolk. Realizing how much his parents disapproved of Canaanite women as wives for their sons, Esau himself took another wife, Mahalath, who was the daughter of Ishmael, Isaac's half-brother.

Esau settled in the land of Seir, south of the Dead Sea. After many years had gone by, messengers arrived from Jacob, to say he had returned to Canaan with his wives and children. Esau set out to meet him, at the head of four hundred men. Jacob was fearful that the twin brother he had wronged might be coming to slay him. He therefore sent ahead many choice sheep, goats, cattle and camels as gifts for Esau.

The meeting took place near the ford of Jabbok (where the Jabbok river joins the Jordan river, to the north of Jericho). Jacob walked forward with his two wives, his two concubines, and their children, and bowed down to the ground before Esau. But his fears were unfounded. Esau ran to meet his brother and embraced him, and they kissed each other and wept.

At first Esau refused the gifts of livestock, saying he had enough animals of his own, but he was finally persuaded to accept them.

Esau wanted Jacob to return with him to the land of Seir. Jacob pleaded that he could only travel slowly as his children were of tender years and his animals were with young, and he prevailed on Esau and his men to go ahead. Jacob did not follow Esau but turned away and remained in Canaan.

Esau's character seems open and straightforward, without a trace of his brother Jacob's guile. His emotions are strong and spontaneous, whether he is weeping and pleading before his father when cheated of his blessing – or threatening to kill Jacob in revenge – or rushing to embrace his brother when they meet again in later life.

Esau is also called Edom in the Bible, and was regarded as the forefather of the Edomites, the people inhabiting the rugged semi-desert terrain of Seir or Edom, below the Dead Sea. [Gen. 25–8; 32–3; 35:1; 36; Josh. 24:4; 1 Chr. 1:34–5; Mal. 1:2–3]

Eshbaal *see* ISHBOSHETH

Eshban date unknown. Son of Dishon and a grandson of Anah. [Gen. 36:26; 1 Chr. 1:41]

Eshcol (Heb. 'cluster of grapes') *c.* 18 century BC. One of three Amorite brothers who were neighbours of Abraham at Hebron, and helped him to rescue the captured Lot.

Eshcol may have given his name to a fertile valley near Hebron from which Moses's spies brought back grapes, figs and pomegranates. [Gen. 14:13, 24; Num. 13:23, 24; 32:9; Deut. 1:24]

Eshek (Heb. 'oppression') *c.* 9 century BC. Son of Eleasah of the tribe of Benjamin and a descendant of King Saul. [1 Chr. 8:39]

Eshtemoa date unknown. The Maacathite leader of the tribe of Judah whose grandmother was an Egyptian princess. [1 Chr. 4:19]

Eshton date unknown. Son of Mehir and a leader of the tribe of Judah. [1 Chr. 4:11, 12]

Esther (Pers. 'star') 5 century BC. Jewish queen of King Ahasuerus (Xerxes I). The tale of Esther, the Jewish queen of King Ahasuerus of Persia (486–65), and the way she foiled the wicked designs of Haman, the Vizier (chief minister), forms one of the Books of the Old Testament. It is connected with the Feast of Purim, in early spring.

The story shows a remarkable familiarity with the atmosphere and usages of the Persian court, though there are scholastic doubts as to its authenticity. Nevertheless, this uncertainty did not prevent Purim from becoming an immensely popular Jewish folk festival, completely identified with the Book of Esther, the Megillah (scroll) of which is read in every synagogue to the accompaniment of noise and stamping at each mention of Haman's name. It is the only gay carnival of the Jewish calendar, a time for masquerades, fancy dress parades for the children, and the baking of three-cornered poppyseed cakes which are colloquially called in Hebrew 'Haman's ears'.

The Book of Esther relates that in the third year of his reign King Ahasuerus gathered together all the leading men of his empire at Shushan (Susa), the capital. On the seventh day of feasting in the palace grounds, the king, under the influence of wine, sent his court chamberlains to fetch Queen Vashti, so that her beauty could be displayed to his guests. When she refused to come, the angry king consulted his chief counsellors. They advised him to take drastic action against the queen, otherwise her example would encourage other wives to disobey their husbands. The king, they said, should issue a decree banning Vashti from his presence, and confer her position on a worthier woman.

Beautiful maidens were brought to the capital from all the provinces for a new queen to be chosen from among them. They were kept under the charge of the chief eunuch, and each of them received special beauty treatment for a year with oils and spices before being brought into the king. None of them appealed to him as a suitable queen.

In Susa lived a sage and devout Jew called Mordecai, one of the exiles from Jerusalem. He had adopted as his own daughter a young orphaned cousin, Hadassah, whose Persian name was Esther, for 'the maiden was beautiful and lovely' (Esther 2:7). She was one of the girls brought to the king's palace, and so appealed to the chief eunuch that he gave her seven maids to attend on her and the best quarters in the harem. When she was summoned to the king, he was immediately attracted by her beauty and intelligence, 'so that he set the royal crown on her head and made her queen instead of Vashti' (Esther 2:17). On Mordecai's advice she did not reveal her Jewish origins.

Mordecai himself had an official position at the court. One day he overheard two of the king's chamberlains plotting to assassinate their master. He asked Esther to warn the king, who had the conspirators seized and executed. This service by Mordecai was recorded in the official court annals.

THE EDICT OF HAMAN

Shortly afterwards the king appointed Haman, the Agagite, as his chief minister and gave orders that all the palace officials were to prostrate themselves before him. Mordecai alone refused to abase himself in this fashion. Haman's anger at Mordecai, the Jew, turned into hatred of the Jewish race, and a resolve to wipe it out. In the twelfth year of the reign of Ahasuerus, Haman had the magicians cast the 'pur' or sacred lot to pick a propitious day for his evil design. Haman then went to the king and denounced the Jewish minority: 'There is a certain people scattered abroad and dispersed among the peoples in all the provinces of your kingdom; their laws are different from those of every other people, and they do not keep the king's laws, so that it is not for the king's profit to tolerate them.' (Esther 3:8) He offered to pay a large sum of money into the royal treasury if he got his way – perhaps from the Jewish property that would be confiscated. The king declined the contribution but gave Haman permission to act as he saw fit about the Jews and gave him his signet ring for issuing the necessary royal decrees.

Haman had these orders drawn up, translated into all the languages of the empire and sent by special runners to the authorities in each province. On the appointed day they were to have all the local Jews slaughtered and their possessions seized.

The Jews were thrown into consternation at the news of the pending pogrom. They fasted, prayed and tore their clothes in mourning. Dressed in sackcloth, Mordecai stood in the square in front of the palace. When Esther sent to ask him what had happened, Mordecai produced a copy of Haman's edict and told her to approach the king and beg for the lives of her people.

After fasting for three days, Esther dressed herself up in her regal robes and went into the king, who was sitting on his throne. He addressed her kindly and agreed to come and dine in her quarters together with Haman. At the meal she invited them to come again the following day. Haman went home in high spirits at the unusual honour paid him. But his anger was aroused again at the sight of Mordecai in the palace square. Encouraged by his wife and friends he ordered a gallows to be constructed, intending to ask the king next morning to have Mordecai hanged on it. However, being unable to sleep the previous night, the king had called for the court records to be read to him, and came across the entry about Mordecai's having revealed the plot to assassinate him. He discovered that Mordecai's act had gone unrewarded. Thus, when Haman arrived in the morning to see the king, Ahasuerus promptly asked him 'What shall be done to the man whom the king delights to honour?' (Esther 6:6) Believing that the reference was to himself, Haman eagerly advised that such a man should be dressed in royal robes, placed upon the king's horse and led by a high official through the streets of the capital. To Haman's dismay, he was ordered to do just that for Mordecai.

When the king and Haman sat at Queen Esther's table for her second banquet, she appeared downcast, and the king asked her whether there was anything she wanted. Esther pleaded that the lives of herself and her people should be spared: 'For we are sold, I and my people, to be destroyed, to be slain, and to be annihilated.' (Esther 7:4) She then accused the terrified Haman of having organized this mass murder. Overcome with anger, the king rushed out into the garden. Haman flung himself down on the couch next to the queen and begged her to save his life. At that moment the king stalked in again and, seeing Haman on the couch, cried out: 'Will he even assault the queen in my presence, in my own house?' (Esther 7:8) The attendants seized Haman and the king ordered him to be hanged on the gallows he had constructed for Mordecai.

Haman's house and possessions were confiscated and given to Esther, while Mordecai was appointed chief minister in his place. He left the palace clothed in 'royal robes of blue and white, with a great golden crown and a mantle of fine linen and purple, while the city of Susa shouted and rejoiced' (Esther 8:15).

Esther again appeared weeping before the king and begged him to have Haman's decree cancelled. That could not be done, since Persian law made a formal edict of the ruler irrevocable even by himself. Instead Mordecai was authorized to send out another decree, which was taken on fast horses, mules and camels to all the 127 provinces of the empire. It gave the Jews the right to carry arms in self-defence. On the day Haman had appointed for their destruction, they turned on their enemies and slew them. This happened on the thirteenth day of Adar, the twelfth month by the Jewish calendar, and on the fourteenth they celebrated their survival. Mordecai, and later also Esther, sent letters to all the Jews, laying down that their deliverance from their persecutor should be commemorated each year with the Feast of Purim: 'Therefore the Jews of the villages, who live in the open towns, hold the fourteenth day of the month of Adar as a day for gladness and feasting and holiday-making, and a day on which they send choice portions to one another.' (Esther 9:19) (In walled cities the feast was held a day later because in Susa the fighting had lasted two days.) [Book of Esther]

Etam (Heb. 'lair') date unknown. A leader of the tribe of Judah and father of Jezreel, Ishma, Idbash and their sister Hazzelelponi. [1 Chr. 4:3]

Ethan (Heb. 'strong') *1. c.* 16 century BC. Son of Zerah and a grandson of Judah. [1 Chr. 2:6, 8]
2. c. 10 century BC. Son of Zimmah and a Levite descended from Gershom. [1 Chr. 6:42]
3. date unknown. The Ezrahite son of Mahol, famed for his wisdom which was exceeded only by that of King Solomon. [1 Kgs. 4:31; Ps. 89]
4. c. 10 century BC. Son of Kushaiah, one of the Levites appointed to sing while the Ark of God was brought into Jerusalem by King David. [1 Chr. 6:44; 15:17, 19]

Ethbaal (Heb. 'man of Baal') *c.* 9 century BC. King of the great Phoenician port city of Sidon, he was father of Jezebel, who was married to Ahab, king of Israel.

The important alliance between the Israelites and the seafaring Phoenicians was started by David, developed by Solomon, and revived by Ahab's father King Omri. [1 Kgs. 16:31]

Ethnan (Heb. 'hire') date unknown. Son of Helah and a leader of the tribe of Judah. [1 Chr. 4:7]

Ethni (Heb. 'gift') date unknown. A Levite descended from Gershom, he was an ancestor of King David's musician, Asaph. [1 Chr. 6:41]

Eve (Heb. 'life') date unknown. The first woman. When Adam had been created and placed in the Garden of Eden, the Lord decided that he should have a helpmate. Adam was put into a deep sleep, and one of his ribs was removed and turned into a woman. Adam declared that 'This at last is bone of my bones and flesh of my flesh.' (Gen. 2:23) He called her Eve (in Hebrew 'Chava') because she was 'the mother of all living' (Gen. 3:20).

The serpent, the most subtle of the beasts, talked Eve into tasting the fruit of the tree of the knowledge of good and evil, which she gave to Adam as well. 'Then the eyes of both were opened, and they knew that they were naked; and they sewed fig leaves together and made themselves aprons.' (Gen. 3:7)

When the Lord discovered what they had done Eve pleaded that the serpent had 'beguiled' her. The Lord inflicted punishments on the serpent, on Eve and on Adam. Eve's curse was to bear children in pain and sorrow, and to be ruled by her husband.

After Adam and Eve had been expelled from the Garden of Eden she bore him three children – Cain, Abel and Seth. *see* ADAM [Gen. 3; 4:1]

Evi (Heb. 'desire') *c.* 13 century BC. One of the five chiefs of Midian slain by the army of the Children of Israel in the wilderness under Phinehas's command. [Num. 31:8; Josh. 13:21]

Evil-Merodach (Bab. 'man of Merodach [a god]') 6 century BC. Successor to Nebuchadnezzar as king of Babylon, he dealt kindly with King Jehoiachin of Judah whom Nebuchadnezzar had taken captive to Babylon. King Evil-merodach released Jehoiachin from prison, treated him as a distinguished guest at court,

and granted him a regular allowance for the rest of his life. [2 Kgs. 25:27; Jer. 52:31]

Ezbai 10 century BC. The father of Naarai, a warrior in the army of King David. [1 Chr. 11:37]

Ezbon (Heb. 'finger') *1. c.* 16 century BC. Son of Gad and grandson of Jacob. Also called Ozni. [Gen. 46:16; Num. 26:16]
2. c. 16 century BC. Son of Bela and a grandson of Benjamin. [1 Chr. 7:7]

Ezekiel (Heb. 'the strength of God') *c.* 6 century BC. A Hebrew prophet of the Exile. Ezekiel the son of Buzi ranks as one of the three major figures among the latter prophets, together with Isaiah and Jeremiah. Above all, he is the prophet of the Babylonian exile, that started with Nebuchadnezzar's first deportations from Judah in 598 BC and was swelled with the fall of Jerusalem in 587 BC.

The record of Ezekiel's ministry covers a span of twenty-two years, starting in 593 BC. Although some of the earlier chapters have a Jerusalem setting, the majority of scholars believe that his work was wholly in Babylon, and that his apparent presence in Jerusalem was visionary.

The Book of Ezekiel is more unified and systematic than those of Isaiah and Jeremiah. It contains forty-eight chapters grouped round four themes. After an introduction describing how Ezekiel receives his call in a vision, the first part contains God's warnings and threats against the population of Judah for their faithlessness. Then come the oracles against the surrounding nations – chiefly Tyre and Egypt, and to a lesser extent Sidon, Philistia, Ammon, Moab and Edom. After the fall of Jerusalem his addresses to the exiles bring a message of comfort and a promise of return to their land. The final section lays down detailed provisions for the restored Isra-elite state of the future, including the rebuilding of the Temple and the regulations for worship.

The Book of Ezekiel is almost devoid of biographical and personal details. It is known that he had been a priest, was one of the first group of deportees to Babylonia, and lived there in a refugee community at Tel-Abib on the river Chebar, a large irrigation canal leading from the Euphrates north of the city of Babylon. The only reference to his family is that the death of his wife on the eve of the fall of Jerusalem was for him a personal symbol of the national disaster.

What emerges from the Book is a versatile and complex mind. One part of Ezekiel is the ordained priest, deferring to the formal commandments of the Mosaic Code and absorbed by the details of temple ritual and architecture. The other Ezekiel is a mystic-prophet given to ecstatic visions and bizarre symbols. His four visions spring from the subconscious mind rather than the intellect, and are expressed in images that are precise and powerful but at times baffling. These visions found later echoes in the apocalyptic passages of Daniel and the Book of Revelations, and in such painters as Hieronymus Bosch in 15th-century Flanders, and William Blake in late 18th- and early 19th-century England.

THE FOUR VISIONS

The Book of Ezekiel opens with the vision in which he receives his call from God. (He is addressed by the Lord as 'Son of man', which recurs eighty-seven times throughout the Book, though the expression is almost unknown elsewhere in the Old Testament.) He sees the Lord in a kind of chariot that moves on four creatures, each having a human form, two pairs of wings, a head with four faces – man, eagle, lion and ox – and the burnished hoofs of a calf. Above them stretches an irridescent arch. The whole tableau is bathed in blinding light and flames and the whirring of the wings is like the noise of rushing water. A hand is stretched forth towards Ezekiel holding a scroll written on both sides with words of 'lamentation and mourning and woe' (Ezek. 2:10), and he is commanded to eat the scroll, which tastes of honey. The voice of the Lord warns Ezekiel that he is being sent to minister a people 'of a hard forehead and of a stubborn heart' (Ezek. 3:7). '... nor be afraid of their words, though briars and thorns are with you and you sit upon scorpions' (Ezek. 2:6). Ezekiel records that for seven days after this revelation he was like a man stunned.

Another vision concerns the idolatrous practices which he so vehemently and constantly denounced. He feels that the hand of the Lord lifts him up by the hair and transports him to Jerusalem. Through a hole in the wall, he is shown seventy elders inside the Temple, burning incense on the altars and worshipping wall reliefs of '... creeping things, and loathsome beasts, and all the idols of the house of Israel' (Ezek. 8:10). (These were apparently the sacred creatures of Assyrian and Babylonian cults.) The men are also prostrating themselves to the sun, while a group of women are weeping for the death of the Canaanite spring god Tammuz. Ezekiel then sees seven angels. Six of them are armed as soldiers while the seventh wears the white linen garb and inkhorn of a scribe. The scribe marks crosses on the foreheads of those inhabitants who are still righteous enough to be saved, and all the rest are then put to the sword.

After the fall of Jerusalem, Ezekiel has a vision of the Return in which he finds himself in a valley filled with dry bones. The Lord commands him to prophesy, and then 'there was a noise, and behold, a rattling; and the bones came together, bone to its bone ... flesh had come upon them, and skin had covered them; ... and the breath came into them, and they lived ... an exceeding great host.' (Ezek. 37:7, 8, 10)

In the twenty-fifth year of Ezekiel's exile and fourteen years after Jerusalem was destroyed, Ezekiel sees in a vision the city and the kingdom restored. He is guided round the new Temple by an angel architect equipped with a cord and a measuring rod. The detailed plans of the Temple and the adjacent structures are given, with the exact measurements of the wooden altar. (The design of the gateways, with three guard rooms on each side, was apparently modelled on the gateways to Solomon's destroyed Temple, and corresponds to the city gates excavated at Hazor, Megiddo and Gezer, dating from Solomon's time.)

The life-giving force that flows from the sanctuary is symbolized by the sacred river the celestial guide shows Ezekiel. It starts from a spring beneath the Temple and flows eastward into the Dead Sea. The waters of the river are teeming with fish and its banks are green and fruitful. (This picture would be a striking one for the prophet's audience of exiled Judeans, who would remember the bleakness of the wilderness of Judea.)

In the vision the kingdom is reunited and its boundaries restored more or less to those in David's time. Its territory is divided again among the twelve Israelite tribes, by horizontal strips without regard to geography. The ordinances are specified for sacrifices, festivals, dietary restrictions and the functions of the priests and Levites.

It was in character for Ezekiel to portray the future commonwealth with a mixture of fantasy and concrete detail. This no doubt made the hope of the Return much more tangible to the exiles in distant Babylon. His blueprint inspired those who went back in the time of Ezra and Nehemiah and laid the foundations for the Second Temple and a renewed nationhood.

PICTORIAL IMAGES AND ORACLES

Ezekiel's love of visual imagery expressed itself at times in 'acting out' his message. This use of mime may have been connected with his disclosure that at times the Lord made him dumb.

For instance, the prophet describes the elaborate enactment of the siege and fall of Jerusalem, before the event took place. He was instructed to draw a map of the city on a clay tablet, place it on the ground, and draw round it furrows and other indications of siege. Playing the role of God, he flung out his bare arm and condemned the city. After that he lay for some time on his left side and then on his right side, to indicate the periods during which first Israel and then Judah had sinned against the Lord. His next act was to cook various grains in a pot, make himself bread, and ration out this food to himself with very little water. This was done to indicate the hardship of the siege. Finally he was told to shave off his hair and his beard, to place a third of it inside the map of Jerusalem for its residents who would be slain; to spread another third around Jerusalem with a tip of a sword for the inhabitants who would be killed outside the city, and to scatter the last third to the wind for those who would be taken into exile.

On another occasion Ezekiel was told to pack a refugee's knapsack, make a hole in the wall, and go out into the dark at a time when everybody could see him. This would bring home to them the fate that awaited the sinners in Jerusalem.

On the day that Nebuchadnezzar commenced the siege of Jerusalem, Ezekiel was commanded to put flesh and bones in a cooking pot and set it on the fire. The food was reduced to cinders, the pot became red-hot but the rust and filth was not completely burnt away. This action dramatized the failure of the Lord to purge the inhabitants of Jerusalem of their wickedness and the consequent destruction of the city.

Apart from these symbolic actions, the text of the Book is studded with verbal similes and parables, mostly drawn from nature. The kingdom is compared to a vine; Babylon and Egypt are vultures, a symbol of power; the Judean kings Jehoiakim and Zedekiah are lion cubs that become man-eaters and are captured; Egypt is a crocodile; and Judah and Israel are two sticks that are tied together as a sign of reunion.

Ezekiel seems strongly attracted by a very human simile, that of the harlot. The history of Israel is told as a parable: a traveller finds a newborn girl baby by the wayside and brings her up to womanhood, but she becomes corrupted and sells her favours, to neighbouring peoples. In another parable, Israel and Judah appear as two lascivious sisters who are first defiled in Egypt and then become prostitutes.

In the millennium he prophesies, Ezekiel imagines an invasion of the country by an army from the extreme north, led by King Gog of Magog, an unknown country somewhere in the Black Sea region. The barbarian hordes on horseback would sweep down on the peaceful countryside and undefended towns of Israel. But they would be destroyed by the convulsion of nature the Lord would unleash on them: '... On that day there shall be a great shaking in the land of Israel; ... and the mountains shall be thrown down, and the cliffs shall fall, and every wall shall tumble to the ground.' (Ezek. 38:19, 20) Fire, brimstone and hail would rain down on the invaders. Their corpses would be scattered over the whole country, and it would take seven months to gather them and bury them in the steep gorge of the Arnon river, leading into the Dead Sea from the east. Their weapons would provide the Israelites with firewood for seven winters. This demonstration of the Lord's power would exalt his name among all the nations.

Ezekiel's vivid pictorial imagination is not matched by the quality of his literary style. Much of it is rather prosaic, compared to the sublime poetry of Isaiah or the fervent eloquence of Jeremiah. There are, however, passages of sharp invective, and others of brilliant descriptive power. Some of the best of these occur in the oracles against Tyre and Egypt.

It is likely that he learnt about Tyre, the great Phoenician seaport on the Mediterranean coast, from the Tyrian captives he met in Babylon. He vividly describes the city's almost impregnable location, on a rocky offshore island. (It took the Babylonians thirteen years to capture it.) Its far-ranging merchant fleet was the source of its wealth and power: 'The ships of Tarshish travelled for you with your merchandise. So you were filled and heavily laden in the heart of the seas. Your rowers have brought you out into the high seas.' (Ezek. 27:25, 26) He deplored the arrogance of its king who thought of himself as a divinity. 'Because your heart is proud, and you have said, "I am a god, I sit in the seat of the gods, in the heart of the seas", yet you are but a man, and no god ...' (Ezek. 28:2) The city-state of Tyre was like a glittering Garden of Eden. Yet no earthly city could withstand the Lord. 'They shall destroy the walls of Tyre, and break down her towers; and I will scrape her soil from her, and make her a bare rock.' (Ezek. 26:4)

The haughtiness of the ruler of Egypt is also offensive to God. 'Behold, I am against you, Pharaoh king of Egypt, the great dragon that lies in the midst of his streams, that says, "My Nile is my own; I made it." ... I will put hooks in your jaws, ... And I will cast you forth into the wilderness, you and all the fish of your streams.' (Ezek. 29:3, 5)

EZEKIEL'S CREED

Unlike other prophets, who stood outside the priestly establishment and were often in conflict with it, Ezekiel respected organized religious observance and established religious laws. The regulations for worship set out in his fourth vision for the future common-wealth draw a clear line between the sacred and the profane.

At the same time, Ezekiel broke with tradition by rejecting the concept of collective guilt and retribution. He asserted that each individual was solely responsible for his own actions: 'The soul that sins shall die. The son shall not suffer for the iniquity of the father, nor the father suffer for the iniquity of the son; the righteousness of the righteous shall be upon himself, and the wickedness of the wicked shall be upon himself.' (Ezek. 18:20)

Ezekiel's religious creed has two main sources: his intense and mystical personal revelation of the glory of God; and his belief that the Hebrew nation has a holy calling which cannot be betrayed without punishment. The independence of his people has been wiped out because its covenant with God has been broken; but it will be offered a fresh start and a new covenant. 'I will take the stony heart out of their flesh and give them heart of flesh, that they may walk in my statutes and keep my ordinances and obey them; and they shall be my people, and I will be their God.' (Ezek. 11:19, 20) [Book of Ezekiel]

Ezer (Heb. 'help') *1.* date unknown. Son of Seir the Horite and an Edomite leader. [Gen. 36:21, 27, 30; 1 Chr. 1:38, 42]
2. c. 16 century BC. One of the sons of Ephraim who was killed by the men of Gath for trying to steal their cattle. [1 Chr. 7:21]
3. date unknown. A leader of the tribe of Judah descended from Hur. [1 Chr. 4:4]
4. c. 11 century BC. Leader of a group of warriors of the tribe of Gad who deserted from King Saul's army and rallied to David's support. [1 Chr. 12:9]
5. 5 century BC. A priest who helped rebuild the walls of Jerusalem in the time of Nehemiah. [Neh. 3:19]
6. 5 century BC. A priest who took part in the service for the rebuilt walls of Jerusalem in the time of Nehemiah. [Neh. 12:42]

Ezra (Heb. 'help') *1.* 6 century BC. A leading priest who returned with Zerubbabel to Judah from exile in Babylon. [Neh. 12:1]
2. 5 century BC. Hebrew priest and scribe. Ezra was a Hebrew priest and scribe who played a notable role in the restoration of Judea by exiles returning from Babylonia.

The first Judean deportees, including the young King Jehoiachin, had been taken to Babylon by Nebuchadnezzar in 598 BC. Their number was swelled in 587 BC when Jerusalem was destroyed and the kingdom of Judah came to an end.

In 539 BC Babylon was captured by King Cyrus of Persia, who then became the master of the Near East. Cyrus issued a decree in 538 BC permitting the Jews to return to their homeland and rebuild it. Some forty thousand of them did so, and the Temple was restored on the original site in Jerusalem.

The community of exiles who remained in Babylon seems to have prospered under the benign Persian rule, and some of its members gained influential positions. However, they clung to their own faith and traditions encouraged by notable prophets like Ezekiel, as well as by such scholars and teachers as Ezra. They also kept in touch with their brethren in Judea, collected funds to help them and felt themselves involved with the progress of the restoration. Ezra resolved to go to Jerusalem, investigate the conditions there, and reform the religious life of the settlers. There is reason to believe that he had attained an official position at the Persian Court, as a commissioner for the affairs of the Jewish minority. At any rate, he was able to obtain palace sponsorship and aid for his trip. The time was 458 BC in the seventh year of the reign of Artaxerxes I and eighty years after the edict of Cyrus had started the movement back to the Holy Land.

The Hebrew bible quotes in Aramaic the royal document authorizing Ezra's mission. It states that he is being sent by the king and his seven counsellors '... to make inquiries about Judah and Jerusalem according to the law of your God, which is in your hand' (Ezra 7:14). Any of the Israelites in the kingdom, including priests and Levites, who wish to accompany Ezra may do so. With the official money grant, as well as voluntary offerings by Ezra's fellow-Jews, he is to buy animals to sacrifice in the Jerusalem Temple on behalf of the king. Any funds left over may be spent at Ezra's discretion. For whatever else may be necessary for the Temple, Ezra is authorized to draw on the royal treasury. The treasurers of the beyond-the-river region (west of the Euphrates) are commanded to supply Ezra with stated amounts of money, wheat, wine, oil and salt for the Temple. The priests and staff of the Temple are to be exempt from taxes. Ezra is to appoint scribes and judges to administer and teach the Jewish Law. 'Whoever will not obey the law of your God and the law of the king, let judgment be strictly executed upon him, whether for death or for banishment or for confiscation of his goods or for imprisonment.' (Ezra 7:26)

In the diary contained in Chapters 7 to 9, Ezra records that the number of persons who gathered together to accompany him numbered some fifteen hundred men, or about five thousand souls in all, divided into twelve family clans.

Ezra assembled the whole party on the banks of a river, where they camped for three days. In reviewing his mixed contingent of settlers, Ezra realized that though it included a group of priests,

there were no Levites, the traditional Temple staff. He sent a deputation to Iddo, the head priest of the Jewish shrine at Casiphia, who recruited several Levite families for the expedition. Ezra chose twelve of the priests to serve as trustees of the gold and silver Temple vessels and the money donations for the Temple. They were to be responsible for handing them over at the journey's end in accordance with the inventory.

THE JERUSALEM MISSION

On arrival in Jerusalem they rested for three days. After that the treasure was delivered at the Temple, the sacrifices were offered that the king had commanded, and Ezra's royal letter of instructions was handed over to the local authorities.

Ezra now set about promoting the central purpose of the mission – to restore strict religious observance and revive the national identity of the repatriate congregation, which had been weakened in the decades since the original Return. The most immediate and sensitive issue was that of the mixed marriages between the leading Jewish families, including priests, and the 'foreign women' belonging to other local ethnic groups. Ezra was determined to break these unions and to restore the exclusiveness of the Hebrews.

Using the powers vested in him, Ezra ordered all the men of Jerusalem and the Judean towns to attend a mass meeting in the Temple compound within three days, on pain of exclusion from the community and confiscation of property. The gathering shivered with apprehension – and also from the heavy rain and cold. Ezra addressed them sternly, 'You have transgressed and married foreign women, ... Now then make confession ... separate yourselves from the peoples of the land and from the foreign wives.' (Ezra 10:10,11) The people sadly agreed to this drastic measure. A commission of two priests and two Levites was set up to supervise the multiple divorce proceedings which lasted for two months.

Nothing more is recorded of Ezra's actions for the next thirteen years. In the meantime a new Jewish governor, Nehemiah, had been sent to Jerusalem from the Persian court to administer what was now the province of 'Yahud'. He was an able and energetic man, who restored the fortifications of the city and increased its population by drawing on the smaller Judean towns and villages.

The time had come for Ezra to establish the religious law more firmly as the basis of daily life. He had brought with him from Babylon the codified Scriptures. On the first day of the seventh month the whole community gathered in the square at the water-gate, while Ezra, standing on a wooden dais, and in the presence of Nehemiah, the governor, read out to them the sacred book, and they wept with emotion. He called to them not to weep but to eat, drink and be glad of heart 'for this day is holy to our Lord; do not be grieved, for the joy of the Lord is your strength' (Neh. 8:10).

The next day Ezra continued the study of the Law together with the Levites and heads of families. When they read that 'the people of Israel should dwell in booths during the feast of the seventh month' (Neh. 8:14), it was decided immediately to revive the festival of Succoth (Tabernacles), commemorating the time when their ancestors were led out of Egypt by Moses and wandered for forty years in the wilderness. (In the cycle of the agricultural year this was the autumn harvest festival.) From every Judean town the menfolk went out to collect branches of olive, pine, myrtle and palm for constructing booths on the flat roof-tops and in the courtyards and public squares. The festival lasted seven days and on the eighth day another solemn assembly was held.

Ezra consolidated the religious and legal code of the small Jewish community in the Holy Land, and thereby laid the foundations for the later development of Judaism as a creed and a way of life.

EZRA AND NEHEMIAH

The precise date of Ezra's mission to Jerusalem is problematical – in particular, whether it took place before, during or after Nehemiah's governorship, that started in 446 BC.

Ezra states that he made his journey in the seventh year of the reign of Artaxerxes, but this date creates difficulties in the sequence of events. Two other theories have been put forward: that the word 'seventh' is a corruption for 'thirty-seventh', so that the date of Ezra's return would be 428 and not 458 BC; or that the monarch referred to is not Artaxerxes I Longimanus (465–24 BC) but Artaxerxes II Mnemon (404–358 BC), which would give 397 BC as the date for Ezra.

In their respective personal memoirs Ezra and Nehemiah do not refer to each other at all. In the third person narrative in the Book of Nehemiah, describing the reading of the Law by Ezra, Nehemiah's name appears as being present, but this could have been inserted by a later chronicler.

There is reason to believe that Ezra-Nehemiah originally formed a single Book, continuing the Book of Chronicles and compiled by the same chronicler. That is the way it appeared in the Greek and Latin bibles. However, Ezra and Nehemiah were later split into two Books in the Hebrew bible, and consequently in the Protestant versions. This division is an unsatisfactory one, as the most important part of Ezra's work – the reading of the Book of the Law and the religious reforms which followed it – remain in Chapters 8, 9 and 10 of the Book of Nehemiah. [Books of Ezra and Nehemiah]

Ezrah (Heb. 'help') date unknown. A leader of the tribe of Judah descended from Caleb, son of Jephunneh. [1 Chr. 4:17]

Ezri (Heb. 'my help') *c.* 10 century BC.

Son of Chelub, he was appointed by King David to supervise the work of tilling the soil on the royal estates. [1 Chr. 27:26]

G

Gaal (Heb. 'contempt') *c.* 12 century BC. Son of Ebed, he organized a revolt among the inhabitants of Shechem against Abimelech, king of the district of Shechem and challenged him to battle. Gaal was defeated and driven out of Shechem by the governor, Zebul. [Judg. 9:26–41]

Gabbai (Heb. 'gatherer') 5 century BC. A Benjaminite chief who settled in Jerusalem after the return from exile in Babylon. [Neh. 11:8]

Gabriel (Heb. 'man of God') An angel who appeared to the prophet Daniel bringing him the word of God. [Dan. 8:16; 9:21]

Gad (Heb. 'fortune') *1. c.* 16 century BC. Seventh son of Jacob. Gad was the eldest son of Zilpah, the maid of Jacob's wife Leah. Believing herself past childbearing age, Leah gave Zilpah to her husband as a concubine.

Together with his brothers, Gad was involved in the events that led to the selling of their brother Joseph into slavery in Egypt. Later he was one of the ten sons sent by Jacob to buy corn in Egypt where Joseph had become a leading figure at Pharaoh's court. When Jacob went to settle in Egypt with all his family, it included Gad's seven sons.

On his deathbed Jacob blessed his sons in turn. Of Gad he said, 'Raiders shall raid Gad, but he shall raid at their heels.' (Gen. 49:19)

Centuries later in the conquest of Canaan under Joshua, the tribe of Gad was allocated an extensive territory east of the Jordan on condition they took part in the conquest west of the river. In the blessing attributed to Moses, it is said that 'Gad couches like a lion. ... He chose the best of the land for himself.' (Deut. 33:20, 21) [Gen. 30:11; 35:26; 46:16; 49:19; Exod. 1:4; Deut. 33:20, 21]

2. c. 10 century BC. A prophet in the time of King David. When David was hiding from King Saul, Gad advised him not to remain in the cave of Adullam because Saul might capture him there but to go into the land of Judah. Later, when David was king and angered the Lord by taking a census, Gad told him that God had offered him a choice of punishments – famine, military defeat or pestilence. David chose pestilence but after many thousands of people had died, he prayed to God to stop the plague and Gad came to him and told him to build an altar on the threshing floor of Araunah, the Jebusite. Gad is referred to in the Book of Chronicles as the author of a book on the acts of King David. [I Sam. 22:5; 2 Sam. 24:11–18; 1 Chr. 21:9–19; 29:29; 2 Chr. 29:25]

Gaddi (Heb. 'my fortune') *c.* 13 century BC. A leader of the tribe of Manasseh and the son of Susi, he was one of the twelve men sent by Moses to spy out the land of Israel. [Num. 13:11]

Gaddiel (Heb. 'fortune of God') *c.* 13 century BC. Son of Sodi of the tribe of Zebulun, he was one of the twelve men sent by Moses to spy out the land of Israel. [Num. 13:10]

Gadi (Heb. 'my fortune') 8 century BC. Father of Menahem who assassinated King Shallum and reigned in his stead for ten years. [2 Kgs. 15:14–17]

Gaham *c.* 18 century BC. A son of Abraham's brother Nahor by his concubine Reumah, he became the founder of a desert tribe. [Gen. 22:24]

Gahar date unknown. Ancestor of a family of temple servants that returned with Zerubbabel to Judah from exile in Babylon. [Ezra 2:47; Neh. 7:49]

Galal (Heb. 'God has removed [my shame]') *1.* 6 century BC. One of the first Levites to settle in Jerusalem following the return from exile in Babylon. [1 Chr. 9:15] *2.* 5 century BC. Father of Shemaiah, head of a family of Levites who served in Jerusalem after the return from Babylon in the time of Nehemiah. [1 Chr. 9:16; Neh. 11:17]

Gamaliel (Heb. 'recompense of God') *c.* 13 century BC. Leader of the tribe of Manasseh appointed by Moses to take a census of the men of his tribe fit for war. [Num. 1:10; 2:20; 7:54–9; 10:23]

Gamul (Heb. 'is rewarded') 10 century BC. A Levite and head of the twenty-second of the priestly course who served in the Tabernacle at the time of King David. [1 Chr. 24:17]

Garmite *see* KEILAH

Gareb (Heb. 'potter') 10 century BC. An Ithrite, he was one of King David's outstanding warriors. [2 Sam. 23:38; 1 Chr. 11:40]

Gatam (Heb. 'small and thick') *c.* 16 century BC. A son of Eliphaz and a grandson of Esau, he was an Edomite leader. [Gen. 36:11, 16; 1 Chr. 1:36]

Gazez (Heb. 'sheep-shearer') *1. c.* 13 century BC. Son of Caleb of the tribe of Judah, by his concubine Ephah. [1 Chr. 2:46] *2.* 13 century BC. The son of Haran and a grandson of Caleb. [1 Chr. 2:46]

Gazzam (Heb. 'wood-cutter') date unknown. Ancestor of a family of temple servants who returned with Zerubbabel to Judah from exile in Babylon. [Ezra 2:48; Neh. 7:51]

Geber (Heb. 'man') 10 century BC. Son of Uri, he was one of the twelve officers appointed by King Solomon to supply the provisions of the royal household. [1 Kgs. 4:19]

Gedaliah (Heb. 'God is great') *1.* 10 century BC. Son of Jeduthun, one of King David's chief musicians. Gedaliah and his brothers took the second turn of service in the Tabernacle under their father's direction. [1 Chr. 25:3, 9]
2. c. 7 century BC. Grandfather of the prophet Zephaniah. [Zeph. 1:1]
3. c. 6 century BC. Governor of Judah. On the fall of Jerusalem in the summer of 587 BC and the capture of King Zedekiah, the Babylonians appointed Gedaliah the son of Ahikam as governor. Some of the surviving Judean officers and their men came to see him at Mizpah, just north of Jerusalem, and he urged them to cooperate with the conquerors: 'Do not be afraid because of the Chaldean officials; dwell in the land, and serve the king of Babylon, and it shall be well with you.' (2 Kgs. 25:24) This advice went unheeded. Soon after a small group of political exiles assassinated Gedaliah and fled to Egypt. [2 Kgs. 25:22–5; Jer. 39:14; 40:5–16; 41:1–10, 16; 43:6]
4. 6 century BC. Son of Pashhur, he was one of the nobles of Judah who threw Jeremiah into a pit for prophesying that those who surrendered to the Babylonians would be saved but those who stayed in Jerusalem would die. [Jer. 38:1–6]

5. 5 century BC. A priest who divorced his non-Jewish wife at the request of Ezra. [Ezra 10:18]

Gedor (Heb. 'wall') *c.* 11 century BC. One of the ten sons of Jeiel and Maachah, and an ancestor of Saul, the first king of Israel. [1 Chr. 8:31; 9:37]

Gehazi (Heb. 'valley of vision') *c.* 9 century BC. Gehazi was the manservant of the prophet Elisha. When the prophet wanted to reward the lady of Shunem for her kindness to him, it was Gehazi who pointed out that she was childless. Elisha blessed her and the following year she gave birth to a boy. She rushed to Elisha when the child died. Gehazi was sent ahead with the prophet's staff, but the boy could not be revived till Elisha came personally and performed a miracle.

Later, after a long absence because of the drought, the woman was able to recover her property because Gehazi identified her to the king. 'My lord, O king, here is the woman, and here is her son whom Elisha restored to life.' (2 Kgs. 8:5) [2 Kgs. 4, 5, 8:5]

Gemalli (Heb. 'my recompense from God') *c.* 13 century BC. A member of the tribe of Dan, his son Ammiel was one of the twelve spies sent by Moses to reconnoitre the land of Israel. [Num. 13:12]

Gemariah (Heb. 'perfected by God') *1.* *c.* 7 century BC. Son of Shaphan the scribe, he was a leader of Judah. His son Micaiah told the leaders of Jeremiah's dire prophecies about the people of Judah. [Jer. 36:10–12, 25]
2. 6 century BC. Son of Hilkiah, he was sent from Jerusalem with a letter of comfort from Jeremiah the prophet to the exiles in Babylon. [Jer. 29:3]

Genubath (Heb. 'theft') 10 century BC. Son of Hadad the Edomite who fled to Egypt after David's attack on Edom. His mother was the sister of Tahpenes, queen of Egypt, and he was brought up together with Pharaoh's sons. [1 Kgs. 11:20]

Gera (Heb. 'stranger') *1.* *c.* 16 century BC. One of the ten sons of Benjamin. [Gen. 46:21; 1 Chr. 8:3, 5, 7]
2. *c.* 16 century BC. Son of Bela and a grandson of Benjamin. Also called Heglam. [1 Chr. 8:3, 7]
3. *c.* 12 century BC. Father of Ehud who delivered the children of Israel from subservience to Eglon, king of Moab, by slaying him and then leading a successful expedition against the confused Moabites. [Judg. 3:15]
4. *c.* 10 century BC. A Benjaminite who was a member of the royal family of King Saul. His son Shimei cursed King David and threw stones at him at the time of Absalom's revolt. [2 Sam. 16:5; 19:16, 18:1 Kgs. 2:8]

Gershom (Heb. 'exiled') *1.* *c.* 16 century BC. Sometimes called Gershon, he was the eldest of Levi's three sons. During the Exodus, his Levite descendants were given the task of carrying the Tabernacle, and had charge of its coverings and hangings. [Gen. 46:11; Exod. 6:16, 17; Num. 3:21-6; 4:22-6; 7:7; 10:17; 26:57; Josh. 21:6; 1 Chr. 6:43; 15:7]
2. *c.* 13 century BC. Moses's first child born to his wife Zipporah during the sojourn of Moses in Midian. Moses gave him that name for he said, 'I have been a stranger in a strange land' (Exod. 2:22). (The Hebrew word 'ger' means a stranger.) Zipporah performed a dramatic circumcision on the boy with a sharp stone, to avert Moses being killed by God. One of Gershom's descendants served as a priest to the graven image set up by the tribe of Dan. [Exod. 2:22; 4:25; 18:3; Judg. 18:30; 1 Chr. 23:15, 16; 26:24]
3. *c.* 5 century BC. A descendant of the high priest Phinehas, he returned with

Ezra to Jerusalem from the Babylonian exile. [Ezra 8:2]

Gershon *see* GERSHOM I.

Geshan date unknown. One of the six sons of Jahdai of the tribe of Judah, he was a descendant of Caleb. [1 Chr. 2:47]

Geshem (Heb. 'rain') 5 century BC. An Arab prince who derided Nehemiah's work of rebuilding the walls of Jerusalem and tried to hinder it by spreading the rumour that the Jews would revolt against Persian rule when Jerusalem was rebuilt. He also plotted to assassinate Nehemiah. [Neh. 2:19; 6:1-6]

Gether date unknown. One of the four sons of Aram and a grandson of Shem. [Gen. 10:23; 1 Chr. 1:17]

Geuel (Heb. 'majesty of God') *c.* 13 century BC. Son of Machi of the tribe of Gad, he was one of the twelve spies sent by Moses to reconnoitre the land of Israel. [Num. 13:15]

Gibbar (Heb. 'strong') date unknown. Ancestor of a family who returned with Zerubbabel to Judah from exile in Babylon. Also called Gibeon. [Ezra 2:20; Neh. 7:25]

Gibea (Heb. 'hill') date unknown. A grandson of Caleb of the tribe of Judah. [1 Chr. 2:49]

Gibeon *see* GIBBAR

Gibeonites Inhabitants of the town of Gibeon, north-west of Jerusalem, they made a treaty with Joshua by a ruse and thereby saved their city from attack. King Saul failed to respect the agreement and King David later made atonement for this breach. The Bible refers to them as Hivites and also as 'the remnant of

the Amorites' (2 Sam. 21:2). [Josh. 9; 10; 11; 2 Sam. 21:1-4, 9]

Giddalti (Heb. 'I have praised') 10 century BC. Son of Heman, one of King David's chief musicians. Giddalti and his brothers played musical instruments in the Tabernacle services under their father's direction. His family was responsible for the twenty-second turn of service. [1 Chr. 25:4, 29]

Giddel 1. (Heb. 'praised') 10 century BC. A servant of King Solomon whose descendants returned with Zerubbabel to Judah from exile in Babylon. [Ezra 2:56; Neh. 7:58]
2. date unknown. Ancestor of a family of Temple servants who returned with Zerubbabel from exile in Babylon. [Ezra 2:47; Neh. 7:49]

Gideon (Heb. 'hewer') *c.* 12 century BC. Judge of Israel and military commander. The story of Gideon belongs to the period after Joshua's invasion when the Israelite tribes were struggling to hold their allotted territories against the pressure of neighbouring peoples. From time to time, a tribal leader or hero would emerge to free his people from the oppressors. These spontaneous leaders in times of stress were known as judges, since they acquired the moral authority to settle disputes.

Gideon was the fifth of the judges listed in the book of that name, and one of the most outstanding. The enemy he fought was the Midianites, one of the lean and hungry nomad tribes that roamed the uncharted wasteland of Arabia and periodically erupted into the fertile areas. Gideon's battle was one episode in the immemorial struggle between the 'Desert' and the 'Sown'. In the previous century, the Israelites themselves had been tent-dwelling nomads from the eastern desert who had fought their way into the Promised Land.

The Midianites were not the only

nomads penetrating into Canaan in Gideon's time. The Bible refers to the Amalekites pressing in from the south as far as the Gaza area, and to 'the people of the East' (Judg. 6:3). They may have been driven by drought to seek food, pasture and water. Also, there was a breakdown of authority in Canaan. Egypt's control had faded, while local conflicts had weakened the security of the country against outside invaders. Earlier, Deborah's victory had relieved the pressure of local Canaanite kings on the Israelites. But the Jezreel valley region remained exposed to the camel-riding Midianite raiders from the east. By the time Gideon challenged them, they had for seven years been harassing this area, coming in across the river like locust swarms, looting, killing and destroying the harvests.

Gideon was the youngest son of Joash, a farmer of the Abiezer clan in the tribe of Manasseh. The family lived at Ophrah, in the hills between Shechem (Nablus) and the Jezreel valley. One day Gideon was threshing wheat, concealed in the winepress for fear of roving Midianite bandits. A stranger was suddenly seen sitting under a nearby oak tree. It was an angel who told him that the Lord wanted him to rescue Israel from the power of Midian. Gideon demurred, saying: '... how can I deliver Israel? Behold, my clan is the weakest in Manasseh, and I am the least in my family.' (Judg. 6:15) Gideon went into the house, prepared a young goat, made unleavened cakes and a pot of broth, and brought the food to his visitor, who asked him to place it on a rock. The angel then touched the meat and unleavened cakes with the tip of his staff. Fire sprang from the rock and consumed the offering, while the angel vanished. Gideon was convinced that the message was authentic, and built an altar to the Lord on that spot.

That night the Lord commanded him to break down the local altar to Baal, to cut down the sacred grove next to it, and to sacrifice a young bullock, using the wood from the grove for the fire. This Gideon did under cover of darkness, with the help of ten servants. Next morning the townspeople learned that Gideon had destroyed the pagan altar and grove, and came to his father to demand his death. Joash retorted: 'Will you contend for Baal? ... If he is a god, let him contend for himself, because his altar has been pulled down.' (Judg. 6:31) That day his father gave Gideon the additional name of Jerubbaal, meaning 'Let Baal contend against him.' (Judg. 6:32)

THE BATTLE OF AIN HAROD

The Midianites pitched their camp in the valley of Jezreel near the hill of Moreh, and Gideon issued a call to arms. First his own clan of Abiezer rallied round him, followed by the rest of the tribe of Manasseh. He then sent messengers to the three Galilee tribes of Asher, Zebulun and Naphtali and they joined him. Before proceeding further, Gideon requested the Lord to give him further signs of divine approval. Twice he put a sheep's fleece out on the threshing floor at night. The first time the fleece was soaked with dew while the ground around it remained dry; while the second time the ground was wet and the fleece dry. Since these were the proofs Gideon had requested beforehand, he was reassured.

Altogether thirty-two thousand men mustered at the spring of Harod, at the foot of Mount Gilboa on the southern edge of the Jezreel valley. The position faced the Midianite camp a few miles across the valley. Gideon set about reducing his forces drastically. The scriptural reason was that the Lord wanted the Israelites to realize that victory would be gained by his strength and not their own strength of numbers. Actually, Gideon's own battle tactics called for a small, mobile picked force rather than an unwieldy mass of men.

It was proclaimed that everyone who was fearful of battle could go home, and twenty-two thousand promptly left. The remaining ten thousand were sent to the pool at the spring, to quench their thirst. Three hundred of them did not fling themselves down on the ground and put their faces in the water like the rest, but scooped it up and lapped it out of their hands – thereby proving themselves to be wary and alert in the face of the enemy. These three hundred were then held for the operation and the rest dismissed. Gideon had pinned his faith on a commando attack at night, exploiting surprise and psychological weapons.

That night the commander carried out a personal reconnaissance. Accompanied only by his servant Purah, Gideon stole into the slumbering Midianite camp, and overheard two soldiers talking to each other. One told about a dream he had in which a loaf of barley-bread came rolling through the camp and knocked down a tent. The other interpreted the dream as prophesying that they would be defeated by the Israelites. Gideon fell to his knees in thankfulness at this good omen.

He returned to his own camp, aroused his men and organized them for the assault. He divided them into three companies of a hundred each, and issued each man with a trumpet and a lighted torch inside an empty pitcher. They crept up to the enemy camp and spread themselves around its edge. At a given signal from Gideon, the Israelites rushed in from all sides. They shouted, 'A sword for the Lord and for Gideon!' (Judg. 7:20), blew their trumpets, smashed the pitchers and waved the torches – which were no doubt also used to set fire to the tents. The Midianites were thrown into panic and in the dark started striking each other down. They then fled in confusion down the Beth-shean valley towards the Jordan river fords.

The three hundred who carried out the attack were probably Gideon's own clansmen. The men from the other northern tribes joined in the pursuit of the fleeing Midianites. Gideon sent messengers to the tribesmen of Ephraim asking them to seize the crossing-places along the Jordan and harass the retreat. They did so, capturing two Midianite chiefs, Oreb ('the raven') and Zeeb ('the wolf'). The two were killed and their heads sent to Gideon.

The Ephraimites were indignant because Gideon had not summoned them to fight from the beginning of the battle. They were sensitive about their standing as the leading tribe in the north. Gideon soothed them down with flattery, maintaining that their role had been decisive, especially in disposing of the two Midianite leaders.

The remnant of the Midianite army streamed down the Jordan valley, managed to get across the river, and sought to escape eastward. Gideon and his three hundred crossed behind them. They reached the town of Succoth exhausted and hungry, and Gideon asked for some provisions to feed his men. He was refused, as the local inhabitants were afraid of the Midianites and distrustful of Gideon's victory claims. Referring to the Midianite kings Gideon was pursuing, they asked, 'Are Zebah and Zalmunna already in your hand, that we should give bread to your army?' (Judg. 8:6) (This was a reference to the practice of chopping off the hands of slain enemies, as tangible proof.) Gideon was given the same churlish rebuff at Penuel, the next town. He angrily swore to deal with them when he came back, and pressed on with the pursuit.

He caught up with the Midianites two hundred miles away at Karkor, travelling the ancient route of the nomads and caravans. Feeling that they had shaken off their pursuers and could relax, the Midianites had bivouacked in a valley between rocky ridges. Here Gideon's men again sprang a surprise attack on them and routed them, capturing the two kings.

Before returning across the Jordan, Gideon settled accounts with the two towns that had refused him help. Approaching Succoth before dawn, they caught a young man who drew up a list for them of the important men of the town, seventy-seven of them. Gideon rounded them up, showed them the two captive Midianite kings, and had them beaten with thorn-bushes. At Penuel he demolished the city tower and slew some of the men.

Interrogated by Gideon, the Midianite kings admitted to killing Israelites at Mount Tabor who had resembled Gideon and had carried themselves as proudly as princes. Gideon said they had been his own brothers; if they had been spared, he would have spared the kings. He ordered his eldest son, Jether, to kill the captives but the lad shrank from drawing his sword. As a matter of honour, the kings implored Gideon himself to strike the mortal blow, which he did.

After Gideon had broken the power of the Midianites, his own people pressed him to become king over them and establish a dynasty. Gideon refused, saying that their king was the Lord. His only request was that from the booty he should be given the gold earrings and other ornaments worn by the Midianites, as well as the gold collars of their camels. He spread a garment on to which these contributions were thrown. From the gold Gideon fashioned an ephod or sacred object that was set up in Ophrah, his home town, to commemorate his victory. But the ephod proved a snare, for the common people came from all around to worship it as an idol.

By subduing the Midianites, Gideon had won security for his people for the next generation. He himself retired to private life in Ophrah where he lived as a man of wealth and honour, with many wives who bore him seventy sons.

Gideon reached a ripe old age and on his death was buried in the tomb of his father Joash at Ophrah. Also known as Jerubbaal and Jerubbeshetho. [Judg. 6:11–39; 7; 8:4–35; 9:1, 5, 16, 19, 24, 28, 57; 1 Sam. 12:11; 2 Sam. 11:21]

Gideoni (Heb. 'hewer') *c.* 13 century BC. Father of Abidan who was chosen by Moses as a leader of the tribe of Benjamin. [Num. 1:11; 2:22; 7:60–5; 10:24]

Gilalai 5 century BC. A Levite musician who played at the dedication ceremony in Jerusalem in the time of Nehemiah. [Neh. 12:36]

Gilead (Heb. 'rocky') *1.* date unknown. Son of Machir and a grandson of Manasseh, he gave his name to the area of Gilead east of the river Jordan and was the founder of the tribe of Gileadites. [Num. 26:29, 30; 27:1; 36:1; Josh. 17:1–3; 1 Chr. 2:21–3; 5:14; 7:14, 17]
2. c. 12 century BC. Father of Jephthah, one of the judges of Israel. [Judg. 11:1, 2]
3. date unknown. Son of Michael, recorded in the genealogy of the tribe of Gad. [1 Chr. 5:14]

Ginath (Heb. 'garden') *c.* 9 century BC. Father of Tibni who contested the throne of Israel with Omri after the death of King Zimri, and was eventually put to death by Omri. [1 Kgs. 16:21, 22]

Ginnethoi 6 century BC. The head of a priestly family that returned to Judah with Zerubbabel from exile in Babylon. [Neh. 12:4]

Ginnethon 5 century BC. Head of a priestly family who returned to Judah from captivity in Babylon, he signed the solemn covenant in the time of Nehemiah. [Neh. 10:6; 12:16]

Gishpa *c.* 5 century BC. One of the two

Levites who supervised the work of the Temple servants after the return from exile in Babylon. [Neh. 11:21]

Gog *1.* date unknown. The son of Shemaiah and a leader of the tribe of Reuben. [1 Chr. 5:4]
2. date unknown. The symbolic leader of Meshech and Tubal whom Ezekiel prophesied would join forces with other nations against the land of Israel 'in the latter years' (Ezek. 38:8) and be utterly destroyed in the ensuing battle. [Ezek. 38; 39:1–16]

Goliath *c.* 11 century BC. The Philistine slain by David.

King Saul and his army faced the Philistine troops in the Vale of Elah across a narrow valley, through which ran a stream. Neither side would risk an attack. In this stalemate, the Philistines produced a fearsome champion named Goliath, from the city of Gath, a giant of a man clad in brass helmet and armour, equipped with a massive spear and sword, and preceded by a shield bearer. Every day he paraded up and down between the lines scornfully challenging any Israelite soldier to meet him in single combat. Goliath cried out, 'choose a man for yourselves, and let him come down to me. If he is able to fight with me and kill me, then we will be your servants: but if I prevail against him and kill him, then you shall be our servants and serve us.' (1 Sam. 17:8, 9)

Saul was in a humiliating position, for he had no man who could match the giant in size and strength. At this point David, the shepherd lad, arrived in the camp with provisions for his brothers, and prevailed on Saul to let him face Goliath. The giant was dumbfounded when the Israelite 'champion' who came out to fight him was a mere youth armed only with a stave, a sling and a pouch into which he put a few round pebbles from the brook. He bellowed at David, 'Am I a dog, that you come to me with

sticks? ... Come to me, and I will give in your flesh to the birds of the air and to the beasts of the field.' (1 Sam 17:43, 44)

In the combat, Goliath's vastly superior power was pitted against David's nimbleness and unorthodox tactics. Each time the giant lumbered forward, David slipped out of reach towards his own lines. When the sweating Goliath paused, David's sling whipped round and the stone hit his opponent square in the forehead, so that he fell down stunned. In a flash David leapt upon him, and using Goliath's sword, severed his head. Overcome with dread at this abrupt end, the Philistines turned and fled, with the Israelites pursuing them across the border.

The story of David and Goliath has remained the classic parable of superior odds being overcome by faith, daring and skill. [1 Sam. 17; 21:9; 22:10]

Gomer (Heb. 'ember') *1.* date unknown. Eldest son of Japheth and a grandson of Noah. Ezekiel prophesied that Gomer's descendants would be destroyed in the battle 'in the latter years' (Ezek. 38:8) between Gog and Israel. [Gen. 10:2, 3; 1 Chr. 1:5, 6; Ezek. 38:6]
2. c. 8 century BC. Wife of the prophet Hosea, Gomer was the daughter of Diblaim. She was a loose woman but bore him three children to whom he gave names of bitter rejection. Hosea divorced her but continued to love her and at some later stage appeared to have forgiven her and taken her back. She is obviously a symbol of the relation between God and Israel. [Hos. 1:3]

Guni *1. c.* 16 century BC. One of the four sons of Naphtali, and the head of the Gunite family. [Gen. 46:24; Num. 26:48; I Chr. 7:13]
2. c. 8 century BC. A leader of the tribe of Gad and the father of Abdiel. [1 Chr. 5:15]

H

Haahashtari date unknown. Son of Ashhur and a leader of the tribe of Judah. [1 Chr. 4:6]

Habaiah (Heb. 'God hides') date unknown. Ancestor of a family of priests who returned with Zerubbabel to Judah from exile in Babylon but were barred from officiating as priests because their genealogy could not be satisfactorily traced. Also called Hobaiah. [Ezra 2:61; Neh. 7:63]

Habakkuk (Ass. 'basil plant') *c*. end of 7 century BC. A Hebrew prophet in the kingdom of Judah. Habakkuk probably lived in Jerusalem in the last phase of the kingdom of Judah. The short prophetical Book bearing his name has been dated soon after the defeat of the Egyptians by the Babylonians at Carchemish in 605 BC, when Nebuchadnezzar became the new master of the Near East.

The first part of the Book is a dialogue between the prophet and God, in the form of two complaints answered by two oracles. The reflective Habakkuk is troubled by what appears to be divine indifference to evil and oppression: '... the law is slacked and justice never goes forth. For the wicked surround the righteous, so justice goes forth perverted.' (Hab. 1:4) The Lord indicates that worse is yet to come, and vividly describes the coming invasion of the Chaldeans (Babylonians), '... that bitter and hasty nation, who march through the breadth of the earth, to seize habitations not their own' (Hab. 1:6). They are an arrogant people who scoff at kings and princes, and scoop up prisoners like sand. Their horses are swifter than leopards and fiercer than wolves in the dark.

The prophet returns to his protest that God should not permit his people to suffer unjustly. 'Thou who art of purer eyes than to behold evil and canst not look on wrong, why dost thou look on faithless men, and art silent when the wicked swallows up the man more righteous than he?' (Hab. 1:13)

God does not explain, but instructs the prophet to write down his vision on clay tablets and to wait patiently for its fulfilment, which will come without fail.

The middle part of the Book contains five curses, each starting with the words 'Woe to him'. Their common theme is that the oppressor will himself suffer what he does to others. The Babylonians are described as plunderers and exploiters, killers and drunkards. The many peoples they have ruined cry out against them. 'Woe to him who builds a town with blood, and founds a city on iniquity!' (Hab. 2:12) They make for themselves dumb idols of wood and stone; 'But the Lord is in his holy temple; let all the earth keep silence before him.' (Hab. 2:20)

The Book ends with a psalm or hymn that appears to be taken from the Temple liturgy. It extols the power and the glory of the Lord, from whom comes salvation for his people. The prophet reaffirms his own faith: 'God, the Lord, is my strength; he makes my feet like hinds' feet, he makes me tread upon my high places.' (Hab. 3:19)

One of the Dead Sea Scrolls discovered by Bedouin shepherds in 1947 was a Hebrew commentary on the Book of Habakkuk, written about the 1st century BC. The writer finds an analogy between the Babylonians of Habakkuk and the Romans who were the master race of his own time. [Book of Habakkuk]

Habazziniah (Heb. 'the Lord has made me rich') 7 century BC. A leader of the Rechabites who was invited by Jeremiah to drink wine with him but firmly refused because of his pledge. [Jer. 35:3]

Hacaliah (Heb. 'waits for God') 5 century BC. Father of Nehemiah. [Neh. 1:1; 10:1]

Hachmoni (Heb. 'wise') c. 10 century BC. Father of Jehiel who was a friend of King David's sons. Also called 'the Hachmonite'. [1 Chr. 11:11; 27:32]

Hachmonite see HACHMONI

Hadad (Heb. 'sharp') *1. c.* 18 century BC. The sixth son of Ishmael. [Gen. 25:15; 1 Chr. 1:30]
2. (name of a god) date unknown. Son of Bedad, he was king of the desert kingdom of Edom and defeated the Midianites in Moab. [Gen. 36:35; 1 Chr. 1:46]
3. c. 10 century BC. A son of the royal house of Edom, he escaped as a child when David and Joab conquered the Edomites and slew every male. He was brought up in Egypt at Pharaoh's court and married the queen's sister. When Hadad heard that both David and Joab were dead, he returned to his hill kingdom whence he made raids on Israel. [1 Kgs. 11:14–22]

Hadad see HADAR

Hadadezer (Heb. 'Hadad is help') *c.* 10

century BC. Son of Rehob, he was king of Zobah, at that time the leading state in the Aram-Syrian area to the northeast of Israel. Hadadezer was defeated by David, and Zobah became a vassal-state paying tribute to Israel.

Later Hadadezer sent an army into Transjordan under his general Shobach. It was again defeated by David, and the Aramean kingdoms remained under Israelite domination. [2 Sam. 8; 10:16, 19; 1 Kgs. 11:23; 1 Chr. 18:3–11]

Hadar (Heb. 'grandeur') date unknown. King of Edom, he married Mehetabel and set up his capital in the city of Pau or Pai. Also called Hadad. [Gen. 36:39; 1 Chr. 1:50]

Hadassah see ESTHER

Hadlai *c.* 8 century BC. A chief of the tribe of Ephraim and the father of Amasa who objected to holding the men of Judah as prisoners of Pekah, king of Israel. [2 Chr. 28:12]

Hadoram (Heb. 'Hadad is exalted') *1.* date unknown. Son of Joktan and a descendant of Shem. [Gen. 10:26, 27; 1 Chr. 1:21]
2. c. 10 century BC. Taskmaster over forced labour in the reign of King Rehoboam, he was stoned to death by the people of Israel as a sign of rebellion against Rehoboam's authority. [2 Chr. 10:18]
3. see ADONIRAM
4. see JORAM *1.*

Hagab (Heb. 'locust') date unknown. Ancestor of a family of Temple servants who returned with Zerubbabel to Judah from exile in Babylon. [Ezra 2:46]

Hagaba see HAGABAH

Hagabah (Heb. 'locust') date unknown. Ancestor of a family of Temple servants who returned with Zerubbabel to Judah from exile in Babylon. Also called Hagaba. [Ezra 2:45; Neh. 7:48]

Hagar ('one who fled') *c.* 18 century BC. Sarah's Egyptian slave-maid. The story of Hagar is one of the most human and poignant in the Old Testament.

Her mistress Sarah proposed to Abraham that he should have a child by Hagar since she herself was barren and old. (Such a suggestion was not regarded as unusual by the customs of that time, which permitted a man to have more than one wife and as many concubines as his wealth and inclination allowed.)

When Hagar conceived, Sarah became jealous. She complained to Abraham that Hagar now despised her. Abraham replied (as any husband would) that she should deal with her servant herself. Sarah vented her resentment on Hagar, who finally ran away into the desert. At a well near Beersheba, an angel of the Lord prevailed upon her to go back, promising that she would bear a son and he would father 'a great nation'. Hagar returned and gave birth to Ishmael. Abraham was then eighty-six years old.

When Sarah's own son Isaac was born, Ishmael was more than thirteen, and fresh friction arose between the two women. At the feast Abraham gave for Isaac's weaning, the ninety-year-old Sarah felt that Hagar and Ishmael were mocking her and demanded of Abraham that he cast them out, 'for the son of this slave woman shall not be heir with my son'. Caught between his angry wife and his paternal feelings for Ishmael, Abraham could not this time avoid the issue, and sought the Lord's counsel. He was told to do as Sarah wanted, but Abraham was reassured that no harm would come to Hagar and Ishmael. Early in the morning Abraham gave Hagar a supply of bread and water and sent them away.

Hagar and the boy wandered in the Beersheba desert till the water was used up. Unable to bear watching her son die, Hagar left him crying under a bush and moved a bowshot away, where she wept in anguish. The angel of God called out to her from heaven and told her not to fear, for God had heard the voice of the lad. She looked up and saw a well of water nearby, and thus they were saved.

They remained in the part of the Sinai desert known as the wilderness of Paran. When Ishmael grew up Hagar had a wife brought for him from her own country, Egypt.

Ishmael is regarded by the Arabs as their ancestor, and there is a Moslem legend that he and his mother Hagar are buried in the sacred Ka'aba in Mecca. [Gen. 16; 21; 25:12]

Haggai (Heb. 'festal') 6 century BC. Post-exilic Hebrew prophet who played a part in the life of Jerusalem after the return of the Jews from Babylonian captivity in the time of Cyrus, king of Persia.

In the summer of 520 BC Haggai and his fellow-prophet Zechariah succeeded by their moral pressure in getting work resumed on the destroyed Temple. Haggai linked the struggles of the community to the fact that the Lord's house still remained a ruin. It was for that reason that their harvests were poor, and their fields drought-stricken. If they wanted prosperity to be restored, he told them, 'Go up to the hills and bring wood and build the house' (Hag. 1:8).

In the short Book bearing his name, Haggai's thoughts went beyond the immediate aim of reconstructing the Temple. He predicted the coming of a day of divine judgment – 'and to overthrow the throne of kingdoms; I am about to destroy the strength of the kingdoms of the nations and overthrow the chariots and their riders; and the horses and their riders shall go down, every one by the sword of his fellow.' (Hag. 2:22) When that liberation came, the Jews would again be an independent nation, and perhaps Zerubbabel the leader of the returnees would be their king. The new Temple would then shine with a glory greater than that of Solomon's Temple. [Ezra 5:1; Book of Haggai]

Haggedolim (Heb. 'the great') 5 century BC. Father of Zabdiel. [Neh. 11:14]

Haggi (Heb. 'festive') c. 16 century BC. A son of Gad, he went down to Egypt at the same time as his grandfather, Jacob. [Gen. 46:16; Num. 26:15]

Haggiah (Heb. 'Lord's feast') c. 10 century BC. A Levite from the family of Merari, whose descendants were appointed by King David to conduct the musical service in the Tabernacle. [1 Chr. 6:30]

Haggith (Heb. 'festive') c. 10 century BC. A wife of King David and the mother of Adonijah. [2 Sam. 3:4; 1 Kgs. 1:5, 11; 2:13; 1 Chr. 3:2]

Hagri (Heb. 'who fled') c. 10 century BC. Father of Mibhar, a warrior in the armies of King David. [1 Chr. 11:38]

Hakkatan (Heb. 'the little one') c. 5 century BC. Father of Johanan who returned with Ezra to Judah from exile in Babylon. [Ezra 8:12]

Hakkoz (Heb. 'thorn') *1.* c. 10 century BC. A priest in the reign of King David, who took the seventh turn of service in the Tabernacle. [1 Chr. 24:10]
2. date unknown. Ancestor of a family of priests who returned with Zerubbabel from exile in Babylon. Perhaps the same as the grandfather of Meremoth. [Ezra 2:61; Neh. 3:4, 21; 7:63]

Hakupha (Heb. 'bent') date unknown. Ancestor of a family of Temple servants who returned with Zerubbabel from

exile in Babylon. [Ezra 2:51; Neh. 7:53]

Hallohesh (Heb. 'enchanter') 5 century BC. One of the leaders of Judah in the days of Nehemiah who signed the covenant to observe the Laws of God. His son Shallum ruled over half of the district of Jerusalem. [Neh. 3:12; 10:24]

Ham (Heb. 'hot') date unknown. Second son of Noah. Ham and his wife were in the ark with Noah and the rest of the family. After the great flood had subsided, Noah had become a farmer and planted a vineyard. One day, Ham saw his father lying naked in a drunken stupor in his tent, and he went to tell his two brothers what he had seen. Shem and Japheth promptly took a garment, entered the tent backwards so as not to see their father's nakedness, and covered him. When Noah awoke and heard what had happened, he blessed Shem and Japheth but cursed Ham: 'a slave of slaves shall he be to his brothers' (Gen. 9:25).

Ham had four sons, Egypt, Canaan, Cush and Put, who were the legendary founders of these countries and peoples. [Gen. 5:32; 6:10; 7:13; 9:18–27 10:1, 6, 20; 1 Chr. 1:4, 8; 4:40; Ps. 78:51; 105:23, 27; 106:22]

Haman c. 5 century BC. Chief minister of King Ahasuerus. Haman the Agagite, son of Hammedatha, was made the chief minister of King Ahasuerus of Persia, who commanded all the king's staff and courtiers to bow down before him. Everyone obeyed except Mordecai the Jew who also served at the court. Haman's anger at Mordecai turned into a hatred of the Jewish race. He obtained permission from the king to deal with the Jewish minority and had a royal decree despatched to the authorities throughout the empire, ordering them to slaughter all their Jews on a certain day the court magicians selected by lot as propitious.

The Jews were thrown into consternation at the news of the impending pogrom. Mordecai instructed his niece, now Queen Esther, to intercede with the king. Ahasuerus agreed to dine with her together with Haman, who was gratified at the unusual honour but complained, 'Yet all this does me no good, so long as I see Mordecai the Jew sitting at the king's gate.' (Esther 5:13) His wife Zeresh and friends then suggested that he should build a gallows and persuade the king to have Mordecai hanged on it.

That night the king was unable to sleep and had the court records read to him. He came across an entry that Mordecai had foiled a plot on the king's life. Next morning the king asked Haman what he would do for a man he wanted to honour. Haman, thinking it was for himself, suggested that such a man should be led through the city square on the king's horse, and dressed in royal robes with a crown on his head. To his dismay, he was told to arrange such honours for Mordecai.

At dinner with Queen Esther, she accused Haman of having organized a mass murder against the Jews and pleaded for the lives of her people. The king in a rage rushed into the garden. The terrified Haman flung himself down on the couch and begged the queen to save his life. At that moment the king stalked in again and thinking that Haman was assaulting the queen, ordered the attendants to seize him. 'So they hanged Haman on the gallows which he had prepared for Mordecai.' (Esther 7:10) Ahasuerus gave Haman's house to Queen Esther, and Mordecai was appointed chief minister in his place. [Esther 3:1–9:24]

Hammath (Heb. 'hot spring') date unknown. An ancestor of Rechab. [1 Chr. 2:55]

Hammedatha (Pers. 'given by the moon') c. 5 century BC. Father of Haman whom the Persian king Ahasu-

erus made his chief minister. [Esther 3:1; 8:5; 9:10]

Hammolecheth (Heb. 'who is queen') c. 16 century BC. Daughter of Machir and the granddaughter of Manasseh. [1 Chr. 7:18]

Hammuel (Heb. 'God's protection') date unknown. Son of Mishma and a leader of the tribe of Simeon. [1 Chr. 4:26]

Hamor (Heb. 'ass') c. 16 century BC. A Hivite chief who ruled over the area of the city of Shechem in the days of Jacob. His son, also named Shechem, raped Jacob's daughter Dinah and then asked Hamor to obtain her family's consent to his marrying Dinah. Hamor suggested to Jacob's sons that the two families should trade together and intermarry and that his son Schechem should marry their sister Dinah. The brothers agreed provided that Hamor, Schemem and the entire male population of the city would be circumcised. The people of Shechem agreed. However, while Hamor, Shechem and the males of Shechem were recovering from the operation, Simeon and Levi, two of Dinah's brothers, rushed into the city, killed all the males and looted their property. [Gen. 33:19; 34; Josh. 24:32; Judg. 9:28]

Hamran see HEMDAN

Hamul (Heb. 'pity') date unknown. Son of Perez and a grandson of Judah, his descendants were an important branch of the tribe of Judah. [Gen. 46:12; Num. 26:21; 1 Chr. 2:5]

Hamutal (Heb. 'protection') c. 7 century BC. Daughter of Jeremiah of Libnah, she became the wife of Josiah, king of Judah, and the mother of Jehoahaz and Zedekiah, kings of Judah. [2 Kgs. 23:31; 24:18; Jer. 52:1]

Hanamel (Heb. 'given of God') c. 7 century BC. Son of Shallum and a cousin of the prophet Jeremiah, he asked Jeremiah to redeem a plot of land for seventeen shekels of silver to demonstrate his faith that the people of Judah would eventually return in peace to their land. [Jer. 32:7–12]

Hanan (Heb. 'merciful') *1.* date unknown. Son of Shashak and a chief of the tribe of Benjamin living in Jerusalem. [1 Chr. 8:23]
2. date unknown. A son of Azel of the tribe of Benjamin and a descendant of King Saul. [1 Chr. 8:38; 9:44]
3. c. 10 century BC. Son of Maachah and a warrior in the army of King David distinguished for his bravery. [1 Chr. 11:43]
4. date unknown. Ancestor of a family of Temple servants who returned to Judah with Zerubbabel from exile in Babylon. [Ezra 2:46; Neh. 7:49]
5. c. 6 century BC. Son of Igdaliah, a man of God, his sons had a room in the Temple where the prophet Jeremiah met the Rechabites. [Jer. 35:4]
6. 5 century BC. A Levite who helped explain the Law to the people of Judah after Ezra had read it to them. He later signed the solemn covenant. [Neh. 8:7; 10:10]
7. 5 century BC. Two of the leaders of Judah with the same name who signed the covenant to keep the Laws of God, in the days of Nehemiah. [Neh. 10:22; 10:26]
8. 5 century BC. Son of Zaccur, the Levite, he was one of four trustworthy men appointed by Nehemiah to distribute the offerings among the priests and Levites. [Neh. 13:13]

Hanani (Heb. 'gracious') *1. c.* 9 century BC. Father of Jehu, he was a holy man who reproved King Asa of Judah for entering into an alliance with Syria instead of relying only on the Lord. The king had him flung into prison. [1 Kgs. 16:1, 7; 2 Chr. 16:7; 19:2; 20:34]

2. c. 10 century BC. A son of Heman, King David's musician, he and his fourteen brothers played musical instruments in the Tabernacle. Hanani was responsible for the eighteenth turn of service. [1 Chr. 25:4, 25]
3. 5 century BC. Descendant of Immer the priest, he divorced his non-Jewish wife in the time of Ezra. [Ezra 10:20]
4. 5 century BC. Brother of Nehemiah, he came to Nehemiah in the Persian palace at Shushan and told him that the people living in Judah were in great poverty, that the walls of the city were broken and the gates burned down. Later after the walls of the city were rebuilt, Nehemiah made Hanani keeper of the gates of Jerusalem together with Hananiah, the governor of the palace. [Neh. 1:2; 7:2]
5. 5 century BC. A priest who played musical instruments in the dedication service for the rebuilt walls of Jerusalem in the time of Nehemiah. [Neh. 12:36]

Hananiah (Heb. 'the Lord is gracious') *1.* date unknown. A son of Shashak and a leader of the tribe of Benjamin living in Jerusalem. [1 Chr. 8:24]
2. c. 10 century BC. A son of King David's musician, Heman, he and his brothers played musical instruments in the Tabernacle services under their father's direction; and Hananiah was responsible for the sixteenth turn of service. [1 Chr. 25:4, 23]
3. c. 8 century BC. An army commander of Uzziah, king of Judah. [2 Chr. 26:11]
4. c. 7 century BC. Hananiah the son of Azzur was a prophet from Gibeon and appeared in the Temple before Zedekiah the king, the priests and the people, in the time of Jeremiah. The Lord, he proclaimed, had broken the yoke of the king of Babylon; within two years the holy vessels carried off by Nebuchadnezzar would be returned, and the Lord would bring back Jehoiachin, the cap-

tive king of Judah, with all the other Judean deportees.

Jeremiah disagreed with him, but Hananiah illustrated his point with a symbolic act. He smashed the yoke that Jeremiah had taken to wearing, and prophesied in the name of the Lord: 'Even so will I break the yoke of Neb-uchadnezzar king of Babylon from the neck of all the nations ...' (Jer. 28:11). Jeremiah answered the false prophet, 'Listen, Hananiah, the Lord has not sent you and you have made this people trust in a lie.' (Jer. 28:15) Jeremiah prophesied that Hananiah would be dead within the year. He died two months later. [Jer. 28]

5. c. 6 century BC. Father of Zedekiah who was a leader of Judah to whom Jeremiah's prophecy of doom was read. [Jer. 36:12]

6. c. 6 century BC. The grandfather of Irijah, a Benjaminite army captain who arrested the prophet Jeremiah on a charge of defecting to the Chaldeans. [Jer. 37:13]

7. see SHADRACH

8. 6 century BC. Son of Zerubbabel who led the children of Israel from exile in Babylon back to Judah. [1 Chr. 3:19, 21]

9. c. 5 century BC. A descendant of Bebai who divorced his non-Jewish wife in the time of Ezra. [Ezra 10:28]

10. 5 century BC. A perfumer who helped rebuild the walls of Jerusalem in the time of Nehemiah. [Neh. 3:8]

11. 5 century BC. Son of Shelemiah and a leader of Judah who helped rebuild the walls of Jerusalem in the days of Nehemiah. [Neh. 3:30]

12. 5 century BC. Governor of the reno-vated king's palace in Jerusalem in the days of Nehemiah, he was jointly respon-sible with Nehemiah's brother Hanani for opening and closing the gates of the city. [Neh. 7:2]

13. 5 century BC. One of the leaders of Judah in the time of Nehemiah who signed the covenant to obey the Laws of God. [Neh. 10:23]

14. 5 century BC. A chief priest of Judah when Joiakim was high priest in the time of Nehemiah. [Neh. 12:12]

15. 5 century BC. A chief priest of Judah in the days of Nehemiah, he blew a trumpet at the dedication ceremony for the rebuilt walls of Jerusalem. [Neh. 12:41]

Hannah (Heb. 'grace') *c.* 11 century BC. Mother of the prophet Samuel.

Hannah lived in the town of Ramathaim-zophim, in the hill country of Ephraim. She grieved at being child-less and her husband Elkanah was unable to console her. His other wife Peninnah taunted Hannah.

The next time the family went to Shiloh on the pilgrimage, she stayed longer and prayed to the Lord to give her children. Eli, the chief priest, saw the woman's lips moving, though she did not utter a sound. Deciding she was drunk he reproached her. Hannah ex-plained her trouble, and vowed that if God 'wilt give to thy maidservant a son, then I will give him to the Lord all the days of his life' (1 Sam. 1:11). Eli encour-aged her to believe that the Lord would grant her prayer.

In due time Hannah bore a child which she called Samuel, 'the Lord heard'. When she had weaned him she took him with her to Shiloh, together with a gift of three bullocks, flour and a bottle of wine, and left him with Eli.

Though Hannah had five other chil-dren she never forgot her first-born. Each year she made him a coat and brought it to him when she came on the annual pilgrimage. [1 Sam. 1; 2]

Hanniel (Heb. 'grace of God') *1. c.* 13 century BC. Son of Ephod, he was the leader of the tribe of Manasseh ap-pointed by Moses to help divide the land of Canaan among the children of Israel. [Num. 34:23]

2. date unknown. Son of Ulla of the

tribe of Asher, he was a great warrior and a leader of the tribe. [1 Chr. 7:39]

Hanoch (Heb. '[God's] follower') *1. c.* 16 century BC. Son of Midian and a grandson of Abraham and Keturah. [Gen. 25:4]
2. *c.* 16 century BC. Eldest son of Reuben, he went down to Egypt at the same time as his grandfather Jacob. [Gen. 46:9; Exod. 6:14; Num. 26:5; 1 Chr. 5:3]

Hanun (Heb. 'gracious') *1. c.* 10 century BC. King of the Ammonites, he received a message of condolence from David on the death of his father King Nahash. Hanun 'took David's servants, and shaved off half the beard of each, and cut off their garments in the middle, at their hips, and sent them away' (2 Sam. 10:4). This insult was regarded as an invitation to a war, in which Joab, David's commander, defeated the Ammonites and their Aramean allies. [2 Sam. 10; 1 Chr. 19]
2. 5 century BC. A Judean who repaired the Valley Gate of Jerusalem in the time of Nehemiah. [Neh. 3:13]
3. 5 century BC. Son of Zalaph, he repaired part of the walls of Jerusalem in the time of Nehemiah. [Neh. 3:30]

Happizzez (Heb. 'hasty') *c.* 10 century BC. A priest in the reign of King David who took the eighteenth turn of service in the Tabernacle. [1 Chr. 24:15]

Haran (Heb. 'mountainous') *1. c.* 18 century BC. Brother of Abraham and Nahor, he died at an early age and left three children, Lot, Milcah and Iscah. [Gen. 11:26–32]
2. date unknown. Son of Caleb and Ephah and a leader of the tribe of Judah. [1 Chr. 2:46]
3. *c.* 10 century BC. Son of Shimei, a Levite descended from Gershon. [1 Chr. 23:9]

Harbona *c.* 5 century BC. One of the seven chamberlains of King Ahasuerus who was commanded by the drunken king on the seventh day of a feast to bring Queen Vashti before his guests to show off her beauty. Later he told the king of the gallows Haman had prepared for Mordecai. [Esther 1:10; 7:9]

Hareph (Heb. 'sharp') date unknown. Son of Hur, he was a leader of Judah and regarded as the founder of Bethgader. [1 Chr. 2:51]

Harhaiah 5 century BC. Father of Uzziel, a goldsmith, who helped repair the walls of Jerusalem in the time of Nehemiah. [Neh. 3:8]

Harhas *c.* 7 century BC. Ancestor of Shallum, the husband of the prophetess Huldah. Also called Hasrah. [2 Kgs. 22:14; 2 Chr. 34:22]

Harhur date unknown. Ancestor of a family of Temple servants who returned with Zerubbabel to Judah from captivity in Babylon. [Ezra 2:51; Neh. 7:53]

Harim (Heb. 'dedicated to God') *1. c.* 10 century BC. A priest who served in the Tabernacle during the reign of King David. [1 Chr. 24:8]
2. 6 century BC. Head of a family who returned with Zerubbabel to Judah from exile in Babylon. One of his sons, Malchijah, helped rebuild the walls of Jerusalem in the days of Nehemiah. [Ezra 2:32; 10:31; Neh. 3:11; 7:35]
3. date unknown. Ancestor of a family who returned to Judah with Zerubbabel from exile in Babylon. Some of his descendents married foreign wives. [Ezra 2:39; 10:21; Neh. 7:42; 12:15]
4. 5 century BC. A chief priest of Judah in the time of Nehemiah who signed the covenant to observe the Laws of God. [Neh. 10:5]
5. 5 century BC. A leader of Judah who signed the covenant to observe the Laws

of God in the time of Nehemiah. [Neh. 10:27]

Hariph (Heb. 'sharp') *1. see* JORAH
2. 5 century BC. He was a leader of Judah at the time of Nehemiah who signed the covenant to observe the Laws of God. [Neh. 10:19]

Harnepher (Heb. 'God is good') date unknown. One of the five sons of Zophah of the tribe of Asher, he was a leader of the tribe and a mighty warrior. [1 Chr. 7:36]

Haroeh (Heb. 'seer') date unknown. Son of Shobal, a leader of the tribe of Judah. Also called Reaiah. [1 Chr. 2:52; 4:2]

Harsha date unknown. Ancestor of a family of Temple servants who returned with Zerubbabel from exile in Babylon. [Ezra 2:52; Neh. 7:54]

Harum (Heb. 'high') date unknown. Father of Aharhel of the tribe of Judah. [1 Chr. 4:8]

Harumaph (Heb. 'slit-nosed') 5 century BC. Father of Jedaiah who helped rebuild the walls of Jerusalem in the time of Nehemiah. [Neh. 3:10]

Haruz (Heb. 'gold') *c.* 7 century BC. Father of Meshullemeth and the grandfather of Amon, king of Judah. [2 Kgs. 21:19]

Hasadiah (Heb. 'beloved of God') 6 century BC. A son of Zerubbabel who led the return to Judah from captivity in Babylon. [1 Chr. 3:20]

Hashabiah (Heb. 'considered') *1.* date unknown. Son of Amaziah, a Levite, descended from Merari. [1 Chr. 6:45]
2. *c.* 10 century BC. A son of Jeduthun, one of King David's musicians, he and his brothers were taught to play the harp in the thanksgiving service in the

Tabernacle, and he had the twelfth rota in the service. [1 Chr. 25:3, 19]
3. *c.* 10 century BC. A Levite of one of the Hebronite families who served King David on the west bank of the river Jordan. [1 Chr. 26:30]
4. *c.* 10 century BC. Son of Kemuel, and head of the tribe of Levi in the reign of King David. [1 Chr. 27:17]
5. *c.* 7 century BC. A chief Levite who donated large quantities of cattle for the special Passover service celebrated by King Josiah of Judah. [2 Chr. 35:9]
6. date unknown. Son of Bunni, the Levite, his great-grandson Shemaiah returned to Jerusalem in the days of Nehemiah and ministered in the Tabernacle. [1 Chr. 9:14; Neh. 11:15]
7. 5 century BC. A leader of the priests who answered Ezra's call to return to Jerusalem to serve in the Tabernacle. He and his family helped bring back the treasure and the precious vessels from Babylon, and later he became a priest. [Ezra 8:19, 24; Neh. 12:21]
8. 5 century BC. Descendant of Parosh, he returned from exile in Babylon with Ezra. [Ezra 10:25]
9. 5 century BC. A chief Levite of Judah and ruler of half of the district of Keilah, he helped repair the walls of Jerusalem and signed the solemn covenant in the time of Nehemiah. [Neh. 3:17; 10:11; 12:24]
10. 5 century BC. Son of Mattaniah, the Levite, his grandson Uzzi supervised the service of the Levites in Jerusalem in the days of Nehemiah. [Neh. 11:22]

Hashabnah (Heb. 'regarded') 5 century BC. A leader of Judah who signed the covenant to observe the Laws of God in the time of Nehemiah. [Neh. 10:25]

Hashabneiah (Heb. 'God has considered me')
1. 5 century BC. Father of Hattush who helped repair the walls of Jerusalem in the time of Nehemiah. [Neh. 3:10]
2. 5 century BC. A Levite who exhorted

the people of Judah to praise God on the fast day proclaimed by Ezra and to confess their sins. [Neh. 9:5]

Hashbaddanah 5 century BC. A leader of Judah who stood at the side of Ezra when he read the Law of Moses to the people. [Neh. 8:4]

Hashem *see* JASHEN

Hashubah (Heb. 'important') *c.* 6 century BC. A son of Zerubbabel who led the return to Judah from captivity in Babylon. [1 Chr. 3:20]

Hashum *1.* date unknown. Ancestor of a family who returned with Zerubbabel from exile in Babylon. Seven of his descendants married non-Jewish wives whom they later divorced. [Ezra 2:19; 10:33; Neh. 7:22]
2. 5 century BC. A leader of Judah who stood at the side of Ezra when he read the Law of Moses to the people in the market-place. [Neh. 8:4]
3. 5 century BC. One of the leaders of Judah who signed the covenant in the time of Nehemiah to observe the Laws of God. [Neh. 10:18]

Hasrah *see* HARHAS

Hassenaah *see* SENAAH

Hassenuah (Heb. 'hated') *1.* date unknown. Ancestor of Sallu, one of the first Benjaminites to settle in Jerusalem after the return from exile in Babylon. [1 Chr. 9:7]
2. c. 5 century BC. Father of Judah, the deputy governor of Jerusalem after the return from exile in Babylon. [Neh. 11:9]

Hasshub (Heb. 'respected') *1.* 5 century BC. Father of Shemaiah, one of the Levites who settled in Jerusalem after the return from exile in Babylon. [1 Chr. 9:14; Neh. 11:15]
2. 5 century BC. Descendant of Pahath-moab, he helped repair the walls of Jeru-

salem in the time of Nehemiah. [Neh. 3:11]
3. 5 century BC. A man of Judah who helped repair the walls of Jerusalem in the time of Nehemiah. [Neh. 3:23]
4. 5 century BC. A leader of Judah who signed the covenant to observe the Laws of God in the time of Nehemiah. [Neh. 10:23]

Hassophereth *see* SOPHERETH

Hasupha (Heb. 'stripped') date unknown. Ancestor of a family of Temple servants who returned with Zerubbabel from exile in Babylon. [Ezra 2:43; Neh. 7:46]

Hathach *c.* 5 century BC. The servant of Queen Esther who brought her Mordecai's message of how Haman planned to destroy the Jews. [Esther 4:5–10]

Hathath (Heb. 'fear') 12 century BC. Son of Othniel, leader of the tribe of Judah. [1 Chr. 4:13]

Hatipha (Heb. 'captive') date unknown. Ancestor of a family of Temple servants who returned with Zerubbabel to Judah from exile in Babylon. [Ezra 2:54; Neh. 7:56]

Hatita date unknown. Ancestor of a family of gatekeepers of the Temple who returned to Judah with Zerubbabel from exile in Babylon. [Ezra 2:42; Neh. 7:45]

Hattil (Heb. 'talkative') *c.* 10 century BC. One of King Solomon's servants whose descendants returned to Judah with Zerubbabel from exile in Babylon. [Ezra 2:57; Neh. 7:59]

Hattush *1.* 6 century BC. One of the priests who returned with Zerubbabel to Judah from exile in Babylon. [Neh. 12:2]
2. 5 century BC. Son of Shemaiah of the

tribe of Judah and a descendant of King David, he returned with Ezra from exile in Babylon. [1 Chr. 3:22; Ezra 8:2]
3. 5 century BC. Son of Hashabneiah, he helped repair the walls of Jerusalem in the days of Nehemiah. [Neh. 3:10]
4. 5 century BC. One of the priests of Judah in the days of Nehemiah who signed the covenant to observe the Laws of God. [Neh. 10:4]

Havilah (Heb. 'stretch of sand') *1.* date unknown. Son of Cush and a grandson of Ham. [Gen. 10:7; 1 Chr. 1:9]
2. date unknown. Son of Joktan and a descendant of Shem. [Gen. 10:29; 1 Chr. 1:23]

Hazael (Heb. 'God sees') *c.* 9 century BC. King of Aram (Syria). When Elisha was on a visit to Damascus, the sick King Ben-hadad II told Hazael, then a senior Syrian commander: 'Take a present with you and go to meet the man of God, and inquire of the Lord through him, saying, "Shall I recover from this sickness?"' (2 Kgs. 8:8) Hazael went off to meet Elisha, taking with him forty camels loaded with all the good things of Damascus. Elisha gave him a cryptic answer: the king would recover from his illness but was about to die. The prophet then seemed to go into a trance and began to weep, explaining that Hazael would become king and do great evil to the children of Israel. The next day Hazael smothered his master and seized the throne.

At this time Assyrian pressure ebbed, and Aram (Damascus) under Hazael became the dominant power in the Palestine-Syrian area. The kingdom of Israel became a feeble vassal of Damascus, and all its territory east of the Jordan was occupied by the ruthless Hazael. The kingdom of Judah also had to pay him heavy tribute, which he received from King Joash at Gath in the coastal plain about 815 BC. [1 Kgs. 19:15–17; 2 Kgs. 8:8–15; Amos 1:4]

Hazaiah (Heb. 'whom God sees') 6 century BC. Son of Adaiah of the tribe of Judah, his grandson Maaseiah settled in Jerusalem in the time of Nehemiah. [Neh. 11:5]

Hazarmaveth (Heb. 'Moth [a god]'s court') date unknown. Son of Joktan and a great-grandson of Shem. [Gen. 10:26; 1 Chr. 1:20]

Haziel (Heb. 'vision of God') *c.* 10 century BC. A Levite leader descended from Shimei, he was appointed by King David to minister in the Tabernacle. [1 Chr. 23:9]

Hazo *c.* 18 century BC. Son of Nahor and Milcah and a nephew of Abraham. [Gen. 22:22]

Hazzelelponi (Heb. 'coming shadows') date unknown. Descendant of Judah, she was the sister of Jezreel, Ishma and Idbash. [1 Chr. 4:3]

Heber (Heb. 'alliance') *1.* date unknown. Son of Beriah and a grandson of Asher, he was one of seventy descendants of Jacob who went with him into Egypt. [Gen. 46:17; Num. 26:45; 1 Chr. 7:31, 32]
2. c. 12 century BC. A Kenite descended from Moses's father-in-law Jethro, and the husband of Jael. [Judg. 4:11–21; 5:24]
3. date unknown. Descendant of Ezrah of the tribe of Judah, and the father of Soco. [1 Chr. 4:18]
4. date unknown. Son of Elpaal and a leader of the tribe of Benjamin living in Jerusalem. [1 Chr. 8:17, 18]

Hebron (Heb. 'league') *1. c.* 13 century BC. A descendant of Kohath of the tribe of Levi, and an uncle of Moses. [Exod. 6:18; Num. 3:19, 27; 1 Chr. 6:2, 18; 15:9; 23:12, 19; 24:23]
2. date unknown. Son of Mareshah, and a leader of the tribe of Judah. [1 Chr. 2:42, 43]

Hegai *c*. 6 century BC. Eunuch of King Ahasuerus of Persia into whose custody were given all the maidens who were candidates to become Queen of Persia. He showed special favour to Esther. [Esther 2:3, 8, 15]

Heglam *see* GERA 2.

Helah (Heb. 'necklace') date unknown. One of the two wives of Ashhur, father of Tekoa, a leader of the tribe of Judah. [1 Chr. 4:5, 7]

Heldai (Heb. 'mole') *1. c*. 10 century BC. Commander of a division in King David's army in the twelfth month of each year. [1 Chr. 27:15]
2. 6 century BC. One of the Judeans who returned from exile in Babylon. God commanded the prophet Zechariah to take them into the house of Josiah, son of Zephaniah and place a crown on Joshua, son of Jehozadak, the high priest. [Zech. 6:10, 14]

Heleb *see* HELED

Heled (Heb. 'passing') *c*. 10 century BC. Son of Baanah, he was a warrior in the army of King David. Also called Heleb. [1 Chr. 11:30; 2 Sam. 23:29]

Helek (Heb. 'portion') date unknown. A leader of the tribe of Manasseh descended from Gilead. [Num. 26:30; Josh. 17:2]

Helem (Heb. 'strength') date unknown. Brother of Shemer and a leader of the tribe of Asher. [1 Chr. 7:35]

Helez (Heb. 'strong') *1*. date unknown. Son of Azariah and father of Eleasah, he was descended from Jarha, an Egyptian servant who married the daughter of a leader of Judah. [1 Chr. 2:39]
2. c. 10 century BC. A warrior in the army of King David described as the 'Paltite' in the Second Book of Samuel

and the 'Pelonite' in the First Book of Chronicles, where he is said to be of the tribe of Ephraim and commander of King David's army in the seventh month. [2 Sam. 23:26; 1 Chr. 11:27; 27:10]

Helkai (Heb. 'portion') *c*. 6 century BC. Head of a family of priests, descended from Meraioth, in the days of King Jeoiakim. [Neh. 12:15]

Helon (Heb. 'strong') *c*. 13 century BC. Father of Eliab, a leader of the tribe of Zebulun who was appointed by Moses to take a census of the men of his tribe fit for war and led the contingent in the army of the children of Israel. [Num. 1:9; 2:7; 7:24, 29; 10:16]

Heman (Heb. 'trusty') *1*. date unknown. Son of Lotan and a grandson of Seir, the Horite. Also called Homan. [Gen. 36:22; 1 Chr. 1:39]
2. date unknown. Son of Zerah and a grandson of Judah, he was known as the Ezrahite. [1 Chr. 2:6; Ps. 88]
3. date unknown. Son of Mahol, he was a wise man whose wisdom was exceeded only by that of King Solomon. [1 Kgs. 4:31]
4. c. 16 century BC. Son of Joel and a grandson of Samuel, he was a Levite musician in the time of King David, who led his fourteen sons in the service in the Tabernacle. [1 Chr. 6:33; 15:17, 19; 16:41, 42; 25:1, 4–6; 2 Chr. 5:12; 29:14; 35:15]

Hemdan date unknown. Son of Dishon and a descendant of Seir the Horite. Also called Hamran. [Gen. 36:26; 1 Chr. 1:41]

Henadad (Heb. 'favour of Hadad') date unknown. Ancestor of a family of Levites who helped supervise the work of repairing the Temple in the time of Zerubbabel. [Ezra 3:9; Neh. 3:18, 24; 10:9]

Hepher (Heb. 'pit') *1. c.* 16 century BC. A son of Gilead and a grandson of Manasseh, he was father of Zelophehad. In the Book of Joshua he is described as a son of Manasseh. [Num. 26:32, 33; 27:1; Josh. 17:2, 3]

2. date unknown. Son of Ashhur of the tribe of Judah and his wife Naarah. [1 Chr. 4:6]

3. c. 10 century BC. A warrior in the armies of King David, he was distinguished for his bravery. [1 Chr. 11:36]

Hephzibah (Heb. 'my delight is in her') *c.* 8 century BC. Wife of King Hezekiah and the mother of King Manasseh. [2 Kgs. 21:1]

Heresh (Heb. 'carpenter') 6 century BC. A Levite descended from Asaph who settled in Jerusalem after the return from exile in Babylon. [1 Chr. 9:15]

Heth date unknown. Son of Canaan and a grandson of Ham, he was the acknowledged ancestor of the Hittite tribe. [Gen. 10:15; 23:7; 25:10; 1 Chr. 1:13]

Hezekiah (Heb. 'strength of God') *1.* Thirteenth king of Judah after the monarchy split, he reigned 716–687 BC.

Hezekiah was the son of King Ahaz of Judah and Abijah. He succeeded his father on the throne at the age of twenty-five. Judah at that time was shrunken in size, a mere satellite of Assyria – a small bark kept afloat on rough seas by two remarkable men: King Hezekiah, and the great prophet-statesman Isaiah.

For a number of years Hezekiah was careful to avoid giving offence to the Assyrians, and devoted himself to strengthening his kingdom. His first task was to restore the force and purity of the Hebraic religion and cleanse it of the idolatrous practices that had been prevalent in his father's reign. The local shrines or 'high places' (2 Kgs. 21:3) around the country were closed down, as were the street shrines Ahaz had erected in various parts of Jerusalem. The Temple was cleaned out, reconsecrated and restored to its primacy as the national centre of worship. From all over Judah, the people gathered in Jerusalem for the Passover as had been the custom before; and the king also sent special messengers to the towns of conquered Israel, now an Assyrian province, inviting them to worship once more in Jerusalem. In all the long array of the kings of Judah and Israel, Hezekiah is one of the very few who are commended on religious grounds. He received powerful backing from Isaiah, who was concerned with the spiritual health of the nation rather than with Temple rituals.

Hezekiah also streamlined the administration and tax-gathering structure of the kingdom, and built stables and large storehouses in which he amassed wealth for the state treasury in the form of grain, wine, oil and livestock. The border areas were consolidated and expanded, especially on the frontier with Philistia, in the western Negev as far as the town of Gerar, and southwards in the direction of Mount Seir (Edom).

THE ASSYRIAN INVASION

The defences of Jerusalem, and its capacity to withstand siege, were of special concern to Hezekiah: he 'built up all the wall that was broken down, and raised towers upon it, and outside it he built another wall; and he strengthened the Millo in the city of David. He also made weapons and shields in abundance. And he set combat commanders over the people ...' (2 Chr. 32:5, 6) The most vital step the king took concerned the water supply, a step to ensure access to the water source from inside the city in time of siege, and to deny access by the enemy. The only natural spring was that of Gihon, emerging from a cave outside the city wall. Hezekiah had a six-hundred-yard tunnel constructed from the spring through the rock of the hillside and underneath the south-eastern part of the city wall to discharge into a reservoir called the Pool of Siloam [Shiloah]. At the same time the cave at the source was sealed up so as to prevent the enemy from using or tampering with the water supply. The tunnel has remained intact to this day.

In 704 BC the Assyrian ruler Sargon II died and was succeeded by Sennacherib. At that time Assyrian supremacy was being challenged from two directions, Babylonia and Egypt. The king of Babylon sent envoys to Jerusalem to stimulate the spirit of rebellion against Assyria. For its part Egypt incited the Philistine towns against their Assyrian masters, in order to regain its own traditional influence. The banner of revolt was raised in the Philistine city of Ashkelon. Hezekiah took the calculated risk of joining in the anti-Assyrian movement, and played a leading role in it. Isaiah apparently felt serious misgivings about this venture into power-politics. The event proved him right.

In 701 BC, after the defeat of Babylon, Sennacherib marched an army down the coastal plain and easily suppressed the Philistine rebels as well as routing Egyptian forces that had come to their aid. He then turned his attention to Judah. According to the Assyrian records, he occupied forty-six Judean towns, deported a great number of inhabitants and took a huge amount of booty. As for Hezekiah, Sennacherib records: '... himself, I imprisoned in Jerusalem, his residence, like a bird in a cage.'

The main Assyrian force was thrown against the strategic fortified city of Lachish in the foothills east of Gaza. In his palace at Nineveh Sennacherib afterwards had a detailed bas-relief made, depicting in four panels the siege and capture of Lachish. These panels have survived nearly intact, and provide one of the most graphic descriptions ever found of an ancient battle.

Realizing the ill-fated rebellion was over, Hezekiah sent a message of submission to Sennacherib at Lachish: 'I have done wrong; withdraw from me; whatever you impose on me I will bear.' (2 Kgs. 18:14) The Assyrian ruler exacted a tribute of three hundred talents of silver and thirty talents of gold, which exhausted the treasury of the palace and the Temple.

But Sennacherib was not satisfied with tribute alone. He sent one of his chief aides with a detachment of troops to demand the surrender of Jerusalem. A meeting took place outside the city where Hezekiah was represented by the master of the palace, the official scribe and the herald. No agreement was reached. The Assyrian envoy shouted out in Hebrew to the spectators on the ramparts that their king was deluding them if he relied on their God to save them: had all the other peoples conquered by Assyria, including the kingdom of Israel, been saved by their deities?

The king and his ministers were thrown into fear and confusion by these threats, and Isaiah was consulted. The prophet's counsel was that they should stand firm and resist the demand to open the gates. Isaiah said: 'Therefore thus says the Lord concerning the king of Assyria, He shall not come into this city ... By the way that he came, by the same he shall return.' (2 Kgs. 19:32, 33) Sennacherib did not in fact lay siege to Jerusalem but withdrew his forces – the Bible suggests they were smitten by a sudden plague and returned to Nineveh. After this deliverance Judah reverted to its vassal status.

Not long after, Hezekiah became deathly ill with ulcers, which, on the Lord's advice, were cured with a fig poultice. Hearing of his sickness, the king of Babylon sent an envoy with a letter and gift affecting solicitude for Hezekiah's health. The king received the envoy warmly, and showed him round the palace, the treasure-house, the armoury and the city. When Isaiah heard about this visit he predicted grimly that Judah would be destroyed in the future by the Babylonians. The king shrugged his shoulders and remarked, 'Why not, if there will be peace and security in my days?' (2 Kgs, 20:19)

The remaining fourteen years of Hezekiah's reign were uneventful. When he died 'all Judah and the inhabitants of Jerusalem did him honour' (2 Chr. 32:33). He was succeeded by his son Manasseh. [2 Kgs. 16:20; 18; 19; 20; 21:3; 1 Chr. 3:13; 4:41; 2 Chr. 28:27; 29; 30; 31; 32; 33:3; Prov. 25:1; Isa. 1:1; 36; 37; 38; 39; Jer. 15:4; 26:18, 19; Hos. 1:1; Mic. 1:1]

THE SILOAM INSCRIPTION
A discovery one hundred and ten years ago confirmed the biblical record concerning Hezekiah's measures to ensure the water supply of Jerusalem when faced by the threat of siege by Sennacherib. The Bible says that Hezekiah 'made the pool and the conduit and brought water into the city' (2 Kgs. 20:20). He also 'closed the upper outlet of the waters of Gihon and directed them down to the west side of the city of David' (2 Chr. 32:30). Gihon, the main source of the city's water, lay at the foot of what in Hezekiah's time was the eastern wall of Jerusalem, and Hezekiah's tunnel brought the water by gravity flow to a reservoir inside the city at its southwestern point.

The discovery in 1880 concerned an inscription in the rock wall of the tunnel on how it was excavated. The language is perfect classical Hebrew prose, its content, script and style pointing to the reign of Hezekiah. The words are inscribed on a prepared surface of the wall, so that it looks like the surface of a tablet, but the upper part of the inscription was missing. However, six lines remained, and they describe how the tunnel was dug by two teams of miners starting at opposite ends, working towards each other and meeting in the middle. The plaque, now in the Istabul Museum, is known as the 'Siloam Inscription', and in its standard English translation it read as follows:

'... when [the tunnel] was driven through. And this was the way in which it was cut through: - while ... [were] still ... axe[s], each man toward his fellow, and while there were still three cubits to be cut through, [there was heard] the voice of a man calling to his fellow, for there was an overlap in the rock on the right [and on the left]. And when the tunnel was driven through, the quarrymen hewed [the rock], each man toward his fellow, axe against axe; and the water flowed from the spring toward the reservoir for 1,200 cubits, and the height of the rock above the head[s] of the quarrymen was 100 cubits.'

2. date unknown. Father of Amariah and an ancestor of the prophet Zephaniah. [Zeph. 1:1]

3. date unknown. Father of Ater whose family returned with Zerubbabel to Judah from exile in Babylon. [Ezra 2:16; Neh. 7:21]

4. 5 century BC. A leader of Judah in the days of Nehemiah who signed the covenant to observe the Laws of God. [Neh. 10:17]

Hezion (Heb. 'light') c. 10 century BC. Father of Tabrimmon and grandfather of Ben-hadad 1, king of Aram. [1 Kgs. 15:18]

Hezir (Heb. 'boar') **1.** c. 10 century BC. A priest during the reign of King David responsible for the seventeenth turn of service in the Tabernacle. [1 Chr. 24:15]
2. 5 century BC. A leader of Judah who signed the covenant to observe the Laws of God in the time of Nehemiah. [Neh. 10:20]

Hezro c. 10 century BC. A Carmelite warrior in the armies of King David. [2 Sam. 23:35; 1 Chr. H:37]

Hezron *1. c.* 16 century BC. A son of Reuben, he went down to Egypt with his grandfather Jacob. [Gen. 46:9; exod. 6:14; Num. 26:6; 1 Chr. 5:3]
2. date unknown. Elder son of Perez and a grandson of Judah, he was an ancestor of King David. [Gen. 46:12; Num. 26:21; Ruth 4:18, 19; 1 Chr. 2:5, 9, 18, 21, 24, 25; 4:1]

Hiddai (Heb. 'leader') *c.* 10 century BC. One of King David's warriors who came from the 'brooks of Gaash' (2 Sam. 23:30). Also called Hurai. [2 Sam. 23:30; 1 Chr. 11:32]

Hiel (Heb. 'God lives') *c.* 9 century BC. Born in Bethel in the time of King Ahab, he rebuilt the city of Jericho which had been destroyed by Joshua. Hiel's two sons, Abiram and Segub, died in fulfilment of Joshua's curse upon the man who rebuilt Jericho. [Josh. 6:26; 1 Kgs. 16:34]

Hilkiah (Heb. 'God's portion') *1.* date unknown. A Levite descended from Merari, he was an ancestor of Ethan the musician of King David. [1 Chr. 6:45]
2. c. 10 century BC. Son of Hosah the Levite, he and his family served in the Tabernacle during the reign of King David. [1 Chr. 26:11]
3. c. 8 century BC. Father of Eliakim, head of King Hezekiah's household. [2 Kgs. 18:18, 26, 37; Isa. 22:20; 36:3, 22]
4. c. 7 century BC. The high priest in the time of King Josiah, he found a 'book of the law' (2 Kgs. 22:8) during the renovations to the Temple. The king was distressed at finding out from the book that the Laws of Moses were being neglected, and sent Hilkiah and four others to consult the prophetess Huldah, who predicted a grim fate for the Israelites. Hilkiah and his fellow-priests were ordered to destroy profane vessels and to purify the Temple. [2 Kgs. 22:4-14; 23:4, 24; 1 Chr. 6:13; 9:11; 2 Chr. 34:9-22; Ezra 7:1]
5. c. 7 century BC. Father of the prophet Jeremiah, he was a priest in Anathoth in the territory of Benjamin, and may have been a descendant of Abiathar, the priest banished to Anathoth by King Solomon. [Jer. 1:1, 2]
6. c. 6 century BC. Father of Gemariah whom King Zedekiah sent to Babylon with a message to the Emperor Nebuchadnezzar. [Jer. 29:3]
7. 6 century BC. A head priest who returned with Zerubbabel from exile in Babylon. His descendant Hashabiah was one of the chief priests of Judah when Joiakim was high priest. [Neh. 12:7, 21]
8. c. 5 century BC. A leader of Judah who stood on the right side of Ezra when he read from the Law of Moses to the people of Judah after the return from Babylon. [Neh. 8:4]

Hillel (Heb. 'praise') *c.* 12 century BC. Father of Abdon who was judge over Israel eight years. [Judg. 12:13, 15]

Hinnom date unknown. A man or family whose name was given to a valley at the southern and western edges of Jerusalem. It was here that child sacrifices were offered and the name Gehenna was derived from the word Gei (Heb. 'valley of') Hinnom. The valley is also called Ben-hinnom. [Josh. 15:8; 18:16; 2 Kgs. 23:10; 2 Chr. 28:3; 33:6; Neh. 11:30; Jer. 7:31, 32]

Hirah (Heb. 'noble') *c.* 16 century BC. An Adullamite shepherd and friend of Judah who was sent to find Judah's daughter-in-law Tamar. [Gen. 38:1; 20-2]

Hiram (Heb. 'my brother is exalted') *1. c.* 10 century BC. Hiram was king of Tyre on the Phoenician coast in succession to Abibaal. When David established Jerusalem as his capital, Hiram 'sent messengers to David, and cedar trees, also carpenters and masons who built David a house' (2 Sam. 5:11). A warm friendship existed between the two men 'for Hiram always loved David' (1 Kgs. 5:1).

Solomon also made an agreement with Hiram for the supply of cedar and for logs and gold for the building of the Temple, in exchange for wheat and olive oil. To balance accounts, Solomon ceded to Hiram twenty towns in Galilee. Another joint venture was the trade in the Red Sea area through the port of Eziongeber (modern Eilat). 'And Hiram sent with the fleet his servants, seamen who were familiar with the sea, together with the servants of Solomon.' (1 Kgs. 9:27) Also called Huram. [2 Sam. 5:11; 1 Kgs. 5:1–18; 9:11–27; 10:11–22; 1 Chr. 14:1; 2 Chr. 8:2–18; 9:10, 21]

2. *c.* 10 century BC. Hiram was the son of a widow from the tribe of Naphtali and his father was a man of Tyre. Solomon sent to Tyre for him in connection with the building of the Temple, 'and he was full of wisdom, understanding, and skill, for making any work in bronze' (1 Kgs. 7:14). Hiram cast the two great bronze pillars in front of the Temple, also the 'sea' (1 Kgs. 7:23), a great metal basin mounted on the backs of twelve oxen, and all the smaller basins and Temple implements. Also called Huram and Huram-abi. [1 Kgs. 7; 2 Chr. 2:13; 4–11, 16]

Hittites An ancient Canaanite tribe descended from Heth who were driven out of the land of Canaan by the children of Israel under Joshua. [Gen. 10:15; 25:9; Exod. 23:23; Deut. 7:1; Josh. 3:10; 2 Sam. 11:3]

Hivites 13 century BC. An ancient Canaanite tribe most of whom were driven out of Canaan by the children of Israel under Joshua. [Exod. 23:23; Deut. 7:1; Josh. 3:10; 1 Chr. 1:15]

Hizki (Heb. 'strong') date unknown. Son of Elpaal and a leader of the tribe of Benjamin living in Jerusalem. [1 Chr. 8:17]

Hizkiah (Heb. 'my strength is God') date unknown. Son of Neariah of the tribe of Judah and a descendant of King David. [1 Chr. 3:23]

Hobab *see* JETHRO

Hobaiah *see* HABAIAH

Hod (Heb. 'splendour') date unknown. Son of Zophah, he was a leader of the tribe of Asher and a mighty warrior. [1 Chr. 7:37]

Hodaviah (Heb. 'praise') *1.* date unknown. A leader of a portion of the tribe of Manasseh living east of the river Jordan. [1 Chr. 5:24]

2. date unknown. Son of Hassenuah, the Benjaminite, his grandson Sallu returned to Jerusalem from captivity in Babylon in the time of Nehemiah. [1 Chr. 9:7]

3. date unknown. Ancestor of a family of Levites who returned to Judah with Zerubbabel from captivity in Babylon. Also called Hodevah. [Ezra 2:40; Neh. 7:43]

4. date unknown. Son of Elioenai of the tribe of Judah and a descendant of King David. [1 Chr. 3:24]

Hodesh (Heb. 'new moon') date unknown. Third wife of Shaharaim of the tribe of Benjamin who bore him seven sons. [1 Chr. 8:9]

Hodevah *see* HODAVIAH *3.*

Hodiah (Heb. 'splendour of God') *1.* date unknown. A leader of the tribe of Judah, he was the grandfather of Keilah the Garmite and Eshtemoa the Maacathite. [1 Chr. 4:19]

2. 5 century BC. A Levite in the time of Ezra who explained the Law to the assembled people of Judah on the public fast day, and who called upon the people to praise God and confess their sins. He also signed the covenant to observe the Laws of God. [Neh. 8:7; 9:5; 10:10]

3. 5 century BC. Another Levite who signed the covenant to observe the Laws of God. [Neh. 10:13]

4. 5 century BC. A leader of Judah who also signed the covenant to obey the Laws of God. [Neh. 10:18]

Hoglah (Heb. 'partridge') *c.* 13 century BC. One of the five daughters of Zelophehad who appealed to Moses, claiming their father's patrimony since he had no sons. [Num. 26:33; 27:1; 36:11; Josh. 17:3]

Hoham *c.* 13 century BC. Hoham, king of Hebron, made an alliance with four other Amorite kings to attack the city of Gibeon for having made a peace treaty with Joshua. Defeated by Joshua, the five kings hid themselves in a cave but were discovered. Later they were taken out, put to death, and buried in the same cave. [Josh. 10]

Homam *see* HEMAN *1.*

Hophni *c.* 11 century BC. Hophni and his brother Phinehas were priests at the sanctuary of Shiloh, where their father Eli was the chief priest. They abused their office by seducing women who came to the Temple, and by taking for themselves the best part of the sacrificial meat. Eli remonstrated with them, but they took no notice.

The two priests were sent with the Ark of the Covenant to rally the Israelite forces being hard pressed in battle by the Philistines at Aphek. The Israelites were defeated and the Ark captured, and Hophni and Phinehas were among the slain. The shock of their death and the loss of the Ark killed their aged father. [1 Sam. 1:3; 2:34; 3:13; 4:11]

Hophra *see* PHARAOH 10.

Horam (Heb. 'hill') *c.* 13 century BC. King of Gezer, he went to the aid of the town of Lachish when it was besieged by Joshua and was defeated. [Josh. 10:33]

Hori (Heb. 'noble') *1.* date unknown. Eldest son of Lotan and a grandson of Seir, the Horite. [Gen. 36:22; 1 Chr. 1:39]

2. c. 13 century BC. Father of Shaphat of the tribe of Simeon, one of the twelve men sent by Moses to spy out the Promised Land. [Num. 13:5]

Horites Inhabitants of Seir, the northwest region of Edom, south of the Dead Sea. They took their name from Hori, grandson of Seir who gave his name to the territory. (Modern scholars consider that the Horites were Hurrians whose original home was in the mountains of Armenia and who then thrust down into northern Mesopotamia. Some of them moved south into Edom in the early centuries of the 2nd millennium BC.) [Gen. 14:6; 36:20, 21, 29, 30; Deut. 2:12, 22]

Hosah (Heb. 'refuge') *c.* 10 century BC. A Levite descended from Merari, he was gatekeeper at the west gate of the Tabernacle during the reign of King David. [1 Chr. 16:38; 26:10, 11, 16]

Hosea (Heb. 'salvation') *c.* 8 century BC. A Hebrew prophet in the Kingdom of Israel. Hosea, the son of Beeri, prophesied in the northern kingdom of Israel for a period starting towards the end of the reign of Jeroboam II (783–43 BC). From the death of that illustrious king until the fall of Samaria in 721 BC, the kingdom went through a decline marked by political assassinations and moral and religious laxity. Hosea vigourously denounced these evils, particularly the prevailing idolworship, and prophesied the disasters that would come as a punishment from the Lord.

Nothing is known about Hosea's personal life, except for his own revelations about his disastrous family life. He was married to Gomer, the daughter of Diblaim, who turned out to be a loose woman, 'a wife of harlotry' (Hos. 1:2). To the three children she bore, he gave names of bitter rejection: Jezreel, after the valley where Jehu, founder of the hated royal house, had carried out his bloody coup; Loruhamah, 'not pitied' (Hos. 1:8); Loammi, 'not of my people' (Hos. 1:9). The two latter names at least suggest that he did not regard them as his own offspring. He probably divorced Gomer by the formal declaration that 'she is not my wife, and I am not her husband' (Hos. 2:2). But he continued to love his erring wife, and at some later stage appeared to have forgiven her and taken her back.

His domestic experience strongly influenced Hosea's concept of the Lord's relationship with His people. He saw Israel as a spouse betraying God her husband, and committing adultery with pagan cults. Israel would be punished and driven out by God, but one day she would purge herself of sin and be forgiven.

Hosea fiercely attacked the Canaanite practices which crept into the 'high places', the local shrines on hilltops and under sacred trees. He was caustic too about the golden calves introduced into the sanctuaries of Bethel and Dan by the breakaway northern kingdom of Israel. Hosea did not hesitate to attack the priesthood for failing to set an example to the people: 'I reject you from being a priest to me. And since you have forgotten the law of your God, I also will forget your children.' (Hos. 4:6)

But the prophet does not call for mere observance of the formal tenets of religion. For him, true faith is a matter of the heart and not of external ritual: 'For I desire steadfast love and not sacrifice, the knowledge of God, rather than burnt offerings.' (Hos. 6:6) Hosea here struck a note that was echoed by Isaiah and Jeremiah and became one of the basic themes of the Hebrew prophetic strain.

In a period of turbulence in the Near East, Hosea warned the rulers of his little land against seeking safety in weapons or in alliances with great powers: 'Ephraim is like a dove, silly and without sense, calling to Egypt, going to Assyria.' (Hos. 7:11) Only faith in God could save his people from destruction.

Hosea has been regarded as a fierce prophet of disaster, who told his fellow-countrymen that 'they sow the wind, and they shall reap the whirlwind' (Hos. 8:7). But his God of wrath was also a God of love and mercy, who felt about his chosen people like a father does about a son whom he held in his arms in infancy, and is reluctant to punish. He is a God who says: 'I will not execute my fierce anger, I will not again destroy Ephraim; for I am God and not man, the Holy One in your midst.' (Hos. 11:9) The Book of Hosea ends with an idyllic picture of future happiness for the Israelites, when they have been reconciled with the Lord. 'O Ephraim, what have I to do with idols? It is I who answer and look after you. I am like an evergreen cypress.' (Hos. 14:8) [Book of Hosea]

Hoshaiah (Heb. 'helped by God') *1.* 6 century BC. Father of Azariah, a leader of Judah in the time of Jeremiah. [Jer. 42:1; 43:2]
2. 5 century BC. A leader of Judah in the time of Nehemiah who led half the princes of Judah at the ceremony of dedicating the walls of Jerusalem. [Neh. 12:32]

Hoshama (Heb. 'when God hears') *c.* 6 century BC. Seventh son of Jeconiah of the royal house of Judah and a descendant of King David. [1 Chr. 3:18]

Hoshea (Heb. 'salvation') *1.* see JOSHUA *1.*
2. c. 10 century BC. Son of Azaziah, he

was head of the tribe of Ephraim in the days of King David. [1 Chr. 27:20]

3. Nineteenth and last king of Israel after the monarchy split, he reigned 732–24 BC. Hoshea, son of Elah, was the last king of Israel before the kingdom was finally engulfed by the rising tide of Assyrian imperialism.

Already in the reign of his predecessor, Pekah, the Assyrian forces had invaded Israel, occupied the Galilee, the coastal district and the Transjordan territory of Gilead, and converted them into provinces under Assyrian governors. Hoshea had then murdered Pekah and replaced him on the throne. Whether this was done with the connivance of the Assyrians is not clear, but what is clear is that Hoshea was a puppet king subservient to his Assyrian masters, and paying tribute to them. That was the price for retaining the nominal independence of a rump kingdom that had shrunk to little more than the capital Samaria and the Ephraim hill-region around it.

After the death of the Assyrian monarch Tiglathpileser III, Hoshea made a rash attempt to throw off the Assyrian yoke by invoking the rival imperial power of Egypt. The new Assyrian ruler, Shalmaneser V, reacted by invading what was left of Israel, capturing and imprisoning Hoshea, and laying siege to the capital Samaria. Its surrender in 721 BC and the deportation of its inhabitants marked the end of the northern kingdom of Israel. [2 Kgs. 15:30; 17:1–6; 18:1, 9, 10]

4. 5 century BC. A leader of Israel who signed the covenant to observe the Laws of God in the time of Nehemiah. [Neh. 10:23]

Hotham (Heb. 'seal') *1.* date unknown. Son of Heber and a leader of the tribe of Asher. [1 Chr. 7:32]

2. c. 11 century BC. Father of two of King David's distinguished warriors, Shama and Jeiel. [1 Chr. 11:44]

Hothir (Heb. 'fullness') *c.* 10 century BC. Son of Heman, King David's musician. He and his brothers played musical instruments in the Tabernacle service under their father's direction, and Hothir was responsible for the twenty-first turn of service. [1 Chr. 25:4, 28]

Hul date unknown. Son of Aram and a grandson of Shem. [Gen. 10:23; 1 Chr. 1:17]

Huldah (Heb. 'weasel') *c.* 7 century BC. Huldah, a respected prophetess, was the wife of Shallum, keeper of the royal wardrobe. King Josiah sent a deputation to consult with her on what was to be done about the 'book of the law' (2 Kgs. 22:8) found during the repairs to the Temple. She replied: 'Thus says the Lord, Behold, I will bring evil upon this place and upon its inhabitants ... Because they have forsaken me and have burned incense to other gods ...' (2 Kgs. 22:16, 17) However, Josiah himself would die in peace. [2 Kgs. 22:14–20; 2 Chr. 34:22–8]

Hupham *see* HUPPIM *1.*

Huppah (Heb. 'covered') *c.* 10 century BC. A leader of the priestly family who took the thirteenth rota of service in the Tabernacle in the reign of King David. [1 Chr. 24:13]

Huppim *1. c.* 16 century BC. Son of Benjamin, he went down to Egypt with his grandfather Jacob. Also called Hupham. [Gen. 46:21; Num. 26:39]

2. date unknown. A descendant of Benjamin and a leader of the tribe. [1 Chr. 7:12, 15]

Hur (Heb. 'noble') *1. c.* 13 century BC. Hur was one of the children of Israel in the desert. In the battle against the Amalekites, Moses had to keep his rod lifted 'and Aaron and Hur held up his hands, one on one side, and the other on the other side; so his hands were steady until the going down of the sun' (Exod. 17:12).

Later when Moses went up Mount Sinai, he left Aaron and Hur in charge of the encampment.

Because of his intimacy with Moses and Aaron, Jewish tradition holds that he was the husband of Miriam, their eldest sister. [Exod. 17:10–12; 24:14]
2. *c.* 13 century BC. Grandfather of Bezalel of the tribe of Judah, and a descendant of Hezron or Perez. [Exod. 31:2; 35:30; 38:22; 1 Chr. 2:19, 20, 50; 4:1–4; 2 Chr. 1:5]
3. *c.* 13 century BC. One of the five Midianite kings killed by the children of Israel in the wilderness on their way to the land of Israel. [Num. 31:8; Josh. 13:21]
4. *c.* 5 century BC. Father of Rephaiah, the ruler of half of Jerusalem in the time of Nehemiah, who helped rebuild the walls of Jerusalem. [Neh. 3:9]

Hurai *see* HIDDAI

Huram (Heb. 'my brother is exalted') *1.* date unknown. Son of Bela and a grandson of Benjamin. [1 Chr. 8:5]
2. *see* HIRAM 1.
3. *see* HIRAM 2.

Huram-abi *see* HIRAM 2.

Huri (Heb. 'noble') date unknown. Son of Jaroah and a grandson of Gilead of the tribe of Gad. [1 Chr. 5:14]
Hushah (Heb. 'haste') date unknown. Son of Ezer and a leader of the tribe of Judah, he was descended from Hur. [1 Chr. 4:4]

Hushai (Heb. 'my brother's gift') *c.* 11 century BC. Hushai the Archite (from a village west of Bethel) was an intimate friend and adviser of King David. When David fled from Jerusalem after the revolt of Absalom, Hushai came to join him 'with his coat rent and earth upon

his head' (2 Sam. 15:32). David persuaded him to remain behind and gain Absalom's confidence. In this way he would be able to counteract the advice that would be given by Ahithophel, David's leading counsellor who had gone over to Absalom's camp.

When Absalom entered Jerusalem he was surprised to be met by Hushai who greeted him warmly: 'Long live the king! Long live the king!' (2 Sam. 16:16) Absalom took him to task for having deserted David: 'Is this your loyalty to your friend? Why did you not go with your friend?' (2 Sam. 16:17) Hushai answered him by explaining that his duty was to serve the man chosen by the Lord and the people of Israel, and Absalom took him at his word.

Absalom knew that even with Jerusalem in his hands his power could not be secure as long as David was at large and free to strike back. He asked for advice. Ahithophel urged immediate pursuit that same night so that David could be caught before he had a chance to organize a counter-thrust. Hushai argued in favour of greater caution. To engage David and his men in a hurry would entail too great a risk for Absalom's cause. 'And Absalom and all the men of Israel said, "The counsel of Hushai the Archite is better than the counsel of Ahithophel."' (2 Sam. 17:14) Hushai then sent a trusted runner to David telling him not to spend that night on the Jericho plain but to cross the Jordan, where he could rebuild his forces. Realizing that Absalom had made a fatal blunder and that his own career was wrecked, Ahithophel went home and hanged himself.

Hushai thus successfully carried out the task entrusted to him by David. The gratitude of David's house was reflected in the fact that Hushai's son Baana was later appointed by King Solomon as the commissioner in charge of one of the twelve administrative and tax districts of the king. [2 Sam. 15:32, 37; 16:16–18; 17:516; 1 Kgs. 4:16; 1 Chr. 27:33]

Husham (Heb. 'haste') date unknown. The Yemanite king of Edom. [Gen. 36:34, 35; 1 Chr. 1:45, 46]

Hushim (Heb. 'haste') *1. c.* 16 century BC. Son of Dan and the grandson of Jacob and Bilhah, he went down with Jacob into Egypt. Also called Shuham. [Gen. 46:23; Num. 26:42]

2. date unknown. A leader of the tribe of Benjamin descended from Aher. [1 Chr. 7:12]

3. date unknown. One of the wives of Shaharaim, a leader of the tribe of Benjamin. [1 Chr. 8:8, 11]

I

Ibhar (Heb. 'he will choose') *c.* 10 century BC. A son born to King David in Jerusalem. [2 Sam. 5:15; 1 Chr. 3:6; 14:5]

Ibneiah (Heb. 'God builds') 5 century BC. Son of Jeroham, he was one of the first men of Benjamin to settle in Jerusalem after the return from exile in Babylon. [1 Chr. 9:8]

Ibnijah (Heb. 'God builds') date unknown. Ancestor of Ibneiah, one of the first men of Benjamin to settle in Jerusalem after the return from exile in Babylon. [1 Chr. 9:8]

Ibri (Heb. 'Hebrew') *c.* 10 century BC. A Levite descended from Merari, he served in the Tabernacle in the reign of King David. [1 Chr. 24:27]

Ibsam (Heb. 'balsam') *c.* 16 century BC. Son of Tola and a grandson of Issachar, he was a leader of the tribe and a mighty warrior. [1 Chr. 7:2]

Ibzan *c.* 12 century BC. Judge of Israel for seven years, he succeeded Jephthah. His sixty children married outside the tribe of Zebulun. [Judg. 12:8–10]

Ichabod (Heb. 'inglorious') *c.* 11 century BC. Grandson of Eli and son of Phinehas a corrupt priest, he was born after the death of his father and grandfather. His mother lived long enough to call her son Ichabod – because the 'glory has departed from Israel' (1 Sam. 4:21) – and then she herself died. [1 Sam. 4:21; 14:3]

Idbash (Heb. 'honey-sweet') date unknown. A leader of the tribe of Judah. [1 Chr. 4:3]

Iddo (Heb. 'God's friend') *1.* 10 century BC. Father of Ahinadab, one of King Solomon's twelve officers responsible for supplying the provisions of the royal household. [1 Kgs. 4:14]
2. c. 10 century BC. Son of Zechariah, he was appointed by King David as ruler of the half-tribe of Manasseh in Gilead, east of the Jordan. [1 Chr. 27:21]
3. date unknown. Son of Joah, a Levite, he was descended from Gershom. Also called Adaiah. [1 Chr. 6:21, 41]
4. c. 10 century BC. The seer who prophesied against the kings Jeroboam, Rehoboam and Abijah. His writings are referred to in the Second Book of Chronicles but have not survived to our day. [2 Chr. 9:29; 12:15; 13:22]
5. c. 6 century BC. Father of Berechiah and grandfather of the prophet Zechariah, who describes him as a prophet. In the Book of Ezra he is described as Zechariah's father. [Ezra 5:1; 6:14; Zech. 1:1, 7]
6. 6 century BC. A priest of Judah who returned with Zerubbabel from exile in Babylon. His descendant, Zechariah, was one of the chief priests in the days of Nehemiah. [Neh. 12:4, 16]
7. 5 century BC. A leader of Judah and chief of the exiles at Casiphia, at Ezra's request he sent priests and Levites to serve in the Tabernacle in Jerusalem. [Ezra 8:17]

Iezer *see* ABIEZER *1.*

Igal (Heb. 'may God redeem') *1. c.* 13 century BC. Son of Joseph, he represented the tribe of Issachar among the twelve spies chosen by Moses. He was one of the majority of the spies who felt that the Canaanite people who lived there in their walled cities were too strong for the Israelites to drive out. [Num. 13:7–33]

2. c. 10 century BC. Son of Nathan of Zobah, he was a warrior in the armies of King David. Also known as Joel. [2 Sam. 23:36; 1 Chr. 11:38]

3. c. 5 century BC. A son of Shemaiah of the tribe of Judah and a descendant of King David. [1 Chr. 3:22]

Igdaliah (Heb. 'may God be glorified') *c.* 6 century BC. Father of Hanan, he is described by the prophet Jeremiah as 'a man of God' and his descendants occupied rooms in the vicinity of the Temple. [Jer. 35:4]

Ikkesh (Heb. 'stubborn') *c.* 10 century BC. Father of Ira, who was a heroic warrior and one of David's twelve army commanders. [2 Sam. 23:26; 1 Chr. 11:28; 27:9]

Ilai (Heb. 'exalted') *c.* 10 century BC. An Ahohite warrior in the army of King David, distinguished for his bravery. Also known as Zalmon the Ahohite. [2 Sam. 23:28; 1 Chr. 11:29]

Imlah (Heb. 'full') *c.* 9 century BC. Father of the prophet Micaiah consulted by Ahab and Jehoshaphat, kings of Israel and Judah. [1 Kgs. 22:8, 9; 2 Chr. 18:7, 8]

Immanuel (Heb. 'God is with us') *c.* 8 century BC. The symbolic name given by Isaiah to the child he predicted would be born unto the royal family of Judah, and who would choose good and reject evil. [Isa. 7:14]

Immer (Heb. 'lamb') *1. c.* 10 century BC. Head of a family of priests who served in the Tabernacle in the reign of King David. [1 Chr. 9:12; 24:14; Ezra 2:37; 10:20; Neh. 3:29; 7:40; 11:13]

2. c. 7 century BC. Father of Pashhur, the chief priest in the Temple who beat the prophet Jeremiah and put him in the stocks. [Jer. 20:1]

Imna date unknown. Son of Helem, he and his family were leaders of the tribe of Asher and mighty warriors. [1 Chr. 7:35]

Imnah (Heb. 'may God defend') *1. c.* 16 century BC. Son of Asher, he went down to Egypt at the same time as his grandfather Jacob. [Gen. 46:17; Num. 26:44; 1 Chr. 7:30]

2. c. 8 century BC. Father of Kore, the Levite responsible for distributing the tithes and offerings in the reign of King Hezekiah. [2 Chr. 31:14]

Imrah (Heb. 'stubborn') date unknown. Son of Zophah, he and his family were leaders of the tribe of Asher and mighty warriors. [1 Chr. 7:36]

Imri (Heb. 'my lamb') *1.* date unknown. An ancestor of Uthai who was one of the first members of the tribe of Judah to return to Jerusalem after the Babylonian exile. [1 Chr. 9:4]

2. 5 century BC. Father of Zaccur who helped rebuild the walls of Jerusalem in the time of Nehemiah. [Neh. 3:2]

Iob *c.* 16 century BC. Son of Issachar, he went down to Egypt with his grandfather Jacob. Also called Jashub. [Gen. 46:13; 1 Num. 26:24; 1 Chr. 7:1]

Iphdeiah (Heb. 'may God redeem') date unknown. Son of Shashak, he was one of the leaders of the tribe of Benjamin living in Jerusalem. [1 Chr. 8:25]

Ir *see* IRI

Ira *1. c.* 10 century BC. A court officer

of King David and a priest of Israel. [2 Sam. 20:26]

2. *c*. 10 century BC. Son of Ikkesh of Tekoa, he was one of the warriors in King David's army distinguished for his bravery and appointed one of the twelve commanders. [2 Sam. 23:26; 1 Chr. 11:28; 27:9]

3. *c*. 10 century BC. An Ithrite in the army of King David, distinguished for his bravery. [2 Sam. 23:38; 1 Chr. 11:40]

Irad (Heb. 'fleet') date unknown. Son of Enoch and a grandson of Cain. [Gen. 4:18]

Iram date unknown. An Edomite leader descended from Esau. [Gen. 36:43; 1 Chr. 1:54]

Iri *c*. 16 century BC. Son of Bela and a grandson of Benjamin, he and his brothers were leaders of the tribe of Benjamin and mighty warriors. Also known as Ir, the father of Shuppim and Huppim. [1 Chr. 7:7, 12]

Irijah (Heb. 'may God see') *c*. 6 century BC. Son of Shelemiah, he was an army captain in Jerusalem in the days of King Zedekiah who imprisoned the prophet Jeremiah after accusing him of deserting to the Babylonian army. [Jer. 37:13]

Irnahash (Heb. 'serpent city') date unknown. Son of Tehinnah, a leader of the tribe of Judah. [1 Chr. 4:12]

Iru *c*. 13 century BC. Son of Caleb, and a leader of the tribe of Judah. [1 Chr. 4:15]

Isaac (Heb. 'he laughed') *c*. 18–16 centuries BC. The second patriarch son of Abraham.

Abraham was ninety-nine years old when the Lord told him that his barren wife Sarah would bear him a son. According to the account in Genesis, Abraham laughed in his heart, and Sarah

was also bitterly amused because she was ninety and long past child-bearing age. The son was called Isaac (Hebrew *Yitzchak*) meaning 'he laughed'.

When Isaac was a young lad, Abraham's obedience to God was put to a fearful test. He was told to take the boy to a distant mountain top and sacrifice him to the Lord. They set out with two young servants and a load of firewood. When they neared the place, the servants and the ass were left behind and father and son went forward on foot. Isaac asked, 'Behold, the fire and the wood; but where is the lamb for a burnt offering?' (Gen. 22:7) Abraham replied evasively that the Lord would provide the lamb.

At the spot for the sacrifice, Abraham erected an altar, arranged the wood on it, and laid the bound boy on top. When he stretched his hand for the knife an angel of the Lord intervened, and a ram that was seen in a nearby thicket was sacrificed instead of Isaac.

Stricken in years, Abraham concerned himself with finding a wife for Isaac, then forty years old. Abraham did not want him to marry a local Canaanite girl, so he sent a trusted servant to his own kinsmen in Haran (northern Syria). The servant returned with Rebekah, the daughter of Abraham's nephew. One evening Isaac was strolling through the fields when he saw the camel caravan approaching. Rebekah modestly veiled herself and alighted to greet him. 'Then Isaac brought her into the tent, and took Rebekah, and she became his wife; and he loved her. So Isaac was comforted after his mother's death.' (Gen. 24:67)

Nearing the end of his days, Abraham declared that Isaac would be the heir to his estate. To avoid trouble later, Abraham gave gifts to the sons he had had by concubines and sent them to live further east. Abraham died and was buried next to Sarah in the Cave of Machpelah by Isaac and his half-brother

Ishmael, the son of Hagar, Sarah's Egyptian slave-maid.

At first Rebekah was barren but after Isaac had appealed to the Lord, she gave birth to twins. The first to be born was Esau, covered with red hair, and then Jacob, clutching his brother's heel.

There was a famine in the land and Isaac started moving with his flocks and herds towards Egypt, as his father Abraham had done in an earlier famine. He reached Gerar, ruled over by his father's friend (or his friend's namesake) Abimelech. Here the Lord appeared to him and told him not to go down to Egypt but to stay in that area. The Lord recalled his covenant with Abraham and repeated to Isaac the promise that he would be blessed and multiply and the land would belong to his seed. So Isaac remained in Gerar.

As Abraham had done with Sarah, Isaac passed Rebekah off as his sister for fear that he might be killed for her sake, as she too was fair to look upon. Looking through a window Abimelech saw Isaac and Rebekah together and realized they were husband and wife. He was angry at first at the deception but gave orders that anyone who molested them would be put to death.

Isaac re-opened the wells that Abraham had dug in this area and that had been filled in again. He reaped good crops from his sowing; his herds and flocks multiplied and he became wealthy and important. This aroused local envy. At Abimelech's suggestion, Isaac moved further away, though remaining in the region of Gerar and Beersheba. Again he located and restored some of Abraham's wells. There was friction with local shepherds over two of these watering places, but at the third, Rehoboth, they were left in peace. Isaac said, 'For now the Lord has made room for us, and we shall be fruitful in the land.' (Gen. 26:22) Isaac built an altar at Beersheba as his father had done.

ISAAC'S BLESSING

Being aged and practically blind, Isaac sent for his favourite son Esau who was a skilled hunter. He asked him to take his quiver and bow, shoot a deer and prepare some of the venison he loved. He would then bless him before he died. Rebekah overheard this, and determined to secure the blessing for Jacob whom she loved more. She told Jacob to slaughter two young goats, made a savoury stew of the meat, and sent it in to Isaac with Jacob pretending to be Esau. To make the deception more effective, she covered Jacob's smooth hands and neck with bits of the fleece of the slain kids (for Esau was a hairy man) and she put Esau's garment on Jacob. Isaac was suspicious at first, saying, 'The voice is Jacob's voice, but the hands are the hands of Esau.' (Gen. 27:22) But when he asked Jacob to come near and kiss him, the smell of the fields clinging to Esau's garment convinced him. He then gave Jacob his blessing, declaring that he would be the head of the family when Isaac died and his brethren would serve him

Esau came in with the venison he had prepared for his father, and Isaac realized he had been deceived. But he could not now take back the blessing bestowed on Jacob. Esau, wailing with anger and grief, pressed Isaac to bless him as well. The old man replied that Esau would have to serve Jacob, but he too would prosper and become independent.

Fearing that Esau would kill Jacob in revenge, Rebekah persuaded Isaac to send Jacob to her brother Laban in Haran so that he too should marry someone of his own kin.

Isaac died at the age of one hundred and eighty and was buried by his twin sons Esau and Jacob in the Cave of Machpelah at Hebron, with his father and mother and his wife Rebekah.

Of the three patriarchs, Isaac is a less striking figure than either his father Abraham or his son Jacob.

In the dramatic episode of the

sacrifice, he shows a touching faith and docility towards his father. In his later life, moving through the southland with his flocks, he stays in his father's footsteps, re-digging Abraham's abandoned wells. As soon as there is friction with the local inhabitants, he chooses to move elsewhere.

In his old age, he is not only deceived by his wife and his son Jacob, but seems helpless to undo the wrong done to the first-born son Esau, cheated of the paternal blessing.

The character that emerges from the story is not strong, but benign, pious and gentle. [Gen. 17–28]

Isaiah (Heb. 'God's salvation') *c.* second half of 8 century BC. A Hebrew prophet in the kingdom of Judah. Isaiah the son of Amoz was the greatest of the Hebrew prophets, and the author of the most sublime religious poetry in the Old Testament. The force and beauty of his message is best appreciated in the original Hebrew, a terse and sonorous language, rich in concrete similes.

Isaiah was born in Jerusalem about 765 BC. At the age of twenty-five he had a vision of God: 'In the year that King Uzziah died I saw the Lord sitting upon a throne, high and lifted up; and his train filled the temple ... And I heard the voice of the Lord saying, "Whom shall I send, and who will go for us?" Then I said, "Here am I! Send me."' (Isa. 6:1, 8) From that day he devoted himself to the vocation of prophecy.

The Hebrew prophets were inspired men who preached the word of God and fearlessly attacked the evils of men, not even sparing kings. They acted as the moral conscience of the community. Being able to predict future events was not their main attribute. The discourses of some of them were preserved and later collected in separate books of the Bible.

The little that is known about Isaiah is contained in the book that bears his name, and from the parallel account in the Second Book of Kings. It appears that he was a man of position in the capital, with access to the king and a voice in affairs of state. He had a wife and two sons, both of whom are given symbolic names: Shear-jashub ('the remnant will return') and Mahershalal-hash-baz ('the booty and shame are imminent' – a reference to the impending doom of Samaria). His prophecies covered about half a century, during the reigns of the Judean kings Jotham, Ahaz and Hezekiah.

His whole life was bound up with Jerusalem, that 'faithful city' he loved and chided. In his vision of the future it was from this city, remote in the Judean hills, that men would gain inspiration: '... and many peoples shall come, and say: "Come, let us go up to the mountain of the Lord, to the house of the God of Jacob; that he may teach us his ways and that we may walk in his paths." For out of Zion shall go forth the law, and the word of the Lord from Jerusalem.' (Isa. 2:3)

It was a turbulent period in the history of the Near East. The two small Hebrew kingdoms, Israel and Judah, often at odds with each other, were being caught up in the clash of empires. In Isaiah's time, the dominant power was Assyria, located on the Upper Orontes river in Mesopotamia. Four times in Isaiah's life the Assyrian cohorts rolled southward 'like a wolf on the fold' (Byron), threatening the small states in their path. The northern kingdom of Israel was wiped out with the fall of Samaria in 721 BC. In Judah's struggle to survive, its rulers sought to insure the kingdom by makeshift alliances. Isaiah strongly disapproved of this game of power politics. As a statesman, he did not believe that Judah's safety lay in pacts of expediency. As a man of deep religious conviction, he insisted on faith in God alone. He saw the enemy before the gate as an instrument of God's will, to punish the chosen people for its transgressions.

Soon after Ahaz came to the throne of Judah, Pekah king of Israel and Rezin king of Aram-Damascus formed an alliance in an attempt to halt the Assyrian advance. They wanted Ahaz to join them, and when he refused they invaded Judah to depose him. When they reached Jerusalem, there was panic in the city. The king sent to consult Isaiah, who replied firmly, 'do not fear, and do not let your heart be faint because of these two smouldering stumps of firebrands ...' (Isa. 7:4). The Lord would not permit the attempt to succeed.

Against Isaiah's counsel, Ahaz sent messengers with gifts to the king of Assyria, asking for his help. The Assyrians advanced, took Damascus, and occupied part of Israel. The pressure was relieved on Judah, but she remained a subservient vassal of Assyria.

Thirty years later, King Hezekiah joined in a revolt against the Assyrians, who marched to quell it. Isaiah derided Hezekiah's feverish preparations for the defence of Jerusalem: '... and you saw that the breaches of the city of David were many, and you collected the waters of the lower pool, and you counted the houses of Jerusalem, and you broke down the houses to fortify the wall ... But you did not look to him who did it, or have regard for him who planned it long ago.' (Isa. 22:9–11)

Isaiah was even more scornful of the mission Hezekiah sent to Egypt to gain support against the Assyrians. '"Woe to the rebellious children," says the Lord, "who carry out a plan, but not mine ... Therefore shall the protection of Pharaoh turn to your shame, and the shelter in the shadow of Egypt to your humiliation."' (Isa. 30:1, 3) He pointed out that 'The Egyptians are men, and not God; and their horses are flesh, and not spirit' (Isa. 31:3).

In 701 BC the Assyrian monarch Sennacherib swept through Judah and de-manded the surrender of Jerusalem. It was again Isaiah who persuaded Hezekiah to stand firm: 'Therefore thus says the Lord concerning the king of Assyria, He shall not come into this city or shoot an arrow there ... By the way that he came, by the same he shall return ... For I will defend this city to save it.' (2 Kgs. 19:32–4)

A pestilence struck the camp of the Assyrians and they withdrew. The deliverance of Jerusalem was regarded as a divine miracle.

THE MESSAGE OF ISAIAH

In vivid phrases Isaiah foretold the fate of each of Judah's enemies. About Babylon he thundered: 'wild beasts will lie down there, and its houses will be full of howling creatures; ... Fallen, fallen is Babylon; and all the images of her gods he has shattered to the ground.' (Isa. 13:21; 21:9)

Isaiah's strongest invective however was reserved for his own people. They were a 'sinful nation, a people laden with iniquity, offspring of evildoers ...' (Isa. 1:4). 'How the faithful city has become a harlot, she that was full of justice! Righteousness lodged in her, but now murderers. Your silver has become dross, your wine mixed with water.' (Isa. 1:21, 22)

Isaiah railed against religious hypocrisy: 'What to me is the multitude of your sacrifices? says the Lord; I have had enough of burnt offerings of rams and the fat of fed beasts; ... When you spread forth your hands, I will hide my eyes from you; even though you make many prayers, I will not listen; your hands are full of blood.' (Isa. 1:11, 15) What the Lord wanted, he said, was not rituals and prayers but simply that each man should 'cease to do evil, learn to do good' (Isa. 1:16, 17).

It was not only the prophets of humble origin, like Amos and Hosea, that lashed out against the greed and luxury of the establishment and the exploitation of the poor. This social concern was deeply indebted in the Hebrew prophetic strain, and was shared by men of birth and position like Isaiah and Jeremiah. Isaiah abhorred the ostentation and moral laxity he saw around him, especially at the court. 'Your princes are rebels and companions of thieves. Every one loves a bribe and runs after gifts. They do not defend the fatherless, and the widow's cause does not come to them.' (Isa. 1:23)

He had no respect for men of property as such: 'Woe to those who join house to house, who add field to field.' (Isa. 5:8)

He was especially caustic about ladies of fashion who were solely concerned with their own beauty and adornment. He stripped them of their finery in one of the most precise and biting passages in the Bible: 'Because the daughters of Zion are haughty and walk with outstretched necks, glancing wantonly with their eyes, mincing along as they go, tinkling with their feet; the Lord will smite with a scab the heads of the daughters of Zion, and the Lord will lay bare their secret parts. In that day the Lord will take away the finery of the anklets, the headbands, and the crescents; the pendants, the bracelets, and the scarfs; the headdresses, the armlets, the sashes, the perfume boxes, and the amulets; the signet rings and nose rings; the festal robes, the mantles, the cloaks and the handbags; the garments of gauze, the linen garments, the turbans, and the veils. Instead of perfume there will be rottenness; and instead of a girdle, a rope; and instead of well-set hair, baldness; and instead of a rich robe, a girding of sack-cloth; instead of beauty, shame.' (Isa. 3:16–24)

Isaiah's pessimism about the pending fate of his country was tempered by hope. It was not God's design to destroy utterly his chosen but erring people. Some would survive and would return to Zion and to righteousness. 'In that day the remnant of Israel and the survivors of the house of Jacob will no more lean upon him that smote them, but will lean upon the Lord, the Holy One of Israel, in truth. A remnant will return, the remnant of Jacob, to the mighty God.' (Isa. 10:20, 21)

The Immanuel passage in Chapter 7 is celebrated but its meaning is obscure. It opens with the words 'Behold, a young woman shall conceive and bear a son, and shall call his name Immanuel. He shall eat curds and honey when he knows how to refuse the evil and choose the good.' (Isa. 7:14, 15) The name Immanuel means in Hebrew 'God is with us' which was very relevant to Isaiah's argument at the time with King Ahaz about resistance to the invasion by Pekah, king of Israel. The Hebrew word translated in the Authorized Version as 'virgin' was 'almah', which means a young woman, single or married. Nevertheless Christian theologians regard the passage as a prediction of the birth of Jesus. The same applies to another famous passage in Chapter 9: 'For to us a child is born, to us a son is given; and the government will be upon his shoulder, and his name will be called "Wonderful Counsellor, Mighty God, Everlasting Father, Prince of Peace."' (Isa. 9:6) To the Jews, the promised Messiah is yet to come.

The ideal world of Isaiah's Messianic kingdom is one in which man and nature at long last live in peace and brotherhood. 'The wolf shall dwell with the lamb, and the leopard shall lie down with the kid, and the calf and the lion and the fatling together, and a little child shall lead them.' 'They shall not hurt or destroy in all my holy mountain; for the earth shall be full of the knowledge of the Lord as the waters cover the sea.' (Isa. 11:6, 9)

When the United Nations was born into a war-weary human race, it was fitting that on a stone wall facing the entrance to its building in New York there should be inscribed Isaiah's vision of a better world: '... and they shall beat their swords into ploughshares, and their spears into pruning hooks; nation shall not lift up sword against nation, neither shall they learn war any more.' (Isa. 2:4)

THE SECOND ISAIAH

The Book of Isaiah is a compilation that reached its present form many centuries after the prophet's time. Of its sixty-six chapters, the first thirty-five are undoubtedly the authentic voice of the great prophet, with perhaps some scattered additions by his disciples.

Chapters 36 to 39 correspond to Chapters 18 and 20 of the Second Book of Kings and are devoted mainly to the story of the Assyrian threat to Jerusalem in 701 BC in the reign of King Hezekiah. Isaiah is referred to in the third person, and these chapters may have been composed in part by his disciples.

From the beginning of Chapter 40, one is suddenly transferred into a work of consolation relating to the exile in Babylon after the fall of Jerusalem in 587 BC, more than a century after Isaiah. The thought and style are still lofty, but the language is gentler and more diffuse. The tone is set by the opening words of Chapter 40:

'Comfort, comfort my people, says your God, speak tenderly to Jerusalem, and cry to her that her warfare is ended, that her iniquity is pardoned, that she has received from the Lord's hand double for all her sins. A voice cries: "In the wilderness prepare the way of the Lord, make straight in the desert a highway for our God."' (Isa. 40:1–3)

For a long time, the scholars have been perplexed by this strange transition. Had Isaiah's vision projected itself forward more than a century, after the calamity of which he had so often warned? Or did the second part of the Book of Isaiah contain the utterances of an unknown comforter-prophet close in spirit to Isaiah, though removed from him in time?

For the last 150 years, the problem of the Second Isaiah, or Deutero-Isaiah, has been one of the central themes of Biblical dispute. Modern scholarship, however, has come to accept that the second part was not the work of the great 8th-century prophet. This view seems to have been scientifically verified by a rather unexpected instrument of biblical research. In 1970 a lecturer at the Haifa Technion obtained his doctorate at the Hebrew University of Jerusalem for a thesis based on a computer analysis of the Book of Isaiah. On such criteria as word frequency and sentence construction, the statistics showed odds of 100,000 to 1 against the two parts having derived from the same author.

Dividing the authorship has clarified the message. The later part of the Book (at any rate Chapters 40–55) was written not only by a different prophet, but in a profoundly different historical context. The original Isaiah addressed himself to his fellow-citizens in a Jewish State. The later unknown prophet preached to a community uprooted from its homeland and flung down onto the alien soil of the Babylonian diaspora. What mattered at that stage was that the Israelites should cling to their identity and ancestral faith until they should return.

The authorities tend to regard Chapters 56–66 as relating to a still later period, after the return and the reconstruction of the Temple – that is, in the period of Ezra and Nehemiah. If so, this 'Third Isaiah' may be the work of disciples of the Second Isaiah, whose style and thought are generally maintained, though the setting appears to be Jerusalem and no longer the Babylonian exile. [Book of Isaiah]

THE DEAD SEA SCROLLS

On 29 November 1947, Dr Eleazar Sukenik, Professor of Archaeology at the Hebrew University in Jerusalem, bought three scrolls through an Armenian dealer in the Old City. They turned out to be some two thousand years old, older than any Hebrew biblical documents known till then.

Five years later, Dr Sukenik's son and successor, Professor Yigael Yadin, bought four more scrolls that had been in the possession of the Syrian Metropolitan of the Monastery of St Mark in the Old City of Jerusalem.

These priceless manuscripts had been discovered in 1946 by Bedouin shepherds in a cave overlooking the Dead Sea. They had belonged to a Jewish sect living about the 1st century BC in a nearby monastery at Qumran on the shore of the Dead Sea, close to the fresh-water springs of Ein Feshka. The remains of the monastery have been excavated, and thousands of fragments of other scrolls have been gathered from the floor of the original cave, and other caves in the vicinity.

The scrolls include:
Isaiah (MS 1) (complete and in good state of preservation)
Isaiah (MS 2) (incomplete and in poor state of preservation)
The Thanksgiving Scroll
The War of the Sons of Light and Darkness
Habbakuk Commentary
Manual of Discipline
Genesis Apocryphon (formerly called the Lamech Scroll).

Two copper scrolls were also found, and purport to a number of places where a great quantity of gold and silver treasure was buried.

The complete Isaiah scroll (MS 1) is 24 feet long, and is made of seventeen leather sheets sewn to each other with linen thread. It contains all sixty-six chapters, set out in fifty-four columns. The scribe made a number of mistakes, which he corrected later, while several passages carelessly omitted by him were later added by someone else.

The second Isaiah scroll (MS 2) was very difficult to unroll, for the columns were stuck together and the leather parchment partially decomposed. It

could be partly deciphered by the use of infra-red photography.

Before the discovery of these scrolls, the earliest known version of the Hebrew Bible was the Masoretic Text, completed in the 9th century AD. Written a thousand years earlier, the Isaiah scrolls are nearly identical with the Masoretic version.

The Dead Sea Scrolls are on display in the specially built Shrine of the Book at the Israel Museum in Jerusalem.

Iscah (Heb. 'who looks') c. 18 century BC. Daughter of Abraham's brother Haran. [Gen. 11:29]

Ishbah (Heb. 'praising') date unknown. A leader of the tribe of Judah, he was the father of Eshtemoa. [1 Chr. 4:17]

Ishbak c. 18 century BC. A son of Abraham and his wife Keturah, he became a desert chief east of Canaan. [Gen. 25:2; 1 Chr. 1:32]

Ishbi-Benob (Heb. 'man sitting in Nob') c. 10 century BC. A Philistine giant who, armed with a new sword, sought to kill David but was himself killed by Abishai. [2 Sam. 21:16]

Ishbosheth (Heb. 'a man of shame') c. 11 century BC. The fourth son of Saul. When Saul was killed in battle, his commander-in-chief Abner took Ishbosheth, Saul's forty-year-old son, over the Jordan to Mahanaim and made him king. David had meanwhile become king of Judah, with his capital in Hebron. A long-drawn conflict developed between north and south.

One day Ishbosheth took Abner to task for having an affair with Rizpah, one of Saul's concubines. Abner was furious. He lost patience with the puppet king he had set up and made his peace with David. David insisted on the return of Saul's daughter Michal who had been his first wife. Her brother Ishbosheth sent her with Abner, ignoring the distress of the second husband Saul had given her.

Ishbosheth heard that Abner had been murdered and 'his courage failed, and all Israel was dismayed' (2 Sam. 4:1). Two of Saul's officers, Baanah and his brother Rechab, decided to murder Ishbosheth. At noon, while the king lay on his bed, they managed to get to his room and 'they smote him' (2 Sam. 4:7). The brothers then hacked off his head and escaped. Expecting a reward they brought the head to David at Hebron. The shocked David turned on them for having slain 'a righteous man in his own house upon his bed' (2 Sam. 4:11), and commanded his men to kill them. He then had the head of Ishbosheth buried in the tomb of Abner in Hebron. The way was now open for David to become ruler over the whole kingdom. Also called Eshbaal. [2 Sam. 2:8, 10, 12; 3:1; 4; 1 Chr. 8:33; 9:39]

Ishhod (Heb. 'famed') *c.* 15 century BC. Son of Hammolecheth who was the sister of Gilead, a leader of the tribe of Manesseh. [1 Chr. 7:18]

Ishi (Heb. 'saving') *1.* date unknown. Son of Appaim of the tribe of Judah, and the father of Sheshan, a leader of the tribe. [1 Chr. 2:31]
2. date unknown. A leader of the tribe of Judah, descended from Caleb. [1 Chr. 4:20]
3. date unknown. One of the leaders of the tribe of Manasseh living east of the Jordan and a mighty warrior. [1 Chr. 5:24]
4. c. 8 century BC. Head of a family of Simeon in the days of King Hezekiah of Judah. [1 Chr. 4:42]

Ishma date unknown. A leader of the tribe of Judah. [1 Chr. 4:3]

Ishmael (Heb. 'God hears') *1. c.* 18 century BC. Son of Abraham by Hagar.

When Sarah's Egyptian slave Hagar became pregnant by Abraham, Sarah's jealousy was aroused. Hagar fled into the desert, but the angel of the Lord persuaded her to return. He told her that she would bear a son called Ishmael and that 'He shall be a wild ass of a man, his hand against every man and every man's hand against him' (Gen. 16:12).

When Ishmael was thirteen, he was circumcised together with his father Abraham and the other males of the household, as a physical mark of the covenant between God and Abraham.

In her old age, Sarah bore a son Isaac. She felt Hagar was mocking her, and in order to placate his wife, Abraham sent Hagar and Ishmael away. They wandered in the desert, and when their water was finished Hagar left the boy under a shrub to die. But they were saved by the miraculous appearance of a well.

They settled down in that part of the Sinai desert known as the wilderness of Paran, where Ishmael became a noted archer. His mother obtained a wife for him from her own native land, Egypt. Ishmael had twelve sons, who became the 'princes' of the tribes (rather like the sons of Jacob who are identified with the twelve Tribes of Israel). Ishmael died at the age of one hundred and thirty-seven years.

By Jewish and Moslem tradition Ishmael came to be regarded as the ancestor of the nomad desert tribes, particularly those inhabiting the area from the Sinai desert across the Negev to southern Jordan. The Hebrews considered themselves superior to these primitive (and usually hostile) desert kinsmen, descended from the common forefather. Abraham. The Arabs on their part venerate Ishmael as their forefather, and there is a Moslem legend that he and his mother Hagar are buried in the sacred Ka'aba at Mecca. It is interesting that in some Arab tribes male children are circumcised at the age of thirteen, as

Ishmael was in the Bible story. [Gen. 16, 17, 25, 36:3; 1 Chr. 1:28–31]

2. date unknown. Son of Azel of the tribe of Benjamin and a descendant of King Saul. [1 Chr. 8:38; 9:44]

3. *c.* 9 century BC. Father of Zebadiah who was in charge of King Jehoshaphat's affairs. [2 Chr. 19:11]

4. *c.* 9 century BC. Son of Jehohanan, he was one of the five army commanders of Judah to obey the orders of the high priest Jehoiada to crown Joash king and execute Queen Athaliah who had usurped the throne. [2 Chr. 23:1]

5. *c.* 6 century BC. The murderer of Gedaliah, governor of Jerusalem.

Ishmael, the son of Nethaniah, was a member of the royal house of Judah. After the fall of Jerusalem and the appointment by the Babylonians of Gedaliah as governor, Ishmael and a group of commanders, still roaming the countryside with their men, came to see him in his residence at Mizpah, just north of Jerusalem. Gedaliah urged them to co-operate with the Babylonian conquerors. But two months later Ishmael 'came with ten men, attacked and killed Gedaliah and the Jews and the Chaldeans who were with him ...' (2 Kgs. 25:25). The following day, before anyone knew of the murder, eighty men arrived at Mizpah, bringing offerings for the Temple. Ishmael lured them into Gedaliah's house where he and his men killed them and threw their bodies into a cistern. Only ten men were allowed to live as they promised to show Ishmael where great stores of wheat, barley, oil and honey were hidden. Ishmael then took prisoner everyone left at Mizpah and set out to cross the Jordan river to the Ammonites.

When the news of Ishmael's crimes reached the other army commanders, headed by Johanan, they set out with a force and caught up with Ishmael at Gibeon. As soon as the prisoners saw Johanan, they broke away and joined him but Ishmael and eight men escaped and crossed the river. Johanan, fearing he and his comrades would be blamed for Ishmael's crimes, fled to Egypt, taking Jeremiah and Baruch with him. [2 Kgs. 25:23–25; Jer. 40, 41]

6. 5 century BC. Son of Pasphur, the priest, he divorced his non-Jewish wife in the time of Ezra. [Ezra 10:22]

Ishmaiah (Heb. 'may God hear') *1.* *c.* 11 century BC. A mighty warrior of Gibeon who deserted from the army of King Saul and rallied to David at Ziklag. [1 Chr. 12:4]

2. *c.* 10 century BC. Son of Obadiah, he was appointed by King David as ruler over the tribe of Zebulun. [1 Chr. 27:19]

Ishmerai (Heb. 'God guards') date unknown. Son of Elpaal, he was a leader of the tribe of Benjamin living in Jerusalem. [1 Chr. 8:18]

Ishpah date unknown. Son of Beriah, he was a leader of the tribe of Benjamin living in Jerusalem. [1 Chr. 8:16]

Ishpan date unknown. Son of Shashak, he was a leader of the tribe of Benjamin living in Jerusalem. [1 Chr. 8:22]

Ishvah (Heb. 'resembles') *c.* 16 century BC. Son of Asher, he went down to Egypt with his grandfather Jacob. [Gen. 46:17; 1 Chr. 7:30]

Ishvi (Heb. 'quiet') *1.* *c.* 16 century BC. Son of Asher, he went down to Egypt at the same time as his grandfather Jacob. [Gen. 46:17; Num. 26:44; 1 Chr. 7:30]

2. *c.* 11 century BC. Son of King Saul and a younger brother of Jonathan. [1 Sam. 14:49]

Ismachiah (Heb. 'may God support') *c.* 9 century BC. A Levite who supervised the bringing of offerings and tithes to the Temple in the reign of Hezekiah, king of Judah. [2 Chr. 31:13]

Israel *see* JACOB

Issachar (Heb. 'rewarded') *1. c.* 16 century BC. Issachar was the ninth son of Jacob and the fifth son born to Leah. Thinking she was past childbearing age, his mother had given her maid Zilpah to Jacob as a concubine, so when this child was born she said, 'God has given me my hire because I gave my maid to my husband.' (Gen. 30:18) Together with his brothers he was involved in the events that led to the selling of their brother Joseph into slavery in Egypt. Later he was one of the ten sons sent by Jacob to buy corn in Egypt, where Joseph had become a leading figure at the court of Pharaoh. When Jacob went to settle in Egypt with all his family it included Issachar and his four sons.

On his deathbed Jacob blessed all his sons in turn, and said, 'Issachar is a strong ass, crouching between the sheepfolds.' (Gen. 49:14)

In the blessing attributed to Moses, it is said: 'They shall call peoples to their mountain; there they offer right sacrifices.' (Deut. 33:19)

In the conquest of Canaan under Joshua, the tribe of Issachar was allocated an area across the eastern end of the valley of Jezreel. [Gen. 30:18; 35:23; 46:13; 49:14; Exod. 1:3; 1 Chr. 2:1; 7:1]
2. c. 10 century BC. Seventh son of Obed-edom, a Levite, who, like his father and his family, was a gatekeeper of the Tabernacle in the reign of King David. [1 Chr. 26:5]

Isshiah (Heb. 'there is God') *1.* date unknown. The son of Izrahiah and a leader of the tribe of Issachar. [1 Chr. 7:3]
2. c. 11 century BC. One of the soldiers who deserted from the army of King Saul and joined David at Ziklag. [1 Chr 12:6]
3. c. 10 century BC. A Levite descended from Uzziel who ministered in the Tabernacle in the reign of King David. [1 Chr. 23:20; 24:25]
4. c. 10 century BC. A Levite descended from Rehabiah who served in the Taber-

nacle in the reign of King David. [1 Chr. 24:21]

Isshijah (Heb. 'there is God') 5 century BC. A descendant of Harim who divorced his non-Jewish wife in the time of Ezra. [Ezra 10:31]

Ithai (Heb. 'God is with me') *c.* 10 century BC. A Benjaminite warrior in the army of King David distinguished for his bravery. Also called Ittai. [2 Sam. 23:29; 1 Chr. 11:31]

Ithamar (Heb. 'island of the palm tree') *c.* 13 century BC. Youngest son of Aaron and Elisheba, he was consecrated as a priest by Moses together with his father and his three brothers. He was given the task of listing the gifts brought for the tabernacle, and of supervising its transport and erection.

Ithamar became the founder of a line of priests, though it was smaller than that of his brother Eleazar. The priest Eli traced his ancestry to Ithamar. His descendants came back from exile in Babylon with Ezra. [Exod. 6:23; 28:1; 38:21; Lev. 10:6, 16; Num. 3:2, 4; 4:28, 33; 7:8; 26:60; 1 Chr. 6:3, 24:1–6]

Ithiel (Heb. 'God is with me') *1.* date unknown. An ancestor of Sallu, one of the first Benjaminites to settle in Jerusalem after the return from exile in Babylon. [Neh. 11:7]
2. date unknown. One of the two men to whom Agur, son of Jakeh, directed his teachings. [Prov. 30:1]

Ithmah *c.* 10 century BC. A Moabite warrior who fought in the armies of King David and was distinguished for his bravery. [1 Chr. 11:46]

Ithra *see* JETHER *5.*

Ithran *1.* date unknown. Son of Dishon and a grandson of Seir the Horite. [Gen. 36:26; 1 Chr. 1:41]

2. date unknown. Son of Zophah and a leader of the tribe of Asher. [1 Chr. 7:37]

Ithream (Heb. 'populous') *c.* 10 century BC. Son of King David and his wife Eglah, he was born in Hebron. [2 Sam. 3:5; 1 Chr. 3:3]

Ittai (Heb. 'with me') *1. c.* 10 century BC. A Philistine who joined David in exile, when Absalom staged his revolt against his father David. His followers included a detachment of six hundred Gittites from the Philistine city of Gath, led by Ittai. David tried to persuade Ittai to return 'for you are a foreigner, and also an exile' (2 Sam. 15:19). Ittai answered with a ringing declaration of loyalty: '... wherever my lord the king shall be, whether for death or for life, there also will your servant be.' (2 Sam. 15:21) So Ittai and his men joined David at Mahanaim in the land of Gilead across the Jordan river. When David reorganized his forces to meet Absalom, he divided his army into three parts and placed them under the command of Joab, Abishai and Ittai. Absalom was defeated and killed and David's kingdom was saved. [2 Sam. 15:19–22; 18:2–12]
2. *see* ITHAI

Izhar (Heb. 'oil') *c.* 13 century BC. Son of Kohath and head of an important family of Levites who served in the Tabernacle in the wilderness. Izhar's son Korah led a rebellion against Moses and Aaron. [Exod. 6:18; Num. 3:19, 27; 16:1; 1 Chr. 6:2, 18, 38; 23:12,18]

Izliah date unknown. Son of Elpaal and a leader of the tribe of Benjamin living in Jerusalem. [1 Chr. 8:18]

Izrahiah (Heb. 'may God shine forth') date unknown. Son of Uzzi of the tribe of Issachar, he and his family were mighty warriors and leaders of the tribe. [1 Chr. 7:3]

Izri *see* ZERI

Izziah 5 century BC. A descendant of Parosh, he divorced his non-Jewish wife in the time of Ezra. [Ezra 10:25]

J

Jaakan date unknown. A descendant of Seir the Horite who became an Edomite leader. Also called Akan. [Gen. 36:27; 1 Chr. 1:42]

Jaakobah (Heb. 'will protect') *c.* 8 century BC. One of the leaders of the tribe of Simeon in the reign of King Hezekiah of Judah, who drove out the native population from the Gedor valley and settled there. [1 Chr. 4:36]

Jaala (Heb. 'wild goat') *c.* 10 century BC. A servant of King Solomon whose descendants returned with Zerubbabel from exile in Babylon. Also called Jaalah. [Ezra 2:56; Neh. 7:58]

Jaalah *see* JAALA

Jaareoregim *see* JAIR *3.*

Jaareshiah date unknown. Son of Jeroham, he was a leader of the tribe of Benjamin living in Jerusalem. [1 Chr. 8:27]

Jaasiel (Heb. 'made by God') *1. c.* 10 century BC. The Mezobaite warrior in the armies of King David distinguished for his bravery. [1 Chr. 11:47]
2. c. 10 century BC. Son of Abner, he was leader of the tribe of Benjamin in the reign of King David. [1 Chr. 27:21]

Jaasu (Heb. 'created') 5 century BC. One of the descendants of Bani who divorced his non-Jewish wife in the time of Ezra. [Ezra 10:37]

Jaazaniah (Heb. 'may God hear') *1. c.* 6 century BC. One of the four army captains who promised loyalty to Gedaliah when the Babylonians made him governor of Judah. Also called Jezaniah. [2 Kgs. 25:23; Jer. 40:8]
2. 6 century BC. Head of the ascetic family of Rechabites in the days of the prophet Jeremiah who refused to drink wine with him, holding to his vow of abstinence. [Jer. 35:3]
3. c. 6 century BC. Son of Shaphan, he was one of the seventy elders of Israel seen by the prophet Ezekiel committing idolatry in a cellar in the Temple building. Jaazaniah is the only person mentioned by name and was probably the most important of them. [Ezek. 8:11]
4. c. 6 century BC. Son of Azzur, he was one of the men condemned by Ezekiel for their false prophecies concerning Judah. [Ezek. 11:1]

Jaaziah (Heb. 'may God strengthen') *c.* 10 century BC. A Levite whose descendants served in the Tabernacle during the reign of King David. [1 Chr. 24:26, 27]

Jaaziel (Heb. 'may God strengthen') *c.* 10 century BC. A Levite in the reign of King David who played a musical instrument when the Ark of God was brought to Jerusalem. Also called Aziel. [1 Chr. 15:18, 20]

Jabal (Heb. 'stream') date unknown. Son of Lamech and his wife Adah, he is described as 'the father of those that dwell in tents and have cattle'. [Gen. 4:20]

Jabesh (Heb. 'dry') *c.* 8 century BC.

Father of Shallum, one of the last kings of Israel. [2 Kgs. 15:10, 13–14]

Jabez (Heb. 'sorrow') date unknown. A leader of the tribe of Judah and a pious man, he is described as being 'more honourable than his brothers'. [1 Chr. 4:9, 10]

Jabin (Heb. 'he understands') *1. c.* 13 century BC. Jabin was the Canaanite king of Hazor in the north of the country who organized a confederation of local kings to fight against the Israelites. They met at the Waters of Merom but, with the Lord's help, Joshua defeated them. Then Joshua 'turned back at that time, and took Hazor, and smote its king with the sword' (Josh. 11:10). [Josh. 11:1–15]
2. c. 12 century BC. The Canaanite king of Hazor in the time of the Judges who oppressed the Israelites and whose general Sisera was defeated by Deborah and Barak. 'And the hand of the people of Israel bore harder and harder on Jabin the king of Canaan.' (Judg. 4:24) [Judg. 4; Ps. 83:9]

Jacan (Heb. 'affliction') date unknown. Head of a family of the tribe of Gad living in Bashan. [1 Chr. 5:13]

Jachin (Heb. 'established') *1. c.* 16 century BC. A son of Simeon and grandson of Jacob and Leah. Also called Jarib. [Gen. 46:10; Exod. 6:15; Num. 26:12; 1 Chr. 4:24]
2. c. 10 century BC. A priest in the Tabernacle in the reign of King David, he took the twenty-first turn of service. [1 Chr. 24:17]
3. 5 century BC. A priest living in Jerusalem in the days of Nehemiah. [1 Chr. 9:10; Neh. 11:10]

Jacob (Heb. 'supplanted') *c.* 16 century BC. Third patriarch.

After years of childlessness, Isaac's wife Rebekah had twin sons. While still in their mother's womb 'The children struggled together' (Gen. 25:22). Esau, the first-born, was at birth covered with red hair. He grew up to be a hunter and the favourite of his father. Jacob was born clutching his brother's heel. (The Hebrew name *Ya'acov* is derived from *ekev*, 'the heel of the foot'.) He became a herdsman and cultivator and his mother loved him more than she did Esau.

One day Esau came back from hunting, faint with hunger. In exchange for a meal of bread and red lentil soup, Jacob obtained from Esau his birthright, that is, his rights as the eldest son.

When Isaac was old and practically blind, he sent for Esau and asked him to go hunting, and to prepare a dish of venison, which Isaac loved. He would then bestow the paternal blessing on Esau. Rebekah overheard this, and decided to obtain the blessing for Jacob instead. She sent Jacob to select two kids from the flock, cooked them to taste like venison and told Jacob to take them into his father, pretending to be Esau. Jacob demurred, pointing out that 'My brother Esau is a hairy man, and I am a smooth man.' (Gen. 27:11) To overcome this difficulty Rebekah wrapped pieces of the fleece of the kids over his hands and the back of his neck and dressed him in Esau's garments.

Even after Isaac had touched Jacob, he was still suspicious and said, 'The voice is Jacob's voice, but the hands are the hands of Esau.' (Gen. 27:22) But the smell of the field clinging to Esau's clothes satisfied Isaac and he blessed Jacob saying: 'Let peoples serve you, and nations bow down to you. Be lord over your brothers.' (Gen. 27:29) Esau hated Jacob because of the stolen blessing and threatened to kill him after Isaac's death. Rebekah felt it would be prudent to get Jacob out of the way. She persuaded Isaac to send the young man to her brother Laban in Haran (northern Syria) where he would find a bride among Laban's daughters, instead of marrying a Canaanite girl as Esau had already done.

On his way northward from Beersheba to his uncle Laban, the weary Jacob sank down on the ground to sleep at night, with his head against a stone. Here he dreamt he saw a ladder rising up to heaven, with angels going up and down on it. The Lord stood at the top and spoke to him, reaffirming the promise made to Abraham that his seed would multiply. 'Behold, I am with you and will keep you wherever you go, and will bring you back to this land.' (Gen. 28:15) Jacob woke from this dream and said with awe, 'Surely the Lord is in this place; and I did not know it.... This is none other than the house of God, and this is the gate of heaven.' (Gen. 28:16, 17) Early next morning he set up and anointed with oil the stone that had served as his pillow and called the place Bethel ('the House of the Lord'). It was the same spot where Abraham had earlier made a sacrifice to the Lord. Bethel remained a holy place for the Israelites. The site is some twelve miles north of Jerusalem off the main highway.

THE STAY IN HARAN

Jacob went on his way and reached Haran. He stopped at a well where flocks of sheep were waiting to be watered. In answer to his question the shepherds said they knew Laban and pointed out his daughter Rachel approaching with her father's sheep. Jacob introduced himself, kissed his cousin and helped her draw water for the sheep. Rachel ran and told Laban, who came out to embrace this kinsman from a distant land.

Jacob fell in love with Rachel who was 'beautiful and lovely' (Gen. 29:17); but he was told he would have to work for seven years for her father before he could marry her. At the end of that time Laban arranged a wedding feast. Jacob spent the wedding night with his bride and was shocked to find next morning that Laban had substituted for Rachel her older and plainer sister, Leah. When reproached, Laban claimed that by the custom of his country the elder daughter should be wedded first. Jacob was allowed to marry Rachel as well a week later, on undertaking to work another seven years for his father-in-law.

When that period had gone by, Jacob continued to serve Laban. As payment he asked to be allowed to keep for himself all the speckled and streaked goats, and all the dark-coloured sheep. Laban agreed to these terms but that day sent off with his sons all the animals marked in such a way. Jacob cut wands of poplar, hazel and chestnut trees, peeled white streaks in them and stuck them at the watering troughs. As a result of the visual suggestion, the goats conceived at the trough were born speckled or streaked. Jacob used this device to breed from the stronger animals, leaving the offspring of the weaker ones to Laban. After several years, Jacob owned large flocks of his own and acquired his own servants, camels and asses. It was not surprising that Laban and his sons resented the fact that Jacob had gained so much of the family wealth.

By now twenty years had gone by since Jacob had first met Rachel at the well, and he decided the time had come to return to his own country. He departed quietly when Laban was away sheep-shearing and moved southward towards Canaan with his two wives, his two concubines (the handmaids of his wives) and his children mounted on camels, and his flocks.

At this time Jacob had eleven sons and one daughter. The children of Leah were Reuben, Simeon, Levi, Judah, Issachar, Zebulun and Dinah; Leah's maid Zilpah bore Gad and Asher; the two sons of Bilhah, Rachel's maid, were Dan and Naphtali; Rachel herself gave birth to Joseph, after she had been childless for many years.

When Laban discovered that Jacob had gone, he and his kinsmen set out in pursuit. They caught up with Jacob's caravan seven days later in the mountains of Gilead, east of the Jordan river. Laban protested against the surreptitious way Jacob had gone off with his daughters and his grandchildren. He also accused Jacob of stealing the 'teraphim', the images of his household gods. Jacob indignantly denied this charge and invited Laban to go through his tents. He did not know that the images had been taken by Rachel, who hid them in the saddlebag of her camel and sat upon them while her father searched in vain. Rachel and Leah had felt cheated of their dowries by their father: 'Are we not regarded by him as foreigners? For he has sold us, and he has been using up the money given for us.' (Gen. 31:15)

Jacob and Laban agreed to part in peace, and in accordance with custom, sealed their pact by assembling a heap of stones, and partaking of food together upon them. Jacob called the place Galeed ('the heap of witness'), which explains the name of Gilead given to that region.

Laban and his party turned back, and Jacob continued southward. He had a vision of a host of angels welcoming him and called the place Mahanaim ('hosts' or 'camps'). Jacob's party descended from the plateau of Gilead into the deep gorge of the Jabbok river, a tributary flowing into the lower Jordan. His family and retainers crossed at the ford before sundown, but Jacob lingered behind and suddenly found himself wrestling in the dark with a mysterious stranger. The struggle continued until daybreak, when the other tried to get away, but Jacob held on to him until he obtained his blessing. The stranger said to Jacob that henceforth he would be known as Israel ('who prevails with God') 'for you have striven with God and with men, and have prevailed' (Gen. 32:28). During the fight Jacob's adver-

sary had struck the inside of his thigh, causing the sinew to shrink. (Since then Jews are forbidden to eat that sinew in animals.) Jacob called the place Peniel ('the face of God').

This strange experience at the ford is related by some scholars to the primitive legends of river gods that accost travellers, but that, like all spirits, must vanish again before dawn.

Jacob's twin brother Esau had settled in the land of Seir, the rugged, semi-arid country of Edom to the east and south of the Dead Sea. Jacob sent messengers to inform Esau that he had returned, and suggesting that they meet. The messengers came back to report that Esau was advancing towards him with four hundred men, and Jacob was afraid that his wronged brother was seeking revenge. He turned to the Lord for protection; but also sent ahead a large number of choice sheep, goats, cattle and camels to placate Esau. Jacob divided his servants and the rest of his flock into two groups, so that if Esau attacked one group, the other might escape.

His fears proved groundless. When Esau arrived, Jacob bowed down to the ground before him: 'But Esau ran to meet him, and embraced him, and fell on his neck and kissed him, and they wept.' (Gen. 33:4) After Jacob had presented his women and children, Esau courteously declined the gift of livestock, saying he already had enough animals of his own. Jacob insisted that he keep them as a mark of goodwill.

RETURN TO CANAAN

Esau invited his brother to return with him to Seir but Jacob pleaded that he had to travel slowly because of his young children and the lambs. Esau rode ahead, but Jacob did not follow, continuing instead on his way to Canaan. He lived for some while at Succoth ('booths'), at the edge of the Jordan valley; then he moved across the river to Shalem, near the town of Shechem (present-day Nablus) in the hills of

Samaria. Here he bought a parcel of land from Hamor, the leader of the local Hivite clan, and erected an altar on it.

Jacob's daughter Dinah became friendly with the local girls and was seen by Hamor's son Shechem, who seized and raped her. Hamor sought permission from Jacob for Shechem to marry Dinah, and further proposed that his clan and Jacob's should intermarry and merge with each other. Concealing their rage at Dinah's seduction, her brothers pretended to agree to Hamor's proposal provided that he, Shechem and all the other males of their clan would first be circumcised, as the Israelites were. This was done, but before the men had recovered from the painful operation, Jacob's sons Simeon and Levi killed them all and despoiled the town.

Jacob bitterly reproached his two sons for this bloody act of vengeance, and was afraid it would arouse the population of the surrounding area against them. He decided to move to the sanctuary at Bethel, twelve miles further south. But first he insisted that all the members of his household should purify themselves, change their clothes, and surrender to him their idolatrous images and magic amulets, which he buried under an oak tree at Shechem. To his relief, the local inhabitants did not pursue or attack him during this anxious journey – perhaps because word of the killing at Shechem had already spread, and they were afraid. At Bethel, Jacob restored the altar he had erected twenty years previously, after his dream of the ladder ascending to heaven.

They proceeded on their way towards Hebron, where the aged Isaac, Jacob's father, was still alive. Near Bethlehem, Rachel died in giving birth to a boy, whom Jacob named Benjamin ('son of my right hand'). Rachel was buried there, and Jacob erected a pillar as a monument over her grave.

Soon after, Isaac died at the age of a hundred and eighty and his two sons,

Jacob and Esau, buried him in the Cave of Machpelah, the family tomb. This was the last time the twin brothers saw each other.

Jacob's favourite son was Joseph, born in his old age of his beloved Rachel, and the youngest of the twelve brothers except for the baby Benjamin. His father pampered him and dressed him in a coat of many colours; but he incurred the envy and dislike of his brothers.

When Joseph was seventeen, Jacob sent him to find his brothers, who had trekked northwards with the flocks in search of pasture. They sold the youth to a passing caravan, stained his coat with the blood of a slaughtered kid and produced it to Jacob, saying they had found it in the fields. Jacob assumed that Joseph had been killed by a wild beast, and mourned him in deep grief.

Many years later, during a famine, Jacob sent his ten sons to Egypt to buy wheat, keeping at home young Benjamin. Pharaoh's powerful governor allowed them to buy the wheat only on the undertaking that they would return with their younger brother. Simeon was held in Egypt as a hostage. They had no inkling that the governor was their long-lost brother Joseph. Jacob refused to part with Benjamin. However, when they had consumed the food brought from Egypt and the famine continued, his sons prevailed upon him to yield. This time Joseph revealed his identity to the brothers, and there was a tearful reunion. Joseph proposed they should fetch Jacob and the rest of the family from Canaan and settle in the fertile Egyptian province of Goshen, in the eastern corner of the Nile delta. He would then be able to care for them in the five years of famine which he knew were still to come. Pharaoh gave his approval, and ordered that wagons should be provided for the purpose.

Jacob at first refused to believe that the youth thought slain so long ago had suddenly reappeared in Egypt. Persuaded by the sight of the wagons and the lavish gifts of food Joseph had sent, the old man said simply, 'It is enough; Joseph my son is still alive; I will go and see him before I die.' (Gen. 45:28)

Three generations of Jacob's family, numbering seventy souls, set out from Hebron together with his servants, flocks, herds and household goods. They stopped at Beersheba where Jacob's father Isaac had dwelt, and here he offered parting sacrifices to God before leaving the land of Canaan. The Lord renewed to him the promise first made to his grandfather Abraham, saying: '... do not be afraid to go down to Egypt; for I will there make of you a great nation. I will go down with you to Egypt, and I will also bring you up again.' (Gen. 46:3, 4)

(This promise of a return was to be redeemed some four centuries later in the time of Moses.)

They crossed the Sinai desert and reached Goshen. Judah was sent to inform Joseph, who came by chariot to meet them and flung himself weeping on his father's neck. Joseph presented his father and five of his brothers to Pharaoh, on whom Jacob bestowed a blessing. Pharaoh was told that Joseph's family had been shepherds and cattlemen for generations, and suggested that they might take charge of the royal flocks.

Jacob dwelt for seventeen years in Goshen. Having heard that his father was failing, Joseph went to see him, and took with him his two sons Manasseh and Ephraim. Jacob adopted the boys as his own.

On his deathbed Jacob gathered all his sons around him and charged them to bury him with his forefathers in Canaan. The celebrated blessing attributed to him is composed of vivid poetic similes, and refers to the qualities in each of his twelve sons that would distinguish the Israelite tribe named after him:

Reuben, the first born, was dignified but unstable as water.

Simeon and Levi were cruel and angry men.

Judah was a lion's whelp and would rule.

Zebulun would dwell on the coast and be a seafarer.

Issachar was strong as an ass and would serve others.

Dan would judge his people.

Gad would be overcome but would win in the end.

Asher would be a successful tiller of the soil.

Naphtali was a hind let loose (a venturesome spirit).

Joseph was a fruitful bough, blessed by the Almighty.

Benjamin would be as aggressive as a wolf.

Jacob died at the age of one hundred and forty-seven, and Joseph arranged to have his body embalmed by Egyptian physicians. An impressive funeral caravan wound its way out of Egypt and included all Jacob's sons and, as a special mark of respect, members of Pharaoh's household and other leading Egyptians. It reached Hebron where Jacob was interred in the Cave of Machpelah, together with Abraham and Sarah, Isaac and Rebekah, and Jacob's first wife Leah. Joseph returned to Pharaoh's court and his brothers to their homes in Goshen.

THE CHARACTER OF JACOB

Jacob belongs to the patriarchal, pastoral society from which the Hebrew people originated two thousand years before the Christian era. Like his grandfather Abraham and his father Isaac, he was a tent-dwelling nomad who moved slowly in search of grazing and water, with his wives and concubines, his many children, his servants, flocks and herds.

Later writers – including the learned rabbis of the Talmud – were hard put to explain the contradictions in Jacob's character. By the standards of a later age, it was embarrassing that so re-spected a patriarch should in his youth have outwitted his brother, his father and his uncle for his own gain. But the ancient chroniclers of the Old Testa-ment made no attempt to idealize their forefathers. The deviousness of the young Jacob did not seem wicked to the nomad world in which he lived, nor did it detract from his stature or his many virtues.

The Bible calls Jacob an 'ish tam' – a plain or quiet man. In all his long life he was peaceable and never resorted to vio-lence – on the contrary he was fearful lest his aggrieved and more turbulent brother Esau might attack him. He sub-mitted to Laban's substitution of Leah for Rachel, and agreed to work another seven years for the latter. His diligence and skill in tending his father-in-law's flocks greatly increased their numbers and value. To his wives and children Jacob was kind and affectionate, with a tender love for Rachel and for Joseph and Benjamin, the two sons she bore him in his old age.

Above all, Jacob inherited from Abra-ham and Isaac their intimate commun-ion with God, and the promise that Canaan would belong to their seed. With Jacob this covenant was singularly marked by his dream at Bethel, and by his wrestling with the angel at the ford of Jabbok. Jacob's devotion to God made him spurn the household images and magic amulets to which members of his family clung. (At Shechem he made them bury all these objects under a tree and purify themselves.)

Jacob has a pivotal role in the Hebrew saga. The twelve Israelite tribes that occu-pied Canaan from Joshua's conquest traced their descent and their names back to his sons. The Hebrews were referred to collectively as the House of Jacob or the Children of Israel. The name of the biblical kingdom of Israel was adopted for the newly-proclaimed State of Israel in 1948. [Gen. 25; 27–37; 42; 45–50]

Jada (Heb. '[God] has cared') date un-known. Younger son of Onam and a leader of the tribe of Judah. [1 Chr. 2:28, 32]

Jaddai (Heb. 'God's friend') 5 century BC. A descendant of Nebo who divorced his non-Jewish wife in the time of Ezra. [Ezra 10:43]

Jaddua (Heb. 'known') *1.* 5 century BC. A leader of Judah who signed the coven-ant to follow the Laws of God in the time of Nehemiah. [Neh. 10:21]
2. 5 century BC. Son of Jonathan, a Levite of Judah after the return from exile in Babylon. [Neh. 12:11, 22]

Jadon (Heb. 'he will judge') 5 century BC. A Meronothite who helped rebuild the walls of Jerusalem in the time of Nehemiah. [Neh. 3:7]

Jael (Heb. 'deer') *c.* 12 century BC. A Kenite woman who killed Sisera.

Jael was the wife of Heber, a Kenite, whose family had peaceful relations with Jabin, king of Hazor. After the defeat of Jabin's army under Sisera by the Chil-dren of Israel, inspired by the prophetess Deborah and led by Barak, Sisera es-caped eastward and came to Heber's encampment. Jael came out and invited him into her tent, gave him milk to drink, covered him up and stood guard outside. After he fell asleep she 'took a tent peg ... and drove the peg into his temple' (Judg. 4:21). When Barak came in pursuit of Sisera, Jael showed him Sisera lying dead in her tent.

According to Deborah's song of vic-tory, Jael struck Sisera down when he came to her tent door and not while he was sleeping inside the tent. Neither account offers any explanation for her deed. [Judg. 4:17–22; 5:24–27]

Jahath (Heb. 'may [God] allay his fear') *1.* date unknown. Son of Reaiah of the tribe of Judah. [1 Chr. 4:2]

2. date unknown. A Levite descended from Gershom. [1 Chr. 6:20, 43]

3. c. 10 century BC. Eldest son of Shimei the Levite, he served in the Tabernacle in the reign of King David. [1 Chr. 23:10, 11]

4. c. 10 century BC. Son of Shelomoth, the Levite, he served in the Tabernacle in the reign of King David. [1 Chr. 24:22]

5. 7 century BC. A Levite descended from Merari, he supervised the work of repairing the Temple in the days of King Josiah. [2 Chr. 34:12]

Jahaziel (Heb. 'seen of God') *1. c.* 10 century BC. A warrior of the tribe of Benjamin who left the army of King Saul and joined David at Ziklag. [1 Chr. 12:4]

2. c. 10 century BC. A priest who blew a trumpet during the celebrations following the bringing of the Ark of God to Jerusalem in the reign of King David. [1 Chr. 16:6]

3. c. 10 century BC. A descendant of Hebron, he and his family were leaders of the tribe of Levi who served in the Tabernacle. [1 Chr. 23:19; 24:23]

4. c. 9 century BC. Son of Zechariah of the tribe of Levi who prophesied that King Jehoshaphat would win a great victory against the invading armies of Moab and Ammon without needing to fight since God would fight the battle on Judah's behalf. His prophecy came true for the invading armies attacked each other and destroyed themselves. [2 Chr. 20:14–17]

5. 5 century BC. Father of Shecaniah who returned to Judah with Ezra from exile in Babylon. [Ezra 8:5]

Jahdai (Heb. 'God leads') date unknown. A leader of the tribe of Judah descended from Caleb. [1 Chr. 2:47]

Jahdiel (Heb. 'may God cause to rejoice') date unknown. A leader and warrior of the half-tribe of Manasseh east of the river Jordan. [1 Chr. 5:24]

Jahdo (Heb. 'joyful') date unknown. Son of Buz, a leader of the tribe of Gad living in Bashan east of the river Jordan. [1 Chr. 5:14]

Jahleel (Heb. 'waiting for God') *c.* 16 century BC. A son of Zebulun who went down to Egypt with his grandfather Jacob. [Gen. 46:14; Num. 26:26]

Jahmai (Heb. 'guarded') date unknown. Son of Tola and a grandson of Issachar, he was one of the leaders of the tribe and a mighty warrior. [1 Chr. 7:2]

Jahzeel (Heb. 'may God grant a portion') *c.* 16 century BC. A son of Naphtali, he went down to Egypt with his grandfather Jacob. Also called Jahziel. [Gen. 46:24; Num. 26:48; 1 Chr. 7:13]

Jahzeiah (Heb. 'may God see') 5 century BC. Son of Tikvah, he was present when Ezra called on those inhabitants of Judah who had married non-Jewish wives to divorce them. [Ezra 10:15]

Jahzerah date unknown. Ancestor of Maasai, who was one of the first priests to settle in Jerusalem after the return from exile in Babylon. Also called Ahzai. [1 Chr. 9:12; Neh. 11:13]

Jahziel *see* JAHZEEL

Jair (Heb. 'enlightened') *1.* date unknown. Son of Manasseh and a grandson of Joseph, his descendants took possession of Gilead and Bashan, east of the river Jordan and called the territory Havvoth-jair in his honour. [Num. 32:41; Deut. 3:14; Josh. 13:30; 1 Kgs. 4:13]

2. c. 12 century BC. The eighth judge of Israel who ruled for twenty-two years. Born in Gilead he had thirty sons who rode on thirty asses and ruled over thirty cities in Gilead called Havvoth-jair. [Judg. 10:3–5]

3. *c.* 10 century BC. Father of Elhanan who killed one of the Philistine giants. Also called Jaareoregim. [2 Sam. 21:19; 1 Chr. 20:5]

4. date unknown. Son of Segub of the tribe of Judah, he was ruler over twenty-three cities in the land of Gilead. [1 Chr. 2:22]

5. *c.* 5 century BC. An ancestor of Mordecai. [Esther 2:5]

Jakeh (Heb. 'pious') date unknown. Father of Agur whose words appear in the thirtieth chapter of Proverbs. [Prov. 30]

Jakim (Heb. 'established') **1.** date unknown. A son of Shimei, he was a leader of the tribe of Benjamin living in Jerusalem. [1 Chr. 8:19]

2. *c.* 10 century BC. A priest in the reign of King David who was responsible for the twelfth turn of service in the Tabernacle. [1 Chr. 24:12]

Jalam (Heb. 'young') *c.* 16 century BC. Son of Esau and Oholibamah, he became a leader of a desert tribe in Edom. [Gen. 36:5, 14, 18; 1 Chr. 1:35]

Jalon (Heb. 'seeks shelter [in God]') date unknown. One of the four sons of Ezrah of the tribe of Judah. [1 Chr. 4:17]

Jamin (Heb. 'lucky') **1.** *c.* 16 century BC. A son of Simeon, he went down to Egypt with his grandfather Jacob. [Gen. 46:10; Exod. 6:15; Num. 26:12; 1 Chr. 4:24]

2. date unknown. Son of Ram and a grandson of Jerahmeel, he was a leader of the tribe of Judah. [1 Chr. 2:27]

3. 5 century BC. A leader of Judah who explained the law of Moses to the people after Ezra had read out the law in the market-place. [Neh. 8:7]

Jamlech (Heb. 'God gives dominion') *c.* 8 century BC. One of the leaders of the tribe of Simeon, in the reign of King Hezekiah of Judah, who drove out the indigenous population from the Gedor valley and settled there instead. [1 Chr. 4:34]

Janai (Heb. 'answered') date unknown. A leader of the tribe of Gad living in Bashan, east of the river Jordan. [1 Chr. 5:12]

Japheth (Heb. 'he enlarges') date unknown. Third son of Noah, Japheth and his family were in the ark with Noah during the great flood. When Noah was in a drunken sleep, Japheth and Shem discreetly 'covered the nakedness of their father' (Gen. 9:23). As a result Noah blessed Japheth and told him he would 'enlarge', that is, have many descendants.

He had seven sons: Gomer, Magog, Madai, Javan, Tubal, Meshech and Tiras. These sons became the legendary founders of northern peoples that inhabited areas from the Caspian Sea to the Greek islands. [Gen. 5:32; 6:10; 7:13; 9:18–27; 10:1–5; 1 Chr. 1:4–5]

Japhia (Heb. 'splendour') **1.** *c.* 13 century BC. King of Lachish in the days of Joshua, he joined the Canaanite alliance against Joshua and was defeated in battle and executed. [Josh. 10:3, 23]

2. *c.* 10 century BC. One of the sons of King David born to him in Jerusalem. [2 Sam. 5:15; 1 Chr. 3:7; 14:6]

Japhlet (Heb. 'delivered') date unknown. Eldest son of Heber, he was a leader of the tribe of Asher and a mighty warrior. [1 Chr. 7:32, 33]

Jarah (Heb. 'honeycomb') date unknown. Son of Ahaz of the tribe of Benjamin, a descendant of King Saul. Also known as Jehoaddah. [1 Chr. 8:36; 9:42]

Jared (Heb. 'descent') date unknown.

Father of Enoch and the grandfather of Methuselah. [Gen. 5:15–20; 1 Chr. 1:2]

Jarha date unknown. An Egyptian servant who married the daughter of his master Sheshan, a leader of Judah. [1 Chr. 2:34, 35]

Jarid (Heb. 'God defends') *1. see* JACHIN *1.*
2. 5 century BC. A leader of Judah sent by Nehemiah to Iddo, with instructions to bring Levites to Jerusalem to serve in the Temple. [Ezra 8:16]
3. 5 century BC. One of the priests who divorced his non-Jewish wife in the time of Ezra. [Ezra 10:18]

Jaroah (Heb. 'is relieved') date unknown. Son of Gilead of the tribe of Gad, he was a leader of the tribe living east of the river Jordan. [1 Chr. 5:14]

Jashen (Heb. 'sleeping') *c.* 10 century BC. Father of Jonathan, a warrior in the armies of King David distinguished for his bravery. Also called Hashem. [2 Sam. 23:32; 1 Chr. 11:34]

Jashobeam (Heb. 'to whom the people turn') *c.* 10 century BC. Son of Zabdiel, he was one of David's veteran commanders, and famous for killing with his spear three hundred Philistines in one battle. When the army was reorganized he was put in charge of one of the monthly contingents of conscripts. [1 Chr. 11:11; 12:6; 27:2]

Jashub (Heb. 'he turns') 5 century BC. One of the descendants of Bani who divorced his non-Jewish wife in the time of Ezra. [Ezra 10:29]

Jashub *see* IOB

Jathniel (Heb. 'God-given') *c.* 10 century BC. Fourth son of Meshelemiah, a Levite, he and his family were gatekeepers of the Tabernacle in the reign of King David. [1 Chr. 26:2]

Javan (Heb. 'Greece') date unknown. Son of Japheth and a grandson of Noah, he was regarded by the Hebrews as the legendary father of the Greeks. [Gen. 10:2, 4; 1 Chr. 1:5, 7]

Jaziz *c.* 10 century BC. The Hagrite officer of King David responsible for the royal flocks of sheep. [1 Chr. 27:30]

Jeatherai date unknown. A Levite descended from Gershom, he was an ancestor of Asaph, the musician of King David. [1 Chr. 6:21]

Jeberechiah (Heb. 'may God bless') *c.* 8 century BC. Father of Zechariah, one of Isaiah's two witnesses to his prophecies of conquest by the Assyrian armies. [Isa. 8:2]

Jebusites date unknown. An ancient tribe of warriors living in Canaan, they ruled over Jerusalem until they were defeated in battle by King David. [Deut. 7:1; Josh. 11:3; 2 Sam. 5:6–10]

Jecoliah (Heb. 'God is mighty') *c.* 8 century BC. Wife of Amaziah, king of Judah, and mother of his successor Uzziah. [2 Kgs. 15:2; 2 Chr. 26:3]

Jeconiah *see* JEHOIACHIN

Jedaiah (Heb. 'known by God') *1.* date unknown. Son of Shimri and father of Allon of the tribe of Simeon. [1 Chr. 4:37]
2. c. 10 century BC. A priest who took the second turn of service in the Tabernacle in the reign of King David. [1 Chr. 24:7; Ezra 2:36; Neh. 7:39; 11:10]
3. c. 6 century BC. One of the first priests to settle in Jerusalem after the return from exile in Babylon. [1 Chr. 9:10; Neh. 12:6, 7, 19, 21]
4. 6 century BC. One of the leaders of Judah who returned from exile in Babylon in the days of the prophet Zechariah. He was ordered by Zechariah to provide

gold and silver for a crown to be put on the head of Joshua, son of Jehozadak, the high priest, who would rebuild the Temple. Jedaiah and his colleagues were then instructed to keep the crowns in the Temple as a memorial of the event. [Zech. 6:10–14]

5. 5 century BC. Son of Harumaph, he helped repair the walls of Jerusalem in the time of Nehemiah. [Neh. 3:10]

Jediael (Heb. 'known of God') *1. c.* 16 century BC. A son of Benjamin, he and his family were leaders of the tribe. [1 Chr. 7:6, 10]

2. c. 11 century BC. One of the eight leaders of the tribe of Manasseh who left the army of King Saul and joined David at Ziklag. [1 Chr. 12:20]

3. c. 10 century BC. Son of Shimri and brother of Joha, he and his brother were warriors in the armies of King David, distinguished for their bravery. [1 Chr. 11:45]

4. 10 century BC. Second son of Meshelemiah, a Korahite of the tribe of Levi, he and his family were gatekeepers of the Tabernacle in the reign of King David. [1 Chr. 26:2]

Jedidah (Heb. 'beloved') *c.* 7 century BC. Wife of King Amon of Judah and mother of King Josiah. [2 Kgs. 22:1]

Jedidiah *see* SOLOMON

Jeduthun (Heb. 'praiseworthy') *c.* 10 century BC. Temple choir leader, he was a Levite and came from the town of Netophah. In the time of David he was put in charge of the sacred music of the Temple service, while his sons were made keepers of the gate to the Temple. Jeduthun's choir sang to the accompaniment of harps, lutes and cymbals. In Solomon's Temple, when the priests came out of the Holy Place, Jeduthun and his sons were among the levitical singers standing to the east of the altar. He is mentioned as being the leader of one of the three music guilds. 'Ethan' is mentioned in some accounts in connection with Temple music and scholars have suggested that this might be a variant of the name of Jeduthun.

The family of Jeduthun is also listed among those taking part in Temple services in the reigns of Hezekiah and Josiah, and among those who returned from exile in Babylon. [1 Chr. 9:16; 16:38–42; 25:1, 3; 2 Chr. 5:12; 29:14; 35:15; Neh. 11:17; Titles of Pss. 39, 62, 77]

Jehallelel (Heb. 'who praises God') *1.* date unknown. A descendant of Caleb, the son of Jephunneh. [1 Chr. 4:16]

2. c. 8 century BC. Father of Azariah, a priest of Judah in the reign of King Hezekiah, who helped cleanse the Temple. [2 Chr. 29:12]

Jehdeiah (Heb. 'may God cause to rejoice') *1. c.* 10 century BC. Son of Shubael, he was a Levite who served in King David's Tabernacle. [1 Chr. 24:20]

2. c. 10 century BC. An official of King David responsible for the king's herds of asses. [1 Chr. 27:30]

Jehezkel (Heb. 'may God strengthen') *c.* 10 century BC. A priest in the reign of King David responsible for the twentieth rota of service in the Tabernacle. [1 Chr. 24:16]

Jehiah (Heb. 'may God live') *c.* 10 century BC. One of the two gatekeepers for the Ark in King David's Tabernacle. [1 Chr. 15:24]

Jehiel (Heb. 'may God live') *1. c.* 10 century BC. One of the Levites who played musical instruments for the services in the Tabernacle during the reign of King David. [1 Chr. 15:18, 20; 16:5]

2. c. 10 century BC. Eldest son of Ladan the Levite, he and his family took charge of the gifts collected for the building of the Temple. [1 Chr. 23:8; 29:8]

3. c. 10 century BC. Son of Hachmoni, he was a tutor to the sons of King David. [1 Chr. 27:32]

4. c. 9 century BC. One of the sons of King Jehoshaphat of Judah who was put to death by his brother Jehoram when he became king. [2 Chr. 21:2]

5. c. 8 century BC. One of the Levites in the reign of King Hezekiah of Judah who supervised the bringing of offerings and tithes to the Temple. [2 Chr. 31:13]

6. c. 7 century BC. A leader of Judah who donated large numbers of animals for the special Passover offering proclaimed by King Josiah. [2 Chr. 35:8]

7. 5 century BC. Father of Obadiah, a leader of Judah who returned from exile in Babylon. [Ezra 8:9]

8. 5 century BC. Father of Shecaniah who publicly confessed to Ezra that many men of Judah had married non-Jewish wives. [Ezra 10:2]

9. c. 5 century BC. One of the sons of Harim the priest, he divorced his non-Jewish wife in the time of Ezra. [Ezra 10:21]

10. c. 5 century BC. One of the sons of Elam, he divorced his non-Jewish wife in the time of Ezra. [Ezra 10:26]

Jehieli (Heb. 'may my God live') *c.* 10 century BC. Son of Ladan, and an ancestor of Gershon, he was a Levite, assigned a post in the sanctuary in the time of King David. [1 Chr. 26:21]

Jehizkiah (Heb. 'may God show his strength') *c.* 8 century BC. Son of Shallum, he was one of the leaders of Ephraim who clothed and fed the men of Judah captured by the army of Pekah, king of Israel, and returned them to Judah. [2 Chr. 28:12]

Jehoaddah *see* JARAH

Jehoaddan (Heb. 'God waters') *c.* 9 century BC. Wife of Joash, king of Judah, and mother of his successor Amaziah. Also called Jehoaddin. [2 Kgs. 14:2; 2 Chr. 25:1]

Jehoaddin *see* JEHOADDAN

Jehoahaz (Heb. 'God possessed') *1. see* AHAZIAH 2.

2. Eleventh king of Israel after the monarchy split, he reigned 814–798 BC.

Jehoahaz succeeded his father Jehu on the throne of Israel at a time when that kingdom was in decline. Before the end of Jehu's reign, the territories east of the Jordan river had been lost to Israel's aggressive northern neighbour Aram (Syria) with its capital at Damascus. Under Jehoahaz, the Israelites became even more dominated by King Hazael of Aram and his predecessor King Ben-hadad II. Israel's army dwindled to ten thousand foot-soldiers, fifty horsemen and ten chariots. Late in this reign, some relief from the Aramean pressure was afforded when Aram had to face a fresh threat from the rising Assyrian empire further north. 'Therefore the Lord gave Israel a saviour, so that they escaped from the hand of the Syrians.' (2 Kgs. 13:5)

Jehoahaz reigned for seventeen years and was buried in the capital Samaria. He was succeeded by his son Joash. Also called Joahaz. [2 Kgs. 10:35; 13:1–10, 22–5; 14:1, 8, 17; 2 Chr. 25:17, 25]

3. The seventeenth king of Judah after the monarchy split, he reigned for three months in 609 BC. Jehoahaz was the son of King Josiah of Judah and Hamutal, daughter of Jeremiah from Libnah. He succeeded to the throne after his father was killed in the battle against the Egyptian forces at Megiddo. The Egyptian Pharaoh Neco, who was now trying to consolidate his position in Syria, summoned Jehoahaz to his headquarters in Riblah. When he arrived, Neco arrested him, put him in chains, deposed him as king and deported him to Egypt, where he died. Neco appointed Jehoahaz's half-brother Eliakim to the throne of Judah, changing his name to Jehoiakim. Jehoahaz is also called Shallum by the prophet Jeremiah. [2 Kgs. 23:30–34; 2 Chr. 36:1–4; Jer. 22:10–12]

Jehoash *see* JOASH *7* and *8*.

Jehohanan (Heb. 'given by God') *1.* 10 century BC. Sixth son of Meshelemiah, a Levite. Together with his family he was a gatekeeper of the Tabernacle during the reign of King David. [1 Chr. 26:3]

2. 9 century BC. An army commander of Jehoshaphat, king of Judah. [2 Chr. 17:15]

3. 9 century BC. Father of Ishmael who helped overthrow Queen Athaliah and set up Joash as king of Judah. [2 Chr. 23:1]

4. 5 century BC. Son of Eliashib. Ezra went into Jehohanan's chamber to pray after deciding that all those who had taken non-Jewish wives should divorce them. [Ezra 10:6]

5. 5 century BC. One of the four sons of Bebai who divorced his non-Jewish wife in the time of Ezra. [Ezra 10:28]

6. 5 century BC. Son of Tobiah, one of the conspirators who tried to prevent Nehemiah from rebuilding the walls of Jerusalem. [Neh. 6:18]

7. 5 century BC. One of the chief priests of Judah when Joiakim was high priest in the time of Nehemiah. [Neh. 12:13]

8. 5 century BC. One of the eight priests who sang hymns of praise at the dedication service for the rebuilding of the walls of Jerusalem in the time of Nehemiah. [Neh. 12:42]

Jehoiachin (Heb. 'God appointed') Nineteenth king of Judah after the monarchy split, he reigned for three months in 598 BC.

Jehoiachin was the son of King Jehoiakim of Judah and of Nehushta, daughter of Elnathan from Jerusalem. Just after succeeding his father, he had to surrender to a Babylonian army led by Nebuchadnezzar. The Babylonian troops carried out vindictive reprisals. The king of Judah and his household were taken to Babylon as captives, together with the leading men of Judah,

the army officers and the craftsmen and smiths: 'none remained, except the poorest people of the land' (2 Kgs 24:14). The palace and the Temple were plundered and their treasure removed.

Nebuchadnezzar installed on the throne of Judah Jehoiachin's uncle Mattaniah, whose name was changed to Zedekiah. According to Jeremiah, the people of Judah continued to regard Jehoiachin as their legitimate ruler and believed he would return. The Second Book of Kings relates that thirty-seven years after his removal Jehoiachin was released from prison by a new ruler in Babylon, who treated him well and 'put off his prison garments. And every day of his life he dined regularly at the king's table.' (2 Kgs. 25:29) The records found in the basement of the palace of Nebuchadnezzar in Babylon mention Jehoiachin, his five sons and a number of Judeans in lists of captives who were issued with rations from the king's stores. Also called Jeconiah and Coniah. [2 Kgs. 24:6–17; 25:27–30; 1 Chr. 3:16, 17; 2 Chr. 36:8–9; Esther 2:6; Jer. 22:24, 28; 24:1; 37:1; 52:31; Ezek. 1:2]

Jehoiada (Heb. 'the Lord knoweth') *1.* 10 century BC. Father of Benaiah, a warrior in the army of King David, he deserted from King Saul's army and rallied to King David at Hebron bringing with him 3,700 men. [2 Sam. 8:18; 20:23; 23:20, 22; 1 Kgs. 1:8, 26, 32, 36, 38, 44; 2:25, 29, 34–5, 46; 4:4; 1 Chr. 11:22, 24; 18:17; 27:5]

2. 10 century BC. Son of Benaiah and an adviser to King David. [1 Chr. 27:34]

3. c. 9 century BC. High priest in Jerusalem, he hid the young prince Joash when King Ahaziah's mother Athaliah murdered his children and seized the throne. When the boy was seven, Jehoiada 'brought out the king's son, and put the crown upon him, and gave him the testimony ... and they clapped their hands and said, "Long live the king!"' (2 Kgs. 11:12) Hearing the trumpet blasts Athaliah rushed to the Temple. The guards seized her and upon orders from Jehoiada took her out of the Temple and killed her.

Jehoiada died at a very advanced age and as a tribute was buried 'in the city of David among the kings, because he had done good in Israel, and toward God and his house' (2 Chr. 24:16). He was succeeded as high priest by his son Zechariah. [2 Kgs. 11, 12; 2 Chr. 23; 24:1–22]

4. *c.* 6 century BC. A priest in the time of Jeremiah who was succeeded by Zephaniah, son of Maaseiah. [Jer. 29:26]

5. *see* JOIADA 2.

Jehoiakim (Heb. 'God established') Eighteenth king of Judah after the monarchy split, he reigned 609–598 BC.

Jehoiakim was the son of King Josiah of Judah and of Zebidah, daughter of Pedaiah from Rumah. When Josiah was defeated and killed by the Egyptians in the battle of Megiddo, he was succeeded by his son Jehoahaz. Three months later the Egyptian king Neco deposed Jehoahaz and instead appointed his twenty-five-year-old half-brother Eliakim as a puppet ruler whose name was changed to Jehoiakim. He had to pay a heavy tribute in gold and silver to his Egyptian masters which he raised by imposing a levy on his subjects. Nevertheless he built himself a palace and the prophet Jeremiah railed at him for doing this at a time of national distress.

At the battle of Carchemish in 605 BC, the Babylonians wrested control of the area from Egypt. Three years later, Jehoiakim rebelled against Babylonian control. At first troops were sent against him from the neighbouring vassal states east of the Jordan: Ammon, Moab and Edom. Apparently they did not crush the rebellion because in 597 BC Nebuchadnezzar himself led an army against Judah. But before he arrived Jehoiakim died, after reigning for eleven years, and was succeeded by his son Jehoiachin.

In 1958 an archaeological dig was begun at Ramat Rahel on the southern outskirts of Jerusalem. The remains of a royal Judean citadel were discovered that date back to the end of the 7th century BC and the beginning of the 6th century and a seal was found of the steward to King Jehoiakim. An inner citadel was uncovered with a hewn stone casemate wall in which there were the remains of fine masonry and decorative capitals similar to those found in the royal palaces at Samaria and Megiddo. The ten-foot-thick outer wall of the citadel was of rough stone. [2 Kgs. 23:34–7; 24:1–6; 1 Chr. 3:15–16; 2 Chr. 36:4–8; Jer. 1:3; 22:18–24; 24:1; 25:1; 26:1, 21–3; 27:20; 28:4; 35:1; 36:1, 9, 20–32; 37:1; 45:1; 46:2; 52:2; Dan. 1:1–2]

Jehoiarib (Heb. 'defended by God') **1.** *c.* 10 century BC. Head of a family of priests in the days of King David, he took the first turn of service in the Tabernacle. [1 Chr. 24:7]

2. *See* JOIARIB 1.

Jehonadab *see* JONADAB

Jehonathan (Heb. 'given by God') **1.** *c.* 9 century BC. One of the Levites sent by Jehoshaphat, king of Judah, to teach the Law of God to the people of Judah. [2 Chr. 17:8]

2. 5 century BC. Descended from Shemaiah, he was one of the chief priests of Judah when Joiakim was high priest in the last years of Nehemiah. [Neh. 12:18]

Jehoram (Heb. 'God is exalted') **1.** *c.* 9 century BC. A priest sent by King Jehoshaphat to teach the Law of God to the people of Judah. [2 Chr. 17:8]

2. Ninth king of Israel after the monarchy split, he reigned 852–41 BC.

Jehoram, son of King Ahab and his Phoenician queen Jezebel, succeeded his elder brother Ahaziah on the throne of Israel. Towards the end of Ahab's rule, King Mesha of Moab successfully revolted against Israel's control of his country, the mountain plateau east of the Dead Sea. Jehoram organized a military expedition against Moab in alliance with King Jehoshaphat of Judah and the king of Edom, a vassal of Judah. They made a detour round the southern end, through the 'Wilderness of Edom', and ran out of water, but were saved by a miracle performed by the prophet Elisha. The expedition moved into Moab, plundering and destroying, but retreated again.

After this abortive attempt to reconquer Moab, the rest of Jehoram's reign was involved in the chronic war with Israel's northern neighbour, the kingdom of Aram (Syria) with its capital at Damascus. An Aramean army under King Ben-hadad II pushed into Israel and besieged the capital, Samaria. The city was so powerfully fortified that Ben-hadad could not take it by storm and settled down to starving it into surrender. Inside the walls there was severe famine, and the dwindling supplies were sold at huge prices. Walking along the city wall one day the king was stopped by two quarrelling women, who had agreed to eat their respective children. The child of the one had been killed and eaten, and its mother bitterly accused the other of breaking the bargain by hiding her son. The king tore his clothes in horror and the passers-by noticed that he wore sackcloth next to his skin in grief for the sufferings of his people.

The king's anguish made him turn on Elisha who was in the city. He threatened to kill the man of God, saying, 'This trouble is from the Lord! Why should I wait for the Lord any longer?' (2 Kgs. 6:33) Unshaken in his faith the prophet predicted that by the following day there would be an abundance of food being sold cheaply in the market place.

That night some lepers who had stolen into the enemy camp found it empty. At dawn Jehoram sent out a reconnaissance patrol of two men mounted on two of the last five surviving horses. The scouts came back to confirm that the Arameans had fled during the night and a trail of abandoned baggage and discarded clothes led all the way to the fords over the Jordan river. The townspeople surged out to fall upon the abandoned stores and supplies.

In the twelfth year of Jehoram's reign, he was defending Ramoth-gilead in the mountains east of the Jordan river, against Hazael who had become king of Aram. Ahaziah, the king of Judah, had joined him in this campaign. Wounded by the Arameans, Jehoram handed over the command to his general, Jehu, and went back to his winter palace at Jezreel to recover. Jehu was encouraged by Elisha to make himself king and wipe out the house of Ahab which the prophet regarded as sinful. He leapt into his chariot, and with a troop of his men made a fifty-mile dash from the front across the Jordan valley to Jezreel. Jehoram went out in a chariot to meet Jehu, with King Ahaziah of Judah accompanying him in another chariot. Jehoram innocently called out to him: 'Is it peace, Jehu?' The soldier flung back: 'What peace can there be, so long as the harlotries and the sorceries of your mother Jezebel are so many?' (2 Kgs. 9:22) Realizing they were faced with treason, the two kings swung their chariots round and tried to escape. Jehu brought Jehoram down with an arrow between the shoulder blades, killing him instantly. Jehu ordered the body to be flung onto the ground of Naboth's vineyard nearby, recalling that many years before he had heard Elijah cursing Jehoram's father Ahab at that spot.

Jehu then hunted down the Judean king and afterwards massacred all Jehoram's family, including his mother Jezebel, as well as all the prophets of Baal. In this way the dynasty founded by Omri, Jehoram's grandfather, came to a

bloody end. Also called Joram. [2 Kgs. 1:17; 3; 8:16, 28, 29; 9; 2 Chr. 22:5–7]
3. Fifth king of Judah after the monarchy split, he reigned 848–1 BC.

Jehoram, the eldest son, succeeded his father Jehoshaphat on the throne of Judah at the age of thirty-two. Jehoshaphat had bequeathed a large part of his treasures to his other six sons as well and had allocated certain towns to them. Jehoram promptly murdered all of them and also some of the court ministers. Before then Jehoram had married Athaliah, the daughter of King Ahab of Israel and his queen Jezebel, in order to cement an alliance between the two Hebrew kingdoms. The military reverses in Jehoram's reign and his own painful end are attributed to his indulgence towards foreign gods, under Athaliah's influence.

When the vassal territory of Edom to the south broke away and once more proclaimed its own king, Jehoram led an unsuccessful military expedition with chariots to conquer it. His forces were encircled and cut off by the Edomites and had to break out in a night attack, in order to escape. With the loss of Edom went the profitable trading route to Arabia and the Red Sea area through the port of Ezion-geber (Eilat), that had been revived by Jehoshaphat.

The weakness of Judah at this time laid it open to raids by the Philistines on the coastal plain to the west, and by nomad tribes from the south. They reached Jerusalem, killed the king's wives and children, and carried off a great deal of plunder. The only survivor of the royal household was Jehoram's youngest son, Ahaziah. The Bible links the wiping out of the royal family with a letter from Elijah in which the doom of Jehoram and his house is prophesied. It is possible that the king and the army were away in the north at the time, engaged together with the forces of Israel and other local rulers in a collective effort to stop the Assyrian advance.

After a reign of eight years, Jehoram died from a disease of the bowels. The text says pointedly that nobody regretted his passing and that he was buried in Jerusalem but not in the tomb of the kings.

Jehoram was succeeded by Ahaziah. Also called Joram. [2 Kgs. 1:17; 8:16–29; 12:18; 1 Chr. 3:11; 2 Chr. 21:1–16; 22:1–11]

Jehoshabeath *see* JEHOSHEBA

Jehoshaphat (Heb. 'God has judged') *1. c.* 10 century BC. Son of Ahilud, he served as recorder of chronicles to King David and King Solomon. [2 Sam. 8:16; 20:24; 1 Kgs. 4:3; 1 Chr. 18:15]
2. *c.* 10 century BC. Son of Parvah, he was one of the twelve officers of King Solomon responsible for supplying provisions for the royal household. [1 Kgs. 4:17]
3. *c.* 9 century BC. Father of Jehu, the army commander who seized the throne of Israel from King Jehoram. [2 Kgs. 9:2, 14]
4. Fourth king of Judah after the monarchy split, he reigned 870–48 BC. Jehoshaphat, the son of King Asa and Azubah daughter of Shilhi, succeeded his father at the age of thirty-five and continued Asa's religious reforms. He destroyed many of the local hill-shrines, and restored the central authority of the Temple in Jerusalem. Five senior officials, eight Levites and two priests were sent round the country as instructors in the Book of the Law. Later, the king personally toured the towns of his realm 'and brought them back to the Lord, the God of their fathers' (2 Chr. 19:4). He appointed local judges, warning them that they should not respect rank nor take gifts. In Jerusalem, Jehoshaphat established a central judicial body and appointed its members from among the priests, the Levites and the heads of leading families. He also strengthened the security of the kingdom, by

reorganizing the army and fortifying strategic towns.

For most of Jehoshaphat's long reign, Judah was at peace with its neighbours and enjoyed rising prosperity. In its customary didactic spirit, the Book of Chronicles states that because of the king's piety the Lord instilled 'dread' into neighbouring peoples. Jehoshaphat collected tribute from the Philistines in gifts and silver, and from nomad Arabian tribes in sheep and goats.

The intervention of the Lord frustrated an incursion by a 'great multitude' of Ammonites, Moabites and hill-men from Edom. They came up into the Hebron hills from the direction of the Dead Sea. The king and a panic-stricken congregation gathered in the Temple and prayed for divine help. One of the Levites, possessed by 'the spirit of the Lord', told them not to fear but to march out towards the invaders. They did so with cantors chanting in the vanguard. The Lord caused the invading bands to turn and fight each other. When the Israelites reached the spot, they saw nothing but corpses and spoil. It took three days to collect the booty.

A more mundane reason for prosperity was the revival of trade with the Red Sea region, through the port of Ezion-geber (Eilat) at the head of the Gulf of Akaba. As in Solomon's time a century earlier, the Judeans became middlemen in the lucrative commerce between Arabia and the Mediterranean coast.

The Bible relates that Jehoshaphat tried to emulate Solomon by constructing 'ships of Tarshish' (1 Kgs. 22:48), but they came to grief in the Gulf of Akaba – presumably shipwrecked in a storm.

In spite of clerical disapproval, Jehoshaphat fostered an alliance with the other Hebrew kingdom, Israel. His crown prince, Jehoram, was married to Athaliah, the daughter of King Ahab. Jehoshaphat came to visit Ahab in Samaria and agreed to join in a campaign to recover Ramoth-gilead, in the highlands east of the Jordan from Aram-Damascus. But he wished to know that the venture had the Lord's blessing. Ahab assembled an impressive gathering of four hundred prophets, who appeared before the two kings sitting in state on thrones outside the city gates. All of them predicted victory against the Arameans.

One prophet, Micaiah, failed to come. He was sent for, and when pressed to speak the truth, predicted that Ahab would be killed in the battle and Israel would be 'scattered upon the mountains, as sheep that have no shepherd' (2 Chr. 18:16). To avert his fate Ahab went into battle in disguise, while Jehoshaphat in his full kingly armour was mistaken for Ahab until he gave his own battle-cry. When Ahab was killed by a stray arrow, the Israelites retreated and Jehoshaphat returned home to Jerusalem.

Jehoshaphat took part in another military expedition jointly with Ahab's son Jehoram (who succeeded his brother Ahaziah). It was directed against King Mesha of Moab, who had rebelled against the suzerainty of Israel. Together with the vassal king of Edom, they made a detour through the desert below the Dead Sea, to attack Moab from the south.

When the army ran out of water, the three kings appealed to the prophet Elisha, who was accompanying them. He rebuffed Jehoram, but agreed to help them out of respect for the God-fearing Jehoshaphat. Elisha's instructions to dig trenches produced water and they were able to defeat the enemy forces and invade Moab. However, the Israelite army did not secure their hold on the country and eventually withdrew to their own borders.

Jehoshaphat was succeeded by his son Jehoram. [1 Kgs. 15:24; 22:1–51; 2 Kgs. 1:17; 3:1–14; 8:16; 12:18; 1 Chr. 3:10; 2 Chr. 17–21]

Jehosheba (Heb. 'oath of God') c. 9

century BC. Daughter of Joram, king of
Judah, she hid her nephew Joash to
prevent his being killed by his grandmother Athaliah who had seized the
throne and murdered all her other grandchildren. Also known as Jehoshabeath.
[2 Kgs. 11:2; 2 Chr. 22:11]

Jehozabad (Heb. 'given by God') *1. c.*
10 century BC. Son of Obed-edom, he
and his family were gate-keepers of the
Tabernacle in the reign of King David.
[1 Chr. 26:4]
2. c. 9 century BC. An army commander
of Jehoshaphat, king of Judah. [2 Chr.
17:18]
3. c. 8 century BC. A servant of Joash,
king of Judah, who assassinated the king
and buried the body in Jerusalem. He
was executed by Amaziah, who succeeded his father as king of Judah. [2
Kgs. 12:21; 2 Chr. 24:26]

Jehozadak (Heb. 'Jehovah is righteous')
c. 6 century BC. A priest descended from
Zadok who went into exile at the time
of Nebuchadnezzar, he was father of
the high priest Jeshua. Also called Jozadak. [1 Chr. 6:14, 15; Ezra 3:2, 8; 10:18;
Hag. 1:1, 12, 14; 2:2, 4; Zech. 6:11]

Jehu (Heb. '[man] of God') *1.* date unknown. Son of Obed and a leader of the
tribe of Judah. [1 Chr. 2:38]
2. c. 11 century BC. A Benjaminite warrior who left the army of King Saul and
rallied to David at Ziklag. [1 Chr. 12:3]
3. c. 9 century BC. Jehu, a prophet, son
of Hanani, he foretold the doom of King
Baasha of Israel. Years later, when King
Jehoshaphat of Judah returned from the
battlefield where King Ahab was killed,
Jehu went out to greet him. [1 Kgs.
16:1; 2 Chr. 19:1–3]
4. Tenth king of Israel after the monarchy split, he reigned 841–14 BC.

King Joram, son of Ahab, was engaged in the defence of Ramoth-gilead,
in the mountains east of the Jordan
river, against the forces of Aram-Damas-

cus (Syria). He handed over the command of the front to his general Jehu,
and went back to his winter palace at
Jezreel to recover from campaign
wounds. Here he was joined by his ally,
King Ahaziah of Judah.

The prophet Elisha now instigated a
revolt against the king. He sent a young
disciple who poured holy oil on Jehu's
head and told him the Lord had appointed him to be king of Israel and to
wipe out the sinful house of Ahab. When
Jehu told them what had happened, his
brother officers instantly hailed him
spreading their cloaks for him on the
steps and having trumpets sounded.
Jehu then leapt into his chariot and
with a mounted escort set out on a
fifty-mile dash for Jezreel.

The sentry on the tower of Jezreel
reported that he saw a troop of men
approaching in the distance, and that
'... the driving is like the driving of
Jehu the son of Nimshi; for he drives
furiously' (2 Kgs. 9:20). The unsuspect-
ing Joram then had his chariot brought
round and himself drove out to meet his
army commander with his guest the king
of Judah in another chariot accompanying him. When they reached Jehu and
Joram gave him the customary greeting:
'Is it peace?' he was taken aback at the
rude answer: 'What peace can there be,
so long as the harlotries and the sorceries of your mother Jezebel are so many?'
(2 Kgs. 9:22) At Joram's shout of
'Treachery, O Ahaziah!' (2 Kgs. 9:23),
the two kings spun their chariots round
and tried to get away. An arrow from
Jehu's bow hit the fleeing Joram between the shoulder blades and killed
him on the spot. Jehu told Bidkar, his
aide, to throw the king's body into
Naboth's vineyard nearby, where Ahab
had been cursed by Elijah. Jehu then
chased after Ahaziah who had fled up
the Jezreel valley. The king, wounded
during the pursuit, sought refuge in the
fortress of Megiddo, where he died.

Jehu now went looking for the hated

Jezebel, the mother of King Joram. She was expecting him, and with the stiff pride of a king's daughter she had carefully made up her face and dressed her hair and stood waiting at an upstairs window of the palace. Jehu ordered her servants to throw her down and drove over her bloodstained body. Later, after he had eaten and drunk, he ordered her buried, for despite her end, 'she is a king's daughter' (2 Kgs. 9:34). But the dogs had already eaten her flesh as Elijah had foretold.

The slaying of the two kings by Jehu had robbed the notables in Samaria of the will to resist, and they were terrified of the ruthless usurper. On receipt of a written challenge from Jehu to Ahab's sons, they replied submitting themselves to Jehu's will. He wrote a second letter demanding that by the following day they should bring to him at Jezreel the heads of Ahab's seventy sons. The word 'heads', in Hebrew 'roshim', may have been ambiguous, meaning 'leaders', but the panicky authorities in the capital took his behest literally. They slew Ahab's sons, put their heads in baskets and sent them to Jehu. He had them placed in two heaps at the city gate. Next morning he appeared there and said to the people, 'You are innocent. It was I who conspired against my master, and slew him; but who struck down all these?' (2 Kgs. 10:9)

The blood-bath was far from over. In Jezreel, Jehu butchered all of King Joram's household including his close friends and his priests. Jehu then set out for Samaria. Along the way he killed a party of kinsmen of the slain King Ahaziah of Judah. In Samaria Jehu wiped out all the remaining members of Ahab's family.

Now firmly in the saddle Jehu set himself to crushing the worship of Baal in the country – the purpose for which the prophet Elisha had originally engineered his coup. Jehu disguised his intentions. Giving out that he would personally offer sacrifice in the great temple of Baal in Samaria, he ordered that all the priests and devotees of the cult from the whole kingdom should assemble there. Armed men waiting outside were turned loose on them, and all of them were killed. The temple and altar were demolished and the images of the god were taken out and burnt. The ruins of the building were converted into a latrine.

By this gory military coup, Jehu not only started a new dynasty but wrenched the country into the religious reformation that had been prepared by the work of Elijah and Elisha.

Jehu remained on the throne for twenty-eight years. Having dealt with the religious issue, the Bible pays little attention to the other events of his reign. It was in fact a period of rapid decline in the fortunes of the kingdom, and of drastic shrinkage of its territory. Phoenicia and Judea had been antagonized, and Hazael, king of Aram-Damascus, now occupied all the Israelite territory east of the Jordan. Jehu was left ruling over not much more than the hill-country of Ephraim. According to Assyrian records, Shalmaneser III marched at this time across Israel to a headland on the coast, probably Mount Carmel.

The decline of Israel reached its lowest ebb towards the end of Jehu's reign and that of his son Jehoahaz. Jehu may have been a seasoned soldier, bold and ruthless in seizing power, but he showed no capacity for statesmanship. [1 Kgs. 19:16, 17; 2 Kgs. 9; 10; 12:1; 13:1; 14:8; 15:12; 2 Chr. 22:7–9; 25:17; Hos. 1:4]

5. *c.* 8 century BC. Son of Joshibiah, he was one of the leaders of the tribe of Simeon in the reign of King Hezekiah who drove out the inhabitants of the rich Gedor valley and dwelt there instead. [1 Chr. 4:35]

Jehubbah (Heb. 'hidden') date unknown. Son of Shemer and a member of the tribe of Asher. [1 Chr. 7:34]

Jehucal (Heb. 'God sustains') *c.* 6 century BC. Son of Shelemiah, he was an official of the court and carried a personal message from King Zedekiah to Jeremiah asking the prophet to pray for him. Also called Jucal. [Jer. 37:3; 38:1]

Jehudi (Heb. 'Judean') 6 century BC. Son of Nethaniah, he was sent to Baruch, the scribe of the prophet Jeremiah, to ask him to read Jeremiah's prophecies to the leaders. Later Jehoiakim, king of Judah, sent Jehudi to fetch the scroll of Jeremiah's prophecies and as Jehudi read from the scroll the king burnt it piece by piece. [Jer. 36:14–23]

Jehuel (Heb. 'may God live') 8 century BC. A Levite, descendant of Heman, he sanctified himself so that he could cleanse the Temple during the reign of Hezekiah. [2 Chr. 29:14]

Jeiel (Heb. 'God's treasure') *1.* date unknown. Head of a family of the tribe of Reuben and a leader of the tribe. [1 Chr. 5:7]
2. date unknown. Leader of the tribe of Benjamin living in Gibeon, and ancestor of Saul. [1 Chr. 8:29; 9:35]
3. c. 10 century BC. Son of Hotham, he and his brother Shama were warriors in the army of King David distinguished for their bravery. [1 Chr. 11:44]
4. c. 10 century BC. A Levite in the reign of King David who played musical instruments to accompany the bringing of the Ark of God to Jerusalem, and took part in the services in the Tabernacle. [1 Chr. 15:18, 21; 16:5]
5. c. 9 century BC. Ancestor of the Levite Jahaziel who prophesied a great victory for King Jehoshaphat of Judah over the invading armies of Moab, Ammon and Seir. [2 Chr. 20:14]
6. c. 8 century BC. Secretary to King Uzziah, he kept the records of the numbers of troops in the army of Judah. [2 Chr. 26:11]
7. c. 7 century BC. A leading Levite in

the reign of King Josiah of Judah who donated large quantities of cattle for the Passover offering. [2 Chr. 35:9]
8. 5 century BC. A son of Nebo who divorced his non-Jewish wife in the time of Ezra. [Ezra 10:43]

Jekameam (Heb. 'who gathers') *c.* 10 century BC. A descendant of Hebron, he was one of the Levites who served in the Tabernacle in the reign of King David. [1 Chr. 23:19; 24:23]

Jekamiah (Heb. 'established by God') *1.* date unknown. Son of Shallum and a leader of the tribe of Judah. [1 Chr. 2:41]
2. 6 century BC. Son of Jeconiah of the tribe of Judah and a descendant of King David. [1 Chr. 3:18]

Jekuthiel (Heb. 'may God sustain') date unknown. Father of Zanoah and a leader of the tribe of Judah. [1 Chr. 4:18]

Jemimah (Heb. 'dove') period of the Patriarchs. Job's eldest daughter born after his trials and tribulations had ended and his fortune restored. [Job. 42:14]

Jemuel (Heb. 'day of God') *c.* 16 century BC. A son of Simeon, he went down to Egypt with his grandfather Jacob. Also called Nemuel. [Gen. 46:10; Exod. 6:15; Num. 26:12; 1 Chr. 4:24]

Jephthah (Heb. 'set free') *c.* 12 century BC. A judge in Israel and leader of the war against the Ammonites.

In the period of the Judges, Jephthah was born in the land of Gilead of a father who was also called Gilead, and a mother who was a harlot. His half-brothers by his father's lawful wife drove him away, lest he should share the inheritance with them. Jephthah fled eastward to the land of Tob, on the edge of the desert. Here he became leader of a robber band of destitute men who had gathered round him. He became known as a skilled and daring fighter, 'a mighty warrior' (Judg. 11:1).

The elders of Gilead sought him out and urged him to lead their forces against the Ammonites, who were encroaching on their territory. Jephthah retorted with some bitterness: 'Did you not hate me, and drive me out of my father's house? Why have you come to me now when you are in trouble?' (Judg. 11:7) He agreed to accept the appointment on condition that if they were victorious, he would remain the tribal leader. The undertaking was solemnly endorsed at Mizpah ('watch-tower') where the Israelite defenders had mustered.

On assuming command, Jephthah at first attempted to come to terms with the Ammonites by peaceful means. He sent a delegation to their king, proposing that their forces be withdrawn. In his reply, the Ammonite ruler laid claim to all the Israelite territory in Transjordan to the south of Gilead, between the Arnon and Jabbok rivers, occupied by the tribes of Gad and Reuben. Jephthah sent his envoys back to prove that there was no historical basis for this claim, since the Children of Israel under Moses had taken the area from the Amorites under King Sihon, who had barred their transit. Since then the Israelites had lived in these territories for three hundred years: 'why did you not recover them within that time? I therefore have not sinned against you, and you do me wrong by making war on me.' (Judg. 11:26, 27)

The king of Ammon rejected Jephthah's diplomatic overtures, and hostilities broke out. Jehphthah marched south in a wide sweep to attack the Ammonites from the rear. Before going into battle, he took a vow that if he won he would sacrifice to the Lord 'whoever comes forth from the doors of my house to meet me, when I return victorious...' (Judg. 11:31).

With the Ammonites repulsed, Jephthah returned in triumph. To his horror, the first person who came to meet him was his daughter, an only child, dancing to the sound of timbrels. Jephthah tore his clothes and cried out in grief; but even his daughter agreed that his sacred oath could not be broken. At her request, 'he sent her away for two months; and she departed, she and her companions, and bewailed her virginity upon the mountains' (Judg. 11:38). On her return, the sacrifice was carried out. From this tragic episode the custom arose for the young women to go out each year for four days, mourning Jephthah's daughter.

A quarrel now broke out between the men of Gilead and the tribe of Ephraim across the river. The Ephraimites advanced eastward into Gilead, but Jephthah drove them back towards the river and sent detachments ahead to cut them off at the fords. Those men who sought to cross and denied that they were Ephraimites were asked to say the word *Shibboleth*, which means an 'ear of wheat'. If they pronounced it *Sibboleth*, according to the dialect of Ephraim, they were slain on the spot. Thousands of Ephraimites lost their lives in this ill-advised expedition.

Jephthah judged for six years and on his death was buried in one of the towns of his native Gilead. [Judg. 11, 12; 1 Sam. 12:11]

Jephunneh (Heb. 'favourably regarded') *1. c.* 13 century BC. Father of Caleb, he was a leader of the tribe of Judah. [Num. 13:6; 14:6; 30, 38; Deut. 1:36; 1 Chr. 4:15]
2. date unknown. Eldest son of Jether, he was a leader of the tribe of Asher and a mighty warrior. [1 Chr. 7:38]

Jerah (Heb. 'moon') date unknown. One of Joktan's thirteen sons and a descendant of Shem. [Gen. 10:26; 1 Chr. 1:20]

Jerahmeel (Heb. 'God's mercy') *1.* date unknown. The eldest son of Hezron and a leader of the tribe of Judah, he was one of the most prominent of the early leaders of the tribe. [1 Chr. 2:9, 25–7, 42]

2. 10 century BC. Son of Kish, a Levite descended from Merari, he ministered in the Tabernacle in the reign of King David. [1 Chr. 24:29]

3. c. 6 century BC. One of the officers sent by King Jehoiakim of Judah to arrest the prophet Jeremiah and his scribe Baruch. [Jer. 36:26]

Jered (Heb. 'descent') date unknown. An ancestor of the members of the tribe of Judah that invaded the valley of Gedor. [1 Chr. 4:18]

Jeremai (Heb. 'exalted') 5 century BC. A descendant of Hashum who divorced his non-Jewish wife in the time of Ezra. [Ezra 10:33]

Jeremiah (Heb. 'God will elevate') *1.* date unknown. A leader of half of the tribe of Manasseh who dwelt in Bashan east of the river Jordan. [1 Chr. 5:24]

2. 11 century BC. One of the Benjaminite warriors who deserted from King Saul's army and joined David at Ziklag. [1 Chr. 12:4]

3. c. 11 century BC. Two of the eleven captains of the tribe of Gad who deserted from King Saul's army and joined David at Ziklag. [1 Chr. 12:10, 13]

4. c. 7 century BC. Father of Hamutal, the wife of Josiah, king of Judah. [2 Kgs. 23:31]

5. 7–6 century BC. Hebrew prophet. Jeremiah and Isaiah were the two giants of Hebrew prophecy, next to Moses himself. They lived in Jerusalem a century apart, in the turbulent period that saw the two small Hebrew kingdoms wiped out with the fall of Samaria in 721 BC and that of Jerusalem in 587 BC. Both men were caught up in the political events of their time.

Like Amos, Hosea, Isaiah and Micah before him, Jeremiah was a God-driven man, fearlessly denouncing the religious laxity and social ills of the nation, and warning of the disasters that would follow. With no other prophet, however, has the inner conflict behind the stern message been so revealed. Jeremiah's agony was echoed more than two thousand years later in the words of Shakespeare's Hamlet:
'The times are out of joint – oh cursed
      spite
that ever I was born to put them right.'

Jeremiah was born in the village of Anathoth, in the territory of Benjamin, three miles north-east of Jerusalem. This was one of the towns set aside for the priestly tribe of the Levites in the time of Joshua. Jeremiah's father Hilkiah was also a priest, and the boy was no doubt reared in a devout and quiet home. At about eighteen, he felt the call to follow the vocation of a prophet:

'Then the Lord put forth his hand and touched my mouth; and the Lord said to me, "Behold, I have put my words in your mouth.

'"See, I have set you this day over nations and over kingdoms, to pluck up and to break down, to destroy and to overthrow, to build and to plant."' (Jer. 1:9, 10)

This took place about 627 BC, in the thirteenth year of Josiah's reign. Josiah carried out a sweeping religious reformation, stamping out idolatry and restoring the Temple in Jerusalem as the central sanctuary of the nation. In 622 BC a 'book of the law' was discovered in the Temple (probably an early version of the Book of Deuteronomy), and it became the focus of the reform movement. Curiously, Jeremiah seemed hardly involved in this development. The forms and rituals of organized worship meant little to him – 'the false pen of the scribes has made it into a lie' (Jer. 8:8). For Jeremiah, faith was an intensely personal matter, and God would judge each man by what was in his heart: 'I the Lord search the mind and try the heart, to give to every man according to his ways, according to the fruit of his doings.' (Jer. 17:10)

THE OUTSPOKEN PREACHER

In 609 BC the good King Josiah was killed in battle against an Egyptian army at the pass of Megiddo. He was succeeded by his son Jehoahaz, whom the Egyptian Pharaoh Neco deposed a few months later in favour of Jehoiakim, another son of Josiah. For some years the kingdom remained subservient to Egypt, while it slid back into religious and moral laxity. Jeremiah's outspoken criticisms brought him into continual trouble with the authorities.

Soon after the beginning of Jehoiakim's reign, Jeremiah planted himself in the courtyard of the Temple and addressed the crowd of worshippers that had gathered from all over the country. He shocked them by a diatribe in which he swore that if they did not mend their ways, God would destroy the very sanctuary itself. 'Will you steal, murder, commit adultery, swear falsely, burn incense to Baal, and go after other gods that you have not known, and then come and stand before me in this house, which is called by my name, and say, "We are delivered!" – only to go on doing all these abominations?' (Jer. 7:9, 10)

The crowd swarmed round him, and some of the priests and people seized hold of him shouting, 'Thou shalt surely die.' Hearing the excitement, some of the king's officials immediately came over from the palace and sat down at the Temple gate to conduct an enquiry. Jeremiah's eloquence persuaded the officials that he had conveyed a message from God calling for repentance while there was yet time. The elders who were present started invoking precedents one way or the other. Some recalled that in the reign of Hezekiah a century earlier, the prophet Micah had made similar predictions which had led to repentance

rather than punishment of the prophet. But others spoke of Uriah, another prophet who had recently been put to death by King Jehoiakim for similar statements. Jeremiah might have suffered the same fate but for the protection of an important man of the court, Ahikam, whose father had been the royal scribe at the time of Josiah's reforms.

Before a crowd of priests and citizens in the valley of Hinnom, Jeremiah denounced their pagan practices, and dramatically smashed an earthenware jar crying out, 'Thus says the Lord of hosts: So will I break this people and this city as one breaks a potter's vessel, so it can never be mended.' (Jer. 19:11)

Jeremiah returned to the city, stood in the court of the Temple and addressed the crowd, shouting out in God's name: 'Behold, I am bringing upon this city and upon all its towns all the evil that I have pronounced against it, because they have stiffened their neck, refusing to hear my words.' (Jer. 19:15)

The angry priest Pashhur had the prophet beaten and then put in the stocks which were at the upper gate to the Temple. Next day, when Pashhur released him, Jeremiah was totally unrepentant. He repeated that the city would be destroyed and plundered and all its inhabitants carried off to Babylon. 'And you, Pashhur, and all who dwell in your house, shall go into captivity; to Babylon you shall go; and there you shall die, and there you shall be buried, you and all your friends, to whom you have prophesied falsely.' (Jer. 20:6)

PRESSURE FROM BABYLON

For centuries the Near East had been dominated by the imperial might of Assyria. That period was now coming to an end. In 612 BC the great capital city of Nineveh was capured by the Babylonians. In 605 BC Nebuchadnezzar of Babylon defeated the Egyptian army of Neco at Carchemish, and became the new overlord of Judah and its neighbours.

Jeremiah's preaching acquired a new note of urgency. For twenty-three years he had called for repentance and prophesied disaster without any effect. With the advent of Babylon, he saw this threat as imminent. Before the citizens of Jerusalem he proclaimed: 'This whole land shall become a ruin and a waste, and these nations shall serve the king of Babylon seventy years.' (Jer. 25:11)

Jeremiah had acquired a devoted disciple and scribe, Baruch, the son of Neriah. He sent for Baruch and dictated a scroll containing his discourses and oracles from the beginning of his ministry. Soon after, there was a special fast day on which people gathered from near and far for prayers in the Temple. Since Jeremiah had been banned from the Temple area (probably after the quarrel with the priest Pashhur), he sent Baruch to read out the scroll to the crowd of worshippers, in the hope that the grim prophecies in it would cause the hearers to repent.

Baruch did this, and then found himself summoned to the palace to read the book again before a meeting of the palace officials. Disturbed at its contents, they advised Baruch to take his master and go into hiding. They then informed the king, who was in his chamber keeping himself warm in front of a brazier. He ordered his secretary Jehudi to read the document to him. Each time a few columns had been read, he hacked that piece off in a rage with the scribe's knife and threw it on the fire until the whole scroll was burned. He then ordered Jeremiah and Baruch to be arrested, but they were not to be found. At the Lord's command Jeremiah dictated the scroll over again to Baruch, with additions.

Some two years later in 602 BC, Jehoiakim joined in a revolt of several vassal kingdoms against the rule of Babylon. At first Nebuchadnezzar tried to quell it with local levies from the subject kingdoms east of the Jordan. When this did

not succeed he marched with a Babylonian army against Judah.

The Rechabite community had taken refuge in Jerusalem from the Babylonian troops. They were a fundamentalist sect of desert nomads, living by the injunctions of an ancestor Jonadab, the son of Rehab, that they should not live in houses, till the soil or touch wine. Jeremiah tested them by bringing them into a chamber of the Temple and offering them glasses of wine which were rejected. He then held them up as an example of fidelity to tradition, as opposed to the lax ways of the Jerusalemites.

Jeremiah lashed out at the spendthrift and impious king who had brought calamity upon his people and said, 'With the burial of an ass he shall be buried, dragged and cast forth beyond the gates of Jerusalem.' (Jer. 22:19) In poignant terms, the prophet described the horrors of war and siege that would attend the decline and fall of Judah.

By the time the Babylonians reached Jerusalem, Jehoiakim was dead and succeeded by his son Jehoiachin (598 BC). The young king surrendered the city and was carried off into captivity in Babylon together with the queen mother, the royal household and three thousand leading citizens of the kingdom. The king's uncle Zedekiah was appointed as ruler by Nebuchadnezzar.

A spirit of revolt against the colonial rule of Babylon continued to simmer under the surface in Judah and the other states in the region. Jeremiah was opposed to the militants, and urged submission until the Lord in his own good time should break the hold of Babylon and bring back their captured brothers. Given to the use of dramatic symbols in his preaching, he walked about with a wooden yoke on his neck. He not only addressed his message to the people but also to the rulers of Edom, Moab, Ammon, Tyre and Sidon, through their ambassadors in Jerusalem, warning that armed resistance would lead to the destruction of their countries.

A leading priest and prophet, Hananiah, the son of Azzur, proclaimed that within two years the Lord would smash Babylon and restore the captives, together with all the sacred vessels that had been removed from the Temple by order of Nebuchadnezzar. He too illustrated his point by a symbolic act. He smashed Jeremiah's yoke and proclaimed in God's name: 'Even so will I break the yoke of Nebuchadnezzar king of Babylon from the neck of all the nations ...' (Jer. 28:11). Jeremiah predicted that this false prophet would be dead within the year. Two months later this came to pass.

In another metaphor used by Jeremiah a basket of good figs denoted the exiles in Babylon whom God would look after and bring back, while a basket of rotten figs stood for King Zedekiah and his nobles who would be discarded.

About this time King Zedekiah sent an official delegation to Babylon. Two of its members were friends of Jeremiah, and he sent with them a remarkable letter to the small community of Israelites that had been brought there as captives together with the young King Jehoiachin. Jeremiah begged them to be patient, and not to be deluded by the false prophets among them who were promising them a speedy return home. He repeated that their exile would last seventy years, but in the end God would bring them back in peace. Meanwhile, they should settle down, lead constructive lives and try to be on good terms with the authorities.

'Build houses and live in them; plant gardens and eat their produce.

'Take wives and have sons and daughters; take wives for your sons, and give your daughters in marriage, that they may bear sons and daughters; multiply there, and do not decrease.

'But seek the welfare of the city where I have sent you into exile, and pray to the Lord on its behalf, for in its welfare you will find your welfare.' (Jer. 29:5, 6, 7)

As for those who remained behind in Jerusalem, their evil-doing would be punished by the 'sword, famine, and pestilence' (Jer. 29:17).

This specific counsel drew a sharp reaction from one of the priests in Babylon called Shemaiah. He wrote a letter of protest to Zephaniah, the chief priest of the Temple in Jerusalem, demanding that Jeremiah should be severely disciplined. When Jeremiah was called in and had the protest read to him, he retorted that because Shemaiah had prophesied falsely, God would not let him or his family take part in the return of the exiles to Jerusalem.

THE FALL OF JERUSALEM

In 589 BC King Zedekiah took the step that Jeremiah had so gravely feared. He joined in an uprising against Babylon. Once more Nebuchadnezzar invaded the country and laid siege to Jerusalem. The king sent priests to Jeremiah, asking him to intercede with the Lord for the safety of the city. The prophet's answer was a grim one. God had decided that the faithless city would fall to the enemy. The only way its inhabitants could save themselves was to surrender.

The siege dragged on, until suddenly it was lifted. The Babylonian forces were diverted to meet an advance by an Egyptian army under the Pharaoh Hophra.

With the enemy at the gate, the king and the well-to-do citizens had made a solemn covenant in the Temple to free all their Hebrew slaves. They now broke their word and enslaved them again, at which Jeremiah expressed great indignation.

During this break in the siege, Jeremiah came to be regarded as a pacifist and a quisling, who should be suppressed in the public interest. When he tried to leave the city to attend to some family property in his native village, he was arrested as a deserter by the sentry at the gate and flung into an under-ground cell, where he remained shut up for a long period of time.

The king sent for him and asked anxiously whether he had received any message from God. Jeremiah answered: 'There is.' Then he said, 'You shall be delivered into the hand of the king of Babylon.' Moreover: 'What wrong have I done to you or your servants or this people, that you have put me in prison?' (Jer. 37:17, 18) The king gave orders he should be moved to the court of the guard and be brought a fresh loaf of bread each day from the 'bakers' street'.

But pressure was brought on the king by senior officials and priests on the ground that Jeremiah's words were un-dermining the morale of the army. The prophet was handed over to them and they had him lowered into a muddy cistern and left to die. He was rescued by one of the palace eunuchs, Ebed-melech, the Ethiopian. The distressed slave ran to tell the king what had hap-pened to the prophet and was given three servants to help him pull Jeremiah out with ropes. For this act, the Lord promised that Ebed-melech would be saved from the Babylonians.

The siege was renewed and nearly two years later, in the summer of 587 BC, the starving city fell. A month later the Babylonian commander had the Temple, the palace and most of the build-ings razed. The inhabitants were either killed or rounded up and deported to Babylon. King Zedekiah escaped with some of his soldiers, but was captured and killed.

Nebuchadnezzar had given orders that Jeremiah should be spared and treated well. The Babylonian com-mander located him among the shackled prisoners awaiting deportation. He had him released, and gave him permission to go to Babylon if he wished or to remain anywhere in the country. Jer-emiah went to Mizpah, just north of Jerusalem, to his friend Gedaliah, whom the Babylonians had appointed as governor of Judah.

Two months later, Gedaliah was assas-sinated. A group of Judean patriots loyal to Gedaliah failed to catch the murderer, and fearing that they would be blamed, fled to Egypt to seek political asylum there. Jeremiah was taken with them together with his scribe Baruch.

Little is known about the last period of the prophet's life in Egypt. It is men-tioned that he predicted the invasion of Egypt by Nebuchadnezzar, an event that took place. There is also a record of an assembly at which Jeremiah remon-strated with the Judean refugees in Egypt for worshipping alien gods, and addressed himself particularly to the women who made offerings to the heav-enly bodies. His audience replied with some bitterness that the ancestral faith had not saved their homeland.

There is a dubious tradition that Jer-emiah met his end by being stoned to death.

JEREMIAH'S PERSONALITY AND BELIEFS

The Book of Jeremiah contains fifty-two chapters, not in a very orderly sequence. It is compiled of various elements. Roughly, the first half consists of the prophet's oracles, sermons and divine messages against Jerusalem and Judah, in the reigns of Jehoiakim and Zedekiah. In addition, there is a group of poetic but hard-hitting 'Oracles against the Nations': chiefly Babylon, but also Egypt, the Philistines, the Phoenicians, Moab, Ammon, Edom, Elam and the Arabian tribes. 'The cla-mour will resound to the ends of the earth, for the Lord has an indictment against the nations; he is entering into judgment with all flesh, and the wicked he will put to the sword, says the Lord.' (Jer. 25:31)

In the second part of the Book there are a number of geographical narratives about Jeremiah, probably recorded by his disciple Baruch. They are inter-spersed with revealing personal confessions by the prophet himself.

From the narratives and the confessions Jeremiah emerges as a lonely and sensitive figure. With no other character in the Old Testament is there so moving a revelation of inner conflict.

At an early age, Jeremiah seemed cut off from the fabric of ordinary life. He states that God told him not to get married and have children, since the times were wicked and the people around him doomed. For this reason he was not to share in the mourning or rejoicing of his fellowmen. He was even denied 'the voice of mirth and the voice of gladness' (Jer. 16:9).

As solitary people with a country upbringing tend to do, he communed with nature, and had an affinity with the world of birds. 'Even the stork in the heavens knows her times; and the turtledove, swallow and crane keep the time of their coming.' (Jer. 8:7) He noted the partridge sitting on its eggs and 'the dove that nests in the sides of the mouth of a gorge' (Jer. 48:28).

Plagued by self-doubt, Jeremiah was at times overcome by a sense of futility about his mission: 'O Lord, do not thy eyes look for truth? Thou hast smitten them, but they felt no anguish; thou hast consumed them, but they refused to take correction. They have made their faces harder than rock.' (Jer. 5:3) At first he was naive enough to believe that if the poor and ignorant failed to respond, he would get a hearing from people of standing and education; 'I will go to the great, and will speak to them; for they know the way of the Lord.' (Jer. 5:5) He was soon disillusioned.

Jeremiah suffered acutely from the ill-will and rejection he seemed to bring upon himself. 'Woe is me, my mother, that you bore me, a man of strife and contention to the whole land! I have not lent, nor have I borrowed, yet all of them curse me.' (Jer. 15:10) He cries out to the Lord, 'Why is my pain unceasing, my wound incurable, refusing to be healed?' (Jer. 15:18) His reactions fluctuate between a human desire to be revenged on his persecutors, a need for reassurance from his divine master, and an urge to withdraw into a 'wayfarer's shelter'. But his life's work was a compulsion from which there was no escape: '... there is in my heart as it were a burning fire shut up in my bones.' (Jer. 20:9)

Jeremiah served an uncompromising God, who demanded repentance – otherwise 'Those who are for pestilence, to pestilence, and those who are for the sword, to the sword; those who are for famine, to famine, and those who are for captivity, to captivity.' (Jer. 15:2) But the prophet delivered this stern message without self-righteousness. He was torn by compassion and was driven to intercede with God even for wrongdoers and enemies. Three times he mentions that the Lord rebukes him for such weakness. 'As for you, do not pray for this people, or lift up cry or prayer for them, and do not intercede with me, for I do not hear you.' (Jer. 7:16) During the great drought in the time of King Jehoiakim, he is sickened at the sight of dead men lying in the fields and hungry people in the city, and remonstrates with God himself: 'Hast thou utterly rejected Judah? Does thy soul loathe Zion? Why has thou smitten us so that there is no healing for us? We looked for peace, but no good came; for a time of healing, and behold, terror.' (Jer. 14:19)

The pacifism and the counsels of surrender which so provoked Jeremiah's fellow-citizens in time of siege sprang from a genuine physical horror of war and blooshed. 'My anguish! my anguish! I writhe in pain! Oh, the walls of my heart! My heart is beating wildly; I cannot keep silent; for I hear the sound of the trumpet, the alarm of war.' (Jer. 4:19) Jeremiah is a prophet who proclaims disaster, and then cries out that 'nor have I desired the day of disaster' (Jer. 17:16). The man of peace comes through clearly in the letter he writes to the exiles in Babylon.

Jeremiah is perplexed by the problem of retribution: 'Righteous art thou, O Lord, when I complain to thee; yet I would plead my case before thee. Why does the way of the wicked prosper? Why do all who are treacherous thrive?' (Jer. 12:1) This vain effort to reconcile faith and reason reached its fullest biblical expression in the Book of Job. It is a theme which has dominated recent centuries, which have witnessed the rationalist, scientific onslaught on religion.

In general the great prophet of the 7th century BC is curiously akin in spirit to the modern world. He lived in a confused and insecure time, in which the old values were crumbling and even a man of God could be assailed by doubt and a sense of alienation from society. With it all, Jeremiah clung to a vision of a happier world beyond disaster, where men would have entered into a new covenant with God: 'For I will satisfy the weary soul, and every languishing soul I will replenish.' (Jer. 31:25) [Book of Jeremiah]

THE LAMENTATIONS OF JEREMIAH
The Book known as 'The Lamentations of Jeremiah' is a sombre work consisting of five dirges on the fall of Jerusalem and the exile, each composed on an acrostic pattern. The mood is set by the opening verses:
'How lonely sits the city that was full of people!
How like a widow has she become,
she that was great among the nations!' (Lam. 1:1)
'Judah has gone into exile because of affliction and hard servitude;
she dwells now among the nations,
but finds no resting place.' (Lam. 1:3)

The Vulgate Bible of St Jerome, following the Greek Bible, inserted an introduction: 'When Israel had been taken into captivity and Jerusalem had become a Wilderness, it happened that the Prophet Jeremiah sat down in tears: he uttered this lamentation over Jerusalem.' The work was printed immediately following the Book of Jeremiah.

Protestant Bibles maintained the title 'The Lamentations of Jeremiah', and the position straight after the Book of Jeremiah, but deleted the introduction.

The Hebrew Bible did not connect this book with Jeremiah and inserted it in the section of 'Writings', not in the section of 'Prophets'.

Both the literary pattern and certain specific passages in the text make the attribution to Jeremiah untenable.

Lamentations is recited by Jews on the fast day of the Ninth of Av, commemorating the destruction of Jerusalem. It was used by Christians in the Holy Week liturgy. [Book of Lamentations]

6. c. 6 century BC. Son of Habazziniah, he was the father of Jaazaniah the Rechabite who refused to drink wine with the prophet Jeremiah. [Jer. 35:3]

7. 6 century BC. A chief priest of Judah who returned with Zerubbabel from exile in Babylon. [Neh. 12:1, 12]

8. 5 century BC. A priest who signed the solemn covenant in the time of Nehemiah. [Neh. 10:2]

9. 5 century BC. A leader of Judah who participated in the ceremony of dedicating the rebuilt walls of Jerusalem in the time of Nehemiah [Neh. 12:34]

Jeremoth (Heb. ('Moth [a god] established') **1.** date unknown. Son of Becher and a grandson of Benjamin, he and his family were leaders of the tribe and mighty warriors. [1 Chr. 7:8]

2. date unknown. Son of Mushi, he was a Levite descended from Merari. Also called Jerimoth. [1 Chr. 23:23; 24:30]

3. date unknown. Descendant of Elpaal and a leader of the tribe of Benjamin. [1 Chr. 8:14]

4. see JERIMOTH **4.**

5. 10 century BC. Son of Azriel, he was appointed by King David to lead the tribe of Naphtali. [1 Chr. 27:19]

6. 5 century BC. One of the descendants of Elam who divorced his non-Jewish wife in the time of Ezra. [Ezra 10:26]

7. 5 century BC. Son of Zattu who divorced his non-Jewish wife in the time of Ezra. [Ezra 10:27]

8. 5 century BC. A descendant of Bani who divorced his non-Jewish wife in the time of Ezra. [Ezra 10:29]

Jeriah (Heb. 'God has established') date unknown. The eldest son of Hebron, the Levite, and a descendant of Kohath. Also known as Jerijah. [1 Chr. 23:19; 24:23; 26:31]

Jeribai (Heb. 'my adversary') c. 10 century BC. Son of Elnaam, he and his brother Joshaviah were warriors in the armies of King David and distinguished for their bravery. [1 Chr. 11:46]

Jeriel (Heb. 'God has established') date unknown. A son of Tola and a grandson of Issachar, he and his family were leaders of the tribe and mighty warriors. [1 Chr. 7:2]

Jerijah see JERIAH.

Jerimoth (Heb. 'Moth [a god] established') *1.* c. 16 century BC. Son of Bela and grandson of Benjamin, he and his family were leaders of the tribe and mighty warriors. [1 Chr. 7:7]

2. see JEREMOTH 2.

3. c. 11 century BC. A Benjaminite warrior who deserted from King Saul's army and rallied to David at Ziklag. [1 Chr. 12:5]

4. c 10 century BC. A son of Heman, King David's musician, Jerimoth and his brothers played music in the Tabernacle under their father's direction, and he was responsible for the fifteenth turn of service. Also called Jeremoth. [1 Chr. 25:4, 22]

5. c. 10 century BC. Father of Mahalath, who was the wife of King Rehoboam of Judah. [2 Chr. 11:18]

6. c. 8 century BC. A Levite who supervised the bringing of offerings and tithes into the Temple in the reign of Hezekiah, king of Judah. [2 Chr. 31:13]

Jerioth (Heb. 'tents') date unknown. One of the two wives of Caleb, son of Hezron, of the tribe of Judah. [1 Chr. 2:18]

Jeroboam (Heb. 'the people increased').
1. Jeroboam I First king of Israel after the monarchy split, he reigned 931–10 BC.

During Solomon's building operations in Jerusalem, he appointed Jeroboam the son of Nebat and Zeruah as overseer of the labour force from his tribal area of Ephraim. At the time there was growing disaffection in the country over the tax and compulsory labour burdens, while the northern tribes were also jealous of the dominant position of Judah.

Jeroboam started plotting against the king, and was encouraged by Ahijah, a priest from the sanctuary of Shiloh in Ephraim. The priest stopped him one day on a deserted stretch of road and went through the symbolic act of tearing his cloak into twelve pieces (denoting the tribes of Israel) and handing ten of them to Jeroboam. Condemned to death by Solomon, Jeroboam fled to Egypt, where he was given political asylum by the Pharaoh Shishak.

On Solomon's death his son Rehoboam succeeded to the throne. The northern tribes seceded, setting up a separate kingdom of Israel. Jeroboam returned from Egypt and was elected its first ruler. The great Hebrew realm of David and Solomon had broken up into two small and quarrelling successor states.

Jeroboam at first resided in Shechem. After a period at Penuel across the Jordan river, he set up his permanent capital in Tirzah, seven miles north-east of Shechem. It was an ancient town in beautiful surroundings and commanded both the highway through the hills and the road down to the Jordan ford at Adam (Damia).

Jeroboam consciously set about fostering the separate identity of Israel. Since religion played a vital role in the life of the nation, it was essential for him to wean his subjects away from Solomon's Temple. 'If this people go up to offer sacrifices in the house of the Lord at Jerusalem, then the heart of this people will turn again to their lord, to Rehoboam king of Judah, and they will kill me.' (1 Kgs. 12:27)

He revived the traditional sanctuaries at Bethel near his southern border and Dan in the extreme north, and set up golden calves in them, as Aaron had done in the desert. He expelled the priestly Levites, who were loyal to the House of David, and in their stead recruited priests from the common people to serve at the two main shrines and the local 'high places'.

Scriptural disapproval was vividly expressed in the person of an unnamed 'man of God' from Judah who condemned the king beside the altar at Bethel, on which burnt-offerings had just been made. Jeroboam pointed at the man and ordered him to be arrested, but the king's outstretched arm became paralysed and he could not move it. At the same moment the altar flew apart and the ashes on it were scattered to the winds. The shaken monarch expressed repentance and his arm was healed.

Jeroboam ran into more religious reaction from an unexpected quarter. His son Abijah became critically ill and he sent the queen to the shrine at Shiloh to consult with the priest Ahijah, without disclosing who she was. The priest was old and nearly blind but, forewarned by the Lord, he immediately identified the woman as Jeroboam's wife. He told her pitilessly that her son would die, and uttered a curse against the king and all his house. The Lord would 'utterly consume the house of Jeroboam, as a man burns up dung until it is all gone' (1 Kgs. 14:10).

When Jeroboam had been on the throne for four years, the country was invaded by the Pharaoh Shishak. The biblical account mentions only his threat to Jerusalem. But Shishak's own version was preserved in the great bas-relief carved into the southern wall of the temple of Amon at Karnak. From this it appears that his forces swept through the kingdom of Israel and returned by the coast.

Jeroboam reigned for twenty-two years, and was succeeded by his son Nadab. [1 Kgs. 11:26–40; 12; 13; 14:1–30; 15:1, 6, 7, 9, 25, 29, 30, 34; 16:2, 3, 7, 19, 26; 2 Kgs. 3:3; 9:9; 10:29, 31; 13:2, 11; 14:24; 15:9, 28; 17:21, 22; 23:15; 2 Chr. 9:29; 10:2–15; 11:4, 14; 12:15; 13:1–20]

2. Jeroboam II Thirteenth king of Israel after the monarchy split, he reigned 783–43 BC. He was the son of Joash and the fourth ruler of the dynasty founded by Jehu.

After a period of decline, Joash had started to recover some of the territory lost to Israel's northern neighbour and hereditary enemy, the kingdom of Aram (Syria) with its capital at Damascus. Jeroboam continued this expansion, until his northern and eastern borders again reached those carved out by King David, when Israelite power had been at its peak. Jeroboam's control extended in Transjordan from Hamath (northern Syria) down to the Dead Sea. At the same time, the sister kingdom of Judah also expanded, regaining control of Edom on both sides of the Wadi Arabah down to the Gulf of Akaba.

Jeroboam's conquests were accompanied by a marked rise in living standards, and a burst of constructive energy within the kingdom. He added new buildings to the hill-top capital of Samaria, which Omri had founded almost a century earlier. The prophet Amos railed against the luxury and selfishness of the well-to-do class and its lack of concern for the poor. He also attacked the false sense of security that arose from the lack of outside pressure: 'Woe to those who are at ease in Zion, and to those who feel secure on the mountain of Samaria.' (Amos 6:1) His prediction of pending disaster came true a generation later when Samaria was taken by an invading Assyrian army and the kingdom of Israel came to an end.

Jeroboam died after forty-one years on the throne and was succeeded by his son Zechariah. [2 Kgs. 13:13; 14:16–29; 15:1, 8; 1 Chr. 5:17; Hos. 1:1; Amos 1:1; 7:9–11]

Jeroham (Heb. 'God will have mercy')
1. date unknown. Son of Elihu of the tribe of Levi, he was the father of Elkanah and grandfather of Samuel. [1 Sam. 1:1; 1 Chr. 6:27, 34]
2. date unknown. A leader of the tribe of Benjamin living in Jerusalem. [1 Chr. 8:27]
3. c. 11 century BC. A leader of Benjamin whose sons Joelah and Zebadiah left the army of King Saul and joined David at Ziklag. [1 Chr. 12:7]
4. c. 10 century BC. Father of Azarel who was appointed ruler over the tribe of Dan in the reign of King David. [1 Chr. 27:22]
5. c. 9 century BC. Father of Azariah, one of the army commanders of Judah who, on the instructions of the high priest Jehoiada, enthroned Joash as king and executed Queen Athaliah who had usurped the throne. [2 Chr. 23:1]
6. 5 century BC. Father of Ibneiah of the tribe of Benjamin who settled in Jerusalem in the days of Nehemiah. [1 Chr. 9:8]
7. 5 century BC. Father of the priest Adaiah who served in the Temple in Jerusalem in the time of Nehemiah. [1 Chr. 9:12; Neh. 11:12]

Jerubbaal *see* GIDEON

Jerubbesheth *see* GIDEON

Jerusha (Heb. 'inheritance') *c.* 8 century BC. Daughter of Zadok, she was the wife of Uzziah, King of Judah, and the mother of King Jotham. Also known as Jerushah. [2 Kgs. 15:33; 2 Chr. 27:1]

Jerushah *see* JERUSHA

Jeshaiah (Heb. 'saved') *1.* date unknown. Father of Ithiel of the tribe of Benjamin, his descendants settled in Jerusalem in Nehemiah's time. [Neh. 11:7]
2. c. 10 century BC. A son of King David's musician Jeduthun. Jeshaiah and his brothers played in the Tabernacle under their father's direction and he took the eighth turn of service. [1 Chr. 25:3, 15]
3. c 10 century BC. Descendant of Rehabiah, he was a Levite responsible for keeping the treasures captured by King David in battle, which were dedicated to the Tabernacle. [1 Chr. 26:25]
4. 6 century BC. A son of Hananiah of the tribe of Judah, and the grandson of Zerubbabel, he was a descendant of King David. [1 Chr. 3:21]
5. 5 century BC. Son of Athaliah and a descendant of Elam, he returned with Ezra from exile in Babylon. [Ezra 8:7]
6. 5 century BC. A Levite descended from Merari who returned to Jerusalem to minister in the Tabernacle in the time of Ezra. [Ezra 8:19]

Jesharelah *see* ASHARELAH

Jeshebeab (Heb. 'father's place') *c.* 10 century BC. A priest of Israel during the reign of King David, he was responsible for the fourteenth turn of service in the Tabernacle. [1 Chr. 24:13]

Jesher (Heb. 'right') date unknown. One of the three sons of Caleb, son of Hezron, and a leader of the tribe of Judah. [1 Chr. 2:18]

Jeshishai (Heb. 'son of old age') date unknown. Son of Jahdo of the tribe of

Gad, he was a leader of the tribe living in Gilead. [1 Chr. 5:14]

Jeshohaiah (Heb. 'bowed') *c*. 8 century BC. A leader of the tribe of Simeon who drove out the inhabitants of the rich valley of Gedor and settled there. [1 Chr. 4:36]

Jeshua (Heb. 'saviour') *1. c*. 10 century BC. A priest in the reign of King David, he took the ninth turn of service in the Tabernacle. [1 Chr. 24:11]

2. c. 8 century BC. A priest in the reign of Hezekiah, he was responsible for the distribution of the holy offerings among the priests in their cities in Judah. [2 Chr. 31:15]

3. c. 6 century BC. Head of a family descended from Pahath-moab who returned with Zerubbabel from exile in Babylon. [Ezra 2:6; Neh. 7:11]

4. 6 century BC. Head of a family of priests who returned from Babylon with Zerubbabel. [Ezra 2:36; Neh. 7:39]

5. 6 century BC. Head of a family of Levites who returned with Zerubbabel from Babylon. [Ezra 2:40; Neh. 12:8]

6. 6 century BC. The son of Jozadak, he was high priest in the time of Zerubbabel, and is symbolically crowned in the Book of Zechariah. Also known as Joshua. [Ezra 3:2; 10:18; Hag. 1:1, 12, 14; 2:2, 4; Zech. 3:1, 3; 6:11]

7. 5 century BC. Father of Jozabad, a Levite in the days of Ezra. [Ezra 8:33]

8. 5 century BC. Father of Ezer, the ruler of Mizpah, who repaired part of the wall of Jerusalem in the time of Nehemiah. [Neh. 3:19]

9. 5 century BC. One of the leaders of Judah who explained the Law of Moses to the people in the market-place after Ezra had read it to them. He called upon the people to confess their sins on the public fast day proclaimed by Ezra. [Neh. 8:7; 9:4]

10. 5 century BC. Son of Azaniah, he was one of the Levites who signed the solemn covenant in the time of Nehemiah. [Neh. 10:9]

Jeshurun (Heb. 'upright') Symbolic name for the Children of Israel in the Book of Deuteronomy. [Deut. 32:15; 33:5, 26; Isa. 44:2]

Jesimiel (Heb. 'God will set up') *c*. 8 century BC. One of the leaders of the tribe of Simeon in the days of King Hezekiah, he drove the occupants out of the rich Gedor valley and settled there. [1 Chr. 4:36]

Jesse (Heb. 'the Lord is') *c*. 11 century BC. Father of David, Jesse was a resident of Bethlehem. He was the grandson of Ruth and Boaz and the father of eight sons, of whom David was the youngest. On a visit to Bethlehem the prophet Samuel received Jesse and his sons and anointed David without explaining why.

Later, when three of his sons were in Saul's army, Jesse sent provisions to them with David, and included a gift of ten cheeses for their commanding officers.

When David had fled from Saul, he sent his father and mother to Moab for safety.

Two of Jesse's daughters, Zeruiah and Abigail, were the mothers of famous warriors. [Ruth 4:17, 22; 1 Sam. 16;17:12–58; 20:27–31; 22; 25:10; 2 Sam. 20:1; 23:1; 1 Kgs. 12:16; 1 Chr. 2:12, 13; 10:14; 12:18; 29:26; 2 Chr. 10:16; 11:18; Isa. 11:1, 10]

Jether (Heb. 'who excels') *1. c*. 12 century BC. Eldest son of Gideon, the judge, he was commanded to kill the captured Midianite kings Zebah and Zalmunna. But Jether was young and afraid, so his father slew them. [Judg. 8:20]

2. date unknown. Son of Jada and a leader of the tribe of Judah who died childless. [1 Chr. 2:32]

3. date unknown. One of the four sons of Ezrah of the tribe of Judah. [1 Chr. 4:17]

4. date unknown. A leader of the tribe

of Asher and a mighty warrior. [1 Chr. 7:38]

5. c. 10 century BC. The husband of King David's sister Abigail, he was the father of Amasa who was killed by David's army commander Joab. Jether is described as an Israelite and as an Ishmaelite. Also called Ithra. [2 Sam. 17:25; 1 Kgs. 2:5, 32; 1 Chr. 2:17]

Jetheth date unknown. One of the chiefs of Edom descended from Esau. [Gen. 36:40; 1 Chr. 1:51]

Jethro (Heb. 'excellence') *c.* 13 century BC. Moses's father-in-law. Jethro was a priest, and leader of a Midianite tribe known as Kenites, who lived in the Sinai desert.

When Moses fled from Egypt after killing Pharaoh's overseer, he lived with Jethro, married his daughter Zipporah, and tended his sheep.

Years later, when Moses was again in the Sinai desert leading the Children of Israel, his father-in-law came to visit him at the Rephidim camp. Moses was delighted to see Jethro and told him how the Lord had delivered them out of the hands of the Egyptians. Jethro said, 'Now I know that the Lord is greater than all gods.' (Exod. 18:11) Jethro offered a burnt sacrifice to God, and Aaron and all the elders came to have a meal with him.

Jethro advised Moses to appoint judges to whom he would teach the laws and delegate some of the work, leaving only the difficult cases for himself. 'Then Moses let his father-in-law depart, and he went his way to his own country.' (Exod. 18:27)

Some scholars have suggested that Jethro, also known as Hobab or Reuel, acted as a guide to Moses in the Sinai desert. Others think that Hobab was Jethro's son. [Exod. 3:1; 4:18; 18:1–12; Num. 10:29; Judg. 1:16;4:11]

Jetur *c.* 18 century BC. Son of Ishmael and a grandson of Abraham, he was a desert chieftain. [Gen. 25:15; 1 Chr. 1:31; 5:19]

Jeuel (Heb. 'treasured') *1.* 5 century BC. A descendant of Zerah of the tribe of Judah, he was head of a family who settled in Jerusalem in the time of Nehemiah. [1 Chr. 9:6]

2. date unknown. A Levite whose ancestors took part in the purification of the Temple in the time of Hezekiah. [2 Chr. 29:13]

3. 5 century BC. An exile who returned to Judah with Ezra and helped to rebuild Jerusalem. [Ezra 8:13]

Jeush *1.* (Heb. 'may God help') *c.* 17 century BC. A son of Esau and Oholibamah, and an Edomite leader. [Gen. 36:4, 14, 18; 1 Chr. 1:35]

2. date unknown. Grandson of Jediael of the tribe of Benjamin, he was a leader of the tribe. [1 Chr. 7:10]

3. c. 10 century BC. A son of Shimei, a Levite. Jeush and his brother Beriah did not have many sons, therefore, in David's census, they counted as one family. [1 Chr. 23:10, 11]

4. c. 10 century BC. Son of King Rehoboam of Judah and his wife Mahalath. [2 Chr. 11:19]

5. c. 9 century BC. Son of Eshek of the tribe of Benjamin and a descendant of King Saul. [1 Chr. 8:39]

Jeuz (Heb. 'assembler') date unknown. Son of Shaharaim and his wife Hodesh, he was a leader of the tribe of Benjamin. [1 Chr. 8:10]

Jezaniah *see* JAAZANIAH *1.*

Jezebel (Heb. 'chaste') *c.* 9 century BC. Phoenician wife of King Ahab of Israel.

Jezebel was the daughter of Ethbaal, king of Sidon, and was married to Ahab, son and successor of Omri, king of Israel. She was a strong-willed woman who clearly dominated her husband. She fostered in Israel the worship of

Melkart, the Phoenician 'baal' (god), and Ashtaroth, the goddess of fertility. Four hundred and fifty priests or 'prophets' of Baal were maintained by Jezebel in the capital Samaria, as part of her household. Shrines to her native gods sprang up on the hill-tops, and a temple to Baal was constructed in the palace. It was said that the king himself was drawn into the alien forms of worship. Those Israelite priests who resisted these inroads into the ancestral faith were eliminated or driven into hiding.

The resistance was led by the prophet Elijah. In a contest of faith on Mount Carmel, Elijah triumphed over Jezebel's priests, and all of them were slain. The furious Jezebel wanted to have Elijah put to death but he managed to escape southward into the desert.

Ahab coveted the vineyard of Naboth next to the winter palace at Jezreel, but the owner refused to part with it. Taking matters into her own hands, Jezebel sent letters in Ahab's name and over his royal seal to the local leaders in Jezreel. They were to arrest Naboth on charges of blasphemy against God and the king, and to have him stoned to death on the evidence of two false witnesses. This judicial murder was carried out. By law, the condemned man's property then passed into the hands of the king. Once more Elijah appeared, and prophesied that Ahab and all his household would be destroyed and 'The dogs shall eat Jezebel within the bounds of Jezreel.' (1 Kgs. 21:23)

A tough army commander called Jehu murdered Ahab's son, King Jehoram, and seized the throne. Jezebel met her death with stiff pride: when Jehu came through the gate of the palace in Jezreel, he saw her standing drawn up at the window with her eyes and face made up and her hair carefully dressed. She called out contemptuously to him, 'Is it peace, you Zimri, murderer of your master?' (2 Kgs. 9:31) (Zimri was another army officer who had murdered an earlier king,

Elah, and seized power.) Jehu shouted out to the attendants of the queen-mother to hurl her down from the window, and they obeyed him; '... some of her blood spattered on the wall and on the horses, and they trampled on her.' (2 Kgs. 9:33)

After Jehu had eaten and drunk in the palace, he told his servants to go and bury Jezebel's body, since she was after all a king's daughter. They reported that all they had found left of the corpse was the skull, hands and feet. Jehu declared that this was the fulfilment of Elijah's prediction that the dogs would eat her.

The biblical editors felt obvious revulsion for Jezebel, whose gruesome end is related almost with gusto. She remains the most notorious of all Old Testament characters, and her name has become a symbol of female depravity. [1 Kgs. 16:31; 18:4, 13, 19; 19:1, 2; 21:5–25; 2 Kgs. 9:22, 30–37]

Jezer (Heb. 'God's creature') c. 16 century BC. A son of Naphtali, he went down to Egypt with his grandfather Jacob. [Gen. 46:24; Num. 26:49; 1 Chr. 7:13]

Jeziel c. 11 century BC. Son of Azmaveth, a Benjaminite, he could shoot an arrow with either hand. He and his brother joined David at Ziklag. [1 Chr. 12:3]

Jezrahiah (Heb. 'may God sparkle') 5 century BC. Leader of the singers at the dedication service for the rebuilt walls of Jerusalem in the days of Nehemiah. [Neh. 12:42]

Jezreel (Heb. 'may God sow') *1.* date unknown. A leader of the tribe of Judah. [1 Chr. 4:3]
2. c. 8 century BC. Son of the prophet Hosea, his name symbolized the destruction of the dynasty of Jehu, king of Israel, in the valley of Jezreel, the place

where Jehu had originally seized the throne. [Hos. 1:4]

Jidlaph (Heb. 'weeping') c. 18 century BC. Son of Abraham's brother Nahor. [Gen. 22:22]

Joab (Heb. 'God his father') *1.* date unknown. Son of Seraiah of the tribe of Judah, he was head of a family of craftsmen. [1 Chr. 4:14]
2. c. 11 century BC. Commander-in-chief to King David. David's eldest sister, Zeruiah, had three sons – Joab, Abishai and Asahel, all of whom became professional soldiers. Joab and Abishai may have been a little older than their uncle David, the youngest of Jesse's sons.

Joab was a tough, brave and skilful army commander, intensely loyal to his master, ruthless towards his enemies, and jealous of rivals to the point of murder. He shared David's fortunes over some half a century, from the time that David fled from Saul's hostility. The common hardships and dangers, and the tight comradeship of a fugitive band, forged bonds between uncle and nephew which David was later unable to break, even when he had been given good cause to rid himself of Joab.

When David became king of Judah in Hebron, after Saul's death, he appointed Joab commander-in-chief of his forces. At the pool of Gibeon, north-west of Jerusalem, the forces of Joab and Saul's general Abner confronted each other. They agreed to a trial of strength between twelve picked men on each side. When all these men were killed in a single combat, leaving the issue undecided, general fighting broke out in which Abner's men were routed. The fleeing Abner reluctantly slew Joab's youngest brother Asahel who pursued him. At sunset Joab and his soldiers caught up with Abner's party and agreed to withdraw in order to avoid more bloodshed. But Joab had a score to settle with Abner.

Joab returned from a successful foray with his men and was taken aback to discover that in his absence David had made a pact with Abner to reunite the kingdom. Joab tried to persuade David that Abner had deceived him, and had come only to spy. When this had no effect he sent messengers after Abner to bring him back to Hebron, and waited for him at the entrance to the town. Here 'Joab took him aside into the midst of the gate to speak with him privately, and there he smote him in the belly, so that he died, for the blood of Asahel his brother.' (2 Sam. 3:27)

The horrified David ordered a state funeral for Abner and himself led the mourning. 'These men the sons of Zeruiah,' David complained, 'are too hard for me.' (2 Sam. 3:39) In spite of that, Joab and his brother Abishai remained in David's service.

Joab was sent to capture Jerusalem, which had remained a Jebusite stronghold. At the critical stage of the attack, the Jebusite defenders brought the blind and the lame out on the walls to bar the way. The superstitious Israelite soldiers shrank back from this pathetic human barricade. David offered promotion to the first soldier who would defy the curse. The one who did so was the commander-in-chief Joab himself, and the city fell. David's tough-minded general feared neither military adversaries nor evil spells.

Joab led an expedition of picked Israelite troops against Raboth-Ammon, the capital city of Hanum, king of Ammon, who had formed a military coalition against David. Joab found himself trapped between the Ammonites drawn up in battle array before their city, and a mobile force of Syrian chariots and cavalry on his southern flank. He acted quickly and boldly. With one half of his men he attacked the Syrian force, while the other half of the Israelite troops under the command of his brother Abishai held the Ammonites at bay. The

Syrians were repulsed, and the Ammonite troops retreated into their city.

The next year, the Israelite army under Joab again marched into Ammon, and laid siege to the capital Rabbah. It was during this siege that Joab received a sealed letter from the king concerning Uriah, a Hittite officer serving at the front. The letter said: 'Set Uriah in the forefront of the hardest fighting and then draw back from him, that he may be struck down, and die.' (2 Sam. 11:15) Joab could not know the reason for this extraordinary order – that David was having a love affair with Uriah's wife Bathsheba who had conceived a child by him. But Joab carried out his master's wishes without question. Uriah was sent to lead a rash attack on the walls and was killed.

Joab captured the key citadel controlling the water supply of Rabbah. He proposed that David himself move up with fresh troops for the final assault 'lest I take the city, and it be called by my name' (2 Sam. 12:28). In this way Joab demonstrated that his king's renown mattered more than his own.

JOAB AND DAVID'S SONS

Three years after David's favourite son Absalom murdered his elder brother Amnon and fled into exile, it was Joab who tried to bring about a reconciliation. He did not presume to broach so sensitive a subject directly. Instead he brought before the king a woman from the town of Tekoah who pretended one of her sons had killed the other. When David's compassion had been aroused she referred to his own banished son. The king relented and sent Joab to fetch Absalom back to Jerusalem.

But the conflict between father and son had not been resolved. Absalom launched a rebellion, and Joab was one of the loyal group that fled with David. In the crucial battle that later took place in the woods of Ephraim, east of the Jordan river, David's forces under Joab's command defeated those of Absalom. David had instructed his commanders that no harm should come to his rebellious son but it was not in Joab's nature to spare even a kinsman who had risen against his master. Finding Absalom dangling in mid-air because his flowing hair had become entangled with an overhanging oak branch, Joab cold-bloodedly plunged three darts into his body and ordered his men to finish him off.

Joab roughly upbraided David for giving way to grief, and demanded that he show himself in public if he did not want to lose the support of his people. David pulled himself together but could not forgive Joab. He confirmed the appointment as army commander in Joab's place of Amasa, another nephew who had led Absalom's army.

As he had done many years before with Abner, Joab approached Amasa in feigned friendship, and suddenly stabbed him to death. Joab then assumed command again, pursued Sheba who had led a Benjaminite revolt against David, and returned with his severed head.

David became old and ailing, and his eldest surviving son Adonijah made an attempt to usurp the throne. Joab threw his powerful support behind Adonijah's claim. But his new master's cause collapsed when David renounced the throne in favour of a younger prince, Solomon, the son of Bathsheba. Joab's life was in danger. On his deathbed David referred to Joab's slaying of Abner and Amasa and charged Solomon, 'do not let his grey head go down to Sheol in peace' (1 Kgs. 2:6).

Joab sought sanctuary at the altar, but on King Solomon's instructions Benaiah, the captain of the palace guard, sought him out there and killed him, 'and he was buried in his own house in the wilderness' (1 Kgs. 2:34). Thus Joab paid with his blood for his deeds of violence, and for wavering at the end in his lifelong devotion to David. [1 Sam. 26:6; 2 Sam. 2:13–32; 3:22–31; 8:16;

10:7–14; 11:1–25; 12:26–7; 14:1, 2, 19–33; 17:25; 18:2–29; 19:1, 5, 13; 20:7–23; 23:18, 24, 37; 24:2–9; 1 Kgs. 1:1–41; 2:5, 22, 28–35; 11:15, 16; 1 Chr. 2:16; 11:6, 8, 20, 26, 39; 18:15; 19:8–15; 20:1; 21:3–6; 27:7, 24, 34]

3. 6 century BC. Head of a family descended from Pahath-moab that returned to Judah with Zerubbabel from exile in Babylon. [Ezra 2:6; 8:9; Neh. 7:11]

Joah (Heb. 'brother of God') *1.* date unknown. Son of Zimmah, he was a Levite descended from Gershom. [1 Chr. 6:21]

2. c. 10 century BC. Son of Obed-edom, he and his family were gatekeepers of the Tabernacle in the reign of King David. [1 Chr. 26:4]

3. c. 8 century BC. Son of Asaph, he was court recorder at the time of the Assyrian siege of Jerusalem, and together with two others delivered the Assyrian terms to King Hezekiah. [2 Kgs. 18:18–37]

4. c. 8 century BC. One of the Levites who obeyed King Hezekiah's command to sanctify themselves and cleanse the Temple. [2 Chr. 29:12]

5. c. 7 century BC. Son of Joahaz, he was court recorder for Josiah, king of Judah, and one of the three men responsible for the repair of the Temple. [2 Chr. 34:8]

Joahaz (Heb. 'held by God') *1. see* JEHOAHAZ 2.

2. c. 7 century BC. Father of Joah, who was court recorder for Josiah, king of Judah. [2 Chr. 34:8]

Joash (Heb. 'given by God') *1.* date unknown. A son of Becher and a grandson of Benjamin, he and his nine brothers were leaders of the tribe and mighty warriors. [1 Chr. 7:8]

2. date unknown. Son of Shelah and a leader of the tribe of Judah, he and his brother Saraph were rulers in Moab. [1 Chr. 4:22]

3. c. 12 century BC. Father of Gideon. Joash worshipped the idol Baal, but Gideon destroyed the altar Joash had made to Baal and cut down the grove next to it. When his townsmen ordered Joash to kill his son for destroying the idol, Joash answered: 'Will you contend for Baal? ... If he is a god, let him contend for himself....' (Judg. 6:31) [Judg. 6:11, 29–31; 8:29, 32]

4. c. 11 century BC. One of the men of Benjamin who left the army of King Saul and rallied to David at Ziklag. [1 Chr. 12:3]

5. c. 10 century BC. The supervisor of the royal oil vats in the reign of King David. [1 Chr. 27:28]

6. c. 9 century BC. Son of King Ahab of Israel, he was commanded by his father to imprison the prophet Micaiah. [1 Kgs. 22:26; 2 Chr. 18:25]

7. Eighth king of Judah after the monarchy split, he reigned 835–796 BC.

Joash was the son of King Ahaziah of Judah and Zibiah of Beersheba. When he was still an infant his father was killed in the revolt of Jehu in the kingdom of Israel. His grandmother Athaliah, who was the daughter of the domineering Phoenician Queen Jezebel, then had all the royal offspring murdered and seized the throne herself. The only one to escape was Joash, who was taken away and hidden by his aunt Jehosheba. She handed him over to the priest Jehoiada who secretly kept him in the Temple and cared for him.

When the child was seven years old, Jehoiada had him crowned king in the Temple under the protection of the palace guard and then presented him to the excited crowd. Athaliah rushed to the scene and was killed by the guards.

In the twenty-third year of Joash's reign, he became aware that the voluntary offerings for the renovation of the Temple were not being used for the intended purpose. He ordered them collected in a special chest at the entrance to the Temple, checked under the supervision of the king's officials and paid over directly to the contractors and workmen.

The priesthood lost its influence on the throne with Jehoiada's death, and the king had Jehoiada's son Zechariah, also a priest, executed for making trouble.

During Joash's reign King Hazael of Aram-Damascus marched across Israel and advanced on Jerusalem. Joash was able to save the city only by handing over to the Arameans a crippling ransom, for which the treasuries of the Temple and the palace had to be virtually emptied. It may have been this display of impotence in the face of an external enemy that led to Joash's downfall. He was murdered by two of his palace officials after he had been forty years on the throne. He was succeeded by his son Amaziah. Also called Jehoash. [2 Kgs. 11; 12; 13:1, 10;14:1, 3, 13, 17, 23; 1 Chr. 3:11; 2 Chr. 22:11; 24:1–24; 25:23, 25]

8. Twelfth king of Israel after the monarchy split, he reigned 798–83 BC. Joash was the grandson of Jehu and the son of Jehoahaz. He came to the throne at a time when Israel's northern neighbour Aram-Damascus (Syria) had come to dominate it, and had stripped it of much of its territory.

At the beginning of his reign, Joash went to visit the aged prophet Elisha, then on his deathbed. The prophet told him to open the eastern window and shoot an arrow in the direction of the enemy, Aram. He did so; and this, predicted Elisha, was a symbol of the victory he would gain. The prophet then told the king to strike the ground with the remaining arrows, and reproved him when Joash stopped after the third strike, which meant that his victory would be incomplete: 'You should have struck five or six times; then you would have struck down Syria until you had made an end of it, but now you will strike down Syria only three times.' (2 Kgs. 13:19)

Joash did not conquer Aram but he won three battles against the Syrian forces and was able to regain the towns his father had lost.

King Amaziah of Judah achieved some success against Edom, and sent a boastful challenge to the king of Israel. Joash replied, 'why should you provoke trouble so that you fall, you and Judah with you?' (2 Kgs. 14:10) But Amaziah would not heed the warning. At the battle of Beth-shemesh, on the Israel-Judah border, Amaziah's forces were defeated by Joash who marched on Jerusalem and attacked it, breaking down part of the city wall. He retired to Samaria, taking with him hostages, gold and silver vessels from the Temple, and much of the royal treasure.

Joash died after a reign of sixteen years and was succeeded by his son Jeroboam II. Also called Jehoash. [2 Kgs. 13:9–25; 14:1–27; 2 Chr. 25:17–25; Hos. 1:1; Amos 1:1]

Job period of the Patriarchs. Central character of the Book of Job.

According to a popular folk-tale dating back to the period of the Hebrew Patriarchs, Job was a prosperous and righteous notable living 'in the land of Uz', probably Edom, south of the Dead Sea. He suffered a number of afflictions to test his faith in God, and proved himself steadfast. This simple story was used by an unknown genius of the 5th or 4th century BC as a framework for a dramatic poem which is one of the great masterpieces of literature. Its theme was the reason for human suffering, and it raised profound questions about divine justice. In both form and content, the Book of Job does not resemble any other portion of the Scriptures.

The original narrative is briefly told in prose in a Prologue and Epilogue. The main body of the Book is the most sustained poetry in the Old Testament, and the only biblical work that is cast in dramatic form. It contains the debates between Job and three of his friends, and is climaxed by a confrontation between Job and God himself.

The Prologue pictures Job as a man who was 'blameless and upright, one who feared God, and turned away from evil' (Job 1:1). He was blessed with seven sons and three daughters, and an abundance of livestock: seven thousand sheep, three thousand camels, five hundred yoke of oxen and five hundred she-asses. Each of the sons in turn would give a family feast and then Job would gather them all together to offer a sacrifice at dawn, lest any one of them had unwittingly sinned.

One day in the heavenly council, the Lord asked Satan whether in the course of his earthly journeys he had come across the pious Job. Satan replied sarcastically that it was easy for a rich and successful man to be God-fearing. 'But put forth thy hand now, and touch all that he has, and he will curse thee to thy face.' (Job 1:11) The Lord agreed that Satan should put Job to the test, provided his person was not touched.

The following day Job's donkeys and camels were carried off by marauders, and his sheep were killed in a hailstorm. What was worse, the roof of his eldest son's house collapsed during a gale, when all his children were gathered there, and none of them was left alive. Job went into mourning, but uttered no word of protest against the Lord.

Satan maintained that Job would react otherwise if he were afflicted in his own body. The Lord gave Satan permission to try Job further, provided his life was spared.

Job then broke out in dreadful sores from head to foot. As he sat in the ash-pit and scraped at himself with a sharp piece of broken pottery, his wife cried out bitterly: 'Do you still hold fast your integrity? Curse God, and die.' (Job 2:9)

Job replied that she was a foolish woman. If they accepted happiness from God, must they not accept sorrow too?

Word of Job's misfortunes reached three of his friends – Eliphaz of Teman, Bildad of Shuah and Zophar of Naamah. (These were towns in Edom.) They came to call on Job and were shocked to find he could hardly be recognized. For seven days and nights they sat with him without speaking.

At this point the Prologue ends, and the main poem begins, with Job cursing his own existence. 'Let the day perish wherein I was born, and the night which said, A man-child is conceived.' (Job 3:3)

JOB PROTESTS HIS INNOCENCE

His friends try to console him, and express the traditional and pious views about his sufferings. God does not punish good men, only bad ones. If evil-doers seem to prosper for a while, their sins will soon catch up with them: '... that the exulting of the wicked is short, and the joy of the godless but for a moment' (Job 20:5). Good people may also suffer, but then nobody is wholly pure and innocent, not even an angel, while man is inherently frail. Job should put his trust in God and appeal to him in humility, then all will be well. 'For he wounds, but he binds up; he smites, but his hands heal.' (Job 5:18)

As Job continues to rail against God, his three friends lose patience with him. Bildad asks him angrily, 'How long will you say these things, and the words of your mouth be a great wind? Does God pervert judgment? Or does the Almighty pervert the right?' (Job 8:2, 3) Zophar also chides him: 'Should a multitude of words go unanswered and a man full of talk be vindicated? Should your babble silence men, and when you mock, shall no one shame you?' (Job 11:2, 3) They suggest that if Job is afflicted, he must be a sinful man, and his protests must be prompted by a guilty conscience. Eliphaz even lists a number of uncharitable acts he falsely attributes to Job.

Job makes no effort to conceal his own exasperation with his friends, whom he calls 'miserable comforters' and 'physicians of no value'. 'Hold your peace,' he storms at them, 'Let me have silence, and I will speak, and let come on me what may.' (Job 13:13) Why should they torment him with their lectures? God does not need them to plead for him. To Bildad's strictures he retorts with irony: 'How you have helped him who has no power! How you have saved the arm that has no strength! How have you counselled him who has no wisdom.' (Job 26:2, 3)

He rejects their advice to bear his trials with silent fortitude. 'But I would speak to the Almighty, and I desire to argue my case with God.... Behold, he will slay me ... I will defend my ways to his face.' (Job 13:3, 15)

Job recalls what a good life he used to have and how respected he was. Now everyone shuns him, and youths spit in his face whose fathers he would not have put with his sheep-dogs: 'those whom I loved have turned against me. My bones cleave to my skin and to my flesh.... Have pity on me, have pity on me, O you my friends, for the hand of God has touched me!' (Job 19:19, 20, 21)

Mournfully Job reflects on the futility of life: 'Man that is born of a woman is of few days, and full of trouble. He comes forth like a flower, and withers; he flees like a shadow, and continues not.' (Job 14:1, 2)

Over and over again, Job protests his innocence, and demands of God to 'make me understand how I have erred.' (Job 6:24) Has he been guilty of vanity or deceit, lusted after other women, failed to respect the rights of his servants, or to take care of the poor or needy? Has he sought after riches, or secretly worshipped pagan gods, or wished evil on his enemies, or turned away strangers from his door, or engaged in unfair dealings?

He is ready to account for all his actions, provided they are weighed in an even balance. What he demands is a fair trial, with the charges against him presented in due form of law. Yet how can he expect justice if God is both accuser and judge? A trial between God and himself is an unequal contest. God's power is absolute, his decrees are final, and there is no way to appeal against them. 'For he is not a man, as I am, that I might answer him, and we should come to trial together.' (Job 9:32)

He wants to defend himself, but who will get him a hearing? God is far away, and cannot be reached. 'Oh, that I knew where I might find him, that I might come even to his seat! I would lay my case before him and fill my mouth with arguments ... I cry to thee and thou dost not answer me; I stand, and thou dost not heed me.' (Job 23:3, 4; 30:20) In despair, Job asks whether God really cares about a world in which wicked men prosper and the poor go naked and hungry.

At one point Job becomes weary of seeking justice, and only wants to be left alone like a hired servant that must finish his day's work and then rest. Yet at the end he once more affirms that he is guiltless, and defiantly calls upon the Lord to hand him the list of charges against him, so that he may wear it as a badge of honour.

A new character now appears, Elihu the son of Barachel the Buzite. An introductory paragraph explains that as a young man he had kept quiet in the presence of his elders. But he could not accept the fact that Eliphaz, Bildad and Zophar had ceased to argue with Job. There follow three long speeches, in which Elihu covers much the same ground as Job's three friends, adding little in the way of fresh argument. (It is suggested that the Elihu chapters are of a later date. Elihu is not mentioned elsewhere in the Book; the style and language do not rise to the same heights; and the intervention separates Job's final plea from God's reply to him, thereby disrupting the natural flow of the dialogue.)

After Job has finished speaking, the Lord answers him out of the whirlwind, by putting questions of his own. 'Who is this that darkens counsel by words without knowledge? Gird up your loins like a man, I will question you, and you shall declare to me. Where were you when I laid the foundation of the earth? ... When the morning stars sang together, and all the sons of God shouted for joy?' (Job 38:2, 3, 4, 7)

What does Job know about control of the seas, the coming of the dawn, the snow and hail, thunder, lightning and rain, the movements of the stars, and the ways of the animals and birds? 'Shall a fault-finder contend with the Almighty? He who argues with God, let him answer it.' (Job 40:2)

Job was overwhelmed at the presence of the Lord, and humbled at the majestic and mysterious working of the universe. He accepted that there were matters beyond his comprehension: 'Therefore I have uttered what I did not understand, things too wonderful for me, which I did not know.... I had heard of thee by the hearing of the ear, but now my eye sees thee; therefore I despise myself, and repent in dust and ashes.' (Job 42:3, 5, 6)

With the main work ended by Job's submission to God, a short prose epilogue picks up the original folktale again, and furnishes it with a happy ending. Eliphaz, Bildad and Zophar are admonished. Job is restored to his position, and given double the wealth he lost before. All his kinsmen and friends come to pay their respects and bring gifts. Again he produces seven sons and three beautiful daughters called Jemimah, Keziah and Keren-happuch. He lives to see his descendants to the fourth generation, and dies at the ripe age of one hundred and forty.

The author of the Book of Job was one of the boldest and most original religious thinkers and literary masters ever to have existed. He was as familiar with the intellectual heritage of his time as with the life of the desert, and he did not hesitate to challenge and probe accepted beliefs. The identity of the man who penned Job's immortal dialogue with God and his fellow-men remains one of the unresolved mysteries of the Old Testament. [Book of Job]

Jobab *1.* date unknown. Son of Zerah of Bozrah, he was the second king of Edom. [Gen. 36:33, 34; 1 Chr. 1:44, 45]
2. date unknown. Son of Joktan and a descendant of Shem. [Gen. 10:29; 1 Chr. 1:23]
3. date unknown. Son of Shaharaim, he was a leader of the tribe of Benjamin. [1 Chr. 8:9]
4. date unknown. Son of Elpaal, he was a leader of the tribe of Benjamin. [1 Chr. 8:18]
5. c. 13 century BC. King of Madon who joined a Canaanite alliance against Joshua and was defeated in battle at the Waters of Merom. [Josh. 11:1]

Jochebed (Heb. 'the Lord is glory') *c.* 13 century BC. Jochebed, one of the Children of Israel living in Egypt, was married to Amram a Levite, and had a daughter Miriam and two sons, Aaron and Moses. Her son Moses was born just after Pharaoh had decreed that all Jewish male infants should be killed. She hid him for three months and then she made him a 'basket made of bulrushes, and daubed it with bitumen and pitch; and she put the child in it' (Exod. 2:3). Jochebed put the baby among the bulrushes at the edge of the river, where the Egyptian princess came daily to bathe. When she found it, Miriam came forward and suggested her mother as a nurse for the child. [Exod. 2:1–10; 6:20; Num. 26:59]

Joed (Heb. 'witnessed') date unknown. Son of Pedaiah of the tribe of Benjamin and grandfather of Sallu, one of the first Benjaminites to settle in Jerusalem after the return from exile in Babylon. [Neh. 11:7]

Joel (Heb. 'the Lord is God') *1.* date unknown. A leader of the tribe of Reuben. [1 Chr. 5:4, 8]

2. date unknown. A leader of the tribe of Gad who settled in the land of Bashan, east of the river Jordan. [1 Chr. 5:12]

3. date unknown. Son of Azariah, a Levite descended from Kohath, he was an ancestor of the prophet Samuel. Also called Shaul. [1 Chr. 6:24, 36]

4. date unknown. A descendant of Uzzi and a leader of the tribe of Issachar. [1 Chr. 7:3]

5. c. 11 century BC. Elder son of the prophet Samuel, he and his brother Abijah were judges in Beersheba. They were known to be corrupt and to take bribes, and the people of Israel demanded a king partly because Samuel's sons were unfit to succeed him [1 Sam. 8:2; 1 Chr. 6:28, 33]

6. c. 10 century BC. A Levite descended from Gershom, he was placed in charge of the treasuries in the Tabernacle in the reign of King David. [1 Chr. 23:8; 26:22]

7. see IGAL 2.

8. c. 10 century BC. Head of the Levites descended from Gershom, who helped to carry the Ark of God to Jerusalem from Kiriath-jearim at the orders of King David. [1 Chr. 15:7, 11, 17]

9. c. 10 century BC. Son of Pedaiah, he was ruler of half of the tribe of Manasseh in the reign of King David. [1 Chr. 27:20]

10. c. 8 century BC. One of the leaders of the tribe of Simeon in the reign of King Hezekiah who drove out the population of the fertile Gedor valley and settled there. [1 Chr. 4:35]

11. c. 8 century BC. One of the Levites who obeyed King Hezekiah's command to sanctify themselves and cleanse the Temple. [2 Chr. 29:12]

12. 5 century BC. One of the descendants of Nebo who divorced his non-Jewish wife in the time of Ezra. [Ezra 10:43]

13. 5 century BC. Son of Zichri, he was the overseer of the Benjaminites who settled in Jerusalem in the time of Nehemiah. [Neh. 11:9]

14. c. 5 century BC. A Hebrew prophet in the Kingdom of Judah. The short prophetic Book of Joel, son of Pethuel, appears from its contents to have been written in Judah in the post-exilic period, probably near 400 BC. Its four chapters fall into two distinct parts. In the first two chapters the country is ravaged by a locust swarm, which the prophet regards as heralding the 'day of the Lord'. The last two chapters describe the judgment executed against enemy nations on that day. The language and style are among the finest in the prophetical writings.

Early commentators on the Bible, both Jewish and Christian, regarded the locust swarm in the Book of Joel as merely a symbolic image, set out with poetic hyperbole. But modern scholars have caught up with the facts of nature and indicated that it is also a realistic picture. Vast swarms of these insects (sometimes covering hundreds of square miles) emerge from their desert breeding grounds in Africa, the Middle East and parts of Asia and can lay waste a whole countryside in a matter of hours. Anyone who has witnessed this terrifying scourge will recognize in Joel's account a documentary record of unequalled precision and literary power.

The three stages of the insect's development, the great cloud darkening the sun and the stars, the noise of the whirring wings and chomping jaws, the fertile landscape turned into a bleached and burnt-up waste-land, even the resemblance of the locust head to that of a horse – all these have a startling realism.

'The land is like the garden of Eden before them, but after them a desolate wilderness, and nothing escapes them.... As with the rumbling of chariots, they leap on the tops of the mountains, like the crackling of a flame of fire devouring the stubble, like a powerful army drawn up for battle.... They leap upon the city, they run upon the walls; they climb up into the houses, they enter through the windows like a thief. The earth quakes before them, the heavens tremble. The sun and the moon are darkened, and the stars withdraw their shining.' (Joel 2:3, 5, 9, 10)

Convinced that the day of the Lord is at hand, Joel calls upon the people to repent, with fasting, weeping and mourning. It must be a true inward return to God: 'And rend your hearts and not your garments' (Joel 2:13). He demands that everyone meet in solem assembly, from the elders to the infants at the breast, even to the bride and bridegroom. Then the Lord will bring good autumn and spring rains so that the land will be restored to fertility and the famine will be over. 'The threshing floors shall be full of grain, the vats shall overflow with wine and oil.' (Joel 2:24)

In Joel's apocalyptic vision in the second part of the Book, it is predicted that on the day of the Lord, he will restore Judah and Jerusalem and punish the nations that have oppressed His people. They will be gathered together in the valley of Jehoshaphat near Jerusalem, and the judgment of the Lord upon them will be accompanied by portents in heaven and earth. 'The sun shall be turned to darkness, and the moon to blood.' (Joel 2:31) Egypt will be desolated and Edom become a wilderness, for shedding the blood of innocent Jews. Tyre and Sidon will suffer for plundering the Jews and for selling their sons and daughters into slavery.

After this judgment a new era will dawn, in which 'I will pour out my spirit on all flesh; your sons and your daughters shall prophesy, your old men shall dream dreams, and your young men shall see visions.' (Joel 2:28). It will be a time when Judah will be a green and pleasant land and Jerusalem a Jewish holy city, 'for the Lord dwells in Zion' (Joel 3:21). [Book of Joel]

Joelah *c.* 11 century BC. Son of Jeroham of Gedor, he and his brother were among the Benjaminites to desert the army of King Saul and rally to David's support. [1 Chr. 12:7]

Joezer (Heb. 'God aided') *c.* 11 century BC. A Benjaminite who left the army of King Saul and joined David at Ziklag. [1 Chr. 12:6]

Jogli (Heb. 'my redemption') *c.* 13 century BC. Father of Bukki, the leader of the tribe of Dan in the time of Moses appointed to help divide up the land of Israel. [Num. 34:22]

Joha *1. c* 10 century BC. Son of Shimri, he and his brother Jediael were warriors in the army of King David and were distinguished for their bravery. [1 Chr. 11:45]
2. date unknown. A son of Beriah, he and his family were leaders of the tribe of Benjamin living in Jerusalem. [1 Chr. 8:16]

Johanan (Heb. 'God's mercy') *1. c.* 11 century BC. One of the archers of the tribe of Benjamin who deserted from King Saul's army and joined David at Ziklag. [1 Chr. 12:4]
2. c. 11 century BC. One of the eleven warriors of the tribe of Gad who left the army of King Saul and joined David in the wilderness. [1 Chr. 12:12]
3. c. 10 century BC. Son of Azariah, a descendant of Aaron the priest. [1 Chr. 6:9, 10]
4. c. 8 century BC. Father of Azariah who was one of the four leaders of the tribe of Ephraim to demand the release of the soldiers of Judah whom the army

of Pekah, king of Israel, had captured in battle. [2 Chr. 28:12]

5. *c.* 7 century BC. Eldest son of Josiah, king of Judah. He may be identical with Jehoahaz who succeeded his father as king. [2 Kgs. 23:30, 31; 1 Chr. 3:15]

6. *c.* 6 century BC. Johanan the son of Kareah was one of the Judean officers left in the field after the fall of Jerusalem. They pledged their loyalty to Gedaliah, who had been appointed governor. He advised them to cooperate with the Babylonians and to go out into the abandoned countryside, gather the summer fruits, and make wine and oil for themselves.

A few months later Johanan warned Gedaliah that another officer, Ismael, was plotting against him. Gedaliah brushed aside the threat and was assassinated. Johanan and his men pursued Ishmael and engaged him at Gibeon, but Ishmael fled to Ammon. Afraid of Babylonian reprisals, Johanan and his men took refuge in Egypt, carrying with them Jeremiah, his scribe Baruch, and Gedaliah's family. [2 Kgs. 25:23; Jer. 40:8–16; 41:11–16; 42:1–8; 43:2–5]

7. 5 century BC. One of the seven sons of Elioenai of the tribe of Judah, and a descendant of King David. [1 Chr. 3:24]

8. 5 century BC. Son of Hakkatan and a descendant of Azgad, he was a leader of Judah who returned with Ezra from Babylon. [Ezra 8:12]

9. 5 century BC. Son of Eliashib and one of the chief Levites in the time of Nehemiah. [Neh. 12:22, 23]

Joiada (Heb. 'favoured') *1.* 6 century BC. Son of Eliashib the high priest. One of his sons married the daughter of Sanballat, the enemy of Nehemiah. Also called Jehoiada. [Neh. 12:10, 11, 22; 13:28]

2. 5 century BC. Son of Paseah, he helped repair the old gate of Jerusalem at the time of Nehemiah. [Neh. 3:6]

Joiakim (Heb. 'exalted') 5 century BC.

Son of Jeshua, the priest, and father of Eliashib, he was high priest in the Temple during the time of Ezra and Nehemiah. [Neh. 12:10, 12, 26]

Joiarib (Heb. 'defended') *1.* 6 century BC. Father of Jedaiah and a chief priest who returned to Judah with Zerubbabel from exile and lived in Jerusalem. Also called Jehoiarib. [1 Chr. 9:10; Neh. 11:10; 12:6, 19]

2. 5 century BC. One of the men of 'insight' sent by Ezra to Iddo with a request to provide Levites to minister in the Temple. [Ezra 8:16]

3. date unknown. Son of Zechariah of the tribe of Judah. Maaseiah, one of his descendants, was one of the first men of Judah to settle in Jerusalem following the return from exile in Babylon. [Neh. 11:5]

Jokim (Heb. 'exalted') date unknown. Son of Shelah and a leader of the tribe of Judah. [1 Chr. 4:22]

Jokshan (Heb. 'birdcatcher') *c.* 17 century BC. A son of Abraham by his wife Keturah, he was a desert chieftain. [Gen. 25:2, 3; 1 Chr. 1:32]

Joktan (Heb. 'small') date unknown. Younger son of Eber and a great-grandson of Shem. [Gen. 10:26–9; 1 Chr. 1:19, 20]

Jonadab (Heb. 'the Lord is bounteous') *c.* 9 century BC. The son of Rechab, Jonadab, a Kenite, like his father was a member of an ascetic nomad clan that refused to touch wine, live in settled abodes or cultivate the soil. He supported Jehu in his revolt against the corrupt Ahab and in the religious reforms he carried out. Jeremiah held up Jonadab and his sons as examples of faithful followers of the Lord: to the house of the Rechabites 'Jeremiah said "Thus says the Lord of hosts ... Jonadab the son of Rechab shall never lack a man to stand before me.'" (Jer. 35:19) Also called Jehonadab. [2 Kgs. 10:15–23; Jer. 35]

Jonah (Heb. 'dove') *c.* 8 century BC. Hebrew prophet. The story of Jonah, the reluctant prophet and hapless mariner, is a brief droll fable. Yet it carries a message serious enough to warrant inclusion among the prophetical books of the Bible. The message is that God's compassion extends to all his creatures, whether Jew or Gentile, human or animal.

According to a one-sentence reference in the Second Book of Kings, there was a prophet in the time of King Jeroboam II of Israel called Jonah, the son of Amittai, and he came from the village of Gath-hepher in the Galilee, near Nazareth. Nothing more is known of him outside the Book named after him. The Book opens with the Lord saying to him: 'Arise, go to Nineveh, that great city, and cry against it; for their wickedness has come up before me.' (Jonah 1:2) Nineveh on the Tigris river was the capital of the Assyrian empire. For the Hebrews, it was a byword for luxury and dissipation, so that the prophet Nahum could cry out about it: 'Woe to the Bloody city, all full of lies and booty ... all who hear the news of you clap their hands over you. For upon whom has not come your unceasing evil?' (Nahum 3:1, 19) The city fell to the Babylonians in 612 BC but the legends of its depravity would have been fresh in the minds of the Jews when the story of Jonah was written.

Jonah shirked the unwelcome assignment, and tried to run away. He went to the seaport of Joppa (modern Jaffa) 'and he found a ship going to Tarshish; so he paid the fare, and went on board' (Jonah 1:3). (Tarshish was probably a Phoenician trading post and ironsmelting centre in Spain.)

The Lord unleashed a violent storm, and the ship threatened to founder. The frightened sailors lightened the vessel by throwing the cargo overboard, and each of them prayed to his own deity. Finding Jonah asleep in the hold, the boatswain angrily woke him and told him to invoke the help of his God.

In desperation the crew drew lots to find out whether the ship was in danger for having a guilty man on board, and the lot fell to Jonah. They questioned him about his background, and he admitted he was a Hebrew fleeing from the Lord. The storm was on his account, and if they threw him into the sea it would become calm.

The sailors were reluctant to consign their passenger to a watery death and rowed hard to reach land, but the wind and waves were too strong. Then, begging Jonah's God to forgive them, they threw him overboard and the storm at once subsided. The fearful sailors offered a sacrifice and made vows to the Lord to appease him.

God sent a great fish to swallow Jonah, who remained alive in its belly for three days before being vomited up on the shore. While in the belly of the fish, Jonah offered up a psalm in praise of the Lord who had rescued him from drowning when 'The waters closed in over me, the deep was round about me; weeds were wrapped about my head.' (Jonah 2:5)

God renewed his call to Jonah to go and preach in Nineveh. This time the prophet obeyed. He entered the city and proclaimed that it would be destroyed within forty days. From the king downwards the inhabitants repented and put on sackcloth. A royal decree was issued ordering a fast for men and animals alike, and calling on all the citizens to renounce their evil ways in the hope that God would spare them. The Lord relented and the doom of the city was averted.

Jonah was indignant at this unexpected result of his mission, and complained to the Lord that he might as well be dead. Refusing to believe that the city would really be spared, he left it and sat down some distance away, waiting to see what would happen.

The Lord arranged for a castor-oil plant to grow rapidly next to Jonah so that it would give him shade. But at dawn the next day God sent a worm to attack the plant, and it withered. The sun beat down on Jonah's head and a scorching east wind added to his misery. He fainted and again wished for death. God brushed aside his self-pity and derided him for being upset about a plant which had cost him no labour, had sprouted in one night and had perished the next day. Should God then not spare the great city of Nineveh with 120,000 people and many animals?

All the average person knows about Jonah is that he was swallowed by a whale. The rationalists of the nineteenth century were quick to point out that the inside of a whale's throat has a kind of net built into it, so that it can swallow small fish but not large humans. Therefore, they said, the Bible could not be believed. But, contrary to popular belief, the Bible does not talk of a whale (a creature unknown in the Mediterranean) but of a 'great fish' which is a literal translation of the Hebrew *dag gadol*. [2 Kgs. 14:25; Book of Jonah]

Jonathan (Heb. 'given by God') *1. c.* 13 century BC. The grandson of Moses and the son of Gershom, he was a priest who served the citizens of Dan when they built their city and set up graven images that had been made by Micah. [Judg. 18:30, 31]

2. c. 11 century BC. Eldest son of King Saul.

Jonathan, son of Saul and Ahinoam, is one of the most open-hearted and likeable human beings in the Bible. It was his misfortune to be caught in the feud between the two men closest to him: his father King Saul and his friend and brother-in-law David.

Jonathan was a daring and successful young officer in Saul's army, and skilled at archery, for which the men of the tribe of Benjamin were noted: '... the bow of Jonathan turned not back ...' (2 Sam. 1:22). He first distinguished himself early in Saul's reign in the attack on the Philistine garrison at Geva, north of Jerusalem. Two thousand Israelites under the king's command cut the garrison off from the rear, while Jonathan led a thousand men in a frontal assault that wiped it out.

The Philistines reacted swiftly. They sent a strong army of chariots, horsemen and foot soldiers back into the hills and occupied Michmash, another nearby town. The Israelites fled and Saul was left in a desperate situation with only a remnant of six hundred men. A personal exploit by Jonathan saved the situation. Taking only his young armour-bearer with him, he climbed up above a rocky pass, and surprised and killed a platoon of Philistine soldiers moving through it. Exaggerated accounts of this sudden attack spread through the Philistine army and threw it into a panic. The Israelites attacked and were able to rout the enemy. This unexpected victory at Michmash was the turning point in Saul's military campaigns.

Ignorant of Saul's orders that his pursuing troops should eat nothing, Jonathan did. 'I tasted a little honey with the tip of the staff that was in my hand,' (1 Sam. 14:43) thereby offending the Lord. Saul reluctantly decreed that his son should die but relented when the people appealed on behalf of their popular hero.

When the young David was brought before Saul after he had slain Goliath, 'the soul of Jonathan was knit to the soul of David, and Jonathan loved him ...' (1 Sam. 18:1). Jonathan impulsively stripped off his own armour and gave it to David together with his sword and bow.

Later Saul came to hate David and tried to kill him. David fled from the court, and secretly contacted Jonathan. Saul even hurled his spear at his own son when Jonathan pleaded for David.

Through a pre-arranged signal, the two friends met again in a lonely field, and Jonathan sadly agreed that David was forced to leave and go into hiding. They swore eternal loyalty and took a moving and tearful farewell of each other.

In the defeat of the Israelite army by the Philistines on Mount Gilboa, Jonathan was slain together with his father and his two younger brothers. Their bodies were mutilated and hung on the wall of the nearby city of Beth-shean. The men of Jabesh-gilead, across the Jordan river, stole up at night, took down the bodies and buried them under a tamarisk tree in their own town.

David, still in exile, poured his anguish into the immortal lament for his beloved friend: 'I am distressed for you, my brother Jonathan; very pleasant have you been to me; your love to me was wonderful, passing the love of women.' (2 Sam. 1:26) [1 Sam. 13; 14; 18–20; 23; 31; 2 Sam. 1:4–26; 4:4; 9:1–7; 21:7–14]

3. c. 10 century BC. Son of Abiathar the priest, he supported King David during Absalom's revolt, and later brought the news to Adonijah that King David had appointed Solomon his successor to the throne. [2 Sam. 15:27, 36; 17:17, 20; 1 Kgs. 1:42, 43]

4. c. 10 century BC. Son of Shimei who was the brother of King David, he killed a Philistine giant at Gath, who had six fingers on each hand and six toes on each foot. He may be identical with Jonathan described as King David's uncle. [2 Sam. 21:21; 1 Chr. 20:7]

5. c. 10 century BC. A warrior in the armies of King David distinguished for his bravery. He is described both as the son of Shammah the Hararite and of Shagee the Hararite. [2 Sam. 23:32, 33; 1 Chr. 11:34]

6. c. 10 century BC. Son of Uzziah, he

was in charge of all treasuries in towns and villages outside Jerusalem in the time of King David. [1 Chr. 27:25]

7. c. 10 century BC. Uncle of King David, he educated the sons of the king. He may be identical with Jonathan, son of Shimei, the brother of David. [1 Chr. 27:32]

8. 6 century BC. Son of Joiada the Levite, he and his family returned with Zerubbabel from exile in Babylon. [Neh. 12:11]

9. c. 6 century BC. A scribe in whose house the prophet Jeremiah was held prisoner at the order of the leaders of Judah. [Jer. 37:15, 20; 38:26]

10. 5 century BC. A chief priest of Judah when Joaikim was high priest in the last years of Nehemiah. [Neh. 12:14]

11. date unknown. Younger son of Jada, of the tribe of Judah [1 Chr. 2:32, 33]

12. 5 century BC. Father of Ebed who returned with Ezra to Judah from exile in Babylon. [Ezra 8:6]

13. 5 century BC. Son of Asahel, he was with Ezra when the latter called on the men of Judah to divorce their non-Jewish wives. [Ezra 10:15]

14. 5 century BC. Father of Zechariah, a priest who played musical instruments at the dedication ceremony for the rebuilding of the walls of Jerusalem in the time of Nehemiah. [Neh. 12:35]

Jorah (Heb. 'rain') 6 century BC. Head of a family who returned to Judah with Zerubbabel from exile in Babylon. Also called Hariph. [Ezra 2:18; Neh. 7:24]

Jorai (Heb. 'taught') date unknown. A leader of the tribe of Gad living in Bashan, east of the river Jordan. [1 Chr. 5:13]

Joram (Heb. 'exalted') *1. c.* 10 century BC. Son of Toi, king of Hamath, he was sent by his father to congratulate King David on defeating Hadadezer, king of Zobah, who had fought with Toi in many battles. Joram brought David vessels of gold, silver and brass as gifts which David dedicated to God. Also called Hadoram. [2 Sam. 8:10;1 Chr. 18:10]

2. *c.* 10 century BC. The grandfather of Shelomoth, the priest responsible for all the treasures captured by King David in battle and dedicated to the Tabernacle. [1 Chr. 26:25]

3. see JEHORM 2

4. see JEHORAM 3

Joseph (Heb. 'may [God] add [children]') *c.* 16 century BC. Eleventh son of Jacob. Down the ages, novelists and painters have dwelt on the romantic story of Joseph, the Israelite lad from Canaan who became the most powerful man at the court of the Egyptian Pharaoh.

The patriarch Jacob was married to Leah and Rachel, the daughters of his uncle Laban, for whom he worked. Jacob had ten sons by Leah and by two concubines, and was already an old man when Rachel bore her first child, Joseph. Soon after Jacob had returned to his own country, Canaan, Rachel died giving birth to the last of Jacob's sons, Benjamin. The family settled in Hebron.

The boy Joseph was pampered by his father, who made him a coat of many colours as a special mark of favour. This was resented by his older brothers. They were made angrier still when Joseph bore tales about them to Jacob, and when he claimed to have dreams in which the whole family bowed down to him.

One day Jacob sent Joseph, then seventeen years old, to locate his brothers pasturing the flocks near Shechem (Nablus), and to bring him word about them. Joseph caught up with them further north, in the broad valley of Dothan (near the present Jenin). When they saw him coming, they conspired to get rid of him, and tell their father that Joseph had been slain by a wild beast – 'and we shall see what will become of his dreams' (Gen. 37:20). Reuben, the eldest, persuaded the others not to kill

him but to leave him at the bottom of an empty well, intending to return to save him. This they did, after stripping him of his coloured coat. While they were eating their food, a party of Ishmaelites came by on camels on their way to Egypt with a load of spices from Gilead. The brothers discussed selling Joseph as a slave to this caravan but were forestalled by some passing Midianite merchants who pulled Joseph out of the well and sold him to the Ishmaelites 'for twenty shekels of silver' (Gen. 37:28). (There is some discrepancy in the narrative here, possibly due to different sources having been combined.)

Reuben came to release Joseph and found he had vanished. Reuben returned in great distress to tell the other brothers, who dipped Joseph's coat in the blood of a kid and reported to their father that they had found the garment in a field, suggesting that Joseph had been torn to pieces by some wild animal.

JOSEPH'S RISE TO POWER

In Egypt, the young Joseph was bought by Potiphar, the captain of Pharaoh's guard. In the course of time, Joseph showed such ability and diligence that Potiphar put him in charge of his household and all his affairs: Joseph was 'handsome and good-looking' (Gen. 39:6) and his master's wife tried to seduce him. He firmly rejected her advances. One day she clutched him by his coat and he fled, leaving the garment in her hand. The spurned woman had her revenge. She told her husband that the Hebrew slave he had brought into the house had tried to violate her, and produced his robe as proof. The angry Potiphar threw Joseph into prison. Joseph gained the trust of the head warden, who put him in charge of the other prisoners.

Pharaoh's chief cupbearer and head baker offended their master and were flung into the gaol. One morning Joseph noticed they were downcast and he asked them what was wrong. It appeared they were troubled about the meaning of the dreams they had had the night before. (In Egypt it was believed that dreams foretold the future.) Joseph said, 'Do not interpretations belong to God? Tell them to me, I pray you.' (Gen. 40:8) The cupbearer had dreamt he had filled his master's cup from the grapes of three vines. Joseph told him that in three days' time he would be released and restored to his position. The baker had dreamt he bore three white baskets on his head and the food in the topmost one was eaten by birds. Joseph foretold that in three days' time he would be hanged. Both predictions proved correct. Once free, however, the cupbearer forgot his promise to intercede with Pharaoh on Joseph's behalf.

Two years later, Pharaoh himself was disturbed by dreams which none of the magicians at the court was able to interpret. The cupbearer then told him about his own experience in prison with the Hebrew slave. Pharaoh had Joseph taken out of the dungeon and brought before him, after he had been shaved, bathed, and provided with clean clothes.

In his dream Pharaoh had seen seven fat cows come out of the river and graze in a meadow. They were followed by seven emaciated cows who devoured the fat ones while remaining just as thin themselves. He also saw seven fat ears of wheat on one stalk, and seven withered ears that devoured the fat ones. Joseph declared, 'The dream of Pharaoh is one; God has revealed to Pharaoh what he is about to do.' (Gen. 41:25) There would be seven years of plenty, which would then be wiped out by seven years of severe famine. He advised Pharaoh to find 'a man discreet and wise, and set him over the land of Egypt' (Gen. 41:33) to collect one-fifth of the crops in the good years and store them as a state reserve, to tide over the lean years.

Pharaoh was so impressed by Joseph that he decided to vest power in him. Joseph now became the most important man in the kingdom after Pharaoh himself. He wore the king's own signet ring and rode in the second chariot in the royal procession. Pharaoh gave him the Egyptian name of Zaphnathpaaneah ('says the god: he will live'), and arranged for him to marry Asenath, the daughter of the high priest of the temple at on. At the age of thirty, after thirteen years as a slave in Egypt, Joseph the Hebrew had become governor of the strongest nation in the region.

During the next seven years there were rich harvests in the Nile Valley. Under Joseph's direction, officials gathered one-fifth of each crop and accumulated wheat in great granaries constructed in all the cities. The period of plenty came to an end, and famine smote the whole region. Joseph started selling wheat to the population from his storehouses after their private reserves had been consumed. When their money gave out, he accepted their livestock in payment. After that, food was bartered for land, all of which became Pharaoh's property, except that of the priests, who were given free rations. Joseph was now able to carry out a programme of agrarian reform. Free land and seed were distributed to the peasants; they delivered one fifth of the crop to Pharaoh as a tax and retained the rest for their own needs.

THE BROTHERS IN EGYPT
The Land of Canaan had also been struck by crop failures and famine. Jacob sent his sons to Egypt to buy corn, keeping at home only the youngest one, Benjamin. The brothers bowed down humbly before the resplendent and powerful governor who controlled all food supplies. Joseph did not reveal that he had recognized them, but spoke roughly to them, accusing them of being spies. In pleading their innocence, they told him about their background, and

about their aged father and youngest brother at home in Canaan. Joseph was overcome with longing to see his dear mother's other child, Benjamin.

After keeping them locked up for three days, Joseph said he would release the brothers and let them go home with corn for their families, provided they proved their story by returning with the youngest. Meanwhile one of them would have to remain in Egypt as a hostage. The brothers discussed the matter among themselves in their own language, not realizing that the governor who had spoken to them through an interpreter was able to understand them. When they asked themselves whether their present troubles were not due to their evil treatment of their young brother many years before, Joseph had to turn away to conceal his feelings. Simeon, the second eldest, was bound and left behind. The others loaded their asses with the corn they had bought, and started out on the long journey home. Stopping at an inn that night, they were even more perturbed when one of the brothers opened a sack of corn to feed the animals and discovered in it the money he had paid for it. On opening the other sacks when they arrived home, the rest of the purchase money was found. (They could not know that this had been done on Joseph's instructions as a gesture to his family.)

Back in Hebron, they told Jacob all that had befallen them, including the detention of Simeon by the Egyptian governor, and his demand that Benjamin be produced to him. Jacob at first refused to let Benjamin go to Egypt, as he still grieved over the loss of Rachel's other son, Joseph. He had to yield, however, when the wheat was used up, and his sons insisted they dared not return to buy more food unless Benjamin went with them. Jacob told them to take back the money found in the sacks, with a gift for the Egyptian lord 'a little balm and a little honey, gum, myrrh, pistachio nuts, and almonds' (Gen. 43:11).

This time Joseph received them graciously, asked after their father, and sent them round to his home. They were full of apprehension till Joseph's steward reassured them and told them they were to be his master's guests for the midday meal, and brought Simeon to join them. When Joseph arrived, they gave him the gift from Jacob, and introduced Benjamin. Again, Joseph had to leave the room to hide his tears. In the dining room the brothers were seated in the exact order of their ages, much to their astonishment. The Egyptians of the household sat separately, for they would 'not eat bread with the Hebrews' (Gen. 43:32). Joseph, who sat alone, had choice morsels from his own table served to the brothers, with the largest portion for Benjamin. The atmosphere became relaxed and merry.

The brothers set out again for home in good spirits, with the fresh supply of corn they had bought. But Joseph was still trying to keep Benjamin with him. This time he not only had the money put in again with the wheat, but ordered his silver divining-cup to be concealed in Benjamin's sack. Joseph sent his steward after the brothers, who were accused of theft and dumbfounded when the cup was found. Joseph scolded them and ordered that Benjamin be held back as his retainer. After a moving plea by Judah, Joseph abandoned any further pretence. Sending everyone else out of the chamber he told his amazed brothers who he was. He did not hold against them what they had done to him in his youth, saying it was God's will that he should become lord over Egypt and be able to save his family. He told them there were still five hungry years ahead. They should fetch their father Jacob, together with all their households and flocks, and come to settle in the land of Goshen (the north-east corner of the fertile Nile delta) where Joseph would take care of them.

Pharaoh was pleased to hear that Joseph's brethren had appeared. He approved the plan to settle the family in Goshen and ordered that wagons should be provided to bring them from Canaan. Joseph added a supply of provisions for the journey, loaded on asses.

When Jacob was persuaded that the wondrous tale brought by his sons was true he exclaimed, 'It is enough: Joseph my son is still alive; I will go and see him before I die.' (Gen. 45:28) His descendants at that time numbered seventy souls. Joseph came to meet the party in Goshen, and there was an emotional reunion between the aged patriarch and his long-lost son.

Joseph brought his father and five of his brothers to the court and presented them to Pharaoh, who was interested to learn they were skilled shepherds and suggested they might take care of the royal flocks. With great dignity Jacob gave Pharaoh his blessing.

When Jacob had lived seventeen years in Egypt and had reached the age of one hundred and forty-seven, Joseph was told that his father was ill. He took Manasseh and Ephraim, the two sons born to him by his Egyptian wife Asenath, and brought them to receive his father's blessing. Jacob was already bedridden and his sight was failing. When the old man placed his right hand on the head of Ephraim, the younger son, Joseph sought to correct him, but Jacob explained that Ephraim's descendants would be more important than those of Manasseh, the elder of the two. Jacob adopted the boys as his own children, to share equally with his sons. Jacob then said to Joseph, 'Behold, I am about to die, but God will be with you, and will bring you again to the land of your fathers.' (Gen. 48:21)

Joseph had promised that his father would be buried in the family tomb in Hebron. He had the Egyptian physicians embalm Jacob's body, and a long funeral procession wended its way across the desert. It included all Jacob's sons, also Egyptian dignitaries as a mark of respect.

The brothers now feared that, with their father dead and buried, Joseph would take his revenge on them. But he said to them, 'Fear not, for am I in the place of God?' (Gen. 50:19)

Joseph lived to see his great-grandchildren and died at the age of one hundred and ten. His body too was embalmed, and remained in Egypt at his request for centuries until Moses led the Children of Israel back to the Promised Land. They brought Joseph's bones with them, in accordance with Joseph's deathbed wish, and when they had settled in Canaan, they buried them 'at Shechem, in the portion of ground which Jacob bought ... for a hundred pieces of money' (Josh. 24:32). Nevertheless, a tradition grew up that one of the large tombs in the Cave of Machpelah in Hebron was that of Joseph. [Gen. 30:24-5; 33:2, 7; 35:24; 37-50; Exod. 1:5-8; 13:19; Josh. 24:32. There are other references in Num., Deut., Josh., Judg., 2 Sam., 1 Kgs., 1 Chr., Pss., Ezek., Amos, Obad.]

2. *c.* 13 century BC. Father of Igal of the tribe of Issachar who was one of the twelve men sent by Moses to spy out the land of Canaan. [Num. 13:7]

3. *c.* 10 century BC. A son of Asaph, King David's musician. He and his family played musical instruments in the Tabernacle, Joseph taking the first rota of service. [1 Chr. 25:2, 9]

4. 5 century BC. One of the descendants of Bani who divorced his non-Jewish wife in the time of Ezra. [Ezra 10:42]

5. 5 century BC. A priest descended from Shebaniah, he was one of the chief priests of Judah when Joiakim was high priest towards the end of Nehemiah's lifetime. [Neh. 12:14]

Joshah (Heb. 'God has given') *c.* 8 century BC. Son of Amaziah, he was one of the leaders of the tribe of Simeon in the reign of King Hezekiah who drove out the native population from the rich Gedor valley and settled there. [1 Chr. 4:34]

Joshaphat (Heb. 'God has judged') *1. c.* 10 century BC. A Mithnite warrior in the army of King David distinguished for his bravery. [1 Chr. 11:43]
2. *c.* 10 century BC. A priest in the time of King David who blew the trumpet at the celebration when the Ark was brought to Jerusalem. [1 Chr. 15:24]

Joshaviah (Heb. 'may God settle') *c.* 10 century BC. Son of Elnaam, he and his brother Jeribai were warriors in the army of King David distinguished for their bravery. [1 Chr. 11:46]

Joshbekashah (Heb. 'dwells in trouble') *c.* 10 century BC. One of the sons of Heman who played music in the Tabernacle in the time of King David. He and his family took the seventeenth turn of service. [1 Chr. 25:4, 24]

Joshibiah (Heb. 'may God settle') *c.* 8 century BC. Father of Jehu, one of the leaders of the tribe of Simeon who settled in the Gedor valley in the reign of King Hezekiah. [1 Chr. 4:35]

Joshua (Heb. 'God is salvation') *1.* 13 century BC. Successor to Moses and leader of the Israelite invasion of Canaan. Moses had taken the Children of Israel out of bondage in Egypt, led them for forty years in their desert wanderings, and moulded them into an organized community based on the legal and religious code he taught them. But Moses himself was not permitted to enter the Promised Land with them. That role was reserved for his disciple and successor Joshua the son of Nun, an Ephraimite. He commanded the invasion and conquest of Canaan in a series of brilliant campaigns, and then dealt with its partition between the Israelite tribes.

Nothing is known of Joshua's early life or family. The first mention of him is some two months after the Israelites had left Egypt and had come to a place called Rephidim, in the southern part of the Sinai Peninsula, on the way to Mount Sinai. Here they were attacked by a tribe of Amalekites, fierce desert nomads. The Israelites had not yet developed any regular system of self-defence. The young Joshua must already have attracted attention as a potential military commander; Moses sent for him and told him to pick a number of men and lead the defence, which he did successfully.

During the sojourn at Mount Sinai, Joshua is mentioned incidentally several times, always in connection with Moses – as if to establish an early link between him and the great leader he was to succeed. Thus Joshua was present when Moses first approached the holy mountain with Aaron and seventy elders, and he is referred to as the 'servant' of Moses (Exod. 24:13). When Moses came down from Mount Sinai with the tablet of the Law, and approached the camp where the Israelites were worshipping the golden calf, Joshua was with him and drew his attention to the strange sounds in the distance. Again, Joshua was said to be in the newly-constructed Tabernacle (tent of worship) when Moses first communed there with the Lord.

The Israelites moved northwards from Mount Sinai, and came to rest at the oasis of Kadesh-barnea. Here they were at the southern edge of their destination, the Land of Canaan. Moses sent forward a scouting party to spy out the land. It consisted of twelve picked men, one from each of the tribes, and Joshua was the representative of his tribe, Ephraim.

After a forty-day trip through the hill country of Canaan as far as Syria and back, the spies returned safely to Kadesh-barnea. They described a populated land, with fortified cities. Of the twelve scouts, only Caleb of the tribe of Judah, supported by Joshua, urged that the Israelites should push forward into Canaan. They said, 'The land, which we passed through to spy it out, is an exceedingly good land ... a land which flows with milk and honey.' (Num. 14:7, 8) But the people were plunged into gloom by the report, and railed against Moses. The Lord decreed that since they had shown so little trust in him, they would remain wandering in the desert for forty years, and none of them would reach the Promised Land except for Joshua and Caleb.

For a generation the Israelites lived the lives of desert nomads, with the oasis of Kadesh-barnea as their tribal centre. They then moved round the southern end of the Dead Sea, and occupied most of the territory east of the Jordan river.

Feeling that his task was done and that death was approaching, Moses handed over the leadership to Joshua, who had been selected by the Lord as a man 'full of the spirit of wisdom' (Deut. 34:9). At a solemn ceremony in the Tabernacle, Moses laid his hands upon Joshua and charged him with the task of leading the Israelites into the Promised Land.

THE INVASION OF CANAAN

They were now encamped in the Jordan Valley opposite Jericho. Joshua gave careful thought to his invasion strategy. He had a good idea of the nature of the country and its inhabitants from his recollections of the scouting party nearly forty years before, and from fresh intelligence reports he now gathered.

Canaan was a corridor between the great empires in the river-basins of the Nile and the Euphrates. It was a land divided up by hills, valleys and streams, and its inhabitants lived in a number of little city-states, each under its own local chieftain or 'king'. For several centuries, it was under the sway of Egypt. By the time of Joshua, the protective power of Egypt had declined, and Canaan was weak and disunited. The local kings bickered with each other, though they might form shifting coalitions against an outside enemy. Joshua was able to exploit these political conditions.

It was clear to Joshua that the Israelites had a better chance of gaining control of the hill country than of the plains. The hills were sparsely inhabited, being mostly grazing slopes and low woods and bushes, with only a few cities: Hebron, Jerusalem, Bethel, Ai and Shechem. Down in the flat, open plains, the poorly-armed foot-soldiers could be mowed down by the horse-chariots of the Canaanites.

Joshua's most severe military obstacle was the massive fortifications of the Canaanite cities. In the report he and the other spies had brought back to Moses in Kadesh-barnea, they had stressed that 'the cities are fortified and very large' (Num. 13:28). It was not surprising that these desert tent-dwellers should be discouraged. The existing remains of that period show that the stone walls of Gezer, for instance, were thirteen feet thick; while Jericho had double brick walls, the outer one six feet and the inner one twelve feet thick.

The conventional means of subduing a fortified city were to scale the walls, or to breach them with battering rams, or to tunnel underneath them, or to starve the inhabitants into submission by a lengthy siege. Joshua lacked the military resources for these methods. The Israelites could succeed with the aid of a miracle (Jericho), or a ruse (Ai), or in cases where the enemy force had already been routed in open battle (Lachish and Hazor). A number of major cities remained unconquered at that time – for instance, Jerusalem, Gezer, Megiddo, Beth-shean, Gaza, Ashkelon, Ashdod, Ekron and Gath. Joshua had to compensate for inferiority in numbers and weapons by the fitness, courage and religious zeal of his desert fighters, and by resourceful generalship: surprise attacks, night marches and stratagems.

THE FALL OF JERICHO AND AI

The first objective was to cross the river and establish a bridge-head beyond it. The strategic key was the city of Jericho, five miles west of the fords. Joshua sent two men to spy out the city. They found lodging with Rahab, a prostitute whose dwelling was 'built into the city wall' (Josh. 2:15). She hid them and helped them to escape down a rope from her window.

On the appointed day the Israelites struck camp and moved forward to the river. The Lord said to Joshua: 'This day I will begin to exalt you in the sight of all Israel, that they may know that, as I was with Moses, so I will be with you.' (Josh. 3:7) It was the time of the winter harvest at the end of the rainy season, and the Jordan flood-waters overflowed its banks. The priests were sent ahead with the Ark of the Law. When they reached the edge of the water, its flow was suddenly blocked higher up. The priests remained standing in the centre of the river-bed until all the Israelites had passed over. Camp was pitched that night at Gilgal, between the river and Jericho. Here Joshua had twelve stones from the Jordan set up in a circle, as a memorial to the miraculous crossing.

At Gilgal the Lord commanded that all the male Israelites should be circumcised, as this had not been done when they had been born in the forty years of wandering. The Lord said, 'This day I have rolled away the reproach of Egypt from you.' (Josh. 5:9) The manna which had nourished them in the desert ceased to appear, as they could now eat of the produce of the land. For the first time in Canaan, they celebrated the Passover Feast, recalling their deliverance from bondage in Egypt. It was here too that Joshua met an angel of the Lord in the guise of a warrior holding a drawn sword. He had come 'as commander of the army of the Lord' (Josh. 5:14), and Joshua was much heartened.

The inhabitants of Jericho had shut themselves in behind the seemingly impregnable walls of their city. Its fall was brought about in a remarkable manner, in accordance with divine instructions. Each morning for six days, the Israelite force circled silently once round Jericho, with seven priests in their midst carrying the Ark and blowing on ram's horns. On the seventh day they went round seven times. The priests blew a long final note, and at a given signal from Joshua all the Israelites gave forth a loud shout. The city walls tumbled down, and the fighting men rushed straight in from all sides. They put all the inhabitants to the sword except for Rahab and her family, whom the two young spies she had sheltered took into safety. Jericho was then burnt to the ground.

From the Jericho plain, Joshua now faced the barren slopes that led up to the hill country nearly four thousand feet above. The most direct route was to the Jebusite city of Jerusalem, but it was strongly fortified, and the ascent steep and exposed. A longer but easier approach lay to the right, up a canyon to the city of Ai, some twelve miles north of Jerusalem. A reconnaissance patrol reported that the town had comparatively few inhabitants and was lightly held, so that a relatively small force of two or three thousand men could take it. This was attempted, but the Israelites were repulsed and chased down the mountain, thirty-six men being killed.

Joshua was disconcerted by his first setback, and feared that the news of it would spread through Canaan and discredit the Israelites as a fighting force. 'O Lord, what can I say, when Israel has turned their backs before their enemies!' (Josh. 7:8) He rent his clothes, prostrated himself in the Tabernacle and sought to know what had gone wrong. The answer was that someone in the

Israelite camp had broken the ban against taking spoil in Jericho, and until that crime was expiated the Lord would not help them. Early next morning, Joshua had lots drawn among all the tribes, and by elimination the guilty person was found – Achan of Judah. He confessed to looting a valuable Babylonian robe, two hundred shekels of silver and a bar of gold, and burying them in the floor of his tent. Achan, his family and animals were taken to the nearby valley of Achor and stoned to death, while his possessions were burnt.

Joshua took the second assault on Ai more seriously. This time he used his complete army, and worked out a careful battle plan designed to lure the defenders out of the walls and into the open. An advance force of five thousand men was sent up the mountain under cover of darkness, and concealed themselves in low ground just to the west of Ai, between it and the city of Bethel a mile away. Next morning Joshua and the rest of his men appeared to the north of the town, facing it across a ravine. The king of Ai ordered his troops to attack, and Joshua's men fled, with the enemy in pursuit, being drawn further and further away from their city. Then, at a given moment, Joshua raised his javelin in the air as a signal, and the ambush group lying in wait in the west dashed into the undefended city and set it alight. They then fell on the men of Ai from the rear, while those who had pretended to flee turned round and attacked from the front. The enemy army, unexpectedly caught in this pincer movement, was overcome and wiped out. The king was captured and hanged and the remaining inhabitants of the city killed. Unlike the orders at Jericho, no ban was put on taking booty at Ai. The town itself was razed, but the cattle and spoils were taken.

CAMPAIGNS IN THE SOUTH AND NORTH

Joshua now held a religious ceremony on Mount Ebal above Shechem. He built an altar of unhewn stone, made sacrifices to the Lord, and solemnly read out the Laws handed down by Moses, in the presence of all the congregation including 'the women, and the little ones, and the sojourners who lived among them' (Josh. 8:35).

At the edge of the hill-plateau some six miles north-west of Jerusalem was the town of Gibeon. It stood on a strategic height looking westward towards the coast, and controlled the route down into the valley of Aijalon in the Shephelah (lowlands). Gibeon led a confederation of four towns in the vicinity, belonging to the Hivites, one of the local Canaanite peoples. It now stood directly in the path of the Israelite advance, and was fearful that it might suffer the fate of Ai, seven miles away.

The Gibeonite elders resorted to guile. They dressed themselves in worn clothes and sandals, and loaded their donkeys with stale bread, patched wineskins, and old sacks. In this guise they came to the Israelite base camp at Gilgal and told Joshua they had travelled a long way from their distant home to make a treaty, since they had heard the Lord would make the Israelites masters of the country. Their story was believed, and oaths of mutual friendship were sworn. A few days later the truth came out. The Israelites were angry at being tricked but were obliged to abide by their oath and left the Gibeonites unharmed. Joshua told them they would be punished in the future by serving as menials in the Israelite sanctuary, 'hewers of wood and drawers of water for the congregation' (Josh. 9:27).

Gibeon's pact with the Israelites undermined the security of all southern Canaan. Adonizedek, king of Jerusalem, formed a hurried military alliance with Hebron and the foothill towns of Lachish, Eglon and Jarmuth. He sent messages to their kings to 'Come up to me, and help me, and let us smite Gibeon; for it has made peace with Joshua and with the people of Israel.' (Josh. 10:4) They besieged Gibeon, whose elders sent urgent calls for help to the Israelite camp at Gilgal. After a forced night march Joshua broke the siege and drove the enemy troops pell-mell down the mountain pass into the vale of Aijalon. During this flight the hapless Canaanites were battered by a savage hailstorm, and 'there were more who died because of the hailstones than the men of Israel killed with the sowrd.' (Josh. 10:11) Fearing that his beaten foe might escape and reorganize under cover of the approaching darkness Joshua prayed: 'Sun, stand thou still at Gibeon, and thou Moon in the valley of Aijalon.' (Josh. 10:12) Having been granted this extension of time, he was able to press home his victory.

The five defeated kings hid themselves in a cave but were discovered and shut in with a large boulder while their forces were pursued by the Israelites. Later they were pulled out and put to death, and their bodies hung on trees until sundown, when they were cut down and buried in the same cave.

After this breakthrough, Joshua's force swept through the foothills, capturing and destroying one town after another: Azekah, Makkedah, Libnah, Lachish, Eglon, Hebron and Debir. In this rapid campaign, the Israelites had gained control of the hill country south of Jerusalem, and the strategic defiles from the lowlands into the hills.

The scene of action now shifted to northern Canaan. The most important of the kings in that region was Jabin of Hazor, a large city in the Huleh Valley of eastern Galilee, astride the 'way of the sea' from Egypt to Damascus. Jabin rallied the neighbouring rulers to form a united front against the Israelites. They concentrated a large army, including a number of the formidable Canaanite chariots, at the Waters of Merom in the

hills near the Sea of Galilee. Here Joshua engaged them in battle and defeated them. He then captured and burnt Hazor.

THE AREAS OF SETTLEMENT

After these successful military campaigns in the south and the north, the time had come to allocate defined districts of settlement to each of the tribes.

The men of Reuben, Gad and part of Manasseh were now allowed to return to the lands on the Transjordan plateau which Moses had agreed to let them have before they had crossed the river with Joshua. Reuben and Gad occupied what had been the Amorite kingdom of Sihon, up to the Jabbok river; and the Machir branch of the tribe of Manasseh settled in the land of Gilead, between the Jabbok and Yarmuk rivers. The Joseph tribes remained in possession of an area in the centre – Ephraim south of Shechem, and the remainder of Manasseh from Shechem northwards to the valley of Jezreel.

Judah was allotted the area south of Jerusalem, with Hebron as its main centre. Hebron itself was given to Caleb and his family.

That left seven tribes for whom provision had to be made. Joshua sent out a team of three persons from each tribe to survey the territory not yet allocated. They were to 'describe the land in seven divisions and bring the description here to me' (Josh. 18:6). On the basis of their report tribal areas were marked out, and lots drawn for them at a gathering of the people called by Joshua at the sanctuary at Shiloh. Benjamin's portion was a narrow belt of hill-country just north of Jerusalem. Dan was given a strip of foothills and coastal plain to the west of Benjamin. Simeon remained in the northern Negev round Beersheba. The north was divided between Asher (western Galilee), Naphtali and Zebulun (eastern and central Galilee), and Issachar (the eastern Jezreel and the Bethshean valley).

It is a moot point how much of the land of Canaan was actually conquered and occupied by the Israelites in Joshua's time. In one passage it is claimed that 'Joshua took the whole land, according to all that the Lord had spoken to Moses; and Joshua gave it for an inheritance to Israel according to their tribal allotments. And the land had rest from war.' (Josh. 11:23) But this statement was more rhetorical than factual. That the conquest was neither rapid nor complete is clear from other passages in the Books of Joshua and Judges, from subsequent history, and from archaeological excavation. After a list is given of thirty-one defeated kings west of the Jordan, the Lord says to Joshua: 'You are old and advanced in years, and there remains yet very much land to be possessed.' (Josh. 13:1)

East of Jordan, five Canaanite kingdoms remained intact: Edom and Moab in the south round the Dead Sea; Ammon in the centre; and Geshur and Maachah east and north-east of the Sea of Galilee. The extreme north of Canaan, extending into what is now Syria and Lebanon, remained occupied by the Amorites. The southern coastal plain, soon to be occupied by the Philistines, stayed unconquered. The northern part of the coastal plain also remained in Canaanite hands, and was settled by the Phoenicians. In the middle of the Israelite territories, there were strongly fortified cities that could not be subdued – such as Jerusalem, which was taken by David two centuries later; Gezer, which fell to David's son Solomon; and the line of Canaanite strongholds along the Jezreel Valley, such as Megiddo and Beth-shean. These facts are borne out by the subsequent history of these cities, and by archaeological evidence.

Generally, it was easier for the Israelites to establish themselves in the hills. Their settlement of this difficult terrain was helped by two technological advances. Iron tools could be obtained from their more developed neighbours, and with these implements it was easier to clear hillsides of trees and boulders than with those made of softer bronze (a mixture of copper and tin). Furthermore, they learned to hold rain-water in rock cisterns lined with a plaster that was waterproof, thus becoming less dependent on local wells. Israelite building methods were still primitive, but unlike the Canaanites they were a patriarchal rural society dispersed in small communities, and not in walled cities.

When the Israelites tried to penetrate the plains they ran into trouble. 'And the Lord was with Judah; and he took possession of the hill country, but he could not drive out the inhabitants of the plain, because they had chariots of iron.' (Judg. 1:19) The tribes of Zebulun and Asher failed to gain control of the coastal strip allotted to them north of Acre. The elders of Manasseh and Ephraim complained to Joshua that they were cramped in a mountainous zone without enough land on which to subsist. 'The hill country is not enough for us.' (Josh. 17:16) Joshua told them to make more room for themselves by clearing the natural woods which then covered these hills.

The territory allotted to the tribe of Dan extended right into the coastal plain towards Jaffa. It was unable to hold it but was pushed out, and moved northwards to settle in the eastern Galilee near Mount Hermon. 'The Amorites pressed the Danites back into the hill country, for they did not allow them to come down to the plain.' (Judg. 1:34)

In the partition of the country, the tribe of Levi was not allotted an area of its own, since it carried out religious duties for the whole nation: 'the Lord God of Israel is their inheritance.' (Josh. 13:33) Instead, the Levites were granted a number of towns scattered through the territory of the other tribes, with some grazing land round each town.

Six cities were designated as places of

refuge for persons who had killed some-one inadvertently. In these cases the city authorities could admit them, and they would be safe from the blood feud. There were three such towns east of the Jordan in the areas of Reuben, Gad and Manasseh; and three west of the Jordan: Hebron (in Judah), Shechem (in Manasseh) and Kadesh (in Naphtali).

At the age of one hundred and ten Joshua felt his end was near. He assem-bled all the important men of the tribes at Shechem, and in a moving farewell address urged them to fear and obey the Lord who had done so much for them and to resist the temptation to inter-marry with the Canaanites and be contaminated by their pagan cults.

Joshua died and was buried at Timnath-serah, his personal estate in the territory of the tribe of Ephraim to which he belonged. This burial place has never been identified, though tradi-tion links it with an ancient tomb at Khirbet Tibna, in the hills twelve miles northeast of Lod. Also called Hoshea. [Exod. 17, 24, 32, 33; Num. 11, 13, 14, 26, 27, 32, 34; Deut. 1, 3, 31, 34; Book of Joshua; Judg. 1, 2; 1 Kgs. 16:34]

ARCHAEOLOGY AND THE CONQUEST
The experts have argued for generations about the account of the Israelite con-quest given in the Book of Joshua. The main problem concerns the most dramatic episode in the story – the fall of Jericho.

Jericho is regarded as the oldest inhab-ited city in the world. It is in the Jordan Valley just north of the Dead Sea. In the middle of a bleak plain 800 feet below sea-level, a spring of fresh water gushes out of the ground, and has created an oasis filled with lush tropical vegetation. Close by, remains of a stone wall, a tower and a moat have been excavated that date back 9,000 years – that is, nearly 6,000 years before Joshua, and thirty centuries before any city fortifications found elsewhere.

The archaeological evidence suggests that Jericho was destroyed by earth-quake and fire in about the 14th century BC. Walls were toppled; houses were burnt; and the charred remains were found of wheat and other foodstuffs. The available data put the devastation of Jericho a hundred years or more before Joshua's invasion in the 13th cen-tury BC. It was restored and resettled only several centuries later, in the period of the Hebrew monarchy. This time gap remains an unresolved puzzle. One theory is that the city may have been taken by Hebrew or kindred tribes at an earlier date, and the event was later attributed to Joshua. Others accept the Bible story, and suggest that the walls destroyed in Joshua's time were erected of brick on top of earlier stone walls, thus confusing the chronology.

Another problem arises over the story of the fall of Ai. According to some archaeologists – if they have correctly identified the site – it was destroyed a thousand years before Joshua. (The Hebrew word *Ai* means 'ruin'.) The town of Bethel then developed little more than a mile away from the site of Ai, and was in turn destroyed about the time of Joshua. It was later restored, and became an important Israelite centre. It is assumed, therefore, that the biblical story of the capture of Ai really related to Bethel, and that the two places were confused by later compilers of the Bible.

On the other hand, the excavated Tel of Hazor, in the Huleh Valley north of the Sea of Galilee, fits perfectly into the biblical account. This city was well known in antiquity, being located on the regular route from Egypt across Canaan to Mesopotamia. It is men-tioned a number of times in Egyptian records from the 19th to 13th centuries BC, particularly in the famous Tel el-Amarna Letters, from the Egyptian royal archives of the 14th century BC.

The Bible records that Joshua 'burned Hazor with fire' (Josh. 11:11) for Hazor 'was the head of all those kingdoms' (Josh. 11:11). The excavations carried out between 1955 and 1959 showed that part of the site contained the remains of a well-built Canaanite city, with houses and a canalization system. The floors of the houses in the uppermost stratum were littered with pottery of the Mycenean type definitely belonging to the 13th century BC, and the city in this stratum was destroyed by fire and never again resettled. The high mound at the southern end of the site revealed similar evidence of the last Canaanite settlement in the 13th century BC. Here, however, there was evidence of subsequent settlement, including remarkable remains of structures and fortifications built by King Solomon in the 10th century BC.

Further corroboration of the Book of Joshua came to light in the excavations at Lachish. The city occupied a strategic location, guarding the approach to the Hebron hills and Jerusalem from the south. Its Canaanite stage came to an end when it was destroyed in the 13th century BC, which would correspond to the period of Joshua.

2. c. 11 century BC. An inhabitant of Beth-shemesh in the days of the prophet Samuel. The Ark of God remained in his field on its return from the Philistines. [1 Sam. 6:14, 18]

3. c. 7 century BC. Governor of Judah in the days of King Josiah. [2 Kgs. 23:8]

4. see JESHUA 6.

Josiah (Heb. 'God-healed') *1.* Sixteenth king of Judah after the monarchy split, he reigned 640–09 BC. Josiah was the son of King Amon of Judah and of Jedidah, daughter of Adaiah of Bozkath. He was eight years old when he succeeded his father on the throne.

In the eighteenth year of Josiah's reign, the high priest Hilkiah showed Shaphan, the royal scribe, a 'Book of the Law' which he had discovered in the Temple during the renovations ordered by the king. (It was probably an early version of the Book of Deuteronomy.) Shaphan read the sacred work to his royal master, who was filled with consternation at finding how far the religious practices of his time had strayed from God's commandments. The prophetess Huldah was consulted, and revealed that the wrathful Lord would destroy Judah, though not in the lifetime of the devout Josiah.

The king called a great assembly in the Temple of '... the priests and the prophets, all the people, both small and great' (2 Kgs. 23:2), and read the whole Book to them. He then carried out sweeping reforms. The Temple was purged of all heathen altars and cult objects, particularly those belonging to the Assyrian worship of the sun, the moon and the stars. These objects were solemnly burnt in the valley of Kidron below the city wall. The practice of child sacrifice in the valley of Hinnom (Gehenna) west of the city was stopped 'that no one might burn his son or his daughter as an offering to Molech' (2 Kgs. 23:10). The idolatrous priests were killed, the pagan house of male prostitutes was pulled down and the local shrines outside Jerusalem were destroyed and defiled by burning human bones on them.

When this purge had been completed from Geba to Beersheba, Josiah summoned the whole country to a great Passover celebration in Jerusalem in the reconsecrated Temple. Thousands of lambs, kids and bullocks were slaughtered for the occasion. 'For no such passover had been kept since the days of the judges. ...' (2 Kgs. 23:22)

It is noteworthy that Josiah included in these activities areas of the northern kingdom of Israel that had been conquered and annexed by Assyria a century earlier. Two other great powers were contending for the domination slipping out of the Assyrian grasp: Babylonia and Egypt. In 612 BC the army of the Babylonians and Medes defeated the

Assyrians, and captured Nineveh the capital. At this point Pharaoh Neco of Egypt led an army to the assistance of the Assyrians, in order to stem the rising might of Babylon and to regain Egypt's traditional hold of Syrian and Israelite territory. Josiah tried to frustrate this design. In 609 BC, as the Egyptian army marched across the country along the ancient Via Maris ('way of the sea'). Josiah intercepted it at the key pass of Megiddo. His forces were defeated and he himself mortally wounded. He was rushed back by chariot to Jerusalem where he died. 'All Judah and Jerusalem mourned for Josiah.' (2 Chr. 35:24)

Josiah was succeeded by his son Jehoahaz. [1 Kgs. 13:2; 2 Kgs. 21:24, 26; 22; 23:1–34; 1 Chr. 3:14, 15; 2 Chr. 33:25; 34; 35; 36:1; Jer. 1:1–3; 3:6; 22:11, 18; 25:1, 3; 26:1; 27:1; 35:1; 36:1, 2, 9; 37:1; 45:1; 46:2; Zeph. 1:1]
2. *c.* 6 century BC. Son of Zephaniah, from whom gold and silver were to be taken to make a crown for Jeshua, the high priest. [Zech. 6:10]

Josiphiah (Heb. 'may God add') 5 century BC. A leader of Judah who returned with Ezra from exile in Babylon. [Ezra 8:10]

Jotham (Heb. 'God is upright') *1. c.* 12 century BC. A judge of Israel.

One of Gideon's sons was Abimelech, whose mother was a concubine from the city of Shechem. When his father died. Abimelech had his seventy brothers murdered with the support of his mother's kinsmen, and declared himself king of the region. The only one to escape was Jotham, the youngest one, who managed to hide himself.

The leaders of Shechem gathered in the town meeting-place to proclaim Abimelech king. Jotham suddenly appeared on the top of Mount Gerizim, overlooking the city, and shouted, 'Listen to me, you men of Shechem, that God may listen to you.' (Judg. 9:7) He then told them the following parable. One day the trees decided to elect a king, and offered the position to the olive tree. It refused, saying, 'Shall I leave my fatness, by which gods and men are honoured, and go to sway over the trees?' (Judg. 9:9) They then turned to the fig tree, who replied, 'Shall I leave my sweetness and my good fruit ...?' (Judg. 9:11) The vine, when invited, said, 'Shall I leave my wine which cheers gods and men...?' (Judg. 9:13) Only the useless bramble accepted. 'If in good faith you are anointing me king over you, then come and take refuge in my shade. ...' (Judg. 9:15) But fire came from the thorny branches of the bramble and burnt the whole forest.

Did they think, went on Jotham, that they had served Gideon's memory well by killing seventy of his sons in order to make Abimelech king? He reminded them that his father had risked his life for Shechem, when he delivered the city from the Midianites. Jotham prophesied: 'let fire come out from Abimelech, and devour the citizens of Shechem ... and devour Abimelech.' (Judg. 9:20)

Having uttered his words of doom, Jotham dashed away and escaped again. He took refuge at Beer, a place distant from Shechem, where he could be out of reach of his half-brother Abimelech. Jotham's double prophecy came true three years later. Abimelech crushed a revolt in Shechem by killing all the people and sacking the town. The following day he moved against the neighbouring town of Thebez which had also taken part in the rebellion. Here he was killed by a millstone dropped on his head by a woman from the city wall. [Judg. 9]
2. Eleventh king of Judah after the monarchy split, he reigned 740–36 BC.

Jotham was the eldest son of the illustrious King Uzziah of Judah and Jerusha, the daughter of Zadok. During the late years of his reign Uzziah suffered from leprosy and remained secluded in his quarters. Jotham acted as a co-regent and administered the kingdom under his father's direction. When Uzziah died, Jotham became king in his own right. He continued his father's successful policies that maintained military strength and economic prosperity. The Bible mentions that Jotham constructed the upper gate of the Temple and carried out considerable work on the city wall. He also added to the number of towns that his father had fortified. Jotham defeated the kingdom of Ammon in Trans-jordan and for three successive years exacted from the Ammonites a heavy tribute of silver, wheat and barley.

Upon his death he was succeeded by his son Ahaz. [2 Kgs. 15:5, 7, 30, 32–8; 16:1; 1 Chr. 3:12; 5:17; 2 Chr. 26:21, 23; 27; Isa. 1:1; 7:1; Hos. 1:1; Mic. 1:1]
3. date unknown. A son of Jahdai and a leader of the tribe of Judah. [1 Chr. 2:47]

Jozabad (Heb. 'given by God') *1. c.* 11 century BC. A Benjaminite warrior who deserted from King Saul's army and joined David at Ziklag. [1 Chr. 12:4]
2. c. 11 century BC. Two army commanders of the tribe of Manasseh who left the army of King Saul and rallied to David on his way to Ziklag. [1 Chr. 12:20]
3. c. 8 century BC. One of the Levites who supervised the bringing of offerings and tithes into the Temple in the reign of King Hezekiah. [2 Chr. 31:13]
4. c. 7 century BC. A Levite who donated large quantities of cattle for the Passover offering in the reign of King Josiah of Judah. [2 Chr. 35:9]
5. 5 century BC. Son of Jeshua, he was one of the Levites present when the gold and silver brought back from Babylon at Ezra's command was weighed in the Temple. [Ezra 8:33]
6. 5 century BC. A son of Pashhur the priest who divorced his non-Jewish wife in the time of Ezra. [Ezra 10:22]

7. 5 century BC. One of the Levites who divorced his non-Jewish wife in the time of Ezra. [Ezra 10:23]
8. 5 century BC. A Levite who explained the Law to the people of Judah after Ezra had read out the Law of Moses in the market-place. [Neh. 8:7]
9. 5 century BC. A leader of the Levites who settled in Jerusalem in the days of Nehemiah and was a supervisor of the Temple. [Neh. 11:16]

Jozacar (Heb. 'the Lord remembered') *c.* 9 century BC. Son of Shimeath, he was one of the royal servants who murdered King Joash of Judah and was later put to death by Joash's son, Amaziah. Also called Zabad. [2 Kgs. 12:21; 2 Chr. 24:26]

Jozadak *see* JEHOZADAK

Jubal (Heb. 'sound') date unknown. Son of Lamech and Adah and a descendant of Cain, he was the first musician. [Gen. 4:21]

Jucal *see* JEHUCAL

Judah (Heb. 'God will lead') *1. c.* 16 century BC. Fourth son of Jacob.

Judah was the fourth son of Jacob's first wife Leah and was born in Paddan-aram where Jacob was working for his father-in-law Laban. Together with his brothers, Judah was involved in the events that led to their brother Joseph becoming a slave in Egypt. It was Judah's idea to sell Joseph to a passing caravan of Midianite traders rather than to let him die in the well into which they had lowered him: '"let not our hand be upon him, for he is our brother, our own flesh." And his brothers heeded him.' (Gen. 37:27)

Judah married a Canaanite woman called Bath-shua who had three sons. The eldest was Er and later Judah married him to Tamar, but Er died soon after without a child. Judah told Onan,

Er's brother, to take Tamar so that according to tradition he would 'perform the duty of a brother-in-law to her, and raise up offspring for your brother.' (Gen. 38:8) But Onan refused to have children that would not be considered his and offended the Lord by spilling his semen on the ground, and he too died. Tamar disguised herself as a prostitute and lured Judah to bed with her and became pregnant. When Judah discovered who she was, he blamed himself because he should have given Tamar to his next son. Tamar had twin sons by Judah.

Later Judah was one of the ten sons sent by Jacob to buy corn in Egypt where Joseph had become a leading figure at Pharaoh's court. Joseph longed to see his full brother Benjamin and insisted that he be brought on the next journey. Joseph then accused Benjamin of stealing a silver cup and as a punishment demanded that Benjamin be left behind as his retainer. Judah made a moving plea, saying that this would kill their father Jacob. Finally Joseph disclosed his identity to his brothers and a tearful reunion took place.

Years later, when Joseph had brought his father Jacob and the rest of the family to Egypt, it included Judah's remaining three sons. Jacob sent Judah ahead to tell Joseph he was coming so that he could come to meet him.

On his deathbed Jacob blessed all his sons in turn. Of Judah he said: 'The sceptre shall not depart from Judah, nor the ruler's staff from between his feet, until he comes to whom it belongs ...' (Gen. 49:10). The blessing of Moses asks the Lord to intercede on behalf of Judah against its enemies. In the conquest of Canaan under Joshua, the tribe of Judah was allocated extensive territory that included the Hebron hill district south of Jerusalem. As Jacob's blessing had foretold, Judah became the dominant Israelite tribe, and produced the royal house of David. [Gen. 29:35; 35:23; 37:26, 27; 38; 43; 44; Exod. 1:2; Num. 26:19; Deut. 33:7; Ruth 4:12; 1 Chr. 2; 4; 5; 9; Neh. 11:24]

2. c. 6 century BC. A Levite who returned to Jerusalem with Zerubbabel from exile in Babylon, and supervised the thanksgiving service in the Tabernacle. [Neh. 12:8]

3. c. 5 century BC. A Levite who divorced his non-Jewish wife in the time of Ezra. [Ezra 10:23]

4. c. 5 century BC. Son of Hassenuah, he was deputy supervisor of the tribe of Benjamin in Jerusalem in the time of Nehemiah. [Neh. 11:9]

5. 5 century BC. A Levite who played musical instruments at the dedication ceremony for the rebuilt wall of Jerusalem in the time of Nehemiah. [Neh. 12:34]

6. c. 5 century BC. One of the leaders of Judah who participated in the dedication ceremony for the rebuilt wall of Jerusalem in the time of Nehemiah. [Neh. 12:36]

Judith (Heb. 'from Judah') c. 16 century BC. Wife of Esau. Judith, daughter of Beeri, was a Hittite woman whom Esau married, to the distress of his parents Isaac and Rebekah. [Gen. 26:34-5]

Jushab-Hesed (Heb. 'may covenant be restored') 6 century BC. A son of Zerubbabel of the tribe of Judah and a descendant of King David. [1 Chr. 3:20]

K

Kadmiel (Heb. 'before God') *1.* 6 century BC. Head of a family of Levites descended from Hodaviah who returned with Zerubbabel to Judah from exile in Babylon. He and his sons helped repair the Temple in Jerusalem. [Ezra 2:40; 3:9; Neh. 7:43; 12:8]
2. 5 century BC. One of the eight Levites who led the prayers at the public fast day proclaimed by Ezra, he was also a signatory of the solemn covenant, and conducted the thanksgiving services in the Temple. [Neh. 9:4, 5; 10:9; 12:24]

Kaiwan A star god. [Amos 5:26]

Kallai (Heb. 'runner') *c.* 5 century BC. Head of a priestly family in the time of Nehemiah. [Neh. 12:20]

Kareah (Heb. 'bold') 6 century BC. Father of Johanan, one of the army commanders who rallied to Gedaliah when he became governor of Judah. [2 Kgs. 25:23; Jer. 40:8, 13, 15, 16; 41:11, 13, 14, 16; 42:1, 8; 43:2, 4, 5]

Kedar (Heb. 'blackness') *c.* 17 century BC. Son of Ishmael and father of the tribe of Kedar. [Gen. 25:13; 1 Chr. 1:29; Ezek. 27:21]

Kedemah *c.* 17 century BC. Son of Ishmael and a desert chieftain. [Gen. 25:15; 1 Chr. 1:31]

Keilah date unknown. A leader of the tribe of Judah and known as 'the Garmite'. [1 Chr. 4:19]

Kelaiah 5 century BC. A Levite who divorced his non-Jewish wife in the days of Ezra. He explained the Law to the people after Ezra had read it to them; and was among the signatories to the covenant to observe the Laws of the Lord. Also called Kelita. [Ezra 10:23; Neh. 8:7; 10:10]

Kelita *see* KELAIAH

Kemuel (Heb. 'raised by God') *1. c.* 18 century BC. Son of Abraham's brother Nahor. [Gen. 22:21]
2. c. 13 century BC. Leader of the tribe of Ephraim at the time of Moses, he helped divide the Promised Land among the tribes. [Num. 34:24]
3. 10 century BC. Father of Hashabiah who was head of the tribe of Levi in the reign of King David. [1 Chr. 27:17]

Kenan (Heb. 'owner') date unknown. Son of Enosh and a great-grandson of Adam, he was the father of Mahalalel. [Gen. 5:9, 12; 1 Chr 1:2]

Kenaz *1. c.* 16 century BC. Son of Eliphaz and a grandson of Esau, he was an Edomite leader. [Gen. 36:11, 15, 42; 1 Chr. 1:36, 53]
2. c. 13 century BC. Brother of Caleb the son of Jephunneh, he was father of Othniel and a leader of the tribe of Judah. [Josh. 15:17; Judg. 1:13; 3:9, 11; 1 Chr. 4:13]
3. c. 13 century BC. Son of Elah and grandson of Caleb the son of Jephunneh. [1 Chr. 4:15]

Kenites A desert clan from the tribes of Midian, their main base was the territory south and south-east of Akaba, but they also wandered throughout Sinai. Moses's father-in-law Jethro, a Midianite priest, was also called a Kenite. After the Israelite conquest and the death of Joshua, members of the clan came north and dwelt peaceably in Judah. Jael, who killed the Canaanite general, Sisera, with a tent peg, was the wife of Heber, the Kenite. Both King Saul and King David dealt kindly with them. The ascetic clan of Rechab, who were commended by the prophet Jeremiah, were descendants of the Kenites. [Gen. 15:19; Num. 24:21; Judg. 1:16; 4:11, 17; 5:24; 1 Sam. 15:6; 27:10; 30:29; 1 Chr. 2:55]

Keren-Happuch (Heb. 'horn of beauty') period of the Patriarchs. Youngest daughter born to Job after the Lord had redressed his fortunes. [Job. 42:14]

Keros (Heb. 'crooked') date unknown. Ancestor of a family of Temple servants who returned with Zerubbabel to Judah from exile in Babylon. [Ezra 2:44; Neh. 7:47]

Keturah (Heb. 'incense') c. 17 century BC. Abraham's third wife; he married her after Sarah's death. [Gen. 25:1; 1 Chr. 1:32]

Keziah (Heb. 'cassia') period of the Patriarchs. The second daughter born to Job after the Lord had redressed his fortunes. [Job. 42:14]

Kish (Heb. 'bow') *1.* date unknown. One of the ten sons of Jeiel, the father of Gibeon, and his wife Maachah. [1 Chr. 8:30; 9:36]
2. 11 century BC. Father of King Saul, Kish was the son of Abiel of the tribe of Benjamin and a wealthy landowner. The loss of his asses and Saul's search for them led to Saul's meeting with the prophet Samuel and his anointing as king. [1 Sam. 9:1, 3; 10:11, 21; 14:51; 2 Sam. 21:14; 1 Chr. 8:33; 9:39; 21:1; 26:28]

3. 10 century BC. A Levite descended from Merari, he was the father of Jerahmeel, a Levite in the time of King David. [1 Chr. 23:21, 22; 24:29]
4. 8 century BC. Son of Abdi and one of the Levites who obeyed the command of King Hezekiah to sanctify themselves and cleanse the Temple. [2 Chr. 29:12]
5. date unknown. Ancestor of Mordecai, cousin of Queen Esther. [Esther 2:5]

Kishi *see* KUSHAIAH

Kittim date unknown. Son of Javan and a great-grandson of Noah. [Gen. 10:4; 1 Chr. 1:7]

Koa (Heb. 'male camel') c. 6 century BC. A leader of the Chaldeans whom Ezekiel prophesied would attack and destroy Judah. [Ezek. 23:23]

Kohath (Heb. 'assembly') c. 16 century BC. The second son of Levi, he went down to Egypt at the same time as his grandfather Jacob. Kohath was head of an important family of Levites which included Moses and Aaron, and which served in the Tabernacle in the wilderness, and later served in the Temple. [Gen. 46:11; Exod. 6:16, 18; Num. 3:17, 19, 27; 26:57; Josh. 21:4–42; 1 Chr.; 2 Chr.]

Kohelet (Heb. 'the preacher') c. 3 century BC. The unknown author of the biblical book known as 'Ecclesiastes'. (See the note on 'Solomon and the Wisdom Books' at the end of the entry on SOLOMON.)

Kolaiah (Heb. 'voice of God') *1.* date unknown. A leader of the tribe of Benjamin whose descendant Sallu was one of the first Benjaminites to settle in Jerusalem after the return from exile in Babylon. [Neh. 11:7]
2. 6 century BC. Father of Ahab, one of the false prophets in the days of Jeremiah who favoured King Zedekiah's revolt against Babylon. [Jer. 29:21]

Korah (Heb. 'baldness') *1. c.* 16 century BC. Son of Esau and an Edomite leader. [Gen. 36:5, 14, 18; 1 Chr. 1:35]
2. c. 16 century BC. Son of Eliphaz and a grandson of Esau. [Gen. 36:16]
3. c. 15 century BC. Son of Hebron and a leader of the tribe of Judah. [1 Chr. 2:43]
4. c. 13 century BC. Son of Izhar a Levite, he rebelled against Moses and Aaron, together with Dathan and Abiram and two hundred and fifty leaders, saying, 'You have gone too far! For all the congregation are holy.' (Num. 16:3) Moses retorted: 'You have gone too far, sons of Levi.' (Num. 16:7) The Lord told Moses and Aaron to move away from the leaders of the revolt, 'And the earth opened its mouth and swallowed them up, with their households.' (Num. 16:32) The two hundred and fifty supporters were then killed by fire from the Lord [Exod. 6:21; 24; Num. 16:1–49; 26:9–11; 27:3; 1 Chr. 6:22, 37; 9:19]

Kore (Heb. 'quail') *1.* 10 century BC. Son of Ebiasaph the Levite and a descendant of Korah, his son Shallum served in the Tabernacle in Jerusalem in the time of King David. [1 Chr. 9:19; 26:1]
2. 8 century BC. Son of Imnah the Levite, he was responsible for the distribution of the freewill offerings in the Temple during the reign of King Hezekiah. [2 Chr. 31:14]

Koz (Heb. 'thorn') date unknown. A leader of the tribe of Judah. [1 Chr. 4:8]

Kushaiah (Heb. 'bow') 10 century BC. Son of Abdi, a descendant of Merari, and father of Ethan, a Levite musician who played in the procession when King David brought the Ark of the Lord to Jerusalem. Also called Kishi. [1 Chr. 6:44; 15:17]

L

Laadah *c.* 16 century BC. Son of Shelah and a grandson of Judah, he was the father of Mareshah and his descendants were famous as the makers of fine linen. [1 Chr. 4:21]

Laban (Heb. 'white') *c.* 18 century BC. Jacob's father-in-law. Laban lived in the city of Nahor in northern Mesopotamia, with his father Bethuel and his sister Rebekah. He took part with his father in the negotiations for Rebekah's marriage to Isaac.

A generation later the young Jacob was sent by his mother Rebekah to stay with Laban in order to escape the resentment of his brother Esau, and to find himself a wife among his own people. After Jacob had worked seven years for the hand of Laban's younger daughter, Laban managed to substitute the elder and plainer sister Leah at the wedding. Jacob was obliged to work another seven years for Rachel.

Jacob served Laban twenty years, then decided to return to his own family. Laban agreed that Jacob should keep for himself as wages all the speckled and streaked goats and all the dark-coloured sheep. But the following day Laban sent off with his sons all the animals marked in such a way. His greediness was foiled by Jacob who, with the Lord's help, turned the best of Laban's flocks into speckled and streaked animals.

When Jacob left, Laban pursued him, protested at the removal of his daughters and grandchildren and accused Jacob of stealing the images of his household gods. Jacob indignantly denied the charge and invited Laban to go through his tents. He did not know that the images had been taken by Rachel, who sat on them while her father searched in her tent.

Laban proposed a covenant of friendship and Jacob agreed. They sealed their pact in accordance with custom by assembling a heap of stones and Laban said, 'The Lord watch between you and me, when we are absent one from the other.' (Gen. 31:49) Next morning he blessed his daughters and departed. [Gen. 24; 25; 27:32; 46:18, 25]

Ladan *1. c.* 16 century BC. Son of Tahan of the tribe of Ephraim, he was the father of Ammihud. [1 Chr. 7:26]
2. see LIBNI 2.

Lael (Heb. 'of God') *c.* 13 century BC. A prominent Levite in the days of Moses, his son Eliasaph was leader of the family of Gershonites. [Num. 3:24]

Lahad date unknown. Son of Jahath of the tribe of Judah and a member of the family of Zorathites. [1 Chr. 4:2]

Lahmi (Heb. 'warrior') *c.* 10 century BC. Brother of Goliath, he was a Philistine warrior killed in battle by Elhanan, son of Jair. [1 Chr. 20:5]

Laish (Heb. 'lion') *c.* 10 century BC. Father of Palti to whom King Saul gave his daughter Michal in marriage, even though she was already David's wife. [1 Sam. 25:44; 2 Sam 3:15]

Lamech (Heb. 'strong') *1.* date unknown.

A descendant of Cain, his two wives Adah and Zillah bore him three sons and a daughter. He boasted to his wives of his vengeful killing of those who had injured him. [Gen. 4:18–24]

2. date unknown. Father of Noah and the son of Methuselah. [Gen. 5:25–31]

Lappidoth (Heb. 'torches') c. 12 century BC. Husband of Deborah the prophetess and judge. [Judg. 4:4]

Leah (Heb. 'gazelle') c. 18 century BC. Wife of Jacob. Leah and Rachel were the daughters of Laban who lived in the city of Nahor in Mesopotamia. 'Leah's eyes were weak, but Rachel was beautiful and lovely.' (Gen. 29:17) When Jacob, Laban's nephew, arrived in search of a wife, he fell in love with Rachel and worked seven years to earn her, but on the night of the wedding Laban substituted Leah and Jacob was forced to work another seven years for Rachel. Leah bore him six sons – Reuben, Simeon, Levi, Judah, Issachar and Zebulun, and a daughter Dinah. When Leah found she could not have any more children, she gave Jacob her maid Zilpah who had two sons, Gad and Asher. Leah was acknowledged as one of the matriarchs of Israel. She was buried in the family tomb in the Cave of Machpelah in Hebron, before Jacob went down to join his sons in Egypt. [Gen. 29:16–35; 30:16–24; 33:1–3; 46: 15, 18; 49:31; Ruth 4:11]

Lebana (Heb. 'white') c. 6 century BC. Head of a family who returned to Judah with Zerubbabel from exile in Babylon. [Ezra 2:45; Neh. 7:48]

Lebanah see LEBANA

Lecah c. 15 century BC. Son of Er and a descendant of Judah. [1 Chr. 4:21]

Lehabim (Heb. 'flames') date unknown. One of the eight sons of Egypt and a

grandson of Ham. [Gen. 10:13; 1 Chr. 1:11]

Lemuel (Heb. 'dedicated') date unknown. King of Maasa mentioned in the Book of Proverbs, who was taught by his mother that kings should not waste their energies pursuing women or taking strong drink but should 'judge righteously', and look after the poor and needy. [Prov. 31:1–9]

Letushim (Heb. 'hammered') c. 16 century BC. Son of Dedan and a great-grandson of Abraham and Keturah. [Gen. 25:3]

Leummim (Heb. 'nations') c. 16 century BC. Son of Dedan and a great-grandson of Abraham and Keturah. [Gen. 25:3]

Levi (Heb. 'joined') c. 16 century BC. Levi, born in Haran, in the fertile crescent, was the third son of Jacob by his wife Leah. Together with his brothers, he was involved in the events that led to the selling of their brother Joseph into slavery in Egypt.

When Jacob was living at Shalem, his daughter Dinah was seduced by Shechem, a local young man. The father came and asked for Dinah's hand in marriage for Shechem. Jacob and his sons, concealing their rage, agreed provided that Shechem, his father and all the men in his town were circumcised. This was done, but before the men could recover from the painful operation, Levi and his brother Simeon killed them all.

Later Levi was one of the ten sons sent by Jacob to buy corn in Egypt where Joseph had become a leading figure at Pharaoh's court.

When Jacob went to settle in Egypt with all his family, included were Levi and his three sons Gershon, Kohath and Merari.

On his deathbed Jacob blessed all his sons in turn but remembering the reprisal of Levi and Simeon over the seduction of their sister, he said: 'Cursed be their anger, for it is fierce; and their wrath, for it is cruel! I will divide them in Jacob and scatter them in Israel.' (Gen. 49:7)

The Levites were given no single territory after the conquest of Canaan under Joshua but were allocated forty-eight cities surrounded by pasture land. Six of these were to be cities of refuge – three in Canaan and three east of the river Jordan.

Levi's descendants through his son Kohath were Moses and Aaron who became the founder of the priestly line. His descendants through his sons Gershon and Merari became the Temple servants and were called Levites. [Gen. 29:34; 34:25–30; 35:23; 46:11; 49:5; Exod. 1:2; 6:16; Num. 3:17; 16:1; 26:59; 1 Chr. 2:1; 6:1–47; Ezra 8:18]

Libni (Heb. 'whiteness') *1.* date unknown. Son of Mahli and a grandson of Merari. One of his descendants, Asaiah, served in the Tabernacle in the reign of King David. [1 Chr. 6:29]
2. *c.* 10 century BC. A Levite descended from Gershon he was appointed by King David to minister in the Tabernacle. Also called Ladan. [Exod. 6:17; Num. 3:18; 1 Chr. 6:17, 20; 23:7; 26:21]

Likhi (Heb. 'learned') *c.* 13 century BC. One of the four sons of Shemida, a leader of the tribe of Manasseh. [1 Chr. 7:19]

Lo-ammi (Heb. 'not my people') *c.* 8 century BC. Second son of the prophet Hosea and his wife Gomer, the name is symbolic of God's rejection of his people Israel for their sins. [Hos. 1:9]

Lo-ruhamah (Heb. 'not pitied') *c.* 8 century BC. Daughter of the prophet Hosea and his wife Gomer, the name is symbolic of God's decision not to have mercy on Israel but to exile them for their sins. [Hos. 1:6]

Lot (Heb. 'a covering') *c.* 18–16 centuries BC. Nephew of Abraham.

Lot was the son of Abraham's deceased brother Haran, and migrated with him to Canaan. Abraham and Lot prospered, but strife broke out between their herdsmen over the limited grazing in the hill country of Canaan. It was agreed that Lot would move further east to the well-watered 'plain of Jordan'.

Lot made his home in Sodom, and was among the captives taken by four raiding kings from the north. Abraham organized a pursuit force and brought Lot back together with the other captives and the plunder.

One evening Lot invited two strangers to return home with him for the night, and protected them from a mob demanding their surrender. They disclosed to Lot that they were angels sent by the Lord to destroy the two evil cities of Sodom and Gomorrah, and they urged him to flee with his family. His sons-in-law did not take the story seriously, and refused to leave. At dawn, Lot, his wife and their two unmarried daughters set out for the small nearby town of Zoar. The Lord then destroyed the two cities with fire and brimstone. Though Lot's family were warned not to look back, his wife did so, and was turned into a pillar of salt. Lot and the two daughters later left Zoar for the mountains.

The daughters believed that no one else was left alive in the world, and in order to 'preserve the seed of our father' they plied Lot with wine and when he was too drunk to know what he was doing, they seduced him. As a result the first daughter gave birth to Moab, from whom the Moabites were descended; and the second daughter gave birth to Ben-ammi, the forefather of the Ammonites.

The story of Sodom and Gomorroh probably derives from an earthquake or volcanic convulsion that may have devastated the Dead Sea area about the time of the patriarchs. The physical setting for the story is spectacular. The steel-blue surface of the Dead Sea lies in a deep and desolate rift thirteen hundred feet below sea-level – the lowest inhabited spot on the earth. The shore is overlooked from the west by cliffs of salt and limestone, and local legend identifies one of the odd salt projections as Lot's wife. [Gen. 11:27; 13; 18; 19]

Lotan (Heb. 'hidden') date unknown. Eldest son of Seir the Horite, he was an Edomite leader. [Gen. 36:20; 22, 29; 1 Chr. 1:38, 39]

Lud date unknown. One of Shem's five sons and a grandson of Noah. [Gen. 10:22; 1 Chr. 1:17; Isa. 66:19; Ezek. 27:10]

Ludim date unknown. One of the eight sons of Egypt and a grandson of Ham. [Gen. 10:13]

M

Maacah *1. c.* 18 century BC. Son of Abraham's brother Nahor by his brother's concubine Reumah. [Gen. 22:24]

2. date unknown. Concubine of Caleb son of Hezron, she bore him five sons who were all leaders of Judah. [1 Chr. 2:48]

3. date unknown. Wife of Machir, the son of Manasseh. She is also called his sister. [1 Chr. 7:15, 16]

4. date unknown. Wife of Jeiel, one of the leaders of Benjamin living in Gibeon. [1 Chr. 8:29; 9:35]

5. see MAOCH

6. c. 10-century BC. Father of Hanan, a warrior in King David's army distinguished for his bravery. [1 Chr. 11:43]

7. c. 10 century BC. Father of Shephatiah who was ruler over the tribe of Simeon in the reign of King David. [1 Chr. 27:16]

8. c. 10 century BC. Wife of King David, she was the daughter of King Talmai of Geshur and the mother of Absalom. [2 Sam. 3:3; 1 Chr. 3:2]

9. c. 10 century BC. Mother of King Asa of Judah, whom he removed from her royal position because she worshipped the idol Asherah. [1 Kgs. 15:10, 13; 2 Chr. 15:16]

10. c. 10 century BC. Daughter of Abishalom, she was the favourite wife of King Rehoboam of Judah and mother of his successor Abijah. Also called Micaiah, where her father is given as Uriel. [1 Kgs. 15:2; 2 Chr. 11:20–22; 13:2]

Maadai (Heb. 'ornament') 5 century BC. A descendant of Bani who divorced his non-Jewish wife in the time of Ezra. [Ezra 10:34]

Maadiah (Heb. 'ornament') 6 century BC. A priest of Judah who returned with Zerubbabel from exile in Babylon. Also called Moadiah. [Neh. 12:5, 17]

Maai (Heb. 'merciful') 5 century BC. A Levite who played a musical instrument at the dedication of the rebuilt walls of Jerusalem in the time of Nehemiah. [Neh. 12:36]

Maasai (Heb. 'works of God') *c.* 6 century BC. Son of Adiel, he was one of the priests who returned to Judah from exile in Babylon and settled in Jerusalem. [1 Chr. 9:12]

Maaseiah (Heb. 'work of God') *1. c.* 10 century BC. A Levite who served as porter at the gates of the Tabernacle when King David brought the Ark of God to Jerusalem, and played musical instruments during the celebrations. [1 Chr. 15:18, 20]

2. c. 9 century BC. Son of Adaiah, Maaseiah was one of five army commanders of Judah who, under the instructions of the high priest Jehoiada, proclaimed Joash king of Judah and executed his grandmother Queen Athaliah who had usurped the throne. [2 Chr. 23:1–15]

3. c. 8 century BC. An officer of Uzziah, king of Judah, who supervised the organization of the king's army. [2 Chr. 26:11]

4. c. 8 century BC. Son of Ahaz, king of Judah, he was killed by Zichri of the tribe of Ephraim when the armies of Israel and Syria invaded Judah. [2 Chr. 28:7]

5. c. 7 century BC. The governor of Jerusalem in the reign of Josiah, king of Judah. [2 Chr. 34:8]

6. c. 6 century BC. Father of the priest Zephaniah, who was sent by King Zedekiah of Judah to the prophet Jeremiah to ask whether God would help him against Nebuchadnezzar, king of Babylon. [Jer. 21:1; 29:25; 37:3]

7. c. 6 century BC. Father of Zedekiah who was accused by Jeremiah of prophesying lies in the name of God. [Jer. 29:21]

8. c. 6 century BC. Son of Shallum, he was a doorkeeper at the entrance to the Temple in the time of Jeremiah. [Jer. 35:4]

9. 5 century BC. A descendant of Jeshua the priest, he divorced his non-Jewish wife in the time of Ezra. [Ezra 10:18]

10. 5 century BC. A descendant of Harim the priest, he divorced his non-Jewish wife in the time of Ezra. [Ezra 10:21]

11. 5 century BC. A descendant of Pashhur, he divorced his non-Jewish wife in the time of Ezra. [Ezra 10:22]

12. 5 century BC. A descendant of Pahath-moab, he divorced his non-Jewish wife in the time of Ezra. [Ezra 10:30]

13. c. 5 century BC. Father of Azariah who helped repair the walls of Jerusalem in the time of Nehemiah. [Neh. 3:23]

14. 5 century BC. One of the leaders of Judah who stood at Ezra's right hand when he read out the Law of Moses to the people in the market-place. [Neh. 8:4]

15. 5 century BC. One of the Levites sent by Ezra to explain the Law of Moses to the people of Judah after Ezra had read it aloud. [Neh. 8:7]

16. 5 century BC. One of the leaders of Judah who signed the solemn covenant in the time of Nehemiah. [Neh. 10:25]

17. c. 5 century BC. Son of Baruch, he was one of the first men of Judah to settle in Jerusalem after the return from exile in Babylon. [Neh. 11:5]

18. c. 5 century BC. Son of Ithiel, he was one of the first men of Benjamin to settle in Jerusalem after the return from exile in Babylon. [Neh. 11:7]

19. 5 century BC. A priest who blew a trumpet at the dedication of the rebuilt walls of Jerusalem in the time of Nehemiah. [Neh. 12:41]

20. 5 century BC. A priest who participated in the dedication of the rebuilt walls of Jerusalem in the time of Nehemiah. [Neh. 12:42]

Maaz (Heb. 'wrath') date unknown. A son of Ram and the grandson of Jerahmeel, he was a leader of the tribe of Judah. [1 Chr. 2:27]

Maaziah (Heb. 'God is a refuge') *1.* 10 century BC. A priest in Jerusalem responsible for the twenty-fourth and last turn of service in the Tabernacle in the reign of King David. [1 Chr. 24:18]

2. 5 century BC. A priest who signed the solemn covenant in the time of Nehemiah. [Neh. 10:8]

Machbannai *c.* 11 century BC. One of the eleven warriors of the tribe of Gad who left the army of King Saul and joined David at Ziklag. [1 Chr. 12:13]

Machbenah date unknown. Son of Sheva, a leader of the tribe of Judah. [1 Chr. 2:49]

Machi (Heb. 'decrease') *c.* 13 century BC. A leader of the tribe of Gad, his son Geuel was sent by Moses to spy out the Promised Land. [Num. 13:15]

Machir (Heb. 'sold') *1.* date unknown. Son of Manasseh and his Aramite concubine, he and his tribe seized the land of Gilead east of the river Jordan from the Amorites, and Moses confirmed their possession of this territory in the division of the Promised Land among the tribes of Israel. [Gen. 50:23; Num. 26:29; 27:1; 32:39, 40; 36:1; Deut. 3:15; Josh. 13:31; 17:1, 3; Judg. 5:14; 1 Chr. 2:21–23; 7:14–17]

2. *c.* 10 century BC. Son of Ammiel from Lo-debar in Gilead, with whom Mephibosheth, son of Jonathan, hid after David became king of Israel, fearing that as a grandson of King Saul he would be killed. Machir brought large quantities of food and equipment to the army of King David at Mahanaim east of the river Jordan, during Absalom's civil war against David. [2 Sam. 9:4; 17:27]

Machnadebai 5 century BC. A son of Bihnui who divorced his non-Jewish wife in the time of Ezra. [Ezra 10:40]

Madai date unknown. Son of Japheth and a grandson of Noah, he was traditionally regarded as the father of the Medes. [Gen. 10:2; 1 Chr. 1:5]

Magbish (Heb. 'gathering') date unknown. Ancestor of a large family that returned with Zerubbabel from exile in Babylon. [Ezra 2:30]

Magdiel (Heb. 'God's choice gift') date unknown. An Edomite chieftain descended from Esau. [Gen. 36:43; 1 Chr. 1:54]

Magog date unknown. Magog is mentioned as one of the seven sons of Japheth and a grandson of Noah. Magog was not clearly identified with any nation or territory, but vaguely came to represent a fierce warrior people (possibly the Scythians) that swept southwards to harass the populations of the fertile crescent. This no doubt inspired Ezekiel's vision of the millennium in which Israel was to be invaded by a horde of fierce warriors from the north led by Gog from the land of Magog.

Under the influence of the Book of Ezekiel, 'Gog and Magog' became symbolic names for the heathen who would unsuccessfully try to destroy the Lord's future kingdom. [Gen. 10:2; 1 Chr. 1:5; Ezek. 38:2; 39:6]

Magplash 5 century BC. A chief of Judah who signed the solemn covenant in the time of Nehemiah. [Neh. 10:20]

Mahalalel (Heb. 'God's praise') *1.* date unknown. Son of Kenan and a descendant of Seth. [Gen. 5:12–17; 1 Chr. 1:2]
2. date unknown. Ancestor of Athaiah, one of the first men of Judah to settle in Jerusalem after the return from exile in Babylon. [Neh. 11:4]

Mahalath (Heb. 'harp') *1. c.* 16 century BC. A wife of Esau, she was the daughter of Ishmael. Also called Basemath. [Gen. 28:9; 36:3]
2. *c.* 10 century BC. A wife of King Rehoboam of Judah, she was the daughter of Jerimoth and a granddaughter of King David. [2 Chr. 11:18]

Maharai (Heb. 'swift') *c.* 10 century BC. A distinguished warrior in the army of King David, he was an army commander in the tenth month of each year. [2 Sam. 23:28; 1 Chr. 11:30; 27:13]

Mahath *1.* date unknown. Son of Amasai of the tribe of Levi, he was the father of Elkanah. [1 Chr. 6:35]
2. *c.* 8 century BC. A Levite who supervised the bringing of tithes and offerings into the Temple in the reign of King Hezekiah. [2 Chr. 29:12; 31:13]

Mahazioth (Heb. 'visions') *c.* 10 century BC. Youngest son of King David's musician Heman, he and his brothers played musical instruments in the Tabernacle under their father's direction, and Mahazioth was responsible for the twenty-third turn of service. [1 Chr. 25:4, 30]

Maher-Shalal-Hash-Baz (Heb. 'the booty and the shame are imminent') *c.* 8 century BC. Symbolic name for the son of Isaiah, signifying the impending destruction of the kingdom of Israel. [Isa. 8:1, 3]

Mahlah *1. c.* 13 century BC. One of the

five daughters of Zelophehad who claimed a share of their father's estate from Moses since their father had no sons. [Josh. 17:3; Num. 26:33; 27:1; 36:11]

2. date unknown. Son of Hammolecheth who was the sister of Gilead, the leader of the tribe of Manasseh. [1 Chr. 7:18]

Mahali see MAHLI 1.

Mahli (Heb. 'sick') 1. date unknown. Elder son of Merari and a grandson of Levi, his descendants were assigned special duties in the Temple. Also called Mahali. [Exod. 6:19; Num. 3:20; 1 Chr. 6:19, 29; 23:21; 24:26, 28; Ezra 8:18]

2. date unknown. Son of Mushi and a prominent Levite whose descendants served in the Tabernacle in the reign of King David. Nephew of Mahli 1. [1 Chr. 6:47; 23:23; 24:30]

Mahlon (Heb. 'sickly') c. 11 century BC. Elder son of Elimelech and Naomi of the tribe of Judah, Mahlon and his brother Chilion left their home in Bethlehem during a famine in the days of the judges and settled in Moab. They married Moabite wives, Ruth and Orpah, but after ten years Mahlon and Chilion died, and Naomi returned to Bethlehem with her daughter-in-law Ruth. [Ruth 1:1–5; 4:9, 10]

Mahol (Heb. 'dance') date unknown. Father of Ethan, Heman, Calcol and Darda, all of whom were famed for their wisdom. [1 Kgs. 4:31]

Mahseiah (Heb. 'God is my refuge') c. 7 century BC. Grandfather of Baruch, Jeremiah's faithful scribe, and of Seraiah, King Zedekiah's quartermaster. [Jer. 32:12; 51:59]

Malachi (Heb. 'my messenger') c. middle of 5 century BC. Post-exilic Hebrew prophet. It is generally considered that Malachi is not a name, but a

Hebrew word meaning 'my messenger'. It is taken from the sentence in the text, 'Behold, I send my messenger to prepare the way before me'. (Mal. 3:1) This prophet appeared in Jerusalem about the middle of the 5th century BC, when the second Temple built in the time of Zerubbabel had already been in existence for some while, but Nehemiah had not yet carried out his religious reforms.

The book of Malachi indicates that the morale of the Jewish settlers in and around Jerusalem was at a low ebb at that time. There is mention of lean harvests, drought and locust swarms. The earlier hopes that an independent and flourishing Jewish commonwealth would follow the restoration of the Temple had not been realized. Judea remained a struggling and obscure corner of the Persian empire. The prophet complains about the religious slackness, the moral erosion, and the cynicism that prevailed in it.

The priests are taken to task for accepting blemished offerings contrary to the law, and treating the Lord with a disrespect they would not dream of showing to the local Persian governor: 'When you offer blind animals in sacrifice, is that no evil? And when you offer those those that are lame or sick, is that no evil? Present that to your governor; will he be pleased with you or show you favour?' (Mal. 1:8)

As for the people, they have sinned by divorcing the Jewish wives they married in their youth and taking foreign wives. They fail to bring their tithes and dues for the support of the Temple. When reproached, they openly doubt whether there is anything to gain by fidelity to the Lord and strict observance of his tenets.

The Lord has always kept his covenant with the Children of Israel, and set his face against their enemies, such as the Edomites to the south. His patience is now exhausted. A day of reckoning will soon come when the wrongdoers will be punished and only the faithful preserved. But the Lord is compassionate and will give to everyone a chance to repent. 'Behold, I will send you Elijah the prophet before the great and terrible day of the Lord comes. And he will turn the hearts of fathers to their children and the hearts of children to their fathers, lest I come and smite the land with a curse.' (Mal. 4:5, 6)

Malachi is the last work in the collection of the Twelve Minor Prophets, and therefore brings to an end the prophetical books of the Old Testament. [Book of Malachi]

Malcam (Heb. 'their king') *1. see* MOLECH.
2. date unknown. One of the four sons of Shaharaim and Hodesh of the tribe of Benjamin. [1 Chr. 8:9]

Malchiah (Heb. 'God is my king') *1. c.* 6 century BC. Owner of a dungeon in Jerusalem into which the leaders of Judah cast the prophet Jeremiah. [Jer. 38:6]
2. see MALCHIJAH *3.*

Malchiel (Heb. 'God is my king') date unknown. Younger son of Beriah and the grandson of Asher. Also described as the father of Birzaith. [Gen. 46:17; Num. 26:45; 1 Chr. 7:31]

Malchijah (Heb. 'God is king') *1.* date unknown. Son of Ethni, a Levite, he was the father of Baaseiah, and his descendant Asaph was one of the chief musicians of King David. [1 Chr. 6:40]
2. c. 10 century BC. A priest who took the fifth turn of service in the Tabernacle in the reign of King David. [1 Chr. 24:9]
3. c. 6 century BC. Father of Pashhur the priest, who was sent by King Zedekiah of Judah to consult the prophet Jeremiah and who later cast Jeremiah into a dungeon. His descendants were among the first men of Judah to return from exile in Babylon. Also called Malchiah.

[1 Chr. 9:12; Neh. 11:12; Jer. 21:1; 38:1]
4. 5 century BC. A descendant of Parosh who divorced his non-Jewish wife in the time of Ezra. [Ezra 10:25]
5. 5 century BC. Descendant of Harim, he divorced his non-Jewish wife, and helped repair part of the walls of Jerusalem in the time of Nehemiah, [Ezra 10:31; Neh. 3:11]
6. 5 century BC. Son of Rechab, he rebuilt the Dung Gate of Jerusalem in the time of Nehemiah. [Neh. 3:14]
7. 5 century BC. Son of a goldsmith, he helped repair the walls of Jerusalem in the days of Nehemiah. [Neh. 3:31]
8. 5 century BC. A leader who stood at the left hand of Ezra when he read from the Law of Moses to the people of Judah in the market-place. [Neh. 8:4]
9. 5 century BC. One of the priests who signed the solemn covenant in the time of Nehemiah. [Neh. 10:3]
10. 5 century BC. A priest who blew a trumpet during the service of dedication of the rebuilt walls of Jerusalem in the time of Nehemiah. [Neh. 12:42]

Malchiram (Heb. 'my king is exalted') 6 century BC. A son of Jehoiachin, the last king of Judah. [1 Chr. 3:18]

Malchishua (Heb. 'king of salvation') 11 century BC. Third son of King Saul and his wife Ahinoam, he was killed in battle by the Philistines with his brothers Jonathan and Abinadab. [1 Sam. 14:49; 31:2; 1 Chr. 8:33; 9:39; 10:2]

Mallothi (Heb. 'fullness') *c.* 10 century BC. One of the fourteen sons of Heman, King David's musician. He and his brothers played musical instruments under their father's direction and his sons took the nineteenth turn of service in the Tabernacle. [1 Chr. 25:4, 26]

Malluch (Heb. 'ruling') *1.* date unknown. A Levite descended from Merari, he was the father of Abdi and his descendant Ethan was a musician in the Tabernacle in the reign of King David. [1 Chr. 6:44]

2. 6 century BC. A priest of Judah who returned with Zerubbabel from exile in Babylon. Also known as Malluchi. [Neh. 12:2, 14]

3. 5 century BC. A descendant of Bani who divorced his non-Jewish wife in the time of Ezra. [Ezra 10:29]

4. 5 century BC. A descendant of Harim who divorced his non-Jewish wife in the time of Ezra. [Ezra 10:32]

5. 5 century BC. A priest who signed the solemn covenant in the time of Nehemiah. [Neh. 10:4]

6. 5 century BC. A leader of Judah who signed the solemn covenant in the time of Nehemiah. [Neh. 10:27]

Malluchi see MALLUCH 2.

Mamre (Heb. 'strength') c. 18 century BC. An Amorite leader who gave his name to the plain near Hebron where Abraham lived. [Gen. 14:13–24; 23:19]

Manahath date unknown. Second son of Shobal and a grandson of Seir the Horite, who had a city near Jerusalem named after him. [Gen. 36:23; 1 Chr. 1:40]

Manasseh (Heb. 'forgetting') 1. c. 16 century BC. Elder son of Joseph.

Manasseh, like his younger brother Ephraim, was born in Egypt where Joseph had married Asenath, the daughter of the Egyptian high priest of the temple at On.

When Jacob was old and ailing, Joseph brought Manasseh and Ephraim to his father's bedside to receive the patriarch's blessing. Jacob's sight was failing and when he placed his right hand on the head of the younger son Ephraim instead of on Manesseh, Joseph sought to correct him. Jacob then explained that Ephraim's descendants would be more important than those of

Manasseh. Jacob gave the same importance to these two grandchildren as he did to his sons, and they too became the founders of tribes.

In the conquest of Canaan under Joshua, the tribe of Manasseh was allocated a large area that stretched from the coastal plain across the central hill area round Shechem (Nablus) to the Jordan valley, with one sub-tribe east of the Jordan.

In the blessing of Moses, Joseph is promised great abundance and power, and it is added that 'such are the thousands of Manasseh' (Deut. 33:17). [Gen. 41:51; 48:1–20; 50:23; Num. 26:28, 29–34; 32:39–41; 36:1; Deut. 3:13; 33:17; Josh. 13:31; 17:1–3; 1 Kgs. 4:13; 1 Chr. 7:14–17]

2. Fourteenth ruler of Judah after the monarchy split, he reigned 687–42 BC.

The son of King Hezekiah of Judah and his wife Hephzibah. He was twelve years old when he came to the throne and reigned for forty-five years. A reaction against Hezekiah's religious reforms set in under Manasseh, for which he is denounced in the Bible. Heathen cults were restored and pagan altars and images were introduced even into the Temple. The indignant prophets cried that the Lord 'will wipe Jerusalem as one wipes a dish, wiping it and turning it upside down.' (2 Kgs. 21:13) The account in Chronicles states that Manasseh was carried off in chains to Babylon. He then repented of his sins and was restored to Judah where he purified the Temple and strengthened the walls. A more prosaic explanation is given in Assyrian records, which include Manasseh in a group of vassal kings summoned to Nineveh, apparently in order to extract more tribute from them. He was succeeded by his son Amon. [2 Kgs. 20; 21; 23; 24:3; 1 Chr. 3:13; 2 Chr. 32:33; 33:1–23; Jer. 15:4]

3. 5 century BC. A descendant of Pahath-moab who divorced his non-Jewish wife in the time of Ezra. [Ezra 10:30]

4. 5 century BC. A descendant of Hashum who divorced his non-Jewish wife in the time of Ezra. [Ezra 10:33]

Manoah (Heb. 'rest') *c.* 12 century BC. Father of Samson whose birth was foretold by an angel. [Judg. 13:2–24]

Maoch *c.* 10 century BC. Father of Achish, king of Gath, to whom David fled with all his family when pursued by King Saul. Also called Maacah. [1 Sam. 27:2; 1 Kgs. 2:39]

Maon (Heb. 'dwelling') date unknown. Son of Shammai and the father of Bethzur, he was a leader of the tribe of Judah. [1 Chr. 2:45]

Mara *see* NAOMI

Mareshah (Heb. 'hill-top') *1.* date unknown. Son of Caleb of the tribe of Judah and a nephew of Jerahmeel. [1 Chr. 2:42]
2. date unknown. Son of Laadah and a leader of the tribe of Judah. [1 Chr. 4:21]

Marsena 5 century BC. One of the seven princes of Persia and Media who sat at the table of King Ahasuerus. [Esther 1:14]

Mash date unknown. One of the four sons of Aram and a grandson of Shem. [Gen. 10:23]

Massa *c.* 17 century BC. Son of Abraham's son Ishmael, he was a leader of a desert clan. [Gen. 25:14; 1 Chr. 1:30]

Matred date unknown. Mother of Mehetabel, the wife of Hadar, king of Edom. [Gen. 36:39; 1 Chr. 1:50]

Matri (Heb. 'rain') date unknown. Head of a family of Benjaminites, he was an ancestor of King Saul. [1 Sam. 10:21]

Mattan (Heb. 'gift') *1. c.* 9 century BC. The priest of the idol Baal in Jerusalem appointed by Athaliah, queen of Judah. When the high priest Jehoiada successfully organized the overthrow and execution of Queen Athaliah, the people of Judah destroyed the temple of Baal and slew Mattan in front of the altars to Baal. [2 Kgs. 11:18; 2 Chr. 23:17]
2. c. 6 century BC. Father of Shephatiah who cast the prophet Jeremiah into prison for prophesying that Jerusalem would fall into the hands of the Babylonians. [Jer. 38:1]

Mattaniah (Heb. 'God's gift') *1. c.* 10 century BC. A son of Heman, one of King David's musicians. He and his brothers sang and played musical instruments under their father's direction, and he was appointed to the ninth turn of service in the Tabernacle. [1 Chr. 25:4, 16]
2. c. 8 century BC. A Levite descended from Asaph who cleansed and sanctified the Temple at the command of Hezekiah, king of Judah. [2 Chr. 29:13]
3. see ZEDEKIAH *3.*
4. date unknown. Son of Mica and a descendant of Asaph, one of King David's chief musicians, he was a Levite who settled in Jerusalem following the return from exile in Babylon. He was the ancestor of Jahaziel, son of Zechariah, who prophesied that Jehoshaphat, king of Judah, would defeat the armies of Moab, Ammon and Mount Seir without having to do battle. [1 Chr. 9:15; 2 Chr. 20:14; Neh. 11:17, 22; 12:8]
5. 5 century BC. Son of Elam who divorced his non-Jewish wife in the time of Ezra. [Ezra 10:26]
6. 5 century BC. Son of Zattu who divorced his non-Jewish wife in the time of Ezra. [Ezra 10:27]
7. 5 century BC. A descendant of Pahath-moab who divorced his non-Jewish wife in the time of Ezra. [Ezra 10:30]
8. 5 century BC. A descendant of Bani

who divorced his non-Jewish wife in the time of Ezra. [Ezra 10:37]

9. 5 century BC. A Levite who was a gatekeeper of the Temple in Jerusalem when Joiakim was high priest in the time of Nehemiah. [Neh. 12:25]

10. 5 century BC. Son of Micaiah of the tribe of Levi and a descendant of Asaph, King David's musician, he was the father of Shemaiah and his descendant Zechariah blew a trumpet at the dedication service for the rebuilt walls of Jerusalem. [Neh. 12:35]

11. 5 century BC. A leader of the tribe of Levi, his grandson Hanan administered the treasuries of Judah in the time of Nehemiah. [Neh. 13:13]

Mattattah *c.* 5 century BC. A descendant of Hashum who divorced his non-Jewish wife in the time of Ezra. [Ezra 10:33]

Mattenai (Heb. 'gift of God') *1.* 5 century BC. Descended from the family of Hashum, he divorced his non-Jewish wife in the time of Ezra. [Ezra 10:33]

2. 5 century BC. A descendant of Bani, he divorced his non-Jewish wife in the time of Ezra. [Ezra 10:37]

3. 5 century BC. Head of a priestly family of Judah descended from the priest Joiarib, he served during the period that Joiakim was high priest in the time of Nehemiah. [Neh. 12:19]

Mattithiah (Heb. 'gift of God') *1. c.* 10 century BC. A Levite who served as a gatekeeper of the Tabernacle in the reign of King David and played the harp in the festivities when the Ark was brought to Jerusalem. [1 Chr. 15:18, 21; 16:5]

2. c. 10 century BC. Son of Jeduthun, a musician of King David, Mattithiah and his brothers, under their father's direction, played the harp in the thanksgiving services, and took the fourteenth turn of service in the Tabernacle. [1 Chr. 25:3, 21]

3. 6 century BC. Eldest son of Shallum, a

Levite descended from Kohath, in the time of Zerubbabel, he was responsible for the baking of flat cakes which were among the food offerings prepared for the Temple. [1 Chr. 9:31]

4. 5 century BC. A descendant of Nebo who divorced his non-Jewish wife in the time of Ezra. [Ezra 10:43]

5. 5 century BC. A leader of Judah who stood at the right hand of Ezra when he read the Law of Moses to the people in the market-place. [Neh. 8:4]

Mebunnai *see* SIBBECAI

Medad (Heb. 'measure') *c.* 13 century BC. A leader of Israel, he began to prophesy in the wilderness and Joshua asked Moses to stop him; whereupon Moses replied that he wished all Israel were prophets. [Num. 11:26, 27]

Medan (Heb. 'strife') *c.* 17 century BC. Son of Abraham by his wife Keturah, he was a leader of a desert tribe. [Gen. 25:2; 1 Chr. 1:32]

Mehetabel (Heb. 'God does good') *1.* date unknown. Daughter of Matred who became the wife of Hadar (Hadad) king of Edom. [Gen. 36:39; 1 Chr. 1:50]

2. 5 century BC. Father of Shemaiah who was a false prophet in the time of Nehemiah. [Neh. 6:10]

Mehida 6 century BC. Head of a family of Temple servants who returned with Zerubbabel to Judah from exile in Babylon. [Ezra 2:52; Neh. 7:54]

Mehir (Heb. 'price') date unknown. Son of Chelub, a leader of the tribe of Judah, he was the father of Eshton. [1 Chr. 4:11]

Mehujael (Heb. 'smitten') date unknown. Son of Irad he was a descendant of Cain, and the father of Methuselah. [Gen. 4:18]

Mehuman (Pers. 'true') 5 century BC.

One of the seven chamberlains of King Ahasuerus who was commanded by the drunken king on the seventh day of a feast to bring Queen Vashti before his guests to show off her beauty. [Esther 1:10]

Melatiah (Heb. 'saved') 5 century BC. One of the Gibeonites who helped repair the walls of Jerusalem in the time of Nehemiah. [Neh. 3:7]

Melchizedek (Heb. 'king of righteousness') c. 18 century BC. King of Salem. When Abraham returned from rescuing his nephew Lot from the four kings who had carried him off, Melchizedek welcomed them with bread and wine. Abraham gave him a tenth of the spoil.

Scholars think that Salem might well have been Jerusalem, which is called Salem in Psalm 76:2 and in the 14th century BC Tel el-Amarna tablets is called Uru-salim.

In Psalm 110:4 Melchizedek is a symbol of an ideal priest-king. [Gen. 14:18–28; Ps. 110:4]

Melech (Heb. 'king') date unknown. Son of Micah of the tribe of Benjamin and a descendant of Jonathan, the son of King Saul. [1 Chr. 8:35; 9:41]

Memucan (Pers. 'dignified') c. 5 century BC. One of the seven princes of Persia and Media who sat at the table of King Ahasuerus, and who advised the king to replace Queen Vashti by another. The advice was accepted. [Esther 1:14; 16, 21]

Menahem (Heb. 'comforter') Sixteenth king of Israel after the monarchy split. He reigned 743–38 BC. Menahem, son of Gadi, possibly the governor of the former capital Tirzah, marched to Samaria, deposed and slew the usurper Shallum and seized power himself. Resistance to his authority from several towns in the area was brutally suppressed.

Menahem preserved Israel from being overrun by the Assyrian forces only by agreeing to paying Tiglath-pileser a huge tribute of one thousand talents of silver. He raised this sum by a levy of fifty shekels of silver from every man of property in the kingdom. The Assyrian inscription which relates the campaigns of Tiglath-pileser refers to Menahem of Samaria among those rulers from whom tribute was collected. A number of ostraca found in the ruins of Samaria dealing with the collection of oil and wine in the kingdom may relate to this tribute.

Menahem was succeeded by his son Pekahiah. [2 Kgs. 15:14–22]

Meonothai (Heb. 'my dwellings') c. 12 century BC. A leader of the tribe of Judah and a son of Othniel, he was the father of Ophrah. [1 Chr. 4:14]

Mephibosheth (Heb. 'contender against shame') *1. c.* 10 century BC. Son of Jonathan, he was five years old when his father and grandfather Saul were killed on Mount Gilboa. Fleeing with the rest of the Israelites, Mephibosheth fell and was crippled in both feet.

When David was proclaimed king he sent for Ziba, a servant of Saul, and asked him if any of Saul's family was left. Ziba told him about Jonathan's crippled son and David, instead of having him killed as was the practice, not only spared his life but gave him all of Saul's personal possessions and moved him into the royal palace. The lame Mephibosheth, overcome by David's generosity, bowed down in front of him and said humbly, 'What is your servant, that you should look upon a dead dog such as I?' (2 Sam. 9:8) David appointed Ziba and all his family the servants of Mephibosheth and the boy was brought up with David's own sons.

After the revolt of Absalom, David was forced to flee from Jerusalem and while leaving the city was met by Ziba who brought him two asses laden with provisions for his journey. When David asked Ziba about his master, Ziba suggested indirectly that Mephibosheth had stayed behind because he was siding with Absalom. David was saddened by this desertion but later when he returned to Jerusalem after the defeat of Absalom, Mephibosheth met him with happiness at his safe return. David asked him why he had not fled and he explained that Ziba had maligned him, that he had mourned the king's departure but was now overjoyed at his return. David forgave him but divided Saul's property between Mephibosheth and Ziba in payment for the servant's loyalty to the king. Also called Meribbaal. [2 Sam. 4:4; 9:6–13; 16:1–4; 19:24–30; 21:7;1 Chr. 8:34, 9:40]

2. *c.* 10 century BC. A son of King Saul by his concubine Rizpah, he was one of seven descendants of King Saul who were handed over to the Gibeonites by King David to be hanged as revenge for Saul's slaying of many of the Gibeonites. [2 Sam. 21:8]

Merab (Heb. 'increasing') 11 century BC. Eldest daughter of King Saul and his wife Ahinoam, she was promised to the man who killed Goliath the Philistine. When David came to claim her he found Saul had given her to Adriel and he was given her sister Michal. Later when David became king, he handed over Merab's five sons to the Gibeonites to be killed in expiation of Saul's crimes against them, and in the belief that the current famine would cease. [1 Sam. 14:49; 18:17–19]

Meraiah (Heb. 'rebellion') 5 century BC. Head of a priestly family in Judah when Joiakim was high priest in the time of Nehemiah. [Neh. 12:12]

Meraioth (Heb. 'rebellious') *1.* date unknown. Son of Zerahiah of the tribe of Levi and the father of Amariah, he was

an ancestor of Ezra the scribe. [1 Chr. 6:6, 7, 52; Ezra 7:3]

2. date unknown. Father of Zadok and son of Ahitub, a priest in the Temple, he was an ancestor of Azariah, a priest who settled in Jerusalem in the time of Ezra. [1 Chr. 9:11; Neh. 11:11]

3. *see* MEREMOTH 2.

Merari (Heb. 'bitter') *c.* 16 century BC. A son of Levi, he accompanied his grandfather Jacob when he went down to Egypt. His sons Mahli and Mushi and their families joined Moses in the Exodus, and their descendants became priests in the Temple in Jerusalem. [Gen. 46:11; Exod. 6:16–19; Num. 3:17–36; 4:29–45; 7:8; 10:17; 26:57; Josh. 21:7–40; 1 Chr. 6:1–77; 9:14; 15:6, 17; 23:6, 21; 24:26, 27; 26:10, 19; 2 Chr. 29:12; 34:12; Ezra 8:19]

Mered (Heb. 'revolt') date unknown. Son of Ezrah of the tribe of Judah, he was a descendant of Caleb, son of Jephunneh. [1 Chr. 4:17]

Meremoth (Heb. 'heights') *1.* 5 century BC. Son of Uriah, he was a priest who returned after the exile, and counted and weighed the gold and precious vessels in the Temple which had been brought back from Babylon; he helped repair the walls of Jerusalem. [Ezra 8:33; Neh. 3:4, 21]

2. 6 century BC. A priest who returned with Zerubbabel to Judah from exile in Babylon, he was related to Helkai, the head of a priestly family when Joiakim was high priest in the time of Nehemiah. Also called Meraioth. [Neh. 12:3, 15]

3. 5 century BC. A descendant of Bani who divorced his non-Jewish wife in the time of Ezra. [Ezra 10:36]

4. 5 century BC. A priest who signed the covenant to observe the Commandments of God in the time of Nehemiah. [Neh. 10:5]

Meres (Pers. 'lofty') *c.* 5 century BC.

One of the seven princes of Persia and Media who sat at the table of King Ahasuerus. [Esther 1:14]

Meribbaal *see* MEPHIBOSHETH *1.*

Merodach *see* BAAL

Merodach-baladan (Ass. 'Merodach [a god] has given a son') *c.* 8 century BC. King of Babylonia, he sent a present to the ailing king Hezekiah of Judah. The king showed the messenger the treasures of the Temple and palace, at which Isaiah the prophet grimly predicted that all these treasures would be despoiled by the Babylonians.

Merodach-baladan was defeated by Sargon the Great of Assyria, made a brief comeback, and was driven out by Sennacherib. [2 Kgs. 20:12; Isa. 39:1]

Mesha (Heb. 'freed') *1.* date unknown. Son of Shaharaim and his wife Hodesh, he was a leader of the tribe of Benjamin. [1 Chr. 8:9]
2. c. 9 century BC. King of Moab, the kingdom on the plateau east of the Dead Sea. In the reign of King Omri of Judah and most of the reign of his son Ahab, Moab was a vassal state of Judah. The tribute she paid was in sheep and wool, since Moab was grazing country.

Mesha carried out a successful revolt, as he relates on the black basalt stele (inscribed monument) that was discovered in southern Jordan a century ago.

Later, King Jehoram of Israel and King Jehoshaphat of Judah invaded Moab from the south and devastated the country. Besieged in his last stronghold, Mesha in desperation sacrificed his son to the Moabite god Chemosh. This drastic act seemed to turn the tide, for the Israelite forces retreated. [2 Kgs. 1:1; 3:4, 5, 27]

Meshach (Pers. 'who is unto Aku, the moon-god') *c.* 6 century BC. The Babylonian name given to Mishael, one of the four young princes of Judah taken off to Babylon by the orders of King Nebuchadnezzar. When the four refused to worship or serve the Babylonian gods, Nebuchadnezzar, in great rage, ordered them cast into the fiery furnace. They were delivered by an angel and walked out unhurt. [Dan. 1–3]

Meshech (Heb. 'drawn out') *1.* date unknown. Son of Japheth and a grandson of Noah, his descendants were a tribe of warriors. [Gen. 10:2; 1 Chr. 1:5; Ezek. 27:13; 32:26; 38:2; 39:1]
2. date unknown. Son of Shem, he was a grandson of Noah. [1 Chr. 1:17]

Meshelemiah *see* SHALLUM *4.*

Meshezabel (Heb. 'God saves') *1.* 5 century BC. Father of Berechiah and the grandfather of Meshullam, he helped repair the walls of Jerusalem in the time of Nehemiah. [Neh. 3:4]
2. 5 century BC. A leader of Judah who signed the solemn covenant in the time of Nehemiah. [Neh. 10:21]
3. 5 century BC. A leader of Judah in the time of Nehemiah, he was the father of Pethahiah, adviser to the Persian king. [Neh. 11:24]

Meshillemith (Heb. 'repaid') date unknown. Son of Immer, and the father of Meshullam and Ahazai, one of his descendants was Maasai who settled in Jerusalem after the return from exile in Babylon. Also called Meshillemoth. [1 Chr. 9:12; Neh. 11:13]

Meshillemoth (Heb. 'repaid') *1. c.* 8 century BC. Father of Berechiah of the tribe of Ephraim, a leader of the kingdom of Israel, who called upon his men to release the prisoners of Judah whom they had captured in the war between King Pekah of Israel and Ahaz, king of Judah. [2 Chr. 28:12]
2. see MESHILLEMITH

Meshobab 8 century BC. A leader of

the tribe of Simeon in the days of Hezekiah, king of Judah, who drove out the inhabitants of the rich valley of Gedor and settled there. [1 Chr. 4:34]

Meshullam (Heb. 'rewarded') *1.* date unknown. A chief of the tribe of Gad in the lands of Gilead and Basham east of the river Jordan. [1 Chr. 5:13]
2. date unknown. Son of Elpaal, a leader of the tribe of Benjamin living in Jerusalem. [1 Chr. 8:17]
3. c. 7 century BC. Grandfather of Shaphan, a scribe who was sent by Josiah, king of Judah, to tell the high priest Hilkiah to hand over the silver collected for the repair of the Temple to the workmen. [2 Kgs. 22:3]
4. c. 7 century BC. A Levite descended from Kohath, he was a supervisor of the work of repairing the Temple in the reign of Josiah, king of Judah. [2 Chr. 34:12]
5. date unknown. Son of Zadok, the priest, he was the father of Hilkiah and the grandfather of Azariah, head of a priestly family who returned from exile in Babylon and settled in Jerusalem. [1 Chr. 9:11; Neh. 11:11]
6. date unknown. Son of Meshillemith the priest, he was an ancestor of Maasai, a priest who settled in Jerusalem after the return from Babylon. [1 Chr. 9:12]
7. 6 century BC. Son of Zerubbabel who led the return to Judah from exile in Babylon. [1 Chr. 3:19]
8. 5 century BC. Father of Sallu, he was a Benjaminite who settled in Jerusalem after the return from Babylon. [1 Chr. 9:7; Neh. 11:7]
9. 5 century BC. Son of Shephathiah, he was a prominent Benjaminite who settled in Jerusalem after the return from Babylon. [1 Chr. 9:8]
10. 5 century BC. A leader of Judah in exile in Babylon, he was sent by Ezra to Iddo, ruler of Casiphia, to bring priests and Levites to Jerusalem to serve in the Temple. [Ezra 8:16]
11. 5 century BC. A leader of Judah who

was present when Ezra called upon the people of Judah to divorce their non-Jewish wives. [Ezra 10:15]
12. 5 century BC. A descendant of Bani who divorced his non-Jewish wife in the time of Ezra. [Ezra 10:29]
13. 5 century BC. Son of Berechiah and the grandson of Meshezabel, he was a leader of Judah who helped repair the walls of Jerusalem in the time of Nehemiah. His daughter married Jehohanan, the son of Tobiah, and although Tobiah was against the work of rebuilding Jerusalem, he gained many supporters among the leaders of Judah because of his relationship with Meshullam. [Neh. 3:4, 30; 6:18]
14. 5 century BC. Son of Besodeiah, he helped repair the Old Gate as part of the work of rebuilding the walls of Jerusalem in the time of Nehemiah. [Neh. 3:6]
15. c. 5 century BC. A leader who stood at the left hand of Ezra when he read out the Law of Moses to the people of Judah in the market-place. [Neh. 8:4]
16. 5 century BC. A priest of Judah who signed the solemn covenant in the time of Nehemiah. [Neh. 10:7]
17. 5 century BC. A leader of Judah who signed the solemn covenant in the time of Nehemiah. [Neh. 10:20]
18. 5 century BC. Head of a priestly family when Joiakim was high priest in the time of Nehemiah. [Neh. 12:13]
19. 5 century BC. Head of a priestly family descended from Ginnethon when Joiakim was high priest in the time of Nehemiah. [Neh. 12:16]
20. 5 century BC. A Levite who was a porter at the gates of the Temple when Joiakim was high priest in Jerusalem in the time of Nehemiah. [Neh. 12:25]
21. 5 century BC. A leader of Judah who took part in the dedication of the rebuilt walls of Jerusalem in the time of Nehemiah. [Neh. 12:33]

Meshullemeth (Heb. 'rewarded') *c.* 7 century BC. Wife of Manasseh, king of

Judah, and the mother of Amon who inherited the throne. She was the daughter of Haruz of Jotbah. [2 Kgs. 21:19]

Methuselah (Heb. 'man of the javelin') date unknown. Methuselah was the son of Mehujael and, according to the Old Testament, lived to the ripe old age of nine hundred and sixty-nine years. He is thus the oldest person in the Bible, and the proverbial symbol of longevity. At the age of one hundred and eighty-seven, he had his first son, Lamech, who was the father of Noah. Methuselah had many other children. Also called Methushael. [Gen. 4:18; 5:21–7; 1 Chr. 1:3]

Methushael *see* METHUSELAH

Meunim (Heb. 'dwelling') *c.* 10 century BC. A Temple servant whose descendants returned with Zerubbabel from exile in Babylon. [Ezra 2:50; Neh. 7:52]

Mezahab (Heb. 'gilded') date unknown. Grandfather of Mehetabel, the wife of King Hadar of Edom. [Gen. 36:39; 1 Chr. 1:50]

Mibhar (Heb. 'chosen') *c.* 10 century BC. Son of Hagri, he was a warrior in the armies of King David distinguished for his bravery. [1 Chr. 11:38]

Mibsam (Heb. 'perfumed') *1. c.* 17 century BC. Son of Abraham's son Ishmael, he was a leader of a desert tribe. [Gen. 25:13; 1 Chr. 1:29]
2. c. 16 century BC. Son of Simeon, he was a grandson of Jacob. [1 Chr. 4:25]

Mibzar (Heb. 'fort') date unknown. An Edomite leader, he was descended from Esau. [Gen. 36:42; 1 Chr. 1:53]

Mica (Heb. 'who is like God?') *1. c.* 10 century BC. Son of Mephibosheth, he was a grandson of Jonathan. Also called Micah. [2 Sam. 9:12; 1 Chr. 8:34]
2. c. 10 century BC. Son of Zabdi and

grandson of Asaph, he was a Levite who lived in Judah. [1 Chr. 9:15; Neh. 11:17, 22]
3. 5 century BC. A Levite who signed the solemn covenant in the time of Nehemiah. [Neh. 10:11]

Micah (Heb. 'who is like God?') *1. c.* 12 century BC. He was a man who lived in the hill country of Ephraim and stole eleven hundred pieces of silver from his mother. When she cursed the thief, Micah gave her back the money. She blessed him and consecrated the money to the Lord, but gave two hundred pieces to a silver-smith with which to make a graven image. Micah set up an altar to the idol and installed one of his sons as the priest, until a wandering Levite from Bethlehem arrived at the house and Micah took him in as priest in place of his son.

At that time the tribe of Dan was dissatisfied with their inheritance and sent out five men to search for a better place. They came to Micah's house and recognizing the Levite, asked him whether their expedition would be successful and he assured them that it would.

Later when six hundred men of Dan set out to conquer Laish in the extreme north of the country, they stopped at Micah's house and took away the idol and the Levite who served it. Micah and some of his neighbours chased after them but the Danites threatened them and they returned home. The men of Dan took Laish, changed the name of the city to Dan and set up Micah's graven image for themselves. [Judg. 17, 18]
2. date unknown. Son of Shimei, he was a leader of the tribe of Reuben who lived east of the river Jordan in the land of Gilead. [1 Chr. 5:5]
3. c. 10 century BC. A descendant of Uzziel, he was a leader of the tribe of Levi who ministered in the Tabernacle in the reign of King David. [1 Chr. 23:20; 24:24, 25]

4. see MICA 1.

5. *c.* 8 century BC. Hebrew prophet of the kingdom of Judah. Micah prophesied in Judah in the first half of the 8th century BC during the reigns of Jotham, Ahaz and Hezekiah. He was therefore a contemporary of Isaiah in Jerusalem, and came a little after the prophets Amos and Hosea in the northern kingdom of Israel.

Micah came from the small country town of Moresheth in the fertile foothills of the Shefelah, which faced across the coastal plain towards the Mediterranean. At its back rose the Judean hills, in which Jerusalem lay a day's journey away. The place is marked on the Madeba mosaic floormap of the 6th century AD with the words 'Moresheth, from which came Micah, the prophet'.

Like Amos, another village son, Micah uses rural imagery, such as the sheaves brought to the threshing floor and the jackals howling at night. He detests the capital cities of Samaria and Jerusalem, which symbolize for him the luxury and graft that have corrupted the body of the nation and aroused God's anger.

He says of Jerusalem, 'your rich men are full of violence; your inhabitants speak lies, and their tongue is deceitful in their mouth.' (Mic. 6:12) In stinging terms he foretells the city's destruction: 'Therefore because of you Zion shall be ploughed as a field; Jerusalem shall become a heap of ruins.' (Mic. 3:12) As for the northern hill capital of Samaria, with its idols and sacred prostitutes, 'I will pour down her stones into the valley, and uncover her foundations. All her images shall be beaten to pieces.' (Mic. 1:6, 7)

Micah is a prophet of social protest, the spokesman of poor and simple men exploited by the upper classes. He denounced the greedy and hypocritical Establishment – 'Its heads give judgment for a bribe, its priests teach for hire, its prophets divine for money: yet they lean upon the Lord and say, "Is not the Lord in the midst of us? No evil shall come upon us."' (Mic. 3:11) He rails against the swindling merchants with their false scales and weights, and against the landowners who 'covet fields, and seize them' (Mic. 2:2).

Like other prophets, Micah believes that true faith comes from the heart, and not from formal sacrifices. 'Will the Lord be pleased with thousands of rams, with ten thousands of rivers of oil? ... what does the Lord require of you but to do justice, and to love kindness, and to walk humbly with your God?' (Mic. 6:7, 8)

Micah looks forward from the sinful and troubled present to the future Messianic kingdom, where the remnant of Israel will be gathered together and live in peace, where every man will sit under his vine and his fig tree: 'For out of Zion shall go forth the law, and the word of the Lord from Jerusalem.' (Mic. 4:2) (This phrase also appears in Isaiah 2:3.) [Isa. 2:3; Jer. 26:18; Book of Micah]

6. *c.* 7 century BC. Father of Abdon who was a leader of Judah sent by King Josiah to the prophetess Huldah to find out what would happen to the people of Judah. Also called Micaiah. [2 Kgs. 22:12; 2 Chr. 34:20]

Micaiah (Heb. 'who is like God?') **1.** see MAACAH 10.

2. *c.* 9 century BC. A Hebrew prophet in the time of Ahab. Micaiah was one of the many professional prophets or holy men who frequented Samaria, the capital of the kingdom of Israel.

Jehoshaphat king of Judah joined forces with Ahab king of Israel to retake the Israelite town of Ramoth–gilead in the land of Gilead, east of the Jordan river. The two monarchs sat on thrones at the entrance to Samaria while a large group of prophets appeared before them and assured them of success in the coming battle. The pious Jehoshaphat was not satisfied and asked if there were not another prophet they might ask. Grudgingly Ahab admitted that 'There is yet one man by whom we may enquire of the Lord, Micaiah, the son of Imlah; but I hate him, for he never prophesies good concerning me, but evil.' (1 Kgs. 22:8)

Micaiah was sent for and at first joined sarcastically in the chorus of encouragement. But when pressed by Ahab he courageously foretold defeat and the death of the king. The leader of the other prophets hit Micaiah in the face and the angry Ahab ordered the blunt-spoken pessimist to be flung into jail and kept on bread and water until his own safe return from the battle. Micaiah's prophecy of disaster came true, but it is not recorded what became of the prophet. [1 Kgs. 22]

3. c. 9 century BC. A leader of Judah whom King Jehoshaphat sent out to teach the Law of God to the people. [2 Chr. 17:7]

4. c. 7 century BC. Son of Gemariah, a leader of Judah in the reign of King Jehoiakim, he heard the prophecies of Jeremiah from his scribe Baruch and had them reread to all the leaders. [Jer. 36:11, 13]

5. date unknown. Son of Zaccur the priest, one of his descendants, Zechariah, son of Jonathan, blew a trumpet at the dedication of the walls of Jerusalem in the time of Nehemiah. [Neh. 12:35]

6. see MICAH *6.*

7. 5 century BC. A Levite priest who took part in the ceremony for the dedication of the rebuilt walls of Jerusalem in the time of Nehemiah. [Neh. 12:41]

Michael (Heb. 'who is like God?') *1. c.* 13 century BC. A leader of the tribe of Asher, his son Sethur was one of the twelve men sent by Moses to spy out the Promised Land. [Num. 13:13]

2. date unknown. A leader of the tribe of Gad who settled in Bashan east of the river Jordan. [1 Chr. 5:13]

3. date unknown. Son of Jeshishai, he was a leader of the tribe of Gad who lived in Gilead east of the river Jordan. [1 Chr. 5:14]

4. date unknown. Son of Baaseiah of the tribe of Levi and the father of Shimea, he was an ancestor of Asaph, King David's musician. [1 Chr. 6:40]

5. date unknown. Son of Izrahiah, he and his brothers were leaders of the tribe of Issachar and mighty warriors. [1 Chr. 7:3]

6. date unknown. Son of Beriah, he was a leader of the tribe of Benjamin living in Jerusalem. [1 Chr. 8:16]

7. c. 11 century BC. One of the six captains of thousands of the tribe of Manasseh who joined the army of David at Ziklag, he became a commander of his army. [1 Chr. 12:20]

8. c. 10 century BC. Father of Omri who was made ruler of the tribe of Issachar in the reign of King David. [1 Chr. 27:18]

9. c. 9 century BC. Son of Jehoshaphat, king of Judah, he was killed by his brother Jehoram who inherited the kingdom. [2 Chr. 21:2]

10. 5 century BC. A descendant of Sephatiah, his son Zebadiah returned to Judah from Babylon. [Ezra 8:8]

11. By tradition, one of the four great archangels, he was the special protector of the Hebrews. Though angels appear many times in the Old Testament as messengers of the Lord, it is only after the exilic period and the Babylonian influence that they are referred to by name. In Daniel's last vision the angel about whom he is told is referred to as 'Michael, the great prince who has charge of your people.' (Dan. 12:1) [Dan. 10:13, 21, 12:1]

Michal (Heb. 'who is like God?') *c.* 11 century BC. Younger daughter of King Saul, Michal fell in love with David, and Saul had to agree to the match when David performed the set task of killing two hundred Philistines.

When Saul tried to kill David, he fled to his house, and Michal helped him escape his pursuers by lowering him out of a window at night. Michal then 'took an image and laid it on the bed and put a pillow of goat's hair at its head, and covered it with clothes.' (1 Sam. 19:13) Saul was furious at the escape.

During the years that David spent as an outlaw, Saul gave Michal in marriage to Phalti, the son of Laish. After Saul's death, his general Abner first supported his weak son Ishbosheth, then made overtures to David, who demanded the return of Michal. Ishbosheth was forced to agree. Abner escorted her to David at Hebron, and ordered her weeping husband to turn back.

The resumed marriage does not seem to have been a success. Michal remained out of sympathy with David and his ambitions. On the day the Ark of God was brought to Jerusalem, Michal watched the excitement through a window of the palace and saw the king 'leaping and dancing before the Lord; and she despised him in her heart.' (2 Sam. 6:16) When he came in she mocked him for the exhibition he had made of himself. David, thoroughly angry, reminded her that he had been chosen by the Lord instead of her father to be king over Israel. 'And Michal the daughter of Saul had no child to the day of her death.' (2 Sam. 6:23) [1 Sam. 14:49; 18:20–28; 19:11–17; 25:44; 2 Sam. 3:13, 14; 6:16–23; 1 Chr. 15:29]

Michri (Heb. 'precious') *c.* 6 century BC. Father of Uzzi of the tribe of Benjamin whose grandson Elah settled in Jerusalem following the return from exile in Babylon. [1 Chr. 9:8]

Midian (Heb. 'strife') *c.* 17 century BC. A son of Abraham by his wife Keturah and the legendary father of the Midianites who warred against the children of Israel. [Gen. 25:2–3; 1 Chr. 1:32]

Mijamin (Heb. 'with good luck') *1. c.*

10 century BC. A priest in charge of the sixth turn of service in the Tabernacle in the reign of King David. [1 Chr. 24:9] *2.* 6 century BC. A priest who returned with Zerubbabel to Judah from exile in Babylon. [Neh. 12:5] *3.* 5 century BC. A descendant of Parosh who divorced his non-Jewish wife in the time of Ezra. [Ezra 10:25] *4.* 5 century BC. One of the priests who signed the solemn covenant in the time of Nehemiah. [Neh. 10:7]

Mikloth (Heb. 'staves') date unknown. Son of Jeiel and a leader of the tribe of Benjamin. [1 Chr. 8:32; 9:37, 38]

Mikneiah (Heb. 'possessed by God') *c.* 10 century BC. A Levite who played musical instruments when the Ark of God was brought up to Jerusalem at the orders of King David. [1 Chr. 15:18, 21]

Milalai (Heb. 'God said') 5 century BC. A priest who followed after Ezra playing a musical instrument during the dedication service for the rebuilt walls of Jerusalem. [Neh. 12:36]

Milcah (Heb. 'queen') *1. c.* 18 century BC. The wife of Abraham's brother Nahor, her son Bethuel was the father of Rebekah who married Abraham's son Isaac. [Gen. 11:29; 22:20; 24:15, 24, 47] *2. c.* 13 century BC. One of the five daughters of Zelophehad who claimed a share of their father's estate since their father had no sons. [Num. 26:33; 27:1; 36:11; Josh. 17:3]

Milcom *see* MOLECH

Miniamin (Heb. 'right hand') *1. c.* 8 century BC. A Levite in the days of Hezekiah, king of Judah, he distributed the tithes and offerings to the priests in the cities of Judah. [2 Chr. 31:15] *2.* 5 century BC. One of the heads of the priestly families when Joiakim was high priest in the time of Nehemiah, who blew a trumpet at the dedication of the rebuilt walls of Jerusalem. [Neh. 12:17, 41]

Miriam (Heb. 'bitterness') *1. c.* 13 century BC. The daughter of Amram and Jochebed, she was the sister of Moses and Aaron and probably the eldest of the three. When Pharaoh's daughter found the infant Moses in the reeds, Miriam, who was keeping watch over the baby, suggested to the princess that she could find a wetnurse for the child and brought her mother to the palace.

After the crossing of the water during the Exodus and the death of the Egyptians, Miriam led the women in the ceremonial dance and song of gratitude. But when Moses married and Ethiopian woman, she and Aaron criticized him in such a fashion that it disclosed their jealousy of his leadership. Miriam was struck by leprosy and the Exodus was delayed until Moses had interceded for her with the Lord and she was cured and allowed to return to the encampment. She died and was buried in Kadesh-barnea in the wilderness. [Exod. 15:20–21; Num. 12:1–15; 20:1; 26:59; Deut. 24:9; 1 Chr. 6:3; Mic. 6:4]
2. date unknown. The daughter of Mered of the tribe of Judah. [1 Chr. 4:17]

Mirmah (Heb. 'fraud') date unknown. A son of Shaharaim, who was a leader of the tribe of Benjamin. [1 Chr. 8:10]

Mishael (Heb. 'who is God's') *1. c.* 13 century BC. Son of Uzziel of the tribe of Levi, and an uncle of Moses and Aaron, he and his brother Elazphan were ordered by Moses to remove the bodies of Aaron's sons Nadab and Abihu from the Tabernacle after they had been struck dead for offering forbidden incense to the Lord. [Exod. 6:22; Lev. 10:4]
2. see MESHACH
3. 5 century BC. A leader of Judah who

stood at the left hand of Ezra as he read out the Law of God to the people. [Neh. 8:4]

Misham (Heb. 'the Lord is [my] uncle') date unknown. One of the sons of Elpaal, a leader of the tribe of Benjamin. [1 Chr. 8:12]

Mishma (Heb. 'hearing') *1. c.* 17 century BC. Son of Abraham's son Ishmael, he was leader of a desert tribe. [Gen. 25:13–14; 1 Chr. 1:30]
2. date unknown. Son of Mibsam and father of Hammuel of the tribe of Simeon. [1 Chr. 4:25, 26]

Mishmannah (Heb. 'fatness') *c.* 11 century BC. One of the warriors of the tribe of Gad who deserted from King Saul's army and joined David at Ziklag. [1 Chr. 12:10]

Mispar (Heb. 'number') *c.* 6 century BC. A leader of Judah who returned to Jerusalem with Zerubbabel from exile in Babylon. Also called Mispereth. [Ezra 2:2; Neh. 7:7]

Mispereth *see* MISPAR

Mithredath (Pers. 'given by Mithra') *1. c.* 6 century BC. Treasurer of Cyrus, king of Persia, he was ordered to hand over to Sheshbazzar all the gold, silver and precious vessels which had been plundered from the Temple in Jerusalem. [Ezra. 1:8]
2. c. 5 century BC. A Persian official in Jerusalem in the days of Ezra, he was one of several conspirators to write a letter to Artaxerxes, king of Persia, falsely accusing the Jews of rebuilding the walls of Jerusalem in order to organize a rebellion against the king and stop paying dues to him. [Ezra 4:7]

Mizzah *c.* 16 century BC. Son of Reuel and a grandson of Esau, he was an Edomite chieftain. [Gen. 36:13, 17; 1 Chr. 1:37]

Moab (Heb. 'progeny of a father') *c.* 18 century BC. Son of Lot by his incestuous relationship with his daughter after the destruction of the two cities Sodom and Gomorrah, he is regarded by Hebrew tradition as the ancestor of the Moabites who lived east of the Jordan river. [Gen. 19:37]

Moadiah *see* MAADIAH

Molech The national god of the Ammonites. This god was worshipped by offering up human sacrifices, usually a child from the family. Worship of Molech was expressly forbidden to the Children of Israel in the Book of Leviticus. Nevertheless, some of them worshipped Molech at various times and King Solomon permitted altars to be built to him. Later, Josiah, king of Judah, as part of the purification of Judah, deliberately defiled the holy places for the worship of Molech. Also known as Moloch, Milcom and Malcam, which suggests identification with the tribal god of the Ammonites. [Lev. 18:21; 1 Kgs. 11:5, 7; 2 Kgs. 23:10, 13; Isa. 30:33; Jer. 32:35; Zeph. 1:5]

Molid (Heb. 'begetter') date unknown. The younger son of Abishur of the tribe of Judah and his wife Abihail. [1 Chr. 2:29]

Moloch *see* MOLECH

Mordecai (Heb. 'consecrated to Merodach') *c.* 5 century BC. Cousin and guardian of Esther.

Mordecai was a devout Jew and an exile from Jerusalem, who lived in Shushan (Susa) the capital of the Persian Empire. He had adopted as his own daughter a young orphaned cousin whose Persian name was Esther. She was chosen by King Ahasuerus to be his queen, and Mordecai advised her not to disclose the fact that she was Jewish.

Mordecai had an official position at the court. One day he heard two of the king's eunuchs plotting to assassinate their master. He asked Esther to warn the king, who had the conspirators seized and executed. This service by Mordecai was recorded in the court annals.

Mordecai fell foul of Haman, the chief minister, by refusing to bow down to him. Haman determined to kill not only Mordecai but all the Jews. He persuaded the king to let him destroy them on the ground that they did not keep the king's laws, and a day of execution was fixed. Mordecai told Esther to intercede with the king. He received her kindly and agreed to dine with her together with Haman.

Haman's wife and friends advised him to prepare a gallows and to persuade the king the following day to let Mordecai be hanged.

That night the king was sleepless and had the court annals read to him. He came across the entry about Mordecai having foiled the plot against the king and discovered that the act had gone unrewarded. He summoned Haman and without disclosing the name, asked him how he would set about paying honour to someone. Thinking it was himself, Haman proposed that the person be conducted through the city square dressed in royal robes with a crown on his head, and seated on the king's horse. To his utter dismay, Haman was ordered to carry out this ceremony for Mordecai.

That night at dinner, Queen Esther denounced Haman and accused him of having organized the mass murder of her people. 'So they hanged Haman on the gallows which he had prepared for Mordecai.' (Esther 7:10) Mordecai was then appointed chief minister in Haman's place. Since by Persian law Haman's decree could not be revoked, Mordecai was authorized to send out another decree giving the Jews the right to carry arms in self-defence. On the day Haman had appointed for their destruction, they turned on their enemies and slew them. Mordecai and Esther sent letters to all the Jews, saying that their deliverance should be commemorated every year with the Feast of Purim.

The king advanced Mordecai until 'Mordecai the Jew was next in rank to King Ahasuerus, and he was great among the Jews ... and spoke peace to all his people.' (Esther 10:3)

The story appears non-historical, since no Persian ruler is known to have had a queen called Esther, a chief minister called Haman, or a Jewish counsellor called Mordecai. [Book of Esther]

Moses (Heb. 'to draw out') *c.* 13 century BC. The great Hebrew leader and lawgiver. Moses is the most majestic figure in the old Testament. His role was so central that the Pentateuch was called the Five Books of Moses, and the code of religious laws, the Law of Moses. To Jews he has remained for all time *Moshe Rabbenu* – 'Moses our Teacher'. No one else in the Old Testament had the same close relationship with God. As it was written, 'the Lord used to speak to Moses face to face, as a man speaks to his friend' (Exod. 33:11).

The story opens in Egypt. Jacob and his family had settled as a pastoral clan in the land of Goshen in the north-east corner of the Nile delta. Here their descendants lived and prospered for four centuries, till 'there arose a new king over Egypt, who did not know Joseph' (Exod. 1:8). (This was possibly the Pharaoh Rameses II, in the 13th century BC – the greatest builder in Egyptian history.) He decided that the Children of Israel had become too numerous and strong. He turned them into slave labourers, and put them to work under Egyptian taskmasters on the construction of two treasure cities, Pithom and Rameses, 'And made their lives bitter with hard service, in mortar and brick, and in all kinds of work in the field.' (Exod.

1:14) When this did not reduce their numbers, Pharaoh ordered the Hebrew midwives to kill every male infant at birth. The midwives evaded this decree on the pretext that 'the Hebrew women are not like the Egyptian women; for they are vigorous and are delivered before the midwife comes to them.' (Exod. 1:19) The frustrated ruler then charged his people to throw the male babies into the river, and drown them.

Amram and Jochebed, the parents of Moses, were of the priestly house of Levi. When the child was born, his mother kept him hidden for three months. She then enclosed him in a basket woven of rushes and sealed with pitch, and concealed him among the reeds at the river's edge.

Pharaoh's daughter came to bathe at this spot and when she saw the basket she sent a maid to fetch it. On opening it, the baby started crying and the princess felt pity for it, realizing that it was one of the Hebrew children her father had ordered killed. Moses's elder sister Miriam had been posted a little distance away to watch. She approached the princess and offered to find a Hebrew nurse to suckle the child. This was agreed, and she ran off to fetch Moses's mother. When he was older, Pharaoh's daughter adopted him and gave him the name of Moses, 'Because I drew him out of the water.' (Exod. 2:10) (The Hebrew form, *Moshe*, means 'to draw out'.)

The boy grew up at the royal court but remained aware of his Hebrew origin. One day Moses, now a grown man, went off alone to find out what was happening to his kinsmen. He saw an Egyptian overseer flogging an Israelite slave. Thinking himself unobserved, Moses slew the Egyptian and buried his body in the sand. Next day he intervened in a fight between two Israelites and was alarmed when one of them said pointedly: 'Who made you a prince and a judge over us? Do you mean to kill me, as you killed the Egyptian?' (Exod.

2:14) Report of his deed reached Pharaoh, and he had to flee for his life eastward into the Sinai desert.

Pausing to rest at a well, Moses assisted some young women to water their flocks. When they told their father Jethro (or Reuel) about the helpful stranger at the well, he invited Moses to eat with them. Jethro was the priest of a tribe of desert nomads from Midian. Moses remained with him and married one of his seven daughters, Zipporah. She bore him a son whom he called Gershom, since Moses was a stranger (Heb. *ger*) in a strange land.

Moving deep into the desert in search of pasture for his father-in-law's flocks, Moses came to the mountain of Horeb (or Sinai). He turned aside to examine a strange sight: a bush that was burning without being consumed. God's voice came out of the bush commanding him to halt and remove his shoes, as he was on holy ground. Moses was told that he had been chosen to lead his brethren out of their oppression and bring them to the Promised Land. Moses shrank from this task, saying: 'Who am I that I should go to Pharaoh, and bring the sons of Israel out of Egypt?' (Exod. 3:11) To reassure him, the name of the Lord ('Jehovah') was revealed to Moses, and he was given certain magic signs to impress Pharaoh and the Israelites: turning his staff into a snake, making his hand white with leprosy and turning water into blood. Still reluctant, Moses pointed out that 'I am slow of speech and of tongue'. (Exod. 4:10) The Lord became impatient with him, and replied that his brother Aaron could be his spokesman.

Moses took leave of Jethro and set out with his wife, his eldest son Gershom and his newly-born second son Eliezer. Along the way Moses became ill, and Zipporah circumcised the infant with a sharp flint in the belief that her husband would die if the rite were neglected.

LET MY PEOPLE GO

Aaron came to meet Moses and was told what the Lord required of them. They called together the Israelite elders, and in Moses's presence Aaron conveyed the Lord's message and performed the magic signs. The people were convinced that God was about to liberate them and sank down in worship.

Moses and Aaron then gained an audience with the reigning Pharaoh (probably the successor of the ruler from whom Moses had fled). In the name of the God of Israel they requested him to 'Let my people go' (Exod. 5:1). They did not dare suggest that the Israelites would leave the country for good. Instead, they claimed that sacrifices had to be made to their God at a place three days' journey into the wilderness.

Pharaoh bluntly rejected the request. He charged the Israelites with laziness, and issued instructions that they should no longer be supplied with straw for making bricks. They would have to seek their own straw, without lowering their daily output. The people reproached Moses for having added to their hardships, and Moses complained to the Lord that his mission had only done harm. 'For since I came to Pharaoh to speak in thy name, he has done evil to this people, and thou hast not delivered thy people at all.' (Exod. 5:23) The Lord declared that he had hardened Pharaoh's heart in order that 'the Egyptians shall know that I am the Lord, when I stretch forth my hand upon Egypt and bring out the people of Israel from among them' (Exod. 7:5).

The whole of Egypt now experienced a series of plagues, except for the land of Goshen where the Israelites lived. As each plague became intolerable Pharaoh agreed to let Moses's people go, but changed his mind when the affliction stopped.

First, Aaron and Moses smote the water of the Nile with the rod and it turned to blood before the eyes of

Pharaoh and his court. 'And the fish in the Nile died; and the Nile became foul, so that the Egyptians could not drink water from the Nile; and there was blood throughout all the land of Egypt.' (Exod. 7:21)

When Pharaoh refused to give way, frogs came swarming out of the river and spread everywhere, as Moses had warned Pharaoh they would, crawling 'into your house, and into your bedchamber and on your bed, and into the house of your servants and of your people, and into your ovens and your kneading bowls.' (Exod. 8:3)

The third plague was one of lice which sprang from the dust and infected man and beast alike. There followed swarms of flies; cattle disease; an epidemic of boils; a fierce hailstorm that smashed the trees and flattened the crops; vast clouds of locusts that devoured all growing things; and three days of pitch darkness.

The tenth calamity was the most dreadful of all – the slaying of the first-born. The Lord commanded Moses and Aaron that on the fourteenth day of the month, at dusk, each Israelite family should slaughter a lamb or kid and roast its flesh for a sacrificial meal. 'In this manner you shall eat it: your loins girded, your sandals on your feet, and your staff in your hand; and you shall eat it in haste. It is the Lord's passover.' (Exod. 12:11) Blood from the slaughtered animal was to be daubed on the lintel and doorposts so that the Lord would recognize and pass over Hebrew homes, while smiting the Egyptians.

At midnight the first-born died in every Egyptian family, and even among the domestic animals. There was grief and panic throughout the country. That same night Pharaoh sent for Moses and Aaron and begged them to leave at once with their people, together with all their herds, flocks and possessions. The Egyptians handed over to them jewels and other valuables to speed their departure.

They set out at once from the city of Rameses that their forced labour had helped to build. In fulfilment of an ancient promise, the remains of Joseph were carried with them for burial in Canaan. 'Four hundred and thirty years', says the Bible (Exod. 12:41), had passed since their ancestor Jacob had first come to live in Egypt. Forty years of wandering lay ahead of them before they would reach their journey's end. Moses was at this time eighty years old and his brother Aaron eighty-three.

Each year Jews commemorate the Exodus in the seven-day spring festival of Passover, as enjoined in Exod. 10. They eat 'matzot' (flat cakes of unleavened bread) to recall the haste with which their ancestors departed. At the 'Seder' or ceremonial meal, bitter herbs are the symbol of the bondage in Egypt, and a roasted shank-bone represents the paschal lamb eaten that fateful night.

IN THE WILDERNESS

The great highway from Egypt to Canaan and beyond lay along the Mediterranean coast of the Sinai desert. From the edge of the Nile delta to Gaza it was but a week's march for armies or trading caravans. But that direct and well-travelled route was the most dangerous for the Israelites; and the coastal plain of Canaan to which it led was held by hostile inhabitants. A mob of runaway slaves would not have been able to fight its way through to the Promised Land. So Moses turned away from the coastal road 'lest the people repent when they see war, and return to Egypt' (Exod. 13:17). Instead, they headed south-east, towards the open desert.

The first halt was at Succoth, thirty-two miles from the city of Rameses, and the next at Etham on the edge of the desert. They were trying to move as fast as they could, fearing that Pharaoh would pursue them. 'And the Lord went before them by day in a pillar of a cloud to lead them along the way, and by night in a pillar of fire to give them light, that they might travel by day and night.' (Exod. 13:21)

Their haste was warranted. Pharaoh's courtiers said to him, 'What is this we have done, that we have let Israel go from serving us?' (Exod. 14:5) He set out in pursuit with a mobile force that included six hundred chariots. When the Israelites saw them coming, they trembled with fear and cried out to Moses, 'Is it because there are no graves in Egypt that you have taken us away to die in the wilderness?' (Exod. 14:11) They were at this time at the edge of the Reed Sea (incorrectly translated into English as the 'Red Sea'). Nothing but a miracle could save them. At the Lord's behest, Moses stretched out his hand over the sea and a strong east wind pushed the water aside, so that the Children of Israel were able to cross dryshod to the other side. Dashing after them, Pharaoh's chariots were engulfed for 'the waters returned' (Exod. 14:28), and men and horses were drowned. (This may have happened in the area of the Bitter Lakes, through which the Suez Canal now passes.)

When the Israelites 'saw the Egyptians dead upon the sea shore' (Exod. 14:30), they sang a song of thankfulness to the Lord, while Moses's sister Miriam played on a timbrel (tambourine) and led the women in dance.

The elation of their new-found freedom was short-lived. They now entered the wilderness of Shur in the Sinai peninsula – a wasteland of sand and gravel, intersected with limestone ridges and dry watercourses, in the beds of which a little sparse scrub could be found for the flocks. The sun scorched them by day and the cold was sharp at night.

The chief problem was water. After trekking for three days, they reached a spring of brackish water at Marah (which means 'bitter'). Moses threw a certain bush into the water which made it drinkable. A day's march further on they were able to camp in the oasis of

Elim, 'where there were twelve springs of water and seventy palm trees' (Exod. 15:27). Soon they ran out of food and railed at Moses and Aaron for taking them away from the 'flesh pots' (Exod. 16:3) of Egypt. The Lord would come to the rescue, Moses promised, and would provide 'in the evening flesh to eat and in the morning bread to the full' (Exod. 16:8). Flocks of migrating quails sank down to rest among the scrub at night and could easily be snared (as the desert Arabs do today).

In the early morning, when the dew vanished, the ground was strewn with manna, and 'it was like coriander seed, white, and the taste of it was like wafers made with honey.' (Exod. 16:31) Moses told them the manna was bread from the Lord. They were to gather and prepare just enough to satisfy their hunger, for what was not eaten would go bad in the heat of the day. On the sixth day a double portion could be gathered, and would remain fresh over the Sabbath. (It has been suggested that the manna may have been the resin-like substance that is exuded by the tamarisk trees in the desert, and drops on the ground when dry.)

The Israelites moved deeper into the southern part of the Sinai desert and came to Rephidim. Once more they were without water, and complained loudly. Moses was told by the Lord to gather the elders together and in their presence smite a rock. He did so and fresh water gushed out. Moses called the place 'Massah and Meribah' ('testing and contention') (Exod. 17:7).

They now faced a human threat, being attacked by a party of Amalekites, fierce desert raiders. The Israelites were not yet organized or trained to fight. Moses sent for Joshua the son of Nun, a young Ephraimite, and told him to select and lead a group of Israelite defenders. Moses himself climbed to the top of a hill together with Aaron and Hur (traditionally Moses's brother-in-law); and from here they witnessed the battle. While Moses held up his hands with the sacred rod, the Israelites gained, but they were pushed back when his arms dropped from weariness. His two companions seated him on a stone and, standing on either side of him, held his arms raised in the air until nightfall, when the battle was won and the Amalekites routed. Moses built an altar to the Lord.

In the third month after leaving Egypt, the Israelites reached the wild and rugged terrain of the wilderness of Sinai. In its centre a cluster of gaunt granite peaks of a dark-red colour rose to a height of eight thousand feet, with deep canyons around them. The Israelites camped on the open ground before a peak called Mount Sinai or Mount Horeb. It was here that Moses had heard the voice of the Lord from the burning bush many years before. Jethro now came to see Moses, bringing Zipporah and their two sons, who had been on a visit to her family. Moses welcomed the old man warmly, and they sat for a long time in the tent talking about all the wondrous things that had happened since Moses had gone back to Egypt. The Midianite priest exclaimed: 'Now I know that the Lord is greater than all gods.' (Exod. 18:11) Jethro offered a sacrifice on the Hebrew altar and Moses invited the elders to a feast in his honour.

Jethro was present next day while Moses gave judgment in the disputes and claims brought before him. In the evening Jethro offered his son-in-law some sage advice. It was too burdensome for Moses to deal personally with every trivial matter, while scores of people stood around awaiting their turn. Why should Moses not delegate authority to able men, and put each in charge of a fixed number of persons? Moses agreed, and appointed 'rulers of thousands, of hundreds, of fifties, and of tens. And they judged the people at all times; hard cases they brought to Moses.' (Exod. 18:25, 26) Moses charged them to 'judge righteously between a man and his brother or the alien that is with him. You shall not be partial in judgment; you shall hear the small and the great alike; you shall not be afraid of the face of man, for the judgment is God's.' (Deut. 1:16–17)

Having instigated this system of administration, Jethro took his leave and returned to his own land.

THE TEN COMMANDMENTS
It was timely for Moses to be relieved of routine duties, for the Lord was about to call on him to fulfil a loftier purpose. The stage was set for one of the most awesome moments in human history: the handing down of the Law on Mount Sinai.

God called Moses up to the mountain and instructed him to tell the Children of Israel that if they would keep his covenant 'you shall be to me a kingdom of priests and an holy nation' (Exod, 19:6). They were ordered to wash and purify themselves for two days, and on the third day they gathered before the mountain that was covered with a thick cloud. Out of it came thunder, lightning and the loud blasts of a trumpet. 'And Mount Sinai was wrapped in smoke, because the Lord descended upon it in fire; and the smoke of it went up like the smoke of a kiln, and the whole mountain quaked greatly.' (Exod. 19:18) Then the voice of God rolled forth, solemnly pronouncing the Ten Commandments:

'I am the Lord your God, who brought you out of the land of Egypt, out of the house of bondage.

'You shall have no other gods before me. You shall not make for yourself a graven image ...

'You shall not take the name of the Lord your God in vain ...

'Remember the sabbath day, to keep it holy. Six days you shall labour, and do all your work; but the seventh day is a sabbath to the Lord your God ...

'Honour your father and your mother ...

'You shall not kill.

'You shall not commit adultery.

'You shall not steal.

'You shall not bear false witness against your neighbour.

'You shall not covet your neighbour's house ... or anything that is your neighbour's.' (Exod. 20:2–17)

A number of other laws were then made known to Moses. He built a stone altar with twelve pillars representing the twelve tribes of Israel, and instructed young men to sacrifice oxen on it. Moses read out 'the book of the covenant' (Exod. 24:7) and sprinkled the blood of the sacrifices on the people as 'the blood of the covenant which the Lord has made with you in accordance with all these words' (Exod. 24:8).

He then left Aaron and Hur in charge of the encampment and disappeared into the cloud that still covered the mountain. There he remained for forty days and forty nights, communing with the Lord. At the end of that time God gave him 'two tables of the testimony, tables of stone, written with the finger of God' (Exod. 31:18).

Down in the camp, the Israelites had lost faith when Moses failed to reappear. They came in a body to Aaron and said, 'Up, make us gods, who shall go before us; as for this Moses, the man who brought us up out of the land of Egypt, we do not know what has become of him.' (Exod. 32:1) Aaron felt obliged to appease them. He asked for all the gold earrings worn by the men and women, melted them down, and moulded a golden calf. The people made burnt-offerings to it, and they sang, feasted and danced naked around it.

On the mountain the Lord told Moses what his 'stiff-necked people' (Exod. 32:9) were doing, and threatened to destroy them. Moses pleaded for them, and the Lord relented. But when Moses came down and saw the spectacle with

his own eyes, he was seized with rage and dashed the two stone tablets to the ground, breaking them. Moses threw the golden calf into the fire, ground it up, mixed it with water and made the Israelites swallow it. He upbraided Aaron, who tried to defend himself, saying, 'you know the people, that they are set on evil' (Exod. 32:22). Moses felt a drastic purge was needed. He rallied round him the men from the priestly tribe of Levi (to which he and Aaron belonged) and ordered them to put to the sword a large number of the idol-worshippers.

This painful experience left Moses with a sense of failure, and he asked the Lord to relieve him of the leadership. The reply was that the journey to the Promised Land should continue as before. Moses again ascended the sacred mountain, carrying two stone tablets he had hewed to replace those smashed. Once more he stayed there forty days and nights without food or water. When he returned with 'the words of the covenant, the ten commandments' (Exod. 34:28) engraved on the tablets for the second time, Aaron and the Israelites observed that his face shone with such light that 'they were afraid to come near him' (Exod. 34:30).

The Lord had given Moses precise instructions for the construction of an Ark of acacia wood covered with gold, and a tabernacle with an open-air altar. They were to form a portable temple for the Israelites' wandering life.

The Ark containing the tablets of the Law was placed in the Tabernacle, which was consecrated by Moses in the presence of all the people. As long as the pillar of cloud or of fire stood still over the Tabernacle, it was a sign that the Israelites should remain at that spot until the pillar moved forward again.

Before the Israelites set out once more, Moses adopted two measures to increase their cohesion and their self-defence: a military census and a marching order. The census covered men of military age from twenty upwards, 'all in Israel who are able to go forth to war' (Num. 1:3), except for the Levites who were exempted because of their religious duties. The order in which Moses organized the tribes for travel gave each family clan its fixed position. The Levites were in the centre of a square, carrying the Ark, the Tabernacle and other sacred objects. On each of the four sides a group of three tribes formed up around a standard. The start of the march was marked by a series of trumpet blasts.

Moses prevailed on his Midianite brother-in-law Hobab to come with the Israelites as guide, since he was born and bred in the desert and familiar with it: 'for you know how we are to encamp in the wilderness, and you will serve as eyes for us.' (Num. 10:31)

FROM SINAI TO KADESH

In the second month of the second year the Children of Israel moved northward from Mount Sinai towards the wilderness of Paran, in the central plateau of the Sinai peninsula. Soon trouble broke out again, this time over the monotonous diet of manna. As refugees are apt to do, they became nostalgic for the land they had fled. Tearfully they asked, 'O that we had meat to eat! We remember the fish we ate in Egypt for nothing, the cucumbers, the melons, the leeks, the onions, and the garlic.' (Num. 11:4, 5)

Moses felt weary of leading the discontented community he had brought out of slavery. He said to the Lord: 'I am not able to carry all this people along, the burden is too heavy for me. If thou will deal thus with me, kill me at once ...' (Num. 11:14, 15) At this cry of distress, the Lord saw that Moses needed help in carrying the burden. He had Moses summon seventy elders to the Tabernacle, and inspired them, so that they would serve as a council to share responsibility with him. As for the people's demand for flesh, the Lord

taught them a lesson. Huge flocks of quail were blown inland from the sea and piled up all round the camp. For two days the Israelites gorged themselves on the meat of the birds until they fell violently ill and a number of them died.

At their next camping place Aaron and Miriam started speaking against Moses, of whom they had become jealous. The Lord was angry at this attack, and Miriam was stricken with leprosy. Moses prayed that she be forgiven, and she recovered after seven days of isolation in the desert outside the camp. Oddly enough Aaron was not punished – perhaps because of his priestly role.

The Israelites resumed their journey northward, and came to rest at Kadeshbarnea, a green and well-watered oasis some fifty miles south of Beersheba. They were now nearing the southern rim of Canaan, but it was for them unknown country. Moses decided to send into it a scouting party of twelve picked men, one from each tribe to 'see what the land is, and whether the people who dwell in it are strong or weak, whether they are few or many' (Num. 13:18) – also, whether the inhabitants lived in fortified towns or in tents, and whether the soil was fertile.

The spies crossed the Negev, passed Arad on the plateau above the Dead Sea, and travelled through the central hill country of Canaan. The party reached Kadesh safely after a forty-day trip and reported that Canaan was truly a land flowing with milk and honey. Nevertheless 'the people who dwell in the land are strong and the cities are fortified and very large; and besides, we saw the descendants of Anak there.' (Num. 13:28) (*Anak* is Hebrew for 'giant'.) They also reported on the Amalekites who dwelt in the arid south of Canaan, and the Hittites, Jebusites, Amorites and other peoples in the settled areas further north. As Moses had requested, they brought back specimens of the fruit they had seen: figs, pomegranates and a bunch of grapes so large that it had to be carried on a pole slung between two men. They had picked it near Hebron at the brook of Eshcol, a name which means 'grape-cluster'.

One of the scouts, Caleb of the tribe of Judah, proposed that in spite of the dangers they should advance into the country without delay and trust the Lord to help them overcome resistance. He was supported only by Joshua from the tribe of Ephraim. The other ten were much more discouraging. They submitted 'an evil report of the land ... that devours its inhabitants; all the people that we saw in it are men of great stature ... and we seemed to ourselves like grasshoppers.' (Num. 13:32, 33) The gathering that listened to the report was cast into gloom. What was the good of bringing them to the Promised Land, they said, in order to be slain in it? It would be better to find a new leader who would take them back to Egypt. A wrathful Lord decreed that for their lack of belief in Him, they would stay wandering in the desert for forty years, till that generation had died out, except for Joshua and Caleb.

The Children of Israel now settled down for some decades to the life of nomad shepherds and cattle-herders roaming the wilderness of Zin, with their base at the oasis. 'So you remained at Kadesh many days.' (Deut. 1:46) During this period Moses developed the religious code and the rituals of worship. The stern discipline with which observance was enforced was illustrated by the case of the man who gathered sticks for firewood on the Sabbath and was ordered to be stoned to death.

The leadership of Moses and Aaron was challenged by a revolt – all the more serious because it started with their own tribe of Levi, which was dedicated to priestly duties. It was led by the Levite Korah the son of Izhar, together with two Reubenite brothers, Dathan

and Abiram, and they were supported by two hundred and fifty respected men. Punishment was swift. The earth split open and swallowed up the three rebel leaders with their households. The two hundred and fifty supporters were consumed by fire from the Lord. Moses felt the need of some act to bolster the status of Aaron and the priests. He collected and placed in the Tabernacle a stave from each of the tribes, with the Levites represented by Aaron's own rod. When they were taken out and shown to the people next morning, it was seen that Aaron's stave had sprouted with blossom and borne almonds.

Miriam, the sister of Moses and Aaron, died at Kadesh and was buried there.

ONWARD TO CANAAN

After nearly forty years had gone by, most of them spent at Kadesh, the time had come to resume the march towards the Promised Land. Unable to penetrate Canaan from the south, the Israelites now set out on a lengthy detour in order to enter from the east, across the Jordan river. The route northward into Transjordan lay along the ancient caravan route known as the King's Highway. Moses sent messengers to the king of Edom, to say, 'Now let us pass through your land. We will not pass through field or vineyard, neither will we drink water from a well; we will go along the King's Highway, we will not turn aside to the right hand or to the left, until we have passed through your territory.' (Num. 20:17) The king refused, and Moses thought it prudent to bypass Edom from the west, travelling up the great rift of Wadi Araba towards the Dead Sea. On the way, Aaron died on top of Mount Hor where he had been taken by Moses and by Aaron's son Eleazar, who succeeded him as high priest.

The Israelites now had a taste of the warfare that lay ahead. They were attacked and a number of them killed and captured by Canaanites from Arad, that lies on the plateau west of the Dead Sea. Further on, they passed through a region infested with venomous snakes and some of them were bitten. Moses stuck a brass serpent on a pole, and looking at it served as a magic cure for snake bite.

From the southern end of the Dead Sea, they turned eastward into the mountains, through the precipitous valley of Zered that divided Edom from Moab. They emerged on the plateau and skirted round Moab to the deep gorge of the river Arnon that entered the Dead Sea from the east.

The country north of the Arnon had recently been conquered by the Amorites under King Sihon. He also refused the Israelites passage and attacked them. He was defeated and his capital Heshbon occupied. The advance continued northward into the fertile land of Gilead, up to the Yarmuk river. Og, the giant king of Bashan (the Golan Heights) gave them battle and was repulsed. Thus ended the first phase of the Israelite invasion.

The Israelites started to cohabit with Moabite women, and were drawn into the cult of the local deity, the Baal of Peor. The Lord smote them with a plague but was mollified by the act of an outraged priest called Phinehas, son of Eleazar and grandson of Aaron. He seized a javelin, rushed into a tent where an Israelite was lying with a Midianite woman and with one blow transfixed them both.

The camel-riding Midianites in the region seem to have been involved in this Israelite immorality. An Israelite expedition was sent against them, with a thousand men from each tribe. They wiped out the Midianite encampments with religious zeal, sparing only the young girls. Moses ruled on the division of the captured livestock: half to the fighting men and half to the rest of the community, with special shares for the priesthood.

Another census was taken and showed that none of the men of the Exodus was left alive, except for Joshua, Caleb and Moses himself. A new breed of Israelites had grown up as free men, hardened by the rigours of desert life and disciplined by the laws Moses had taught them. Out of the craven and unruly bondsmen that had emerged from Egypt, Moses had in forty years moulded a small but stalwart nation, ready to meet its destiny in the Promised Land. He was not to share that destiny; his own task was nearly done.

THE DEATH OF MOSES

In three farewell addresses, recorded in the Book of Deuteronomy, Moses recalled for the Israelites the story of their wandering; expanded their religious and legal code; and instructed them about their coming settlement in Canaan. He climaxed his religious exhortations with the 'Shema Yisrael' – 'Hear, O Israel' – which has remained to this day the most celebrated prayer in the Jewish liturgy.

To a desert-weary people Moses painted a pleasant picture of the country they were about to enter:

'For the Lord your God is bringing you into a good land, a land of brooks of water, of fountains and springs flowing forth in valleys and hills, a land of wheat and barley, of vines and fig trees and pomegranates, a land of olive trees and honey, a land in which you will eat bread without scarcity, in which you will lack nothing, a land whose stones are iron, and out of whose hills you can dig copper.' (Deut. 8:7–9)

Moses composed a song of praise to God, whom he had served so humbly and faithfully, and gave his blessing to each of the tribes in turn.

He asked the Lord to appoint a new leader to whom he could hand over his charge 'that the congregation of the Lord may not be as sheep which have no shepherd' (Num. 27:17). It was indicated that Moses's successor would be Joshua the son of Nun, 'a man in whom is the spirit' (Num. 27:18).

At a solemn ceremony in the Tabernacle before Eleazar the High Priest and all the congregation, with the presence of the Lord in a pillar of cloud over the door, Moses laid his hands upon Joshua and said, 'Be strong and of good courage; for you shall go with this people into the land which the Lord has sworn to their fathers to give them; and you shall put them in possession of it.' (Deut. 31:7)

The men of Reuben and Gad asked whether they could remain in the territory east of the river. They were herdsmen, and these rolling uplands would give good grazing for their cattle and sheep. Moses rebuked them: 'Shall your brethren go to the war while you sit here? Why will you discourage the heart of the people of Israel from going over into the land which the Lord has given them? Thus did your fathers, when I sent them from Kadesh-barnea to see the land.' (Num. 32:6–8) A compromise was reached. They would establish their families and herds in Transjordan, cross the river with the other tribes to fight their way into Canaan, and return when it had been subdued. Part of the tribe of Manasseh joined in this arrangement, as they were attracted by the wooded ridges and fertile dales of Gilead, and wanted to settle there.

Before he died, Moses was given a distant view of the Promised Land from 'Mount Nebo, to the top of Pisgah, which is opposite Jericho' (Deut. 34:1). On a height jutting out from the great escarpment, Moses stood with his back to the Moab plateau, stretching away to the empty desert beyond the eastern horizon. Before him a tremendous panorama unfolded. Thousands of feet below glittered the Dead Sea, the lowest body of water on the earth's surface. Beyond it rose the dun-coloured rampart of the Judean desert, with Jerusalem and Hebron and other Canaanite cities hidden behind its rim. To the right, the Jordan river looped snake-like through lush green banks. And the Lord said: 'I have let you see it with your eyes, but you shall not go over there.' (Deut. 34:4)

After this single view Moses died and was buried by the Lord 'in the valley in the land of Moab, opposite Beth-peor; but no man knows the place of his burial to this day' (Deut. 34:6). At his death he was a hundred and twenty years old, but 'his eye was not dim, nor his natural force abated' (Deut. 34:7). For thirty days the Children of Israel wept and mourned for the great leader and teacher they had lost, 'And there has not arisen a prophet since in Israel like Moses, whom the Lord knew face to face.' (Deut. 34:10).

[There are references to Moses throughout the Old Testament. His history is given: Exod. 2–40; Book of Numbers; Deut. 1–34.]

THE LAW OF MOSES

The body of Hebrew legislation in the Pentateuch was developed over many centuries from many sources, and constituted a unique code. Whatever similarities of detail there might have been with other ancient codes, such as that of Hammurabi in Babylon, the Law of Moses had nothing in common with them in its religious beliefs or in its humanism.

The central message is the monotheism which the Hebrew people were the first to expound – the worship of one single, invisible and just God, and the rejection of every form of idolatry and paganism. The first and most important of the Ten commandments was:

'You shall have no other gods before me.' (Exod. 20:3)

But the Mosaic Code goes far beyond religious observance in the narrow sense. It deals with political, social and family affairs in a progressive spirit well in advance of its period. For example: there must be no arbitrary exercise of power; even a king must fear God and obey the law, 'that his heart may not be lifted up above his brethren, and that he may not turn aside from the commandment, either to the right hand or to the left' (Deut. 17:20).

Justice must be impartially administered, for rich and poor alike:

'You shall appoint judges and officers in all your towns which the Lord your God gives you, according to your tribes; and they shall judge the people with righteous judgment.

'You shall not pervert justice; you shall not show partiality; and you shall not take a bribe, for a bribe blinds the eyes of the wise, and subverts the cause of the righteous.' (Deut. 16:18–19)

Special protection is extended to the needy and the under-privileged, to fugitive slaves, debtors, hired servants, orphans, widows and foreigners. Women must be respected, and a slander against the chastity of a wife is a crime. Even the ox may not be muzzled while it is treading the grain on the threshing floor, and the mother-bird must be spared if eggs are collected from her nest. There must be fair practices in commerce – 'a full and just weight you shall have, a full and just measure you shall have' (Deut. 25:15). Men shall be exempted from military service if they have recently built a house, planted a vineyard or betrothed a wife, or are faint-hearted. Always, in his dealings with others, the Hebrew must say to himself: 'Love the sojourner therefore; for you were sojourners in the land of Egypt.' (Deut. 10:19)

For century after century, the Jewish rabbis and sages discussed and refined the Laws of Moses. Their commentaries were gathered together in the huge tomes of the Talmud, which a learned man might study all his life without exhausting them. In this fashion was shaped the distinctive outlook and way of life which the Jewish people carried with them to all the countries of their dispersion. Through Christianity, the Hebrew code profoundly influenced the civilization of the Western world.

Moza (Heb. 'departing') *1.* date unknown. A son of Caleb of the tribe of Judah, and his concubine Ephah. [1 Chr. 2:46]
2. date unknown. Son of Zimri of the tribe of Benjamin and a descendant of King Saul. [1 Chr. 8:36, 37; 9:42]

Muppim (Heb. 'serpent') *c.* 16 century BC. One of the ten sons of Benjamin and a grandson of Jacob, he went down to Egypt at the same time as Jacob. He is also known as Shephupham and Shephuphan. [Gen. 46:21; Num. 26:39; 1 Chr. 8:5]

Mushi (Heb. 'deserted') date unknown. Younger son of Merari and a grandson of Levi, his descendants were assigned special duties in the Tabernacle in the wilderness in the days of Moses. [Exod. 6:19; Num. 3:20; 4:29–31; 1 Chr. 6:47; 23:21, 23; 24:30]

N

Naam (Heb. 'pleasant') *c.* 13 century BC. Son of Caleb the son of Jephunneh and a leader of the tribe of Judah. [1 Chr. 4:15]

Naamah (Heb. 'pleasing') *1.* date unknown. Daughter of Lamech and Zillah, and the sister of Tubal-cain. [Gen. 4:22]
2. c. 10 century BC. A princess of Ammon who was the wife of King Solomon and the mother of Rehoboam who succeeded him as king of Israel. [1 Kgs. 14:21, 31; 2 Chr. 12:13]

Naaman (Heb. 'pleasantness') *1. c.* 16 century BC. A son of Benjamin and a grandson of Jacob and Rachel, he went down to Egypt at the same time as Jacob. In the Book of Numbers and in the First Book of Chronicles, Naaman is described as a grandson of Benjamin the son of Bela. [Gen. 46:21; Num. 26:40; 1 Chr. 8:4]
2. date unknown. Son of Ehud and a leader of the tribe of Benjamin, he was head of a family in Geba carried off in exile to Manahath. [1 Chr. 8:7]
3. c. 9 century BC. Commander of the Syrian army in the time of King Ben-hadad II, he contracted the dread disease of leprosy. His wife had an Israelite slave who had been taken captive on one of the Syrian incursions into Israel. The girl said there was a prophet called Elisha in Samaria who could cure him. Carrying lavish presents and a letter from his king to Jehoram, king of Israel, Naaman set out for Samaria with a military escort. Jehoram was very distressed at this unwelcome visit, fearing that the Syrians were making an impossible demand on him as a pretext to attack him. Elisha, hearing the story, sent word that the Syrian commander should be brought round to his house. The prophet did not come out to receive the foreign dignitary nor invite him in, but sent a messenger out to tell him that he should bathe seven times in the river Jordan. Naaman was enraged at this curt treatment and snorted that the rivers of Damascus were better than all the waters of Israel and why should he not wash in them. But his staff persuaded him to follow Elisha's advice and he was cured.

Naaman came back to Elisha and offered him a reward which the prophet declined. Now convinced that the Hebrew God was the only true one, Naaman asked leave to take two mule-loads of earth back to Damascus with him so that he could worship the Lord on Israelite soil. He also asked Elisha if the Lord would forgive him if, in the course of his duties to his master the king, he accompanied him to worship at the temple to Rimmon. Elisha told him to go in peace.

Elisha's servant Gehazi was overcome with greed at the thought of the rich gifts his master had spurned. He hurried after Naaman and with a concocted story about a couple of needy priests visiting Elisha, obtained from him two bags of silver and two changes of clothing. When he returned he hid these things in his house, but through his occult powers Elisha knew what had happened. He told Gehazi he may have enriched himself but at the cost of contracting the leprosy of which Naaman had been cured. [2 Kgs. 5]

Naarah (Heb. 'young girl') date unknown. One of the two wives of Ashhur a leader of the tribe of Judah. [1 Chr. 4:5, 6]

Naarai see PAARAI

Nabal (Heb. 'fool') c. 11 century BC. Nabal was a wealthy sheep farmer who lived in Carmel in the Hebron hills with his attractive and intelligent wife Abigail. At shearing time a group of ten young men called on him, asking for provisions for David, then leader of a band of outlaws. They pointed out that Nabal's sheep had grazed all winter unmolested. Nabal answered rudely: 'Who is David? Who is the son of Jesse? There are many servants nowadays who are breaking away from their masters.' (1 Sam. 25:10) David was furious when he heard the story and set out with four hundred men, vowing he would wipe out everyone he found at Nabal's farmstead. He was headed off by Abigail who slipped out to meet him with provisions. On returning, she found her husband drunk from the feast given to celebrate the sheep-shearing. Next morning she told him how narrowly he had escaped David's wrath. The frightened Nabal suffered a heart attack from which he died ten days later. On hearing about this, David sent her a proposal of marriage, which she accepted. [1 Sam. 25:3–39; 27:3; 30:5; 2 Sam. 2:2]

Naboth (Heb. 'fruits') c. 9 century BC. Naboth the Jezreelite had a vineyard adjoining the grounds of the winter palace of King Ahab of Israel. Ahab asked Naboth to give him the vineyard in exchange for another one, or to sell it to him, as he wanted it for a vegetable garden. But Naboth answered Ahab, 'The Lord forbid that I should give you the inheritance of my fathers.' (1 Kgs. 21:3)

Queen Jezebel arranged for Naboth to be charged and convicted of blasphemy, on false evidence. 'So they took him outside the city, and stoned him to death with stones.' (1 Kgs. 21:13) Ahab was then entitled to take possession of the vineyard, presumably because the property of criminals was held to be forfeited to the ruler. [1 Kgs. 21:18; 2 Kgs. 9:25, 26]

Nacon (Heb. 'ready') c. 10 century BC. Owner of the threshing floor where the oxen stumbled while carrying the Ark to Jerusalem and where Uzzah was killed. Also called Chidon. [2 Sam. 6:6; 1 Chr. 13:9]

Nadab (Heb. '[God] is willing') *1. c.* 13 century BC. Eldest son of Aaron the high priest, Nadab and his brothers held priestly office with their father Aaron. After the Tabernacle had been completed, Nadab and Abihu burnt forbidden incense before the Lord and were instantly killed. [Exod. 6:23; 24:1, 9; 28:1; Lev. 10:1, 52; Num. 3:2, 4; 26:60, 61; 1 Chr. 6:3; 24:1, 2]
2. date unknown. A son of Jeiel, Nadab and his family were leaders of the tribe of Benjamin living in Jerusalem. [1 Chr. 8:30; 9:36]
3. date unknown. The elder son of Shammai and a leader of the tribe of Judah. [1 Chr. 2:28, 30]
4. Second king of Israel after the monarchy split, he reigned 910–09 BC. Nadab was the son and successor of Jeroboam I. Just before he became king, Israel had been defeated by the forces of Judah and the southern part of its territory occupied. Thus weakened it came under pressure from the Philistines in the coastal plain. Nadab led his men against the Philistines, and laid siege to the town of Gibbethon, south-west of Gezer. Baasha, of the tribe of Issachar, seized the chance to carry out a successful coup, overthrowing Nadab and putting him and all his offspring to death. [1 Kgs. 14:20; 15:25–31]

Naham (Heb. 'comforter') date unknown. Brother-in-law of Hodiah, from the tribe of Judah. [1 Chr. 4:19]

Nahamani (Heb. 'compassionate') 6 century BC. A leader of Judah who returned to Judah with Zerubbabel from exile in Babylon. [Neh. 7:7]

Naharai c. 10 century BC. A soldier from Beeroth, he was armour-bearer to Joab and one of King David's chosen guard renowned for his bravery. [2 Sam. 23:37; 1 Chr. 11:39]

Nahash (Heb. 'serpent') *1. c.* 10 century BC. King of the Ammonites who lived east of the river Jordan, he besieged the city of Jabesh-gilead. The inhabitants of the city offered to make a treaty and surrender to him. Nahash agreed, provided he could gouge out the right eye of every Jabeshite. Gaining seven days' truce, they sent frantic messages asking for help throughout Israel. Saul was coming in from the fields with his cattle when he learnt the grim plight of Jabesh-gilead. He mobilized a large force and marched to the relief of the beleaguered town. The Ammonite army was routed, and the city saved.

Nahash's son Shobi brought supplies to David when he fled from Absalom, and came to Mahaniam. [1 Sam. 11:1–3; 12:12; 2 Sam. 10:2; 17:27; 1 Chr. 19:1–2] *2. c.* 11 century BC. Sister of Zeruiah, mother of Abigail, she was the grandmother of Amasa who commanded the army of Absalom. [2 Sam. 17:25]

Nahath (Heb. 'rest') *1. c.* 16 century BC. Son of Reuel and a grandson of Esau, he was an Edomite leader. [Gen. 36:13, 17; 1 Chr. 1:37]
2. see TOAH
3. c. 8 century BC. A Levite appointed by King Hezekiah to supervise the bringing of offerings and tithes into the Temple. [2 Chr. 31:13]

Nahbi (Heb. 'secret') *c.* 13 century BC.

Son of Vophsi, a leader of the tribe of Naphtali, Nahbi was one of the twelve men sent by Moses to spy out the Promised Land. [Num. 13:14]

Nahor *1.* date unknown. Son of Serug and grandfather of Abraham. [Gen. 11:22, 23; 1 Chr. 1:26]
2. c. 18 century BC. Brother of Abraham whose granddaughter Rebekah married Abraham's son Isaac. [Gen. 11:26, 27, 29; 22:20; 24:10, 15, 24, 47; 29:5; Josh. 24:2]

Nahshon (Heb. 'diviner') *c.* 13 century BC. Leader of the tribe of Judah in the wilderness and a brother-in-law of Aaron, he was the son of Amminadab. [Exod. 6:23; Num. 1:7; 2:3; 7:12, 17; 10:14; Ruth 4:20; 1 Chr. 2:9–11]

Nahum (Heb. 'comforted') *c.* 7 century BC. Hebrew prophet. In his brief prophetic Book, Nahum the Elkoshite (the place is unknown) is not concerned with the religious and moral welfare of his own people, like other Hebrew prophets. He confines himself to lashing out against Nineveh, the capital of the hated Assyrian empire, that dominated the Near East of his time. He calls it a 'bloody city, all full of lies and booty' (Nah. 3:1), and predicts its coming downfall in some of the most vivid and powerful descriptive passages in the Old Testament. The Book must have been written a few years before the actual fall of the city in 612 BC.

Nahum describes the assault troops – the scarlet uniforms and shields and the flashing steel of the chariots: 'Horsemen charging, flashing sword and glittering spear, hosts of slain, heaps of corpses, dead bodies without end – they stumble over the bodies.' (Nah. 3:3) Fear and panic grip the inhabitants but there is no one to save the city from becoming 'Desolate! Desolation and ruin!' (Nah. 2:10) And when it has been destroyed 'all who hear the news of you clap their hands over you. For upon whom has not come your unceasing evil?' (Nah. 3:19)

Among the fragments of Dead Sea Scrolls found in the Qumran caves were portions of a commentary on Nahum, which has helped to establish the dates of the Scrolls and identify some of the obscure references. [Book of Nahum]

Naomi (Heb. 'my pleasure') *c.* 11 century BC. Mother-in-law of Ruth.

The tender tale of the love between Naomi and her Moabite daughter-in-law Ruth is placed in the period of the judges. Naomi lived with her husband Elimelech in the small town of Bethlehem, where she had two sons, Mahlon and Chilion. When famine swept the country, the family moved to the neighbouring country of Moab on the fertile plateau east of the Dead Sea and settled there. Elimelech died and the two sons married Moabite girls, Orpah and Ruth. After ten years, both sons died and the bereft Naomi, hearing that the famine had ceased in the land of Israel, decided to return to her people.

To her daughters-in-law Naomi said, 'Go, return each of you to her mother's house. May the Lord deal kindly with you, as you have dealt with the dead and with me.' (Ruth 1:8) The two young widows at first refused to leave her. With melancholy sarcasm she asked whether they expected her to marry again and produce sons as husbands for them. Orpah finally went 'back to her people and to her gods' (Ruth 1:15). Naomi tried to persuade the tearful Ruth to do the same; but Ruth refused to part from her.

The two women set out alone along the arduous hundred-mile journey down the mountains, across the floor of the Jordan valley and up through the wilderness of Judea to Bethlehem. When they entered the town the people were very surprised and cried out, 'Is this Naomi?' (Ruth 1:19) Naomi, making a play on

her name, said to them, 'Do not call me Naomi, call me Mara, for the Almighty has dealt very bitterly with me.' (Ruth 1:20) (*Mara* means 'bitter' in Hebrew.)

Ruth went to glean barley in a field belonging to Boaz, a wealthy relative of her dead father-in-law, Elimelech. Boaz treated her kindly and gave her extra food. With Boaz obviously attracted towards the gentle and appealing young widow, Naomi saw a prospect of gaining a happier and more secure life for her beloved daughter-in-law. Naomi said to Ruth, 'My daughter, should I not seek a home for you, that it may be well with you? Now is not Boaz our kinsman ...?' (Ruth 3:1, 2) She had Ruth bathe and perfume herself and put on her best clothes. On Naomi's instructions Ruth waited until Boaz was asleep on the ground at the threshing floor and went to lie trustfully at his feet. When he woke up he was deeply moved to find her there.

Next day Boaz arranged to marry Ruth, in exercise of a kinsman's 'right of redemption' of a widow. A son was born to them called Obed, and to Naomi's great joy the baby was handed over to her care. Her women neighbours assured Naomi that the boy would be 'a restorer of life and a nourisher of your old age' (Ruth 4:15). Obed's son Jesse was the father of King David. [Book of Ruth]

Naphish *c.* 17 century BC. Son of Abraham's son Ishmael, he was a desert leader. [Gen. 25:13–15; 1 Chr. 1:31; 5:18–19]

Naphtali (Heb. 'wrestling') *c.* 16 century BC. The fifth son of Jacob.

Naphtali was the second son born to Bilhah, the maid Rachel gave Jacob her husband as a concubine. Together with his brothers, he was involved in the selling of Joseph into slavery in Egypt. Later he was one of the ten sons sent by Jacob to buy corn in Egypt where Joseph had become a leading figure at the Pharaoh's court. When Jacob went to settle in Egypt with all his family it included Naphtali's four sons.

On his deathbed Jacob blessed his sons in turn. Of Naphtali he said: 'Naphtali is a hind let loose, that bears comely fawns.' (Gen. 49:21)

Centuries later, in the conquest of Canaan under Joshua, the tribe of Naphtali was allocated an extensive territory stretching from the Jezreel valley and the Sea of Galilee to the northern border.

In the blessing attributed to Moses, he referred to Naphtali as 'satisfied with favour, and full of the blessing of the Lord' (Deut. 33:23). [Gen. 30:8; 35:25; 46:24; 49:21; Exod. 1:4; Deut. 33:23; 1 Chr. 2:2; 7:13]

Naphtuhim date unknown. Son of Egypt and a grandson of Ham. [Gen. 10:13]

Nathan (Heb. 'he gave') *1.* date unknown. Son of Ahai, descended from Jerahoneel, he was the father of Zabad. [1 Chr. 2:36]

2. c. 10 century BC. Hebrew prophet.

The prophet Nathan was a trusted adviser to King David. The Lord revealed to Nathan in a dream that he did not want the Temple built by David but by his son Solomon.

After the king had sent Uriah the Hittite to his death in battle, so that he could marry Uriah's wife Bathsheba, Nathan told a parable to the king, concerning 'two men in a certain city, the one rich and the other poor' (2 Sam. 12:1). The rich man had a great many flocks and herds, while the poor man had only one cherished ewe-lamb reared in his home. One day a traveller came to the city and the rich man offered him hospitality. Instead of killing one of his flock for the meal, he slaughtered the poor man's lamb. On hearing this story, David was greatly incensed and said the rich man should die 'because he did this thing, and because he had no pity.' (2 Sam. 12:6) Nathan promptly answered, 'You are the man.' (2 Sam. 12:7) He reminded David how much he had achieved with the Lord's help; yet he had done evil in the sight of the Lord, who now declared that 'Behold, I will raise up evil against you out of your own house.' (2 Sam. 12:11) The child born by Bathsheba fell ill and died.

When David was aged and ailing, the prophet got word that the eldest prince Adonijah planned to usurp the throne. Nathan advised Bathsheba to go to the king, recall his promise that Solomon would succeed him, and tell him of Adonijah's designs. The prophet followed her and confirmed her words. David commanded Nathan and Zadok the priest to take Solomon on the royal mule to the spring of Gihon and anoint him king.

After David's death, Nathan's two sons were given high office by Solomon: Azariah was put in charge of the officials responsible for the twelve tax districts; while Zabud became Solomon's confidential adviser.

It is mentioned that Nathan chronicled the events of David's reign, but no such work has been found. [2 Sam. 7:2–17; 12:1–25; 1 Kgs. 1:8–45; 4:4–5; 1 Chr. 17:1–15; 29:29; 2 Chr. 9:29; 29:25; Ps. 51; Zech. 12:12]

3. c. 10 century BC. Father of Igal, a warrior in the army of King David; in the First Book of Chronicles he is described as the brother of Joel. [2 Sam. 23:36; 1 Chr. 11:38]

4. c. 10 century BC. A son of King David and Bathsheba. [2 Sam. 5:14; 1 Chr. 3:5; 14:4]

5. 5 century BC. A leader of Judah in Babylon, he was sent by Ezra to ask Iddo to send Levites to Jerusalem to minister in the Temple. [Ezra 8:16]

6. 5 century BC. A descendant of Binnui who divorced his non-Jewish wife in the time of Ezra. [Ezra 10:39]

Nathan-Melech *c.* 7 century BC. An official in the time of King Josiah whose name was given to a room in the Temple used for sun-worship. During the reforms Josiah took down the statues of horses – 'chariots of the sun' – that had been set there by earlier kings of Judah. [2 Kgs. 23:11]

Neariah (Heb. 'child of God') *1. c.* 8 century BC. A leader of the tribe of Simeon in the days of Hezekiah, king of Judah, he led an army of 500 men and drove out the Amalekites from Mount Seir, south-east of the Dead Sea, and settled there. [1 Chr. 4:42]
2. date unknown. Son of Shemaiah of the tribe of Judah, he was a descendant of King David. [1 Chr. 3:22, 23]

Nebai (Heb. 'building') 5 century BC. A leader of Judah who signed the solemn covenant in the time of Nehemiah. [Neh. 10:19]

Nebaioth (Heb. 'heights') *c.* 17 century BC. Eldest son of Ishmael and the grandson of Abraham and Hagar, he was one of the twelve leaders who ruled from Egypt to Assyria. [Gen. 25:13; 28:9; 36:3; 1 Chr. 1:29]

Nebat (Heb. 'view') *c.* 10 century BC. Father of Jeroboam, king of Israel, he died before his son's rebellion split the united monarchy. [1 Kgs. 11:26; 12:2, 15; 15:1; 16:3, 26, 31; 21:22; 22:52; 2 Kgs. 3:3; 9:9; 10:29; 13:2, 11; 14:24; 15:9; 17:21; 23:15; 2 Chr. 9:29; 10:2, 15; 13:6]

Nebo (Acc. 'the proclaimer') *1.* A Babylonian god, he was originally the Sumerian deity of wisdom and writing, and the cult of Nebo became very popular in Assyria and the Babylonian empire. His 'wisdom' related to the movement of the stars and the priests of Nebo were astrologers. His 'writing' was associated with the tables of fate upon which were inscribed the names of the people. The main centre of Nebo worship was his shrine at Borsippa, south-west of Babylon. [Isa. 46:1]
2. date unknown. Ancestor of a family who returned to Judah with Ezra and whose descendants divorced their non-Jewish wives. [Ezra 10:43]

Nebuchadnezzar (Ass. 'Nabu protects my boundary stone') King of Babylon, 604–562 BC. The fall of Nineveh in 612 BC marked the end of the mighty Assyrian empire and its replacement by Babylonia as the dominant power of the Near East. In 605 BC a Babylonian army commanded by Nebuchadnezzar, the crown prince, marched into the area and decisively defeated the Egyptians at the battle of Carcemish. He advanced towards Egypt but turned back to assume the throne of Babylon when his father died. Judah became a vassal of Babylon.

In 598 BC Judah attempted to throw off the yoke of Babylon. Nebuchadnezzar advanced on Jerusalem and occupied it. He carried off the young King Jehoiachin and appointed his uncle Zedekiah to the throne.

Nine years later, in 587 BC, Zedekiah was drawn into a rebellion, against the advice of the prophet Jeremiah. Again Nebuchadnezzar besieged Jerusalem, which held out for two years and then fell. The city was destroyed, including the demolition of the Temple, the palace and the walls. Most of the inhabitants were carried off to exile in Babylon. Judah was annexed as a Babylonian province.

Nebuchadnezzar was the most powerful and energetic ruler of the new Babylonian empire. His capital, Babylon, became the greatest centre of trade, architecture, art and astronomy of the time.

The terraced roof gardens on top of his palace, the 'hanging gardens of Babylon', were listed by the Greeks as one of the seven wonders of the world. Also called Nebuchadrezzar. [2 Kgs. 24, 25; 1 Chr. 6:15; 2 Chr. 36; Ezra 1:7; 2:1; 5:12, 14; Neh. 7:6; Esther 2:6; Jer. 21; 22; 24; 25; 27–9; 32; 34; 37; 39; 43; 44; 46; 49–52; Ezek. 26; 29; 30; Dan. 1–5]

Nebuchadrezzar *see* NEBUCHADNEZZAR

Nebushazban (Ass. 'Nabu saves') *c.* 6 century BC. One of the officers in the Babylonian army responsible for the destruction of Jerusalem, he was among those who committed Jeremiah to the care of Gedaliah, son of Ahikam, the Babylonian-appointed governor of Judah. His title was Rabsaris. [Jer. 39:13]

Nebuzaradan (Ass. 'Nabu has given offspring') *c.* 6 century BC. Captain of the guard of Nebuchadnezzar, king of Babylon, he led a successful attack on Jerusalem and burnt the Temple, the king's palace and all the houses, and demolished the city walls. He carried off the people of Jerusalem to exile in Babylon, but left some farmers to look after the vineyards and the field crops. He released the prophet Jeremiah who had advised the people to submit to the Babylonians and appointed Gedaliah, son of Ahikam, to rule over Judah. Five years later Nebuzaradan returned to Jerusalem and took another group of Jews into exile. [2 Kgs. 25:8–20; Jer. 39:9–13; 40:1–5; 41:10; 43:6; 52:12–26]

Neco *see* PHARAOH *9.*

Nedabiah (Heb. 'God is generous') *c.* 6 century BC. Son of Jehoiachin, the last king of Judah, and a descendant of King David. [1 Chr. 3:18]

Nehemiah (Heb. 'God has consoled') *1.* 6 century BC. A leader of Judah who returned with Zerubbabel from Babylon. [Ezra 2:2; Neh. 7:7]

2. 5 century BC. Son of Azbuk, he helped rebuild the walls of Jerusalem in the days of Nehemiah. [Neh. 3:16]
3. c. 5 century BC. Jewish governor of Judea.

Nehemiah the son of Hacaliah was a member of the Judean exile community in Babylonia that came into existence at the time of the fall of Jerusalem. After Babylon had been conquered by the Persians in 539 BC, the Jewish minority was well treated and prospered. Nehemiah was appointed the royal cupbearer to King Artaxerxes I in Susa (Shushan) the capital. This was a position of honour and trust which brought Nehemiah into daily contact with the monarch.

Nearly a century earlier, the Persian king Cyrus had issued a decree permitting the Jewish exiles to return to Judea. Nehemiah relates in his personal memoirs how his kinsman Hanani arrived with some companions from Jerusalem and came to see him. He asked how the settlers in Judea were faring and was told: 'The survivors there in the province who escaped exile are in great trouble and shame; the wall of Jerusalem is broken down, and its gates are destroyed by fire.' (Neh. 1:3) Nehemiah was deeply affected by this report. A devout man, he fasted and prayed, recalling the Lord's promise to Moses to redeem the Children of Israel. That was in 445 BC, the twentieth year of the reign of his master Artaxerxes.

The resolve took shape in Nehemiah's mind to go to Jerusalem himself. A short while later, he was serving wine at the royal table when the king asked him why he looked so downcast. He replied: 'why should not my face be sad, when the city, the place of my fathers' sepulchres, lies waste ...?' (Neh. 2:3) Nehemiah asked for permission to make a trip to Jerusalem, which was granted. The sympathetic ruler also gave him letters to the provincial governors along the route, an instruction to the keeper of the royal parks to provide him with any timber he might need for construction work in Jerusalem, and an armed escort for the journey of over a thousand miles across mountains, rivers and deserts.

On his arrival in Jerusalem, Nehemiah did not make himself known at once to the authorities. He rested three days, then got up at night and with a few men made a secret moonlight inspection tour of the ruined walls and gates of the city. Nehemiah then called together the Jewish leaders, and proposed that the work of rebuilding the fortifications be put in hand at once. They responded eagerly: 'Let us rise up and build.' (Neh. 2:18) The project was organized on a voluntary basis, with specific parts of it allocated to some of the surrounding towns and to guilds such as the goldsmiths and perfume-makers. Each of the leading merchants and priests undertook to be responsible for the section of the wall opposite his own home.

There were leaders in neighbouring territories who objected to the shattered fortifications of Jerusalem being restored. One was Sanballat the provincial governor of Samaria, who claimed general authority over the Judean district as well. The Samaritans had been hostile to the return of the Jewish exiles from Babylon and at an earlier stage had succeeded for a long time in holding up the reconstruction of the Temple.

Sanballat's opposition was supported by Geshem, ruler of the Edomites who had occupied the southern part of Judah; and by Tobiah, head of a wealthy feudal family of Jews in Transjordan, with relatives among the Jerusalem notables. At first the three of them tried to kill the project by ridicule: 'They derided us and despised us and said, "What is this thing that you are doing? Are you rebelling against the king?"' (Neh. 2:19) Nehemiah answered stoutly that the building would go on,

and that 'you have no portion or right or memorial in Jerusalem.' (Neh. 2:20) Sanballat continued to mock them, and asked whether these 'feeble Jews' really wanted to 'revive the stones out of the heaps of rubbish, and burned ones at that?' (Neh. 4:2) Tobiah added that even a fox would be able to break down their stone wall.

But when the wall reached mid-height and the builders were getting tired and discouraged, their opponents threatened to stop them by force. Nehemiah made security arrangements for the work to continue. He posted an armed militia day and night, and also made each of the workers carry a weapon. 'And each of the builders had his sword girded at his side while he built.' (Neh. 4:18) Since the working parties were strung out in different sectors at some distance from each other, he commanded that they should all rally when they heard the trumpet sound. At night they remained within the walls. Nehemiah records that during this period neither he nor the members of his family nor his bodyguard took off their clothes except for washing.

These vigorous precautions had their effect, and the idea of armed intervention was dropped. Instead, his enemies resorted to various intrigues. They invited Nehemiah to meet them for a parley, but he distrusted them and declined. Sanballat then sent Nehemiah a letter, suggesting that the walls were being erected because Nehemiah planned to rebel against the Persian rulers and proclaim himself king. These rumours, the letter stated, would no doubt reach the Persian court, and Nehemiah had better come and discuss matters. Nehemiah replied that the rumours were unfounded, and a figment of Sanballat's imagination.

At this point Shemaiah, the high priest, urged Nehemiah to take sanctuary in the Temple and hide there, as his life was in danger. Nehemiah answered sharply that he had no intention of running away. He notes in his memoirs that the priest was no doubt in the pay of Tobiah, and that they were trying to frighten him.

In spite of every obstacle, the walls and gates were completed. On the appointed day the solemn dedication took place. After the purification ceremonies, two processions marched round the walls in opposite directions, each headed by priests and notables. They met at the Temple, where the thanksgiving service was followed by a feast.

Nehemiah appointed gatekeepers and sentries for the gates. He put his kinsman Hanani in charge of the city with instructions to see that all the gates were to be shut before sundown and reopened in the morning.

With the city secure behind its reconstructed walls, Nehemiah gave thought to increasing its population. He had a census taken of the inhabitants, and compared the results with the original lists of returnees from Babylon. He then invited the leading men of other Judean towns to move to Jerusalem, 'the Holy City'. From the rest of the Judean population, one person selected by lot out of every ten came to settle in the capital.

The list of the towns outside Jerusalem indicates areas of Jewish settlement which were not part of the Jerusalem district at an earlier period of the Return. It is probable that these were border areas of Hebrew settlement in the Negev, the Shephelah and to the north of Jerusalem that remained intact at the time of the fall of the city and the deportations to Babylon. If so, they became integrated again into Judea in Nehemiah's time.

In 433 BC, after twelve years in Jerusalem, Nehemiah returned to Persia and presented himself again to his royal master. During his absence the standards of religious observance declined in Judea and abuses crept in. Some time later Nehemiah came back to Jerusalem and

carried out a series of sweeping reforms. They corresponded to the written covenant which the leading citizens had signed in a formal ceremony, probably under the supervision of Ezra the scribe.

On his return Nehemiah was horrified to find that the high priest Eliashib had placed at the disposal of Tobiah, a wealthy Jewish landowner, a room in the Temple court used for keeping sacrificial food, incense and vessels. Nehemiah ordered the furnishings to be flung out and the room restored to its proper use.

Most of the Levites and cantors in the service of the Temple had gone back to their villages and fields because the dues from the worshippers had not been paid. Nehemiah strongly reprimanded all concerned; the Temple staff returned to work and the tithes were promptly paid into the storehouses in the form of corn, oil and wine. Nehemiah placed four trustworthy officials in charge of gathering and distributing these dues.

He next clamped down on the desecration of the Sabbath. Farmers were bringing their produce into the city market on the holy day, and Phoenician traders were selling fish brought up from the coast. Nehemiah ordered the gates of the city to be shut before the Sabbath started and reopened only after the Sabbath was over. Traders who came and bivouacked next to the walls on the Sabbath were chased away.

Nehemiah denounced the practice of intermarriage with the surrounding peoples. In many cases, the children could only speak the foreign tongue and not Hebrew. To set an example, he expelled from Jerusalem Jehoiada the high priest's son, for having married the daughter of Sanballat the Samaritan leader.

Nehemiah was anxious to get due credit with the Lord for his diligence in restoring the purity of religion and in preserving the identity of the Jews. His memoir ends with the words:

'Remember me, O my God, for good.' (Neh. 13:31) [Book of Nehemiah]

Nehushta (Heb. 'brazen') *c.* 7 century BC. Daughter of Elnathan of Jerusalem, she became the wife of Jehoiakim, king of Judah, and the mother of Jehoiachin, his successor. [2 Kgs. 24:8]

Nehum (Heb. 'comfort') 6 century BC. A leader of the Jewish community in Babylon who returned with Zerubbabel and settled in Jerusalem. Also known as Rehum. [Ezra 2:2; Neh. 7:7]

Nekoda (Heb. 'sheep owner') *1.* date unknown. Ancestor of a family of Temple servants who returned to Judah with Zerubbabel from exile in Babylon. [Ezra 2:48; Neh. 7:50]
2. date unknown. Ancestor of a family of Judah who returned with Zerubbabel from exile but who could not trace their family tree and therefore could not prove that they were Jews. [Ezra 2:60; Neh. 7:62]

Nemuel (Heb. 'God's day') *1.* see JEMUEL
2. c. 13 century BC. A son of Eliab, he was a leader of the tribe of Reuben and the brother of Dathan and Abiram who conspired with Korah against Moses and Aaron in the wilderness. [Num. 26:9]

Nepheg (Heb. 'sprout') *1. c.* 13 century BC. A son of Izhar of the tribe of Levi, he was a brother of Korah who led the revolt against Moses in the wilderness. [Exod. 6:21]
2. c. 10 century BC. A son of King David, born to him in Jerusalem. [2 Sam. 5:15; 1 Chr. 3:7; 14:6]

Nephisim date unknown. Ancestor of a family who returned to Judah with Zerubbabel from Babylon. In the Book of Nehemiah he is called Nephushesim. [Ezra 2:50; Neh. 7:52]

Nephushesim *see* NEPHISIM

Ner (Heb. 'lamp') *c.* 11 century BC. Grandfather or uncle of King Saul. In the First Book of Samuel Ner is described as the son of Abiel and a brother of Saul's father Kish, but in the First Book of Chronicles Ner is described as the father of Kish and the grandfather of Saul. His son was Abner, the commander of King Saul's army. [1 Sam. 14:50, 51; 26:5, 14; 2 Sam. 2:8, 12; 3:23, 25, 28, 37; 1 Kgs. 2:5, 32; 1 Chr. 8:33; 9:36, 39; 26:28]

Nergal The god of sun and war worshipped by the Assyrians and Babylonians and taken over by the men of Cuth who were settled in Samaria after the destruction of the northern kingdom of Israel in 721 BC. [2 Kgs. 17:30]

Nergal–Sharezer (Bab. 'Nergal preserve the king') *c.* 6 century BC. An officer of Nebuchadnezzar who sat down in the middle gate after the fall of Jerusalem. He carried out Nebuchadnezzar's order to release the prophet Jeremiah from jail and treat him well. His title was Rabmag (Babylonian 'most wise prince').

His name was found on a cuneiform tablet excavated at Erech. He succeeded to the throne after killing his brother-in-law Evil-meredoch, became king of Babylon, and reigned four years, 560–56 BC. [2 Kgs. 25:27; Jer. 39:3, 13, 14]

Neriah (Heb. 'God is my light') *c.* 7 century BC. A priest of Judah who was the father of Baruch, disciple of the prophet Jeremiah. He may be identical with Neriah, son of Mahseiah whose son Seraiah was the leader of Judah to whom Jeremiah addressed his prophecies after the fall of Jerusalem. [Jer. 32:12, 16; 36:4, 8, 14, 32; 43:3, 6; 45:1; 51:59]

Nethanel (Heb. 'gift of God') *1. c.* 13

century BC. Son of Zuar, Nathanel was appointed chief of the contingent of Issachar in the army of the children of Israel in the wilderness. [Num. 1:8; 2:5; 7:18, 23; 10:15]

2. *c.* 10 century BC. Fourth son of Jesse of the tribe of Judah and a brother of King David. [1 Chr. 2:14]

3. *c.* 10 century BC. A priest who blew a trumpet during the ceremony of bringing the Ark of God to Jerusalem in the reign of King David. [1 Chr. 15:24]

4. *c.* 10 century BC. A Levite, he was the father of Shemaiah, the scribe who kept the records of the service of the Levites in the Tabernacle in the reign of King David. [1 Chr. 24:6]

5. *c.* 10 century BC. A son of Obededom who, with his seven brothers, served as gatekeepers of the Tabernacle in the reign of King David. [1 Chr. 26:4]

6. *c.* 9 century BC. A leader of Judah sent by King Jehoshaphat to teach the Law of God to the people of Judah. [2 Chr. 17:7]

7. *c.* 7 century BC. A leader of the Levites in the reign of Josiah, king of Judah, who donated large quantities of cattle for the special Passover offering. [2 Chr. 35:9]

8. 5 century BC. A descendant of Pashhur, a priest of Judah, he divorced his non-Jewish wife in the time of Ezra. [Ezra 10:22]

9. 5 century BC. Son of Hilkiah and head of a priestly family who lived when Joiakim was high priest, towards the end of Nehemiah's lifetime. [Neh. 12:21]

10. 5 century BC. A Levite who played musical instruments at the service of dedication of the rebuilt walls of Jerusalem in the time of Nehemiah. [Neh. 12:36]

Nethaniah (Heb. 'given by God') **1.** *c.* 10 century BC. A son of Asaph, chief musician to King David, he and his brothers played musical instruments under their father's direction. Nethaniah

took the fifth turn of service in the Tabernacle. [1 Chr. 25:2, 12]

2. *c.* 9 century BC, One of the Levites sent by King Jehoshaphat to teach the Law of God to the people of Judah. [2 Chr. 17:8]

3. *c.* 7 century BC. Son of Shelemiah, he was the father of Jehudi, the court official who read out Jeremiah's prophecies to the princes of Judah. [Jer. 36:14]

4. 6 century BC. Son of Elishama and a descendant of the royal family of Judah, he was the father of Ishmael who assassinated Gedaliah, the governor of Judah. [2 Kgs. 25:23, 25; Jer. 40:8, 14, 15, 16; 41:1-18]

Neziah date unknown. Ancestor of a family of Temple servants who returned to Judah with Zerubbabel from exile in Babylon. [Ezra 2:54; Neh. 7:56]

Nibhaz One of the gods worshipped by the people of Babylon who were settled in parts of Samaria by the Assyrians after the capture of the northern kingdom of Israel. [2 Kgs. 17:31]

Nimrod date unknown. Son of Cush and a grandson of Noah, he was renowned as a great hunter and ruled over a large kingdom in what is now Iraq. The prophet Micah refers to the destruction of the land of Nimrod by a Jewish king from Bethlehem. [Gen. 10:9; 1 Chr. 1:10; Mic. 5:6]

Nimshi *c.* 9 century BC. Grandfather of Jehu, commander of the army of King Joram who seized the throne of Israel. Jehu is also referred to as the son of Nimshi. [1 Kgs. 19:16; 2 Kgs. 9:2, 20; 2 Chr. 22:7]

Nisroch An Assyrian god in whose temple Sennacherib, king of Assyria, was murdered by two of his sons. [2 Kgs. 19:37; Isa. 37:38]

Noadiah (Heb. 'revealed by God') **1.** 5

century BC. Son of Binnui, he was a Levite who assisted the priest, Meremoth, in weighing the gold, silver and precious vessels which Ezra brought back from Babylon to Judah. [Ezra 8:33]

2. 5 century BC. A prophetess hired by Tobiah and Sanballat to discourage Nehemiah from completing the work of rebuilding the walls of Jerusalem after the return from exile in Babylon. [Neh. 6:14]

Noah (Heb. 'rest') *1. c.* 2000 BC. The son of Lamech, Noah was the tenth generation in descent from Adam. He was a just and God-fearing man, but lived in a period when 'the earth was corrupt ... filled with violence' (Gen. 6:11). God told Noah that He had decided to destroy all living creatures with a great flood. Noah was ordered to build a wooden ark with three decks, according to certain precise measurements. It was stocked with every kind of food.

Before the flood began, Noah went into the ark with his wife, his three sons Shem, Ham and Japheth and their wives, and a male and female of each living creature (in the case of the 'clean' animals there were seven pairs of each). The Bible gives Noah's age at this time as 'six hundred years old' (Gen. 7:6).

Then the rains came: 'on that day all the fountains of the great deep burst forth, and the windows of the heavens were opened.' (Gen. 7:11) It poured for forty days and forty nights and the floodwater rose until it covered the mountain tops. The ark floated on the surface with its strange cargo while all other life perished on earth.

After five months the floodwater started to recede and in the seventh month the ark came to rest on the top of Mount Ararat. Noah waited several more months while the water subsided. He then opened the window of the ark and sent out a raven which 'went to and fro'. (Gen. 8:7) He also despatched a dove which did not find dry land and came back to the ark. A week later the dove went forth the second time and brought back an olive leaf in its beak. The third time the dove did not return, and this meant that the earth was dry. A year after they had entered it, Noah and his family and all the living creatures emerged from the ark.

Noah built an altar and made sacrifices to the Lord, in thankfulness for his deliverance. The Lord made a covenant with him that the flood would not be repeated; that Noah and his descendants would be fruitful and people the earth again; and that all the living creatures that had been preserved in the ark would also multiply and serve man for food. The cycle of nature, the Lord promised, would be restored: 'While the earth remains, seedtime and harvest, cold and heat, summer and winter, day and night, shall not cease.' (Gen. 8:22) Every time there was a rainbow in the clouds, it would serve as a token of God's covenant with Noah.

Noah cultivated a vineyard and became drunk on his own wine. While he lay naked in his tent, his son Ham came in and stared at his father in this undignified position. He told his two brothers, Shem and Japheth, who entered the tent backwards carrying a garment and covered up Noah with their faces averted. When Noah aroused himself from his stupor, he cursed Ham and Ham's son Canaan, saying that they would be servants to their brethren.

Noah died at the age of nine hundred and fifty years.

If Adam was the first Founding Father, Noah was the second, for with him the human race made a fresh start. He had another minor distinction as the first producer of wine recorded in the Bible.

Noah's story is told with such charm and freshness of detail that he and his family, the wooden ark, the animals who went in two by two, and the dove with an olive leaf in its beak, have become the nursery fables and toys of countless generations of children.

The Hebrews believed that the races of the ancient Near East were each descended from one or other of Noah's three sons. Shem was the ancestor of the Semites inhabiting the fertile crescent and the Arabian desert. From Japheth came the Indo-European peoples to the north and west. The Hamites dwelt mainly in Africa (Egypt and Ethiopia). These three groups were represented in the Land of Canaan itself: the Hebrews were Semites, the Philistines in the coastal area were Western invaders identified with Japheth, and the forefather of the local Canaanites was Canaan, the son of Ham.

The story of a great flood that destroyed most of mankind recurs in the folklore of primitive tribes in different parts of the world. The account in the Bible has many similarities with a Babylonian version appearing in the epic Gilgamesh, written on clay tablets in the 7th century BC, but believed to be a copy of a much earlier original. It is possible that the Babylonian story had its origin in a flood disaster in southern Mesopotamia in the 3rd millennium BC. [Gen. 5-10; 1 Chr. 1:4]

2. *c.* 13 century BC. A daughter of Zelophehad who claimed a share of her father's estate before Moses, since her father had no sons. [Num. 26:33; 27:1; 36:11; Josh. 17:3]

Nobah (Heb. 'barking') date unknown. A leader of the tribe of Manasseh who settled east of the river Jordan, captured the region of Kenath and named it after himself. [Num. 32:42; Judg. 8:11]

Nogah (Heb. 'bright') *c.* 10 century BC. One of the sons of King David, born to him in Jerusalem. [1 Chr. 3:7; 14:6]

Nohah (Heb. 'rest') *c.* 16 century BC. Fourth son of Benjamin and a grandson of Jacob and Rachel. [1 Chr. 8:2]

Nun (Heb. 'fish') *c.* 13 century BC. Father of Joshua. *see* JOSHUA *I.*

O

Obadiah (Heb. 'servant of God') *1.* date unknown. A son of Izrahiah, he and his five brothers were leaders of the tribe of Issachar and mighty warriors. [1 Chr. 7:3]

2. c. 10 century BC. One of the eleven army commanders of the tribe of Gad who left the army of King Saul and rallied to David at Ziklag. [1 Chr. 12:9]

3. c. 10 century BC. Father of Ishmaiah who was made ruler of the tribe of Zebulun during the reign of King David. [1 Chr. 27:19]

4. c. 9 century BC. The head of the royal household of King Ahab of Israel. He was a pious man and when Jezebel, the king's wife who was a worshipper of Baal, had begun to kill off the priests of the Lord, Obadiah had hidden a hundred in caves and they had survived. During a famine, Ahab told Obadiah that they would have to find pasture for the livestock or they would die. He went in one direction and sent Obadiah in another. Obadiah met the prophet Elijah and, recognizing him, fell on his face in front of him. Elijah told Obadiah to take him to Ahab but the servant was terrified, knowing that Ahab had placed a price on the head of the prophet and would kill him for having spoken to him. But Eiljah insisted and Obadiah took the message to the king and Ahab agreed to meet Elijah. [1 Kgs. 18]

5. date unknown. Son of Azel of the tribe of Benjamin and a descendant of King Saul. [1 Chr. 8:38; 9:44]

6. c. 9 century BC. A leader of Judah who was sent by King Jehoshaphat to teach the Law of God in the cities of Judah. [2 Chr. 17:7]

7. 7 century BC. A Levite descended from Merari who was a supervisor of the work of repairing the Temple during the reign of Josiah, king of Judah. [2 Chr. 34:12]

8. 5 century BC. A leader of the tribe of Judah descended from Zerubbabel and the royal house of King David. [1 Chr. 3:21]

9. c. 5 century BC. Son of Shemaiah, and a descendant of Jeduthun, he was one of the first Levites who settled in Jerusalem following the return from exile in Babylon. Also called Abda. [1 Chr. 9:16; Neh. 11:17]

10. c. 5 century BC. Son of Jehiel and a descendant of Joab, he was a leader of Judah who returned to Jerusalem from exile in Babylon and brought with him two hundred and eighteen men. [Ezra 8:9]

11. 5 century BC. A priest of Judah who signed the covenant to observe the Laws of God in the days of Nehemiah. [Neh. 10:5]

12. c. 5 century BC. A Levite who was a porter at the gates of the Temple in Jerusalem in the time of Nehemiah. [Neh. 12:25]

13. c. 5 century BC. Post-exilic Hebrew prophet. The Book of the prophet Obadiah is the shortest one in the Old Testament: a single chapter of twenty-one verses. Nothing is known of the personal history of the author, though the text suggests he probably lived in the 5th century BC, some time after the fall of Jerusalem (587 BC).

His oracle is directed against the Edomites, who moved up from the Dead Sea area and occupied the depopulated southern part of Judah, up to Hebron.

Obadiah fiercely denounces them for their behaviour in the darkest hour of his people:

'For the violence done to your brother Jacob, shame shall cover you, and you shall be cut off for ever ... on the day that strangers carried off his wealth, and foreigners entered his gates and cast lots for Jerusalem, you were like one of them ... you should not have looted his goods in the day of his calamity. You should not have stood at the parting of the ways to cut off his fugitives ...' (Obad. 1:10, 11, 13, 14)

Obadiah looked forward to the day of the Lord, when the Hebrew nation would be restored to its independence and its former territory, and the heathen nations that oppressed them would be destroyed. On that day: 'The house of Jacob shall be a fire, and the house of Joseph a flame, and the house of Esau stubble ... and there shall be no survivor to the house of Esau.' (Obad. 1:18)

After that day of judgment 'the kingdom shall be the Lord's' (Obad. 1:21). [Book of Obadiah]

Obal *see* EBAL 2.

Obed (Heb. 'servant') *1. c.* 11 century BC. The son of Boaz and Ruth, he was the father of Jesse and the grandfather of King David. [Ruth 4:17, 21; 1 Chr. 2:12]

2. c. 10 century BC. One of the chosen warriors in the army of King David famous for his bravery. [1 Chr. 11:47]

3. c. 10 century BC. A son of Shemaiah who was a porter at the gates of the Tabernacle during the reign of King David. [1 Chr. 26:7]

4. date unknown. Son of Ephlal of the tribe of Judah and the father of Jehu. [1 Chr. 2:37, 38]

5. c. 9 century BC. Father of Azariah, one of the five army commanders of Judah who, on the orders of the high priest Jehoiada, crowned Joash king of Judah and executed Joash's grand-

mother Athaliah, who had usurped the throne. [2 Chr. 23:1]

Obed-Edom (Heb. 'servant of Edom') *1. c.* 10 century BC. Obed-edom was a Philistine from Gath who lived near Jerusalem in the time of King David. After the death of one of the Israelites for touching the Ark, David left it for three months in the house of Obed-edom: 'and the Lord blessed Obed-edom and all his household.' (2 Sam. 6:11) Obed-edom helped carry the Ark from his house to Jerusalem and later was appointed one of its guards. He had five sons, who also tended the Ark. [2 Sam. 6:10–12; 1 Chr. 13:13–14; 15:18, 21, 24; 16:38; 26:4, 8, 15; 2 Chr. 25:24]

2. 10 century BC. Son of Jeduthun, he was a gatekeeper for the Ark in the time of King David. He also played a musical instrument at the celebration when the Ark was brought to Jerusalem. [1 Chr. 15:18, 24; 16:5, 38; 26:4, 8, 15]

3. 8 century BC. A servant in charge of the gold and silver vessels in the Temple, he was captured by King Joash of Israel together with the vessels. [2 Chr. 25:24]

Obil (Heb. 'camel-keeper') *c.* 10 century BC. The Ishmaelite officer of King David responsible for the king's camels. [1 Chr. 27:30]

Ochran (Heb. 'disturber') *c.* 13 century BC. Father of Pagiel and a member of the tribe of Asher. [Num. 1:13; 2:27; 7:72, 77; 10:26]

Oded (Heb. 'restoring') *1. c.* 10 century BC. Father of Azariah, the prophet who counselled King Asa of Judah. [2 Chr. 15:1–8]

2. c. 8 century BC. A prophet. After King Pekah invaded and defeated the kingdom of Judah, he carried off to Israel a large number of captives. Oded arrived in Samaria and intervened on behalf of the captives. Several of the leaders listened to him, and arranged for the prisoners to be treated well and returned. [2 Chr. 28:9-15]

Og *c.* 13 century BC. Og was the king of Bashan, east of the Sea of Galilee. He fought against Moses at Edrei, one of his main cities, was unexpectedly defeated, 'and they possessed his land' (Num. 21:35). This area was later assigned to the tribe of Manasseh.

In the Book of Deuteronomy they talk of his enormous iron bedstead (probably a black basalt tomb) which could be seen in Rabbath-ammon, the capital of Ammon. [Num. 21:33; 32:33; Deut. 1:4; 3:1-13; 4:47; 29:7; 31:4; Josh. 2:10; 9:10; 12:4; 13:12, 30, 31; 1 Kgs. 4:19; Neh. 9:22; Ps. 135:11; 136:20]

Ohad (Heb. 'strength') *c.* 16 century BC. Son of Simeon and a grandson of Jacob with whom he went down to Egypt. [Gen. 46:10; Exod. 6:15]

Ohel (Heb. 'tent') 6 century BC. Son of Zerubbabel who led the return from Babylon and a descendant of King David. [1 Chr. 3:20]

Oholah (Heb. 'tent') date unknown. Sister of Oholibah and a harlot whose name was used by the prophet Ezekiel to describe Samaria. [Ezek. 23:4, 11]

Oholiab (Heb. 'father is my tent') *c.* 13 century BC. Son of Ahisamach of the tribe of Dan, he was appointed assistant to Bezalel by Moses in the construction of the Tabernacle in the wilderness. [Exod. 31:6; 35:34; 36:1, 2; 38:23]

Oholibah (Heb. 'my tent is in her') date unknown. Sister of Oholah and a harlot whose name was used by the prophet Ezekiel to describe Jerusalem. [Ezek. 23:4, 11]

Oholibamah (Heb. 'my tent is in them') *1. c.* 17 century BC. A wive of Esau, she was the daughter of Anah and the grand-

daughter of Zibeon the Hivite. [Gen. 36:2, 5, 14, 18]
2. date unknown. A leader of Edom descended from Esau. [Gen. 36:41; 1 Chr. 1:52]

Omar (Heb. 'speaker') *c.* 16 century BC. Second son of Eliphaz, and a grandson of Esau, he was a chieftain of an Edomite clan. [Gen. 36:11, 15; 1 Chr. 1:36]

Omri (Heb. 'pupil') *1.* date unknown. Son of Becher and a grandson of Benjamin, he and his brothers were leaders of the tribe and mighty warriors. [1 Chr. 7:8]
2. c. 10 century BC. Son of Michael, he was made ruler over the tribe of Issachar during the reign of King David. [1 Chr. 27:18]
3. Sixth king of Israel after the monarchy split, he reigned 885-74 BC. Omri was one of the ablest and most successful of the Israelite kings. Yet the Bible takes only brief and unsympathetic notice of him. The royal house he founded, continued by his son Ahab, was held in disfavour because of its ties with the pagan Phoenicians, and the religious controversies that swirled around the prophets Elijah and Elisha.

Omri first appeared as commander of the armed forces of Israel during the brief reign of Elah. While engaged in the siege of the Philistine town of Gibbethon, Omri was informed that a senior army officer, Zimri, had murdered the king and his household and seized the throne. Proclaimed king by his men, Omri immediately marched back and occupied the capital, Tirzah. With the collapse of his bid for power, Zimri set part of the palace on fire and was burnt to death.

The kingdom was now flung into a protracted fight for the succession between the supporters of Omri and those of Tibni son of Ginath, and it ended only with the latter's death.

The kingdom had been weakened by

internal strife and lost much territory. As a wise general, Omri freed his hands for the struggle with Aram-Damascus (Syria) by making peace with Judah. This terminated the chronic border warfare between the two Hebrew kingdoms since the death of Solomon.

Omri secured another important ally by renewing the friendship with Tyre on the Phoenician coast. This alignment was strengthened by the marriage of Omri's crown prince Ahab to Jezebel, the daughter of Ethbaal, king of Sidon.

Omri regained lost territory east of the Jordan, and reconquered the kingdom of Moab, the fertile plateau east of the Dead Sea. This is confirmed by the stele of the Moabite king Mesha. It states that 'as for Omri, king of Israel, he humbled Moab many years ...'

There was a growth of security and affluence in Israel in the period of Omri and his son Ahab, as well as in the kingdom of Judah. The palace at Hazor, the extensive stables at Megiddo, and the thick walls and the elaborate tunnels to external water springs at both places probably date from this age.

Omri's greatest achievement was the construction of the new capital, Samaria, later completed by Ahab. For the first six years of his reign Omri had continued to use the capital of Tirzah in the same vicinity. Samaria was constructed on a prominent, solitary hill eight miles north-west of Shechem (Nablus) with a spectacular view to the sea twenty-three miles away. It commanded the ancient road to the coastal plain through the broad Vale of Barley. The site was bought from a certain Shemer for two talents of silver. The name Samaria (Hebrew 'Shomron') was supposed to be derived from Shemer, though it may also come from the Hebrew word for a watchtower. In due course the whole area became known as Samaria, and its inhabitants as Samaritans.

Various motives for the new capital could be attributed to Omri. He was conscious of the lustre of Jerusalem as the centre of Hebrew politics, religion and culture, and wanted his own kingdom to have a capital worthy of comparison with that of Judah. No doubt too, he felt the compulsion of most energetic and affluent monarchs to perpetuate their fame in splendid buildings. Physical security also played a part – the hill Omri bought was very steep on three sides, and could be made almost impregnable. Recent excavations have revealed the remains of the great stone walls, the palaces, courtiers' homes, storehouses, large reservoirs and granaries dating back to Omri's period.

Omri died after twelve years on the throne and was buried in Samaria. He was succeeded by his son Ahab. His reign had been sufficiently important for the kingdom of Israel to be referred to in documents of surrounding countries for more than a century afterwards as 'the house of Omri'. [1 Kgs. 16:16–28; 2 Kgs. 8:26; 2 Chr. 22:2; Mic. 6:16]
4. c. 6 century BC. Son of Imri, he was the father of Ammihud and his grandson Uthai was one of the first men of Judah to settle in Jerusalem after the return from exile in Babylon. [1 Chr. 9:4]

On (Heb. 'strength') *c.* 13 century BC. Son of Peleth and a chief of the tribe of Reuben, he joined Korah's revolt in the wilderness against the leadership of Moses and Aaron. [Num. 16:1]

Onam (Heb. 'strong') *1.* date unknown. Son of Shobal and the grandson of Seir, the Horite, he was a leader of an Edomite clan. [Gen. 36:23; 1 Chr. 1:40]
2. date unknown. Son of Jerahmeel and Atarah, and a leader of the tribe of Judah. [1 Chr. 2:26, 28]

Onan *c.* 16 century BC. A son of Judah. Onan was the second son of Jacob's son Judah and of Bath-shua, a Canaanite woman. According to Jewish law, Judah told Onan that he had to marry his brother Er's widow Tamar and have a son by her that would carry on the line. Knowing the child would not be regarded as his, Onan spilled his seed on the ground. The Lord was displeased and slew him.

This story gave rise to the word 'onanism'. [Gen. 38:4–10; 46:12; Num. 26:19; 1 Chr. 2:3]

Ophir (Heb. 'fruitful') date unknown. Son of Joktan and a descendant of Shem. [Gen. 10:29; 1 Chr. 1:23]

Ophrah (Heb. 'faun') c. 12 century BC. Son of Meonothai and grandson of Othniel, he and his father were leaders of the tribe of Judah. [1 Chr. 4:14]

Oreb (Heb. 'raven') c. 12 century BC. A leader of Midian slain by the men of Ephraim, after Gideon had defeated them. The rock on which Oreb was killed became known as the 'rock of Oreb' and Oreb's head was brought to Gideon. [Judg. 7:24, 25; 8:3; Ps. 83:11]

Oren (Heb. 'pine') date unknown. Son of Jerahmeel and a leader of the tribe of Judah. [1 Chr. 2:25]

Ornan see PHARAOH 7.

Orpah c. 11 century BC. Orpah was a Moabitess who married Chilion the son of Naomi when he and his family lived in Moab. After Chilion died, and Naomi returned to Bethlehem, Orpah remained in Moab. [Ruth 1:4, 14]

Osorkon *1. see* PHARAOH 7.

Othni c. 10 century BC. A son of Shemaiah, he and his brothers, like their father, were gatekeepers of the Tabernacle. [1 Chr. 26:7]

Othniel (Heb. 'my strength is God') c. 13–12 centuries BC. An Israelite judge. Othniel was the son of Kenaz and the nephew of Caleb the son of Jephunneh, whose daughter Achsah he was given in marriage as a reward for capturing the town of Kiriath-sepher.

Later, Othniel defeated Cushun-rishafaim the king of Mesopotamia who had oppressed the Israelites for eight years. Afterwards Othniel judged the people for forty peaceful years. [Josh. 15:17; Judg. 1:13; 3:9–11; 1 Chr. 4:13; 27:15]

Ozem *1. c.* 10 century BC. Sixth son of Jesse and a brother of King David. [1 Chr. 2:15]
2. date unknown. Son of Jerahmeel and a leader of Judah. [1 Chr. 2:25]

Ozni see EZBON 1.

P

Paarai (Heb. 'opening') 10 century BC. The Arbite warrior in the army of King David noted for outstanding bravery. Also called Naarai. [2 Sam. 23:35; 1 Chr. 11:37]

Padon (Heb. 'escape') date unknown. Ancestor of a family of Temple servants whose descendants returned with Zerubbabel to Judah from exile in Babylon. [Ezra 2:44; Neh. 7:47]

Pagiel (Heb. 'allotted by God') c. 13 century BC. Son of Ochran, he was appointed by Moses to count the tribe of Asher for military service and led the contingent of the tribe in the army of the children of Israel. [Num. 1:13; 2:27; 7:72, 77; 10:26]

Pahath-moab (Heb. 'governor of Moab') *1.* date unknown. A leader of Israel and the ancestor of many who returned to Jerusalem from captivity in Babylon. [Ezra 2:6; 8:4; 10:30; Neh. 3:11; 7:11]
2. 5 century BC. One of the leaders who signed the solemn covenant in the time of Nehemiah. [Neh. 10:14]

Palal (Heb. 'God will judge') 5 century BC. Son of Uzai, he helped rebuild the walls of Jerusalem in the days of Nehemiah and repaired the tower of the king's palace. [Neh. 3:25]

Pallu (Heb. 'famous') c. 16 century BC. A son of Reuben and a grandson of Jacob, Pallu was the father of Eliab, ancestor of Dathan and Abiram who joined Korah's revolt against Moses and Aaron. [Gen. 46:9; Exod. 6:14; Num. 26:5, 8; 1 Chr. 5:3]

Palti (Heb. 'deliverance') *1.* 13 century BC. Son of Raphu of the tribe of Benjamin, he was one of the twelve men chosen by Moses to spy out the Promised Land. [Num. 13:9]
2. 10 century BC. Son of Laish from Gallim, he married King Saul's daughter Michal after Saul had driven away her legitimate husband David. When David became king, he forced Ishbosheth to take Michal from Palti and restore her to him. Palti wept at Michal's departure and followed her on her way to David, until ordered to return. Also called Paltiel. [1 Sam. 25:44; 2 Sam. 3:15]

Paltiel (Heb. 'deliverance by God') *1. c.* 13 century BC. Son of Azzan and a member of the tribe of Issachar, he was chosen to make the division of the land allocated to his tribe. [Num. 34:26]
2. see PALTI 2.

Paltite *see* HELEZ 2.

Parmashta (Pers. 'stronger') 5 century BC. A son of Haman who conspired to kill all the Jews in Persia during the reign of Ahasuerus. [Esther 9:9]

Parnach 13 century BC. Father of Elizaphan who represented the tribe of Zebulun and aided Moses in the division of the land of Israel among the tribes. [Num. 34:25]

Parosh (Heb. 'flea') *1.* date unknown.

Ancestor of a large family of Judah, some of whom returned with Zerubbabel and others with Ezra from exile in Babylon. Some helped Nehemiah to rebuild the walls of Jerusalem and joined him in signing the covenant to observe the Law. Several are recorded as having divorced their non-Jewish wives in the time of Ezra. [Ezra 2:3; 8:3; 10:25; Neh. 3:25; 7:8]
2. c. 5 century BC. One of the leaders of Judah in the days of Nehemiah who signed the covenant to observe the Laws of God. [Neh. 10:14]

Parshandatha (Pers. 'prayer given') c. 5 century BC. A son of Haman who was chief minister of Ahasuerus, king of Persia, and who conspired to kill all the Jews in the land. [Esther 9:7]

Paruah (Heb. 'gloomy') c. 10 century BC. Father of Jehoshaphat who was in charge of supplies to the palace for one month a year during the reign of King Solomon. [1 Kgs. 4:17]

Pasach (Heb. 'passed over') date unknown. One of the three sons of Japhlet and a leader of the tribe of Asher. [1 Chr. 7:33]

Paseah (Heb. 'lame') 1. date unknown. Son of Eshton, an early leader of the tribe of Judah. [1 Chr. 4:12]
2. date unknown. Ancestor of a family who returned with Zerubbabel to Judah from exile in Babylon. [Ezra 2:49; Neh. 7:51]
3. 5 century BC. Father of Joiada who helped repair the walls of Jerusalem in the time of Nehemiah. [Neh. 3:6]

Pashhur (Heb. 'freedom') 1. date unknown. Ancestor of a priestly family who returned with Zerubbabel to Judah from exile in Babylon; one descendant was a signatory to the solemn covenant, and others divorced their non-Jewish wives in the time of Ezra. [Ezra 2:38; 10:22; Neh. 7:41]

2. 6 century BC. Son of Immer and chief priest in the Temple, he was angered by Jeremiah's prophecy of the defeat of Judah, and had him put in stocks near the Temple area for a day. When he let him out, Jeremiah cursed him with the name 'Terror on every side' (Jer. 20:3) and prophesied that when Judah would fall to the Babylonians, Pashhur would be taken into captivity and die in exile in Babylon. [Jer. 20:1–6]
3. 6 century BC. A contemporary of Pashhur 1, he was the son of Malchiah. He was sent by King Zedekiah of Judah to ask Jeremiah what the outcome of Nebuchadnezzar's attack on Jerusalem would be. Jeremiah gave them a message of unrelieved gloom. After this Pashhur joined a group of men who complained to Zedekiah that Jeremiah was undermining the morale not only of the citizens of Jerusalem but also of the army. The king gave them permission to deal with the prophet as they saw fit. They tied him up with rope and lowered him into a empty water cistern so 'Jeremiah sank in the mire' (Jer. 38:6), but was later rescued by Ebed-melech the Ethiopian. Pashhur's descendants returned to Jerusalem from Babylonian exile. [1 Chr. 9:12; Neh. 11:12; Jer. 21:1, 3]
4. c. 6 century BC. Father of Gedaliah, one of the leaders of Judah who threw the prophet Jeremiah into a well. [Jer. 38:1]
5. c. 5 century BC. A leader of Judah who signed the covenant to observe the Laws of God in the time of Nehemiah. [Neh. 10:3]

Pathrusim (Egypt. 'from the southern land') date unknown. Son of Egypt and a grandson of Ham. [Gen. 10:14]

Pedahel (Heb. 'saved') c. 13 century BC. Son of Ammihud of the tribe of Naphtali, he was the leader of the tribe in the time of Moses selected to divide the part of Israel given to Naphtali among the members of the tribe. [Num. 34:28]

Pedahzur (Heb. 'saved by the rock') *c.* 13 century BC. A leader of the tribe of Manasseh, he was the father of Gamaliel who was responsible for numbering the tribe of Manasseh for service in the army of Israel in the wilderness. [Num. 1:10; 2:20; 7:54, 59; 10:23]

Pedaiah (Heb. 'saved by God') *1. c.* 10 century BC. Father of Joel who was made ruler of the half-tribe of Manasseh west of the river Jordan in the reign of King David. [1 Chr. 27:20]
2. 7 century BC. Father of Zebidah, who married Josiah king of Judah and gave birth to a son, Jehoiakim. [2 Kgs. 23:36]
3. see SHEALTIEL
4. 5 century BC. Son of Parosh, he helped repair the walls of Jerusalem in the days of Nehemiah after the return from exile in Babylon. [Neh. 3:25]
5. date unknown. Son of Kolaiah and the father of Joed, he was an ancestor of Sallu, one of the first Benjaminites to settle in Judah after the return from exile in Babylon. [Neh. 11:7]
6. 5 century BC. A leader who stood at the side of Ezra when he read the Law of God to the people of Judah in the market-place. [Neh. 8:4]
7. 5 century BC. One of the four trustworthy Levites appointed by Nehemiah to distribute offerings among the Levites. [Neh. 13:13]

Pekah (Heb. 'open-eyed') Eighteenth king of Israel after the monarchy split, he reigned 737–2 BC. Pekah, the son of Remaliah, was an army officer who carried out a coup with fifty Gileadite troopers, murdered King Pekahiah and seized the throne.

He made common cause with Israel's traditional enemy Aram-Damascus (Syria) against the expanding Assyrian power that threatened them both. Pekah and Rezin, king of Aram, tried to draw the kingdom of Judah into the coalition. Ahaz, king of Judah, rejected these overtures. With the support of Rezin, Pekah then invaded and defeated Judah, carrying off to Israel a large number of captives. They were returned due to the intervention of a prophet called Oded.

In 733 BC the Assyrian forces of Tiglath-pileser III invaded Israel from the north, breaking through the line of forts guarding the upper Jordan valley, and occupying Galilee and the coastal region. The invaders annexed the occupied territories and converted them into three Assyrian provinces, with governors stationed at Megiddo (for the Galilee), Dor (for the coast), and Gilead, east of the Jordan river. Many of the inhabitants of these territories were taken away to Assyria as captives. All that was left intact of Israel was the capital Samaria and the hill region of Ephraim round it. This remnant of Israelite independence was to be finally wiped out a decade later.

Pekah did not survive the disastrous outcome of his challenge to Assyrian power. He was murdered and succeeded by Hoshea, son of Elah, who reverted to the policy of submission to Assyria.

The excavations at Hazor and Megiddo show extensive destruction dating from the same period, probably caused by the Assyrians. [2 Kgs. 15:25–32, 37; 16:1, 5; 2 Chr. 28:6; Isa. 7:1]

Pekahiah (Heb. 'God watches') Seventeenth king of Israel after the monarchy split, he reigned 738–7 BC. Pekahiah succeeded his father Menahem on the throne of Israel at a time when the kingdom was rapidly declining. It was internally unstable and already sucked into the orbit of Assyria, to which heavy tribute was paid. Pekahiah maintained this submissive policy for two years until he was murdered and supplanted by one of his army officers, Pekah, the son of Remaliah. [2 Kgs. 15:22–6]

Pelaiah (Heb. 'distinguished') *1.* 5 century BC. A Levite who explained the Law of God to the people of Judah after Ezra had read it in the market-place. He later signed the covenant to observe the Laws of the Lord in the time of Nehemiah. [Neh. 8:7; 10:10]

2. date unknown. Son of Elioenai of the tribe of Judah, he was a descendant of King David. [1 Chr. 3:24]

Peleliah (Heb. 'judged') *c.* 5 century BC. Ancestor of a priest who returned from exile in Babylon and lived in Jerusalem in the time of Nehemiah. [Neh. 11:12]

Pelatiah (Heb. 'saved') *1. c.* 8 century BC. Son of Ishi, during the reign of King Hezekiah of Judah he commanded a force of 500 Simeonites who drove out the Amalekites from the hill-country of Seir south-east of the Dead Sea and settled there. [1 Chr. 4:42]

2. 6 century BC. Son of Benaiah, Pelatiah was one of two leaders in Jerusalem mentioned by name among the twenty-five who appeared in the vision of the prophet Ezekiel standing at the city gate and giving false counsel to the people. Ezekiel prophesied that Jerusalem would be destroyed, and in the vision Pelatiah dropped dead. [Ezek. 11:1–13]

3. 6 century BC. Son of Hananiah and a grandson of Zerubbabel who led the return from Babylon, he was a descendant of King David. [1 Chr. 3:21]

4. 5 century BC. A leader of Judah in the time of Nehemiah who signed the solemn covenant. [Neh. 10:22]

Peleg (Heb. 'divided') date unknown. Elder son of Eber and a great-grandson of Shem, he was called Peleg 'for in his days the earth was divided'. [Gen. 10:25; 11:16–19; 1 Chr. 1:19, 25]

Pelet (Heb. 'refuge') *1.* date unknown. Son of Jahdai of the tribe of Judah and a descendant of Caleb son of Hezron. [1 Chr. 2:47]

2. 11 century BC. Son of Azmaveth, he and his brother Jeziel were among the Benjaminites to desert King Saul and rally to David at Ziklag. [1 Chr. 12:3]

Peleth *1. c.* 13 century BC. A leader of the tribe of Reuben and the father of On, who joined Korah's rebellion against Moses and Aaron in the wilderness. [Num. 16:1]

2. date unknown. Son of Jonathan and a descendant of Jerahmeel, a leader of the tribe of Judah. [1 Chr. 2:33]

Pelonite *see* HELEZ 2.

Peninnah (Heb. 'pearl') 11 century BC. A wife of Elkanah, the father of the prophet Samuel, Peninnah had several children. Elkanah favoured his other wife, Hannah, even though she was childless until the birth of Samuel. Peninnah, jealous of Hannah, scoffed at her because of her childlessness. [1 Sam. 1:2, 4]

Penuel (Heb. 'face of God') *1.* date unknown. An early leader of the tribe of Judah, he was the father of Gedor. [1 Chr. 4:4]

2. date unknown. Son of Shashak he was a leader of the tribe of Benjamin living in Jerusalem. [1 Chr. 8:25]

Peresh (Heb. 'clung') date unknown. Son of Machir and his wife Maachah, and grandson of Manasseh, his descendants settled in Gilead east of the river Jordan. [1 Chr. 7:16]

Perez (Heb. 'a breach') *c.* 16 century BC. A twin son of Judah and Tamar. Perez and his twin brother Zerah were conceived as the result of an incestuous relationship between Judah and his daughter-in-law Tamar. At the birth Zerah's hand appeared first and the midwife tied a scarlet thread round the wrist. But to the midwife's surprise Perez was born first. Later he had two sons and founded a tribe called Pharzites. Boaz the husband of Ruth was a descendant of his, as was King David. [Gen. 38:29; 46:12; Num. 26:20–1; Ruth 4:12, 18; 1 Chr. 2:4, 5; 4:1; 9:4; 27:3; Neh. 11:4–6]

Perida see PERUDA

Perizzites (Heb. 'villagers') An ancient tribe in Canaan at the time of the conquest by the Children of Israel under Joshua. Their land was taken over by the tribes of Ephraim and Manasseh. [Gen. 13:7; Josh. 17:15]

Peruda (Heb. 'gay') 10 century BC. A servant of King Solomon, his descendants were among the first men of Judah to return with Zerubbabel from exile in Babylon. Also called Perida. [Ezra 2:55; Neh. 7:57]

Pethahiah (Heb. 'freed by God') *1.* 10 century BC. A priest in the days of King David who took the nineteenth turn of service in the Tabernacle in Jerusalem. [1 Chr. 24:16]
2. 5 century BC. A Levite who divorced his non-Jewish wife in the time of Ezra. Also among the Levites who called on the people of Judah to confess their sins and praise God on the public fast day proclaimed by Ezra. [Ezra 10:23; Neh. 9:5]
3. 5 century BC. Son of Meshezabel and a leader of the tribe of Judah, he was chief adviser to the king of Persia in the days of Nehemiah, on matters relating to the exiles of Judah who returned to Jerusalem. [Neh. 11:24]

Pethuel (Heb. 'vision') *c.* 5 century BC. Father of the prophet Joel. [Joel 1:1]

Peullthai (Heb. 'my works') 10 century BC. Son of Obed-edom and a gatekeeper of the Tabernacle in Jerusalem in the reign of King David. [1 Chr. 26:5]

Pharaoh (Egypt. 'the great house') *1. c.* 18–16 centuries BC. The Pharaoh who wished to take over Abraham's wife Sarah, who had been passed off as his sister, cannot be identified as the date is conjectural. [Gen 12: 14–20]
2. c. 16 century BC. The Pharaoh at whose court Joseph rose to eminence may have been an early ruler of the Hyksos dynasty (1720–1450 BC) but cannot be identified by name. [Gen. 37:36; 39:1; 40–1; 42:15, 45; 46:33, 47; 50:4–6]
3. Pharaoh Rameses II (1301–234 BC) may have been the 'new king over Egypt, who did not know Joseph' (Exod. 1:8), who started to use the Israelites as forced labour for building the store-cities of Pithom and Rameses. [Exod. 1:8; 11–14; 5:4–19; 10:11, 16, 28]
4 c. 11 century BC. An unknown Pharaoh in the reign of King David (1025–970 BC) who gave political asylum to Hadad, a young Edomite prince. Pharaoh gave him a house and land, and the sister of his principal wife in marriage. [1 Kgs. 11:17–22]
5. The Pharaoh whose daughter was married to King Solomon (970–31 BC) must have been one of the lesser known rulers of Egypt in the last part of the 21st dynasty that ended in 945 BC. [1 Kgs. 3:1; 7:8; 9:16, 24; 11:1; Chr. 8:11; S. of S. 1:9]
6. Pharaoh Shishak I [Sheshonk] (945–25 BC) invaded the kingdoms of Judah and Israel in the fifth year of the reign of Rehoboam, king of Judah, which would be *c.* 926 BC. Jerusalem was spared by payment of a heavy ransom. The names of the towns occupied by Shishak are inscribed in the wall of the Temple of Karnak in Egypt. It was to his court that Jeroboam, later king of Israel, fled during the reign of Solomon. [1 Kgs. 11:40; 14:25, 26; 2 Chr. 12:2–9]
7. Pharaoh Osorkon I, successor to Shishak, may have been 'Zerah the Ethiopian' who invaded Judah from the south about 900 BC and was repulsed by King Asa (911–870 BC). [2 Chr. 14:9–15; 2 Chr. 16:8]
8. Pharaoh Tirhakah (690–64 BC) of the 25th (Nubian) Dynasty, was 'Tirhakah, king of Ethiopia', whom Sennacherib went off to fight during the siege of Lachish in the reign of King

Hezekiah of Judah. [2 Kgs. 18:21; 19:9; Isa. 19:11; 30:2–7]

9. Pharaoh Neco (609–593 BC) defeated and killed King Josiah of Judah at Megiddo in 609 BC and was himself defeated by the Babylonian crown prince Nebuchadnezzar at Carchemish in 605 BC. [2 Kgs. 23:28–35; 2 Chr. 35:20; 36:4]

10. Pharaoh Hophra (Apries) (588–66 BC) was defeated in 587 BC by the Babylonian army under Nebuchadnezzar, who temporarily raised the siege of Jerusalem to encounter the Egyptians. [Jer. 37:5, 11; 44:30]

Phicol (Heb. 'strong') *c.* 17 century BC. The army commander of Abimelech who was king over an area of southern Israel in the days of Abraham. Phicol accompanied Abimelech when the latter made a covenant with Abraham. [Gen. 21:22; 26:26]

Philistines An energetic people from the regions of the Aegean Sea, they reached Canaan in the 12th century BC, after Joshua's conquest, and settled along the coastal plain. They quickly established themselves, and were soon in conflict with the Israelites, a situation which lasted throughout the period of the judges. Their principal base of settlement and of power was the group of five towns near the coast, Gaza, Ashkelon, Ashdod, Ekron and Gath. By the middle of the 11th century BC they had become a formidable force, their control of the manufacture of iron tools and weapons giving them arms superiority over the Israelites. Their destruction in 1050 BC of Shiloh, the centre of Hebrew worship at the time, and the capture of the Ark of the Covenant were grievous blows to Israel, and they were followed by the occupation of additional territory. Not until the reign of Saul were they checked, after suffering a series of defeats at the hands of the king and of his son Jonathan. They were finally subdued by King David. When the kingdom was divided after the death of King Solomon, the Philistines partially reasserted themselves. Following the Assyrian invasion under Sennacherib at the close of the 8th century BC, they vanish from the records. [Books of 1 Sam.; 2 Sam.; 1 Kgs.; 2 Kgs.; 1 Chr.; 2 Chr.]

Phinehas (Egypt. 'negro') *1. c.* 13 century BC. High priest in the time of Moses. Phinehas was the son of Eleazar and the grandson of Aaron, and on his father's death he became high priest in his stead. When the Children of Israel under Moses stopped at Shittim (Abel-shittim) on the east of the Jordan river, they began to dally with the gods of Moab and with Moabite women. This angered the Lord and he threatened to destroy the Israelites, and sent a plague. Moses ordered the judges among his people to sentence to death anyone bowing down to Baal of Peor, the Moabite god. At this moment an Israelite came into the camp with a Midianite woman. Phinehas was so incensed that he 'took a spear in his hand and went after the man of Israel into the inner room, and pierced both of them ...' (Num. 25:8) The plague was stopped but not before twenty-four thousand had died.

After the tribes of Gad, Reuben and half of Manasseh had settled on the east side of the Jordan, they built an altar to the Lord. When the rest of the Israelites who had now settled in the land of Canaan heard about it, they grew afraid that this might anger the Lord again. Phinehas was sent at the head of a delegation to arbitrate. He decided that the altar on the east of the river Jordan had been built with the best motives and that it might remain without causing any harm to the rest of the tribes. Phinehas was given a hill in the Ephraim range in Samaria and brought his father there for burial. [Exod. 6:25; Num. 25:7–11; 31:6; Josh, 22:13, 31;

24:33; Judg. 20:28; 1 Chr. 6:4, 50; 9:20; Ezra 7:5; 8:2; Ps. 106:30]

2. *c.* 11 century BC. Wicked son of the priest Eli. Phinehas and Hophni were priests at the sanctuary of Shiloh, and sons of Eli, the chief priest. They were corrupt enough to be thus described: 'the sons of Eli were worthless men; they had no regard for the Lord.' (1 Sam. 2:12) They abused their office by taking for themselves the best part of the meat for sacrifices and by seducing women who came to the Temple. Eli remonstrated with them in vain, even though another priest prophesied they would both die on the same day.

When the Israelites were being hard pressed in battle by the Philistines at Aphek, the two priests were sent there with the sacred Ark to rally them. They were defeated and the Ark captured, with Phinehas and Hophni among the slain. The shock of their death and the loss of the Ark killed their father.

When Phinehas's wife, who was pregnant, heard the news she began her labour, but when her son was born she refused to look at him. She called him Ichabod – 'inglorious' – since 'The glory has departed from Israel.' (1 Sam. 4:21) She then died. [1 Sam. 1; 2; 4]

3. 5 century BC. Father of Eleazar, a priest who weighed the gold, silver and precious vessels for the Temple brought back to Jerusalem from Babylon by Ezra. [Ezra 8:33]

Pildash *c.* 18 century BC. Son of Abraham's brother Nahor. [Gen. 22:22]

Pilha (Heb. 'worship') 5 century BC. A leader of Judah who joined Nehemiah in signing the solemn covenant. [Neh. 10:24]

Piltai (Heb. 'saved') 5 century BC. Head of a priestly family in Jerusalem when Joiakim was high priest in the time of Nehemiah. [Neh. 12:17]

Pinon date unknown. An Edomite leader. [Gen. 36:41; 1 Chr. 1:52]

Piram (Heb. 'wild ass') 13 century BC. King of Jarmuth in the days of Joshua who joined with four other kings to attack the Gibeonites because Gibeon had made an alliance with the children of Israel. Joshua rushed to the aid of the Gibeonites, destroyed the armies of the five kings and put them to death at Makkedah. [Josh. 10:3]

Pispa date unknown. Son of Jether and a member of the tribe of Asher. [1 Chr. 7:38]

Pithon (Heb. 'harmless') date unknown. Son of Micah of the tribe of Benjamin and a descendant of King Saul. [1 Chr. 8:35; 9:41]

Pochereth-hazzebaim (Heb. 'gazelle-hunter') 10 century BC. Ancestor of a family of Temple servants who returned with Zerubbabel to Judah from exile in Babylon. [Ezra 2:57; Neh. 7:59]

Poratha *c.* 5 century BC. A son of Haman, the chief minister of Persia in the reign of Ahasuerus, who together with his sons was put to death on the discovery of their plot against the Jews. [Esther 9:8]

Potiphar (Egypt. 'belonging to the sun-god Ra') *c.* 16 century BC. Potiphar, an Egyptian officer and captain of the guard, bought Joseph, Jacob's favourite son, as a slave for his household from a band of Midianites who had found him in a well. Joseph proved his worth and Potiphar promoted him to 'overseer of his house and put him in charge of all that he had' (Gen. 39:4). Potiphar's wife made amorous overtures to Joseph, which he rejected. Angrily she complained to her husband that Joseph had made improper suggestions to her and Potiphar had him jailed. [Gen. 37:36; 39]

Potiphera (Egypt. 'belonging to the

sun') *c.* 16 century BC. The Egyptian father-in-law of Joseph, and a priest of On. [Gen. 41:45, 50; 46:20]

Puah (Heb. 'mouth') *1. c.* 16 century BC. A son of Issachar and a grandson of Jacob, he went down to Egypt with his grandfather. Also called Puvah. [Gen. 46:13; Num. 26:23; 1 Chr. 7:1]
2. c. 13 century BC. One of the two Hebrew midwives in the days when the Children of Israel were slaves to Pharaoh in Egypt. She and the other Hebrew midwife deliberately ignored Pharaoh's order to kill all Hebrew boys immediately after birth and excused herself by saying that Hebrew mothers always gave birth before the midwives arrived. The Lord rewarded her with riches. [Exod. 1:15]
3. c. 12 century BC. Father of Tola of the tribe of Issachar who was judge over Israel for twenty-three years. [Judg. 10:1]

Pul *see* TIGLATH-PILESER III

Purah *c.* 12 century BC. Gideon's aide who at God's command secretly crawled with him into the camp of the Midianites and Amalekites and overheard a soldier tell his dream in which he saw the destruction of Midian, Israel's enemy. [Judg. 7:10–14]

Put date unknown. A son of Ham and a grandson of Noah, he was the father of the people of Put, who were famous warriors. [Gen. 10:6; 1 Chr. 1:8]

Putiel *c.* 13 century BC. His daughter married Eleazar, the son of Aaron and nephew of Moses. [Exod. 6:25]

Puvah *see* PUAH *1.*

R

Raama *see* RAAMAH

Raamah (Heb. 'shaking') date unknown. Son of Cush and a descendant
of Ham. Also called Raama. [1 Gen.
10:7 ;1 Chr. 1:9 ; Ezek. 27:22]

Raamiah *see* REELAIAH

Rabmag *see* NERGAL-SHAREZER

Rabsaris (Heb. 'chief of the eunuchs')
1. c. 8 century BC. Title of a commander
of the Assyrian army of King Sennacherib who marched against Jerusalem
and demanded the surrender of King
Hezekiah. [2 Kgs. 18:17]
2. see NEBUSHAZBAN
3. see SARSECHIM

Rabshakeh (Ass. 'chief cupbearer') *c.* 7
century BC. The chief officer of Sennacherib, king of Assyria, he was sent together with the commander-in-chief and
the chief eunuch to demand the surrender of Jerusalem from King Hezekiah.
A Hebrew delegation was sent to meet
them but no agreement was reached.
Rabshakeh shouted out in Hebrew to
the crowd on the ramparts that Hezekiah was deluding them if he relied on
their God to save them. The Assyrian
demand was rejected, and Rabshakeh
returned to report to Sennacherib, who
had been besieging Lachish. [2 Kgs. 18,
19; Isa. 36, 37]

Rachel (Heb. 'ewe') *c.* 18 century BC.
Second wife of Jacob.
Rachel was the younger daughter of
Laban, Jacob's uncle in Nahor, Mesopo-

tamia. Jacob first met and fell in love
with her when she was watering her
father's sheep at a well. He had been
sent there by his mother Rebekah, who
wanted him to escape the anger of Esau
his brother and to find a wife among
her people.

Laban had two daughters: 'Leah's
eyes were weak, but Rachel was beautiful and lovely' (Gen. 29:17). Jacob said
he would work seven years for Laban to
earn the hand of Rachel 'and they
seemed to him but a few days because
of the love he had for her' (Gen. 29:20).
But after the wedding feast, Laban managed to substitute Leah for Rachel and
Jacob did not find this out until next
morning. Jacob had to work another
seven years to earn Rachel.

Though Jacob loved Rachel more
than Leah, she remained childless, while
Leah had four sons. Rachel envied her
sister and reproached Jacob: 'Give me
children, or I shall die!' (Gen. 30:1) He
became angry and asked her, 'Am I in
the place of God, who has withheld
from you the fruit of the womb?' (Gen.
30:2) In desperation Rachel gave Jacob
her maid Bilhah and adopted the two
sons she had, Dan and Naphtali. Then
'God remembered Rachel' (Gen. 30:22),
and she had a son who was called
Joseph.

When Jacob set out for his own land
he was pursued by Laban. Jacob denied
stealing Laban's household images. He
did not know that 'Rachel had taken
the household gods and put them in the
camel's saddle, and sat upon them'
(Gen. 31:34) so that Laban failed to find
them in the tents.

When Jacob and his family reached the outskirts of Bethlehem en route to Hebron, Rachel gave birth to another son, whom she called Benoni ('son of my sorrow') for she died in childbirth. Jacob changed the boy's name to Benjamin, 'son of my right hand'. Rachel was buried there, 'and Jacob set up a pillar upon her grave; it is the pillar of Rachel's tomb, which is there to this day' (Gen. 35:20).

The traditional site of Rachel's tomb is today marked by a small white structure with a cupola, standing at the side of the main road before entering Bethlehem. It is venerated by Jews and Moslems as a holy place, and superstitious women wind threads of cotton round the tomb to secure healthy sons for their daughters.

In the Book of Jeremiah she is pictured as weeping for her children who were taken away in captivity to Babylon. [Gen. 29–31; 33; 35; 46; 48:7; Ruth 4:11; 1 Sam. 10:2; Jer. 31:15]

Raddai (Heb. 'trampling') 11 century BC. Fifth son of Jesse of the tribe of Judah and a brother of King David. [1 Chr. 2:14]

Rahab (Heb. 'wide') c. 13 century BC. A prostitute in Jericho who lived on the city wall. The two spies Joshua sent into the city found lodging in Rahab's house. She hid them from the authorities on a promise that the Israelites would spare her and her family. The spies agreed and instructed her to tie a scarlet thread to her window as a sign. She then lowered them with a rope through her window and down the outside of the wall.

When Jericho fell, the two young men were sent by Joshua to bring Rahab and her family to safety inside the Israelite camp. Jericho was then burnt to the ground. The descendants of Rahab 'dwelt in Israel to this day'. (Josh. 6:25) [Josh. 2:1–21; 6:22–3, 25]

Raham (Heb. 'mercy') date unknown. Son of Shema of the tribe of Judah and descendant of Caleb son of Hezron. [1 Chr. 2:44]

Rakem (Heb. 'woven') date unknown. Son of Sheresh and a leader of the tribe of Manasseh. [1 Chr. 7:16]

Ram (Heb. 'exalted') *1*. date unknown. Son of Hezron of the tribe of Judah, father of Amminadab, and an ancestor of King David. [1 Chr. 2:9, 10; Ruth 4:19]
2. date unknown. Son of Jerahmeel and grandson of Hezron of the tribe of Judah. [1 Chr. 2:25, 27]
3. date unknown. Ancestor of Elihu son of Barachel the Buzite, the young man who debated angrily with Job and his three friends. [Job. 32:2]

Ramiah (Heb. 'God is exalted') 5 century BC. A descendant of Parosh who divorced his non-Jewish wife in the time of Ezra. [Ezra 10:25]

Rapha (Heb. 'tall') c. 16 century BC. Son of Benjamin and grandson of Jacob and Rachel, he was a leader of the tribe born after Jacob's family went down into Egypt. [1 Chr. 8:2]

Raphah (Heb. 'tall') date unknown. Son of Binea of the tribe of Benjamin, and a descendant of King Saul. Also called Rephaiah. [1 Chr. 8:37; 9:43]

Raphu (Heb. 'healed') 13 century BC. Leader of the tribe of Benjamin whose son Palti was appointed by Moses as one of the twelve men sent to spy out the Promised Land. [Num. 13:9]

Reaiah (Heb. 'seen by God') *1*. c. 8 century BC. Son of Micah and grandfather of Beerah who was a Reubenite leader taken into captivity by Tiglath-pileser during the Assyrian conquest of the northern kingdom of Israel. [1 Chr. 5:5]

2. date unknown. Ancestor of a family of Temple servants who returned with Zerubbabel from exile in Babylon. [Ezra 2:47; Neh. 7:50]

3. *see* HAROEH

Reba (Heb. 'fourth') 13 century BC. A leader of Midian killed on the plain of Moab by the children of Israel. [Num. 31:8; Josh. 13:21]

Rebekah *c.* 17 century BC. Wife of Isaac.

Rebekah, the second of the biblical matriarchs, was the daughter of Bethuel and the granddaughter of Nahor, Abraham's brother. This part of the family stayed behind in Paddan-aram (northern Syria) when Abraham moved to the land of Canaan with his wife Sarah and his nephew Lot.

Rebekah went one evening to fill her water-jar at the well. As she was returning, a stranger in charge of a string of laden camels stopped the comely young girl and asked for a drink. She gave it to him and offered to draw water for his camels as well. He bestowed upon her a gold earring and two gold bracelets.

The man was Abraham's trusted servant, sent to find a wife for his master's son Isaac from among his kinsfolk. Having earlier enlisted the help of an angel, he knew that this was the girl he sought. He enquired who her parents were and whether there was room in her home for him to lodge that night. She courteously invited him to do so.

The servant disclosed his mission to her family and gave them the gifts sent by Abraham. After some discussion, and with Rebekah's consent, it was settled that she should travel to distant Canaan to be the bride of her relative Isaac.

On nearing their destination, Rebekah saw a man walking through the fields towards them at dusk, and was told by the servant that this was Isaac. She alighted from the camel and veiled her face to meet him. Rebekah became Isaac's wife and he brought her to the tent of his late mother, Sarah.

Rebekah remained barren for many years, but after Isaac had pleaded with the Lord, she bore him twin sons, Esau and Jacob. During a famine, Rebekah moved with Isaac into the territory of Abimelech, king of the Philistine city of Gerar (between Beersheba and Gaza). Here she was passed off as Isaac's sister for fear that he might otherwise be killed because of her. On learning the truth, Abimelech was angry with Isaac, but gave orders that they should not be harmed.

Old and nearly blind Isaac asked his favourite son Esau, a skilled hunter, to bring him a dish of venison. He would then bestow his patriarchal blessing on Esau, the first-born. Rebekah overheard the conversation and determined to secure the blessing for Jacob, the twin brother she loved best. She ordered Jacob to select two young kids from his flock and prepared a savoury dish of meat. Jacob carried the food to his father, after Rebekah gave him Esau's garment to wear and covered his smooth hands and neck with the fleece of the kids, for Esau was a hairy man. Isaac was misled into bestowing the blessing on Jacob, declaring he would succeed his father as head of the family and that his brethren would serve him. Hearing that Esau had threatened to kill Jacob in revenge, Rebekah persuaded Isaac to send Jacob away to her brother Laban, in distant Paddan-aram, so that he too could find a bride among his own people.

When Rebekah died, she was buried in the family tomb in the Cave of Machpelah in Hebron. [Gen. 22:23; 24:29; 35:8; 49:31]

Rechab (Heb. 'rider') *1. c.* 11 century BC. Rechab and Baanah were the two fierce sons of Rimmon, from Beeroth. They served under Abner when he supported Ishbosheth, Saul's weakling son, against David. After Abner's death, realizing that Ishbosheth's cause was hopeless, Rechab and Baanah entered his house in the middle of the day. They slipped past the doorman, who was dozing over the chore of sorting wheat, and killed their master while he lay sleeping on his bed. The two brothers hacked off his head and brought it to David at Hebron, hoping to be well rewarded. The shocked David ordered his men to kill them both for having 'slain a righteous man in his own house upon his bed' (2 Sam. 4:11). Their hands and feet were cut off and they were hung up over a nearby pool. David ordered the head of Ishbosheth to be buried in the sepulchre of Abner in Hebron. [2 Sam. 4:2, 5–12]

2. 9 century BC. Descendant of the desert tribe of Kenites and father of the redoubtable Jonadab who supported Jehu in wiping out the remnants of the house of King Ahab of Israel and their priests and eradicating Baal worship from Samaria. Rechab's descendants abstained from drinking wine and, opposed to the materialism of city life, dwelt only in tents. Their asceticism was commended by the prophet Jeremiah. [2 Kgs. 10:15–23; 1 Chr. 2:55; Jer. 35]

3. 5 century BC. Father of Malchijah, ruler of the district of Beth-haccherem, who repaired the Dung Gate of Jerusalem. [Neh. 3:14]

Reelaiah (Heb. 'thunder of God') 6 century BC. A leader of Judah who returned to Jerusalem with Zerubbabel from exile in Babylon. Also known as Raamiah. [Ezra 2:2; Neh. 7:7]

Regem (Heb. 'friend') date unknown. Son of Jahdai of the tribe of Judah and a descendant of Caleb son of Hezron. [1 Chr. 2:47]

Regem-Melech (Heb. 'friend of the king') 5 century BC. One of the Jewish leaders during the reign of Darius of Persia who was deputed by the people to enquire of the priests in Jerusalem whether the custom of mourning the destruction of the Temple would be continued since the Temple had been rebuilt. [Zech. 7:2]

Rehabiah (Heb. 'God has broadened') 13 century BC. Only son of Eliezer and a grandson of Moses, he was chief of the Levites. [1 Chr. 23:17; 24:21; 26:25]

Rehob (Heb. 'width') *1. c.* 10 century BC. Father of Hadadezer, king of Zobah, who was defeated and killed in battle by King David. [2 Sam. 8:3, 12]
2. 5 century BC. A leading Levite among the returned exiles who signed the covenant to observe the Laws of God in the time of Nehemiah. [Neh. 10:11]

Rehoboam (Heb. 'increase of the nation') First king of Judah after the monarchy split, he reigned 931–13 BC.

When Solomon died, he was succeeded on the throne by Rehoboam, his forty-one-year-old son by an Ammonite wife, Naamah. The new king immediately ran into trouble with the northern tribes, headed by Ephraim, the traditional rival of Judah. At an assembly in the ancient city of Shechem (Nablus), the northern leaders confronted Rehoboam with a list of demands for relief of taxation and other burdens. He asked for three days to think the matter over, and consulted the courtiers who had been his father's chief counsellors. They urged him to take a conciliatory tone with the restive northerners, and to redress some of their legitimate grievances. But he was influenced by the more hawkish advice of younger men. On the third day he again met the assembly at Shechem and harshly rejected the petition that had been presented to him: 'My father made your yoke heavy, but I will add to your yoke; my father chastised you with whips, but I will chastise you with scorpions.' (1 Kgs. 12:14)

This attempt to browbeat the northern tribes into submission was disastrous. Their accumulated resentment burst into open rebellion. The leaders cried: 'What portion have we in David? We have no inheritance in the son of Jesse. To your tents, O Israel! Look now to your own house, David.' (1 Kgs. 12:16)

Rehoboam realized how serious the revolt was when Adoniram, the court official in charge of the forced levies, was stoned to death by the northerners, and the king himself had to flee back to Jerusalem in his chariot.

The northern kingdom of Israel was proclaimed with Jeroboam as its ruler. Rehoboam's rump kingdom, Judah, was left with only the tribal areas of Judah and Benjamin. The united monarchy had split into two small and warring Hebrew states. Rehoboam prepared to recover the lost provinces by force, but was dissuaded by Shemaiah the prophet.

In the fifth year of Rehoboam's reign, the country was invaded by the Egyptian Pharaoh Shishak. The biblical chronicler attributes this visitation to the religious backsliding of Rehoboam under the influence of his foreign wives. After he had been three years on the throne, he and his people had started to revive pagan forms of worship, erecting 'high places, and pillars, and Asherim on every high hill and under every green tree' (1 Kgs. 14:23).

Shishak approached the capital after capturing the fortified Judean towns on the way. He accepted the treasures of the Temple and the palace as a ransom and the city was spared.

Probably as a result of Shishak's invasion, Rehoboam proceeded to construct a chain of fifteen fortified places to defend the approaches to his country from the east, west and south. The southern line of defence was along the edge of the hills, which implies that Rehoboam had lost control of the Negev

desert, and with it Solomon's Red Sea port of Ezion-geber. The forts did not extend across the disputed northern frontier with Israel, perhaps because Judah hoped to push Israel back in this Benjaminite borderland.

Rehoboam's household was modest compared to that of his father Solomon, but large by any other standard. He had eighteen wives, sixty concubines, twenty-eight sons and sixty daughters. The wife he loved best was Maacah, the daughter of Abishalom. Rehoboam died after a reign of seventeen years and was succeeded by Abijah, his son by Maacah. [1 Kgs. 11:43; 12; 1 Chr. 3:10; 2 Chr. 9:31; 13:7]

Rehum (Heb. 'merciful') *1.* 6 century BC. A leader of Judah who returned with Zerubbabel from exile in Babylon. [Neh. 12:3]

2. see NEHUM

3. 5 century BC. A leading Persian official stationed in Samaria during the reign of King Artaxerxes who wrote to the king falsely accusing the returning Jewish exiles of rebellion. The letter led to a royal decree stopping the work of rebuilding and Rehum and his colleagues hastened to Jerusalem to enforce it. [Ezra 4:8, 9, 17, 23]

4. 5 century BC. Son of Bani of the tribe of Levi, he helped repair the walls of Jerusalem in the time of Nehemiah. [Neh. 3:17]

5. 5 century BC. One of the leaders of Judah who joined Nehemiah in signing the covenant to observe the Laws of God. [Neh. 10:25]

Rei (Heb. 'friendly') 10 century BC. A loyal minister of King David, he did not join David's son Adonijah when he tried to make himself king. [1 Kgs. 1:8]

Rekem (Heb. 'flowered') *1.* 13 century BC. A chief of Midian who was killed when his army was defeated by the children of Israel under Moses in the plain of Moab. [Num. 31:8]

2. date unknown. Son of Hebron, leader of the tribe of Judah, and a descendant of Caleb. [1 Chr. 2:43-4]

Remaliah (Heb. 'exalted by God') *c.* 8 century BC. Father of Pekah, the army general who assassinated King Pekahiah of Israel and usurped the throne. [2 Kgs. 15:25-7; 16:1, 5; 2 Chr. 28:6; Isa. 7:1, 4-5, 9; 8:6]

Rephael (Heb. 'healed by God') 10 century BC. Son of Shemaiah and grandson of Obed-edom, he and his family were gatekeepers of the Tabernacle in the reign of King David and outstanding warriors. [1 Chr. 26:7]

Rephah (Heb. 'wealth') date unknown. Son of Beriah and a grandson of Ephraim. [1 Chr. 7:25]

Rephaiah (Heb. 'healed by God') *1. c.* 16 century BC. Son of Tola, and a grandson of Issachar, he and his family were leaders of the tribe and mighty warriors. [1 Chr. 7:2]
2. see RAPHAH
3. 8 century BC. Son of Ishi of the tribe of Simeon who commanded a band of 500 men which drove the Amalekites out of Mount Seir, south-east of the Dead Sea, and settled there. [1 Chr. 4:42]
4. c. 6 century BC. A descendant of King David and probably a contemporary of Zerubbabel. [1 Chr. 3:21]
5. 5 century BC. Son of Hur, ruler of part of Jerusalem in the days of Nehemiah, he helped to rebuild the walls of Jerusalem. [Neh. 3:9]

Rephaim (Heb. 'giants') Ancient race of giants living east of the land of Canaan. [Gen. 14:5; 15:20; Deut. 2:20]

Resheph (Heb. 'fire') *c.* 16 century BC. Son of Rephah and a leader of the tribe of Ephraim. [1 Chr. 7:25]

Reu (Heb. 'friend') date unknown. Son of Peleg and a descendant of Shem. [Gen. 11:18-21; 1 Chr. 1:25]

Reuben (Heb. 'see a son') *c.* 16 century BC. Reuben was the eldest son of Jacob and Leah. One day he found mandrakes in a field at harvest time and brought them to his mother, who gave them to Rachel, Jacob's favourite wife, in return for Jacob's favour that night.

Later Reuben incurred his father's displeasure by sleeping with Bilhah, one of Jacob's concubines.

When the jealous brothers wanted to kill their brother Joseph, Reuben saved him by having him left in a pit but when Reuben came to take him out, Joseph had disappeared. Reuben was one of the ten sons sent by Jacob to buy corn in Egypt where Joseph had become a leading figure in Pharaoh's court. Joseph demanded that the youngest child, Benjamin, should be brought back with Jacob's sons on their next visit. Jacob objected but Reuben offered to leave his own two sons as hostage for the safe return of Benjamin. When Jacob went to settle in Egypt with all his family, it included Reuben's four sons. On his deathbed Jacob blessed his sons in turn. Reuben he called: 'my might, and the first fruits of my strength, pre-eminent in pride and pre-eminent in power. Unstable as water ...' (Gen. 49:3, 4)

Centuries later in the conquest of Canaan under Joshua, the tribe of Reuben obtained an area east of the Jordan, between the rivers Arnon and Jabbok.

In the blessing attributed to Moses, he said: 'Let Reuben live, and not die, nor let his men be few.' (Deut. 33:6) [Gen. 29:32; 30:14; 35:22, 23; 37:21, 22, 29; 42:22, 37; 46:8, 9; 48:5; 49:3; Exod. 1:2; 6:14; Num. 1:20; 16:1; 26:5; Deut. 11:6; Josh. 15:6; 18:7; 1 Chr. 2:1; 5:1]

Reuel (Heb. 'God is my friend') *1.* 16

century BC. Son of Esau and Basemath, and a leader in Edom. [Gen. 36:4, 10, 13; 1 Chr. 1 Chr. 1:35, 37]

2. date unknown. Son of Ibnijah and an ancestor of Meshullam, one of the first Benjaminites to settle in Jerusalem after the return from Babylon. [1 Chr. 9:8]

3. *see* JETHRO

4. *see* DEUEL

Reumah *c.* 18 century BC. Concubine of Abraham's brother Nahor, and mother of four of Nahor's sons. [Gen. 22:24]

Rezin (Heb. 'firm') *1.* 8 century BC. King of Syria who, together with King Pekah of Israel, attacked King Ahaz of Judah when he refused to join them in revolting against their Assyrian masters. Ahaz called upon the Assyrian king Tiglath-pileser III for help and he marched on Damascus, destroyed Rezin's army and killed Rezin. [2 Kgs. 15:37; 16:5, 7, 9; Isa. 7:1, 4, 8; 8:6]

2. 6 century BC. Head of a family of Temple servants who returned with Zerubbabel from exile in Babylon. [Ezra 2:48; Neh. 7:50]

Rezon 10 century BC. Son of Eliada and commander of the army of Hadadezer, king of Zobah. When King David captured Zobah, Rezon fled with a band of his followers. [1 Kgs. 11:23]

Ribai (Heb. 'pleader') *c.* 10 century BC. A Benjaminite from Gibeah whose son Ittai was a warrior in the army of King David noted for outstanding bravery. [2 Sam. 23:29; 1 Chr. 11:31]

Rimmon (Heb. 'pomegranate') *1. c.* 11 century BC. Father of Baanah and Rechab who murdered Saul's son Ishbosheth in the hope of getting a reward from King David, but were put to death instead. [2 Sam. 4:2, 5, 9]

2. Hebraized form of Ramman, the Babylonian and also Syrian god of thunder.

When the Syrian general Naaman was cured of leprosy by taking the advice of the prophet Elisha, he accepted the God of Israel as all powerful but nevertheless felt he should go with the king of Syria to worship in the temple of Rimmon. [2 Kgs. 5:18]

Rinnah (Heb. 'song') date unknown. One of the four sons of Shimon and a leader of the tribe of Judah. [1 Chr. 4:20]

Riphath (Heb. 'spoken') date unknown. Son of Gomer and a grandson of Japheth. Also called Diphath. [Gen. 10:3; 1 Chr. 1:6]

Rizia (Heb. 'delight') date unknown. Son of Ulla of the tribe of Asher, he and his family were leaders of the tribe and mighty warriors. [1 Chr. 7:39]

Rizpah (Heb. 'hot stone') *c.* 11 century BC. Concubine of King Saul.

Rizpah, the daughter of Aiah, was one of King Saul's concubines and the mother of two sons by him. After Saul's death, his general Abner was angered when Saul's son Ishbosheth charged him with having relations with Rizpah.

Towards the end of David's reign there was a three-year famine in the country. It was regarded as a belated punishment for Saul's slaying of a number of inhabitants of Gibeon, an Amorite hill-town five miles north-west of Jerusalem. The Gibeonites demanded as an act of atonement that David hand over to them Saul's seven children and grandchildren. David felt obliged to yield up to them the two sons Saul had had by Rizpah and five grandsons by Saul's eldest daughter. The Gibeonites hanged all seven. 'Then Rizpah the daughter of Aiah took sackcloth, and spread it for herself on the rock' (2 Sam. 21:10) and she kept watch over the bodies of the children until the harvesting was finished and the rains came.

When this was reported to David, he made peace with his troubled conscience by burying the bones of the children in the family tomb of their grandfather Kish, in the territory of Ephraim. [2 Sam. 3:7; 21:8–12]

Rohgah (Heb. 'clamour') date unknown. Son of Shemer of the tribe of Asher, and one of the leaders of the tribe. [1 Chr. 7:34]

Romamti-Ezer 10 century BC. One of the fourteen sons of Heman, King David's musician. He and his family played musical instruments in the Tabernacle under their father's direction and Romamti-ezer took the twenty-fourth turn of service. [1 Chr. 25:4, 31]

Rosh (Heb. 'head') *c*. 16 century BC. A son of Benjamin and a grandson of Jacob and Rachel, he went down to Egypt at the same time as his grandfather Jacob. [Gen. 46:21]

Ruth (Heb. 'beloved') *c*. 11 century BC. The Moabite ancestress of King David.

The touching story of the love between the Israelite widow Naomi and her Moabite daughter-in-law is set in the time of the judges.

During a period of famine, Naomi with her husband Elimelech and their two sons, Mahlon and Chilion, left their home town of Bethlehem and moved eastwards, beyond the Dead Sea to the mountain plateau of Moab. There Elimelech died. The sons married Moabite girls, Orpah and Ruth. Ten years later, both sons also died, and Naomi decided to return to Bethlehem, but she urged her two widowed daughters-in-law to remain with their own families in Moab. When they clung to her and wept, she gently chided them, pointing out that she could not produce more sons to replace their dead husbands. Orpah went back to her family, but Ruth refused to be parted from Naomi saying

'for where you go I will go, and where you lodge I will lodge; your people shall be my people, and your God my God.' (Ruth 1:16)

The two destitute women reached Bethlehem at the beginning of the wheat and barley harvest. Ruth went into the fields to glean the ears of corn left by the reapers, hoping that a farmer would be kind to her. By chance, her gleaning brought her into a barley patch belonging to Boaz, a well-to-do relative of Naomi's late husband, Elimelech. Coming to the field from Bethlehem Boaz asked his foreman who the unknown young woman was and was told she was the Moabite who had come back with Naomi. Boaz felt drawn towards her. He told her he had heard about her devotion to her mother-in-law whom she had followed to a strange land. He insisted that she remain in his field and share the food and water of his workers. He then quietly ordered the foreman to let Ruth glean even among the bound sheaves, and to leave handfuls of barley for her to gather and to ensure that she was not molested. At the end of the day Ruth returned to the town and handed to Naomi a whole bushel of barley, together with some of the food she had been given. Naomi told her that Boaz was one of her husband's relatives who might have a right of redemption over both of them as widows. (In the Israelite law of the time, a dead man's next-of-kin had the right to marry the widow, or 'redeem' her, and if he renounced that right it would pass on to the next nearest male relative.) Naomi urged Ruth to go on working in Boaz's field where she would be treated kindly and would not be molested. This Ruth did, gleaning the barley and wheat harvests.

Naomi heard that Boaz would be at the winnowing of the barley and would be spending the night on the threshing floor after the customary eating and drinking. On her mother-in-law's advice

Ruth went there and waited until Boaz had laid himself down to sleep next to the barley heap. She quietly turned back the edge of his cloak and lay down at his feet. In the middle of the night Boaz awoke and was surprised to find her there. She told him who she was and added 'spread your skirt over your maid-servant, for you are next of kin.' (Ruth 3:9) He praised her, saying that all Bethlehem knew she was a virtuous woman and did not go after young men poor or rich. He explained that the right of redemption was held by another kinsman closer than he was. If the other did not exercise that right, he Boaz would do so and marry her. Before daybreak he sent her back to Naomi, after filling her cloak with barley.

That morning Boaz waited in the city gate for the other relative to pass by. They sat down together in the presence of ten elders whom Boaz had invited to join them as witnesses. Boaz asked the other man whether he was prepared as the next-of-kin to redeem the piece of land that had belonged to Elimelech and that his widow Naomi now wanted to sell. The other was willing to do so, until Boaz pointed out to him that he would also be required to marry Ruth, the Moabite, the widow of Elimelech's son and heir. The kinsman then renounced his right of redemption in favour of Boaz. The agreement was ratified in the customary way by his taking off one sandal and handing it to Boaz in the presence of the witnesses. Boaz then declared that he was acquiring the property and also Ruth to be his wife 'that the name of the dead may not be cut off from among his brethren ...' (Ruth 4:10) All those present called down the blessings of the Lord upon the union.

Ruth gave birth to a son, Obed. The other women congratulated Naomi and expressed their admiration 'for your daughter-in-law who loves you, who is more to you than seven sons ...' (Ruth 4:15)

In the course of time Obed had a son Jesse, who was the father of David. Ruth, the Moabite girl, was thus the great-grandmother of Israel's most illustrious king. [Book of Ruth]

S

Sabta *see* SABTAH

Sabtah date unknown. Son of Cush and a grandson of Ham, he was a desert chieftain. Also called Sabta. [Gen. 10:7; 1 Chr. 1:9]

Sabteca date unknown. Son of Cush and a grandson of Ham, he was a desert chieftain. [Gen. 10:7; 1 Chr. 1:9]

Sachar (Heb. 'reward') *1. c.* 10 century BC. Father of Ahiam one of David's trusted warriors. Also known as Sharar. [2 Sam. 23:33; 1 Chr. 11:35]
2. c. 10 century BC. Son of Obed-edom a gatekeeper of the Ark in the time of King David. [1 Chr. 26:4]

Sachia date unknown. Son of Shaharaim and a leader of the tribe of Benjamin. [1 Chr. 8:10]

Sallai (Heb. 'basket-maker') *1.* 6 century BC. A leading priest who returned with Zerubbabel from exile in Babylon. His son Kallai was a chief priest of Judah in the days of Nehemiah. Also known as Sallu. [Neh. 12:7, 20]
2. 5 century BC. A chief of the tribe of Benjamin who returned to Judah from exile in Babylon and settled in Jerusalem. [Neh. 11:8]

Sallu (Heb. 'measured') *1. see* SALLAI *1.*
2. 5 century BC. Son of Meshullam and a leader of the tribe of Benjamin who returned to Judah from exile in Babylon and lived in Jerusalem in the time of Nehemiah. [1 Chr. 9:7; Neh. 11:7]

Salma (Heb. 'clothed') *1. c.* 13 century BC. A leader of Judah, son of Hur and grandson of Caleb, he was regarded as the founder of Bethlehem. [1 Chr. 2:51, 54]
2. see SALMON

Salmon (Heb. 'clothed') *c.* 11 century BC. Father of Boaz who married Ruth, the Moabitess, he was an ancestor of King David. Also called Salma. [Ruth 4:20, 21; 1 Chr. 2:11]

Salu (Heb. 'measured') *c.* 13 century BC. A leader of a Simeonite family in the wilderness whose son publicly consorted with a Midianite woman for immoral purposes and was killed by Phinehas the priest. [Num. 25:14]

Samgar-nebo (Bab. 'sword of Nebo') *c.* 6 century BC. A prince of Babylon who sat in triumph in the middle gate of Jerusalem after the Babylonian army had broken through the walls of Jerusalem. [Jer. 39:3]

Samlah (Heb. 'cloth') date unknown. Fifth king of Edom, he succeeded Hadad. [Gen. 36:36, 37; 1 Chr. 1:47, 48]

Samson (Heb. 'man of the sun') *c.* 12 century BC. A judge of the tribe of Dan. It is attempted in the Book of Judges to fit Samson into the pattern of the tribal leaders called 'judges', and it is said that he 'judged Israel in the days of the Philistines twenty years' (Judg. 15:20). However, there is nothing in the narrative to indicate that he actually gave judgments or that he led his people in battle. He was not a judge, a military commander, or a religious leader – but a folk-hero of the kind that has captivated the popular mind down the ages, from Hercules to Superman, with feats of incredible strength.

Samson belonged to the tribe of Dan. At the time of Joshua's conquest of Canaan, that tribe was allocated a strip of territory extending westwards from the Judean hills across the Shephelah (lowlands) and the coastal plain. It thereby encroached into an area occupied by the Philistines, a sea-people recently arrived from the Aegean Islands and Crete (though some scholars say they came from the south and west coasts of Asia Minor). The Danites were unable to secure their hold on that territory, and most of them left and resettled in the north-eastern corner of the country, near Mount Hermon. Remnants of the tribe must have clung to their homes in the Judean foothills and continued to live insecurely side by side with the Philistines, who in Samson's time 'had dominion over Israel' (Judg. 14:4). It was in this context that he carried on his one-man border war, and that he met his death.

Samson's birth, like that of a number of Bible heroes, had a miraculous aspect. His father Manoah lived in the village of Zorah, situated in the undulating foothill region of the Shephelah. It overlooked the valley of Sorek (through which the railway line now climbs up to Jerusalem).

His mother was a pious woman who had been childless for many years. One day an angel appeared before her and told her she would conceive a son. He warned her not to drink wine or eat unclean food during her pregnancy. The child would be dedicated to God's service, and forbidden to cut his hair or touch strong drink. The prophecy was added that when he grew up, he would 'begin to deliver Israel from the hand of the Philistines' (Judg. 13:5).

As a young man Samson fell in love with a Philistine girl from the village of Timnath, four miles from his home. He asked his father and mother to arrange the match. They first protested, urging him to marry someone of his own people, not knowing that Samson's wish 'was from the Lord; for he was seeking an occasion against the Philistines' (Judg. 14:4). But Samson persuaded them to come with him to the girl's home and talk to her family.

During this visit Samson encountered a young lion in the vineyards of Timnath and killed it with his bare hands. Passing there on his next visit he turned off the road to see what had happened to the lion's carcass, and found that a swarm of bees had settled in it. He scooped out the honeycomb, ate some of it and brought the rest home to his parents, without saying where he had got it.

As was the custom, Samson gave in his bride's village a wedding feast that went on for seven days. Thirty young Philistines were invited to attend. Samson put a riddle to them, for a wager of thirty pieces of fine linen and thirty garments. He said to them: 'Out of the eater came something to eat. Out of the strong came something sweet.' (Judg. 14:14) Unable to resolve the riddle, they threatened Samson's wife that if she did not coax the answer out of him and reveal it to them, they would burn her and her father's house. She reproached Samson with tears until he told her.

On the last evening of the wedding feast, the Philistines gleefully produced the answer: 'What is sweeter than honey? What is stronger than a lion?' (Judg. 14:18) Samson was furious and rejoined, 'If you had not ploughed with my heifer, you would not have found out my riddle.' (Judg. 14:18)

EXPLOITS AGAINST THE PHILISTINES
Samson stalked away and paid his wager by killing thirty Philistines at Ashkelon and taking the pieces of linen and garments from them. He then returned to

his father's home. But his longing for his Philistine wife sent him back to her village, bearing a kid as a gift. Her embarrassed father refused to let him enter her room, explaining that she had meantime been given to the Philistine who had acted as the best man at the wedding. He offered Samson her pretty younger sister as a substitute. Samson scorned this proposal, and claimed that this time he was clearly entitled to revenge himself on his wife's people.

He caught three hundred foxes, tied them together in pairs by their tails, put lighted torches between the tails and let them loose into the Philistine wheat-fields. It was harvest time, and the fires destroyed the sheaves and the unreaped corn, as well as vineyards and olive groves.

The Philistines asked in consternation who had caused the damage. They were told that Samson had been getting his own back for what his wife's family had done to him. As a reprisal, the incensed farmers then set fire to the house of the Timnite, and he and his daughter perished in the flames.

Again Samson reacted violently, and 'he smote them hip and thigh with great slaughter' (Judg. 15:8). He then took refuge in a rock cleft at Etam, in the Judean hills.

By now what had started as a family incident at a wedding threatened to escalate into a war. The Philistines sent an armed force into the territory of the tribe of Judah with a demand that Samson be handed over to them. The men of Judah came to Samson's hiding-place and said to him: 'Do you not know that the Philistines are rulers over us? What then is this that you have done to us?' (Judg. 15:11) Samson retorted: 'As they did to me, so have I done to them.' (Judg. 15:11) All the same he agreed to let his fellow-countrymen bind him and hand him over, on a promise they would not try to kill him themselves. They tied him up with two

new ropes and brought him to the place where the Philistines were waiting.

But when his enemies shouted in triumph, the spirit of the Lord came upon Samson and he snapped the cords that bound him, like 'flax that has caught fire' (Judg. 15:14). Catching sight of the jawbone of an ass, he snatched it up, went on a rampage among the Philistines and slew a thousand of them. The place where he tossed away the curious weapon was named Ramath-lehi ('the Hill of the Jawbone'). After these exertions, Samson was overcome with a burning thirst. The Lord opened a hollow in the ground from which water gushed, and he was able to drink his fill and revive.

Some time later, Samson went to spend the night with a harlot in Gaza. Word of his presence got around and a group of Gaza men set an ambush for him near the city entrance, waiting for him to emerge in the early morning (since the city gates were closed at night). Instead, he rose at midnight, wrenched off the gates together with the two posts and bar, and carried them on his back to a hilltop near Hebron, thirty-eight miles away.

SAMSON AND DELILAH

Samson once more indulged in his fondness for Philistine women. He fell in love with Delilah, who lived in the valley of Sorek near his home town. A group of the Philistine chiefs came to her and offered to pay her eleven hundred silver shekels each if she would wheedle out of Samson the secret of his abnormal strength, so that they could capture and hurt him. Pretending to satisfy her curiosity, Samson told her that he would be helpless if tied with seven freshly-made bowstrings. Concealing armed men in her room, Delilah tied her lover while he was sleeping, and then shouted, 'The Philistines are upon you, Samson!' (Judg. 16:9) He jumped up and snapped the cords with ease. The same story was repeated with unused ropes, and again when she wove the locks of his hair into a web of her loom and pegged it down. Each time he laughingly broke free, and the plot was thwarted.

Having failed three times, she nagged him until 'his soul was vexed to death' (Judg. 16:16). In the end he disclosed to her that as he had been dedicated to the service of God from birth, his strength would fail him if his hair was shorn. Convinced this time that she had heard the truth, she sent for the Philistines, who arrived with the money in their hands. When he was asleep, with his head in her lap, Delilah called on one of the men to cut off Samson's hair, 'and his strength left him' (Judg. 16:19). This time the Philistines were able to overcome and capture him. They put out his eyes, brought him to Gaza, and set him to work turning the millstone in the prison.

The legendary strongman had suddenly become an object of derision and sport, led around helplessly by a boy:

'Promise was that I
Should Israel from Philistinian yoke
    deliver:
Ask for this great deliverer now, and
    find him
Eyeless in Gaza at the mill with
    slaves,
Himself in bonds under Philistinian
    yoke.'

(Milton: *Samson Agonistes*)

But some assurance of divine grace crept back to him, as 'the hair of his head began to grow again after it had been shaved' (Judg. 16:22).

All the leading Philistines gathered in the temple of their god Dagon, to offer sacrifices and celebrate the capture of their enemy. (Dagon was a Canaanite corn god, whose cult was absorbed by the Philistines.) 'And when their hearts were merry, they said, "Call Samson, that he may make sport for us."' (Judg. 16:25) The temple was full, and three thousand more men and women crowded onto the roof to jeer at him.

Samson asked the boy to lead him by the hand to the two middle pillars supporting the roof. When he stood between them and felt them on either side with his hands, he entreated the Lord: 'remember me, I pray thee, and strengthen me, I pray thee, only this once, O God, that I may be avenged upon the Philistines for one of my two eyes.' (Judg. 16:28) As his former power came surging back, he grasped the pillars, cried out, 'Let me die with the Philistines' and 'bowed with all his might' (Judg. 16:30). The pillars cracked and collapsed and the building crashed down, killing its occupants together with Samson.

The brawny fighter and the lover of women had become in his death a noble and tragic figure. His kinsfolk came to fetch his body and buried it in the tomb of his father, between Zorah and Eshtaol, in the foothills of his childhood.

Samson's name in Hebrew, Shimshon, is related to the word for the sun, *shemesh*; the locality in which he lived centred on the town of Beth-shemesh, which means 'house of the sun'; and his power resided in the long hair radiating from his head, like the sun's rays. These facts, together with some of his exploits, prompted some Bible scholars to suggest that Samson originated as a mythical sun-god, such as appears in other ancient religions. Legends may have grown up around him; but the biblical story is so specific in time and place that Samson was undoubtedly a real person, pitting his great strength against the oppressors of his people. [Judg. 13–16]

Samuel (Heb. 'name of God') *c.* 11 century BC. The last of the judges. The judges were individuals who exercised influence over the tribes of Israel because of their strong personality, moral stature, and the belief that they had direct access to the Lord. They were able to rally the tribes in self-defence, and to settle disputes. Samuel, the reluctant king-maker, was the last and most dominant of these spontaneous leaders.

Samuel's father was Elkanah, from the town of Ramathaim-zophim, in the hill country of Ephraim. His mother, Hannah, was childless. On one of their annual pilgrimages to the religious centre at Shiloh, she vowed that if she was given a son, he would be given to God's service.

In due time Hannah bore a child she called Samuel, because the Lord had heard her. When he was weaned she brought the infant to the shrine at Shiloh and left him to be reared by the priests, as she had promised. The child Samuel helped with the religious services, wearing a linen ephod or priestly apron. Each year Hannah came with her husband to worship and brought the boy a coat she had made for him.

Twice one night Samuel thought he heard the voice of the aging high priest Eli and went to him, but was sent back to bed. The third time this happened Eli understood that it was the Lord calling to Samuel and told the boy to answer: 'Speak, Lord, for thy servant hears.' (1 Sam. 3:9) When Samuel did this, the Lord told him that Eli and his household would suffer for the misdeeds of his two sons, the corrupt priests Hophni and Phinehas. 'Behold, I am about to do a thing in Israel, at which the two ears of every one that hears it will tingle.' (1 Sam. 3:11) Next morning, at Eli's insistence, Samuel reported to him what he had heard. This experience was a turning point in Samuel's life. For the first of many times, the Lord had spoken directly to him. Samuel continued to serve in the shrine at Shiloh and his reputation spread through the country from Dan to Beersheba.

At the battle of Aphek, in the foothills, the Israelites were heavily defeated by their Philistine foes, and thousands of them were killed. Among the killed were Eli's two sons, who had been sent from Shiloh with the sacred Ark of the Covenant to rally the Israelite warriors. The Ark was captured. On hearing the news, Eli fell over backward with shock and died of a broken neck.

For the Philistines the Ark proved an awkward trophy. In the temple of Dagon at Ashdod, the great idol fell down before it and was broken. Plague broke out, and 'the hand of God was very heavy' (1 Sam. 5:11). The Ark was sent back in a cart drawn by 'two milch cows' to the Israelite town of Beth-shemesh in the foothills. From there it was brought to the sanctuary of Kiriath-jearim near Jerusalem, and remained at that spot for twenty years.

Samuel summoned the people to gather at Mizpah, a hilltop north of Jerusalem. He attributed their misfortunes to religious backsliding and the worship of pagan Canaanite deities, and exhorted them to fasting and prayer. When a Philistine army again advanced upon them, Samuel interceded with the Lord who unleased a violent thunderstorm on the enemy. The Israelites were able to repel the Philistines and regain lost territory. Samuel marked the victory by setting up a stone to the Lord, and called the place Ebenezer ('the Stone of Help'). Samuel's leading position was now established. He settled at Ramah, six miles north of Jerusalem, 'and there also he administered justice to Israel' (1 Sam. 7:17).

SAMUEL THE KINGMAKER

When Samuel became old he appointed his two sons, Joel and Abijah, to be local judges in Beersheba. But they were corrupt, taking bribes and perverting justice. The elders of Israel complained to Samuel, saying: 'Behold, you are old and your sons do not walk in your ways; now appoint for us a king to govern us like all the nations.' (1 Sam. 8:5)

Till that time the twelve Hebrew tribes had had no earthly ruler, and were loosely held together by their common origin, history and religion.

God was their king, and His commandments were their law. Outraged at the demand of the elders, Samuel warned them that a king would take their sons as soldiers and their daughters as servants; he would exact tithes from their herds and produce, and confiscate their best lands for his own use. The elders refused to be put off by this lecture and Samuel had to yield. He called the people together at Mizpah and upbraided them for their ingratitude to the Lord after all he had done for the Hebrew people. He then proceeded with the drawing of lots, whereby the choice was narrowed to the small tribe of Benjamin and finally fell on 'Saul the son of Kish' (1 Sam. 10:21) of Gibeah. Saul, who had hidden himself, was brought forth. He was very tall, 'taller than any of the people from his shoulders upward' (1 Sam. 10:23) and Samuel presented him to the populace. All shouted 'Long live the king.' (1 Sam. 10:24) Samuel then 'told the people the rights and duties of the kingship; and he wrote them in a book' (1 Sam. 10:25) and dispersed the gathering. Saul went quickly back to his father's house in Gibeah.

Into this account intrudes a different version. Looking for strayed asses, Saul came to a town where Samuel was visiting and decided to consult the seer. Guided by the Lord, the prophet took Saul up with him to the place of sacrifice, gave him the seat of honour at the table, and invited him to spend the night. Early next morning Samuel poured oil on Saul's head and told him that 'the Lord has anointed you to be prince over his heritage' (1 Sam. 10:1). After Saul had led a military expedition to relieve the Israelite town of Jabesh-gilead (east of the Jordan river) Samuel called the people together at Gilgal to 'renew the kingdom' (1 Sam. 11:14). There, amid the sacrifice of peace offerings to the Lord and great rejoicing, Saul was publicly acclaimed.

But the imperious old Samuel remained unreconciled to the change. He pointedly reminded the people that even if they now had a king, only the Lord could preserve them, as he had in the past. To drive home the point, he miraculously summoned up thunder and rain although it was still the dry harvest season. Having terrified his audience, he concluded: 'I will instruct you in the good and the right way. Only fear the Lord, and serve him faithfully with all your heart ... But if you still do wickedly, you shall be swept away, both you and your king.' (1 Sam. 12:23, 24, 25) These ominous words were the prelude to a bitter conflict between prophet and king that lasted for the rest of Samuel's life, and even after his death.

THE CONFLICT WITH SAUL

When Saul had reigned two years he felt ready to challenge the Philistines, who had gained a foothold in the hills north of Jerusalem. At Gilgal, down on the Jericho plain, Saul waited seven days for Samuel to come and make the ritual sacrifices to the Lord before battle. Then, feeling that he dared not tarry any longer, Saul made the burnt-offerings himself. The prophet then appeared, angrily denounced him and hinted that he would be replaced by someone else.

Having pushed back the Philistines, Saul sent an expedition against the Amalekites, the fierce nomad tribes of the southern desert. Samuel gave explicit instructions, in the Lord's name, to wipe out all of them, together with all their herds and flocks. Saul failed to obey these instructions to the letter. After vanquishing the Amalekites, he took captive their king, Agag, and allowed his men to bring back the pick of the cattle and sheep. He tried to appease Samuel's wrath by claiming that the animals were meant to be sacrificed to the Lord. Samuel retorted with scorn, 'Has the Lord as great delight in burnt offerings and sacrifices, as in obeying the voice of the Lord?' (1 Sam. 15:22)

As Samuel turned away Saul clutched at his mantle, which tore. Samuel promptly claimed this was a sign that the 'Lord has torn the kingdom of Israel from you this day' (1 Sam. 15:28). The prophet demanded that Agag be brought before him: 'And Samuel said, "As your sword has made women childless, so shall your mother be childless among women." And Samuel hewed Agag in pieces before the Lord in Gilgal.' (1 Sam. 15:33) After this bloody reproof, Samuel retired to his home in Ramah, and went into mourning for the king as if he were dead.

The Lord now called on Samuel to anoint the boy David the son of Jesse as the future king. The prophet went to Bethlehem, where David lived, on the pretext of conducting a religious ceremony in the town. That gave him a chance to see Jesse, and meet seven of his sons. The youngest one, David, was tending the sheep. He was sent for at the request of the prophet, who anointed him with oil.

Later, when David had become established at court and married Saul's daughter, the moody king became jealous of him and tried to kill him. David fled to Ramah and took refuge with Samuel. Saul sent messengers to bring him back and when they failed he went himself. But Saul was caught up in the religious fervour surrounding Samuel: 'And he too stripped off his clothes, and he too prophesied before Samuel, and lay naked all that day and all that night. Hence it is said, "Is Saul also among the prophets?"' (1 Sam. 19:24) This curious episode did not heal the breach between the king and the prophet.

The aged Samuel died and was buried at Ramah, and was mourned by all Israel.

Before his last battle against the Philistines at Mount Gilboa, Saul persuaded an old witch in the hamlet of Endor to summon up from the grave the spirit of Samuel. When the apparition appeared of an old man covered with a mantle, Saul flung himself on the ground before him. The ghost demanded, 'Why have you disturbed me by bringing me up?' (1 Sam. 28:15) Saul replied humbly '... I have summoned you, to tell me what I shall do.' (1 Sam. 28:15)

Samuel's spirit was as unrelenting as the living prophet had been. He reminded Saul that he had disobeyed the Lord, who had rejected him. On the morrow, he revealed, the Israelites would be defeated and Saul slain together with his sons. At these dread tidings, the king swooned away, and had to be revived and fed by his servants and the women of Endor. The next day the prediction came true.

Even in death Samuel had had the last and crushing word to the king he had raised up and then tried to cast down again. Saul had stood in awe of his mentor, and had never argued with him; yet the king had not acted as the docile instrument he was set up to be. The uncompromising dictates of a man of God had clashed with the more flexible attitudes of a ruler coping with political and military realities. The conflict between the two men reflected the oft-repeated conflict between Church and State. [First Book of Samuel]

THE BOOKS OF SAMUEL

The First and Second Books of Samuel were probably a single work later divided into two scrolls for convenience. The whole story of Samuel is confined to the First Book where it overlaps with the reign of Saul and the early part of David's life. The Second Book of Samuel is not concerned at all with him but only with the reign of King David.

Sanballat (Ass. 'Sin save the life') c. 5 century BC. Sanballat was a Horonite who lived in Beth-horon, north of Jerusalem, and held a post in the Persian government. He was vehemently opposed to the rebuilding of Jerusalem by Nehemiah and tried various means to prevent it. He ridiculed the capacity of the 'feeble Jews' to build the walls, but when the work went on and was almost finished, he tried to lure Nehemiah from Jerusalem in order to kill him. When this failed he threatened war against the Jews. This did not stop the work as Nehemiah stationed armed men to protect the builders. Finally Sanballat wrote a letter accusing Nehemiah of conspiring to set himself up as king of Judah. Later, on his second visit to Jerusalem, Nehemiah banished Sanballat's son-in-law from Jerusalem, and Jewish folklore suggests that he became the founder of the Samaritan sect. [Neh. 2:10, 19; 4:1–2, 7; 6:1–14; 13:28]

Saph *c.* 10 century BC. A giant in the Philistine army, killed in battle by a warrior in the army of King David. Also called Sippai. [2 Sam. 21:18; 1 Chr. 20:4]

Sarah (Heb. 'princess') *c.* 18 century BC. Wife of Abraham. Sarah was Abraham's half-sister and became his wife before the family left Ur of the Chaldeans on the long journey to Haran, and from there to Canaan. She was the first of the four biblical matriarchs, the others being Rebekah, Leah and Rachel.

Sarah's unusual beauty gave rise to two similar episodes. When they journeyed to Egypt because of famine, Abraham passed her off as his sister for fear that he might otherwise be killed on her account. Pharaoh took her into his harem, bestowing gifts on her alleged 'brother'. But when the Lord afflicted Pharaoh and his household with plagues, he learnt the truth and hastily restored Sarah to her husband, bidding them go their way in peace. On a later journey into the territory of Abimelech, ruler of Gerar near Gaza, he too acquired Sarah after being told she was Abraham's sister, but handed her back after the Lord had disclosed the truth in a dream. (One of the Dead Sea Scrolls

discovered in 1948 is an apochryphal commentary on the story of Abraham, that dwells on Sarah's beauty.)

The tragedy of Sarah's life was that she was barren. Her childless state was particularly ironical because the Lord kept telling Abraham that 'I will make your descendants as the dust of the earth' (Gen. 13:16) and that the whole land of Canaan would belong to his descendants. Sarah suggested a solution that fitted in with the customs of the period. She offered Abraham her Egyptian slave-maid Hagar, who bore him a son called Ishmael. Sarah could not conceal her jealousy when Hagar conceived, and at one stage the pregnant maid 'fled from her' (Gen. 16:6) but was persuaded to return by an angel of the Lord.

When Abraham was ninety-nine, the Lord announced to him that Sarah would bear him a son. He was incredulous, for Sarah was then ninety, and long past child-bearing age. The announcement was later repeated by three strangers, angels in disguise, who visited Abraham at Mamre. Listening to the conversation from inside the tent, Sarah laughed scornfully to herself. But in due time the child was born and named Isaac, which in Hebrew means 'he laughed'.

Sarah remained sensitive about having a child in her old age. She wanted also to secure the inheritance for Isaac. When Hagar and Ishmael mocked her at Isaac's weaning feast, Sarah demanded of Abraham that he send them away. This he did reluctantly, after consulting the Lord.

Sarah lived to the ripe old age of one hundred and twenty-seven, and was buried by Abraham in the Cave of Machpelah at Hebron, which he bought to serve as a family tomb. Also called Sarai. [Gen. 11, 12, 16–18, 20, 21, 23; 49:31; Isa. 51:2]

Sarai *see* SARAH

Saraph (Heb. 'burning') date unknown.

A descendant of Shelah and leader of the tribe of Judah, he ruled over parts of Moab, east of the Dead Sea. [1 Chr. 4:22]

Sargon II (Ass. 'lawful king') King of Assyria, 721–04 BC. Sargon was an Assyrian general who seized the throne when King Shalmaneser v died during the siege of Samaria. The city fell to Sargon, thus ending the northern kingdom of Israel. According to Assyrian records, 27,290 Israelites were deported to other parts of the Assyrian empire, while colonists were brought in from elsewhere and settled in Israel, which then became a province of Assyria.

Judah and other neighbouring kingdoms remained vassal states paying tribute to Assyria. In 711 BC Sargon sent an army into the coastal plain of Philistia to quell a revolt at Ashdod, whose king was deposed and a governor appointed. Judah, as well as the Transjordan kingdoms of Edom and Moab, were probably linked with this revolt but seemed to have submitted to the Assyrians. Sargon was killed in 704 BC and was succeeded by his son Sennacherib. [2 Kgs. 17; Isa. 20:1]

Sarsechim (Bab. 'master of wardrobes') *c.* 6 century BC. One of the Babylonian army commanders who conquered Jerusalem and sat in triumph at the middle gate of the city following its capture. His title was Rabsaris. [Jer. 39:13]

Saul (Heb. 'loaned') *c.* second half of 11 century BC. First Hebrew king.

Saul was the son of Kish, a man of substance in the tribe of Benjamin, and his wife Ahinoam. The family home was at Gibeah, three miles north of Jerusalem. Saul himself is described as 'a handsome young man ... from his shoulders upward he was taller than any of the people' (1 Sam. 9:2). The kingly office was bestowed upon him by the prophet Samuel at a time when the Israel-ites were being hard pressed by their enemies, and felt desperately in need of a single leader under whom they could unite.

There are two different accounts in the First Book of Samuel of how Saul became king. According to the first, he was sent by his father with a servant to look for some asses that had strayed in the hill country north of Gibeah. They came to a town where Samuel was on a visit, and decided to consult him, since he was a renowned seer. Samuel had already been apprised by the Lord that Saul was destined to be king. He therefore showed the young man special favour, inviting him to eat with him and stay the night. At daybreak, Samuel sent him on his way after anointing him with oil and telling him the Lord had chosen him 'to be prince over his heritage' (1 Sam. 10:1). On the road Saul encountered various signs foretold by Samuel: two men told him the missing asses had been found, and three passing prophets gave him bread. When he met a company of prophets coming down from the high places with music, the spirit of God came upon him and he prophesied among them to the astonishment of all who knew him – hence the saying 'Is Saul also among the prophets?' (1 Sam. 10:11) On his return Saul encountered his uncle and told him about his meeting with Samuel but kept to himself what the prophet had said about the kingship.

The other account of Saul's selection pictures Samuel as yielding to popular pressure against his will. He called the people to a gathering where the drawing of lots determined that the choice should be from the tribe of Benjamin, then narrowed it down to Saul. The young man had hidden himself but was fetched and presented by Samuel to the people, who shouted, 'Long live the king.' (1 Sam. 10:24) Saul then went back to his home.

It took a military emergency to propel Saul into the leadership for which he had been marked. The Hebrew town of Jabesh-gilead, east of the Jordan river in the tribal area of Manasseh, was being heavily attacked by the Ammonites from further to the east. The townspeople sought surrender terms. Nahash the Ammonite king bluntly replied that he would spare them but take out their right eyes, in order to humiliate Israel. The elders prayed for time while they sent out appeals for help. Saul was coming from the fields with his cattle when he learnt of the grim plight of Jabesh-gilead. He mobilized a large force and marched to the relief of the beleaguered town. Approaching at night, he launched a surprise attack at dawn. The Ammonite army was routed, and Jabesh-gilead was saved.

SAUL BECOMES KING

This victory established Saul as a military leader. Samuel assembled all the people at Gilgal and Saul was crowned with ceremonial sacrifices and public rejoicing.

When Saul had been king two years, he felt ready to challenge the power of the Philistines. They were a formidable enemy – an alliance of five wealthy tribes, possessing an effective army equipped with chariots. The Israelites at this time were relatively poor and backward, and did not know how to smelt iron. 'Now there was no smith to be found throughout all the land of Israel; for the Philistines said, "Lest the Hebrews make themselves swords or spears"' (1 Sam. 13:19). In fact only Saul and his son Jonathan possessed these weapons; their men were a people's militia armed with pitchforks and other farm tools.

Saul decided to attack the Philistine garrison at Geba, just a few miles north of his capital of Gibeah. He selected and trained a force of three thousand men, left a thousand of them under the command of his eldest son Jonathan, and with the rest cut off the rear line of the Philistines. Jonathan's task force then struck at the enemy garrison and wiped it out.

The Philistine leaders reacted swiftly to this bold challenge. With an army of chariots, horsemen and foot-soldiers, they marched upon the occupied Michmash, not far from Saul's capital. The Israelites were overcome with fear. They hid in mountain caves and bushes, and many of them fled across the Jordan river. Saul's forces melted away, and he was left with only six hundred men.

It was Jonathan who saved the situation. Unknown to his father, he slipped away with his young armour-bearer, climbed up above a rocky pass, and surprised and killed a group of twenty Philistine soldiers moving through it. After this sudden counter-attack, panic spread among the Philistines, and the Hebrews came out of hiding and fell upon them as they fled.

The victory at Michmash relieved the Philistine pressure for some time, and Saul was able to campaign against other neighbouring peoples that had been harassing the Israelites. They included the Amorites and the Zobahites, Aramean peoples pressing down from the north; the Ammonites on the Transjordan plateau to the east; and the Amalekites in the southern desert.

THE CONFLICT WITH SAMUEL

From the beginning of Saul's reign, his relations with Samuel were strained. The moment the king deviated from what he was told to do, the prophet turned fiercely upon him and rejected him. It was a one-sided quarrel. However strong and courageous Saul was in battle against his people's enemies, he was cowed by Samuel's wrath, and stood in awe of Samuel's claim to speak for God. He did not argue or resist when attacked by the prophet.

The trouble had started when the Philistine army had occupied Michmash. Saul waited for Samuel at Gilgal for seven days; then, unable to tarry any longer, Saul himself made the ritual burnt-offerings before battle. Samuel denounced him for this, and declared that the Lord 'has sought out a man after his own heart' (1 Sam. 13:14) to replace Saul.

It was perhaps to atone for this transgression and demonstrate his piety that Saul ordered his men to fast all day during the battle of Michmash that followed. Jonathan unwittingly broke the order by tasting some wild honey, and encouraged the hungry soldiers to kill and eat captured animals. Because of this sin, when Saul asked counsel of God 'he did not answer him that day' (1 Sam. 14:37). Saul declared that Jonathan must die, but readily yielded to the pleas of the people for the beloved son whose single-handed exploit had turned the tide of battle.

The next clash with Samuel took place after Saul's successful expedition against the Amalekites. Contrary to Samuel's injunction, Saul had spared and brought back as his captive the Amalekite king, Agag, and had allowed his men to take as booty the pick of the enemy's sheep and cattle. When Saul claimed that the animals were intended as a sacrifice to the Lord, Samuel scornfully replied, 'Behold, to obey is better than sacrifice, and to hearken than the fat of rams.' (1 Sam. 15:22) Saul begged Samuel to pardon him and appear at his side before the elders. The prophet refused, and turned to leave. Saul clutched at the edge of his robe; it tore, and Samuel promptly called this a sign that the Lord had rent the kingdom of Israel from Saul. Samuel relented about departing but demanded that the captive king be brought to him; and he 'hewed Agag in pieces before the Lord in Gilgal' (1 Sam. 15:33). After this bloody lesson, Samuel retired to his abode at Ramah, and did not see Saul again in his lifetime. Meanwhile, Samuel had secretly anointed someone else on the Lord's behalf to be the future king. He was the young David.

SAUL AND DAVID

Two different accounts are given of how the young David first came to the notice of the king. According to one, Saul had become increasingly subject to fits of depression, for 'an evil spirit from the Lord tormented him' (1 Sam. 16:14). He was told by his servants that David the son of Jesse the Bethlehemite was a skilled player on the harp, and might be able to relieve his mood. Saul sent for the youth, was charmed by his music and his comely looks, and made him the king's armour-bearer. The other account suggests that David met Saul when he killed Goliath, and was then taken into the king's service.

Saul's jealousy was aroused when David's exploits made him popular. The women turned out to greet them on their return from battle, singing 'Saul has slain his thousands, and David his ten thousands.' (1 Sam. 18:7) This rankled with the king; 'And Saul eyed David from that day on.' (1 Sam. 18:9) In one of his black moods, Saul actually hurled a javelin at David who was playing for him. After that Saul tried to get rid of him by sending him out against the Philistines in command of a unit.

David handled himself wisely and his fame grew. Saul said, 'Let not my hand be upon him, but let the hand of the Philistines be upon him.' (1 Sam. 18:17) He offered David the hand of his daughter in marriage, provided David slew a hundred Philistine soldiers and brought back their foreskins as evidence. David and his men slew two hundred, and he married Michal, the younger daughter.

One night Jonathan warned David to hide himself because his father Saul again intended to kill him. Jonathan interceded with Saul on David's behalf and the king appeared to relent and welcome David back. But Saul again tried to kill David, who escaped. Saul's men were sent in pursuit to David's home. Michal saved her husband by lowering him down through a window, and putting a dummy figure in his bed. David made his way to Ramah where he told Samuel what had happened. After the king's messenger had failed to capture David, the king came in person. But David was saved by the religious streak coming to the surface in Saul, who 'prophesied before Samuel' (1 Sam. 19:24).

From now on David was a fugitive from the king. He found refuge in the mountain caves of Adullam, south-west of Jerusalem, and became the leader of a band of about four hundred outcasts. When Saul heard that David had slipped out of his hands, he railed bitterly at his attendants and accused everyone of disloyalty, including Jonathan. Hearing the priests of the Shrine of Nob had helped David, he had them brought before him and killed, and their village wiped out.

Saul heard that David and his band were in the town of Keilah in the Adullam area, and saw a chance to trap them inside the walls. But the wily David slipped away again into the hills. At one point David was surrounded, but Saul had to abandon the chase and hurry back to meet a threat from the Philistines.

Saul resumed the hunt into the Engedi wilderness near the Dead Sea. By chance, Saul took shelter in a cave where David and some of his men were hiding. David could easily have killed the king, but all he did was to cut a piece from the hem of Saul's robe. On learning of this, Saul was deeply moved and said, 'You are more righteous than I; for you have repaid me good, whereas I have repaid you evil.' (1 Sam. 24:17) Saul made David swear that when he became king of Israel, he would not injure Saul's descendants or try to wipe out his name.

On another occasion, David penetrated into Saul's camp at night, but refrained from killing the sleeping king. On being awakened Saul called out, 'return, my son David, for I will no more do you harm, because my life was precious in your eyes this day; behold, I have played the fool, and have erred exceedingly.' (1 Sam. 26:21) This was the last encounter between them. David decided to put himself out of the king's reach by going into exile, and joined Achish, the Philistine king of Gath.

THE DEATH OF SAUL

When Saul had reigned for twenty years, the Philistines once more massed an army to attack Israel, and advanced into the valley of Jezreel. The Israelite forces faced them from Mount Gilboa. Unable to reach the Lord for his guidance, Saul felt abandoned and fearful. In disguise, and accompanied by two trusted menservants, he sought out a woman at Endor who was a famous medium. Though she pointed out that a royal decree had banned practices of witchcraft and magic in the kingdom, Saul persuaded her to summon the spirit of Samuel from the dead. What Samuel foretold was shattering. The Israelites would be defeated and Saul and his sons killed in battle. Saul lay on the ground in a swoon, till the woman and his two servants picked him up, seated him on the bed and made him eat some food. From his grave, Samuel had had the last word.

The Israelite forces were disastrously defeated on Mount Gilboa and put to flight. Saul's three sons, Jonathan, Abinadab and Melchishua were among the slain. The king himself was wounded by the Philistine archers and begged his armour-bearer to kill him rather than let him fall into the hands of the enemy. The armour-bearer was afraid to do so and Saul 'took his own sword, and fell upon it' (1 Sam. 31:4). The armour-bearer did likewise and died with his master.

Next day the Philistines found Saul's body on the battlefield. They cut off his head, hung his corpse and those of his sons on the wall of Beth-shean city, and exhibited his armour as a trophy in their main temple. When the grim tidings reached the men of Jabesh-gilead (the town Saul had saved at the beginning of his reign), they journeyed all night, recovered and brought back the bodies of Saul and his sons, cremated them and buried their bones under a tree, and fasted seven days in mourning.

David had in the meantime returned to the southern part of Judah, and was in the town of Ziklag when he was told of the disaster on Mount Gilboa. His lament for Saul and Jonathan is one of the most eloquent and moving passages in the Bible. (2 Sam. 1:19–27)

The valley of Jezreel, the scene of Saul's defeat and death, was the classic battleground of the Old Testament, and associated also with the stories of Deborah and Gideon. It was here that Bible prophecy located the final battle of the world at 'Armageddon' – a corruption of the Hebrew *Har Megiddo*, the Mount of Megiddo.

The Bible narrative gives King Saul less than due credit. The two decades of his reign fully justified the first Hebrew experiment in kingship. He gave the weak and poorly organized Israelite tribes the military and political cohesion needed to hold their enemies at bay. He thereby paved the way for the expansion of the kingdom under David. But his achievements are overshadowed in the story by personal conflicts: with his spiritual mentor, the aging and resentful Samuel; with his brilliant young protégé and rival David; and the conflict within himself, that made him erratic, unstable and subject to outbursts of violence. Though the later biblical chroniclers tended to favour David at Saul's expense, the latter emerges as a kingly figure and a leader of men, although a tragic prisoner of his own 'evil spirit'.

Archaeological excavations carried out from 1921 to 1933 at Tel el-Hosen, the 'mound of the fortress', which was the location of the Canaanite city of Bethshean, brought to light the remains of six temples. Four were in the stratum belonging to the period when the city was subject to Egyptian rule. In them were found victory steles of Pharaoh Seti I and a monument and statue of Rameses II. Two temples date to the time when it was under Philistine authority, and are associated by scholars with the account of the death of Saul and Jonathan at nearby Mount Gilboa. [1 Sam. 9–11; 13–29; 31; 2 Sam. 1–7; 9; 12; 16; 19; 21; 22; 1 Chr. 5:10; 8:33; 9:39; 10; 15:29; 26:28]

Seba date unknown. Son of Cush and a grandson of Ham, he was a leader of a desert tribe and an ancestor of the Sabeans. [Gen. 10:7; 1 Chr. 1:9; Ps. 72:10; Isa. 43:3]

Segub (Heb. 'lifted up') *1.* date unknown. Son of Caleb the son of Hezron, he was the father of Jair, a leader of Judah who ruled over twenty-three cities in Gilead, east of the river Jordan. [1 Chr. 2:21, 22]
2. c. 9 century BC. Son of Hiel of Bethel, he died in fulfilment of Joshua's curse when his father rebuilt Jericho, during the reign of King Ahab. [Josh. 6:26; 1 Kgs. 16:34]

Seir (Heb. 'the rugged') date unknown. The Horite ruler of the part of the land of Edom named after him. [Gen. 36:20, 21; 1 Chr. 1:38; 2 Chr. 25:11, 14]

Seled (Heb. 'lifted up') date unknown. Son of Nadab of the tribe of Judah and a descendant of Jerahmeel, he died childless. [1 Chr. 2:30]

Semachiah (Heb. 'sustained by God') *c.* 10 century BC. Son of Shemaiah and a grandson of Obed-edom, he and his family were gatekeepers of the Tabernacle in the reign of King David and renowned for their strength. [1 Chr. 26:7]

Senaah (Heb. 'brambly') date unknown.

Ancestor of the men of Judah who rebuilt the Fish Gate of Jerusalem in the time of Nehemiah. Also called Hassenaah. [Ezra 2:35; Neh. 3:3; 7:38]

Sennacherib (Acc. 'Sin [a god] replace the brothers') King of Assyria, 704–681 BC. Sennacherib succeeded to the throne of the Assyrian empire in 704 BC when his father Sargon II was killed. In 701 BC he invaded Judah, and took forty-six towns. The siege and capture of the fortified Judean city of Lachish is depicted in detail on four wall panels from the palace in Nineveh, Sennacherib's great capital city.

Hezekiah, king of Judah, sent a message of submission to Sennacherib at Lachish, with a huge sum in tribute. The Assyrian monarch was not satisfied but demanded the surrender of Jerusalem. This was refused, and for reasons which are not clear, Sennacherib withdrew without laying siege to the city.

The rest of his reign was spent in constant campaigns in parts of the empire closer to Assyria. He was murdered by two of his sons in 681 BC. [2 Kgs. 18:13; 19:16; 20; 2 Chr. 32; Isa. 36, 37]

Seorim (Heb. 'bearded') c. 10 century BC. A priest in the reign of King David who took the fourth turn of service in the Tabernacle in Jerusalem. [1 Chr. 24:8]

Serah (Heb. 'lady') c. 16 century BC. Daughter of Asher and the granddaughter of Jacob and Zilpah, she went down to Egypt at the same time as her grandfather Jacob. Serah was the only woman mentioned in the genealogy of the tribes of Israel in the wilderness. [Gen. 46:17; Num. 26:46; 1 Chr. 7:30]

Seraiah (Heb. 'warrior of God') *1. c.* 13 century BC. Son of Kenaz, brother of Othniel of the tribe of Judah, he was head of a family of craftsmen. [1 Chr. 4:13, 14]
2. c. 10 century BC. He was appointed

secretary by David when he became king. Seraiah's two sons were secretaries to King Solomon. Also called Sheva, Shisha and Shavsha. [2 Sam. 8:17; 20:25; 1 Kgs. 4:3; 1 Chr. 18:16]
3. 9 century BC. Grandfather of Jehu who was a leader of the tribe of Simeon. [1 Chr. 4:35]
4. c. 6 century BC. Chief priest of Judah in the reign of King Zedekiah, he was taken before the king of Babylon following the destruction of the Temple and put to death. [2 Kgs. 25:18, 21; 1 Chr. 6:14; Jer. 52:24, 27]
5. 6 century BC. A captain of the army who joined Gedaliah when he was made governor over the cities of Judah after the Babylonian conquest. [2 Kgs. 25:23; Jer. 40:8]
6. c. 6 century BC. One of the men King Jehoiakim ordered to seize the prophet Jeremiah and his scribe Baruch. [Jer. 36:26]
7. 6 century BC. Son of Neriah and quartermaster to King Zedekiah, he went with his master into exile in Babylon. The prophet Jeremiah ordered him to take with him a book containing the evil prophecies that would befall Babylon. When he finished reading this book, Seraiah was to tie a stone round the scroll and throw it into the Euphrates where it would sink. This would be a symbol of the coming destruction of the Babylonians. [Jer. 51:59–64]
8. 6 century BC. A leader of the Jewish captives in Babylon who returned to Jerusalem with Zerubbabel. Also called Azariah. [Ezra 2:2; Neh. 7:7; 12:1, 12]
9. 5 century BC. Father of Ezra the scribe. [Ezra 7:1]
10. 5 century BC. A priest who signed the solemn covenant in the days of Nehemiah. [Neh. 10:2]
11. 5 century BC. One of the priests who returned to Jerusalem following the exile in Babylon. Also called Azariah. [1 Chr. 9:11; Neh. 11:11]

Sered c. 16 century BC. A son of Zebulun

and the grandson of Jacob and Leah, he went down to Egypt with his grandfather Jacob. [Gen. 46:14; Num. 26:26]

Serug (Heb. 'branch') date unknown. Son of Reu and ancestor of Abraham. [1 Gen. 11:20–23; 1 Chr. 1:26]

Seth (Heb. 'founder') date unknown. Seth was the third son of Adam and Eve. He was born after his oldest brother Cain had killed Abel. In the Book of Genesis it is said that Seth was born when Adam was one hundred and thirty years old. He was the father of Enosh. [Gen. 4:26; 5:3–8; 1 Chr. 1:1]

Sethur (Heb. 'hidden') c. 13 century BC. Son of Michael and a leader of the tribe of Asher, he was chosen by Moses as one of the twelve men sent to spy out the Promised Land. [Num. 13:13]

Shaaph (Heb. 'division') *1.* date unknown. Son of Caleb and his concubine Maacah, he was a leader of the tribe of Judah and the father of Madmannah. [1 Chr. 2:49]
2. date unknown. Son of Jahdai and a leader of the tribe of Judah descended from Caleb. [1 Chr. 2:47]

Shaashgaz (Pers. 'lover of beauty') 5 century BC. Chamberlain of Ahasuerus, king of Persia, into whose custody the king's concubines were delivered, he took charge of all the young girls from whom the king was to choose a new wife. [Esther 2:14]

Shabbethai (Heb. 'my rest') 5 century BC. A prominent Levite in the time of Ezra who helped explain the Law of God to the people of Judah after Ezra had read it out in the market-place, and supervised the administration of the Temple. [Ezra 10:15; Neh. 8:7; 11:16]

Shadrach (Pers. 'command of Aku') c. 7 century BC. The Babylonian name given

to Hananiah, one of the four princes of Judah taken off to Babylon by the orders of King Nebuchadnezzar in 607 BC. When the four refused to worship or serve the Babylonian gods, Nebuchadnezzar, in great rage, ordered them cast into the fiery furnace. They were delivered by an angel and walked out unhurt. [Dan. 1:7; 2; 3]

Shagee (Heb. 'erring') c. 10 century BC. Father of Jonathan, a warrior in the army of King David who was distinguished for his bravery. [1 Chr. 11:34]

Shaharaim (Heb. 'double warning') date unknown. Leader of the tribe of Benjamin, he sent away two of his wives, Hushim and Baara, and had seven sons by his wife Hodesh with whom he lived in Moab east of the river Jordan. [1 Chr. 8:8–11]

Shallum (Heb. 'reward') *1. see* SHIL-LEM.
2. c. 16 century BC. A grandson of Simeon and the father of Mibsam, he and his family were leaders of the tribe. [1 Chr. 4:25]
3. date unknown. Son of Sismai of the tribe of Judah and the father of Jekamiah. [1 Chr. 2:40, 41]
4. c. 10 century BC. Son of Kore the Levite and a descendant of Korah, he was chief of the porters at the gates of the Tabernacle in the reign of King David. His descendants performed similar services in the time of Ezra and Nehemiah. Also called Meshelemiah and Shelemiah. [1 Chr. 9:17, 19, 31; 26:1, 2, 9, 14; Ezra 2:42; Neh. 7:45]
5. 8 century BC. Fifteenth king of Israel after the monarchy split, he reigned for one month in 743 BC. This brief reign of Shallum the son of Jabesh was inglorious. Nothing is known about his background. He assassinated King Zechariah and seized the throne, but a month later was murdered and succeeded by Menahem, son of Gadi. [2 Kgs. 15:10–15]

6. c. 8 century BC. Father of Jehizkiah, a leader of Ephraim who insisted that the prisoners of Judah captured in battle by the army of Israel in the reign of Pekah should be returned to Judah. [2 Chr. 28:12]

7. c. 7 century BC. Husband of Huldah the prophetess, he was the son of Tikvah and the grandson of Harhas who was keeper of the king's wardrobe. [2 Kgs. 22:14; 2 Chr. 34:22]

8. c. 7 century BC. Son of Zadok and father of Hilkiah, the high priest in the reign of King Josiah, he was an ancestor of Ezra. [1 Chr. 6:12; Ezra 7:2]

9. c. 7 century BC. An uncle of Jeremiah, he was the father of Hanamel whose field in Anatoth Jeremiah redeemed though he knew the land of Israel was about to be conquered by the Babylonians. [Jer. 32:7]

10. see JEHOAHAZ 3.

11. c. 6 century BC. Father of Maaseiah who was a gatekeeper of the Temple in Jerusalem in the time of the prophet Jeremiah. [Jer. 35:4]

12. 5 century BC. A Levite who was a porter at the gates of the Temple and who divorced his non-Jewish wife in the time of Ezra. [Ezra 10:24]

13. 5 century BC. A descendant of Binhui who divorced his non-Jewish wife in the time of Ezra. [Ezra 10:42]

14. 5 century BC. Son of Hallohesh and a ruler of part of Jerusalem, he and his daughters helped repair the walls of Jerusalem in the days of Nehemiah. [Neh. 3:12]

15. 5 century BC. Son of Colhozeh and ruler of the district of Mizpah, he repaired the Fountain Gate of Jerusalem and the wall of the Pool of Siloam in the time of Nehemiah. [Neh. 3:15]

Shalmai (Heb. 'thanks') date unknown. Ancestor of a family of Temple servants who returned with Zerubbabel to Judah from exile in Babylon. Also called Shamlai. [Ezra 2:46; Neh. 7:48]

Shalman 8 century BC. An eastern ruler who captured and despoiled the city of Beth-arbel. It is thought by some scholars to be a reference to the Assyrian emperor Shalmaneser V. [Hos. 10:14]

Shalmaneser V (Ass. 'Sulman is leader') King of Assyria, 727–2 BC. When Tiglath-pileser III, king of Assyria, died in 727 BC, the throne was seized by Ululai, the governor of Babylon, who became Shalmaneser V.

At that time most of the kings in Palestine were tributaries of the Assyrian empire, including Hoshea, king of Israel. With Egyptian encouragement, he revolted against Assyrian domination. In 724 BC Shalmaneser invaded Israel and took Hoshea captive. The Assyrians then besieged the strongly fortified hill capital of Samaria, which held out for two years. Before its fall, Shalmaneser died and was succeeded by Sargon II. (Possibly he is Shalman referred to by Hosea, Hos. 10:14.) [2 Kgs. 17:3–6; 18:9, 10]

Shama (Heb. 'heard') *c.* 10 century BC. One of the two sons of Hotham who were warriors in King David's army and distinguished for their bravery. [1 Chr. 11:44]

Shamgar (Heb. 'sword') *c.* 12 century BC. Son of Anath, and the third judge of Israel, he delivered Israel from the Philistines and once killed six hundred Philistines with an ox-goad. [Judg. 3:31; 5:6]

Shamhuth (Heb. 'destruction') *c.* 10 century BC. A captain in King David's army who commanded the army for the fifth month of each year. Also known as Shammah and Shammoth. [2 Sam. 23:25; 1 Chr. 11:27; 27:8]

Shamir (Heb. 'thorn') *c.* 10 century BC. Son of Micah of the tribe of Levi and a descendant of Izhar, he served in the Tabernacle in the reign of King David. [1 Chr. 24:24]

Shamlai *see* SHALMAI

Shamma (Heb. 'desolation') date unknown. Son of Zophah, he and his family were leaders of the tribe of Asher and mighty warriors. [1 Chr. 7:37]

Shammah *1.* 16 century BC. Son of Reuel and a grandson of Esau, he was an Edomite leader. [Gen. 36:13, 17; 1 Chr. 1:37]
2. c. 11 century BC. Son of Jesse and a brother of David, he fought in Saul's army against the Philistines. Also known as Shimei and Shimea. [1 Sam. 16:9; 17:13; 2 Sam. 13:3, 32; 21:21; 1 Chr. 2:13; 20:7]
3. c. 10 century BC. One of the three mighty men of King David, he fought the Philistines single-handed at Lehi in a lentil patch after all the men of Israel had fled. [2 Sam. 23:11, 33]
4. see SHAMHUTH

Shammai (Heb. 'assessor') *1.* date unknown. Son of Onam and grandson of Jerahmeel, a leader of the tribe of Judah, he was the father of Nadab and Abishur. [1 Chr. 2:28]
2. date unknown. Son of Rekem of the tribe of Judah and the grandson of Hebron, he was the father of Maon. [1 Chr. 2:44, 45]
3. date unknown. Son of Mered of the tribe of Judah by his wife Bithiah, the daughter of a Pharaoh. [1 Chr. 4:17]

Shammoth *see* SHAMHUTH

Shammua (Heb. 'heard') *1. c.* 13 century BC. Son of Zaccur and a leader of the tribe of Reuben, he was appointed by Moses as one of the twelve men sent to spy out the Promised Land. [Num. 13:4]
2. c. 10 century BC. One of the sons of King David born to him when he was king in Jerusalem. Also called Shimea. [2 Sam. 5:14; 1 Chr. 3:5; 14:4]
3. see SHEMAIAH *17.*

4. 5 century BC. The head of a priestly family descended from Bilgah, he was a chief priest of Judah towards the end of Nehemiah's lifetime. [Neh. 12:18]

Shamsherai (Heb. 'hero') date unknown. Son of Jeroham, he was a leader of the tribe of Benjamin living in Jerusalem. [1 Chr. 8:26]

Shaphan (Heb. 'bare') date unknown. A leader of the tribe of Gad living in Bashan, east of the river Jordan. [1 Chr. 5:12]

Shaphan (Heb. 'rabbit') *1. c.* 7 century BC. Son of Azaliah and secretary of Josiah, his son Ahikam saved the prophet Jeremiah from being put to death at the order of King Jehoiakim. [2 Kgs. 22:3; 2 Chr. 34:8; Jer. 26:24; 36:10–12]
2. c. 6 century BC. Father of Jaazaniah, a leader of Judah condemned by Ezekiel for offering sacrifices to idols near the Temple. [Ezek. 8:11]

Shaphat (Heb. 'judge') *1. c.* 13 century BC. Son of Hori and a leader of the tribe of Simeon, he was one of the twelve men chosen by Moses to spy out the Promised Land. [Num. 13:5]
2. c. 10 century BC. The official of King David in charge of the royal herds that fed in the valleys. [1 Chr. 27:29]
3. c. 9 century BC. Father of the prophet Elisha. [1 Kgs. 19:16, 19; 2 Kgs. 3:11; 6:31]
4. c. 5 century BC. Son of Shemaiah and a member of the royal family of Judah descended from King David. [1 Chr. 3:22]
5. date unknown. A leader of the tribe of Gad living in Bashan, east of the river Jordan. [1 Chr. 5:12]

Sharai (Heb. 'set free') 5 century BC. A descendant of Binnui who divorced his non-Jewish wife in the time of Ezra. [Ezra 10:40]

Sharar see SACHAR *1.*

Sharezer (Heb. 'prince') *1. c.* 7 century
BC. One of the two sons of Sennacherib,
king of Assyria, who murdered their
father while he was at worship in the
temple of Nisroch at Nineveh. [2 Kgs.
19:37; Isa. 37:38]
2. c. 6 century BC. One of the two
leaders of a delegation of men of Judah
who asked the prophet Zechariah if the
people were still obliged to commemorate the destruction of the Temple even
after it had been rebuilt. [Zech. 7:2]

Shashai (Heb. 'noble') 5 century BC. A
descendant of Binnui who divorced his
non-Jewish wife in the time of Ezra.
[Ezra 10:40]

Shashak date unknown. Son of Elpaal
and a leader of the tribe of Benjamin. [1
Chr. 8:14, 25]

Shaul (Heb. 'asked') *1.* date unknown.
A king of Edom who came from Rehoboth on the Euphrates. [Gen. 36:37,
38; 1 Chr. 1:48, 49]
2. c. 16 century BC. Son of Simeon and his
Canaanite wife, he went down to Egypt
with his grandfather Jacob. [Gen. 46:10;
Exod. 6:15; Num. 26:13; 1 Chr. 4:24]
3. see JOEL *3.*

Shavsha see SERAIAH *2.*

Sheal (Heb. 'asking') 5 century BC. A
descendant of Bani, he divorced his
non-Jewish wife in the time of Ezra.
[Ezra 10:29]

Shealtiel (Heb. 'asked of God') *c.* 6 century BC. Father of Zerubbabel who led
the return to Judah from exile in Babylon. In the First Book of Chronicles,
Zerubbabel's father is given as Pedaiah.
[1 Chr. 3:17, 18, 19; Ezra 3:2, 8; 5:2;
Neh. 12:1; Hag. 1:1, 12, 14; 2:21]

Sheariah (Heb. 'God's gate') date un-

known. Son of Azel of the tribe of Benjamin and a descendant of King Saul. [1
Chr. 8:38; 9:44]

Shear-Jashub (Heb. 'a remnant shall
return') *c.* 8 century BC. The son of the
prophet Isaiah whom God ordered to
go with Isaiah to meet Ahaz, king of
Judah, at the upper pool outside Jerusalem. His name is symbolic of Isaiah's
prophecy that the kingdoms of Israel
and Judah would be destroyed but a
remnant would return to Judah. [Isa.
7:3]

Sheba *1.* date unknown. Son of Joktan,
a descendant of Shem. [Gen. 10:28; 1
Chr. 1:22]
2. c. 16 century BC. Son of Jokshan and
grandson of Abraham and Keturah, he
was a desert chieftain. [Gen. 25:3; 1
Chr. 1:32]
3. date unknown. A leader of the tribe
of Gad, living in Bashan, east of the
river Jordan. [1 Chr. 5:13]
4. c. 10 century BC. Son of Bichri, he
was a Benjaminite who stirred up a rebellion against David after the revolt of
Absalom had been quelled. David sent
his commander Joab after Sheba who
took refuge in the city of Abel-beth-
maacha in northern Galilee. Joab besieged the town and attacked the wall.
A woman renowned for her wisdom
called down to him, reminding Joab that
this city had always been loyal to David.
Joab agreed to withdraw his troops if
she would hand over Sheba. The men of
the city killed him and sent his head to
Joab who immediately left and returned
to King David. [2 Sam. 20]

Shebaniah (Heb. 'grown by God') *1. c.*
10 century BC. A priest who blew a
trumpet during the celebrations when
King David brought the Ark of God to
Jerusalem. [1 Chr. 15:24]
2. date unknown. Ancestor of a priestly
family of Judah that returned from exile
in Babylon, his descendant Joseph was a

priest in the time of Nehemiah. [Neh. 12:14]

3. 5 century BC. A Levite who prayed to God to forgive the people of Judah for their sins on the public fast day proclaimed by Ezra. He later signed the solemn covenant. [Neh. 9:4; 10:10]

4. 5 century BC. A Levite who called upon the people of Judah to praise God during the public fast day called by Ezra. He later signed the solemn covenant. [Neh. 9:5; 10:12]

5. 5 century BC. A priest of Judah who signed the solemn covenant in the time of Nehemiah. [Neh. 10:4]

Sheber (Heb. 'breaking') date unknown. Son of Caleb and Maacah and a leader of the tribe of Judah. [1 Chr. 2:48]

Shebna (Heb. 'may God sit') *c.* 8 century BC. Official scribe to King Hezekiah, he took part in the negotiations between Judah and the attacking Assyrians in which the surrender of Jerusalem was demanded. No agreement was reached.

Hezekiah sent Shebna as part of a delegation to consult the prophet Isaiah, who told them that the Assyrians would not take Jerusalem, but would go away – which is what happened.

Later Shebna carved himself an elaborate rock tomb for which he was attacked by Isaiah. The prophet told him that the Lord would 'whirl you round and round, and throw you like a ball into a wide land; there you shall die' (Isa. 22:18). He also told him he would be replaced by Eliakim, son of Hilkiah, who would fill the post with honour. [2 Kgs. 18:18, 26, 37; 19:2; Isa. 22:15; 36:3, 11, 22; 37:2]

Shebuel (Heb. 'captive of God') *1. c.* 10 century BC. A descendant of Moses and leader of the family of Gershomites in the reign of King David, he was responsible for the administration of the treasury in the Tabernacle. Also called Shubael. [1 Chr. 23:16; 24:20; 26:24]

2. c. 10 century BC. A son of Heman, one of King David's chief musicians, he and his brothers played musical instruments in the Tabernacle under their father's directions and were responsible for the thirteenth turn of the service. Also called Shubael. [1 Chr. 25:4, 20]

Shecaniah (Heb. 'dweller with God') *1. c.* 10 century BC. A priest in the reign of King David who was responsible for the tenth turn of service in the Tabernacle in Jerusalem. [1 Chr. 24:11]

2. c. 8 century BC. A priest of Judah in the reign of King Hezekiah who distributed the freewill offering among the priests and Levites in the cities of Judah. [2 Chr. 31:15]

3. 6 century BC. A leading priest who returned to Judah with Zerubbabel from exile in Babylon. [Neh. 12:3]

4. 5 century BC. A descendant of Zerubbabel, he was the father of Shemaiah and the head of a family which returned with Ezra from exile in Babylon. [1 Chr. 3:21, 22; Ezra 8:3]

5. 5 century BC. Son of Jahaziel, he was head of a family which returned with Ezra from exile in Babylon. [Ezra 8:5]

6. 5 century BC. Son of Jehiel, he suggested that the people of Judah could begin to make atonement for their sins by promising to divorce their non-Jewish wives. [Ezra 10:2]

7. 5 century BC. Father of Shemaiah, the priest who repaired the East Gate of Jerusalem in the time of Nehemiah. [Neh. 3:29]

8. 5 century BC. Son of Arah he was a leading citizen of Judah. His daughter married Tobiah the Samaritan leader who attempted to interfere with Nehemiah's work of rebuilding Jerusalem and whose relationship with Shecaniah brought him many allies among the leading families of Judah. [Neh. 6:18]

Shechem (Heb. 'shoulder') *1. c.* 16 century BC. Son of Hamor, a Canaanite leader, he fell in love with Jacob's daughter Dinah and seduced her. Shechem sent his father Hamor to Jacob to ask for her hand in marriage. Jacob and his sons agreed provided that all the males in his family and in his city were circumcised. This was done but before the men could recover from this painful operation, Simeon and Levi, full brothers of Dinah, entered the city and killed them all. [Gen. 33:19; 34:2, 4, 13; Josh. 24:32; Judg. 9:28]

2. date unknown. A leader of the tribe of Manasseh descended from Gilead, his family was numbered among the children of Israel in the wilderness. [Num. 26:31; Josh. 17:2]

3. *c.* 13 century BC. Son of Shemidah, he and his family were leaders of the tribe of Manasseh living in Gilead, east of the river Jordan. [1 Chr. 7:19]

Shedeur (Heb. 'God is my light') *c.* 13 century BC. Father of Elizur who was chosen by Moses in the wilderness to number the men of Reuben who were fit for the army. [Num. 1:5; 2:10; 7:30–35; 10:18]

Sheerah (Heb. 'relation') *c.* 16 century BC. Daughter of Beriah and the granddaughter of Ephraim, her descendants built the towns of Lower and Upper Bethhoron and Uzzen-sheerah. [1 Chr. 7:24]

Shehariah (Heb. 'seeks God') date unknown. Son of Jeroham, he was one of the leaders of the tribe of Benjamin living in Jerusalem. [1 Chr. 8:26]

Shelah (Heb. 'prayer') *1.* date unknown. Son of Arpachshad and a grandson of Shem. [1 Chr. 1:18, 24]

2. *c.* 16 century BC. Youngest son of Judah, he went down to Egypt with his grandfather Jacob. [Gen. 38:5, 11, 26; 46:12; Num. 26:20; 1 Chr. 2:3; 1 Chr. 4:21]

Shelemiah (Heb. 'God rewards') *1.* see SHALLUM *4.*

2. *c.* 7 century BC. Son of Cushi and father of Nethaniah, his grandson Jehudi read out Jeremiah's prophecies of doom to Jehoiakim, king of Judah. [Jer. 36:14]

3. *c.* 7 century BC. Son of Abdeel, he was an officer of Jehoiakim, king of Judah, commanded to arrest the prophet Jeremiah and his scribe Baruch after the king had heard the prophecies of doom concerning Judah. [Jer. 36:26]

4. *c.* 6 century BC. Father of Jehucal who was sent by Zedekiah, king of Judah, to ask the prophet Jeremiah to pray for Judah during the Babylonian siege of Jerusalem. Later, he was among the Judean leaders who demanded the death of the prophet for spreading alarm and despondency and threw him in prison. [Jer. 37:3; 38:1]

5. *c.* 6 century BC. Son of Hananiah and the father of Irijah, a captain in the army of Zedekiah who falsely accused the prophet Jeremiah of deserting to the Babylonians during the siege of Jerusalem. [Jer. 37:13]

6. 5 century BC. Two descendants of Binnui who divorced their non-Jewish wives in the time of Ezra. [Ezra 10:39, 41]

7. 5 century BC. Father of Hananiah who helped repair the walls of Jerusalem in the time of Nehemiah. [Neh. 3:30]

8. 5 century BC. A priest of Judah who was appointed by Nehemiah to supervise the distribution of corn, wine and oil among the priests and Levites. [Neh. 13:13]

Sheleph date unknown. One of Joktan's thirteen sons and a great-grandson of Shem. [Gen. 10:26; 1 Chr. 1:20]

Shelesh (Heb. 'strength') date unknown. Son of Helem, he and his family were leaders of the tribe of Asher and mighty warriors. [1 Chr. 7:35]

Shelomi (Heb. 'my peace') *c.* 13 century BC. Father of Ahihud, a leader of the tribe of Asher who was chosen by Moses to divide up the area of the land of Israel allotted to his tribe. [Num. 34:27]

Shelomith (Heb. 'peace') *1.* date unknown. Daughter of Dibri of the tribe of Dan who married an Egyptian. Their son cursed God during a fight with a man of Israel and as a punishment was stoned to death. [Lev. 24:11]
2. see SHELOMOTH 2.
3. c. 10 century BC. Son of Rehoboam king of Judah and his favourite wife Maacah. [2 Chr. 11:20]
4. 6 century BC. Daughter of Zerubbabel of the tribe of Judah who led the return from exile in Babylon. [1 Chr. 3:19]
5. c. 5 century BC. Son of Josiphiah, he returned with Ezra from exile in Babylon. [Ezra 8:10]

Shelomoth (Heb. 'peace') *1. c.* 10 century BC. A Levite descended from Gershom, he and his family ministered in the Tabernacle during the reign of King David. [1 Chr. 23:9]
2. c. 10 century BC. The head of a family of Levites, he and his son Jahath ministered in the Tabernacle in the reign of King David. Also known as Shelomith. [1 Chr. 23:18; 24:22]
3. c. 10 century BC. Son of Zichri the Levite, during the reign of King David he was in charge of the precious vessels taken in battle, which were dedicated to the Tabernacle. [1 Chr. 26:25–8]

Shelumiel (Heb. 'God's peace') *c.* 13 century BC. Son of Zurishaddai, he was head of the tribe of Simeon who helped Moses with the census in the wilderness. [Num. 1:6; 2:12; 7:36, 10:19]

Shem (Heb. 'renown') date unknown. Eldest son of Noah. Shem and his wife went into the ark with his father Noah and the rest of the family. When they left the ark, Noah became a farmer, planted a vineyard, made wine out of his grapes and became drunk. Shem,

together with his brother Japheth, covered their father as he lay in a drunken stupor in his tent, and tactfully turned their heads away so they should not see his nakedness. When Noah heard what Shem and Japheth had done for him he blessed them. Noah said: 'Blessed by the Lord my God be Shem.' (Gen. 9:26) Shem lived for five hundred years and had many sons who gave their names to states and cities in the region. He came to be regarded as the legendary ancestor of the Semites. [Gen. 5:32, 6:10, 9:18–27, 10:1, 21, 22, 31; 11:10, 11; 1 Chr. 1:1, 17, 24]

Shema (Heb. 'hearing') *1.* date unknown. Son of Hebron and a leader of the tribe of Judah. [1 Chr. 2:43–4]
2. date unknown. Grandfather of Bela, he was a leader of the tribe of Reuben. Also called Shemaiah. [1 Chr. 5:4, 8]
3. date unknown. A leader of the tribe of Benjamin who 'put to flight the inhabitants of Gath' (1 Chr. 8:13). Also known as Shimei. [1 Chr. 8:13, 21]
4. 5 century BC. A leader of Judah who stood at the side of Ezra when he read out the Law of Moses to the people. [Neh. 8:4]

Shemaah (Heb. 'God hears') *c.* 11 century BC. Father of Ahiezer and Joash, leaders of a band of Benjaminite archers who deserted from King Saul's army and joined David at Ziklag. [1 Chr. 12:3]

Shemaiah (Heb. 'God hears') *1.* date unknown. Father of Shimri, he was an ancestor of Ziza, one of the leaders of Simeon in the reign of Hezekiah, king of Judah. [1 Chr. 4:37]
2. see SHEMA 2.
3. c. 10 century BC. A prophet during the reign of Rehoboam. Shortly after succeeding his father, King Solomon, Rehoboam faced a revolt of the northern tribes, who seceded and established a separate kingdom of Israel under the

rule of Jeroboam. When Rehoboam assembled an army from the tribes of Judah and Benjamin to suppress the revolt and restore the united kingdom, Shemaiah warned him against it, calling upon him in the name of the Lord not to fight his 'kinsmen the people of Israel' (1 Kgs. 12:24). His words were heeded; there was no war; and Rehoboam ruled over a truncated kingdom, the kingdom of Judah.

Five years later, when the Egyptian Pharaoh Shishak attacked Judah, ravaged several of its cities and was marching on Jerusalem, Shemaiah again came to Rehoboam and told him that since he had deserted the ways of the Lord, the Lord had abandoned him. However, because Rehoboam took the prophet's words to heart and repented, Jerusalem did not fall but Judah became a tributary of Egypt. It is recorded that Shemaiah together with Iddo wrote an account of Rehoboam's reign. [1 Kgs. 12:22; 2 Chr. 11:2; 12:5, 7, 15]

4. *c.* 10 century BC. The head of a family of Levites descended from Elizaphan who took part in the ceremony of bringing the Ark of God to Jerusalem in the reign of David. [1 Chr. 15:8, 11]

5. *c.* 10 century BC. Son of Nethanel the Levite, he was a scribe in the reign of King David who wrote out the rota of service for the priests in the Tabernacle. [1 Chr. 24:6]

6. *c.* 10 century BC. Eldest son of Obededom, a family of porters at the gates of the Tabernacle in Jerusalem in the reign of King David. His sons were strong men dedicated to the service of the Tabernacle. [1 Chr. 26:4, 6, 7]

7. *c.* 9 century BC. A Levite sent by Jehoshaphat, king of Judah, to teach the Law of God to the people in the cities of Judah. [2 Chr. 17:8]

8. *c.* 8 century BC. A Levite descended from Jeduthun who obeyed the command of King Hezekiah to sanctify himself and cleanse the Temple. [2 Chr. 29:14]

9. *c.* 8 century BC. A Levite in the reign of Hezekiah, king of Judah, entrusted with the distribution of the offerings among the priests in the cities of Judah. [2 Chr. 31:15]

10. *c.* 7 century BC. A leading Levite who donated large quantities of cattle as part of the Passover sacrifice in the fourteenth year of King Josiah's reign. [2 Chr. 35:9]

11. 6 century BC. A priest of Judah who returned with Zerubbabel from exile in Babylon, and was the ancestor of Jehonathan, head of a priestly family in the days of Nehemiah. [Neh. 12:6, 18, 34]

12. *c.* 6 century BC. Father of the prophet Uriah of Kiriath-jearim who predicted the destruction of Jerusalem and was put to death by Jehoiakim, king of Judah. [Jer. 26:20]

13. *c.* 6 century BC. A false prophet of Judah who was taken into captivity in the days of the prophet Jeremiah. He wrote to the priest Zephaniah, son of Maaseiah, telling him that the exile in Babylon would soon end and asking him to rebuke Jeremiah for prophesying that the exile would last a long time. Jeremiah foretold that Shemaiah and his descendants would never live to see the return of the exiles to Zion. [Jer. 29:24–32]

14. *c.* 6 century BC. Father of Delaiah, one of the leaders of Judah who reported Jeremiah's prophecies of doom to King Jehoiakim. [Jer. 36:12]

15. *c.* 5 century BC. Son of Shecaniah and a leader of the tribe of Judah descended from King David. Shecaniah was keeper of the East Gate of Jerusalem and Shemaiah helped repair the walls at the time of Nehemiah. [1 Chr. 3:22; Neh. 3:29]

16. 5 century BC. Son of Hasshub the Levite and a descendant of Merari, he was one of the first Levites to settle in Jerusalem following the return from Babylon, and ministered in the Temple. [1 Chr. 9:14; Neh. 11:15]

17. 5 century BC. Son of Galal the Levite,

he was the father of Obadiah, who was responsible for conducting the thanksgiving prayer in the Temple in the time of Nehemiah. Also called Shammua. [1 Chr. 9:16; Neh. 11:17]

18. 5 century BC. A descendant of Adonikam who returned with Ezra to Judah from exile in Babylon. [Ezra 8:13]

19. c. 5 century BC. One of the men sent by Ezra to Iddo at Casiphia to ask him to send Levites to Jerusalem to serve in the Temple. [Ezra 8:16]

20. 5 century BC. A descendant of Harim, the priest, who divorced his non-Jewish wife in the time of Ezra. [Ezra 10:21]

21. 5 century BC. A descendant of Harim, a man of Israel, who divorced his non-Jewish wife in the time of Ezra. [Ezra 10:31]

22. 5 century BC. Son of Delaiah, he invited Nehemiah to meet him in secret inside the Temple, claiming that conspirators planned to kill Nehemiah. Guessing that Shemaiah had been hired by his enemies to frighten him, Nehemiah declined the invitation. [Neh. 6:10]

23. 5 century BC. A priest of Judah who signed the solemn covenant in the time of Nehemiah. [Neh. 10:8]

24. 5 century BC. One of the leaders of Judah who took part in the dedication of the rebuilt walls of Jerusalem at the time of Nehemiah. [Neh. 12:34]

25. 5 century BC. Grandfather of Zechariah, one of the priests who blew a trumpet at the ceremony dedicating the walls of Jerusalem in the days of Nehemiah. [Neh. 12:35]

26. 5 century BC. A Levite who played musical instruments during the dedication service for the rebuilt walls of Jerusalem in the days of Nehemiah. [Neh. 12:36, 42]

Shemariah (Heb. 'preserved by God') *1. c.* 11 century BC. One of the Benjaminite archers who deserted the army of King Saul and rallied to David at Ziklag. [1 Chr. 12:5]

2. c. 10 century BC. A son of Rehoboam, king of Judah, by his wife Mahalath. [2 Chr. 11:19]

3. 5 century BC. A descendant of Harim, he divorced his non-Jewish wife in the time of Ezra. [Ezra 10:32]

4. 5 century BC. Son of Binnui, he divorced his non-Jewish wife in the time of Ezra. [Ezra 10:41]

Shemeber *c.* 18 century BC. King of Zeboiim in the days of Abraham, he was one of the five kings defeated in battle by Chedorlaomer, king of Elam, and his three confederate kings. [Gen. 14:2]

Shemed date unknown. One of the three sons of Elpaal, a leading Benjaminite, whose descendants built the towns of Ono and Lod. [1 Chr. 8:12]

Shemer (Heb. 'keeper') *1.* date unknown. A leader of the tribe of Levi descended from Merari, he was an ancestor of Ethan who served in the Tabernacle in the reign of King David. [1 Chr. 6:46]

2. c. 9 century BC. The owner of the hill which King Omri of Israel bought for two talents of silver and on which he built his capital city. He called it Samaria (Heb. *Shomron*) after Shemer. [1 Kgs. 16:24]

3. see Shomer *1.*

Shemida (Heb. 'wise') *c.* 13 century BC. A leader of the tribe of Manasseh and the son of Gilead, he was head of a family who were numbered among the children of Israel with Moses in the wilderness. [Num. 26:32; Josh. 17:2;1 Chr. 7:19]

Shemiramoth (Heb. 'heights of heaven') *1. c.* 10 century BC. A Levite who ministered in the Tabernacle in the reign of King David and played musical instruments when the Ark of the Lord was brought up to Jerusalem. [1 Chr. 15:18, 20; 16:5]

2. *c.* 9 century BC. A Levite sent by Jehoshaphat, king of Judah, to teach the Law of God in the cities of Judah. [2 Chr. 17:8]

Shemuel (Heb. 'heard by God') **1.** date unknown. Son of Tola and a grandson of Issachar, he and his family were leaders of the tribe and mighty warriors. [1 Chr. 7:2]
2. *c.* 13 century BC. Son of Ammihud and a leader appointed by Moses to divide up the part of the land of Israel allotted to the tribe of Simeon. [Num. 34:20]

Shenazzar (Ass. 'Sin [a god] protected') *c.* 6 century BC. Son of Jehoiachin, king of Judah, he and his family were taken into captivity when Judah was conquered by the Babylonians. [1 Chr. 3:18]

Shephatiah (Heb. 'God judges') **1.** date unknown. An ancestor of Zebadiah, son of Michael, who returned with Ezra to Judah from exile in Babylon. [Ezra 8:8]
2. date unknown. Son of Mahalalel of the tribe of Judah and the father of Amariah, he was an ancestor of Athaiah, who settled in Jerusalem in the days of Nehemiah. [Neh. 11:4]
3. date unknown. Ancestor of a family of Temple servants who returned with Zerubbabel from exile in Babylon. [Ezra 2:57; Neh. 7:59]
4. date unknown. Ancestor of a family that returned with Zerubbabel to Judah from exile in Babylon. [Ezra 2:4; Neh. 7:9]
5. *c.* 11 century BC. One of several archers of the tribe of Benjamin who deserted the army of King Saul and rallied to David at Ziklag. [1 Chr. 12:5]
6. *c.* 10 century BC. A son of King David and Abital, he was born in Hebron. [2 Sam. 3:4; 1 Chr. 3:3]
7. *c.* 10 century BC. Son of Maachah, he was appointed ruler over the Simeonites in the reign of King David. [1 Chr. 27:16]

8. 9 century BC. A son of Jehoshaphat, king of Judah, who was killed by his eldest brother Jehoram when he succeeded to the throne. [2 Chr. 21:2]
9. *c.* 6 century BC. Son of Mattan and a leader of Judah, he was one of four who pressed King Zedekiah to put the prophet Jeremiah to death for urging surrender to the invading Babylonians. When the king gave them freedom to do what they liked with Jeremiah, they threw him into a cistern with the intention of letting him die there. [Jer. 38:1]
10. *c.* 5 century BC. Son of Reuel of the tribe of Benjamin and the father of Meshullam, one of the first men to settle in Jerusalem after the return from Babylon. [1 Chr. 9:8]

Shephi *see* SHEPHO

Shepho (Heb. 'bareness') date unknown. Son of Shobal and a grandson of Seir, the Horite. Also called Shephi. [Gen. 36:23; 1 Chr. 1:40]

Shephupham *see* MUPPIM

Shephuphan *see* MUPPIM

Sherebiah (Heb. 'God's burning heat') 5 century BC. A Levite who returned from Babylon following Ezra's appeal to Iddo to send Levites to minister in the Temple in Jerusalem. He was entrusted with carrying the gold and silver vessels from Babylon back to Jerusalem and was responsible for the thanksgiving services in the Temple. He helped to explain the Law to the people and called upon them to repent of their sins. He signed the solemn covenant in the time of Nehemiah. [Ezra 8:18, 24; Neh. 8:7; 9:4, 5; 10:12; 12:24]

Sheresh (Heb. 'root') date unknown. Son of Machir and Maacah, and a grandson of Manasseh, he was a leader of the tribe. [1 Chr. 7:16]

Sheshai (Heb. 'princely') *c.* 13 century

BC. A descendant of the giant Anak, he was killed by Caleb following the invasion of the land of Israel under Joshua, and Caleb took possession of his lands at Hebron as part of his inheritance. [Num. 13:22; Josh. 15:14; Judg. 1:10]

Sheshan (Heb. 'princely') date unknown. Son of Ishi and a leader of the tribe of Judah, he married his daughter to his Egyptian servant, Jarha. [1 Chr. 2:31–5]

Sheshbazzar (possibly Pers. 'fire-worshipper') c. 6 century BC. A member of the Judean royal house, he became leader of the first group of repatriated exiles after the decree of Cyrus, king of Persia, in 538 BC. He received the vessels of silver and gold that had been pillaged from the Temple by the Babylonians and were sent back by Cyrus with the returning Jews. There were forty-two thousand, three hundred and sixty of them, and Sheshbazzar was in charge of bringing them up to Jerusalem.

Although it is stated in one passage that he became governor of Jerusalem, his name fades out at the beginning of the account of the return from Babylon in the Book of Ezra, while Zerubbabel emerges as the leader of the settler community in Jerusalem. Since both of them were, of royal blood, had Babylonian names and figured in the return, some scholars suggest that Sheshbazzar and Zerubbabel were really the same person. [Ezra 1:8, 11; 5:14, 16]

Sheshonk see PHARAOH 6.

Shethar (Pers. 'star') c. 5 century BC. One of the seven princes of Persia and Media who sat at the table of King Ahasuerus. [Esther 1:14]

Shethar-Bozenai (Pers. 'star of splendour') c. 6 century BC. A Persian official in Judah who wrote to Darius, king of Persia, telling him that the Jews under

Zerubbabel were rebuilding the Temple in Jerusalem, and asking the king if they had authority to do so, as they claimed. When Darius replied that the Jews had permission and ordered that help be given to them, the Persian official hastened to carry out the order. [Ezra 5:3, 6; 6:6, 13]

Sheva (Heb. 'warrior of God') *1.* date unknown. Grandson of Caleb and son of Hezron and Maacah, he was a leader of the tribe of Judah and the father of Machbenah. [1 Chr. 2:49]
2. see SERAIAH *2.*

Shilhi (Heb. 'armed') c. 9 century BC. Grandfather of Jehoshaphat, king of Judah. [1 Kgs. 22:42; 2 Chr. 20:31]

Shillem (Heb. 'paid') c. 16 century BC. Son of Naphtali, he was a grandson of Jacob and Bilhah. Also called Shallum. [Gen. 46:24; Num. 26:49; 1 Chr. 7:13]

Shilshah (Heb. 'third') date unknown. Son of Zophah, he and his family were leaders of the tribe of Asher and mighty warriors. [1 Chr. 7:37]

Shimea (Heb. 'hearing') *1.* date unknown. Son of Uzzah the Levite, he was a descendant of Merari. [1 Chr. 6:30]
2. c. 11 century BC. Grandfather of Asaph, King David's musician. [1 Chr. 6:39]
3. see SHAMMAH *2.*
4. see SHAMMUA *2.*

Shimeah (Heb. 'hearing') date unknown. Son of Mikloth, he was one of the leaders of the tribe of Benjamin living in Jerusalem. Also called Shimeam. [1 Chr. 8:32; 9:38]

Shimeam see SHIMEAH

Shimeath (Heb. 'hearing') c. 9 century BC. Ammonite mother of Jozacar, an officer of Joash, king of Judah, who assassinated the king in revenge for the execution of Zechariah, son of the high priest Jehoiada. [2 Kgs. 12:21; 2 Chr. 24:26]

Shimei (Heb. 'famed') *1.* date unknown. Son of Gog, a Reubenite who lived in Aroer, east of the Jordan. [1 Chr. 5:4]

2. date unknown. Younger son of Gershom and the grandson of Levi, his descendants were leading Levites who ministered in the Tabernacle of King David in Jerusalem. [Exod. 6:17; Num. 3:18; 1 Chr. 6:17, 42; 23:7, 10]

3. date unknown. Son of Zaccur, he was a leader of the tribe of Simeon. [1 Chr. 4:26, 27]

4. date unknown. Son of Libni of the tribe of Levi, he was a descendant of Merari. [1 Chr. 6:29]

5. date unknown. Son of Jahath of the tribe of Levi and a grandson of Gershom, he was the father of Zimmah and an ancestor of Asaph, one of King David's chief musicians. [1 Chr. 6:42]

6. date unknown. Leader of the tribe of Benjamin who lived in Jerusalem. [1 Chr. 8:21]

7. see SHEMA *3.*

8. see SHAMMAH *2.*

9. c. 10 century BC. Shimei, the son of Gera, was a Benjaminite and a member of Saul's family, living at Bahurim, southeast of Jerusalem. When David came through the town fleeing from Absalom, Shimei threw stones and dirt at him, shouting, 'Begone, begone, you man of blood, you worthless fellow!' (2 Sam. 16:7) David restrained his men from killing the old man, and said, 'Behold, my own son seeks my life; how much more now may this Benjaminite!' (2 Sam. 16:11)

After the defeat of Absalom, Shimei came down to the Jordan ford to greet David, and begged for forgiveness. Again, David spared his life. But David did not forget the incident, and on his deathbed instructed Solomon: 'You shall bring his grey head down with blood to Sheol.' (1 Kgs. 2:9)

Three years later, Shimei went off to Gath after two runaway slaves. This broke his undertaking not to leave Jerusalem, and Solomon ordered him to be put to death. [2 Sam. 16:19; 19:16; 1 Kgs. 2:8, 9, 36–46]

10. c. 10 century BC. A leader of Israel who remained loyal to King David when Adonijah proclaimed himself king before his father was dead. [1 Kgs. 1:8]

11. c. 10 century BC. Son of Ela, he was one of the twelve officers of King Solomon responsible for supplying the provisions of the royal household. [1 Kgs. 4:18]

12. c. 10 century BC. An officer of King David who was responsible for supervising the king's vineyards. [1 Chr. 27:27]

13. c. 8 century BC. A Levite descended from Heman, King David's musician, he obeyed the call of Hezekiah, king of Judah, to sanctify himself and cleanse the Temple. [2 Chr. 29:14]

14. c. 8 century BC. Brother and deputy of Conaniah, leader of the Levites in charge of the offerings and tithes brought to the Temple in the reign of Hezekiah, king of Judah. [2 Chr. 31:12, 13]

15. 6 century BC. Son of Pedaiah of the tribe of Judah and the brother of Zerubbabel who led the Return of the Jews to Judah from exile in Babylon. [1 Chr. 3:19]

16. 5 century BC. A Levite, he divorced his non-Jewish wife in the time of Ezra. [Ezra 10:23]

17. 5 century BC. A descendant of Hashum, he divorced his non-Jewish wife in the time of Ezra. [Ezra 10:33]

18. 5 century BC. A descendant of Binnui, he divorced his non-Jewish wife in the time of Ezra. [Ezra 10:38]

19. c. 5 century BC. Son of Kish of the tribe of Benjamin and the father of Jair, his grandson Mordecai thwarted the plot during the reign of King Ahasuerus to kill all the Jews in the Persian empire. [Esther 2:5]

Shimeon (Heb. 'one who hears') 5

century BC. A descendant of Harim, he divorced his non-Jewish wife in the time of Ezra. [Ezra 10:31]

Shimon (Heb. 'wasteland') date unknown. A leader of the tribe of Judah, descended from Caleb son of Jephunneh. [1 Chr. 4:20]

Shimrath (Heb. 'watcher') date unknown. Son of Shimei, he was a leader of the tribe of Benjamin living in Jerusalem. [1 Chr. 8:21]

Shimri (Heb. 'vigilant') *1.* date unknown. Father of Jedaiah, he was the ancestor of Ziza, a leader of the tribe of Simeon who settled in the rich valley of Gedor in the reign of Hezekiah, king of Judah. [1 Chr. 4:37]
2. c. 10 century BC. Father of Jediael who was one of the warriors in the army of King David and distinguished for his bravery. [1 Chr. 11:45]
3. c. 10 century BC. Son of Hosah, a Levite descended from Merari who served as a gatekeeper of the Tabernacle in the reign of King David. [1 Chr. 26:10]
4. c. 8 century BC. A Levite descended from Elizaphan who obeyed the command of Hezekiah, king of Judah, to sanctify himself and cleanse the Temple. [2 Chr. 29:13]

Shimrith (Heb. 'vigilant') 8 century BC. The Moabite mother of Jehozabad, an officer of Joash, king of Judah, who assassinated the king in revenge for the execution of Zechariah, son of the high priest Jehoiada. Also known as Shomer. [2 Kgs. 12:21; 2 Chr. 24:26]

Shimron (Heb. 'watch-place') *c.* 16 century BC. A son of Issachar and a grandson of Jacob and Leah, he went down to Egypt with his grandfather Jacob. [Gen. 46:13; Num. 26:24; 1 Chr. 7:1]

Shimshai (Heb. 'bright') 5 century BC.

A Persian scribe who served under Rehum, the Persian governor in Judah, he was one of the authors of a letter to King Artaxerxes calling upon him to order the Jews to stop rebuilding the walls of Jerusalem and suggesting they planned to rebel against the authority of Persia as soon as the walls were rebuilt. [Ezra 4:8, 17, 23]

Shinab (Heb. 'splendour') *c.* 18 century BC. King of Admah in the days of Abraham, he was one of five kings defeated in battle by Chedorlaomer, king of Elam, and his three confederate kings. [Gen. 14:2]

Shiphi (Heb. 'many') 8 century BC. Son of Allon of the tribe of Simeon, he was the father of Ziza, a Simeonite leader in the time of King Hezekiah who invaded and settled the Gedor valley. [1 Chr. 4:37]

Shiphrah (Heb. 'handsome') *c.* 13 century BC. One of the two Hebrew midwives in Egypt who did not obey Pharaoh's orders to kill all Hebrew boys at birth. [Exod. 1:15]

Shiphtan (Heb. 'judging') *c.* 13 century BC. Father of Kemuel, a leader of the tribe of Ephraim who was appointed by Moses to share out the part of the Promised Land allotted to his tribe. [Num. 34:24]

Shisha *see* SERAIAH 2.

Shishak *see* PHARAOH 6.

Shitrai (Heb. 'scribe') *c.* 10 century BC. A herdsman living in the Sharon plain in the reign of King David who was responsible for tending the royal herds in the Sharon area. [1 Chr. 27:29]

Shiza *c.* 10 century BC. Father of Adina, commander of a force of men of the tribe of Reuben in King David's army who was renowned for his bravery. [1 Chr. 11:42]

Shobab (Heb. 'hostile') *1.* date unknown. Son of Caleb and his wife Jerioth, he was a leader of the tribe of Judah. [1 Chr. 2:18]
2. c. 10 century BC. Son of King David born to him when he was king in Jerusalem. [2 Sam. 5:14; 1 Chr. 3:5; 14:4]

Shobach (Heb. 'enlarging') *c.* 10 century BC. The general commanding the army of Hadadezer, king of Zobah in Syria, who was defeated and killed in battle by King David. Also called Shophach. [2 Sam. 10:16, 18; 1 Chr. 19:16–18]

Shobai (Heb. 'captive') date unknown. Ancestor of a family of Levites who returned with Zerubbabel to Judah from exile in Babylon and who served as gatekeepers of the Temple in Jerusalem. [Ezra 2:42; Neh. 7:45]

Shobal *1. c.* 16 century BC. Youngest son of Judah and a grandson of Jacob. [1 Chr. 4:1, 2]
2. date unknown. Son of Seir, the Horite, and an Edomite chieftain. [Gen. 36:20, 23, 29; 1 Chr. 1:38, 40]
3. date unknown. Son of Hur and grandson of Caleb, he was a leader of Judah and regarded as the founder of Kiriath-jearim. [1 Chr. 2:50, 52]

Shobek (Heb. 'forsaken') 5 century BC. A leader of Judah who signed the solemn covenant in the time of Nehemiah. [Neh. 10:24]

Shobi (Heb. 'captive') *c.* 10 century BC. Son of Nahash from Rabbah in Ammon, he brought food and equipment to King David and his army when they crossed the river Jordan to avoid attack from Absalom's rebel forces. [2 Sam. 17:27]

Shoham (Heb. 'onyx') *c.* 10 century BC. Son of Jaaziah, the Levite descended

from Merari, he and his family ministered in the Tabernacle in Jerusalem in the reign of King David. [1 Chr. 24:27]

Shomer (Heb. 'watchman') *1.* date unknown. Son of Heber, he and his family were leaders of the tribe of Asher and mighty warriors. Also known as Shemer. [1 Chr. 7:32, 34]
2. see SHIMRITH

Shophach *see* SHOBACH

Shua (Heb. 'wealth') *1. c.* 16 century BC. A Canaanite whose daughter Bath-shua married Judah and bore him three sons. [Gen. 38:2, 12; 1 Chr. 2:3]
2. date unknown. Daughter of Heber, a leader of the tribe of Asher. [1 Chr. 7:32]

Shuah (Heb. 'pit') *c.* 17 century BC. A son of Abraham and his wife Keturah, he was a leader of a desert tribe. [Gen. 25:2; 1 Chr. 1:32]

Shual (Heb. 'fox') date unknown. Son of Zophah, he and his family were chiefs of the tribe of Asher and mighty warriors. [1 Chr. 7:36]

Shubael *see* SHEBUEL *1.* and *2.*

Shuhah (Heb. 'pit') date unknown. A chief of the tribe of Judah and the brother of Chelub. [1 Chr. 4:11]

Shuham *see* HUSHIM I.

Shuni (Heb. 'resting') *c.* 16 century BC. A son of Gad and grandson of Jacob and Zilpah, he went down to Egypt with his grandfather Jacob. [Gen. 46:16; Num. 26:15]

Shuppim (Heb. 'serpents') *1. c.* 16 century BC. A descendant of Benjamin and a leader of the tribe. [1 Chr. 7:12, 15]
2. c. 10 century BC. A Levite in the reign of King David who served as a

gatekeeper of the Tabernacle in Jerusalem. He and Hosah were chosen by lot to be posted on the western side near the gate of Shallecheth. [1 Chr. 26:16]

Shuthelah (Heb. 'discord') *1. c.* 16 century BC. A son of Ephraim and grandson of Joseph. [Num. 26:35, 36; 1 Chr. 7:20] *2.* date unknown. Son of Zabad and a leader of the tribe of Ephraim. [1 Chr. 7:21]

Sia *see* SIAHA

Siaha (Heb. 'assembly') date unknown. Ancestor of a family of Temple servants who returned with Zerubbabel to Judah from exile in Babylon. Also called Sia. [Ezra 2:44; Neh. 7:47]

Sibbecai (Heb. 'weaver') *c.* 10 century BC. A warrior in the army of King David who killed the Philistine giant, Saph. Sibbecai was commander of David's army for the eighth month of the year. Also called Mebunai. [2 Sam. 21:18; 23:27; 1 Chr. 11:29; 20:4; 27:11]

Sidon date unknown. Elder of Canaan's two sons and a grandson of Ham, he was the traditional founder of the great Phoenician port city of Sidon. [Gen. 10:15; 1 Chr. 1:13]

Sihon (Heb. 'sweeping away') *c.* 13 century BC. Amorite king in Transjordan in the time of Moses. When the Children of Israel reached the Arnon river east of the Dead Sea, they found that the country beyond it had recently been conquered by the Amorites under King Sihon. Moses sent messengers asking for leave to pass through and promising to stay on the King's Highway. Not only was his request turned down, but 'He gathered all his men together, and went out against Israel ...' (Num. 21:23) The battle took place at Jahaz and Sihon was beaten. The Israelites overran his land from the Arnon river to the Jabbok

river, including Heshbon, Sihon's capital. His territory, together with that of Og, king of Bashan, who was also defeated, was allocated to the tribes of Reuben, Gad and half of Manasseh. Frequent references to the defeat of Sihon occur in the Old Testament. [Num. 21:21–34; 32:33; Deut. 1:4; 2:24–32; 3:2, 6; 4:46; 29:7; 31:4; Josh. 2:10; 9:10; 12:2; 13:8; Judg. 11:19–22; 1 Kgs. 4:19; Neh. 9:22; Ps. 135:11; 136:19; Jer. 48:45]

Simeon (Heb. '[God] has heard') *c.* 16 century BC. Simeon was the second son of Jacob, by his wife Leah. Together with his brothers he was involved in the events that led to the selling of their brother Joseph into slavery in Egypt.

When Jacob was living at Shalem, his daughter Dinah was seduced by Shechem, a local young man. The father came and asked for Dinah's hand in marriage for Shechem. Jacob and his sons, concealing their rage, agreed provided that Shechem, his father, and all the men in the town should be circumcised. This was done, but before the men had recovered from the painful operation, Simeon and his brother Levi killed them all.

Later he was one of the ten sons sent by Jacob to buy corn in Egypt, where Joseph had become a leading figure at Pharaoh's court. Simeon was selected as the hostage to be left behind as a guarantee that the brothers would return with Benjamin, the youngest of Jacob's sons and Joseph's full brother. He was duly released when they all returned.

When Jacob went to settle in Egypt with all his family, it included Simeon and his six sons.

On his deathbed Jacob blessed all his sons in turn, but remembering the reprisal of Simeon and Levi over the seduction of their sister, he said: 'Simeon and Levi are brothers; weapons of violence are their swords ... I will divide them in Jacob and scatter them in Israel.' (Gen. 49:5, 7)

In the conquest of Canaan under Joshua, the tribe of Simeon was allocated an area in the south that included Beer-sheba. It seems to have disappeared soon after, perhaps by merging with local tribes. [Gen. 29:33; 34:25, 30; 35:23; 42:24, 36; 43:23; 46:10; 48:5; 49:5; Exod. 1:2; 6:15]

Sippai see SAPH

Sisera (Canaanite 'leader') *1. c.* 12 century BC. Sisera was the Canaanite commander of the army of Jabin, king of Hazor, who had conquered the Israelites and had treated them harshly for twenty years. The prophetess Deborah roused the Israelites to fight Sisera under Barak and he was defeated at the Kishon river. Sisera fled northwards on foot and arrived at the tent of a Kenite woman, Jael. She invited him in, fed him and, when he fell asleep, she killed him by driving a tent peg through his head.

In Deborah's song of victory, which is considered as an earlier version of the same story, there is a moving account of Sisera's mother looking through her lattice window, watching for her son's return. Her maids try and divert her by chattering about the booty Sisera will bring back with him. This account refers to Sisera as the king and not the commander. [Judg.4:5–23; 5:20, 26–30; 1 Sam. 12:9; Ps. 83:9]
2. date unknown. Ancestor of a family of Temple servants who returned with Zerubbabel to Judah from exile in Babylon. [Ezra 2:53; Neh. 7:55]

Sismai (Heb. 'famous') date unknown. Son of Eleasah of the tribe of Judah he was the father of Shallom. [1 Chr. 2:40]

Sithri (Heb. 'protected') *c.* 13 century BC. Son of Uzziel and a grandson of Kohath, he was a Levite leader in Egypt in the days of Moses and Aaron. [Exod. 6:22]

So *c.* 8 century BC. 'So, king of Egypt', whose help King Hoshea of Israel (732–24 BC) sought against the Assyrians, was apparently not a Pharaoh but an Egyptian general or prince. [2 Kgs. 17:4]

Soco date unknown. Son of Heber and a leader of the tribe of Judah. [1 Chr. 4:18]

Sodi (Heb. 'secret') *c.* 13 century BC. A leader of the tribe of Zebulun, he was the father of Gaddiel who was chosen by Moses as one of the twelve men sent to spy out the Promised Land. [Num. 13:10]

Solomon (Heb. 'peaceable') Son and successor of King David, he reigned from 970–31 BC. In all the long array of Israelite kings, Solomon shares with David the pinnacle of renown. Yet father and son emerge from the biblical narrative with markedly different lives and personalities. David's story is a vivid human document of a shepherd boy's struggle to power. In contrast, Solomon was reared as a royal prince, had the sceptre thrust into his boyish hand by an aging father and an ambitious mother, and kept his realm free of war and internal strife. Compared to David, Solomon seems an aloof and intellectual figure.

Solomon's mother was the beautiful Bathsheba, with whom King David fell in love when he saw her bathing herself on a moonlit rooftop below the palace. He caused her husband Uriah the Hittite to be killed in battle, then married her. As retribution, the first child of David and Bathsheba died in infancy. Solomon was the second child of this marriage. As a mark of divine forgiveness, Nathan the court prophet gave him the additional name of Jedidiah, 'beloved of God'.

When David was aged and ailing, his eldest surviving son Adonijah made a bid for the throne, supported by two of the most powerful figures at the court:

Joab the commander of the army and Abiathar, one of the two high priests. Bathsheba rushed to David to tell him that Adonijah was attempting to supplant him, and she was supported by Nathan. The king agreed that Solomon should at once be crowned. He sent Solomon on the royal mule to the spring of Gihon in the Kidron valley where the youth was anointed with oil from the sacred Tabernacle. The trumpets sounded, and everyone shouted, 'Long live King Solomon.' (1 Kgs. 1:39)

The dying David gave Solomon his last counsel. 'I am about to go the way of all the earth. Be strong, and show yourself a man.' (1 Kgs. 2:2) If Solomon wished to be a successful ruler, he should above all obey the Lord and observe his Laws. 'Then David slept with his fathers, and was buried in the city of David.' (1 Kgs. 2:10)

As a young and untried king, Solomon acted with surprising forcefulness in crushing the men who had turned against his father and had remained a threat to his own throne.

Adonijah had been spared, but now played into Solomon's hands. Through the queen-mother Bathsheba, he asked permission to marry Abishag of Shunam, the young girl who had nursed David in his old age. Solomon reacted sharply. Adonijah might as well have asked for the kingdom, he said. (To take a woman from the household of a dead or deposed king symbolized a claim to the succession.) Benaiah the captain of the palace guard was immediately sent to kill Adonijah.

Solomon told Abiathar the high priest that he too deserved to die for his support of Adonijah's attempt to take the throne, but his life would be spared because of the years of hardship he had shared with David. Instead, he was banished from the capital to the small village of Anathoth, near Jerusalem.

When the news reached David's nephew and general Joab, who had also supported Adonijah, he realized his danger and fled for sanctuary to the altar. Benaiah was sent to dispose of him too, but shrank from violating the sanctuary until Solomon firmly ordered him to do so. Joab was then struck down. Solomon justified this unprecedented act on the grounds that the blood-guilt was being wiped out for Joab's murder of Abner and Amasa during David's reign.

Shimei, the old Benjaminite who had cursed David, had been ordered to live in Jerusalem on pain of death if he should leave the city. One day he went to the Philistine city of Gath to look for two runaway slaves, and Solomon had him executed when he returned.

By these vigorous actions, 'the kingdom was established in the hand of Solomon' (1 Kgs. 2:46).

He went to Gibeon, an important sanctuary some six miles north-west of Jerusalem, and made a thousand burnt-offerings to the Lord. In a dream God asked him what he would like to be given. Solomon replied that he was a very young man, unskilled in leadership. 'Give thy servant therefore an understanding mind to govern thy people, that I may discern between good and evil.' (1 Kgs. 3:9) The Lord was pleased that the young king had not asked for long life, riches, and triumph over his enemies, and promised him these boons as well.

Solomon soon gave dramatic proof of his wisdom in judgment. There appeared before him two prostitutes living in the same house, each of whom had given birth to a son. One child died, and both claimed the surviving one as hers. The king ordered that a sword be brought in and the baby cut in two, with half to be given to each of the women. At this one of them cried out: 'Oh, my Lord, give her the living child, and by no means slay it.' (1 Kgs. 3:26) The other one declared: 'It shall be neither mine nor yours; divide it.' (1 Kgs. 3:26) The king decreed that the first woman was the real mother and should have the baby. The story of this judgment spread through the land and established Solomon's fame.

The Bible states categorically that 'Solomon's wisdom surpassed the wisdom of all the people of the east, and all the wisdom of Egypt. For he was wiser than all other men.' (1 Kgs. 4:30, 31) It is further claimed that he composed three thousand proverbs and a thousand and five songs; and that he could discourse learnedly about all plants, animals, birds, reptiles and fish.

The borders of the Israelite empire had been firmly established by David, and Solomon did not add to them. They extended up to the Euphrates in the north and to the desert in the east and south. Aram (Syria) and the Transjordan kingdoms of Ammon, Moab, and Edom had been conquered by David and remained vassal states under Solomon. Two skilled and energetic peoples had retained their independence in enclaves along the coast: the Philistines to the south and the Phoenicians further north. Hiram, king of the Phoenician port-city of Tyre, had been a friend and ally of David, and this special relationship was retained by Solomon.

ADMINISTRATION AND TRADE

From the list of chief ministers in Chapter 4 of the First Book of Kings, it appears that Solomon ensured continuity in the conduct of the kingdom's affairs by relying mostly on the men who had served David, or by appointing their sons.

For administrative and tax purposes, the kingdom was divided into twelve districts, about half of them corresponding to the old tribal areas. Each district was placed in charge of a commissioner who was provided with an official residence, and thick-walled storehouses for the grain, oil and other products that served as taxes. Judah, which was the most important tribe and that of the royal house, was left out of this arrange-

ment, and was presumably governed directly from Jerusalem.

Each district was to provide the food for the palace for one month a year. The text specifies the daily quota of flour and meal, oxen, sheep, deer, gazelles, roebucks and fowl, as well as barley and straw for the horses and other animals. It is reckoned that the quantity of food specified was sufficient for a household of five to six thousand persons.

Solomon's foreign policy rested on securing political alliances and developing trade with the surrounding countries. As had always been the custom with monarchs, diplomatic relations were cemented with suitable marriages. Solomon was a notable exponent of this harem statecraft, and early in his reign he brought off a political coup of the first magnitude by marrying the daughter of the Egyptian Pharaoh.

The kingdom of Israel lay astride the great trade routes between the Nile valley and the Euphrates basin, and lucrative revenue was derived from tolls and supplies for the laden caravans passing to and fro. Israelite merchants expanded their own foreign trade; the Bible mentions that they bought chariots in Egypt and horses in Cilicia (now southern Turkey), reselling them to the Hittites and the Syrians in the north-east.

Solomon's partnership with Hiram, king of Tyre, also opened up a southern sea route through the Gulf of Akaba into the Red Sea area. The Israelites were essentially a hill people, with a desert background, and they had no real knowledge of seafaring. But with the help of Hiram's shipwrights, Phoenician-type wooden vessels with flat bottoms and square sails were constructed at Solomon's port of Ezion-geber near Eilat, at the head of the Gulf. They were suitable for transporting the copper ore from King Solomon's mines, a few miles north of Ezion-geber, for export southwards. (These mines are being worked again in modern Israel three thousand years later.) Carrying Solomon's traders, and manned by Hiram's crews, the vessels reached the coasts of southern Arabia and East Africa. The richest country in that region was the land of Ophir, the exact location of which is still uncertain. Once in three years, the fleet of ships brought back cargoes of 'gold, silver, ivory, apes, and peacocks' (1 Kgs. 10:22). It is these voyages that figure in John Masefield's poem *Cargoes*:

'Quinquireme of Nineveh from
    distant Ophir
Rowing home to haven in sunny
    Palestine,
With a cargo of ivory,
And apes and peacocks,
Sandalwood, cedarwood and sweet
    white wine.'

There is also a suggestion that Solomon may have sent ships with the Phoenician trading fleets along the Mediterranean coasts.

In the Red Sea region now penetrated by Israelite shipping and commerce, there was a kingdom called Sheba. It may have occupied the south-west corner of the Arabian peninsula at the southern entrance to the Red Sea in what is now Yemen; though the Ethiopians maintain that Sheba was on the African side in a locality now included in Ethiopia. Its inhabitants, the Sabeans, took advantage of their strategic position to become an enterprising trading nation along the sea-lanes and the inland caravan routes. They dealt in gold, gems, spices and other valuable commodities from the East and from Africa. In Solomon's time Sheba was ruled by a queen. She was intrigued by the reports of Solomon's legendary wisdom, and the growing wealth and power of Israel; and she no doubt also saw prospects of extending her people's commercial activities. The Queen of Sheba decided to pay a royal visit to the Israelite court in

Jerusalem, and set out by camel caravan on the arduous fifteen-hundred-mile overland trek across deserts and mountains.

Solomon received the queen with due pomp, and she was dazzled by the brilliance and luxury of his household. She had come armed with cunning riddles and difficult questions to test him, and found him able to deal easily with them. She declared that 'Your wisdom and prosperity surpass the report which I heard.' (1 Kgs. 10:7) She then presented him with the lavish gifts she had brought – a great quantity of gold and precious stones and more spices than had ever been seen at one time in Israel. Solomon made gifts in return from the royal treasury and the queen set out again on the long journey home.

The story of King Solomon and the Queen of Sheba has given rise to much romantic folk-lore in Jewish, Moslem and Christian writings. Some of these tales suggest that the relations between them were less platonic than might appear from the biblical account. In Ethiopia it is a national legend that the Queen of Sheba bore Solomon a son, Menelek, who settled in what was then the land of Cush and became the founder of the royal house. The Emperor of Ethiopia bears the official title 'The Lion of Judah'; and the national emblem is a six-pointed star, corresponding to the Shield of David on the Israel flag.

SOLOMON THE BUILDER
Growing wealth, and freedom from external pressures, enabled Solomon to launch an ambitious building programme. In this he was fortunate in being able to draw on the aid of his Phoenician ally Hiram for designers, craftsmen, lumber and gold.

Solomon set about embellishing Jerusalem, the city David had captured from the Jebusites and had made the political and religious centre of the nation. On the rising ground to the north of David's city, Solomon laid out a series of terraces and courtyards holding a complex of sumptuous buildings, and enclosed by a great stone wall. In the complete programme the Temple stood at the highest point, on the site of the threshing floor that David had bought for this purpose for fifty shekels of silver. (It is today the platform known as the Haram-esh-Sharif, holding the Dome of the Rock and the El-Aksa Mosque.)

The Temple itself took seven years to build. Its dedication was one of the most solemn days in the history of Israel. The elders from all over the country assembled in Jerusalem to be present. The priests carried the sacred Ark from the Tabernacle where David had brought it after the capture of Jerusalem, and placed it in the Temple courtyard. The king offered sacrifices on the bronze altar. The chief priests then bore the Ark into the Holy of Holies. When they emerged, a dark cloud filled the Temple, denoting God's presence.

The palace complex took another thirteen years to build. Solomon also built fortresses at strategic points along the main highways passing through the country. Three regional centres for his chariot forces were the sites of important archaeological excavations in this century. They were Hazor, north of the Sea of Galilee, commanding the historic road to Damascus; Megiddo, controlling the pass from the coastal plain into the Jezreel Valley; and Gezer, lying astride the road from Joppa to Jerusalem.

Solomon's extensive building operations required a huge labour force. Eighty thousand men are stated to have worked on the buildings, in the stone quarries and as porters; while thirty thousand more were sent to Phoenicia in shifts of ten thousand a month, to fell timber from the cedar and pine forests in the Lebanese mountains, and transport it to the coast. Hiram's men floated the log-rafts down to the Israelite port of Joppa, and from there the timber was hauled up to Jerusalem.

Under the treaty arrangements between Solomon and Hiram, lumber and gold were bartered for Israelite wheat and oil. During twenty years a deficit accumulated, which Solomon was obliged to meet by ceding to Hiram a strip of territory in western Galilee along the plain of Acre, containing twenty towns. This area was known as the land of Cabul.

Revenue flowed into the royal exchequer from various sources: the heavy taxes, the profits from trade, tribute monies from the vassal states, tolls levied on the passing caravans, and the lavish gifts brought by distinguished foreign visitors. These resources were drained out again by Solomon's building programme, and by the luxury and splendour of the court. The biblical chronicler records with awe the king's throne of ivory and gold, and the golden drinking vessels. For an oriental potentate, an even more impressive status symbol was the size of his harem, given as seven hundred wives and three hundred concubines. 'Now King Solomon loved many foreign women: the daughter of Pharaoh, and Moabite, Ammonite, Edomite, Sidonian, and Hittite women.' (1 Kgs. 11:1) Even if the statistics are inflated, it was clearly an expensive household to maintain in royal style.

EROSION OF THE KINGDOM

In the later years of Solomon's reign, the kingdom ran into increasing difficulties. In the Bible, they are ascribed to a lack of religious piety on the king's part, for which his foreign wives are held to blame. Solomon was broad-minded enough to give them facilities for worshipping their own assorted heathen gods. This could hardly have commended itself to the faithful. What was worse, they felt that the king himself did not remain immune to these idolatrous practices. 'For when Solomon was old his wives turned away his heart after other gods; and his heart was not wholly true to the Lord his God, as was the heart of David his father.' (1 Kgs. 11:4) He was accused of being drawn towards Ashtaroth the Phoenician goddess, and to the 'abominations' that were the gods of Ammon and Moab, building shrines for them in the hills round Jerusalem. The Lord was angry with him and declared that the kingdom would be torn apart when he died. However, the historian would link to more mundane factors the erosion that started to show itself.

The vassal states became troublesome. Edom, the desert kingdom in the south, was less tractable than it had been under David. The revived Aram-Damascus kingdom in the north was a constant source of harassment. The Egyptians were regaining their influence over the Philistine part of the coastal plain.

Inside the country, discontent was growing. Solomon's subjects were proud of his fame, the splendour of his court and the magnificent new Temple and palace in Jerusalem. They had enjoyed decades of peace and prosperity. But they groaned under the burden of heavy taxes and forced labour. In addition, the traditional rivalry between Judah and the other tribes (especially Ephraim in the centre) still smouldered under the surface. An abortive plot against the king was instigated by Jeroboam, a young Ephraimite of good birth whom Solomon had put in charge of the labourers engaged in the Jerusalem construction work. The king learnt of the plot, and Jeroboam fled for his life to Egypt. (He later returned to become ruler of the northern kingdom.)

Solomon died after nearly forty years on the throne, and was buried in Jerusalem with David. His son Rehoboam succeeded to the throne, but the ten northern tribes revolted. The united monarchy started by Saul, expanded by David and consolidated by Solomon,

irretrievably split apart. The two small successor states of Judah and Israel were to co-exist or clash for centuries, until each in turn was wiped out by imperial invaders from the north. [The main story of Solomon is told in 1 Kgs. 1–11 and 2 Chr. 1–9]

SOLOMON'S ARCHITECTURE
The Temple
No remains of Solomon's Temple have as yet been excavated; but the Bible account describes it with such loving detail that it can be visualized. The building itself was famous not for size (it was only about 100 feet by 30 feet), but for beauty and the splendour of its material and decoration. It was built of stone lined on the inside with cedarwood and gold. The interior was divided into three parts: the vestibule; the nave; and the inner sanctuary or Holy of Holies. The latter contained the sacred Ark of the Law, under the outstretched wings of two fifteen-foot cherubim of olive wood overlaid with gold leaf. In the space above their wings, the invisible spirit of God was said to hover. The entrance to the Temple was flanked by two great bronze pillars. In the courtyard in front of the building stood the bronze altar, and an enormous bronze bowl or 'molten sea' supported on the figures of twelve oxen. The pillars and the bowl were fashioned and cast by an artist of genius from Tyre, whose name was also Hiram.

Solomon's Temple stood for nearly four hundred years, until it was destroyed in the sack of Jerusalem in 587 BC by the Babylonian army under Nebuchadnezzar. Half a century later, in the reign of Cyrus, king of Persia, the Jews started returning from the Babylonian exile and began to build the Second Temple, completed in 515 BC. Herod the Great set out to reconstruct it on a grander scale in 20 BC. His temple was completed after his death, and just four years before the Romans razed it to the ground in AD 70. The Temple has never been rebuilt, and its most notable relic remains the Western (Wailing) Wall.

The Palace

The palace complex was just south of the Temple. First came the king's quarters and the quarters for the Egyptian Queen and the harem. Below that were the 'Porch of Pillars'; the 'Porch for the Throne'; and the large 'House of the Forest of Lebanon'. The latter buildings were used for official purposes: halls for meetings and special assemblies, the hall in which Solomon gave judgment, and the administrative offices.

The Chariot Cities

The excavations at Hazor, Megiddo and Gezer disclosed Solomonic fortifications of identical plan, presumably built by the same engineer. The casemate walls were eighteen feet wide, with the chambers within it used as guests' quarters or stores. The entrance gateway was fifty-five feet wide and of elaborate design. It was flanked by two square towers and led into a long vestibule with three rooms on either side. Both at Megiddo and Hazor the digs revealed underground tunnels leading to springs of fresh water. They were constructed in order to withstand a siege, like Hezekiah's tunnel in Jerusalem.

SOLOMON AND THE WISDOM BOOKS

Solomon was Israel's greatest sage, renowned for his judicial insight, learning and literary skill, so that it could be said that 'he was wiser than all other men' (1 Kgs. 4:30, 31). It is not surprising that he came to be regarded as the father of Hebrew wisdom literature.

This kind of writing flourished in the ancient cultures of the Near East, in the form of proverbs, parables, fables, riddles, and poems. It was common in Egypt, Mesopotamia, and Assyria, and was associated with the local sages of Canaan, Edom and Arabia. The earliest Hebrew proverbs derived much from these sources in the area, but developed their own unique character.

It is not easy to define 'wisdom' in this context. Where the prophets were concerned with the covenant between God and his chosen people, and the priests with formal worship, the sages (Heb. hachamim) were more concerned with the individual human predicament. Their domain was the practical morality of daily life rather than abstract theology.

The Wisdom Books in the Hebrew Bible are Proverbs, Job and Ecclesiastes. Two more works – the Wisdom of Solomon (also known as the Book of Wisdom) and the Wisdom of Jesus the Son of Sirach (also known as Ecclesiasticus) – were included in the Greek and Latin Bibles, but classified as Apocrypha in the Protestant bible. Of these works, Solomon's name is associated with Proverbs, Ecclesiastes and Wisdom. The Song of Songs (or Song of Solomon) has also been attributed to his authorship; it appears together with the wisdom books in the Old Testament, but is of a different genre.

Proverbs

The Book as a whole is headed 'The proverbs of Solomon, son of David, king of Israel'. It is compiled from several collections of proverbs made at different times. The two main anthologies are introduced as 'The proverbs of Solomon' (375 maxims) and 'Proverbs of Solomon, which the men of Hezekiah king of Judah copied out' (128 maxims). The contents of these two collections may well go back to the time of Solomon, or even earlier.

Other sections of the Book include an introduction in which a father commends wisdom to his son; smaller groups of 'sayings'; and an alphabetical poem at the end in praise of the good wife whose 'price is far above rubies'.

The standard form of the proverb (Heb. mashal) is a single sentence with the second half balancing the first. In the Hebrew, a very condensed language, the usual length of a proverb is from six to eight words. The main themes are the virtues of piety, industry, thrift, moderation, honesty and charitableness. A few familiar examples are:

'Go to the ant, O sluggard; consider her ways, and be wise.' (6:6)

'Like a gold ring in a swine's snout is a beautiful woman without discretion.' (11:22)

'He who spared the rod hates his son, but he who loves him is diligent to discipline him.' (13:24)

'A soft answer turns away wrath, but a harsh word stirs up anger.' (15:1)

'Better is a dinner of herbs where love is than a fatted ox and hatred with it.' (15:17)

'Pride goes before destruction, and a haughty spirit before a fall.' (16:18)

'Let a man meet a she-bear robbed of her cubs, rather than a fool in his folly.' (17:12)

'Wine is a mocker, strong drink a brawler; and whoever is led astray by it is not wise.' (20:1)

'If you have found honey eat only enough for you, lest you be sated with it and vomit it.' (25:16)

'If your enemy is hungry, give him bread to eat; and if he is thirsty, give him water to drink.' (25:21)

'Where there is no prophecy the people cast off restraint, but blessed is he who keeps the law.' (29:18)

Ecclesiastes

The unknown writer of this book refers to himself in Hebrew as Kohelet, meaning one who appears before an assembly or *kahal*. The word was translated in the Greek bible (Septuagint) as 'Ecclesiastes' and in English as 'the Preacher'.

Up to the first century AD the rabbis hesitated to accept into the Hebrew bible a work which seemed to many of them heretical and impious. It was included mainly because King Solomon was supposed to be the author. Solomon's name is not actually used, but the title reads 'The Words of the Preacher, the son of David, king in Jerusalem'. In the text the writer refers to himself as a king who has reigned in Jerusalem, is exceptionally wise and has enjoyed great wealth and luxury. However, it is now considered that these references are only literary allusions, meant to give the work the prestige attached to Israel's royal sage.

From the contents and language of the Book, it appears to have been written by a Jewish intellectual of the 3rd century BC during the Hellenistic period, before the Maccabean Revolt put fresh faith and confidence into the people. Kohelet has a brilliant but pessimistic and sceptical mind. He is obviously influenced by the contemporary Greek philosophers, such as Epicurus.

The tone is set in the opening passage: 'Vanity of vanities, says the Preacher, vanity of vanities! All is vanity. What does man gain by all the toil at which he toils under the sun?' (Eccles. 1:2, 3)

Injustice is rife in the world. The pursuit of power, wealth or pleasure cannot gain any lasting happiness, nor does achievement bring reward. Whatever is to happen to any man is predetermined. No man can comprehend God's will. Only one thing is certain – that death will come to all. 'For who knows what is good for man while he lives the few days of his vain life, which he passes like a shadow? For who can tell man what will be after him under the sun?' (Eccles. 6:12) His advice therefore is: 'So I say that there is nothing better than that a man should enjoy his work, for that is his lot; who can bring him to see what will be after him?' (Eccles. 3:22)

Whatever its meaning, life should be accepted as a fact: 'But he who is joined with all the living has hope, for a living dog is better than a dead lion.' (Eccles. 9:4) Kohelet's views are not all negative, and at times he contradicts his own pessimism. The aphorisms in the Book contain much sage counsel, based on worldly experience.

Ecclesiastes is one of the five

Megilloth (Scrolls) that form part of the Jewish service on certain festivals. It is read in synagogues on the Feast of Tabernacles (Succoth).

The Song of Solomon
This dazzling love poetry, the only work of its kind in the Bible, opens with the words: 'The Song of Songs, which is Solomon's' (Heb. *Shir ha-Shirim*). Here the identification is with Solomon not as a sage but as a writer of songs and an oriental monarch credited with having a thousand wives and concubines in his harem.

However, the suggested link with Solomon is clearly no more than a poetic fiction. The work was probably woven together about the 3rd century BC though it must have drawn on more ancient oral sources. Its form is that of a series of short songs or poems designed to be chanted in turn by the bride and bridegroom at a wedding feast, in part as a dialogue and in part separately.

Religion has no visible place in the work and its inclusion in the bible is at first glance puzzling. But the attribution to Solomon had become an accepted tradition by the time the canon of the Hebrew bible was settled. Moreover, the rabbis read into the work an elaborate allegory of the relations between God (the bridegroom) and the people of Israel (the bride). For their part, the Christian Fathers saw in it an allegory of Jesus's relations with the Church.

However valid these religious interpretations may be, the Song of Songs has been cherished for its own sake – above all for the sensuous delight of the language and imagery. It is filled with the rapture of love between man and woman, and with the lyricism of the Israel countryside in the springtime:

'O that you would kiss me with the
    kisses of your mouth!
For your love is better than wine.'
                                    (S. of S. 1:2)

'Sustain me with raisins,
    refresh me with apples;

for I am sick with love.
O that his left hand were under my
    head,
    and that his right hand embraced
    me!'
                                (S. of S. 2:5, 6)
'Your two breasts are like two fawns,
    twins of a gazelle,
    that feed among the lilies.'
                                    (S. of S. 4:5)
'for lo, the winter is past,
    the rain is over and gone.
The flowers appear on the earth,
    the time of singing has come,
and the voice of the turtledove
    is heard in our land.
The fig tree puts forth its figs,
    and the vines are in blossom;
    they give forth fragrance.
Arise, my love, my fair one,
    and come away.'
                                (S. of S. 2:11–13)

The Wisdom of Solomon
Certain passages in this book are written as if Solomon were speaking in the first person; but again, these references are a mere literary device. The work is a philosophical treatise written anonymously in the Greek language by a cultivated Alexandrian Jew, about the middle of the 1st century BC. The theme is traditional wisdom and its role in the history and outlook of the Jewish people. The author's object is plainly to counteract among his educated fellow-Jews the attraction of Hellenistic culture, philosophy and rationalism. This work is included in the Apocrypha.

Sophereth (Heb. 'scribe') *c.* 10 century BC. A servant of King Solomon, his descendants were among the people of Judah who returned with Zerubbabel from exile in Babylon. Also known as Hassophereth. [Ezra 2:55; Neh. 7:57]

Sotai (Heb. 'fickle') *c.* 10 century BC. A servant of King Solomon, and ancestor of a family who returned with Zerubbabel from exile. [Ezra 2:55; Neh. 7:57]

Suah (Heb. 'sweeping') date unknown. Son of Zophah of the tribe of Asher, he and his family were chiefs of the tribe and mighty warriors. [1 Chr. 7:36]

Succoth-benoth A deity worshipped by the Babylonians who were settled in Samaria by the conquering Assyrian empire after the fall of the northern kingdom of Israel. [2 Kgs. 17:30]

Sukkiim A tribe (possibly African) who joined Pharaoh Shishak of Egypt in his invasion of Judah during the reign of Rehoboam, king of Judah. [2 Chr. 12:3]

Susi (Heb. 'my horse') *c*. 13 century BC. A leader of the tribe of Manasseh, he was the father of Gaddi who was appointed by Moses as one of the twelve men sent to spy out the Promised Land. [Num. 13:11]

T

Tabbaoth (Heb. 'rings') date unknown. Ancestral head of a family of Temple servants who returned to Judah with Zerubbabel from exile in Babylon. [Ezra 2:43; Neh. 7:46]

Tabeel (Heb. 'God is good') *1. c.* 8 century BC Father of a pretender to the throne of Judah whom the kings of Syria and Israel planned to crown when they had overthrown King Ahaz. [Isa. 7:6]
2. c. 5 century BC. A Samarian leader who wrote a letter to Artaxerxes, king of Persia, protesting against the rebuilding of Jerusalem by the Jews. [Ezra 4:7]

Tabrimmon (Ass. 'Rimmon is good') *c.* 10 century BC. King of Syria, he was the son of Hezion and father of Ben-Hadad I who allied himself with King Asa of Judah against King Baasha of Israel. [1 Kgs. 15:18]

Tahan (Heb. 'camp') *1. c.* 16 century BC. Son of Ephraim and head of the family of Tahanites. [1 Num. 26:35]
2. date unknown. Son of Telah and the father of Ladan, he and his family were chiefs of Ephraim. [1 Chr. 7:25, 26]

Tahash (Heb. 'porpoise') *1. c* 17 century BC Son of Abraham's brother Nahor by his concubine Reumah and by Hebrew tradition the founder of an Aramean clan. [Gen. 22:24]

Tahath (Heb. 'compensation') *1. c.* 16 century BC Son of Bered of the tribe of Ephraim, he was father of Eleadah. [1 Chr. 7:20]
2. c. 15 century BC. Son of Eleadah of the tribe of Ephraim and the father of Zabad. [1 Chr. 7:20, 21]
3. c. 13 century BC Son of Assir, a Levite descended from Kohath and the father of Uriel and Zephaniah, he was an ancestor of the prophet Samuel. [1 Chr. 6:24, 37]

Tahpenes (Heb. 'Egyptian wife of the king') *c.* 10 century BC. Queen of Egypt during the reign of King David, her sister married Hadad, the Edomite leader who fled from David to Egypt. [1 Kgs. 11:19, 20]

Tahrea see TAREA

Talmai (Heb. 'makes furrows') *1.* date unknown. A descendant of the giant Anak from Hebron, he was killed by Caleb, leader of the tribe of Judah, after the invasion of Canaan by the Children of Israel under Joshua. [Num. 13:22; Josh. 15:14; Judg. 1:10]
2. c 10 century BC. Father of Maacah who married King David and bore him Absalom. When Absalom killed his half-brother Amnon, he fled to his grandfather, Talmai. [2 Sam. 3:3; 13:37; 1 Chr. 3:2]

Talmon 6 century BC. Head of a family of Levites who returned to Judah with Zerubbabel from Babylon. Members of his family became gatekeepers of the Tabernacle in Jerusalem in the days of the high priest Joiakim. [1 Chr. 9:17; Ezra 2:42; Neh. 7:45; 11:19; 12:24]

Tamar (Heb. 'date') *1. c.* 16 century BC. The wife of Judah's elder sons Er and Onan. Both men died before she had children, so when Judah refused to give her his third son in marriage, Tamar tricked Judah into sleeping with her by disguising herself as a prostitute, and bore him twin sons Perez and Zerah. [Gen. 38:6, H, 13–30; Ruth 4:12; I Chr. 2:4]

2. c. 10 century BC. She was the beautiful daughter of King David and his wife Maacah, and a full sister of Absalom.

Her eldest half-brother Amnon fell in love with her and, pretending to be ill, he received David's permission for her to look after him. Amnon sent everyone out of his room, raped her and, suddenly hating her, had her thrown out of his house. Tamar went in great distress to Absalom who looked after her. Two years later Absalom gave a feast, invited Amnon and killed him in revenge for the honour of his sister. [2 Sam. 13; 1 Chr. 3:9]

3. c. 10 century BC. Daughter of Absalom and the granddaughter of King David, she was known for her beauty. [2 Sam. 14:27]

Tammuz (Syrian 'sprout') An Accadian god whose worship spread throughout the ancient world – Babylonia, Assyria, Palestine and Phoenicia. He was worshipped by the people of Judah shortly before the destruction of the Temple. The prophet Ezekiel in his vision of 'abominations' describes women weeping for Tammuz at the very gates of the Temple in Jerusalem. [Ezek. 8:14]

Tanhumeth (Heb. 'comfort') c. 6 century BC. Father of Seraiah, one of the army commanders of Judah who rallied to Gedaliah when the Babylonians made him governor of Judah. [2 Kgs. 25:23; Jer. 40:8]

Taphath (Heb. 'drop') c. 10 century BC. Daughter of King Solomon, she married Ben-abinadab, one of the leaders of Israel who ruled over the area of Dor. [1 Kgs. 4:11]

Tappuah (Heb. 'apple') date unknown. Son of Hebron of the tribe of Judah and a descendant of Caleb son of Hezron. [1 Chr. 2:43]

Tarea c. 10 century BC. Son of Micah of the tribe of Benjamin and a descendant of King Saul. Also called Tahrea. [1 Chr. 8:35; 9:41]

Tarshish (Heb. 'gold-coloured stone') date unknown. Son of Javan and a great-grandson of Noah, he was by Hebrew tradition the legendary founder of Tarshish. [Gen. 10:4; 1 Chr. 1:7]

2. date unknown. Son of Bilhan and a leader of the tribe of Benjamin. [1 Chr. 7:10]

3. c. 5 century BC. One of the seven princes of Persia and Media who sat at the table of King Ahasuerus. [Esther 1:14]

Tartak One of the gods worshipped by the Avvites, an eastern tribe settled in Samaria by the Assyrians after they had exiled the population of the northern kingdom of Israel. [2 Kgs. 17:31]

Tartan (Ass. 'officer') c. 8 century BC. A commander of the Assyrian army sent against the kingdom of Judah in the reign of King Hezekiah. Tartan had previously commanded the Assyrian army which captured the Philistine city of Ashdod. [2 Kgs. 18:17]

Tattenai c. 6 century BC. The Persian governor of Judah in the days of Zerubbabel who questioned the right of Zerubbabel to repair the Temple and the walls of Jerusalem and wrote to the Persian Emperor, Darius, asking for instructions. When ordered by Darius to assist in repairing the Temple, he hastened to carry out the emperor's command. [Ezra 5:3, 6; 6:6, 13]

Tebah (Heb. 'slaughter') c. 17 century BC. A son of Abraham's brother Nahor by his concubine Reumah and by Hebrew tradition the founder of an Aramean clan. [Gen. 22:24]

Tebaliah (Heb. 'purged') *c*. 10 century BC. Son of Hosah, and a Levite descended from Merari, he was a gatekeeper of the Tabernacle in the days of King David. [1 Chr. 26:11]

Tehinnah (Heb. 'entreaty') date unknown. Son of Eshton, a leader of the tribe of Judah who lived in Recah. [1 Chr. 4:12]

Telah date unknown. Son of Resheph of the tribe of Ephraim and the father of Tahan, he was an ancestor of Joshua who led the Children of Israel into the Promised Land. [1 Chr. 7:25]

Telem *c*. 5 century BC. A Levite gatekeeper at the Temple in the days of Ezra, who divorced his non-Jewish wife. [Ezra 10:24]

Tema (Heb. 'desert') *c*. 18 century BC. Son of Ishmael, and a grandson of Abraham, he was leader of a desert clan. [Gen. 25:13–15; 1 Chr. 1:30]

Temah (Heb. 'mirth') date unknown. Ancestral head of a family of Temple servants who returned with Zerubbabel from exile in Babylon. [Ezra 2:53; Neh. 7:55]

Teman (Heb. 'south') *c*. 16 century BC. Eldest son of Eliphaz and a grandson of Esau, he was an Edomite leader. [Gen. 36:11, 15; 1 Chr. 1:36, 53]

Temeni (Heb. 'southern') date unknown. Son of Ashhur, a leader of the tribe of Judah, and his wife Naarah. [1 Chr. 4:6]

Terah *c*. 18 century BC. Father of Abraham, he left his native city of Ur in Babylonia intending to go to Canaan but settled in Haran in Syria. Terah worshipped idols and did not adopt his son's faith in God. [Gen. 11:24–32; Josh. 24:2; 1 Chr. 1:26]

Teresh *c*. 5 century BC. One of the two doorkeepers who plotted to assassinate King Ahasuerus of Persia. Their plot was discovered by Mordecai and the two conspirators were put to death. In the Greek Additions to the Book of Esther, in the Apocrypha, he is called Tharra. [Esther 2:21; 6:2]

Tibni *c*. 9 century BC. Son of Ginath he tried to make himself king of the northern kingdom of Israel after the suicide of King Zimri. Some of the people supported Tibni and the rest supported the army commander Omri who eventually triumphed, and Tibni was put to death. [1 Kgs. 16:21, 22]

Tidal *c*. 18 century BC. Tidal was king of Goiim (a word meaning 'nations') and one of the four Mesopotamian kings who defeated an alliance of five local kings from the Dead Sea area in the time of Abraham. They carried off a number of captives, including Abraham's nephew Lot, and much booty. Abraham pursued them and rescued the captives and booty.

None of these nine kings have been identified, and none of their countries or cities except Elam. [Gen. 14]

Tiglath-pileser III (Ass. 'my confidence is the son of Esarra') King of Assyria 745–27 BC. Assyria, on the Upper Tigris river in Mesopotamia, was for centuries the dominant imperial power in the Near East. Tiglath-pileser III, also known as Pul or Tilgath-pilneser, was one of its greatest conquerors. In 733–2 BC his armies swept westward, and in a series of campaigns conquered Philistia on the Mediterranean coastal plain, destroyed Damascus, and occupied most of the kingdom of Israel, turning Gilead, the Galilee and the coastal district into Assyrian provinces. Many of the inhabitants were deported to other parts of the Assyrian empire.

This took place in the reign of Pekah, king of Israel, who was murdered by Hoshea who then ruled over the rump of the kingdom as a vassal paying tribute to the Assyrians. Ahaz, the king of Judah, also came to present himself to Tiglath-pileser in Damascus, and to tender him tribute.

Tiglath-pileser died in 727 BC and the throne was seized by Ululai, the governor of Babylonia, who became Shalmaneser v. [2 Kgs. 15:19, 29; 16:7, 10; 1 Chr. 5:6; 2 Chr. 28:20, 21]

Tikvah (Heb. 'hope') *1. c.* 7 century BC. Son of Harhas, keeper of the wardrobe of the king of Judah, he was the father-in-law of the prophetess, Huldah. Also called Tokhath. [2 Kgs. 22:14; 2 Chr. 34:22]
2. 5 century BC. Father of Jahzeiah who opposed Ezra in his appeal to the people of Judah to divorce their non-Jewish wives. [Ezra 10:15]

Tilgath-pilneser *see* TIGLATH-PILESER

Tilon date unknown. Son of Shimon of the tribe of Judah, he was descended from Caleb son of Jephunneh. [1 Chr. 4:20]

Timna *1. c.* 16 century BC. Concubine of Esau's son, Eliphaz, she bore him Amalek. [Gen. 36:12]
2. c. 16 century BC. Son of Eliphaz, he was the grandson of Esau. [1 Chr. 1:36]
3. date unknown. Daughter of Seir, leader of the Edomite warriors, she was the sister of Lotan. [Gen. 36:22; 1 Chr. 1:39]
4. date unknown. One of the Edomite chiefs descended from Esau. [Gen. 36:40; 1 Chr. 1:51]

Tiras (Heb. 'longing') date unknown.

Son of Japheth, he was a grandson of Noah. [Gen. 10:2; 1 Chr. 1:5]

Tirhakah *see* PHARAOH *8.*

Tirhanah (Heb. 'favour') date unknown. Son of Caleb the son of Hezron and his concubine Maacah, he and his family were leaders of the tribe of Judah. [1 Chr. 2:48]

Tiria (Heb. 'dread') date unknown. Son of Jehallelel, he was a leader of the tribe of Judah descended from Caleb son of Jephunneh. [1 Chr. 4:16]

Tirzah (Heb. 'pleasing') *c.* 13 century BC. One of the five daughters of Zelophehad who successfully claimed a share of their father's estate before Moses, since their father had no sons. [Num. 26:33; 27:1; 36:11; Josh. 17:3]

Toah (Heb. 'bent') date unknown. Son of Zuph of the tribe of Levi and the father of Eliab, he was an ancestor of the prophet Samuel. Also known as Tohu and Nahath. [1 Sam. 1:1; 1 Chr. 6:26, 34]

Tobadonijah (Heb. 'good is the Lord my God') *c.* 9 century BC. A Levite sent by Jehoshaphat, king of Judah, to teach the Law of Moses to the people of Judah. [2 Chr. 17:8]

Tobiah (Heb. 'the Lord is good') *1. c.* 5 century BC. A Transjordan Jew in the time of Nehemiah. Tobiah was the head of a wealthy family of landowners, with relatives among the Jerusalem notables. Together with Sanballat, the governor of Samaria, and Geshem, an Edomite chief, he opposed Nehemiah's plans to rebuild the walls of Jerusalem and suggested that it would be interpreted as a rebellious act against the king of Persia. The Judeans persisted and Tobiah sneered at their handiwork: 'if a fox goes up on it he will break down their stone wall!' (Neh. 4:3) As the work progressed Tobiah and his friends grew angry and tried to lure Nehemiah out of Jerusalem, but he felt they would harm him and refused to go.

Later, when Nehemiah returned from a visit to Babylon, he was horrified to find that the high priest had installed Tobiah in a room in the Temple courtyard. Nehemiah ordered all the household gear thrown out of the room and had it thoroughly cleansed and returned to its former function. [Neh. 2:10, 19; 4:3, 7; 6:1–19; 13:4–8]

2. date unknown. Ancestor of a family which returned from exile with Zerubbabel but could not trace their ancestry and therefore could not prove that they were Jewish. [Ezra 2:60; Neh. 7:62]

Tobijah (Heb. 'God's goodness') *1. c. 9* century BC. A Levite sent by Jehoshaphat, king of Judah, to teach the Law of Moses to the people of Judah. [2 Chr. 17:8]

2. *c.* 6 century BC. A leader of Judah who returned from exile in Babylon and was commanded by the prophet Zechariah to provide gold and silver for a crown to be put on the head of Joshua, son of Jehozadak, the high priest, who would rebuild the Temple. He was told to keep the crown as a memorial in the Temple. [Zech. 6:10, 14]

Togarmah (Heb. 'bony') date unknown. Son of Gomer and a great-grandson of Noah. [Gen. 10:3; 1 Chr. 1:6; Ezek. 27:14; 38:6]

Tohu *see* TOAH

Toi (Heb. 'wandering') *c.* 10 century BC. The king of Hamath in the reign of King David, who sent his son Joram to congratulate David on his victory over his enemy Hadadezer, king of Syria. Also known as Tou. [2 Sam. 8:9; 1 Chr. 18:9, 10]

Tokhath *see* TIKVAH.

Tola (Heb. 'worm') *1. c.* 16 century BC. A son of Issachar and a grandson of Jacob and Leah, he went down to Egypt with his grandfather Jacob. [Gen. 46:13; Num. 26:23; 1 Chr. 7:1, 2]

2. *c.* 12 century BC. The son of Puah of the tribe of Issachar, he became judge and ruler over Israel after the death of Abimelech. He ruled for twenty-three years from Shamir in the hills of Ephraim, then died and was buried in Shamir. [Judg. 10:1]

Tou *see* TOI

Tubal (Heb. 'tumult') date unknown. Son of Japheth and a grandson of Noah, and by Hebrew tradition the father of the people Tubal, referred to in the Books of Isaiah and Ezekiel. [Gen. 10:2; 1 Chr. 1:5; Isa. 66:19; Ezek. 27:13; 32:26; 38:2; 39:1]

Tubal-Cain date unknown. Son of Lamech and Zillah a descendant of Cain, he was the 'forger of all instruments of bronze and iron'. [Gen. 4:22]

U

Ucal (Heb. 'power') date unknown. One of the two men to whom Agur's words were addressed. [Prov. 30:1]

Uel (Heb. 'God's will') 5 century BC. One of the twelve descendants of Bani who married a non-Jewish woman and divorced her in the time of Ezra. [Ezra 10:34]

Ulam (Heb. 'porch') *1.* date unknown. Eldest son of Eshek, a Benjaminite chief descended from King Saul. His descendants were renowned as mighty archers. [1 Chr. 8:39, 40]
2. date unknown. A chief of the tribe of Manasseh descended from Machir. [1 Chr. 7:16, 17]

Ulla (Heb. 'yoke') date unknown. A leader of the tribe of Asher, he and his three sons were mighty warriors. [1 Chr. 7:39]

Unni (Heb. 'afflicted') *c.* 10 century BC. A Levite who played musical instruments in the celebrations when the Ark of God was brought by King David to Jerusalem. [1 Chr. 15:18, 20]

Unno (Heb. 'afflicted') *c.* 6 century BC. One of the Levites who participated in the thanksgiving services in the Temple after the return from exile in Babylon. [Neh. 12:9]

Ur (Heb. 'light') *c.* 10 century BC. Father of Eliphal, one of the warriors in the army of King David distinguished for his bravery. Also called Ahasbai. [2 Sam. 23:34; 1 Chr. 11:35]

Uri (Heb. 'fire') *1. c.* 13 century BC. Son of Hur of the tribe of Judah and the father of Bezalel, the craftsman who constructed the Tabernacle of the Children of Israel in the wilderness. [Exod. 31:2; 35:30; 38:22; 1 Chr. 2:20; 2 Chr. 1:5]
2. c. 10 century BC. Father of Geber who was one of King Solomon's twelve officers responsible for providing the royal supplies. [1 Kgs. 4:19]
3. 5 century BC. One of the Levites who was a Temple gatekeeper and who divorced his non-Jewish wife in the time of Ezra. [Ezra 10:24]

Uriah (Heb. 'God is my light') *1. c.* 10 century BC. First husband of Bathsheba. Uriah, the Hittite, was one of the thirty chosen men who commanded David's army. While the king's army under Joab was besieging Rabbah, the Aramean capital, David took advantage of Uriah's absence to have an affair with his wife Bathsheba. When he discovered she was pregnant he sent a secret message to Joab, asking him to send Uriah home, so that he should be regarded as the father. Uriah, however, did not join his wife and spent that night and the next with the palace guard.

Fearful of the scandal if the adultery became known, David sent Uriah back to the front with a sealed letter to Joab, saying, 'Set Uriah in the forefront of the hardest fighting, and then draw back from him, that he may be struck down, and die.' (2 Sam. 11:15) Joab accordingly arranged a dangerous sortie and in this engagement Uriah was killed. David was then able to marry Bathsheba. [2

Sam. 11; 1 Kgs. 15:5; 1 Chr. 11:41]

2. c. 8 century BC. The high priest of Judah in the reign of King Ahaz. At the king's request he designed an altar in Jerusalem on the model of the altar Ahaz had seen in Damascus, when he went to pay tribute to the Assyrian emperor, Tiglath-pileser. Uriah also carried out the king's command to offer sacrifices on the altar. When the prophet Isaiah denounced the iniquities of Israel he referred to Uriah as one of the witnesses to his prophecy of doom. [2 Kgs. 16:10–16; Isa. 8:2]

3. c. 6 century BC. Son of Shemaiah, he was a prophet from Kiriath-jearim. He foretold the destruction of Jerusalem at the same time as Jeremiah, and fled to Egypt to escape arrest by the enraged King Jehoiakim. The king sent agents to seize him in Egypt and he was brought back to Judah where he was executed. [Jer. 26:20–23]

4. c. 5 century BC. A Levite who stood at the right-hand of Ezra when he read the Law of Moses to the people of Judah after the return from exile in Babylon. [Neh. 8:4]

5. 5 century BC. Son of Hakkoz and the father of Meremoth, the priest who was head of the four leaders of Judah appointed by Ezra to weigh the gold and silver and precious vessels brought back from Babylon, and who also helped repair the walls of Jerusalem. [Ezra 8:33; Neh. 3:4]

Uriel (Heb. 'God is my light') *1.* 13 century BC. Son of Tahath, a Levite descended from Kohath, he was an ancestor of the prophet Samuel. [1 Chr. 6:24]

2. c. 10 century BC. Head of a family of Levites descended from Kohath who ministered in the Tabernacle in the reign of King David. He was one of the Levites ordered by King David to carry the Ark of God to Jerusalem. [1 Chr. 15:5, 11]

3. see ABISHALOM

Uthai (Heb. 'helpful') *1. c.* 6 century

BC. Son of Ammihud of the tribe of Judah, he was one of the first men of Judah to settle in Jerusalem following the return from exile in Babylon. Also called Athaiah. [1 Chr. 9:4; Neh. 11:4]

2. c. 6 century BC. Son of Bigvai he returned to Judah from exile in Babylon. [Ezra 8:14]

Uz *1.* date unknown. Grandson of Shem, and son of Aram. [Gen. 10:23; 1 Chr. 1:17]

2. c. 18 century BC. Son of Nahor and Milcah, he was a nephew of Abraham. [Gen. 22:21]

3. date unknown. Son of Dishan, a Horite. [Gen. 36:28]

Uzai 5 century BC. Father of Palal who repaired part of the walls of Jerusalem in the days of Nehemiah. [Neh. 3:25]

Uzal (Heb. 'wanderer') date unknown. Son of Joktan and a descendant of Shem, he was a leader of a desert tribe. [Gen. 10:27; 1 Chr. 1:21]

Uzza (Heb. 'strength') *1.* date unknown. Son of Gera, a leader of the tribe of Benjamin. [1 Chr. 8:7]

2. date unknown. A Temple servant whose descendants returned with Zerubbabel from exile in Babylon. [Ezra 2:49; Neh. 7:51]

3. c. 7 century BC. Owner of the garden in which the kings of Judah, Manasseh and Amon, were buried. [2 Kgs. 21:18, 26]

Uzzah (Heb. 'strength') *1.* date unknown. Son of Shimei, a Levite descended from Merari, he was the father of Shimea. [1 Chr. 6:29]

2. c. 10 century BC. Son of Abinadab of Gibeah, he took hold of the Ark of God to steady it while it was being transported to Jerusalem on King David's orders; he was killed immediately. [2 Sam. 6:3–8; 1 Chr. 13:7–10]

Uzzi (Heb. 'my strength') *1. c.* 16

century BC. Son of Tola and a grandson of Issachar, he and his brothers were leaders of the tribe of Issachar and mighty warriors. [1 Chr. 7:2]

2. c. 16 century BC. Son of Bela and a grandson of Benjamin, he and his brothers were leaders of the tribe of Benjamin and mighty warriors. [1 Chr. 7:2]

3. date unknown. Son of Bukki, the priest, and father of Zerahiah, he was an ancestor of Ezra. [1 Chr. 6:5, 6, 51; Ezra 7:4]

4. 6 century BC. Son of Michri and father of Elah who was one of the first Benjaminites to settle in Jerusalem following the return from Babylon. [1 Chr. 9:8]

5. 5 century BC. Son of Bani, he was the overseer of the Levites in Jerusalem after the return from Babylon in the time of Nehemiah. [Neh. 11:22]

6. 5 century BC. Head of a priestly family descended from Jedaiah, he was a chief priest of Judah when Joiakim was high priest and took part in the ceremony of dedication of the walls of Jerusalem in the days of Nehemiah. [Neh. 12:19, 42]

Uzzia (Heb. 'God is [my] strength') c. 10 century BC. An Ashterathite who was a warrior in the army of King David distinguished for his bravery. [1 Chr. 11:44]

Uzziah (Heb. 'God is [my] strength') 1. date unknown. Son of Uriel of the tribe of Levi and a descendant of Kohath. Also called Azariah. [1 Chr. 6:24; 36]

2. c. 10 century BC. Father of Jonathan who supervised the storehouses of King David. [1 Chr. 27:25]

3. Tenth king of Judah after the monarchy split, he reigned 781–40 BC.

Uzziah was the son of King Amaziah of Judah and his wife Jecoliah of Jerusalem. He succeeded to the throne at the age of sixteen after his father was assassinated.

During Uzziah's long reign, Judah enjoyed greater military prowess and mate-rial progress than it had done for generations. This was paralleled by the expansion of the northern kingdom of Israel under Jeroboam II. At the peak of this period, in the middle of the 8th century BC, the two Hebrew states together controlled an area roughly corresponding to that of King David's empire of over two centuries earlier.

Uzziah was statesmanlike enough to repair the relationship with the kingdom of Israel after the brief war in his father's reign when the army of Israel had taken the Judean king captive and battered the walls of Jerusalem. With peace and cooperation between the two kingdoms, Israel was free to expand eastwards across the Jordan river and northward into Aram (Syria); while Judah could expand to the south and west.

Uzziah re-established control over the desert kingdom of Edom, in the Negev and southern Jordan. He could therefore rebuild the harbour town and copper-smelting centre of Ezion-geber (Eilat) originally constructed by King Solomon. Evidence of this period has been found, including a signet ring inscribed with the name Jotham, in the excavations at Tel el-Kheleifeh in this vicinity.

Uzziah also extended the borders of the kingdom into the Philistine area of the coastal plain, capturing and annexing the cities of Gath, Jabneh and Ashdod. He repulsed the nomad tribes in the south, and defeated the Ammonites east of the Jordan, on whom he levied tribute. This extension of Judah's power and influence brought about a large programme of military fortification.

In Jerusalem he strengthened the walls and constructed towers at the 'Corner Gate and at the Valley Gate and at the Angle' (2 Chr. 26:9). Devices were installed on the walls for discharging arrows and hurling rocks. Along the borders and the main highways, large forts were erected. Three such desert forts have been excavated at

Kadesh-barnea on the Sinai border, at Tel Arad in the eastern Negev and at Khirbet Ghazzeh five miles south-east of Tel Arad. These stood on the ancient road to Edom. The army was re-organized, with full-time professional cadres of officers and instructors under the command of Hananiah. It is mentioned that the troops were equipped with shields, spears, helmets, coats of mail, bows and slings.

Uzziah put much effort into the development of the kingdom's agriculture, including the settlement of farming of some of the semi-arid areas he had acquired: 'He built towers in the wilderness, and hewed out many cisterns, for he had large herds, both in the Shephelah and in the plain, and he had farmers and vinedressers in the hills and in the fertile lands, for he loved the soil.' (2 Chr. 26:10)

The building activity and busy commerce in Jerusalem, and the rising standard of luxury are depicted in the disapproving utterances of the great contemporary prophets Isaiah, Amos and Hosea.

Uzziah's importance and prestige were demonstrated by his assuming leadership of a coalition of the kings of the region formed to block the Assyrian advance from the north under Tiglathpileser III. This effort was unsuccessful. Assyrian power subdued Aram and Israel, and Uzziah had to concern himself with preserving the borders of his own kingdom. Judah was left as the strongest local state still holding out against Assyrian pressure. After the death of Jeroboam II of Israel, Judah under Uzziah filled to some extent the vacuum left by the rapid decline of Israel.

During his reign Uzziah was smitten with the dread disease of leprosy. According to the Second Book of Chronicles, this was a punishment for his presumption in personally burning incense on the altar in the Temple, a sacred function reserved for the priests. From then on Uzziah no longer appeared in public but remained secluded in his quarters. He remained in control of the affairs of the kingdom, together with his son and crown prince Jotham, who acted as co-regent and master of the household. This odd father-and-son rule continued for a number of years, until the death of Uzziah, when Jotham became king in his own right.

In the last century, the re-internment stone of King Uzziah was discovered in Jerusalem, and is now in the Israel Museum. Its Aramaic inscription in Hebrew letters reads: 'Hither were brought the bones of Uzziah, king of Judah. Do not open.' It dates to the 1st century BC, when Jerusalem was undergoing its expansion under Herod, and all graves, except for the tombs of the kings, were moved outside the city walls; but as a leper, Uzziah had not been buried in the royal tombs, and so his remains were re-interred at that time and appropriately marked by this limestone plaque. Also called Azariah. [2 Kgs. 14:21; 15:1–8, 13, 17, 23, 27; 2 Chr. 26; 27:2; Isa. 1:1; 6:1; 7:1; Hos. 1:1; Amos 1:1; Zech. 14:5]

4. see AMMIHUD *5.*

5. 5 century BC. Son of Harim the priest he divorced his non-Jewish wife in the time of Ezra. [Ezra 10:21]

Uzziel (Heb. 'God is my strength') *1. c.* 16 century BC. A son of Bela and a grandson of Benjamin, he and his brothers were leaders of the tribe and mighty warriors. [1 Chr. 7:7]

2. date unknown. Son of Kohath and a grandson of Levi, one of his descendants of the same name was an uncle of Moses and Aaron and another was prominent in the reign of King David. [Exod. 6:18, 22; Lev. 10:4; Num. 3:19, 30; 1 Chr. 6:2; 15:10; 23:12, 20; 24:24]

3. see AZAREL *2.*

4. c. 8 century BC. A son of Ishi of the tribe of Simeon, he and his brothers commanded a band of 500 men, which drove out the Amalekites from Mount Seir, south-east of the Dead Sea, and settled there in the time of Hezekiah, king of Judah. [1 Chr. 4:42]

5. c. 8 century BC. A descendant of Jeduthun, the musician in the time of King David, he and his brother Shemaiah were among the Levites to carry out the command of Hezekiah, king of Judah, to repair and sanctify the Temple. [2 Chr. 29:14]

6. 5 century BC. Son of Harhaiah and a member of a Judean family of goldsmiths, he helped repair the walls of Jerusalem in the time of Nehemiah. [Neh. 3:8]

V

Vaizatha *c.* 5 century BC. Youngest son of Haman the Agagite who plotted to kill all the Jews in the Persian empire in the reign of King Ahasuerus. When the plot was discovered Haman and his sons were put to death. [Esther 9:9]

Vaniah 5 century BC. A descendant of Bani who divorced his non-Jewish wife in the time of Ezra. [Ezra 10:36]

Vashti (Pers. 'beautiful') 5 century BC. The queen of Persia who was ordered by her husband, King Ahasuerus, to appear before him at a feast to show off her beauty to his guests. She refused and as a punishment for her disobedience the king divorced her. [Esther 1:9–22; 2:1, 4, 17]

Vophsi *c.* 13 century BC. Father of Nahbi of the tribe of Naphtali, who was one of the twelve scouts sent by Moses to reconnoitre the Promised Land. [Num. 13:14]

Z

Zaavan (Heb. 'unquiet') date unknown. Son of Ezer and a grandson of Seir the Horite, he was a leader of an Edomite tribe. [Gen. 36:27; 1 Chr. 1:42]

Zabad (Heb. 'gift') *1.* date unknown. Son of Tahath and a leader of the tribe of Ephraim. [1 Chr. 7:21]
2. date unknown. Son of Nathan and father of Ephlal, he was a great-grandson of Jarha, the Egyptian slave who married the daughter of his master Sheshan of the tribe of Judah. [1 Chr. 2:36, 37]
3. c. 10 century BC. Son of Ahlai, he was a valiant warrior in the army of King David. [1 Chr. 11:41]
4. see JOZACAR
5. 5 century BC. A descendant of Zattu who divorced his non-Jewish wife in the time of Ezra. [Ezra 10:27]
6. 5 century BC. A descendant of Hashum who divorced his non-Jewish wife in the time of Ezra. [Ezra 10:33]
7. 5 century BC. A descendant of Nebo who divorced his non-Jewish wife in the time of Ezra. [Ezra 10:43]

Zabbai (Heb. 'limpid') *1.* 5 century BC. A son of Bebai who divorced his non-Jewish wife in the time of Ezra. [Ezra 10:28]
2. 5 century BC. Father of Baruch who helped repair part of the walls of Jerusalem in the time of Nehemiah. [Neh. 3:20]

Zabdi (Heb. 'gift') *1. c.* 13 century BC. Son of Zerah of the tribe of Judah, his grandson Achan disobeyed Joshua and took booty from Jericho after it was destroyed. Also called Zimri. [Josh. 7:1, 17; 1 Chr. 2:6]
2. date unknown. Son of Shimhi, he was a leader of the tribe of Benjamin who lived in Jerusalem. [1 Chr. 8:19]
3. c. 10 century BC. An official of King David who was in charge of the royal vineyards. [1 Chr. 27:27]
4. c. 5 century BC. Son of Asaph and father of Mica, his grandson Mattaniah was a Levite responsible for the thanksgiving prayer in the time of Nehemiah. Also called Zichri. [1 Chr. 9:15; Neh. 11:17]

Zabdiel (Heb. 'gift of God') *1. c.* 10 century BC. Father of Jashobeam who was commander of the army which served in the first month of the year during the reign of King David. [1 Chr. 27:2]
2. c. 5 century BC. Head of a group of priests who served in Jerusalem in the days of Nehemiah. [Neh. 11:14]

Zabud (Heb. 'gift') *c.* 10 century BC. Son of the prophet Nathan, he was an important official and the king's friend in the reign of Solomon. [1 Kgs. 4:5]

Zaccai (Heb. 'pure') 6 century BC. Head of a family who returned to Judah with Zerubbabel from exile in Babylon. [Ezra 2:9; Neh. 7:14]

Zaccur (Heb. 'mindful') *1. c.* 13 century BC. Father of Shammua of the tribe of Reuben who was one of the twelve men sent by Moses to spy out the Promised Land. [Num. 13:4]
2. c. 10 century BC. Son of Jaaziah, a

Levite descended from Merari, he ministered in the Tabernacle in the reign of King David. [1 Chr. 24:27]

3. date unknown. Son of Hammuel, he was a leader of the tribe of Simeon. [1 Chr. 4:26]

4. c. 10 century BC. Son of Asaph, one of King David's leading musicians, he took the third turn of service in the Temple. He was the ancestor of Zechariah. [1 Chr. 25:2, 10; Neh. 12:35]

5. 5 century BC. A descendant of Bigvai, he returned to Judah from Babylon with Ezra. [Ezra 8:14]

6. 5 century BC. Son of Imri, he helped rebuild the walls of Jerusalem in the time of Nehemiah. [Neh. 3:2]

7. 5 century BC. A Levite who signed the covenant in the time of Nehemiah. [Neh. 10:12]

8. 5 century BC. Father of Hanan, a treasurer appointed by Nehemiah to distribute tithes. [Neh. 13:13]

Zadok (Heb. 'just') **1.** c. 10 century BC. High priest in the time of King David. Zadok, the son of Ahitub, was from a priestly family claiming Eleazar, Aaron's son and successor, as their ancestor. When David became king of the united monarchy Zadok was made one of his two high priests.

At the time of Absalom's revolt, Zadok and the other high priest Abiathar carried the Ark of the Covenant out of Jerusalem in readiness to follow David into the wilderness. But at David's request they turned back, and arranged to keep him informed of Absalom's actions, using their sons as runners.

Absalom entered Jerusalem and after a debate between his counsellors decided not to pursue David immediately. Zadok and Abiathar sent their sons secretly to find David and tell him not to tarry in the plains, but to cross the Jordan river at once.

After the defeat and death of Absalom, David used Zadok and Abiathar to encourage the leaders of Judah to ask for his return.

When David chose his younger son Solomon as his successor, he sent for Zadok and the prophet Nathan and told them to take Solomon on the royal mule and anoint him 'king at Gihon' (1 Kgs. 1:45). In reward for Zadok's faithful service to his father, King Solomon appointed Azariah, one of his sons, as high priest.

From that time until the Maccabees eight centuries later the high priests were drawn from the Zadokian line. In his vision of the ideal commonwealth Ezekiel insists that the Zadokites are the only legitimate priests. [2 Sam. 8:17; 15:24–36; 17:15; 18:19, 22, 27; 19:11; 20:25; 1 Kgs. 1:26, 32–9; 44–5; 2:35; 4:2, 4; 1 Chr. 6:8, 53; 15:11; 16:39; 18:16; 24:3, 6, 31; 27:17; 29:22; 2 Chr. 31:10; Ezra 7:2; Ezek. 40:46; 43:19; 44:15; 48:11]

2. c. 10 century BC. A young officer who led twenty-two warriors from his clan to join David at Hebron and help him secure the kingdom of Israel from the house of King Saul. [1 Chr. 12:28]

3. c. 8 century BC. Father of Jerusha, wife of King Uzziah of Judah, and grandfather of Uzziah's successor, King Jotham. [2 Kgs. 15:33; 2 Chr. 27:1]

4. c. 8 century BC. A priest, son of Ahitub and father of Shallum, he was probably a descendant of Zadok and an ancestor of Jehozadak, a priest who was taken into Babylonian captivity. [1 Chr. 6:12]

5. c. 6 century BC. Son of Meraioth, he was an ancestor of Azariah, the first priest to settle in Jerusalem after the return of the Jews from Babylon. [1 Chr. 9:11]

6. 5 century BC. Son of Baana, he helped Nehemiah rebuild the walls of Jerusalem. [Neh. 3:4]

7. 5 century BC. Descendant of Immer, he was a priest and scribe who also helped rebuild the walls of Jerusalem in the days of Nehemiah, and was one of four trusted officers appointed to distribute the tithes of corn, wine and oil among the Levites. [Neh. 3:29; 13:13]

8. *c.* 5 century BC. A leader of Judah who signed the covenant to observe the Laws of God in the time of Nehemiah. [Neh. 10:21]

Zaham (Heb. 'hateful') *c.* 10 century BC. Son of Rehoboam, king of Judah, and a grandson of King Solomon, his mother was Mahalath, a granddaughter of King David. [2 Chr. 11:19]

Zalaph (Heb. 'caper plant') 5 century BC. Father of Hanun who helped repair the walls of Jerusalem in the time of Nehemiah. [Neh. 3:30]

Zalmon *see* ILAI.

Zalmunna (Heb. 'shadow') *c.* 12 century BC. One of the two Midianite chieftains who fled after the bulk of the Midianite army had been routed at Ain Harod by Gideon. Gideon caught up with them at Karkor, destroyed their forces and personally executed them in retaliation for their murder of his brother. [Judg. 8:5–21; Ps. 83:11]

Zanoah (Heb. 'swamp') date unknown. Son of Jekuthiel, a leader of the tribe of Judah. [1 Chr. 4:18]

Zattu *1.* 6 century BC. Ancestor of a family of several hundreds who returned to Judah with Zerubbabel from captivity in Babylon. [Ezra 2:8; 10:27; Neh. 7:13]
2. 5 century BC. A leader of Judah who signed the covenant to keep the Laws of the Lord in the time of Nehemiah. [Neh. 10:14]

Zaza (Heb. 'moving') date unknown. Son of Jonathan, a descendant of Jerahmeel of the tribe of Judah. [1 Chr. 2:33]

Zebadiah (Heb. 'portion of God') *1.* date unknown. Son of Beriah, he was a leader of the tribe of Benjamin living in Jerusalem. [1 Chr. 8:15]
2. date unknown. Eldest son of Elpaal, he was one of the leaders of the tribe of Benjamin living in Jerusalem. [1 Chr. 8:17]
3. *c.* 11 century BC. Son of Jeroham of the tribe of Benjamin, he and his brother joined David at Ziklag where he had taken refuge from Saul. [1 Chr. 12:7]
4. *c.* 10 century BC. Son of Meshelemiah, he and his family were gatekeepers at the Tabernacle in the reign of King David. [1 Chr. 26:2]
5. *c.* 10 century BC. Son of Asahel and nephew of Joab, he succeeded his father as commander of the army of King David which served in the fourth month of the year. [1 Chr. 27:7]
6. *c.* 9 century BC. A Levite sent by King Jehoshaphat to teach the Law of God to the people of Judah. [2 Chr. 17:8]
7. *c.* 9 century BC. Son of Ishmael, he was governor of the house of Judah 'in all the king's matters' in the reign of King Jehoshaphat. [2 Chr. 19:11]
8. 5 century BC. Son of Michael and a descendant of Shephatiah, he returned to Judah from exile in Babylon with Ezra. [Ezra 8:8]
9. 5 century BC. Descendant of Immer the priest, he divorced his non-Jewish wife in the time of Ezra. [Ezra 10:20]

Zebah (Heb. 'sacrifice') *c.* 12 century BC. One of the two kings of Midian who were defeated by Gideon and fled with the remnant of their army to Karkor. There Gideon captured the kings and put them to death. [Judg. 8:5–21; Ps. 83:11]

Zebidah (Heb. 'given') *c.* 7 century BC. Daughter of Pedaiah of Rumah, she was the mother of Jehoiakim, king of Judah. [2 Kgs. 23:36]

Zebina (Heb. 'buying') 5 century BC. A descendant of Nebo, he divorced his non-Jewish wife in the time of Ezra. [Ezra 10:43]

Zebul (Heb. 'habitation') c. 12 century BC. Head of the city of Shechem during the reign of Abimelech. When Gaal the son of Ebed roused the Shechemites against Abimelech, Zebul sent secret word to the ruler who took timely action to crush the revolt. [Judg. 9:26–41]

Zebulun (Heb. 'dwelling') c. 16 century BC. Zebulun was the tenth son of Jacob and the sixth born to Leah. Together with his brothers he was involved in the events that led to the selling of their brother Joseph into slavery in Egypt. Later he was one of the ten sons sent by Jacob to buy corn in Egypt, where Joseph had become a leading figure at the court of Pharaoh. When Jacob went to settle in Egypt with all his family it included Zebulun and his three sons.

On his deathbed Jacob blessed all his sons in turn, and said: 'Zebulun shall dwell at the shore of the sea.' (Gen. 49:13)

In the blessing attributed to Moses, it is said: 'for they suck the affluence of the seas and the hidden treasures of the sand.' (Deut. 33:19)

In the conquest of Canaan under Joshua, the tribe of Zebulun was allocated the western Jezreel valley. [Gen. 30:20; 35:23; 46:14; 49:13; Exod. 1:3; 1 Chr. 2:1]

Zechariah (Heb. 'God has remembered') *1.* date unknown. A leader of the tribe of Reuben related to Joel, chief of the tribe. [1 Chr. 5:7]

2. date unknown. Son of Pashhur, the priest, and father of Amzi, his descendant Adaiah lived in Jerusalem in the time of Nehemiah and served in the Temple. [Neh. 11:12]

3. date unknown. Son of Amariah of the tribe of Judah and father of Uzziah, his descendant Athaiah settled in Jerusalem after the return from exile in Babylon. [Neh. 11:4]

4. c. 11 century BC. Son of Jeiel and a leader of the tribe of Benjamin, he was an uncle of King Saul. Also called Zecher. [1 Chr. 8:31; 9:37]

5. c. 10 century BC. Eldest son of Meshelemiah the Levite, he was a gate-keeper at the northern entrance to the Tabernacle in the time of King David. [1 Chr. 9:21; 26:2, 14]

6. c. 10 century BC. A musician during the reign of King David who played the harp when the Ark of God was brought to Jerusalem, he was one of the Levites appointed by David to minister before the Ark of God. [1 Chr. 15:18, 20; 16:5]

7. c. 10 century BC. A priest who blew a trumpet to celebrate the bringing of the Ark of the Lord into Jerusalem by King David. [1 Chr. 15:24]

8. c. 10 century BC. Son of Isshiah, he was a Levite serving in the Tabernacle in King David's reign. [1 Chr. 24:25]

9. c. 10 century BC. Son of Hosah, he was a Levite who served as gatekeeper of the Tabernacle in the reign of King David. [1 Chr. 26:11]

10. c. 10 century BC. Father of Iddo who ruled over the half-tribe of Manasseh in Gilead in the reign of King David. [1 Chr. 27:21]

11. c. 9 century BC. One of the five princes of Judah who were sent by King Jehoshaphat to teach the Law in the cities of Judah. [2 Chr. 17:7]

12. c. 9 century BC. Father of Jahaziel who prophesied in the reign of King Jehoshaphat of Judah that God would defeat the Ammonites and Moabites, and that King Jehoshaphat would not need to fight them. [2 Chr. 20:14]

13. c. 9 century BC. A son of Jehoshaphat, he and his five brothers were killed by their eldest brother, Jehoram, when he succeeded his father as king of Judah. [2 Chr. 21:2]

14. c. 9 century BC. Son of Jehoiada, the priest, in the reign of Joash, king of Judah. After his father's death he admonished the people for transgressing the Laws of God, and the angry king ordered him to be stoned to death in the Temple courtyard. [2 Chr. 24:20–22]

15. Fourteenth king of Israel after the monarchy split, he reigned for six months in 743 BC. Zechariah succeeded his father Jeroboam II and was assassinated six months later by Shallum, the son of Jabesh, who seized the throne. Zechariah's death ended the dynasty of Jehu which had reigned over Israel for nearly a century. [2 Kgs. 14:29; 15:8–12]

16. c. 8 century BC. Father of Abi who was the mother of Hezekiah, king of Judah. [2 Kgs. 18:2; 2 Chr. 29:1]

17. c. 8 century BC. A prophet consulted by Uzziah, king of Judah, who instructed the king how to serve God faithfully. [2 Chr. 26:5]

18. c. 8 century BC. A Levite descended from Asaph who obeyed King Hezekiah's command to sanctify himself and cleanse the Temple. [2 Chr. 29:13]

19. c. 8 century BC. Son of Jeberechiah, he was one of the reliable witnesses who attested to Isaiah's inscription of *Maher-shalal-hash-baz* (Heb. 'booty and shame are imminent') which Isaiah then gave as a name to his newborn son. The inscription signified the impending destruction of Israel and Damascus by the Assyrians. [Isa. 8:2]

20. c. 7 century BC. A Levite descended from Kohath who helped supervise the work of repairing the Temple in the time of Josiah, king of Judah. [2 Chr. 34:12]

21. c. 7 century BC. A head priest serving in the Temple during the reign of Josiah, king of Judah, he received the Passover offerings donated by the leaders of Judah. [2 Chr. 35:8]

22. Second half of 6 century BC. Postexilic Hebrew prophet. Zechariah the son of Berechiah prophesied in Jerusalem after the return from Babylonia. In 520 BC, in the second year of the reign of Darius the Great, he and the prophet Haggai pressed for the work to be resumed on the ruined Temple. It was completed within five years.

In the earlier chapters of the Book of Zechariah, the prophet has eight mystical visions full of symbolic images, as Ezekiel before him and Daniel afterwards. Mysterious horsemen come back from patrolling the earth; four horns represent hostile kingdoms and are destroyed; a man with a measuring rod comes to measure Jerusalem; the high priest Joshua is tried before a heavenly court and his filthy clothes are replaced by splendid robes; a golden lamp stands between two olive trees; an immense scroll flies through the air over the land; a woman representing wickedness sits in a great bowl and is carried off to Babylonia; four chariots are drawn by red, black, white and piebald horses and go to the four points of the compass. These visions are interpreted to reflect the political turmoil in the Persian empire that followed the accession of Darius, and the Messianic hopes for a restored and purified Jewish kingdom.

In one of the visions Zechariah sees a crown placed, on the head of Zerubbabel, who is called a 'branch', because he was a scion of the house of David.

Zechariah sees a future in which the Jews will live in peace in their land, under the protection of the Lord: 'I will return to Zion, and will dwell in the midst of Jerusalem, and Jerusalem shall be called the faithful city, and the mountain of the Lord of hosts, the holy mountain.' (Zech. 8:3)

The coming of the Messianic age is elaborated in the last six chapters. Enemy nations will be subdued, and a third of the Jewish nation will survive and live in freedom, and the Lord will be king over all the earth. This part of the Book has no reference to the historical events of Zechariah's time, and appears to have been written by someone else at a much later date. [Neh. 12:16; Book of Zechariah]

23. c. 6 century BC. Father of Joiarib, his descendant Maaseiah was one of the first men of Judah to settle in Jerusalem after the return from Babylon. [Neh. 11:5]

24. 5 century BC. A descendant of Parosh and a leader of Judah who returned with Ezra from exile in Babylon. [Ezra 8:3]

25. 5 century BC. Son of Bebai, he was one of the leaders of Judah who returned with Ezra from exile in Babylon. [Ezra 8:11]

26. 5 century BC. A leader of Judah sent by Ezra to Iddo at Casiphia to ask him to send Levites to Jerusalem to minister in the Temple. [Ezra 8:16]

27. 5 century BC. A descendant of Elam who divorced his non-Jewish wife in the time of Ezra. [Ezra 10:26]

28. 5 century BC. A leader of Judah who stood at the side of Ezra when he read the Law of Moses to the people of Judah. [Neh. 8:4]

29. c. 5 century BC. A priest of the family of Iddo when Joiakim was high priest over Judah, after the return from exile in Babylon. [Neh. 12:16]

30. 5 century BC. Son of Jonathan and a descendant of Asaph, he was a priest who blew a trumpet at the dedication ceremony for the rebuilt walls of Jerusalem in the time of Nehemiah. [Neh. 12:35, 41]

Zecher see ZECHARIAH 4.

Zedekiah (Heb. 'God is [my] righteousness') **1.** 9 century BC. Son of Chenaanah, he was one of the four hundred 'prophets' of King Ahab of Israel who favoured the joint attack by Ahab and King Jehoshaphat of Judah on the Arameans occupying Ramoth-gilead. When the true prophet Micaiah (correctly) predicted disaster, Zedekiah struck him in the face. [1 Kgs. 22:11, 24; 2 Chr. 18:10, 23]

2. c. 7 century BC. Son of Hananiah, he was one of the princes of Judah who ordered Baruch, son of Neriah, to read out Jeremiah's prophecies of doom and then repeated them before King Jehoiakim. [Jer. 36:12]

3. Twentieth and last king of Judah after the monarchy split, he reigned 598–87 BC. The son of King Josiah and Hamutal, daughter of a certain Jeremiah from Libnah. Zedekiah (called Mattaniah till he mounted the throne) was appointed to the throne by the Babylonians when his nephew King Jehoiachin surrendered Jerusalem and was carried off into captivity. Zedekiah was then twenty-one years old. A Babylonian inscription from the reign of Nebuchadnezzar, referring to these events, states that 'he captured the city and took the king prisoner. A king of his own choice was set up in his midst.'

The Babylonians stripped away much of the territory held by Judah, and carried on a harsh indirect rule of the country. In 589 BC, when Zedekiah had been a puppet king for nine years, he revolted against the Babylonian overlords, together with two neighbouring states, Tyre and Ammon, with Egyptian encouragement. For the second time Nebuchadnezzar advanced on Jerusalem with a large army. This time the city did not surrender and was kept under tight siege for two years. In the year 587, in the heat of midsummer, the northern wall of the starving city was breached by battering rams, and further resistance became hopeless.

That night, under cover of darkness, the king and some of his fighting men escaped through a gateway next to the royal garden and fled eastwards. They were pursued and captured on the Jericho plain. Zedekiah was brought before Nebuchadnezzar and forced to witness the slaying of his children. His eyes were then put out and he was hauled off in chains to Babylon, where he died. The city was sacked, the Temple destroyed and most of the inhabitants taken off into captivity. The independence of Judah had come to an end. [2 Kgs. 24:17–20; 25:1–7; 1 Chr. 3:15; 2 Chr. 36:10–21; Jer. 1:3; 21:1–7; 24:8; 27:3, 12; 28:1; 29:3; 32:1–5; 34:2–8, 21; 37:1, 3, 17, 18, 21; 38:5, 14–26; 39:1–7; 44:30; 49:34; 51:59; 52:1–11]

THE 'LACHISH LETTERS'

The remarkable 'Lachish Letters' relating to the Babylonian invasion of Judah, at the beginning of the 6th century BC, were discovered at the archaeological excavations of the fortified Judean city of Lachish (Tel ed-Duweir) carried out between 1932 and 1938. Eighteen ostraca – inscribed potsherds – were found among the burnt debris in a guard-room of a bastion in the outer city wall. Three more were found elsewhere on the site. The writing, in black ink on broken pottery, is classical Hebrew prose, and the lettering in early Hebrew script. They consist for the most part of reports written in the years 588–7 BC to Yaosh, military commander of the Lachish fortress, one of the last to fall to the Babylonians before the conquest of Jerusalem, by his subordinate officer Hoshaiah, who was in command of an outpost to the north of the city.

The letters reflect the pessimism evident in Jerusalem at the time, when king Zedekiah had Jeremiah brought from prison and 'questioned him secretly' about the immediate prospects. Referring to letters sent to him from Jerusalem, Hoshaiah is much alarmed and writes to 'my lord Yaosh':

'Who is thy servant but a dog that my Lord hath sent the letter of the king and the letters of the princes, saying, "Pray read them": And behold the words of the princes are not good, but to weaken our hands and to slacken the hands of the men who are informed about them ... truly since thy servant read the letters there hath been no peace for thy servant ....'

Other items of this Lachish correspondence deal with purely military matters.

4. 6 century BC. Son of Maaseiah, he was among those deported to Babylon with King Jehoiachin by Nebuchadnezzar, and he, together with Ahab, son of Kolaiah, aroused the anger of the prophet Jeremiah by their immorality and by raising false hopes among the exiles. Jeremiah cursed them and foretold that Nebuchadnezzar would have them burnt to death. [Jer. 29:21, 22]

5. 5 century BC. A leader of Judah who signed the solemn covenant in the time of Nehemiah. [Neh. 10:1]

Zeeb (Heb. 'wolf') c. 12 century BC. A prince of Midian who was killed by the men of Ephraim at the wine press of Zeeb, at the orders of Gideon. [Judg. 7:25; 8:3; Ps. 83:11]

Zelek (Heb. 'chasm') 10 century BC. An Ammonite, he was a warrior in the army of King David distinguished for his bravery. [2 Sam. 23:37; 1 Chr. 11:39]

Zelophehad (Heb. 'protection from fear') c. 13 century BC. A leader of the tribe of Manasseh who died in the wilderness leaving six daughters but no sons. His daughters asked Moses to give them their father's inheritance since they did not want their father's name to die out and Moses, after consulting God, agreed. [Num. 26:33; 27:1, 7 36:2–11; Josh. 17:3; 1 Chr. 7:15]

Zemirah (Heb. 'song') date unknown. Son of Becher, he was a leader of the tribe of Benjamin and a mighty man of valour. [1 Chr. 7:8]

Zephaniah (Heb. 'God has protected')
1. c. 13 century BC. Son of Tahath, a Levite descended from Kohath, he was an ancestor of Heman, musician to King David. [1 Chr. 6:36]
2. c. second half of 7 century BC. Hebrew prophet in the kingdom of Judah. Zephaniah the son of Cushi lived in the reign of King Josiah (640–09 BC), and was a contemporary and fellow-citizen of the great prophet Jeremiah. His words are recorded in the short Book bearing his name.

Since he was vehement against the idolatrous practices in Jerusalem – the star-worship copied from the Assyrians and the infiltration of local Canaanite deities – Zephaniah must have prophesied before the religious reforms of Josiah that started about 622 BC. He denounced the king's deceitful counsellors, dressed in foreign styles; the merchants in the new quarter of the town; the rapacious judges and the false men of religion: 'Her prophets are wanton, faithless men; her priests profane what is sacred, they do violence to the law.' (Zeph. 3:4)

The prophet also pronounced oracles against the neighbouring pagan peoples. The cities of the Philistines would be destroyed, 'The seacoast shall become the possession of the remnant of the house of Judah' (Zeph. 2:7). Moab and Ammon would be reduced to 'nettles and salt pits, and a waste for ever' (Zeph. 2:9). As for the mighty Assyrians, their capital Nineveh would be reduced to a ruin in which sheep would graze and birds would roost.

All this would happen in the 'day of the Lord' that loomed ahead, when the divine wrath would overtake Judah and the other nations: 'I will bring distress on men, so that they shall walk like the blind, because they have sinned against the Lord; their blood shall be poured out like dust, and their flesh like dung.' (Zeph. 1:17) After that great purge, Zion would be restored for the humble and penitent remnant of God's people. The pagan nations would also turn to the Lord, and his worship would become the universal faith of mankind. [Book of Zephaniah]

3. 6 century BC. Son of the priest Maaseiah and himself a priest and adviser to King Zedekiah in the final days of the kingdom of Judah, he opposed the policy of the prophet Jeremiah and favoured revolt against Babylon. With the Babylonian victory, he was among those carried off to Riblah and executed. [2 Kgs. 25:18; Jer. 21:1; 29:25, 29; 37:3; 52:24]

4. 6 century BC. Father of Josiah in whose home in Jerusalem the prophet Zechariah ordered that Joshua son of Jehozadak, the high priest, should be crowned as leader of the return to Judah. [Zech. 6:10, 14]

Zephi *see* ZEPHO

Zepho (Heb. 'watch') *c.* 16 century BC. Son of Eliphaz and a grandson of Esau, he was an Edomite leader of a desert tribe. Also called Zephi. [Gen. 36:11; 1 Chr. 1:36]

Zephon *see* ZIPHION

Zerah (Heb. 'God's shine') *1. c.* 16 century BC. Son of Reuel and a grandson of Esau, he was an Edomite leader of a desert tribe. [Gen. 36:13; 1 Chr. 1:37]
2. c. 16 century BC. One of the twins born to Judah and Tamar. Just before he was born he thrust forth his hand and the midwife put a scarlet thread round his wrist. Actually his brother Perez was born first. [Gen. 38:28–30; Num. 26:20; Josh. 7:1, 24; 22:20; 1 Chr. 2:4, 6; 9:6; Neh. 11:24]
3. c. 16 century BC. Son of Simeon and a grandson of Jacob. Also called Zohar. [Gen. 46:10; Exod. 6:15; Num. 26:13; 1 Chr. 4:24]
4. date unknown. Father of Jobab, king of Edom. [Gen. 36:33; 1 Chr. 1:44]
5. date unknown. Son of Iddo and a descendant of Levi's son Gershom. [1 Chr. 6:21]
6. date unknown. Son of Adaiah the Levite, and an ancestor of King David's musician Asaph. [1 Chr. 6:41]
7. see PHARAOH *7.*
8. c. 9 century BC. An Ethiopian commander who fought against Asa, king of Judah, with a huge army but was completely defeated. [2 Chr. 14:9]

Zerahiah (Heb. 'rising of God') *1.* date unknown. Son of Uzzi, he was a descendant of Aaron, the priest. [1 Chr. 6:6, 51; Ezra 7:4]

2. 5 century BC. Father of Eliehoenai, a leader of Israel who returned from exile in Babylon with Ezra. [Ezra 8:4]

Zeresh (Pers. 'gold') 5 century BC. Wife of Haman, chief minister of King Ahasuerus of Persia. When Mordecai refused to bow down to him, Haman plotted to kill all the Jews in the kingdom. Zeresh encouraged him to build a special gallows on which Mordecai would be hanged. The following day instead of persuading the king to order Mordecai hanged on a trumped-up charge, Haman was ordered by Ahasuerus to pay special honour to the Jew. That evening when Haman told Zeresh what he had been forced to do, she and their friends at once prophesied the fall of Haman and the success of Mordecai. [Esther 5:10, 14; 6:13]

Zereth date unknown. Son of Ashhur, a leader of the tribe of Judah. [1 Chr. 4:7]

Zeri (Heb. 'balsam') *c.* 10 century BC. Son of Jeduthun, a chief musician in the Tabernacle during King David's reign, Zeri and his brothers played musical instruments under their father's direction; Zeri took the fourth turn of service. Also called Izri. [1 Chr. 25:3, 11]

Zeror (Heb. 'tied') 11 century BC. Great-grandfather of King Saul, of the tribe of Benjamin. [1 Sam. 9:1]

Zeruah (Heb. 'leprous') 10 century BC. Mother of King Jeroboam of the northern kingdom of Israel, she was the widow of Nebat an Ephraimite. [1 Kgs. 11:26]

Zerubbabel (Heb. 'seed of Babylon') *c.* 6 century BC. Judean prince associated with the return from the Babylonian exile.

Zerubbabel the son of Shealtiel (called 'son of Pedaiah' in the First Book of Chronicles) was a member of the royal house of King Jehoiachin of Judah who was carried off into captivity to Babylon in 598 BC. Forty years after the fall of Jerusalem, Babylon was captured by Cyrus king of Persia, and Judah became part of the Persian empire. The following year, in 538 BC, Cyrus issued an edict permitting the Judean exiles to return to their homeland if they wished, and to rebuild the Temple. Those who remained behind were to assist the repatriates with money and goods, and to give them voluntary donations for the Temple. A total of 42,360 Jews gathered together for the return, under the leadership of Sheshbazzar, also of the Judean royal dynasty. In listing the other prominent persons going on the journey, Zerubbabel's name is the first one mentioned. (Some scholars believe that he and Sheshbazzar were the same person.) When everything was ready, the caravan moved off slowly on the six-hundred-mile trek across the desert.

The two men who shared authority over the settler community were Zerubbabel and Jeshua the high priest. They now started to organize the rebuilding of the Temple. Masons and carpenters were gathered, and set to work under the supervision of the Levites. Cedar logs from Phoenicia (Lebanon) were imported by sea to Joppa, and paid for in foodstuffs and olive oil – as Solomon had done with the building of the First Temple more than four centuries earlier. When the foundations had been laid, a celebration took place. The priests were robed in their vestments, trumpets and cymbals were sounded, and prayers of thanksgiving loudly chanted. The shouts of joy mingled with the weeping of the old men who remembered the First Temple before it had been destroyed.

Before the work could proceed beyond the foundations, it was interrupted by the Samaritans. They were the mixed offspring of the Hebrews who had survived the destruction of the northern kingdom of Israel a century and a half earlier and the deportees brought in from other parts of the Assyrian empire. At first some of them claimed the right to help rebuild the Temple. But Zerubbabel bluntly refused: 'You have nothing to do with us in building a house to our God.' (Ezra 4:3)

After this rebuff, the Samaritans harassed and disrupted the work. Rehum the local governor of Samaria wrote a letter to the king of Persia. He contended the archives would show that Jerusalem had always been a trouble spot, and would be so again if it was restored: 'and learn that this city is a rebellious city, hurtful to kings and provinces ...' (Ezra 4:15). The palace accepted this plea, and orders were given that the work was to be suspended.

Eighteen years later, after King Darius I had mounted the Persian throne, Zerubbabel and Jeshua called the leading citizens together and initiated another effort to resume the building of the Temple. This was done under strong moral pressure from two Jerusalem prophets, Haggai and Zechariah. Again complaints were made to higher authority. This time Tattenai the satrap (regional governor) came with his staff from Damascus to investigate the dispute personally. Tattenai's report to King Darius was objective. The Jewish settlers claimed, he wrote, that King Cyrus had expressly given authority to reconstruct the Temple that had stood on the site, and he asked for confirmation that this was true.

The reply from the king stated that Cyrus's permission was confirmed by a copy of a memorandum found at Ecbatana (the summer capital in Media of the Persian kings). Darius ordered that the building was to proceed and be paid for out of the revenue of the satrapy. What was more, the animals and supplies that would be needed for the sacrifices were to be provided from official sources. In return, prayers were to be offered for the welfare of the king and the royal family. Anybody who disobeyed these orders would be severely punished.

After the work was resumed, Zerubbabel seems to have disappeared and his end is unknown.

The construction of the Second Temple took five years and was completed in 515 BC. It lasted for 585 years. The Temple was sumptuously remodelled by Herod the Great (37–4 BC) and destroyed by the Roman legions under Titus in AD 70. [1 Chr. 3:19; Ezra 2:2; 3:2, 8; 4:2, 3; 5:2; Neh. 7:7; 12:1, 47; Hag. 1:1, 12, 14; 2:2, 4, 21, 23; Zech. 4:6–10]

Zeruiah (Heb. 'guarded') c. 11 century BC. Sister of King David, she was the mother of Joab, Asahel and Abishai. The name of her husband is not mentioned. [1 Sam. 26:6; 2 Sam. 2:13, 18; 3:39; 8:16; 14:1; 16:9, 10; 17:25; 18:2; 19:21, 22; 21:17; 23:18, 37; 1 Kgs. 1:7; 2:5, 22; 1 Chr. 2:16; 11:6, 39; 18:12, 15; 26:28; 27:24]

Zetham (Heb. 'olive') c. 10 century BC. Son of Ladan, he was a leader of the Gershom branch of Levites in the time of King David. [1 Chr. 23:8; 26:22]

Zethan (Heb. 'olive') date unknown. Son of Bilhan and a grandson of Jediael, he was a leader of the tribe of Benjamin and a mighty man of valour. [1 Chr. 7:10]

Zethar (Pers. 'star') c. 5 century BC. One of the seven chamberlains of King Ahasuerus who was commanded by the drunken king on the seventh day of a feast to bring Queen Vashti before his guests to show off her beauty. [Esther 1:10]

Zia (Heb. 'moving') date unknown. A leader of the tribe of Gad who dwelt east of the Jordan. [1 Chr. 5:13]

Ziba (Heb. 'statue') *c.* 10 century BC. A servant in the household of King Saul. After the death of Saul and Jonathan, David adopted Jonathan's crippled child Mephibosheth, and put Ziba in charge of the boy's property.

When David fled from Jerusalem after the rebellion of Absalom, Ziba met him with asses laden with provisions, and suggested that his master Mephibosheth had sided with Absalom. The angry David promptly told him he could have all Mephibosheth's property. After the defeat of Absalom, David discovered that Ziba had misled him and ordered half the lands to be returned to Mephibosheth. [2 Sam. 9:2–12; 16:1–4; 19:17–29]

Zibeon (Heb. 'hyena') *c.* 16 century BC. Grandfather of Esau's wife, Oholibamah, he was a leader of a Horite tribe. [Gen. 36:2, 14, 20, 24, 29; 1 Chr. 1:38, 40]

Zibia (Heb. 'deer') date unknown. Son of Shaharaim of the tribe of Benjamin and his wife Hodesh, he was an early clan leader. [1 Chr. 8:9]

Zibiah (Heb. 'deer') 9 century BC. Wife of King Ahaziah of Judah and mother of King Joash, she was born in Beersheba. [2 Kgs. 12:1; 2 Chr. 24:1]

Zichri (Heb. 'my memorial') *1.* date unknown. Youngest son of Izhar of the tribe of Levi, he was a leader of the tribe. [Exod. 6:21]
2. date unknown. Son of Shimei, he was a leader of the tribe of Benjamin living in Jerusalem. [1 Chr. 8:19]
3. date unknown. Son of Shashak, he was a leader of the tribe of Benjamin living in Jerusalem. [1 Chr. 8:23]
4. date unknown. Youngest son of Jeroham, he was a leader of the tribe of Benjamin living in Jerusalem. [1 Chr. 8:27]
5. c. 10 century BC. A Levite, father of Shelomoth who was responsible for the treasures in the Tabernacle in the reign of King David. [1 Chr. 26:25]
6. c. 10 century BC. Father of Eliezer who was ruler over the tribe of Reuben in the reign of King David. [1 Chr. 27:16]
7. c. 9 century BC. Father of Amasiah, one of the army commanders of the kingdom of Judah in the days of King Jehoshaphat. [2 Chr. 17:16]
8. c. 9 century BC. Father of Elishaphat who joined the conspiracy organized by the priest Jehoiada to overthrow Athaliah, queen of Judah, and crown her grandson Joash as king. [2 Chr. 23:1]
9. c. 8 century BC. A warrior of the tribe of Ephraim in the army of Pekah, king of Israel, in his war against King Ahaz of Judah, he killed Maaseiah, the king's son, Azrikam, governor of the palace and Elkanah, the chief minister to the king of Judah. [2 Chr. 28:7]
10. 5 century BC. Father of Joel, he was a leader of those of the tribe of Benjamin who lived in Jerusalem in the days of Nehemiah. [Neh. 11:9]
11. 5 century BC. Head of a priestly family when Joiakim was high priest towards the end of Ezra's lifetime. [Neh. 12:17]
12. see ZABDI *4.*

Ziha (Heb. 'dried') *1.* 6 century BC. Head of a family who returned with Zerubbabel from Babylonian exile and who served in the Temple. [Ezra 2:43; Neh. 7:46]
2. 5 century BC. One of the two supervisors of those ministering in the Temple in the days of Nehemiah. [Neh. 11:21]

Zillah (Heb. 'shadow') date unknown. A wife of Lamech and mother of Tubal-Cain. [Gen. 4:19, 23]

Zillethai (Heb. 'shadow') *1.* date unknown. Son of Shimei, a leader of the tribe of Benjamin. [1 Chr. 8:20]

2. 11 century BC. One of the commanders of the tribe of Manasseh who left the army of King Saul and joined David at Ziklag. [1 Chr. 12:20]

Zilpah (Heb. 'dropping') *c.* 18 century BC. The maid whom Laban gave to his daughter Leah when she married Jacob. Later when Leah thought she was past childbearing age she gave Zilpah to Jacob as a concubine. She became the mother of two of his sons, Gad and Asher. [Gen. 29:24; 30:9–12; 35:26; 37:2; 46:18]

Zimmah (Heb. 'wickedness') *1.* date unknown. Son of Jahath, he was a Levite descended from Gershom. [1 Chr. 6:20]
2. date unknown. Son of Shimei and father of Ethan, he was a Levite descended from Gershom. [1 Chr. 6:42]
3. c. 8 century BC. Father of Joah, a Levite who sanctified the Temple in the days of Hezekiah, king of Judah. [2 Chr. 29:12]

Zimran (Heb. 'sung') *c.* 18 century BC. Son of Abraham by his wife Keturah, he was leader of a desert tribe. [Gen. 25:2; 1 Chr. 1:32]

Zimri (Heb. 'singer') *1. c.* 13 century BC. Son of Salu, a leader of the tribe of Simeon, he took a Midianite woman into his tent in front of Moses and the people of Israel. They were both killed by Phinehas. [Num. 25:14]
2. see ZABDI *1.*
3. Fifth king of Israel after the monarchy split, he reigned for seven days in 885 BC. During the brief reign in the northern kingdom of Israel of King Elah, Zimri was the 'commander of half his chariots' (1 Kgs. 16:9). In 885 BC, Zimri murdered Elah while he was drunk in the house of his steward in Tirzah, the capital. Zimri proclaimed himself king, but his rule lasted only seven days. When Omri, the general of the army, occupied the capital, Zimri set fire to

the keep of the palace and died in the flames. Omri mounted the throne after a struggle for the succession. [1 Kgs. 16:9–20]
4. date unknown. Son of Jehoaddah of the tribe of Benjamin, he was a descendant of King Saul. [1 Chr. 8:36; 9:42]

Zina *see* ZIZAH

Ziph (Heb. 'that flows') *1.* date unknown. Son of Mareshah and a leader of the tribe of Judah. [1 Chr. 2:42]
2. date unknown. Son of Jehallelel, he was a leader of the tribe of Judah and the brother of Ziphah. [1 Chr. 4:16]

Ziphah (Heb. 'that flows') Son of Jehallelel and leader of the tribe of Judah, he was the brother of Ziph. [1 Chr. 4:16]

Ziphion (Heb. 'watchman') *c.* 16 century BC. Eldest son of Gad, he went down to Egypt together with his grandfather Jacob. Also called Zephon. [Gen. 46:16; Num. 26:15]

Zippor (Heb. 'bird') *c.* 13 century BC. Father of Balak, king of Moab, who hired the prophet Balaam to curse the children of Israel under Moses before they entered the Promised Land. [Num. 22:2, 10, 16; 23:18; Josh. 24:9; Judg. 11:25]

Zipporah *c.* 13 century BC. Wife of Moses.

Zipporah was one of the seven daughters of Jethro, the Midianite priest with whom Moses found refuge after he killed an Egyptian and fled into the desert. He met Zipporah when she and her sisters were at the well near their home struggling to water their father's flocks. Moses drove off the rest and helped them draw the water from the well. In gratitude Jethro invited Moses to stay with him and gave him Zipporah in marriage.

When Moses set out for Egypt with

his wife, his elder son Gershom and his newly-born second son Eliezer (who had not yet been circumcised), he became ill. Zipporah hastily circumcised the infant with a sharp flint, believing that the Lord was angry with Moses and he would die if the rite were neglected.

Later Moses sent her and the children back to live with her father. They rejoined him when he returned to the desert, leading the Children of Israel towards the Promised Land. [Exod. 2:21; 4:25; 18:2]

Ziza (Heb. 'plenty') *1. c.* 10 century BC. A son of King Rehoboam of Judah by his favourite wife, Maacah. [2 Chr. 11:20]
2. c. 8 century BC. Son of Shiphi, he was a leader of the tribe of Simeon in the days of King Hezekiah, who drove out the inhabitants of the rich Gedor valley and settled there. [1 Chr. 4:37]

Zizah (Heb. 'plenty') *c.* 10 century BC. Son of Shimei of the tribe of Levi, he served in the Tabernacle in the time of King David. Also called Zina. [1 Chr. 23:10, 11]

Zobebah (Heb. 'slothful') date unknown. Son of Koz, a leader in the tribe of Judah. [1 Chr. 4:8]

Zohar (Heb. 'white') *1. c.* 18 century BC. Father of Ephron the Hittite from whom Abraham bought the field near Hebron containing the Cave of Machpelah. [Gen. 23:8; 25:9]
2. see ZERAH *3.*

Zoheth date unknown. Son of Ishi of the tribe of Judah, he was a descendant of Caleb son of Jephunneh. [1 Chr. 4:20]

Zophah (Heb. 'vial') date unknown. Son of Helem, a descendant of Asher, he was one of the leaders of the tribe. [1 Chr. 7:35, 36]

Zophai *see* ZUPH

Zophar period of the Patriarchs. One of the three friends who remonstrated with Job.

Zophar the Naamathite joined two other friends to visit the afflicted Job. They were shocked at his changed appearance, and rent their clothes and put dust on their heads. They sat silently next to him for seven days and seven nights.

Then Job began to curse the day he had been born, and protest that his suffering was undeserved. Zophar and the others tried to console him, but when he persisted they pointed out that he must have committed sins to have so heavy a punishment to bear. As Job continued to rail against the Lord, Zophar said to him sternly: 'oh, that God would speak, and open his lips to you.... Know then that God exacts of you less than your guilt deserves.' (Job 11:5, 6) Job made no effort to conceal his impatience with his pious friends. 'So these three men ceased to answer Job, because he was righteous in his own eyes.' (Job. 32:1)

Finally the Lord spoke to Job out of a whirlwind and he was completely overwhelmed and humbled. Then the Lord turned on the three friends and told them he was angry with them 'for you have not spoken of me what is right, as my servant Job has' (Job 42:7). The Lord instructed them to offer up a burnt sacrifice 'and my servant Job shall pray for you, for I will accept his prayer' (Job 42:8). [Job 2:11; 11; 20; 42]

Zuar (Heb. 'little') 13 century BC. Father of Nethanel who represented his tribe of Issachar when Moses selected one chief of each tribe to help him take a census of the children of Israel fit for military service. [Num. 1:8; 2:5; 7:18–23; 10:15]

Zuph (Heb. 'honeycomb') *c.* 12 century BC. A Levite, son of Elkanah and ancestor of the prophet Samuel. Also called Zophai. [1 Sam. 1:1; 1 Chr. 6:26, 35]

Zur (Heb. 'rock') *1. c.* 13 century BC. Father of Cozbi, a Midianite woman who was brought into the Israelite camp by Zimri. Cozbi and Zimri were killed by Phinehas the priest and Zur was killed in the subsequent war with the Israelites. [Num. 25:15; 31:8; Josh. 13:21]

2. c. 11 century BC. Son of Jeiel and a leader of the tribe of Benjamin living in Gibeon. [1 Chr. 8:30; 9:36]

Zuriel (Heb. 'my rock is God') *c.* 13 century BC. Son of Abihail, a Levite descended from Merari, he was chief of the Merari Levites in the days of Moses, and his people were in charge of specific items of the Tabernacle including the equipment needed for its maintenance in the wilderness. [Num. 3:35]

Zurishaddai (Heb. 'my rock is the Almighty') *c.* 13 century BC. Father of Shelumiel who represented his tribe of Simeon when Moses selected one chief of each tribe to help him take a census of the children of Israel fit for military service. [Num. 1:6; 2:12; 7:36, 41; 10:19]

The Apocrypha

Introduction to the Apocrypha

'The Apocrypha' is the name given to a collection of fifteen Jewish books, or portions of books, written in the last two centuries BC and the 1st century AD. They were not included in the Hebrew canon of the Bible. The Greek Bible (Septuagint) included all of them except 2 Esdras. After centuries of uncertainty, it was laid down in the 16th century AD that these works should be accepted as part of the Latin (Vulgate) Bible, except for the Prayer of Manasseh and 1 and 2 Esdras, which were placed in an appendix after the New Testament. In the Protestant Bible, the Apocrypha were not treated as scriptural. They were printed as a separate section between the Old and New Testaments, and in modern editions usually appear in a separate volume. (On the position of the Apocrypha in the canon of various Christian Bibles, see also the main introduction to this volume, *The Books of the Old Testament*.)

A brief description follows of the Apocrypha, with the order, full titles and abbreviations as used in the Revised Standard Version.

The First Book of Esdras (1 Esd.)

A re-written Greek version of parts of Chronicles, Ezra and Nehemiah. It probably dates from the 2nd century BC. (Since they would be mainly repetitions, no entries from 1 Esd. have been included in the Apocrypha section.)

The Second Book of Esdras (2 Esd.)

An apocalyptic work, with its main part consisting of seven visions attributed to Ezra. It was written in Hebrew or Aramaic, probably at the end of the 1st century AD after the destruction of Jerusalem. (It has not been necessary to include any entries from 2 Esd. in this section.)

Tobit (Tob.)

A tale about a Jewish captive in Babylon who was blinded and had his sight miraculously restored. It was written in Hebrew or Aramaic about 200 BC.

Judith (Jdt.)

A story about a devout and patriotic young Jewish widow who delivered her people from the Assyrians. It was written in Hebrew in the late 2nd century BC.

The Additions to the Book of Esther (Ad. Est.)

Six additional passages inserted in the Book of Esther. They were probably written in Greek about the end of the 2nd century BC, in order to give the Book a more religious character, and to fill out the story by quoting documents.

The Wisdom of Solomon (Wis.)

A book in praise of traditional Hebrew wisdom, written in Greek in the 1st century BC by an unknown Alexandrian Jew. (See the note on the Wisdom Books under SOLOMON.)

Ecclesiasticus, or the Wisdom of Jesus the Son of Sirach (Sir.)

A treatise stressing the value of wisdom in the Hebrew way of life. It was written in Hebrew about 180 BC and was translated into Greek by the author's grandson about 130 BC. (See under JESUS, SON OF SIRACH in this section.)

Baruch (Bar.)

A prophetic work attributed to Jeremiah's scribe and disciple Baruch, prophesying the return of the Jewish exiles to their homeland. It was compiled from several Hebrew elements about the end of the 1st century AD. The work is placed in the Greek and Latin Bibles after Jeremiah and Lamentations.

The Letter of Jeremiah (Let. Jer.)

A document purporting to be an epistle from Jeremiah to his fellow-Jews, warning them against idolatry during their exile. The original was probably written in Hebrew or Aramaic not later than the 2nd century BC. Fragments in Greek have been found among the Dead Sea Scrolls. In the Latin Bible this Letter forms Chapter 6 of the Book of Baruch.

The Prayer of Azariah and the Song of the Three Young Men (S. of 3 Y.)

Liturgical insertions in Chapter 3 of the Book of Daniel. They were probably written in Hebrew in the 2nd century BC.

Susanna (Sus.)

A tale about the beautiful and virtuous wife of a Babylonian Jew who resisted the advances of two elders. The work was probably composed in Greek in the 2nd or 1st century BC. It appears in the Latin Bible as Chapter 13 of the Book of Daniel.

Bel and the Dragon (Bel)

These two popular tales ridicule idolatry. Daniel exposed the priests of the temple of Bel, slew a sacred reptile, and was miraculously delivered from the lions' den. The work was probably written in Greek in the 2nd or 1st century BC. It appears in the Latin Bible as Chapter 14 of the Book of Daniel.

The Prayer of Manasseh (Man.)

A fine penitential psalm attributed to Manasseh the sinful king of Judah. It was composed at some time during the last two centuries BC – whether in Hebrew, Aramaic or Greek is uncertain.

The First Book of the Maccabees (1 Macc.)

An important historical work concerning the Maccabean Revolt against Seleucid rule, covering the period 175–35 BC. The book was originally written in Hebrew about 100 BC, but survives only in a Greek translation.

The Second Book of the Maccabees (2 Macc.)

A different and more fervid account of the Maccabean Revolt, the book covers the period 175–61 BC, and starts with two letters to the Jews of Alexandria from their brethren in Jerusalem. It was written in Greek about 60 BC, and the author states it is condensed from a work in five volumes by one Jason of Cyrene.

The Apocrypha section contains characters that do not appear in the Old Testament, or about whom there is additional material in the Apocrypha – such as Daniel and Esther.

Who's Who in the Old Testament

Absalom (Heb. '[my] father is peace')
1. 2 century BC. The father of two captains in the Maccabean army – Mattathias and Jonathan. [1 Macc. 11:70; 13:11]
2. 2 century BC. An envoy sent by Judas Maccabeus to Lysias carrying a letter for King Antiochus. [2 Macc. 11:17]

Abubus *c.* 2 century BC. The father of Ptolemy, who was married to the daughter of Simon the high priest. [1 Macc. 16:11, 15]

Accos (a form of Heb. *hakkos*, 'thorn') *c.* 3 century BC. Grandfather of Eupolemus, who was sent by Judas Maccabeus on a mission to Rome about 162 BC. [1 Macc. 8:17]

Achior (Heb. 'brother of light') *c.* 5 century BC. An Ammonite chief.

Achior was the leader of a group of Ammonite auxiliary forces, attached to the Assyrian army under Holofernes that was besieging Bethulia, where Judith lived. He advised Holofernes that the Israelite nation could not be defeated as long as it remained faithful to the Lord. The angry commander ordered him to be bound and left outside the gate of Bethulia, so that he would share its fate.

He was taken into the city and treated well by the inhabitants. When Judith returned with the severed head of Holofernes, Achior identified it. He then decided to become converted to the Jewish faith and was circumcised. [Jdt. 5:5–22; 6; 14:5–10]

Aduel (Heb. 'God is an ornament') date unknown. Ancestor of Tobit, the son of Tobiel. [Tob. 1:1]

Ahikar (possibly Aramaic 'precious brother') *c.* 8 century BC. Nephew of Tobit, and Assyrian royal treasurer.

Ahikar was the son of Tobit's brother Anael, and became one of the leading men at the Assyrian court, serving King Sennacherib and his successor Esarhaddon as chief cupbearer and royal treasurer.

Tobit had to flee from Sennacherib's anger when it became known that he had been retrieving and burying the bodies of Jews put to death by the king. When Esarhaddon ascended the throne, Ahikar was able to intervene on his uncle's behalf so that he could return to his home.

Tobit became blind and for the next two years was cared for by Ahikar who then moved to Elemais.

Biblical scholars have been struck by the resemblances between the Book of Tobit and a work called 'The Wisdom of Ahikar', that enjoyed a great vogue throughout the ancient Near East. It has been suggested that the Ahikar story was one of the main sources of the Tobit story, and that Tobit's puzzling deathbed reference to Ahikar and his brother Nadab can only be understood as an echo of the earlier work. [Tob. 1:21; 11:18; 14:10, 11]

Alcimus (from the Heb. 'God sets up') 2 century BC. High priest in Jerusalem in the reign of Demetrius I Soter.

Alcimus, a member of the priestly clan, aspired to become high priest in

Jerusalem, and urged the new Seleucid ruler Demetrius I Soter to crush the Maccabean revolt. The king appointed him high priest, and sent a large force under his general Bacchides to instal him in office.

At first Alcimus by conciliatory talk and promises won over the orthodox sect of the Hasideans, who had supported the Maccabeans. But once he was established he had sixty of the Hasideans seized and killed, while Bacchides put a number of other Jews to death. These harsh measures made Alcimus unpopular, and Judas Maccabeus fanned the embers of revolt throughout Judea. Bacchides had returned to Antioch, leaving some of his troops in Jerusalem.

During the next few years, Alcimus was maintained in office only by the direct military support of the Seleucid armed forces. Alcimus remained high priest until 159 BC when he had a stroke and died. According to legend, Alcimus's death was a divine punishment for breaking down the inner wall of the Temple. [1 Macc. 7:5–25; 9:1–4, 54–57; 2 Macc. 14:3–13, 26]

Alexander the Great (Gk. 'defender of men') 356–23 BC. Alexander the Great is mentioned in the First Book of Maccabees since one of his generals founded the Seleucid kingdom of which Judea was a part at the time of the Maccabean revolt. [1 Macc. 1:1–9]

Alexander Balas (Epiphanes) 2 century BC. King of the Seleucid Empire, 150–45 BC.

Alexander Balas, a claimant to the Seleucid throne, landed at Ptolemais (Acre) in 152 BC and gained control of the country by 150 BC. The high priest Jonathan, who had supported him, was made ethnarch (provincial governor) of Jerusalem. In 145 BC Alexander was in turn defeated by another claimant, Demetrius II, with the help of Ptolemy VI of Egypt, whose daughter Cleopatra

was married to Alexander. He fled into Arabia where he was killed by a tribal sheikh. [1 Macc. 10:1, 15–21, 23, 47–59, 68, 88; 11:1, 2, 8–12, 14–17, 39]

Anael c. 8 century BC. Brother of Tobit, he was the father of Ahikar, the royal treasurer of Esarhaddon. [Tob. 1:21]

Ananias (from the Heb. 'the Lord has been gracious')
1. Date unknown. Ancestor of Judith. [Jdt. 8:1]
2. c. 8 century BC. Descendant of the prophet Shemaiah. [Tob. 5:13]
3. c. 8 century BC. A relative of Tobit claimed as his father by the angel Raphael. [Tob. 5:12]

Ananiel (from the Heb. 'God is gracious') date unknown. An ancestor of Tobit, he was of the tribe of Naphtali. [Tob. 1:1]

Andronicus (Gk. 'conqueror of men') *1.* 2 century BC. One of the ministers of King Antiochus IV Epiphanes.

He was left in charge of affairs when the king hurried to Cilicia to restore order in the towns of Tarsus and Mallus. Menelaus, who had bought himself into the office of high priest in Jerusalem, was summoned at this time to Antioch for failing to pay the monies he owed. He purloined gold plate from the Temple and handed it to Andronicus as a bribe.

Onias, the venerable high priest who had been deposed, was living in the sanctuary at Daphne near Antioch, and denounced the sacrilege committed by Menelaus. The latter persuaded Andronicus to lure Onias out of the sanctuary and have him murdered. This crime stirred up great popular anger, and on his return the king sentenced Andronicus to death. [2 Macc. 4:31–8]
2. 2 century BC. A governor who was left at Gerizim by Antiochus Epiphanes when he fled to Antioch. [2 Macc. 5:23]

Anna (from the Heb. 'grace') *c.* 8 century BC. The wife of Tobit.

Anna, like Tobit, was of the tribe of Naphtali. They were carried off as captives to Nineveh where Anna obtained work with a weaver after Tobit became blind. When she brought home a kid her employer had given her and Tobit accused her of stealing it, she jeered at him. Anna was filled with anxiety when their son Tobias set out on the long journey to Medea, and was the first to see him return with his bride Sarah. Anna lived to a ripe old age and was buried in Nineveh next to her husband. [Book of Tobit]

Antiochis 2 century BC. A concubine of King Antiochus IV Epiphanes, who gave her the revenues from the Cilician towns of Tarsus and Mallus as a gift. The inhabitants of these towns revolted, and Antiochus had to hurry off to restore order. [2 Macc. 4:30]

Antiochus (from the Gk. 'the opposed')
1. Antiochus III ('the Great') King of the Seleucid Empire, 223–187 BC, he was the father of Antiochus Epiphanes. [1 Macc. 1:10; 8:8]
2. Antiochus IV Epiphanes (Gk. 'manifest [God]') King of the Seleucid Empire, 175–63 BC.

In the history of the Maccabean revolt, Antiochus IV is the villain of the piece. The First Book of Maccabees details his religious persecution of the Jews which brought about the revolt; while the Second Book of Maccabees, a more emotional document, pictures him as a vicious tyrant. He seems to have been an able, dynamic and ambitious ruler, vain enough to adopt the title of Epiphanes 'god-manifest'. His detractors suggested that his additional name should have been Epimanes, 'the madman'.

Antiochus belonged to the Seleucid dynasty founded by one of the generals of Alexander the Great. The Seleucid empire covered, with its capital at Antioch in northern Syria, most of Asia Minor and finally, from 198 BC, included Judea.

Having been born and brought up in Athens, Antiochus was an intense admirer of all things Greek, and determined to impose the Greek religion, language and culture upon all his subject peoples. Many of the Jews assimilated the Hellenistic customs and way of life, but the more orthodox among them strongly resisted it, and clung to the ancestral faith and traditions.

Antiochus's greatest ambition was to conquer Egypt, which he tried to do in several campaigns from 170–67 BC. But he was frustrated by the rising power of Rome, which was reaching into the eastern Mediterranean. On returning from his first Egyptian campaign, he marched into Jerusalem and pillaged the Temple, carrying away its gold vessels and even stripping the gold ornaments from the walls. In a second campaign, a Roman envoy curtly ordered Antiochus to withdraw his forces from Egypt, and he was obliged to submit. This repulse sharpened his fear of Roman domination, and his compulsive urge to stamp out religious separatism and enforce a uniform worship of the Greek deities. The harsh steps he took to destroy the Jewish faith provoked armed resistance.

One of his generals was sent to occupy Jerusalem. He butchered many of its inhabitants, razed the walls, and constructed a fortified citadel near the Temple. The practice of Judaism was banned, including observance of the Sabbath and the rite of circumcision. His desecration of the Temple was termed by Daniel 'the abomination of desolation'. The Greek soldiers sacrificed swine on the altar, tore up the sacred scrolls of the Law, and held drunken feasts to Bacchus. A statue of Jupiter was set up in the Holy of Holies. Through intrigue and bribery, a certain Menelaus had got himself appointed to the key office of high priest, and served as a willing tool of Antiochus's repressive religious policy.

The Second Book of Maccabees, more an indictment than a sober history, relates a series of atrocities alleged to have been committed by Antiochus and his subordinates during this period. One story concerns two Jewish mothers who had circumcised their babies. They were driven through the streets with the infants hanging at their breasts, and then hurled over the city wall. In another case, a mother was forced to witness her seven sons tortured to death in turn for refusing to eat pork and then she herself was murdered. A respected ninety-year-old teacher of the Law, Eleazar, chose to be bludgeoned to death rather than make even a pretence of swallowing the forbidden meat.

Officials were sent around Judea to oversee observance of worship of Greek gods by the inhabitants. In the village of Modi'in, one such official was defied and killed by the local Jewish priest, Mattathias, who fled into the Judean hills with his five sons, and operated as a guerrilla band. The banner of revolt had been raised.

During the remaining years of Antiochus's rule, a series of military expeditions failed to crush the Maccabean rebellion or to relieve the Syrian garrison cut off in the citadel in Jerusalem. The Seleucid generals who led the successive campaigns were Apollonius, Seron, Ptolemy Macron, Nicanor, Gorgias, and Lysias.

In 165 BC, two years after the revolt started, Antiochus led a campaign eastwards into Persia and Medea to exact tribute and replenish the empty royal coffers. Lysias was left in charge of the kingdom, and as tutor of the young crown prince.

In 163 BC, Antiochus fell ill and died at Tabae, in Persia, after sacking the Temple of Artemis at Elymais.

On his deathbed Antiochus appointed his close friend Philip as guardian of his young son and regent of the kingdom until he came of age. In Antioch, Lysias ignored this appointment and had the twelve-year-old boy immediately crowned king as Antiochus V Eupator. [1 Macc. 1–6:16; 2 Macc. 4:7; 9:5–28; 10:9]

3. 2 century BC. Father of Numenius, the envoy sent by Judas Maccabeus to Rome. [1 Macc. 12:16; 14:22]

4. Antiochus V Eupator (Gk. 'born of a noble father') Son of Antiochus IV Epiphanes, he was king of the Seleucid Empire, 163–2 BC. [1 Macc. 6:15, 17, 55; 7:2; 2 Macc. 9:25, 29; 10:10–13; 11:1, 14–36; 12:1; 13; 14:2]

5. Antiochus VI King of the Seleucid Empire, 145–39 BC. Antiochus VI, son of Alexander Balas, succeeded to the Seleucid throne as a boy after a confused power struggle. He made a number of concessions to Jonathan, the Maccabean high priest in Jerusalem, in order to win Jewish support. After three years Antiochus was killed by Trypho, a general who usurped the throne. [1 Macc. 11:40, 57–59; 13:31, 32]

6. Antiochus VII Sidetes (Gk. 'from Side [in Pamphylia]') King of the Seleucid Empire, 138–29 BC.

Antiochus VII Sidetes was the younger brother of the Seleucid king Demetrius II, who had been ousted by his general Trypho.

Antiochus landed on the coast of Syria with a large army, quickly gained control, and besieged Trypho at Dor on the west coast of Palestine.

Before his invasion Antiochus had written to Simon the high priest in Jerusalem, offering him a number of concessions in exchange for his support. But the king later repudiated these promises. Pursuing Trypho from Dor, he left behind one of his generals, Cendebeus, who was defeated by Simon's two sons.

After the death of Antiochus VII in 129 BC, his successors were involved in bitter family feuds and lost control of

Judea and the rest of Palestine. [1 Macc. 15:1–38]

Antipater 2 century BC. Son of Jason, he was one of two envoys sent to Rome by Jonathan to renew the pact of friendship. [1 Macc. 12:16; 14:22]

Apollonius (from the Lat. 'of Apollo')
1. 2 century BC. Son of Gennaeus, he was a governor of a Jewish province in the time of Judas Maccabeus. [2 Macc. 12:2]
2. 2 century BC. A Seleucid general who was the military governor in Samaria at the time of the Maccabean revolt in 167 BC. He led a force to crush the insurgents. It was ambushed and routed by Judas Maccabeus on the steep incline of Lebonah along the main road through the hills from Samaria to Jerusalem. Apollonius was killed in this engagement, and Judas took his sword which he used for the rest of his life. The Maccabeans were greatly elated at this first success against regular troops. [1 Macc. 3:10–12]
3. 2 century BC. The son of Menestheus and governor of Coelsyria and Phoenicia. Apollonius of Tarsus was sent by Antiochus IV to Egypt for the coronation of Ptolemy VI Philometer. [1 Macc. 3:5, 7; 4:4, 21]
4. 2 century BC. A captain of the Mysians, he was sent by Antiochus IV to Jerusalem with 22,000 men and had a number of the Jewish inhabitants massacred by his troops on the Sabbath day. [2 Macc. 5:24–6]
5. 2 century BC. General of the Seleucid ruler Demetrius II (147–38 BC), he was sent with a strong army against Judea, then under the leadership of Jonathan, brother of Judas Maccabeus.

Apollonius camped at Jamnia on the coast plain, and challenged Jonathan to meet him in battle in open ground 'where there is no stone or pebble, or place to flee' (1 Macc. 10:73), that is, where Jews could not fight as guerrillas

in familiar hill terrain. Jonathan felt strong enough to accept this challenge. He led a force of 10,000 men into the coastal plain, with his brother Simon bringing up reinforcements. The wily Apollonius feigned a retreat and drew the Israelites into a trap. They were attacked from the rear by cavalry units that had been concealed but stood their ground all day until Simon was able to counter-attack and rout the cavalry. Apollonius and his troops were pursued into Azotus (Ashdod), the outlying defences of which were captured and burnt.

After this victory the Maccabean army was regarded as the strongest military force in the area. [1 Macc. 10:69–87]

Apollophanes 2 century BC. A commander in the Syrian army of Antiochus V Eupator. He was captured and killed when the fortress of Gazara was taken by Judas Maccabeus. [2 Macc. 10:37]

Apphus (possibly from the Heb. 'cunning') see JONATHAN

Aretas (from the Gk. 'goodness') 2 century BC. An Arabian prince who captured the high priest Jason when he was deposed and fled across the Jordan river, during the reign of Antiochus IV Epiphanes. [2 Macc. 5:8]

Ariarathes 2 century BC. King of Cappadocia, he was one of the rulers who received a letter from the Roman consul Lucius, indicating Roman protection for Judea at the time when Simon the Maccabean was high priest in Jerusalem. [1 Macc. 15:22]

Arioch 6 century BC. King of the Elymeans who lived along the plain between the rivers Euphrates and Tigris. [Jdt. 1:6]

Aristobulus *c.* 2 century BC. Member of

a Jewish priestly family in Egypt and tutor to Ptolemy VII Physcon.

The second of the two letters to the Jews in Egypt which form a foreword to the Second Book of The Maccabees is addressed to him. The letter is undated and was probably written early in the 1st century BC. [2 Macc. 1:10]

Arius *c.* 3 century BC. King of Sparta, he sent an envoy with a letter to Onias I the high priest in Jerusalem, to conclude an agreement of alliance and friendship with the Jews. This was probably in the reign of the Seleucid king Seleucus IV. Jonathan the Maccabean leader and high priest later wrote to Sparta to renew this alliance. [1 Macc. 12:7, 20]

Arphaxad *c.* 6 century BC. King of Media.

According to the Book of Judith, Nebuchadnezzar king of Assyria is described as waging war against Arphaxad king of the Medes. Arphaxad fortified his capital Ecbatana with huge walls and towers and massive gates. He was defeated in battle by Nebuchadnezzar who captured the city and pursued Arphaxad into the mountains, where he slew him with a spear.

This account is imaginary. Nebuchadnezzar was in fact king of Babylon, after the end of the Assyrian empire; he did not wage a war against Media, and there is no record of a Median king called Arphaxad. The story of Judith was written in the 2nd century BC and the historical references are inaccurate. [Jdt. 1:1, 5, 13–15]

Arsaces 2 century BC. King of the Parthians, he was one of the rulers who received a letter from the Roman consul Lucius, indicating Roman protection for Judea at the time when Simon the Maccabean was high priest in Jerusalem.

He Later defeated and captured the Seleucid Demetrius II, after the latter had been ousted from his throne. [1 Macc. 15:22]

Artaxerxes see AHASUERUS (O.T. section)

Asiel date unknown. An ancestor of Tobit and a member of the tribe of Naphtali. [Tob. 1:1]

Astyages *c.* 6 century BC. King of Babylon, he was succeeded by Cyrus the Persian in 538 BC. [Bel. 1:1]

Athenobius 2 century BC. An official of the Seleucid ruler Antiochus VII. The king had demanded from Simon the high priest in Jerusalem the return of certain cities and areas captured and annexed by Judea. Athenobius was sent to negotiate these demands. Simon rejected them on the ground that the places in question were part of the ancestral Jewish territory and that their occupation by others had been unlawful. Athenobius returned and reported to his royal master who was very angry at the failure of the mission. [1 Macc. 15:28–36]

Attalus 2 century BC. King of Pergamum, he was one of the rulers who received a letter from the Roman consul Lucius, indicating Roman protection for Judea at the time when Simon the Maccabean was high priest in Jerusalem. [1 Macc. 15:22]

Auranus 2 century BC. Described as 'a man advanced in years and no less advanced in folly' (2 Macc. 4:40), he was used by Lysimachus, brother of the corrupt high priest Menelaus, in an attempt to suppress the angry mob that attacked and killed Lysimachus for plundering the Temple. [2 Macc. 4:40]

Avaran see ELEAZAR *4.*

Azariah (Heb. 'whom God aids') 2 century BC. One of the two senior commanders left in charge in Jerusalem in 163 BC while Judas Maccabeus and his brother Jonathan were campaigning east of the Jordan, and another brother Simon was in Galilee. Azariah and Joseph were eager to prove themselves as generals, and contrary to Judas's instructions, they led an expedition against Jamnia in the coastal plain. Here they were routed by the redoubtable Seleucid general Gorgias, and fled back to Jerusalem. [1 Macc. 5:18, 55–62]

Azarias (from the Heb. 'whom God aids') *c.* 8 century BC. The name assumed by the angel Raphael.

The angel Raphael was sent by the Lord to Nineveh to cure Tobit of his blindness, and to help Sarah the daughter of Tobit's kinsman Raguel. Her seven successive husbands had been killed on the wedding night by the demon Asmodeus.

Pretending to be Azarias, a distant kinsman, he acted as companion and guide to Tobias, Tobit's son, who travelled to Media to reclaim some silver left there by his father twenty years before.

That night he and Tobias camped on the bank of the river Tigris. When Tobias bathed his feet, a huge fish appeared. The angel told Tobias to catch the fish and keep its liver, heart and gall as medicine.

At Ecbatana in Media Tobias married Sarah, the daughter of his father's kinsman Raguel. On the angel's advice, Tobias burnt the heart and liver of the fish and thereby drove away the demon Asmodeus. The demon fled to Upper Egypt where the angel caught and bound him.

At Tobias's request, Azarias travelled on by himself to fetch the silver.

On their return to Nineveh, Tobit's blindness was cured with the gall of the fish. He and his son wished to reward Azarias who revealed himself as an angel and refused their gift. He urged them to praise the Lord instead. [Book of Tobit]

Bacchides 2 century BC. Military com-mander under Seleucid kings Antiochus IV and Demetrius I.

Bacchides, a leading general and governor of the western part of the Seleucid kingdom, led three expeditions into Judea to subdue the Maccabean revolt. In 162 BC he established a garrison in Jerusalem. In 161 BC he defeated the Maccabeans in the battle of Elasa and Judas was killed. In 157 BC Bacchides failed to round up the Jewish partisans under Jonathan, but fortified the area around Jerusalem. [1 Macc. 7:8–20; 9:1–34, 43–53, 57–64, 68–73; 10:12; 2 Macc. 8:30]

Bacenor 2 century BC. Officer under Judas Maccabeus who fought against Gorgias. [2 Macc. 12:35]

Bagoas (possibly from the Persian 'eunuch') *c.* 5 century BC. A eunuch, who was in charge of the personal household of Holofernes, commander of the Assyrian army invading Judea. It was he who took care of Judith in the Assyrian camp, and who discovered the headless corpse of Holofernes after Judith had killed him. [Jdt. 12:11–15; 13:1, 14:14–18]

Baruch (Heb. 'blessed') *c.* 6 century BC. Disciple and scribe of the prophet Jeremiah.

The prophetic book attributed to Baruch, the disciple and scribe of Jeremiah, was probably written in Hebrew about the end of the 2nd century BC. According to the introduction, it purports to have been written by Baruch from exile in Babylonia after the fall of Jerusalem. It contains several sections to be read in temples on feast days. It includes a prayer on behalf of the exiles, a poem on the nature of wisdom; and a poem of complaint and hope spoken by a personified Jerusalem, to which the author replies with a promise of messianic recovery.

In the Greek and Latin Bibles, the

Book of Baruch appears together with Jeremiah and Lamentations.

The letter of Jeremiah is a separate work, probably written in Hebrew in the Hellenic period. In the Latin Bible it appears as Chapter 6 of the Book of Baruch. see also BARUCH (O.T. section) [Book of Baruch]

Ben sira see JESUS, SON OF SIRACH

Callisthenes 2 century BC. A Syrian who with others set fire to the sacred gates of the Temple in the time of Antiochus IV Epiphanes. After the capture of Jerusalem by Judas Maccabeus, he was burnt to death in retaliation. [2 Macc. 8:33]

Cendebeus 2 century BC. A general under the Seleucid ruler Antiochus VII. The king beseiged Dor, on the coast, where the usurper Trypho had taken refuge. Trypho escaped and was pursued by Antiochus, who left Cendebeus in command of the coastal area, with a force of infantry and cavalry. He established his headquarters at Jamnia and fortified the town of Kidron as a forward position. From this area he started to raid and harass the adjacent districts of Judea. Simon, the high priest and Maccabean leader in Jerusalem, sent troops under his two eldest sons, Judas and John, against Cendebeus, who was defeated and chased into Azotus (Ashdod). see JOHN [1 Macc. 15:38–41; 16:1–10]

Chabris c. 5 century BC. The son of Gothoniel, he was one of the three magistrates or elders of the town of Bethulia where Judith lived. When the town was about to surrender to the Assyrian general Holofernes because of famine and thirst, Judith sent for the magistrates and berated them for their lack of faith in God. That night they let her out of the city gate, and she saved the country by beheading Holofernes. [Jdt. 6:15, 8:10, 10:6]

Chaereas 2 century BC. Commander of the fortress of Gazara, stormed by the forces of Judas Maccabeus, he was killed together with his brother Timothy after they were found hiding in a cistern. [2 Macc. 10:32–37]

Chalphi (from the Heb. 'a child replacing one who has been lost') c. 2 century BC. Father of Judas, who was a captain in the Maccabean army under Jonathan the high priest. [1 Macc. 11:70]

Charmis c. 5 century BC. The son of Melchiel, he was one of the three magistrates or elders of the town of Bethulia where Judith lived. When the town was about to surrender to the Assyrian general Holofernes because of famine and thirst, Judith sent for the magistrates and berated them for their lack of faith in God. That night they let her out of the city gate, and she saved the country by beheading Holofernes. [Jdt. 6:15; 8:10; 10:6]

Cleopatra (Gk. 'sprung from a famous father') c. 2 century BC. Daughter of Ptolemy VI Philometer, she married Alexander Balas, a pretender to the Seleucid throne.

In a footnote to the Greek translation of the Book of Esther, it is stated that the translation was brought to Egypt in the fourth year of the reign of 'Ptolemy and Cleopatra'. There were four Ptolemies who had wives called Cleopatra, but the reference appears to be to Ptolemy VIII, and the date has, therefore, been fixed at 114 BC [Ad. Est. 11:1; 1 Macc. 10:57, 58]

Crates 2 century BC. Deputy to Sostratus, the commander of the Syrian garrison in the citadel in Jerusalem, in the reign of Antiochus IV Epiphanes, he was a Cypriot and was transferred back to that island when it came under the control of Antiochus. [2 Macc. 4:29]

Daniel (Heb. 'God is my judge') c. 6

century BC. Hebrew official at the Babylonian court.

Among the Apocrypha are two short works containing additional legends about the prophet Daniel – the story of Susanna; and Bel and the Dragon. They were originally written in Hebrew or Aramaic in the second century BC. These two works were included in the Septuagint (Greek Bible) and later in the Vulgate (Catholic Bible), where they were added to the Book of Daniel as Chapters 13 and 14.

SUSANNA

Susanna was the beautiful and virtuous wife of Joakim, a respected leader of a Jewish community in Babylon. She aroused the lust of two elders or judges. When she repulsed their advances in Joakim's garden, they falsely accused her of adultery with an unknown young man, and she was condemned to death. The young Daniel was inspired by the Lord to intervene, and had the trial reopened. He then had the two elders brought forward separately. Under his interrogation they contradicted each other about the kind of tree under which they claimed to have seen Susanna lying with the young man. Her innocence was established, and the elders were put to death as perjurers.

'And from that day onward Daniel had a great reputation among the people.' (Sus. 64)

BEL AND THE DRAGON

The story of the god Bel opens with Daniel already established as the friend and confidant of the king of Babylon. The king worshipped at the temple of Bel, and asked Daniel why he did not do so as well. Daniel replied that he worshipped the living God, not idols made with human hands. The king insisted that Bel was a living god, and pointed out that he consumed every day the quantities of food and wine placed before him (12 bushels of fine flour, 40 sheep, and 50 gallons of wine). Daniel smiled and said, 'Do not be deceived, O

king; for this is but clay inside and brass outside, and it never ate or drank anything.' (Bel 7)

The indignant king took Daniel to the temple to test his blasphemous statement. The priests retired and the king himself set out the food and wine in the chamber of the god. He then sealed the door. But before that Daniel had instructed his servants to strew ashes over the floor. Next morning the king removed the seals, opened the door and saw that the food and wine had disappeared. However, Daniel pointed to the floor where the footprints of the seventy priests, with their wives and children, were clearly visible. When the king had them arrested, they confessed that there was a secret entrance under the table, and that they came in every night with their families to eat the offerings. The king ordered them to be put to death, and authorized Daniel to destroy the idol and the temple.

THE DRAGON

In Babylon a sacred dragon or snake was worshipped as a god. As had happened with the god Bel, Daniel ridiculed this cult and affirmed the faith of his Lord. When the king remonstrated with him, Daniel obtained authority to try and kill the dragon, without using any weapon. He mixed pitch, fat and hair, baked cakes with them, and fed these cakes to the dragon until it burst and died.

The destruction of the temple of Bel, followed by the killing of the sacred dragon, aroused popular anger against the king, who found himself and his family threatened. To appease the mob, the king agreed that Daniel should be thrown into the lion-pit – a method then used to execute wrongdoers. The seven lions were accustomed to feed on two condemned men and two sheep each day, but this ration stopped while Daniel was in the pit.

In Judea, the prophet Habakkuk was on his way to the fields with a bowl of bread for the reapers. An angel appeared, took him by the hair, and carried him through the air to Babylon, putting him down next to the lion-pit. He called out 'Daniel! Daniel! Take the dinner which God has sent you.' (Bel 37) Daniel ate the food while Habakkuk was taken home the same way.

On the seventh day, the king came to the lion-pit to mourn his friend. To his astonishment Daniel was sitting in it, alive and well. The king draw him out, and gave praise to the Hebrew God who had saved him. Those who had accused Daniel were cast into the pit on the order of the king, 'and they were devoured immediately before his eyes'. (Bel 42) [Sus. 45–59, 60, 69; Book of Bel and the Dragon]

Darius III Codomannus (from the Persian 'he who upholds the good') 4 century BC. The last king of Persia, 336–1 BC, he was defeated by Alexander the Great at Arbela in 331 BC, thereby bringing the Persian empire to an end. [1 Macc. 1:1]

Demetrius   *1. Demetrius I Sober* (GK. 'saviour') Ruler of the Seleucid kingdom, 162–50 BC.

Demetrius seized the Seleucid throne in 162 BC from his cousin Antiochus V.

Judea was in the throes of the Maccabean revolt, led by Judas. Demetrius appointed a loyal and pro-Hellenist high priest in Jerusalem, Alcimus, and sent a military force under his general Bacchides to install Alcimus. Part of the troops were left behind in Jerusalem as a garrison.

During the next few years Demetrius sent several more military expeditions against Judas and later against his brother and successor Jonathan.

From 155 BC, Demetrius tried to win over Judea in his struggle against a rival claimant Alexander Balas, who finally ousted him in 150 BC when Demetrius

was killed in battle. [1 Macc. 7:1–9, 26; 8:31; 9:1, 57; 10:2–9; 15:22–50, 52, 67]
2. Demetrius II Nicator Ruler of the Seleucid kingdom, 145–38 BC and 129–5 BC.

Demetrius II, son of Demetrius I, wrested the Seleucid throne from his cousin Alexander Balas, with the help of an Egyptian army led by Ptolemy VI.

Demetrius marched south to Ptolemais (Acre) and summoned Jonathan, the high priest, who was besieging the Seleucid garrison in Jerusalem. Arriving with lavish gifts, Jonathan made a good impression on the king and was confirmed in his office, as well as being granted tax exemptions. Jonathan later came to the military aid of Demetrius, when the king was in trouble due to a revolt in his army. The disaffection was led by an ambitious general, Trypho, who subsequently succeeded in overthrowing Demetrius and installing in his stead Antiochus VI, the young son of Alexander Balas (145–2 BC).

Demetrius continued his struggle to regain the throne and succeeded in doing so in 129 BC, after ten years' captivity in Medea. This time he reigned for four years during the period that John Hyrcanus, the son of Simon the Maccabee, was high priest in Jerusalem. [1 Macc. 10:67, 69; 11:9–12, 19, 28–53, 55, 63; 12:24, 34; 13:34–40; 14:1–3, 38; 15:1, 22]

Demophon 2 century BC. A Syrian military governor in Palestine in the reign of Antiochus V who harassed the Jews. [2 Macc. 12:2]

Dositheus   *1.* 2 century BC. A fighting commander in the Maccabean army, he distinguished himself in the campaign of Judas Maccabeus against Timothy in Gilead. He and another commander captured Timothy but released him for fear of reprisals against Jewish hostages. [2 Macc. 12:19, 24]
2. 2 century BC. In a later battle with

the Idumeans, 'a certain Dositheus one of Bachenor's men' is described as a Jew of powerful physique, fighting on horseback. He seized Gorgias, the Syrian general, by his cloak and started to drag him away. A Thracian horseman rescued Gorgias by lopping off the arm of Dositheus. It is not clear whether he is the same person referred to in *1.* above. [2 Macc. 12:35]

3. c. 2 century BC. A Jewish priest who, together with his son Ptolemy, brought the Greek translation of the Book of Esther to Egypt in the fourth year of the reign of Ptolemy VIII and Cleopatra (probably 114 BC). The document is referred to in the text as 'Letter of Purim'. [Ad. Est. 11:1]

Edna (Heb. 'delight') *c.* 8 century BC. Edna was married to Raguel, a kinsman of Tobit. Their home was in the city of Ecbatana in Media. They had an only child, Sarah, who had been married seven times, but each time the bridegroom had been killed on the wedding night by the demon Asmodeus. When Tobias, the son of Tobit, arrived on a visit, he too married Sarah, but with the help of an angel exorcized the demon.

After the death of Tobit and his wife Anna in Nineveh, Tobias and Sarah rejoined Raguel and Edna in Ecbatana and took care of them until they died. [Tob. 7:2, 8, 14–18; 8:12; 10:12; 11:1; 14:13]

Eleazar (Heb. 'God has helped') *1. c.* 3 century BC. The father of Sirach who was the father of Jesus the sage and scribe. [Sir. 50:27]

2. c. 2 century BC. The father of Jason who was sent by Judas Maccabeus as an envoy to Rome. [1 Macc. 8:17]

3. c. 2 century BC. A venerable and dignified teacher of the Law in Jerusalem. When Antiochus IV Epiphanes decreed the suppression of the Jewish faith and forcible conversion to Greek paganism, the ninety-year-old sage was ordered to eat pork in public, or undergo flogging. Out of respect for him, the officials in charge privately offered to let him swallow meat acceptable to him, while only pretending to eat the pork. He proudly rejected this subterfuge, declaring that in any case he only had a little while to live, and was not prepared to appear in the eyes of the younger generation as a traitor to his faith. He died of the effects of the flogging then meted out to him. [2 Macc. 6:18–31]

4. 2 century BC. The fourth son of Mattathias the priest who started the Maccabean revolt in the village of Modi'in in 167 BC. Also called Avaran.

Five years after the start of the revolt, the Maccabeans were defeated by the Seleucid general Lysias at the battle of Beth-zechariah, south of Jerusalem. During the battle, Eleazar wrongly concluded that the largest of the war elephants, which was richly decorated in the royal colours, carried the young king Antiochus V, who had accompanied Lysias on the campaign. Eleazar carried out a bold single-handed attack on the animal. He fought his way through the phalanx of soldiers surrounding it, reached the elephant and from below rammed his spear into its belly. The great beast toppled over dead, and Eleazar was crushed beneath it. [1 Macc. 2:5; 6:43–48; 2 Macc. 8:23]

Eliab (Heb. 'God is father') date unknown. Ancestor of Judith. [Jdt. 8:1]

Elijah (Heb. 'my Lord is Jehovah') date unknown. Ancestor of Judith. [Jdt. 8:1]

Elkiah date unknown. Ancestor of Judith. [Jdt. 8:1]

Esdrias 2 century BC. A commander under Judas Maccabeus, mentioned in the battle in Idumea against the Syrian general Gorgias. [2 Macc. 12:36]

Esther (Pers. 'star') *c.* 5 century BC.

Jewish queen of King Artaxerxes (Xerxes I).

In the Greek or Septuagint version of the Book of Esther, additional passages were inserted in order to give the work a stronger religious tone, and to place more emphasis on the help of God in saving the Jews.

After Haman's edict ordering the extermination of the Jews, Mordecai asked Esther not only to speak to the king but also to 'invoke the Lord'. Esther took off her sumptuous robes, put on mourning, covered her head with ashes and dung, tore out her hair and addressed a fervent prayer to God, beseeching his intervention. In this inserted prayer Esther claimed that she got no pleasure out of her high position and the luxurious life of the court: 'thou knowest that I hate the splendour of the wicked and abhor the bed of the uncircumcised ...' (Ad. Est. 14:15)

Esther then took off her mourning attire and went in to the king, leaning on the arm of a maid because she felt weak and fearful. The added passage describes her interview with the king in greater detail, making Esther fall down in a faint, and God making the king well disposed towards her. This enabled Esther to bring about Haman's downfall and save her people. [Additions to the Book of Esther]

Eumenes (Gk. 'well-disposed') 2 century BC. King of Pergamum, 197–58 BC, he was an ally of the Romans when they defeated the Seleucid ruler Antiochus III at the battle of Magnesia (190 BC), and certain territories were ceded to him. He is mentioned in the eulogy to the Romans by Judas Maccabeus. [1 Macc. 8:8]

Eupolemus (Gk. 'skilful in war') 2 century BC. Eupolemus, son of John, and grandson of Accos, was one of two envoys sent by Judas Maccabeus to propose an alliance with Rome; the other

was Jason. They appeared before the Roman Senate about 162 BC, and a treaty of friendship and alliance was approved and inscribed on bronze for the envoys to take back as a permanent record. [1 Macc. 8:17–22; 2 Macc. 4:11]

Gabael *1.* date unknown. Gabael was an ancestor of Tobit, of the tribe of Naphtali [Tob. 1:1]

2. c. 8 century BC. Gabael, the son of Gabrias, was a relative of Tobit and lived in the Median town of Rages. Tobit, who had been employed by the king as a buyer of supplies in Media, had deposited ten talents of silver with Gabael. Then Assyria lost control of the trade routes to Media, and Tobit stopped journeying there.

Twenty years later, when Tobit was stricken with blindness and prayed for death, he sent his son to Media to collect the bags of silver. Tobias set out accompanied by the angel Raphael in the guise of a Jew called Azarias. They reached Ecbatana in Media, where Tobias married Sarah, the daughter of another kinsman of his father. Azarias travelled on his own to Rages, where Gabael produced and handed over the bags of silver with the seals still intact. He accompanied Azarias back to Ecbatana and took part in the wedding celebrations. [Tob. 1:14; 4:1, 20; 5:6; 9:2–6; 10:2]

Gaddi *see* JOHN *3.*

Gennaeus *c.* 2 century BC. Father of Apollonius, a Syrian governor and general in the reigns of Antiochus IV and Antiochus v. [2 Macc. 12:2]

Gideon (Heb. 'hewer') date unknown. Ancestor of Judith. [Jdt. 8:1]

Gorgias 2 century BC. Assyrian general under the Seleucid rulers Antiochus IV and Antiochus V.

Gorgias was one of three generals in command of the Seleucid army sent in

166 BC to crush the Maccabean revolt. While the main force remained in camp at Emmaus, in the Judean foothills, Gorgias led a detachment on a night march into the hills. But Judas Maccabeus and his men slipped away and captured the camp at Emmaus. Gorgias retreated southwards without giving battle.

Gorgias remained in command in the coastal district, and ignominiously repulsed an attack at Jamnia made by two Judean commanders, contrary to the orders of Judas.

In the Second Book of Maccabees, Gorgias is described as operating against Judea from the south, with the Idumeans. In battle, he was seized by the coat and dragged off by one of the Jews, but was saved by a Thracian horseman, who slashed off the arm of the assailant. [1 Macc. 3:38–40; 4:1–5; 5:59; 2 Macc. 8:9; 10:14; 12:32–37]

Hasadiah (Heb. 'beloved of God') date unknown. Ancestor of Baruch the disciple and scribe of Jeremiah. [Bar. 1:1]

Hegemonides (possibly from the Gk. 'guide') 2 century BC. A senior officer in the Syrian army who was left in command of the district from Ptolemais (Acre) to Gerar, when King Antiochus V and his general Lysias had to rush back to Antioch from their Judean campaign. [2 Macc. 13:24]

Heliodorus 2 century BC. Chief minister of the Seleucid ruler Seleucus IV Philopater, he was sent by the king to Jerusalem to confiscate the gold and silver in the Temple, but was driven off by an apparition in the form of a man on horseback in golden armour, and was severely flogged by two supernatural youths.

In 175 BC Heliodorus murdered his royal master and made an unsuccessful attempt to seize the throne. [2 Macc. 3:7–40; 4:1; 5:18]

Hieronymus 2 century BC. A Syrian military governor in Palestine in the reign of Antiochus V, he is mentioned as harassing the Jews. [2 Macc. 12:2]

Hilkiah (Heb. 'God's portion') *1.* date unknown. Ancestor of Judith. [Jdt. 8:1] *2.* date unknown. Ancestor of Baruch the disciple and scribe of Jeremiah. [Bar. 1:1]
3. c. 6 century BC. Father of Susanna, the beautiful and virtuous young wife who was falsely accused of adultery by two elders, but was acquitted when the young Daniel proved her innocence. This charming short tale is supposed to have taken place in a Jewish community in Babylon. [Sus. 1:2, 29, 63]

Holofernes (from the Gk. 'to be deceitful') *c.* 5 century BC. Assyrian general in the Book of Judith.

Holofernes, the Assyrian commander-in-chief, reached Bethulia in Judea at the head of a huge army and laid siege to it. Judith, who lived in the town, came into the Assyrian camp with her maid and was brought before the general. Captivated by her beauty, he believed her story that she had fled the city to escape its fate. He gave orders that she and her maid should be allowed to cross through the lines at night in order to pray. Judith had told him she would know from God when her fellow-townsmen had sinned by eating polluted food, thus exposing them to defeat.

Four days after Judith reached his camp, Holofernes gave a banquet for his retinue. He told his steward to persuade her to join them, 'For it will be a disgrace if we let such a woman go without enjoying her company, for if we do not embrace her she will laugh at us.' (Jdt. 12:12) Judith came to the feast dressed in all her finery, and the commander was filled with lust for her. He drank copiously, and by the time his staff withdrew and left the two of them alone, he was sprawled on the couch in a drunken sleep. Judith seized his sword and with two blows at the neck severed his head. She and her maid stole away with it, and safely reached Bethulia again.

The Assyrian troops panicked and fled, and Judea was saved. [Book of Judith]

Hyrcanus 2 century BC. The son of Tobias, a member of the wealthy Jewish land-owning family of Tobias, he had funds on deposit in the Temple. Onias the high priest explained this to Heliodorus, who had been sent by the Seleucid king to seize the Temple treasury. [2 Macc. 3:11]

Israel (Heb. 'who prevails with God') date unknown. Ancestor of Judith. [Jdt. 8:1]

Jason (Gk. 'to heal') *1.* 2 century BC. Son of Eleazar, he was one of two envoys sent by Judas Maccabeus to Rome to propose an alliance; the other envoy was Eupolemus. They appeared before the Roman Senate in about 162 BC, and a treaty of friendship and alliance was approved and inscribed on bronze for the envoys to take back as a permanent record.

This may be the same Jason mentioned as the father of Antipater, who was later sent by Jonathan on a similar mission to Rome. [1 Macc. 8:17–22; 12:16; 14:22]

2. c. 2 century BC. High priest in Jerusalem (175–2 BC)

Jason was the son of the high priest Simon II and the younger brother of the high priest Onias III. On the accession to the throne of Antiochus IV in 175 BC, Jason had himself appointed in place of his brother, by offering the new king a large sum of money.

Jason collaborated in introducing Hellenistic customs and undermining strict adherence to the ancestral Jewish faith. He constructed a gymnasium in the Temple area, and sent a sacrifice to the shrine of Hercules at Tyre in Phoenicia.

When Antiochus came to Jerusalem, he was lavishly entertained by Jason, although he was generally detested by the Jews for his repressive religious measures.

Three years after becoming high priest Jason was in his turn ousted by the corrupt Menelaus, who had heavily bribed the provincial governor. Jason took refuge across the Jordan river among the Ammonites, from where he made an abortive attempt to regain his position in Jerusalem by force. Taking refuge again over the Jordan, he was captured by the Arabian chief Aretas, but escaped and reached Egypt. From there he went to Sparta where he died. [2 Macc. 1:7, 4:7–27; 5:5–10]

Jathan *c.* 8 century BC. Descendant of the prophet Shemaiah. [Tob. 5:13]

Jeconiah *c.* 6 century BC. The name given in the Book of Baruch to the son of Jehoiakim, the Judean king carried away to captivity in Babylonia. In the introduction to his Book, Baruch claims to have read his work to Jeconiah (Jehoiachin). [Bar. 1:3]

Jehoiakim (Heb. 'God established') *c.* 6 century BC. High priest in Jerusalem in the time of the Babylonian exile. [Bar. 1:7]

Jeremiah (Heb. 'God will elevate') 7–6 century BC. The prophet Jeremiah appeared in a dream to Judas Maccabeus and handed him a golden sword from the Lord with which to crush the enemies of the Jews. [2 Macc. 15:14, 15]

Jesus, son of Sirach (Heb. 'God is salvation') *c.* 2 century BC. Author of the Wisdom Book that bears his name.

The work known as the Wisdom of Jesus the son of Sirach (or Joshua Ben Sira in the Hebrew form) was originally written in Hebrew in Palestine, early in the 2nd century BC. From the 3rd century AD the book also became known in the Christian church as 'Ecclesiasticus', a Latin word that simply means 'church book' – an indication of the liturgical importance attached to it.

In the preface added to the Greek version by the anonymous translator from the Hebrew, he states that he is a grandson of the author and that he settled in Egypt in the thirty-eighth year of the reign of King Euergetes. This would no doubt be Ptolemy VII Euergetes, and the date would thus correspond to 132 BC. The original may therefore have been written about half a century earlier. This would have enabled Jesus son of Sirach to know the renowned high priest Simon II, to whom a glowing tribute is paid in the book.

In his preface, the translator sums up the nature of the work: '... my grandfather Jesus, after devoting himself especially to the reading of the law and the prophets and the other books of our fathers, and after acquiring considerable proficiency in them, was himself also led to write something pertaining to instruction and wisdom, in order that, by becoming conversant with this also, those who love learning should make even greater progress in living according to the law.' (Sir., Prologue)

Jesus son of Sirach lived at a time when Judea was part of the Seleucid kingdom, ruled from Antioch. Among the Jews there was a strong current of assimilation to the Hellenistic way of life, in language, dress, customs, religious practices and philosophical ideas. Jesus son of Sirach was clearly a learned teacher and devout Jew, not unfamiliar with Greek ideas, but keen to reaffirm the traditional Jewish concepts and values. His work is a synthesis of the trends in Hebrew thought that had evolved down the centuries: the formal system of the Mosaic Code, the deep religious emotion of the prophets, and the practical sagacity of the sages. The relationship of wisdom to religion is stated in the opening verse of the Book, 'All wisdom comes from the Lord and is with him for ever' (Sir. 1:1).

This Book belongs to the Hebrew wisdom literature, that includes Proverbs, Job, Ecclesiastes, and another apocryphal work written in Alexandria, the Wisdom of Solomon. Like Proverbs and Ecclesiastes, the Wisdom of Jesus son of Sirach does not form a unified and organic work. It is a loose anthology in fifty-one chapters containing short discourses, sayings and maxims on a variety of unrelated topics, and eulogies of national figures in Israelite history. It ends with a poem in which the author speaks of his lifelong quest for wisdom:

'My heart was stirred to seek her,
    therefore I have gained a good
    possession.
The Lord gave me a tongue as my
    reward, and I will praise him with it.
Draw near to me, you who are
    untaught, and lodge in my school.'
                        (Sir. 51:21–3)

Until recently the book was known only in its Greek translation. In 1896, an astounding collection of old Hebrew manuscripts came to light in the 'genizah' or storehouse for discarded sacred books, belonging to a Cairo synagogue. Two learned English ladies acquired some pages from the genizah, which included portions of Sirach in Hebrew. Some scholars maintained that these pages were not a copy of the original Hebrew, but were translated back from the Greek. However, in Professor Yigael Yadin's 1963–5 archaeological expedition on the Masada Rock next to the Dead Sea, one of the finds was twisted fragments of a scroll which turned out to be from the Wisdom of Jesus son of Sirach in Hebrew. It obviously belonged to the Zealots who died defending the Masada fortress against the Romans in AD 73. Since the text was almost identical with the genizah fragments, the latter may now be regarded as copied from the original Hebrew. [Book of Sirach]

Joakim *1. c.* 6 century BC. Husband of Susanna, he was a rich and respected member of a Jewish community in Babylon. His home was a meeting place for the important members of the community and two of them, who were elders and judges, fell in love with Susanna. When she repulsed them, they falsely accused her of adultery. Her innocence was proved by the young Daniel and she was restored to Joakim and their children. [Sus. 1, 4, 6, 28, 29, 63]

2. c. 5 century BC. High priest in Jerusalem, and as such the national leader of Judea, he governed with the aid of an assembly of elders referred to as the Senate.

When the Assyrian army under Holofernes appeared in the northern part of the country, Joakim and the elders decided to resist. They issued orders that the towns and villages on the heights should be fortified, supplies of food stored, and the narrow passes into the hills defended.

The Assyrians besieged the town of Bethulia where Judith lived, and cut off the water supply. The situation was saved by her beauty and courage. She gained Holofernes's confidence, and cut off his head while he was in a drunken sleep. The Assyrian troops fled in panic and were pursued and slaughtered by the Israelites.

Joakim and the members of the senate travelled to Bethulia to help celebrate this victory, and to bestow praise on Judith for saving the country. In addressing her Joakim said: 'You are the exaltation of Jerusalem, you are the great glory of Israel, you are the great pride of our nation!' (Jdt. 15:9) [Jdt. 4:6–15;15:8–10]

John (from the Heb. 'the Lord has been gracious') *1. c.* 3 century BC. Father of Mattathias. [1 Macc. 2:1]

2. c. 3 century BC. Father of Eupolemus, he obtained concessions for the Jews from Antiochus III. [I Macc. 8:17; 2 Macc. 4:11]

3. 2 century BC. Eldest son of Mattathias. John (also known as Joseph and as Gaddi, meaning 'fortunate'), was the eldest of five sons of Mattathias the priest, the others being Simon, Judas, Eleazar and Jonathan. When Mattathias raised the banner of revolt in the village of Modi'in, in 167 BC, all his sons fled with him into the Judean hills, where they operated as a guerrilla band.

John does not seem to have possessed the qualities of leadership. After his father's death, he served first under Judas and then under Jonathan. John was sent by Jonathan to ask the friendly Nabateans, east of the Dead Sea, to take care of the baggage. His convoy was attacked by local tribesmen, who killed John and his men and made off with the baggage. Jonathan took his revenge by attacking a marriage procession of that tribe. [1 Macc. 2:2; 9:35–8; 2 Macc. 8:22]

4. 2 century BC. An envoy sent by Judas Maccabeus to Lysias with a letter for Antiochus v. [2 Macc. 11:17]

5. 2 century BC. High priest and ruler of Judea from 134–04 BC.

John Hyrcanus was the son of Simon, the last surviving brother of Judas Maccabeus, who was high priest and ethnarch of Judea from 143–34 BC. Simon made John commander of the Judean armed forces. John and his brother Judas routed the forces of Antiochus VII Sidetes, commanded by the Syrian general Cendebeus in the coastal plain near Jamnia. Not long after, Simon and two of his sons, Judas and Mattathias, were murdered by his son-in-law Ptolemy who was the military commander in Jericho. Ptolemy sought to make himself ruler of Judea. But John Hyrcanus, who was in charge of the garrison at Gazara, foiled an attempt to assassinate him. He became high priest and ruler in succession to his father.

By military and political successes, John was able to expand the territory of Judea, and to strengthen its autonomy.

The first Book of Maccabees ends with the death of Simon, the high priest and his succession by John Hyrcanus. [1 Macc. 13:53, 16]

Jonathan (Heb. 'given by God') *1*. 2 century BC. Youngest son of Mattathias and Maccabean leader after Judas.

Jonathan (also called Apphus meaning 'favoured') was the youngest son of Mattathias, the priest of Modi'in who started the Maccabean revolt against Antiochus IV, in the year 167 BC. With his father and his brothers John, Simon, Judas and Eleazar, Jonathan fled into the hills and took part in the partisan activities. When Judas was defeated and killed in 161 BC, the surviving Maccabeans elected Jonathan as their new leader. They took refuge in the wilderness of Tekoa between the Hebron hills and the Dead Sea.

The Seleucid general Bacchides led a strong force in search of the Maccabeans, and trapped them at the northern end of the Dead Sea, between the Jordan river and the marshes. Jonathan and his supporters fought their way out and swam across the river to safety. After fortifying the area round Jerusalem, Bacchides returned to Antioch, and for the next two years the military pressure on the Maccabeans was relaxed. They took advantage of this respite to occupy the abandoned stronghold of Bethbasi, just south of Bethlehem. Bacchides returned and laid siege to this fortress. Jonathan slipped away with some of his men, and attacked the Seleucid force from the rear, with the help of local tribes. At the same time, Simon led a sortie from the fortress and set fire to the siege engines. After this setback Bacchides again withdrew to Syria. Jonathan sent envoys to negotiate a truce. As a result, he was able to establish his headquarters at Michmash, north of Jerusalem, and

gradually to gain control of Judea, except for Jerusalem and the Beth-zur fortress south of it. 'And Jonathan began to judge the people, and he destroyed the ungodly out of Israel.' (1 Macc. 9:73)

During the next few years, Jonathan skilfully exploited the dynastic struggle in the Seleucid kingdom between Demetrius I and the rival claimant Alexander Balas. Both sides sought Judean support by making far-reaching concessions to Jonathan. He was able to regain Jerusalem, become recognized as high priest and governor and expand the borders of Judea from Lydda to beyond the Jordan river. An army sent against Judea by a new ruler, Demetrius II, was defeated at Jamnia by Jonathan and Simon. Judea had become practically autonomous with its Seleucid power marked only by a small annual tribute and by the continued presence of a small garrison in the Jerusalem citadel.

In 144 BC, Jonathan fought another crucial battle against the forces of Demetrius II, which advanced into the Galilee highlands. At Hazor, in northeastern Galilee, the Seleucid army set an ambush and caught the Judean forces in a pincer movement. A large part of Jonathan's army was routed, but he and his two commanders rallied the rest and fought back until the day was won.

Jonathan now sent two envoys to Rome, and obtained from the Senate a renewal of the treaty of alliance that had been negotiated at the time of his brother Judas. On their way home, the envoys stopped in Sparta (Greece) and delivered a message from Jonathan to his Spartan 'brothers' recalling a friendly letter that had been received from the Spartan king by an earlier high priest in Jerusalem.

Demetrius again despatched a large force against Judea. Jonathan marched up into Syria in order to meet the enemy in the district of Hamath, before they reached his own borders. They withdrew and Jonathan marched back through Damascus, collecting on the way a small Jewish community that was in distress.

A ruthless and ambitious army commander called Trypho emerged as the strong man in Antioch, and planned to seize the throne. He decided that a strong Judea would be a threat to him, and led an army southward through Syria to subdue the Jews. On reaching Scythopolis (Beth-shean), he found Jonathan waiting for him with 40,000 men, and shrank from the military confrontation. Instead, he lured Jonathan into Ptolemais (Acre) with false protestations of friendship, and there took him prisoner, killing his bodyguard.

This blow left the Jews confused and dejected. Simon, the second of the Maccabean brothers, now took command and rallied his people. Trypho advanced on Jerusalem from the south, but then abandoned the Judean campaign. On his way back, he had Jonathan put to death. It was the year 142 BC. The Jewish struggle for independence was to be carried on by Simon, the last of the five Maccabean brothers left alive. Simon had the body of Jonathan exhumed and brought to the family tomb at Modi'in for burial. [1 Macc. 2:5; 5:17, 24, 25; 9; 10; 11; 12:53; 13:8–25; 2 Macc. 8:22]

2. 2 century BC. Son of Absalom, who was an officer under Simon the Maccabean. [1 Macc. 13:11]

Joseph (Heb. 'may [God] add [children]') *1.* date unknown. An ancestor of Judith, he was the son of Oziel. [Jdt. 8:1]

2. 2 century BC. Judean commander under Judas Maccabeus.

Son of Zechariah, he was one of two senior commanders who were left in charge in Jerusalem in 163 BC, while Judas Maccabeus and his brother Jonathan were campaigning east of the Jordan, and another brother, Simon, was in Galilee. Joseph and Azariah were eager to prove themselves as generals, and contrary to Judas's instructions, they led an expedition against Jamnia in the coastal plain. Here they were routed by the redoubtable Seleucid general Gorgias, and fled back to Jerusalem. [1 Macc. 5:18, 55–62]
3. see JOHN *3.*

Judas (Gk. from Heb. *Judah*)
1. Judas Maccabeus (probably from the Heb. 'hammer') 2 century BC. Third son of Mattathias and leader of the Maccabean revolt.

Judas (the Greek form of *Judah*) was the third of five remarkable brothers, the others being John, Simon, Eleazar and Jonathan. Their father Mattathias was the priest of the village of Modi'in situated on the coastal plain seventeen miles north-west of Jerusalem. Judas afterwards acquired the nickname of Maccabeus ('the hammer') and as a result, the family and their followers became known as the Maccabeans.

Judea at that time was part of the realm of the able and ambitious Seleucid king Antiochus IV Epiphanes, who ruled from Antioch on the Syrian coast from 175–63 BC. He belonged to the dynasty founded by Seleucus, one of the generals amongst whom Alexander the Great had divided his empire 150 years earlier. From Alexander's time, Hellenistic influence had steadily increased in the whole region. The Greek language became fashionable as well as Greek dress, social customs, athletic pursuits and religious cults. In Judea this assimilationist trend was resisted by orthodox groups that clung firmly to the ancestral faith and the traditional way of life. Antiochus, an intense admirer of all things Greek, was determined to Hellenize the peoples over whom he ruled. This urge was sharpened by his abortive attempt to gain control of Egypt.

Antiochus took harsh measures to stamp out the Jewish faith. Its practice was banned, including Sabbath observance and the right of circumcision. Jerusalem was occupied and many of its inhabitants butchered. The Temple was desecrated with swine sacrificed on the altar and a statue of Jupiter set up in the Holy of Holies.

When one of the king's officials came to Modi'in to enforce worship of the Greek gods, he was killed by Mattathias who then fled into the hills with his sons and followers and launched a partisan movement. In this year of 167 BC the banner of revolt had been raised.

The Maccabeans established a guerrilla base in the Gophna hills, a rugged area of boulders, ravines and bush halfway between Jerusalem and Samaria, then the Seleucid provincial centre. They were joined by other outlaws, and raided the Jewish villages in the region, knocking down pagan altars, circumcising male children and fanning the spirit of rebellion.

In this mountain refuge, the dying Mattathias appointed Judas as the military leader. The old man was buried in the ancestral tomb at Modi'in. (Eighteen rock-cut tombs in the vicinity are by tradition associated with the Maccabeans.)

Apollonius, the military governor in Samaria, led out a force to crush the insurgents. It was ambushed and routed by Judas and his men on the steep incline of Lebonah at the edge of the Gophna hills. Apollonius was killed; Judas took his sword and used it for the rest of his life. The Maccabeans were greatly elated at this first success against regular troops.

After this startling blow, the Seleucid authorities began to take the rebellion seriously. The countryside was aflame and Jerusalem practically cut off. The regional commander, Seron, now led an army against the Maccabeans. As the troops toiled up the path of Beth-horon from the coastal plain, the hearts of Judas's men sank at the overwhelming disparity in numbers. He said to them firmly, 'It is not on the size of the army that victory in battle depends, but strength comes from Heaven ... we fight for our lives and our laws.' (1 Macc. 3:19, 21) Judas launched a surprise attack, broke through the advancing force, and pursued it southward towards the coast. The day was won and only then did Judas allow his followers to be diverted by the plunder: 'much gold and silver, and cloth dyed blue and sea purple, and great riches' (1 Macc. 4:23). This was in 165 BC, two years after the revolt had started in Modi'in.

In the following year, Lysias the regent himself commanded another expedition. He skirted round the foothills of the Shephelah and advanced towards Jerusalem from the south, where the terrain was easier and occupied by the loyal Idumeans. Judas waited for the Seleucid force at Beth-zur, on the highway between Bethlehem and Hebron. Here he launched a swift attack and the enemy was repulsed.

The access to Jerusalem from the south now lay open to the Maccabeans. They entered the city and cut off the garrison in the citadel. Judas devoted himself to restoring and purifying the Temple, which had been disused for three-and-a-half years and was in a state of neglect. 'And they saw the sanctuary desolate, the altar profaned, and the gates burned. In the courts they saw bushes sprung up as in a thicket, or as on one of the mountains. They saw also the chambers of the priests in ruins.' (1 Macc. 4:38)

When the building had been restored and a new stone altar constructed in place of the one that had been defiled, a day was set aside for the rededication of the Temple. This took place on the twenty-fifth day of Chislev, the ninth month of the Hebrew calendar. It was a joyous occasion, with music, singing and prayers of thanksgiving and praise. It was ordained that every year on that day the feast of Hanukkah (dedication) would commence and would be observed for eight days.

A dramatic moment in the celebration was the rekindling of the great eight-branched Temple candelabrum. According to the accepted Jewish legend, a search in the Temple revealed only one small jar of the specially prepared oil that was used for the candelabrum, and had to be sealed by the high priest himself. It was only sufficient for one night, but by a miracle the oil replenished itself and lasted for the eight days. Hanukkah is also called the Feast of Lights.

Judas had Mount Zion fortified to withstand another attack, and also built a fortress at Beth-zur to block the road from Idumea. He then carried out a series of swift campaigns against hostile neighbours. First he marched southward against the Idumeans (Edomites), the 'sons of Esau' who had occupied southern Judea after the fall of Jerusalem. Having defeated them and taken booty, he attacked the Beonites, a marauding tribe near the Dead Sea, and swung eastward across the Jordan against the Ammonites.

The main expedition east of the Jordan was aimed at Gilead, to relieve and evacuate the Jewish communities trapped in a number of fortified cities there. They had written to Judas appealing for help. With his brother Jonathan and eight thousand men, Judas crossed the river and marched three days across the desert, through an area inhabited by friendly Nabateans. He conquered the town of Bozrah, in the land of Nob east of Gilead. The defending army commanded by Timothy fled towards the north-east, in the direction of the Sea of Galilee. The Maccabean forces followed them, and took and ravaged one town after another. In another pitched battle at Raphon, Timothy's reorganized troops were again routed.

The Jewish inhabitants of Gilead were assembled, and evacuated through the Beth-shean valley and the Samarian hills to Jerusalem. At the same time, Simon with three thousand men swung through the Galilee highlands and brought the Jews to safety from that district.

Judas won one more battle against Timothy at Jazer, to the east of the Jericho ford, and the enemy commander was killed.

After his return from the successful Transjordan campaign, Judas carried out expeditions to the south and south-west of Jerusalem, capturing Hebron, destroying a pagan temple at Azotub near the coast, and setting fire to the ships in the ports of Joppa and Jamnia.

Antiochus Epiphanes died during a campaign in Persia, in 163 BC. Lysias had the young prince declared king as Antiochus V Eupator.

In Jerusalem, Judas laid siege to the citadel, which was still held by his Hellenist opponents. They appealed for help to the new king, and Lysias arrived in Judea with a large army, including some of the royal elephants brought from India after the death of Alexander. Once again, Lysias made a detour in order to march on Jerusalem from the south through Idumean territory, where the hills were less rugged. Battle was joined at Beth-zechariah, half-way between Hebron and Jerusalem. Eleazar, the fourth of the Maccabean brothers, attacked and slew one of the war elephants, but was crushed when it toppled over on top of him. The Judeans had to retreat before an overwhelming force. Judas and his followers abandoned Jerusalem, and took to the hills again in the Gophna region.

In 162 BC the throne was seized by another claimant, Demetrius I. His general Bacchides occupied Jerusalem and installed a Jewish priest Alcimus, as high priest and governor. Later, a force commanded by the Seleucid general Nicanor was sent to the aid of Alcimus. In 161 BC Nicanor was surprised by Judas at Adasa, and fell in battle. The remnants of his men fled into the royal fortress at Gazara in the foothills, pursued by the Maccabeans and the local villagers. This victory was later celebrated in Jewish tradition as 'the Day of Nicanor'.

Realizing that he and his followers would not be able to hold out indefinitely against Seleucid armies, Judas decided to invoke the power of the Romans. He sent two envoys to Rome, who appeared before the Roman Senate and said: 'Judas, who is also called Maccabeus, and his brothers and the people of the Jews have sent us to you to establish alliance and peace with you ...' (1 Macc. 8:20) The Romans were not averse to backing a rebellion that weakened and disrupted the Seleucid kingdom from within. The Senate approved a treaty and a mutual defence pact with the Jews. At the same time, a Roman message was sent to King Demetrius warning him that further attempts to crush Judea might lead to Roman intervention.

This development made it urgent for Demetrius to quell the revolt and assert his authority over the Judean province. Bacchides was despatched again with powerful forces. He marched through Galilee, Samaria and Judea to Jerusalem, with Judas keeping out of his way. Bacchides then set out to destroy the Maccabean stronghold in the Gophna hills. Judas was left with no option but to attack greatly superior forces. At the battle of Elasa, north of Jerusalem, Judas forced the Seleucid right wing to retreat. The left wing counter-attacked and cut off the Maccabeans, who were then overrun. Judas himself was killed and his followers scattered. His brothers Simon and Jonathan were able to retrieve his body, and buried it in the family tomb at Modi'in. 'And all Israel made great lamentation for him; they mourned many days, and said "How is the mighty fallen, the saviour of Israel!"' (1 Macc. 9:20–1) In his place, his brother Jonathan was chosen as leader.

After the defeat and death of Judas, less determined men would have given up what seemed a hopeless struggle. But the Maccabeans remained inspired by Judas's dauntless spirit, and were to carry on the fight in the years ahead.

For the Jews, Judas Maccabeus has remained a national hero and a symbol of a never-ending struggle for political and religious freedom. [1 Book of Maccabees; 2 Book of Maccabees]

2. 2 century BC. Son of Chalphi, he was one of the commanders under Jonathan the high priest and Maccabean leader. When Jonathan's forces were routed by the army of Demetrius II in the battle of Hazor in the Galilee, Judas was one of the few who fought on with him, until the others rallied and the enemy was defeated. [1 Macc. 11:70]

3. 2 century BC. Son of Simon the high priest. Together with his brother John, he commanded the Judean force that defeated the Syrian general Cendebeus near Jamnia on the coastal plain in the year 138 BC. Judas was wounded in this engagement. He was later murdered together with his father Simon and brother Mattathias by his ambitious brother-in-law Ptolemy the son of Abubus. [1 Macc. 16:2, 9, 14]

Judith (Heb. 'from Judah') c. 5 century BC. A patriotic widow who saved her people.

Judith was the young wife of Manasseh, a well-to-do farmer of the town of Bethulia, in the northern part of the hills of Ephraim in Judea. She was beautiful, intelligent and devout. One day her husband died of sun-stroke during the reaping of the harvest. Judith did not remarry but remained in mourning, and lived quietly on the farm. She spent much of her time secluded in a shelter she had constructed on the roof of the house.

A huge Assyrian army, commanded by Holofernes, invaded Judea from the north and camped in the Esdraelon valley before Bethulia. The Judeans were in a state of great alarm, but the high priest Joakim and the senate in Jerusalem decided to resist. The Samarian towns and villages on the mountain tops were fortified; food was stored, and the narrow passes through the hill-country were guarded. For several days the high priest and the people, dressed in sackcloth and ashes, prayed and fasted at the Temple. 'So the Lord heard their prayers and looked upon their affliction.' (Jdt. 4:13)

Holofernes asked the leaders of his local auxiliary forces, 'Tell me, you Canaanites, what people is this that lives in the hill country? What cities do they inhabit? How large is their army, and in what does their power or strength consist? Who rules over them as king, leading their army? And why have they alone, of all who live in the west, refused to come out and meet me?' (Jdt. 5:3–4)

Achior, the Ammonite chief, related the history of the Hebrew nation and explained that it was under God's protection and could not be defeated. The angry Holofernes had him bound and thrown down near the gate of Bethulia so that he should share its fate. The city was surrounded and its water supply cut off. The invaders then settled down to wait for the inhabitants to surrender from hunger and thirst.

In Bethulia the water available from cisterns was strictly rationed, but gave out after thirty-four days of blockade. 'Their children lost heart, and the women and young men fainted from thirst and fell down in the streets of the city and in the passages through the gates; there was no strength left in them any longer.' (Jdt. 7:22)

The magistrates agreed to surrender if the Lord did not send help within five days. Judith upbraided them, pointing out that if Bethulia fell, the whole of Judea would be conquered and laid waste. She had her own plan to save

them. After praying fervently to the Lord, she discarded her widow's weeds, dressed in her brightest clothes, put on her jewelry and perfumed herself. She then left the house with her maid and persuaded the city elders to open the gate for them. They were seen to cross the valley in the direction of the enemy camp.

The two women reached the Assyrian outposts and were seized and questioned by the sentries. Judith told them that she had fled from the town to escape its fate. She had important information for the general, since she could tell him of secret routes whereby all the hill country could be occupied without losses. They were escorted to the tent of Holofernes who was lying down under a mosquito net richly decorated with jewels. He rose to greet her; Judith prostrated herself and was raised up by the attendants.

Judith told the commander that the hungry citizens of Bethulia would soon lose divine protection by eating prohibited food. They would then be helpless before the Assyrian advance. She would herself guide Holofernes all the way to Jerusalem and see him crowned king there. Captivated by her beauty, he believed her story. He promised that she would be properly treated and gave instructions to the guards to let Judith and her maid pass freely through the lines to pray to the Lord in the open. In this way she would find out when the Israelites had sinned.

For the next three days Judith went out each evening to the spring, bathed herself and prayed. She refused Holofernes's invitation to share his meals, as she had brought her own food prepared in accordance with Jewish dietary laws.

On the fourth day Holofernes invited his personal retinue to feast with him. Judith readily agreed to join them. Dressed in all her finery, she reclined in front of Holofernes on the fleeces her maid had spread for her. The Assyrian general could hardly control his passion for her. He ate and drank with abandon, and by the time all the attendants retired and left Judith alone with him, he lay sprawled drunk on the couch.

Praying silently for strength, Judith drew Holofernes's sword from the scabbard hung at the bed-head, grasped his hair and with all her force struck twice at his neck, lopping off the head. She rolled the body on to the floor and pulled down the rich canopy to take with her. As she went out, she handed the severed head to the waiting maid, who put it in the food-bag. The two of them left the camp unhindered, as if they were going out to pray as usual. They made their way across the valley and up the hill to the city gate of Bethulia.

Judith called out to the sentries, who let her in. Ussiah and the other elders were hurriedly summoned from their homes. Judith held up Holofernes's head and praised the Lord who had delivered her people through her. She swore that 'it was my face that tricked him to his destruction, and yet he committed no act of sin with me, to defile and shame me'. (Jdt. 13:16)

At dawn a number of armed Israelites sallied out from the gate, pretending they were about to attack the enemy camp. As Judith had foreseen, the Assyrians sprang to arms and the senior officers ran to the tent of the commander-in-chief. The steward went in to arouse him, and rushed out screaming that his master's body was lying on the floor decapitated. Consternation spread through the camp, and the men started running away in panic. A great number were slaughtered in the pursuit, and huge quantities of abandoned baggage and supplies were distributed as booty.

The high priest Joakim and the members of the senate came personally from Jerusalem to visit Bethulia after the victory. They added their voices in praise of Judith, calling her 'the great glory of Israel' (Jdt. 15:9). Judith led the women in a dance of thanksgiving and sang a hymn to God: 'Woe to the nations that rise up against my people! The Lord Almighty will take vengeance on them in the day of judgment.' (Jdt. 16:17) The silver, furnishings and other belongings in Holofernes's tent were given to Judith. Having come to Jerusalem to share in the rejoicing, she handed these costly possessions over to the Temple as a gift.

Judith returned to Bethulia and resumed her quiet way of life on the farm, refusing all offers of marriage. The maid who had accompanied her in her amazing exploit was given her liberty. During the rest of Judith's lifetime Judea remained at peace and was not invaded by foreign armies. She died at the ripe age of 105 and was buried at the side of her husband Manasseh.

It is probable that the story was composed in the time of the Hasmonean ruler and high priest John Hyrcanus I (134–04 BC). In 108–7 BC John Hyrcanus besieged the city of Samaria, and a Seleucid (Syrian) army sent to relieve it was defeated. The Book of Judith may have been inspired by this episode, which would account for its patriotic theme and spirit. Bethulia is an imaginary name. [Book of Judith]

Lasthenes 2 century BC. When Demetrius II, ruler of the Seleucid kingdom, reached an agreement with the Maccabean leader Jonathan, whereby Judea was exempted from tax levies, he sent Jonathan a copy of a letter of instruction to 'our kinsman Lasthenes' about the matter. He was presumably a high official in charge of the royal finances. The historian Josephus later suggested that Lasthenes was the Cretan commander of the mercenaries who helped Demetrius gain the throne by ousting King Alexander Balas. The word 'kinsman' in the letter was only a courtesy term used for a close associate. [1 Macc. 11:31, 32]

Lucius 2 century BC. Roman consul in the time of Simon the Maccabee.

When Simon succeeded his brother Jonathan as high priest and leader in Jerusalem, he sent a special envoy to Rome, with the gift of a gold shield, to renew the alliance maintained with the Romans by his brothers Judas and Jonathan. The envoy came back with the copy of a letter sent by Lucius to the rulers of the surrounding countries, including King Ptolemy in Egypt and King Demetrius in Antioch. The letter warned against making war upon 'our friends and allies the Jews' or harbouring traitors from Judea. The powerful protection of Rome assisted Simon in gaining autonomy for Judea under the Hasmonean dynasty to which he belonged. [1 Macc. 15:16–24]

Lysias 2 century BC. A Seleucid general in the reigns of Antiochus IV and Antiochus V.

When Antiochus IV was preparing a campaign against Persia in 165 BC, he left his kinsman Lysias in charge of the kingdom and as tutor to his young son Antiochus. The king died during this expedition, and Lysias had the boy assume the throne immediately as Antiochus V, while himself wielding the real power.

Lysias despatched an army to subdue the Maccabean revolt in Judea. Judas Maccabeus defeated this force at the battle of Emmaus.

In the next year, 164 BC, Lysias himself headed an expeditionary force against Judea. He marched down the coastal plain and made a detour in order to reach Jerusalem from the south through the Hebron hills, where the terrain was less difficult and the area was occupied by friendly Idumeans. Judas waited for the Seleucid force at Bethzur, on the highway between Bethel and Hebron. Here he launched a swift attack and the troops of Lysias were repulsed. The Maccabeans were now able to enter Jerusalem, and rededicate the Temple.

Two years later, Lysias again marched into Judea at the head of a large army. In the battle of Beth-zechariah, to the north of Beth-zur, the Maccabean forces under Judas were defeated, and his brother Eleazar was killed. Lysias occupied Jerusalem but withdrew northwards when his rival Philip seized Antioch, the capital. Later, he was defeated by another claimant to the throne, Demetrius I Soter, and both he and Antiochus V were killed by their own troops. [1 Macc. 3:32–60; 4:1–35; 6; 7:1–4; 2 Macc. 11:1–26; 12:1; 13:26; 14:1, 2]

Lysimachus *1.* 2 century BC. He was the brother of Menelaus the corrupt high priest in Jerusalem, in the reign of Antiochus IV Epiphanes. When Menelaus was summoned to Antioch, Lysimachus was left in charge of the Temple and plundered its treasury. In the public riots provoked by his actions, he was killed by the mob. [2 Macc. 4:29, 39–42]
2. c. 2 century BC. Lysimachus, an Alexandrian Jew, translated the canonical Book of Esther from Hebrew into Greek. [Ad. Est. 11:1]

Maccabeus *see* JUDAS *1.*

Macron *see* PTOLEMY *2.*

Manasseh (Heb. 'forgetting') *c.* 5 century BC. Husband of the beautiful and brave Judith, he was a well-to-do farmer of the town of Bethulia, in Ephraim. During the time of the barley harvest, he suffered sunstroke and died. Judith was faithful to his memory, and refused to remarry. [Jdt. 8:2, 3, 7; 16:22–4]

Mattathias (Heb. 'gift of the Lord') *1.* 2 century BC. Jewish priest of Modi'in who started the Maccabean Revolt.

Mattathias, the son of John, was a priest of the Joarib family in Jerusalem. He settled in the village of Modi'in, situated on the coastal plain half-way between the sea and the Judean hills. (It is not far from the present Lod airport.) He had five sons: John, Simon, Judas, Eleazar and Jonathan.

At that time there was religious persecution of the Jews by the Seleucid ruler Antiochus IV Epiphanes. The Temple in Jerusalem had been defiled, the practice of the Jewish faith banned, and the worship of Greek gods made compulsory.

Special commissioners were sent around the districts of Judea to enforce this programme of Hellenizing the Jews. One such official came to Modi'in. The villagers gathered in the square where an altar had been placed for a sacrifice to the Greek gods. Mattathias and his sons stood sullenly to one side. The officer called out to him, promising him riches and the favour of the king if he would set a lead as a respected figure in the community. Mattathias flung back defiantly: 'We will not obey the king's words by turning aside from our religion to the right hand or to the left.' (1 Macc. 2:22) At that moment an obsequious villager sidled forward to comply. This was too much for Mattathias who leapt upon him and killed him at the altar. He then spun round and killed the king's official. Mattathias rushed along the street shouting to the faithful to follow him. He and his sons and some of the townspeople fled into the Judean hills, abandoning their homes and possessions. Thus, in the year 167 BC, the banner of revolt was raised.

The Maccabeans (so named after the most famous of the sons, Judas Maccabeus), established a guerrilla base in the Gophna hills, north-west of Jerusalem. From here they raided the surrounding countryside, destroying pagan altars and arousing a spirit of resistance among the people.

It was in their mountain refuge that Mattathias died the following year, 166 BC. On his deathbed he exhorted his sons to carry on with the struggle for freedom: 'show zeal for the law, and give your lives for the covenant of our fathers' (1 Macc. 2:50). He told them to heed the counsel of the wise Simon, and to accept the strong and brave Judas as their military commander.

Mattathias was buried by his sons in the family tomb in Modi'in, and they carried on with the fight he had launched.

The descendants of Mattathias who ruled over Judea for more than a century, from 141 BC onwards, became known as the Hasmonean dynasty, from the name associated with Mattathias's grandfather Simeon. [1 Macc. 2]
2. 2 century BC. The son of Absalom, he was one of the commanders under Jonathan the high priest and Maccabean leader. When Jonathan's forces were routed by the army of Demetrius II in the battle of Hazor in Galilee, Mattathias was one of the few who fought on with him, until the others rallied and defeated the enemy. [1 Macc. 11:70]
3. 2 century BC. Mattathias and his brother Judas were murdered together with their father Simon, the high priest, in the year 138 BC by their ambitious brother-in-law Ptolemy, the son of Abubus. [1 Macc. 16:14-16]
4. 2 century BC. One of three envoys sent by the Syrian general Nicanor to come to terms with Judas Maccabeus. [2 Macc. 14:19]

Melchiel c. 5 century BC. Father of Charmis, a city magistrate in the time of Judith. [Jdt. 6:15]

Menelaus 2 century BC. High priest in Jerusalem, 172-62 BC.

In the reign of Antiochus IV, Menelaus succeeded by bribery in ousting the high priest Jason and getting himself appointed instead. He arranged for the murder of the revered former high priest Onias III who had denounced him.

Menelaus helped Antiochus IV despoil the Temple and carry off its treasures. Later, charges were laid against him before the king by leading citizens of Jerusalem, but he saved himself by bribery.

Menelaus was apparently dismissed when Judas Maccabeus entered Jerusalem and purified the Temple. Eventually he was condemned to death by the Seleucid general Lysias and executed by being thrown from a a high water tower into hot ashes. [2 Macc. 4:23–34, 39, 43–50; 5:15, 23; 11:29–32; 13:3–8]

Menestheus *c.* 2 century BC. Father of Apollonius who was sent to Egypt for the coronation of Ptolemy VI Philometor. [2 Macc. 4:21]

Merari (Heb. 'bitter') *c.* 5 century BC. The father of Judith. [Jdt. 8:1]

Micah (Heb. 'who is like the Lord?') *c.* 5 century BC. Father of Uzziah, chief city magistrate in the time of Judith. [Jdt. 6:15]

Mordecai (Heb. 'consecrated to Merodach') *c.* 5 century BC. Cousin and foster-father of Esther.

In the Septuagint (Greek) translation of the Book of Esther, a number of additional passages were inserted, some of which concern Mordecai (Gk. *Mardochaeus*).

In an introductory passage, Mordecai has an apocalyptic dream: the nations plan to destroy God's people but the humble overcome the mighty.

The Greek text contains a prayer by Mordecai, asking God for deliverance from Haman's edict. It also includes the text of a letter written by Mordecai in the name of the king ordering provincial governors to give the Jews arms for self-defence.

In a final passage, Mordecai recalls his dream, and praises the Lord for safeguarding the Jews.

The object of these additions was clearly to inject a religious note lacking in the canonical story of Esther. *see also*

MORDECAI (O.T. section) [Ad. Est. 11:2–12; 12; 13:8–17; 16:1–24; 10:4–13]

Nadab (Heb. 'God is willing') *c.* 8 century BC. Nephew of Tobit and younger brother of Ahikar, he was the son of his brother Anael. Tobit's deathbed instruction to his son Tobias contains an inexplicable reference to an attempt by Nadab to murder his elder brother Ahikar by shutting him up in a grave, but it is Nadab who gets killed instead in the trap. This allusion has no relation to anything else in the Tobit story, and is probably an echo of an earlier Near Eastern work, *The Wisdom of Ahikar*, which scholars regard as one of the main sources of the Book of Tobit. [Tob. 11:18; 14:10]

Nathanael (Heb. 'God has given') date unknown. Ancestor of Judith. [Jdt. 8:1]

Nebuchadnezzar (Ass. 'Nabu protects my boundary stone') date unknown. In the Book of Judith, Nebuchadnezzar, king of Assyria, sent an army under his general Holofernes to punish the Jews, who had failed to help him in a war against Arphaxad the king of Media.

This reference has no historical basis. Nebuchadnezzar was in fact the king of Babylon after the end of the Assyrian empire, and he did not have a general called Holofernes. [Jdt. 1; 2:1–13; 3:2, 8; 4:1; 6:2, 4; 11:1,4,7; 12:13, 14:18]

Nicanor (Gk. 'conqueror') 2 century BC. A Seleucid general under Antiochus IV Epiphanes and Demetrius I Soter. Nicanor, the son of Patroclus, was one of three generals appointed by Lysias in command of an army sent in 166 BC to crush the Maccabean revolt. This Syrian force was defeated by Judas Maccabeus at the battle of Emmaus, near the foot of the Judean hills, and Nicanor escaped in disguise.

In 162 BC, in the reign of Demetrius I Soter, Nicanor was sent to cut through to Jerusalem and reinforce the garrison there. He was driven back in the battle of Capharsalama. The following year, Nicanor was surprised by Judas at Adasa, and fell in battle. This victory was later celebrated in Jewish tradition as 'the Day of Nicanor', the 13th day of the Hebrew month of Adar. [1 Macc. 3:38–41; 7:27–50; 2 Macc. 8:9–35; 14:12–34, 37–40; 15:1, 6, 25–37]

Numenius 2 century BC. Son of Antiochus, he was one of two envoys sent to Rome by Jonathan to renew the pact of friendship. [1 Macc. 12:16; 14:22–24]

Odomera 2 century BC. Nomad leader defeated by Jonathan. [1 Macc. 9:66]

Onias *1. Onias I* c. 4 century BC. High priest in Jerusalem and ancestor of Simon the Just, a later high priest, he received a letter of friendship from Arius, king of Sparta. [1 Macc. 12:7, 8, 19; Sir. 50:1]
2. Onias III 2 century BC. Son of the high priest Simon II, he was himself high priest in Jerusalem during the reign of the Seleucid ruler Seleucus IV Philopator, 187–75 BC. He was venerated for his learning and piety; after his murder he appeared in a vision related by Judas Maccabeus to inspire his men before battle.

The king's chief minister Heliodorus was sent to Jerusalem to confiscate the gold and silver in the Temple, but was foiled through divine intervention in response to Onias's prayers.

When Antiochus IV Epiphanes came to the throne in 175 BC, Onias was ousted by his corrupt brother Jason, and retired to the sanctuary at Daphne, near Antioch. He was later murdered at the instigation of another high priest Menelaus. [2 Macc. 3:1, 31–35; 4:1–6, 7, 33–38; 15:12–16; Sir. 50:1]

Ox c. 6 century BC. Grandfather of Judith. [Jdt. 8:1]

Oziel date unknown. Ancestor of Judith. [Jdt. 8:1]

Patroclus 3 century BC. Father of Nicanor, the Syrian general, who was killed in a battle against Judas Maccabeus. [2 Macc. 8:9]

Perseus 2 century BC. Last king of Macedonia, he was mentioned by Judas Maccabeus as having been defeated by the Romans. (This was at the battle of Pydna in 168 BC.) [1 Macc. 8:5]

Phasiron date unknown. His descendants were killed in their tents by Jonathan Maccabeus. [1 Macc. 9:66]

Philip *1.* 4 century BC. King of Macedonia, 359–36 BC, he was father of Alexander the Great. [1 Macc. 1:1]
2. 3 century BC. King of Macedonia, 220–179 BC, father of Perseus, he was conquered by the Romans. [1 Macc. 8:5]
3. c. 2 century BC. He was a trusted friend of Antiochus IV Epiphanes and accompanied him on the expedition to Persia in 165 BC. Antiochus IV fell ill in this campaign and before he died, he appointed Philip regent of the Seleucid kingdom, until his young son Antiochus should come of age. But Lysias, who had been left in the capital Antioch in charge of the kingdom, promptly had the boy crowned as Antiochus V Eupator, under his guidance.

In 162 BC, after Lysias had defeated Judas Maccabeus and entered Jerusalem, together with the king, they received news that Philip had returned from Persia with troops and occupied Antioch. Lysias hurried back and recaptured the city. Philip was either killed, or escaped to Egypt. [1 Macc. 6:14–18, 55–63; 2 Macc. 9:29]
4. c. 2 century BC. A Phrygian appointed by Antiochus IV Epiphanes as governor of Jerusalem. He is said to have been a brutal man, who had a number of Jews

burnt alive for having secretly observed the Sabbath against the decrees of Antiochus.

After the Maccabean revolt, when Judas and his men were raiding the countryside round Jerusalem, Philip appealed for military aid. A Syrian army was despatched which Judas defeated at Emmaus in 165 BC. [2 Macc. 5:22; 6:11; 8:8]

Posidonius 2 century BC. One of three envoys sent by the Syrian general Nicanor to come to terms with Judas Maccabeus. [2 Macc. 14:19]

Ptolemy

1. Ptolemy VI Philometor King of Egypt, 180–45 BC. Ptolemy VI succeeded to the Egyptian throne in 180 BC, at the age of seven. His mother Cleopatra acted as regent until he was enthroned in 172 BC.

The Seleucid ruler Antiochus IV twice invaded Egypt. Ptolemy was defeated and taken prisoner but Antiochus was ordered to withdraw by the Romans.

After the death of Antiochus IV, Ptolemy took an active part in the dynastic struggle that followed: initially acknowledging Alexander Balas, to whom he then married his daughter Cleopatra, three years later. He led his forces into Palestine and helped Demetrius II to defeat his own son-in-law near Antioch in 145 BC. Shortly afterwards Ptolemy himself died of wounds, and was succeeded by his younger brother Ptolemy VII Physcon.

Ptolemy VI was friendly towards the Jews, and is favourably mentioned in the Two Books of Maccabees. He permitted the high priest Onias IV to found a Jewish temple at Leontopolis (Tel el-Yehudiyeh), near modern Cairo. It survived until about AD 73. [1 Macc. 1:18; 10:51–58; 11:1–18; 2 Macc. 4:21]

2. 2 century BC. Son of Dorymenes (also called Ptolemy Macron in 2 Macc.), he was made Governor of Cyprus by the Egyptian ruler Ptolemy VI Philometor (180–45 BC). He defected to the Seleucid ruler Antiochus Epiphanes who invaded Egypt.

He was one of the generals put in command of the Seleucid forces sent to crush the Maccabean revolt. This force was defeated by Judas Maccabeus at the battle of Emmaus in 165 BC.

Ptolemy was offered a large bribe to intercede with the King Antiochus IV on behalf of Menelaus, the corrupt high priest accused by several leading Jews.

After the death of Antiochus IV, Ptolemy appears to have been out of favour with the young successor Eupator. Having urged a more liberal policy towards the Jews, Ptolemy was accused by his enemies of disloyalty to the throne, and took his own life by poison. [1 Macc. 3:38; 2 Macc. 4:45, 46; 10:12, 13]

3. 2 century BC. Son of Abubus, he was married to the daughter of Simon the high priest and Maccabean leader. Simon appointed him military commander of the Jericho district. Simon arrived there on a visit, and at a banquet for him Ptolemy treacherously had him murdered together with two of his sons, Mattathias and Judas, and his retinue.

He then sent a message to King Antiochus VII, the Seleucid ruler in Antioch, offering to govern Judea under his rule.

John, the eldest son of Simon, was at the time in Gazara. Having received word of Ptolemy's treachery, he was able to forestall an attempt to assassinate him too. He then appointed himself as the ruler in succession to his father, under the name of John Hyrcanus I.

The fate of Ptolemy is unknown. [1 Macc. 16:11–22]

4. Ptolemy VII Physcon King of Egypt, 145–16 BC. Brother of Ptolemy VI. [2 Macc. 1:10]

5. Ptolemy VII, Soter II, Lathyrus *c.* 2 century BC. In a footnote to the Greek translation of the Book of Esther, it is stated that the translation was brought to Egypt in the fourth year of the reign of 'Ptolemy and Cleopatra'. There were four Ptolemies who had wives called Cleopatra but the reference appears to apply to Ptolemy VIII, and the date has therefore been fixed at 114 BC. [Ad. Est. 11:1]

6. *c.* 2 century BC. With his father Dositheus the priest, he brought the Greek translation of the Book of Esther to Egypt in the fourth year of the reign of Ptolemy and Cleopatra (probably 114 BC).[Ad. Est. 11:1]

Quintus Memmius 2 century BC. One of the two Roman legates who wrote a letter to the Jews at the time of Judas Maccabeus, confirming certain concessions made to them by the Seleucid general Lysias. [2 Macc. 11:34]

Raguel *c.* 8 century BC. Kinsman of Tobit.

Raguel was a relative of Tobit and lived in the city of Ecbatana, in Media. He was married to Edna, and their only child was the beautiful and intelligent Sarah. Their great tragedy was that Sarah had been possessed by the demon Asmodeus. She had been married seven times and each time the demon had killed the respective husband when he entered the bridal chamber on the wedding night.

Tobias, the son of Tobit, arrived in Ecbatana and was betrothed to Sarah. On the wedding night Raguel feared the worst, but the demon was exorcized with the help of the angel Raphael. Tobias returned to Nineveh with his bride. Many years later, after the death of Tobit and Anna, Tobias and Sarah went back to Ecbatana and took care of Raguel and his wife Edna for their remaining years. [Tob. 3:7, 17; 6:10, 12; 7; 8; 10:7-10; 11:1; 14:12, 13]

Raphaim date unknown. Ancestor of Judith. [Jdt. 8:1]

Razis 2 century BC. A devout and re-

spected elder of Jerusalem, he was honoured with the title 'Father of the Jews'. In the persecution under Antiochus IV Epiphanes, the Syrian general Nicanor sent a detachment of troops to arrest Razis. The tower in which he had taken refuge was set alight and stormed. He stabbed himself with his sword, jumped off the tower wall into the street below and, bleeding profusely, dragged himself on to a rock. Tearing out his entrails, he flung them at the crowd, calling upon the Lord to give them back to him again. 'This was the manner of his death.' (2 Macc. 14:46) [2 Macc. 14:37-46]

Rhodocus 2 century BC. A Maccabean soldier who gave military information to the enemy when the Jewish fortress of Beth-zur was being besieged by Syrian forces; he was caught and imprisoned. [2 Macc. 13:21]

Salamiel (possibly from the Heb. 'God is friendly') date unknown. Ancestor of Judith. [Jdt. 8:1]

Sarah (Heb. 'princess') *c.* 7 century BC. Wife of Tobias the son of Tobit.

Sarah, described as 'fair and wise', was the only child of Raguel, a kinsman of Tobit, and his wife Edna. They lived in Ecbatana, a city in Media. Sarah was married seven times but on each occasion when her husband entered the bridal chamber on the wedding night, he was killed by the demon Asmodeus.

Sarah's despair was brought to a head when her maid jeered at her, accusing her of strangling her seven husbands. 'Why do you beat us? If they are dead, go with them!' [Tobit 3:9]

Tobias the son of Tobit arrived in Ecbatana, accompanied by the angel Raphael who was pretending to be a relative called Azarias. Tobias obtained Raguel's permission to marry Sarah. Acting on the angel's advice, he entered the room on the wedding night and drove away the demon by burning the heart and liver of a fish. He and Sarah then prayed to God to keep them safe. Later that night, when a maid was sent into the room with a light to see whether Tobias was still alive, she found the young couple sleeping soundly.

Two weeks later, after the wedding celebrations, Sarah set out with her husband on the journey back to Nineveh. She was met at the city gate by Tobit, whose sight had been miraculously restored.

Tobias and Sarah remained in Nineveh until after her parents-in-law had died, and then went back to her own parents in Ecbatana, together with their children. [Tob. 3:7–15; 6:10–12; 7; 8; 10:10–12; 11:7; 14:12]

Sarasadai (from the Heb. 'Shaddai [a name of God] is a rock') date unknown. Ancestor of Judith. [Jdt. 8:1]

Seleucus IV Philopator 2 century BC. Ruler of the Seleucid kingdom, 187–75 BC.

Seleucus IV succeeded his father Antiochus III (the Great) on the Seleucid throne in Antioch.

The king respected the religion of the Jews and the sanctity of the Temple, which he helped to maintain from his own revenues. However, on getting a report of great riches concealed in the Temple in Jerusalem, Seleucus sent his chief minister Heliodorus with an armed guard to collect the gold and silver for the royal treasury. Heliodorus returned to report that his attempt to do so had been thwarted by divine intervention and he himself severely flogged by two supernatural beings.

At one stage Onias the high priest came personally to appeal to the king against the intrigues of one Simon, who had instigated the story about the Temple treasure.

Seleucus was killed by Heliodorus in 175 BC, and the throne seized by his brother Antiochus IV Epiphanes. [2 Macc. 3:3; 4:7]

Sennacherib (Acc. 'Sin [a god] replace the brothers') 8 century BC. King of Assyria, 704–681 BC.

According to the Book of Tobit, Sennacherib succeeded Shalmaneser as king of Assyria. Tobit had to flee from him, because he had secretly buried Jewish bodies, and returned when Sennacherib was succeeded by Esarhaddon. This order of succession is historically inaccurate. [Tob. 1:15, 16, 18, 21]

Seron 2 century BC. Seleucid general under Antiochus IV. After Judas Maccabeus had defeated and killed Apollonius, the military governor of Samaria, in 166 BC, a larger Seleucid army was sent to crush the Maccabean revolt. It was led by Seron, the commander of the forces in Syria. His troops established a base in the coastal plain and advanced into the Judean hills up the steep pass of Beth-horon, in an effort to relieve the garrison cut off in Jerusalem. Judas and his men launched a surprise attack on the vanguard and routed it. The Seleucid army was pursued towards the coast. [1 Macc. 3:13–24]

Shallum date unknown. Ancestor of Jehoiakim the high priest. [Bar. 1:7]

Shalmaneser V (Ass. 'Sulman is leader') 8 century BC. King of Assyria, 726–2 BC.

Tobit was a member of the tribe of Naphtali in eastern Galilee and was taken captive in the time of Shalmaneser, king of Assyria. This may be a reference to Shalmaneser V who laid siege to Samaria the capital of the kingdom of Israel in 723 BC. It actually fell to his successor Sargon II in 721 BC, and after that the inhabitants were deported to other parts of the Assyrian empire.

Tobit states that his piety won him the favour of Shalmaneser, and he was employed by the king as a buyer of supplies in Media. This is an improbable statement, as Tobit's captivity could not have coincided with the short reign of Shalmaneser V. [Tob. 1:2, 13, 16]

Simeon (Heb. '[God] has heard') *1. c.* 3 century BC. Grandfather of the priest Mattathias who started the Maccabean revolt, to whom the Jewish historian Josephus and later writers attached the name of Hasmon. Thus the descendants of Mattathias who ruled over Judea became known as the Hasmonean dynasty. [1 Macc. 2:1]
2. see SIMON 2.

Simon (Heb. '[God] has heard') *1. c.* 3 century BC. High priest known as 'the Just'. [Sir. 50:1]
2. 2 century BC. Second son of Mattathias and leader of the Maccabean revolt after Jonathan.

Simon (also called Thassi and Simeon) was the second son of Mattathias, the village priest of Modi'in who started the revolt against Antiochus IV Epiphanes in 167 BC. With his father and his four brothers John, Judas, Eleazar and Jonathan, Simon fled into the hills and took part in the partisan movement. On his deathbed the next year, Mattathias made Judas the military commander and told the brothers to heed the wise counsel of Simon. For the next fourteen years Simon faithfully served first under Judas and then under Jonathan. From time to time, he took command of military expeditions such as that in 163 BC to rescue the oppressed Jews of Galilee, and another to capture the port of Joppa (Jaffa).

In 146 BC, Jonathan was captured through the deceit of the Seleucid general Trypho. Simon took charge and rallied the dejected Judeans. Trypho advanced on Jerusalem but then abandoned his Judean campaign and returned to Antioch, killing the captive Jonathan along the way.

The leading citizens of Jerusalem declared to Simon, 'You are our leader in place of Judas and Jonathan your brother. Fight our battles ...' (1 Macc. 13:9) He was to lead them for the next twelve years, until 134 BC.

The power struggle for the Seleucid throne continued and, as Jonathan had done, Simon was able to take advantage of it. Trypho had proclaimed himself king, and Simon sent a message of support to the rightful ruler Demetrius II. In exchange, he obtained from Demetrius recognition of his status as high priest and ethnarch (governor), also suspension of the annual tribute and remission of the taxes. Judea was now autonomous, and in the year 142 BC 'the yoke of the Gentiles was removed from Israel, and the people began to write in their documents and contracts, "In the first year of Simon the great high priest and captain and leader of the Jews".' (1 Macc. 13:41, 42) Simon marked the new independence by beginning to mint and issue Judean coins.

Simon's next military step was the capture of the strongly fortified city of Gazara, on the edge of the coastal plain. He spared the inhabitants but evicted them, and resettled the place with loyal Judean subjects. In the next year, 141 BC, the citadel in Jerusalem was assaulted, and the starving garrison surrendered. This eliminated the last vestige of foreign rule, and was the occasion for public rejoicing 'because a great enemy had been crushed and removed from Israel'. (1 Macc. 13:51) Simon built himself a residence on the site. His son John had reached manhood and was made commander of the armed forces, with his headquarters in Gazara.

Like his brothers had done, Simon sent his ambassadors to Rome and to Sparta, to ensure that the alliances with these two powers remained in force. To the Romans he sent a golden shield as a gift.

In the meantime, Demetrius II had been succeeded by his son Antiochus VII, who deposed and pursued Trypho.

He repudiated previous promises to Simon, and sent an envoy to him in Jerusalem with an ultimatum. Either Joppa, Gazara and the citadel in Jerusalem were to be handed over, or a huge sum of compensation was to be paid. Failing that, war would be declared. Simon rejected the demand, pointing out that the areas he had taken were part of the ancestral territory of the Jews that had wrongfully been occupied by their enemies.

The Seleucid general Cendebeus based an army in the coastal plain and harassed the adjacent Jewish districts. His troops were routed by the Judean forces led by Simon's two eldest sons, John and Judas. Simon did not long survive this success. He was treacherously murdered together with his two sons Judas and Mattathias by his son-in-law Ptolemy, whom he had appointed military commander of Jericho. Ptolemy's bid for power was frustrated by Simon's eldest son John Hyrcanus, who became the new ruler.

The murder of Simon ended the story of the five remarkable Maccabean brothers, all of whom had been killed in battle or been murdered. The Hasmonean dynasty that derived from Mattathias lasted for 120 years, until Herod the Great.

Simon himself remains in Jewish tradition an example of a wise and statesmanlike national leader. He is eulogized for enlarging the borders of the nation, making peace in the land, providing for the needy, and strengthening the Law. [1 Macc. 2:3, 65; 9:33–42, 65–68; 10:74–83; 11:63–66; 12:33, 34, 38; 13; 14; 15; 16:1–3, 11–17]

3. 2 century BC. Simon, of the clan of Benjamin, was the administrator of the Temple under the high priest Onias III. He quarreled with Onias about the regulation of the city market. In order to cause trouble for Onias, he went to Apollonius, the governor, and told him that a huge amount of treasure was hoarded in the Temple. Apollonius passed on this information to the king Seleucus IV, who sent his minister Heliodorus with an armed guard to seize the wealth. The attempt was foiled by divine intervention.

Later Onias went personally to see the king in the capital, Antioch, and asked him to put a stop to Simon's intrigues and slanders so that peace could be restored to Jerusalem. [2 Macc. 3:4; 4:1]

Sosipater (Gk. 'saving one's father') 2 century BC. A fighting commander in the Maccabean army who distinguished himself in the campaign of Judas Maccabeus against Timothy in Gilead. He and another commander captured Timothy but released him for fear of reprisals against Jewish hostages. [2 Macc. 12:19, 24]

Sostratus 2 century BC. A Syrian commander of the garrison in Jerusalem under Antiochus IV Epiphanes. He was entrusted with the collection of taxes and of the money promised by Menelaus for his appointment as high priest. For neglecting his duties Sostratus was recalled by the king. [2 Macc. 4:28, 29]

Susanna c. 6 century BC. A virtuous wife falsely accused of adultery.

Susanna the daughter of Hilkiah was 'a very beautiful woman and one who feared the Lord' (Sus. 2). She was married to Joakim, a wealthy and respected member of a Jewish community in Babylon. Their home was a meeting place for the important men of the community.

Two elders or judges who frequented the house conceived a passion for Susanna. One day they pretended to go home for the noon-day meal but each sneaked back again. Coming face to face, they revealed their secret to each other. They both knew that Susanna was accustomed to walk in the garden at that time of day, and hid themselves so that they could spy on her.

It was a hot day. Susanna decided to bathe in the garden and sent the maids back into the house to fetch soap and olive oil. Unable to restrain their lust, the elders approached her and said, 'we are in love with you; so give your consent, and lie with us' (Sus. 20).

Susanna rejected their advances rather than sin against the Lord. She shouted for help and the servants rushed back. The elders then denounced her, and demanded that she be brought before the communal assembly to answer the charges against her. She came accompanied by her parents, family and children, with her tear-stained face covered by a veil. The two elders insisted that she be unveiled, since they wanted to feast their eyes on her beauty.

They gave evidence that they had been strolling in a corner of Joakim's garden when they saw Susanna enter, dismiss her maids and meet a young man who had been hidden. The two of them then lay together under a tree. The elders claimed they had rushed forward and seized the young man, but he had broken away and escaped. Susanna had refused to disclose his name.

Since the story of two such important citizens could not be doubted, Susanna was immediately condemned to death. She cried out to the Lord that she was innocent, and her appeal was heard. As she was being led out to her death, the young Daniel was inspired to protest. He called the assembly fools for condemning the woman without proper enquiry and demanded that the trial be reopened since the elders had given false evidence. The court reassembled and he was invited to state his case.

Daniel insisted that the accusers should be brought forward separately. He berated the first one for the unjust decisions he had given as a judge. He then asked under what kind of tree he had seen Susanna and the young man

lying together. The witness answered that it was a clove tree. Daniel declared that he lied and his life would be forfeited. He told that elder to stand aside and ordered the other one brought in. Daniel denounced him for frightening women into consorting with him, and declared that this time his lust had betrayed him. When questioned about the kind of tree, this witness replied that it had been a yew.

Daniel's cross-examination convinced the assembly that the two elders had given false evidence. They were put to death, while Susanna was freed and restored to her rejoicing family. 'And from that day onward Daniel had a great reputation among the people.' (Sus. 64)

This charming short tale was written in Palestine about the 2nd century BC. It was included in the Septuagint (Greek Bible) and later in the Vulgate (Latin Bible), and it became attached to the Book of Daniel as Chapter 13 thereof. [Book of Susanna]

Thassi (Gk. 'zealous') *see* SIMON **2**.

Theodotus 2 century BC. One of three envoys sent by the Syrian general Nicanor to come to terms with Judas Maccabeus. [2 Macc. 14:19]

Timothy (Gk. 'man who honours God') 2 century BC. A leader of the Ammonites who fought against Judas Maccabeus.

In 163 BC Judas Maccabeus and his brother Jonathan marched across the Jordan river with an army of 8000 men, to rescue the persecuted Jewish communities in the land of Gilead. They were opposed by an Ammonite army commanded by Timothy. The Maccabeans made a three-day desert march through the territory of the friendly Nabateans, and appeared unexpectedly at the gates of Bozrah, in the land of Tob, east of Gilead, which they captured. They then continued at night towards Dathema, and launched a three-pronged attack on the army of Timothy, which fled. Judas then relieved the Jews in several other fortified towns.

Timothy regrouped his forces, but they were again routed in a pitched battle at Raphon, near the Sea of Galilee.

Judas was victorious in a later battle against Timothy at Jazer, across the Jordan river, east of Jericho. Timothy was killed in this battle. [1 Macc. 5:11, 34, 37–44; 2 Macc. 10:24–38]

Titus Manius 2 century BC. One of the two Roman legates who wrote a letter to the Jews at the time of Judas Maccabeus, confirming certain concessions made to them by the Seleucid commander Lysias. [2 Macc. 11:34]

Tobias (from the Heb. 'God is [my] good')

1. c. 7 century BC. The son and only child of Tobit and Anna, of the tribe of Naphtali in eastern Galilee.

As a child Tobias was carried off with his parents into exile in Nineveh, the capital of Assyria. Here his father became a respected and well-to-do man in the community.

Tobit was stricken with blindness and believed he would soon die. He sent for Tobias, now a young man, and revealed to him that twenty years earlier a substantial sum of silver had been deposited with a kinsman called Gabael, who lived in the town of Rages in Media. Tobias was to find a reliable companion who knew the routes to Media, and travel there to collect the money.

The guide Tobias found called himself Azarias, but was actually the angel Raphael, who had been sent by the Lord to cure Tobit. The two of them set out on the journey, accompanied by the family dog. That night they camped by the river Tigris. Tobias went to bathe his feet in the water and a huge fish tried to grab his foot. On the angel's instructions, Tobias caught the fish and kept its gall, heart and liver to use as medicine.

They reached the city of Ecbatana in Media, where another relative, Raguel, lived. His daughter Sarah, also an only child, was beautiful and wise. As her nearest kinsman Tobias was entitled to claim the hand of Sarah in marriage. The angel undertook to speak to her father about it, but Tobias declined. Sarah had already been married seven times and each husband had been killed on the wedding night by the demon Asmodeus. The angel told Tobias not to be afraid; if he burnt the heart and liver of the fish in the bridal chamber, the demon would be driven away. They were warmly welcomed by Raguel and his wife Edna, though they were distressed to hear that Tobit had gone blind. Raguel agreed that Tobias should marry his daughter, but warned him about the demon. A marriage contract was drawn up and signed, and the bridal chamber prepared.

That night Tobias entered the chamber and burnt the fish's liver and heart on the incense burner. The demon fled to Upper Egypt, where he was caught and bound by the angel Raphael. Tobias and Sarah prayed to the Lord to keep them safe, and went to sleep. Finding that Tobias had survived, Raguel gave praise to the Lord, and prepared the wedding feast.

At Tobias's request, Azarias travelled on by himself to Rages, where Gabael produced the bags of silver Tobit had left with him, and gladly agreed to attend the wedding.

After two weeks, Tobias insisted that he should return to his parents without further delay, taking his wife with him. Raguel handed over to him half of all his possessions, as a wedding gift. On reaching home, Tobias rubbed the gall of the fish into his father's eyes, as the angel had told him to do, and Tobit's sight was restored.

Tobias agreed with his father that

half the wealth he had brought back from Media should be offered to his travelling companion, as a reward for all he had done for them. Azarias disclosed that he was really the angel Raphael, sent by the Lord to cure Tobit and Sarah. They threw themselves on the ground in awe, and when they looked up the angel had disappeared.

Tobit lived on for nearly another half century. On his deathbed, he urged Tobias to depart from Nineveh, which was doomed to destruction for its wickedness. Tobias waited until his mother also died, then buried her with his father, and left with his wife and children to rejoin his parents-in-law in Media. He cared for Raguel and Edna, and buried them at Ecbatana when they died. He himself lived until after the fall of Nineveh to the Medes and Babylonians, and died greatly respected at the age of one hundred and seventeen. [Book of Tobit]

2. *c.* 2 century BC. Father of Hyrcanus, he had money kept on deposit in the Temple in Jerusalem. [2 Macc. 3:11]

Tobiel (Heb. 'God is [my] good') *c.* 8 century BC. Father of Tobit. [Tob. 1:1]

Tobit (Heb. 'my goodness') *c.* 8 century BC. A devout Jewish captive in Assyria.

Tobit the son of Tobiel was a God-fearing young man of the tribe of Naphtali in the eastern Galilee. After the Israelite monarchy divided, this area fell into the northern kingdom of Israel, which broke away from the Temple worship in Jerusalem and developed its own shrines. Tobit expressed disapproval of such apostasy and continued to make the pilgrimage to Jerusalem. When he came of age, he married Anna and had a son called Tobias.

The Assyrians invaded Israel and Tobit was carried off in captivity to Nineveh, the Assyrian capital, together with other members of his tribe. He gained the trust of the king and was employed by him as a buyer of supplies in Media, which lay to the east of Assyria. In connection with these journeys he deposited ten talents of silver – a considerable sum – with his kinsman Gabael, who lived at Rages in Media. When Sennacherib succeeded to the throne of Assyria the routes to Media passed out of Assyrian control and Tobit could no longer travel there.

He remained a devout and charitable man, and claimed with pride that 'I, Tobit, walked in the ways of truth and righteousness all the days of my life, and I performed many acts of charity to my brethren and countrymen ...' (Tob. 1:3) He provided food and clothes for the poor; and would, as an act of piety, give a proper burial to any Jewish body found abandoned outside the city walls. When Sennacherib was repulsed in Judea and killed a number of Nineveh Jews in revenge, Tobit secretly retrieved and buried the bodies. Report of this act enraged the king and Tobit had to flee with his wife and son, leaving behind all his possessions.

Soon afterwards, Sennacherib was murdered and succeeded by his son Esarhaddon. Tobit's nephew Ahikar, who had become the royal treasurer, was able to arrange for his uncle's return.

At the Feast of Pentecost Tobit sent his son Tobias to find a poor man who could be invited to share the family meal. Tobias came back to report that he had seen in the market-place a Jew who had been strangled to death. Tobit rushed off to fetch the body, hid it until dark, and buried it. He was disturbed when the neighbours jeered at him and recalled that he had been forced to flee once for the same offense.

That night it was hot, and Tobit lay down to sleep next to the wall of the courtyard. The droppings from the sparrows on the wall fell right into his eyes, and produced white patches. The doctors treated him, but he went blind, to the distress of all his family.

His wife Anna earned money by weaving cloth for a merchant. One day her employer gave her a young kid as a present, in addition to her wages. When she brought it home the blind Tobit refused to believe her story, accused her of stealing the animal, and ordered her to return it at once. She taunted him: 'Where are your charities and your righteous deeds? You seem to know everything!' (Tob. 2:14) This incident depressed Tobit, and in a fit of despair he prayed to God to end his life.

Believing he might soon die, Tobit sent for his son and commanded him to give his father a decent burial, to take care of his mother, and to live righteously. He then told him about the silver he had deposited in Media with his relative Gabael, twenty years before. Tobias was to find a reliable travelling companion who knew the route, and fetch back the money, which would restore the family's means.

In Ecbatana, a city in Media, Tobit had another kinsman called Raguel. He and his wife Edna had an only child, a beautiful and virtuous daughter called Sarah. She had already been married seven times, but each husband had been killed when he entered the bridal chamber on the wedding night by the demon Asmodeus. Sarah too was in despair, and prayed for death after her serving-maid had jeered at her.

God sent the angel Raphael to help both Tobit and Sarah. Tobias went out to look for someone suitable to journey with him to Media and came face to face with a man who was the angel in human form. When questioned by Tobias, this man said he was a fellow-Jew, knew the routes to Media well, and actually used to lodge with Gabael. Tobias brought him into the house to meet his father, who asked him about his family background. He said his name was Azarias and he was the son of Ananias – another relative of Tobit whom he had known well as a young man in Israel. The delighted Tobit immediately engaged 'Azarias' to accompany Tobias, at a wage of one drachma a day and his travelling expenses. Tobias took leave of his parents and set out with the guide. The family dog ran after him and was taken along.

When some time had gone by without news of their son, Anna started wailing that he was dead. Tobit tried to reassure her, though becoming anxious himself. One day Anna cried out that she saw Tobias approaching with his companion. As the blind Tobias stumbled out through the courtyard door, Tobias came up to him and rubbed into his eyes the gall of a fish caught in the river on the way to Media. (The angel had told him this medicine would restore his father's sight.) Tobias pulled the white patches off the eyes of his father, who burst into tears and blessed the Lord: 'For thou hast afflicted me, but thou hast had mercy upon me; here I see my son Tobias!' (Tob. 11:15)

The young man told his parents all that had happened on his journey. In Ecbatana he had married his relative Sarah, after exorcizing the demon Asmodeus by burning the liver and the heart of the same fish used to cure Tobit's blindness. His father-in-law Raguel, a well-to-do man, had bestowed half his possessions on Tobias. In addition, Gabael had come to the wedding and brought the bags of silver Tobit had once deposited with him. On nearing home Tobias had hurried ahead, and Sarah with the rest of his party were close behind.

Tobit went out to meet his daughter-in-law at the city gate. His fellow-citizens were astonished to see him striding through the streets full of vigour and no longer blind. A sumptuous marriage feast was held. 'So there was rejoicing among all his brethren in Nineveh.' (Tob. 11:17)

Tobit and Tobias offered the travelling companion Azarias half of all the wealth brought back from Media, as a reward for the services he had performed. He then disclosed to them that he was the angel Raphael. All he asked for reward was that Tobit and Sarah should give praise to the Lord and proclaim to everyone what had been done for them. 'It is good to guard the secret of a king, but glorious to reveal the works of God.' (Tob. 12:7) Father and son prostrated themselves to the ground, and when they looked up the angel had disappeared.

Tobit sang hymns of praise to the just and merciful God, prophesying that the Lord would gather his scattered people, and would restore the splendour of Jerusalem and its sanctuary.

He lived on in peace and honour for nearly half a century more, and died at the age of 112. On his deathbed he urged Tobias to depart with his family because Nineveh was doomed to be destroyed for its wickedness. When Anna his mother also died, Tobias buried her with his father in Nineveh, then left to join his parents-in-law in Media.

It is unclear to what period or country the Jewish author of the Book of Tobit belonged. Internal events suggest the 3rd century BC, after the start of the Hellenistic period but before the Maccabean revolt. It is likely that he lived in Egypt. The events are supposed to have taken place in the Assyrian empire several centuries earlier, but the author is curiously vague about the history and the geography which formed the background to the story. Tobit is described as a young man when the Israelite kingdom was split after the death of Solomon (931 BC); he was deported to Assyria (about 734 BC); while his son Tobias died after the fall of Nineveh (612 BC). The town of Rages in Media, where Tobit's kinsman Gabael lived, is stated to be in the hills two days journey from Ecbatana in the plain; in fact, Ecbatana was a winter capital in the mountains at an altitude of 6000 feet; while Rages was 200 miles

away and much lower down. These discrepancies do not detract from a vivid human story mingling Jewish piety, a belief in demons and magic, and warm family sentiment. [Book of Tobit]

Trypho 2 century BC. An army commander who usurped the Seleucid throne.

Trypho was an ambitious army commander under the Seleucid rulers Alexander Balas and Demetrius II. He fomented a mutiny amongst the units that Demetrius was disbanding, seized control of the capital, Antioch, and in 145 BC installed the young son of Alexander Balas on the throne as Antiochus VI.

In an expedition to Judea, Trypho treacherously took Jonathan the Maccabean leader as his prisoner, and later killed him while retreating northwards. Jonathan's brother and successor, Simon the high priest, gave his support to Demetrius II, who continued his struggle to regain the throne. In 143 BC Trypho had Antiochus VI put to death and himself seized the throne.

In 138 BC Trypho was ousted in his turn by Antiochus VII Sidetes who pursued him to Dor on the Palestinian coast and set siege to the town. Trypho escaped by ship to Orthosia but was again pursued by Antiochus, and committed suicide. [1 Macc. 11:39, 40, 54–56; 12:39–49; 13:1, 12–24, 31–34; 15:10–14, 25, 37, 39]

Uzziah (Heb. 'God is [my] strength') c. 5 century BC. Chief magistrate of Bethulia.

Uzziah, the son of Micah, was the chief magistrate or elder of the town of Bethulia in the hills of Ephraim, where Judith lived. It was besieged by an Assyrian army under Holofernes, and its spring of water was seized. After thirty-four days the townspeople, suffering from famine and thirst, demanded that Uzziah surrender to the Assyrians. He promised to do so if help from the Lord did not come within another five days.

Judith, a beautiful and devout young widow living on her deceased husband's farm, was outraged at this undertaking. She reproached Uzziah and his fellow-magistrates for their lack of faith in the Lord. At her request, they let her slip out of the city gate that night, accompanied only by her maid. Four days later, she returned from the Assyrian camp, bearing the severed head of Holofernes. Uzziah was aroused from his sleep and led the crowd in praise of Judith for delivering them. He then sent messengers 'to all the frontiers of Israel' (Jdt. 15:4), telling the men to rush out and destroy the enemy who were now in retreat. [Jdt. 6:15–21; 7:23–32; 8:9, 28–31, 35; 10:6; 13:18–20; 14:6; 15:4]

Zabdiel (Heb. 'gift of God') 2 century BC. Leader of an Arabian tribe, he killed and decapitated King Alexander Balas, after he had been defeated by Ptolemy VI of Egypt, and sent his head to the king. [1 Macc. 11:17]

Zacchaeus (from the Heb. 'pure') 2 century BC. A captain in the Maccabean army, he took part in the siege of two strong Idumean fortresses. [2 Macc. 10:19]

Zedekiah (Heb. 'God is [my] righteousness') date unknown. Ancestor of Baruch who was the disciple and scribe of Jeremiah. [Bar. 1:1]